Careers Outdoors

Careers Outdoors

SALEM PRESS
A Division of EBSCO Information Services, Inc.
Ipswich, Massachusetts

GREY HOUSE PUBLISHING

Publisher's Cataloging-In-Publication Data
(Prepared by The Donohue Group, Inc.)

Title: Careers outdoors.
Other Titles: Careers in--
Description: [First edition]. | Ipswich, Massachusetts : Salem Press, a division of EBSCO
        Information Services, Inc. ; [Amenia, New York] : Grey House Publishing,
        [2018] | Includes bibliographical references and index.
Identifiers: ISBN 9781682176689 (hardcover)
Subjects: LCSH: Outdoor life--Vocational guidance--United States. | Science--Vocational
        guidance--United States. | Building trades--Vocational guidance--United
        States. | Agriculture--Vocational guidance--United States. | Conservation of
        natural resources--Vocational guidance--United States.
Classification: LCC HF5382.5.U5 C37 2018 | DDC 331.7020973--dc23

First Printing

CONTENTS

Publisher's Note vii

Editor's Introduction ix

Agricultural & Food Scientists 1

Animal Caretakers 21

Botanists 36

Bulldozer & Construction Equipment Operators 52

Cement Masons & Masonry Workers 66

Civil Engineers 82

Construction & Building Inspectors 97

Environmental Engineers 114

Farmers, Ranchers & Other Agricultural Managers 128

Firefighters 147

Fish & Game Wardens 161

Fishers/Hunters/Trappers 172

Foresters & Conservation Scientists 187

Gardeners & Groundskeepers 204

Geologists & Geophysicists 218

Insurance Claims Adjusters & Examiners 233

Landscape Architects 248

Marine Biologists 262

Meteorologists 278

Park Rangers 293

Police Officers & Detectives 304

Recreation Program Directors 320

Structural Metal Workers 334

Travel Agents 347

Wildlife Biologists 360

Appendix A: Holland Code 375

Appendix B: Bibliography 379

Index 381

PUBLISHER'S NOTE

Careers Outdoors contains twenty-five alphabetically arranged chapters describing specific fields of interest for those with a desire to work in the great outdoors: in parks, on farms, at construction sites, as a firefighter, or in law enforcement. Merging scholarship with occupational development, this single comprehensive guidebook provides students with the necessary insight into potential careers, and provides instruction on what job seekers can expect in terms of training, advancement, earnings, job prospects, working conditions, relevant associations, and more. *Careers Outdoors* is specifically designed for a high school and undergraduate audience and is edited to align with secondary or high school curriculum standards.

Scope of Coverage

Understanding the wide scope of jobs for those with a passion for the outdoors is important for anyone preparing for a career in which they spend a good portion of their working day out of doors instead of at a desk in an office. *Careers Outdoors* comprises twenty-five lengthy chapters on a broad range of occupations including traditional and long-established jobs such as Animal Caretakers, Fish and Game Wardens, and Park Rangers, as well as in-demand jobs: Forestry and Conservation Scientist, Meteorologist, and Wildlife Biologist. This excellent reference presents possible career paths and occupations within high-growth and emerging fields in this industry.

Careers Outdoors is enhanced with numerous charts and tables, including projections from the US Bureau of Labor Statistics, and median annual salaries or wages for those occupations profiled. Each chapter also notes those skills that can be applied across broad occupation categories. Interesting enhancements, like **Fun Facts**, **Famous Firsts**, and dozens of photos, add depth to the discussion. A highlight of each chapter is **Conversation With** – a two-page interview with a professional working in a related job. The respondents share their personal career paths, detail the potential for career advancement, offer advice for students, and include a "try this" for those interested in embarking on a career in their profession.

Essay Length and Format

Each chapter ranges in length from 3,500 to 4,500 words and begins with a Snapshot of the occupation that includes career clusters, interests, earnings, and employment outlook. This is followed by these major categories:

- **Overview** includes detailed discussions on: Sphere of Work; Work Environment; Occupation Interest; A Day in the Life. Also included here is a Profile that outlines working conditions, educational needs, and physical abilities. You will also find the occupation's Holland Interest Score, which matches up character and personality traits with specific jobs.

- **Occupational Specialties** lists specific jobs that are related in some way, like Geotechnical Engineer, Hazmat Specialist, Seismologist, and Paleontologist. Duties and Responsibilities are also included.
- **Work Environment** details the physical, human, and technological environment of the occupation profiled.
- **Education, Training, and Advancement** outlines how to prepare for this field while in high school, and what college courses to take, including licenses and certifications needed. A section is devoted to the Adult Job Seeker, and there is a list of skills and abilities needed to succeed in the job profiled.
- **Earnings and Advancements** offers specific salary ranges, and includes a chart of metropolitan areas that have the highest concentration of the profession.
- **Employment and Outlook** discusses employment trends, and projects growth to 2026. This section also lists related occupations.
- **Selected Schools** list those prominent learning institutions that offer specific courses in the profiles occupations.
- **More Information** includes associations that the reader can contact for more information.

Special Features

Several features continue to distinguish this reference series from other career-oriented reference works. The back matter includes:
- Appendix A: Guide to Holland Code. This discusses John Holland's theory that people and work environments can be classified into six different groups: Realistic; Investigative; Artistic; Social; Enterprising; and Conventional. See if the job you want is right for you!
- Appendix B: General Bibliography. This is a collection of suggested readings, organized into major categories.
- Subject Index: Includes people, concepts, technologies, terms, principles, and all specific occupations discussed in the occupational profile chapters.

Acknowledgments

Thanks are due to Allison Blake, who took the lead in developing "Conversations With," with help from Vanessa Parks, and to the professionals who communicated their work experience through interview questionnaires. Their frank and honest responses provide immeasurable value to *Careers Outdoors*. The contributions of all are gratefully acknowledged.

EDITOR'S INTRODUCTION

Introduction

Some people can't imagine working inside all day. For them, there's good news: they may be able to join the thousands of workers who call the outdoors their office.

Outdoor careers often don't fit a mold. Some workers spend their time in a single location, unloading cargo or constructing homes. Others may be on the move all day, delivering the mail or walking through nature preserves to catalog plants.

Although working in the open air may offer upsides, it's not all sunshine and blue skies. Keep reading to learn why—and to learn more about some of the possibilities for careers outside.

Working in the open air

If you're interested in working outside, you may have more options than you realize: according to the U.S. Bureau of Labor Statistics (BLS), nearly half of all jobs required outdoor work in 2016. For purposes of this article, an outdoor career is one in which at least some workers spend a large part of their workday doing tasks outside. Industry sectors with opportunities for employment outdoors include:

- Agriculture, forestry, fishing, and hunting
- Construction
- Leisure and hospitality
- Mining, quarrying, and oil and gas extraction
- Transportation and warehousing
- Utilities

Not all workers in these industry sectors are outdoors, of course, but at least some of them are. Even people who work primarily outdoors, however, may spend at least part of their time indoors.

The BLS projects growth in many of the industry sectors with opportunities for employment outdoors. The leisure and hospitality sector—which includes golf courses, nature parks, and recreational camps—is projected to add the most new jobs over the 2014–24 decade. Even in sectors that are projected to have employment declines—such as agriculture, forestry, fishing, and hunting—BLS still expects job openings to arise from the need to replace workers who retire or leave their occupation for other reasons.

Occupations for outdoor employment

If you think you'd like to work outside, where would you most like to be: On the water? In the woods? Surrounded by wildlife—or kids?

Occupations with outdoor opportunities may be grouped by focus or work setting, such as

- on the water
- in the woods
- with people
- with plants and animals
- in cities and towns.

For selected occupations in each of those groups, the tables that follow show data on employment and self-employment in 2014, projected job openings from 2014 to 2024, and median annual wages in 2016. Compare the percentage of self-employed workers in these occupations with 6.2 percent, the proportion of all workers who were self-employed in 2014. And compare the wages with $37,040, the median annual wage for all workers in 2016.

On the water. There are thousands of jobs for people who want to work on the water. Some of these jobs offer opportunities for self-employment or are projected to have lots of openings. Many of the occupations pay above the median, too. Workers may not need formal education to enter some of these occupations. Oil and gas roustabouts, for example, usually learn the skills they need on the job. In other occupations, such as commercial divers, workers typically need a certificate or other postsecondary nondegree award. Work experience in a related occupation also may be important. Ship officers, for example, might need to have first worked as a sailor before qualifying for the higher level position.

In the woods. If the forest is your preferred work locale, consider a career related to forestry and conservation or in logging. Most of these occupations have wages that are higher than the median for all workers.

To enter many of these occupations, you typically need a high school diploma. Forest and conservation technicians usually need an associate's degree. And conservation scientists and foresters generally qualify for entry-level jobs with a bachelor's degree. Forest fire inspectors and prevention specialists may need work experience as a firefighter or police officer to qualify for the occupation.

With people. Occupations that might involve working outdoors with children or adults are projected to have many job openings, and several of these occupations have higher-than-average rates of self-employment.

You typically enter many of these occupations with a high school diploma or less education. Other occupations, such as coaches, may require a college degree at the entry level. Workers also frequently need on-the-job training to become fully competent. And self-enrichment education teachers typically need work experience in an occupation related to the subject matter that they teach.

With plants and animals. Some outdoor jobs, such as those on farms and ranches, involve working with plants and animals. The projected number of job openings over the 2014–24 decade vary for these occupations, as do their wages and rates of self-employment. The education and training usually required to enter or become competent in these occupations vary, too. To qualify as a farmworker or laborer, for example, you typically need no formal education. But to get an entry-level job as a zoologist or agricultural inspector, you usually need a college degree.

Regardless of the level of education required, nearly all of the occupations in table 4 typically involve on-the-job training for workers to become competent. Farmers, ranchers, and other agricultural managers also typically need work experience in a related occupation, such as farmworkers or agricultural equipment operators.

In cities and towns. There are lots of options for working outdoors in residential and commercial areas. In most of these occupations, wages were higher than the median for all workers, and a number of them are projected to have numerous job openings over the 2014–24 decade.

Although outdoor occupations usually require a high school diploma for entry, a few have no formal education requirements. Roofers and construction laborers, for example—two construction trades worker occupations—typically qualify for entry-level jobs with less than a high school diploma. A bachelor's degree typically is needed to become a construction manager, civil engineer, or surveyor.

For some of the occupations, on-the-job training of 1 month or more helps workers attain competency in their jobs. Apprenticeships are common for certain types of construction trades workers, such as carpenters and brickmasons. And surveyors need prior work experience as a survey technician.

Pros and cons of outdoor careers

As with nearly any career, working outside has its upsides and downsides. You need to decide whether the nonstandard schedules, harsh weather, and dangerous conditions prevalent in some of these jobs outweigh the fresh air, love of nature, and sense of pride they may also offer.

Work schedules for outdoor jobs often differ from the standard 9-to-5, Monday-to-Friday hours of many office jobs. For example, boat captains might be away from home for weeks at a time, working night, weekend, and holiday shifts. Certain outdoor occupation workers are more likely than average to be on the job early in the morning.

Outdoor jobs may be seasonal, and work isn't always available year-round. Employment is more plentiful during warmer weather in some industry sectors. And there may be an increase in employment during the winter months in other industries, such as at skiing facilities, even if overall employment dips in that industry sector.

Regardless of the season, people in these jobs must work outdoors frequently in all kinds of weather. In heat, cold, rain, or snow, workers still are expected to perform their tasks. And outdoor work often involves doing physically demanding tasks, such as lifting or digging. As a result, workers in some outdoor jobs incur occupational injuries or illnesses at a higher rate than the average worker. To help prevent accidents and injuries, workers must take precautions and follow safety guidelines.

But the perks of working outside—including being in the open air, enjoying nature, and getting exercise—may outweigh whatever challenges these careers present. In some occupations, working outdoors gives people a chance to appreciate, promote, or protect nature. Whether they ferry commuters across a bay, care for park animals, or help to prevent forest fires, people may be drawn to these careers for the opportunity to interact with the environment positively through their work.

Workers in other outdoor occupations like that their jobs involve hands-on activities that produce tangible results. For example, a civil engineer can take pride in the completion of a bridge that she helped to design, and construction laborers share the satisfaction of having built it.

Learning more

Find out more about the occupations in this article, along with hundreds of others, in the Occupational Outlook Handbook (OOH). The OOH has detailed descriptions of what it takes to enter occupations, as well as information about the job outlook, work environment, and more.

The new Occupational Requirements Survey, conducted by the BLS National Compensation Survey program, gathers information about jobs' environmental conditions—including working outdoors—and other requirements.

—Elka Torpey
July 2017

Elka Torpey is an economist in the Office of Occupational Statistics and Employment Projections, BLS. She can be reached at torpey.elka@bls.gov.

Elka Torpey, "Jobs for people who love being outdoors ," Career Outlook, U.S. Bureau of Labor Statistics, July 2017.

Agricultural & Food Scientists

Snapshot

Career Cluster(s): Agriculture, Food & Natural Resources, Manufacturing, Science, Technology, Engineering & Mathematics
Interests: Agricultural Science, Agronomy, Environmental Science, Biology, Chemistry, Research, Food Science
Earnings (Median Pay): $62,920 per year, $30.25 per hour
Job Growth: As fast as average

OVERVIEW

Agricultural and food scientists may observe the production of field crops and farm animals so that they can research solutions to problems.

Agricultural and food scientists research ways to improve the efficiency and safety of agricultural establishments and products.

Sphere of Work

Agricultural and food scientists play an important role in maintaining and expanding the nation's food supply. Many work in basic or applied research and development. Basic research

seeks to understand the biological and chemical processes by which crops and livestock grow. Applied research seeks to discover ways to improve the quality, quantity, and safety of agricultural products.

Work Environment

Many agricultural and food scientists work with little supervision, forming their own hypotheses and developing their research methods. In addition, they often lead teams of technicians or students who help in their research. Agricultural and food scientists who are employed in private industry may need to travel between different worksites.

Profile

Working Conditions: Work both Indoors and Outdoors
Physical Strength: Light Work
Education Needs: Bachelor's Degree, Master's Degree, Doctoral Degree
Licensure/Certification: Recommended
Opportunities For Experience: Internship, Military Service, Part-time Work
Holland Interest Score*: IRS

* See Appendix A

Occupation Interest

Agricultural and food scientists in private industry commonly work for food production companies, farms, and processing plants. They may improve inspection standards or overall food quality. They spend their time in a laboratory, where they do tests and experiments, or in the field, where they take samples or assess overall conditions. Other agricultural and food scientists work for pharmaceutical companies, where they use biotechnology processes to develop drugs or other medical products. Some look for ways to process agricultural products into fuels, such as ethanol produced from corn.

At universities, agricultural and food scientists do research and investigate new methods of improving animal or soil health, nutrition, and other facets of food quality. They also write grants to organizations, such as the United States Department of Agriculture (USDA) or the National Institutes of Health (NIH), to get funding for their research.

In the federal government, agricultural and food scientists conduct research on animal safety and on methods of improving food and crop production. They spend most of their time conducting clinical trials or developing experiments on animal and plant subjects.

Agricultural and food scientists may eventually present their findings in peer-reviewed journals or other publications.

A Day in the Life—Duties and Responsibilities

The daily responsibilities and duties of agricultural and food scientists vary significantly based on their area of expertise and employer. For example, soil scientists primarily analyze the ground in which crops are grown, while biotechnology specialists study ways to increase crop yields. Government agencies may focus on food safety or sustainable development, while private companies tend to concentrate on maximizing profit yields from agricultural business.

In general, agricultural and food scientists work with commercial agricultural firms, government agencies, small farmers, and food manufacturers, performing in-depth research, collecting samples, and providing technical data and advice for clients. They offer public policy guidance for political leaders, sharing information on ways to produce food, safeguard the environment, and ensure long-term soil fertility and water-use sustainability. Agricultural and food scientists collect water, soil, plant, and animal samples, diagnose diseases and nutrient problems among animals and crops, assess the severity of insect infestations, track breeding trends, monitor weed growth, and examine the effectiveness of new farming techniques and food production technologies. Many agricultural and food scientists conduct controlled experiments in laboratories, trying to generate increased crop growth or healthier foods.

Senior agricultural and food scientists train technicians, research assistants, and other members of their teams. They also perform important administrative tasks, such as completing grant applications and editing research papers.

Duties and Responsibilities

- Conduct research and experiments to improve the productivity and sustainability of field crops and farm animals
- Create new food products and develop new and better ways to process, package, and deliver them
- Study the composition of soil as it relates to plant growth, and research ways to improve it
- Communicate research findings to the scientific community, food producers, and the public
- Travel between facilities to oversee the implementation of new projects

OCCUPATION SPECIALTIES

The following are types of agricultural and food scientists:

Animal Scientists

Animal scientists typically conduct research on domestic farm animals. With a focus on food production, they explore animal genetics, nutrition, reproduction, diseases, growth, and development. They work to develop efficient ways to produce and process meat, poultry, eggs, and milk. Animal scientists may crossbreed animals to make them more productive or improve other characteristics. They advise farmers on how to upgrade housing for animals, lower animal death rates, increase growth rates, or otherwise increase the quality and efficiency of livestock.

Food Scientists and Technologists

Food scientists and technologists use chemistry, biology, and other sciences to study the basic elements of food. They analyze the nutritional content of food, discover new food sources, and research ways to make processed foods safe and healthy. Food technologists generally work in product development, applying findings from food science research to develop new or better ways of selecting, preserving, processing, packaging, and distributing food. Some food scientists use problem-solving techniques from nanotechnology—the science of manipulating matter on an atomic scale—to develop sensors that can detect contaminants in food. Other food scientists enforce government regulations, inspecting food-processing areas to ensure that they are sanitary and meet waste management standards.

Plant Scientists

Plant scientists work to improve crop yields and advise food and crop developers about techniques that could enhance production. They may develop ways to control pests and weeds.

Soil Scientists

Soil scientists examine the composition of soil, how it affects plant or crop growth, and how alternative soil treatments affect crop productivity. They develop methods of conserving and managing soil that farmers and forestry companies can use. Because soil science is closely related to environmental science, people trained in soil science also work to ensure environmental quality and effective land use.

WORK ENVIRONMENT

Physical Environment

Agricultural and food scientists work in laboratories, in offices, and in the field. They spend most of their time studying data and reports in a laboratory or an office. Fieldwork includes visits to farms or processing plants.

Certain positions may require travel, either domestic, international, or both. The amount of travel can vary widely.

Agricultural and food scientists typically work full time.

Relevant Skills and Abilities

Communication Skills
- Speaking effectively
- Writing concisely

Interpersonal/Social Skills
- Being able to work independently
- Working as a member of a team

Organization & Management Skills
- Paying attention to and handling details

Research & Planning Skills
- Solving problems

Technical Skills
- Performing scientific, mathematical and technical work

Work Environment Skills
- Working in a laboratory setting
- Working outdoors

Human Environment

Depending on their areas of specialty, agricultural and food scientists interact and collaborate with a wide range of individuals, including government officials, technologists and technicians, farmers, environmental scientists, business executives, and food manufacturers.

Technological Environment

When visiting a food or animal production facility, agricultural and food scientists must follow biosecurity measures, wear suitable clothing, and tolerate the environment associated with food production processes. This environment may include noise associated with large production machinery, cold temperatures associated with food production or storage, and close proximity to animal byproducts.

EDUCATION, TRAINING, AND ADVANCEMENT

Agricultural and food scientists need at least a bachelor's degree from an accredited postsecondary institution, although many earn advanced degrees. Some animal scientists earn a doctor of veterinary medicine (DVM) degree.

Every state has at least one land-grant college that offers agricultural science degrees. Many other colleges and universities also offer agricultural science degrees or related courses. Degrees in related sciences, such as biology, chemistry, and physics, or in a related engineering specialty also may qualify people for many agricultural science jobs.

Undergraduate coursework for food scientists and technologists and for soil and plant scientists typically includes biology, chemistry, botany, and plant conservation. Students preparing to be food scientists take courses such as food chemistry, food analysis, food microbiology, food engineering, and food-processing operations. Students preparing to be soil and plant scientists take courses in plant pathology, soil chemistry, entomology (the study of insects), plant physiology, and biochemistry.

Undergraduate students in agricultural and food sciences typically gain a strong foundation in their specialty, with an emphasis on teamwork through internships and research opportunities. Students also are encouraged to take humanities courses, which can help them develop good communication skills, and computer courses, which can familiarize them with common programs and databases.

Many people with bachelor's degrees in agricultural sciences find work in related jobs rather than becoming an agricultural or food scientist. For example, a bachelor's degree in agricultural science is a useful background for farming, ranching, agricultural inspection, farm credit institutions, or companies that make or sell feed, fertilizer, seed, or farm equipment. Combined with coursework in business, agricultural and food science could be a good background for managerial jobs in farm-related or ranch-related businesses.

Many students with bachelors' degrees in application-focused food sciences or agricultural sciences earn advanced degrees in applied topics such as toxicology or dietetics. Students who major in a more basic field, such as biology or chemistry, may be better suited for getting their Ph.D. and doing research within the agricultural and food sciences. During graduate school, there is additional emphasis on lab work and original research, in which prospective animal scientists have the opportunity to do experiments and sometimes supervise undergraduates.

Advanced research topics include genetics, animal reproduction, agronomy, and biotechnology, among others. Advanced coursework also emphasizes statistical analysis and experiment design, which are important as Ph.D. candidates begin their research.

Some agricultural and food scientists receive a doctor of veterinary medicine (DVM). Like Ph.D. candidates in animal science, a prospective veterinarian must first have a bachelor's degree before getting into veterinary school.

High School/Secondary

High school students should study biology, physics, chemistry, and other natural sciences. Algebra and applied mathematics are extremely useful as well. High school students should take computer science courses and hone their writing and public speaking skills through English and communications classes. Finally, courses that help students understand agricultural and food systems, such as farm equipment, seeding practices, and food production are

Suggested High School Subjects
- Agricultural Education
- Agricultural Mechanization
- Algebra
- Applied Biology/Chemistry
- Applied Math
- Biology
- Chemistry
- College Preparatory
- English
- Forestry
- Landscaping
- Physics

Famous First

Jethro Tull was an English agricultural pioneer from Berkshire who helped bring about the British Agricultural Revolution. He perfected a horse-drawn seed drill (shown here) in 1700 that economically sowed the seeds in neat rows.

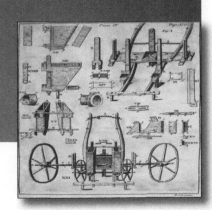

College/Postsecondary

Every state has at least one land-grant college that offers agricultural science degrees. Many other colleges and universities also offer agricultural science degrees or related courses. Degrees in related sciences, such as biology, chemistry, and physics, or in a related engineering specialty also may qualify people for many agricultural science jobs.

Undergraduate coursework for food scientists and technologists and for soil and plant scientists typically includes biology, chemistry, botany, and plant conservation. Students preparing to be food scientists take courses such as food chemistry, food analysis, food microbiology, food engineering, and food-processing operations. Students preparing to be soil and plant scientists take courses in plant pathology, soil chemistry, entomology (the study of insects), plant physiology, and biochemistry.

Undergraduate students in agricultural and food sciences typically gain a strong foundation in their specialty, with an emphasis on teamwork through internships and research opportunities. Students also are encouraged to take humanities courses, which can help them develop good communication skills, and computer courses, which can familiarize them with common programs and databases.

Many people with bachelor's degrees in agricultural sciences find work in related jobs rather than becoming an agricultural or food scientist. For example, a bachelor's degree in agricultural science is a useful background for farming, ranching, agricultural inspection, farm credit institutions, or companies that make or sell feed, fertilizer, seed, or farm equipment. Combined with coursework in business, agricultural and food science could be a good background for managerial jobs in farm-related or ranch-related businesses.

Many students with bachelors' degrees in application-focused food sciences or agricultural sciences earn advanced degrees in applied topics such as toxicology or dietetics. Students who major in a more basic field, such as biology or chemistry, may be better suited for getting their Ph.D. and doing research within the agricultural and food sciences. During graduate school, there is additional emphasis on lab work and original research, in which prospective animal scientists have the opportunity to do experiments and sometimes supervise undergraduates.

Advanced research topics include genetics, animal reproduction, agronomy, and biotechnology, among others. Advanced coursework also emphasizes statistical analysis and experiment design, which are important as Ph.D. candidates begin their research.

Some agricultural and food scientists receive a doctor of veterinary medicine (DVM). Like Ph.D. candidates in animal science, a prospective veterinarian must first have a bachelor's degree before getting into veterinary school.

Related College Majors
- Agriculture/Agricultural Sciences, General
- Agronomy & Crop Science
- Animal Sciences, General
- Dairy Science
- Entomology
- Food Sciences & Technology
- Foods & Nutrition Science
- Foods & Nutrition Studies, General
- Horticulture Science
- International Agriculture
- Plant Sciences, General
- Poultry Science
- Soil Sciences
- Zoology, General

Adult Job Seekers

Qualified agricultural and food scientists may apply directly to government agencies, businesses, or educational institutions with open positions. They may also join and network through a professional organization, such as the American Society of Agronomy or the Soil Science Society of America.

Professional Certification and Licensure

Some states require soil scientists to be licensed to practice. Licensing requirements vary by state, but generally include holding a bachelor's degree with a certain number of credit hours in soil science, working under a licensed scientist for a certain number of years, and passing an exam.

Otherwise, certifications are generally not required for agriculture and food scientists, but they can be useful in advancing one's career. Agricultural and food scientists can get certifications from organizations such as the American Society of Agronomy, the American Registry of Professional Animal Scientists (ARPAS), the Institute of Food Technologists (IFT), or the Soil Science Society of America (SSSA), and others. These certifications recognize expertise in agricultural and food science, and enhance the status of those who are certified.

Qualification for certification is generally based on education, previous professional experience, and passing a comprehensive exam. Scientists may need to take continuing education courses to keep their certification, and they must follow the organization's code of ethics.

Additional Requirements

Internships are highly recommended for prospective food scientists and technologists. Many entry-level jobs in this occupation are related to food manufacturing, and firsthand experience is often valued in that environment.

Agricultural and food scientists must demonstrate exceptional communications skills as well as research and analytical capabilities. Strong knowledge of computer software is also very useful to these scientists. They should enjoy the outdoors, be comfortable working in close proximity to livestock and other animals, and be able to work under varying conditions.

Fun Fact

On average, every hour of every day about $6 million in U.S. agricultural products are consigned for shipment for export to foreign markets.
Source: www.cals.ncsu.edu/CollegeRelations/AGRICU.htm

EARNINGS AND ADVANCEMENT

Agricultural and food scientists in private industry commonly work for food production companies, farms, and processing plants. They may improve inspection standards or overall food quality. They spend their time in a laboratory, where they do tests and experiments, or in the field, where they take samples or assess overall conditions. Other agricultural and food scientists work for pharmaceutical companies, where they use biotechnology processes to develop drugs or other medical products. Some look for ways to process agricultural products into fuels, such as ethanol produced from corn.

At universities, agricultural and food scientists do research and investigate new methods of improving animal or soil health, nutrition, and other facets of food quality. They also write grants to organizations, such as the United States Department of Agriculture (USDA) or the National Institutes of Health (NIH), to get funding for their research.

In the federal government, agricultural and food scientists conduct research on animal safety and on methods of improving food and crop production. They spend most of their time conducting clinical trials or developing experiments on animal and plant subjects.

Agricultural and food scientists may eventually present their findings in peer-reviewed journals or other publications.

Median annual wages, May 2016

Life scientists: $71,950

Agricultural and food scientists: $62,920

Total, all occupations: $37,040

Note: "All Occupations" includes all occupations in the U.S. Economy. Source: U.S. Bureau of Labor Statistics, Occupational Employment Statistics

The median annual wage for agricultural and food scientists was $62,920 in May 2016. The median wage is the wage at which half the workers in an occupation earned more than that amount and half earned less. The lowest 10 percent earned less than $37,660, and the highest 10 percent earned more than $116,520.

Median annual wages for agricultural and food scientists in May 2016 were as follows:

Food scientists and technologists	$63,950
Soil and plant scientists	$62,300
Animal scientists	$60,330

In May 2016, the median annual wages for agricultural and food scientists in the top industries in which they worked were as follows:

Research and development in the physical, engineering, and life sciences	$76,050
Government	$66,110
Management, scientific, and technical consulting services	$63,280
Food manufacturing	$59,210
Colleges, universities, and professional schools; state, local, and private	$52,170

EMPLOYMENT AND OUTLOOK

Agricultural and food scientists held about 43,000 jobs in 2016.
Employment in the detailed occupations that make up agricultural
and food scientists was distributed as follows:

Soil and plant scientists	19,900
Food scientists and technologists	17,000
Animal scientists	6,100

The largest employers of agricultural and food scientists were as
follows:

Food manufacturing	15%
Colleges, universities, and professional schools; state, local, and private	12%
Research and development in the physical, engineering, and life sciences	10%
Government	8%
Management, scientific, and technical consulting services	8%

Overall employment of agricultural and food scientists is projected to
grow 7 percent from 2016 to 2026, about as fast as the average for all
occupations.

Employment of agricultural and food scientists is projected to grow
as research into agricultural production methods and techniques
continues. Challenges such as population growth, increased demand
for water resources, combating pests and pathogens, changes in
climate and weather patterns, and additional demand for agriculture
products, such as biofuels, will continue to create demand for research
in agricultural efficiency and sustainability.

Animal scientists will be needed to investigate and improve the diets, living conditions, and even genetic makeup of livestock. Food scientists and technologists will work to improve food-processing techniques, ensuring that products are safe, waste is limited, and food is shipped efficiently and safely. Soil and plant scientists will continue to try to understand and map soil composition. They will investigate ways to improve soils, to find uses for byproducts, and selectively breed crops to resist pests and disease, or improve taste.

Related Occupations
- Agricultural and Food Science Technicians
- Biochemists and Biophysicists
- Biological Technicians
- Chemical Technicians
- Conservation Scientists and Foresters
- Environmental Scientists and Specialists
- Farmers, Ranchers, and Other Agricultural Managers
- Microbiologists
- Veterinarians
- Zoologists and Wildlife Biologists

Employment Trend,
Projected 2016–26

Life scientists: 10%

Total, all occupations: 7%

Agricultural and food scientists: 7%

Note: "All Occupations" includes all occupations in the U.S. Economy. Source: U.S. Bureau of Labor Statistics, Employment Projections program

Conversation With . . .
HILLARY MEHL, Ph.D.

Assistant Professor, Plant Pathology
Virginia Tech Tidewater
Agricultural Research & Extension Center
Plant Pathologist, 14 years

1. What was your individual career path in terms of education/training, entry-level job, or other significant opportunity?

From a young age, I was fascinated with all aspects of biology; my family would go hiking and camping and collect plants and insects and try to identify them. I majored in botany at Humboldt State University, then went straight into a Ph.D. program at the University of California Davis. I studied plant pathology, which combines my interests in plants, microbiology and fungal biology, and seeks practical ways to manage plant diseases and increase crop yields and quality. As a graduate student, I spent plenty of time in the lab, but I also interacted with growers to identify problems in their crops and conducted field research in grower's fields.

My post-doc was with the U.S. Department of Agriculture in a lab located at the University of Arizona, where I researched biological control of aflatoxin, a toxin produced by a fungus that contaminates food and feed crops. My job here at Virginia Tech is a combination of research and working through the extension service to present the knowledge we gain from research to growers and consultants so they can use it in practice, often through our publications or crop meetings.

I'm working on field crops such as peanuts, cotton, soybeans, small grains and corn, and looking at disease management approaches that combine the use of disease-resistant crops, chemical control, and different cropping practices that can help minimize disease. I'm trying to understand the biology of specific fungal pathogens so we can better understand what they are, what they're doing to plants, and how we can better control them. For example, we're finding strains of frogeye leaf spot of soybean that are resistant to certain fungicides and are trying to find alternative ways to control the disease.

2. What are the most important skills and/or qualities for someone in your profession?

Plant pathology aims to solve real-world problems, so a plant pathologist needs to listen to the needs and concerns of growers and effectively communicate solutions, both verbally and in writing. In addition, analytical skills and curiosity are important to analyze data, make careful observations, and ask good questions. A plant pathologist who does what I do needs to enjoy being outdoors, working in different weather extremes, and traveling to locations with different field conditions.

3. What do you wish you had known going into this profession?

I feel lucky that I got to do what I wanted to do, but there are only so many jobs in academia. It would be beneficial to be aware of other opportunities as an undergraduate so that scientists can train accordingly, rather than go through a doctoral program—where the emphasis is on academic jobs—and find themselves without necessary skills for industry. Knowing this would have given me additional perspective into the field of plant pathology.

4. Are there many job opportunities in your profession? In what specific areas?

A variety of job opportunities are available in academia, industry, and government. In academia, positions include teaching, research, and extension services, and typically require either an M.S. degree (e.g. extension agents, research technicians) or a Ph.D. (researcher, professor, extension specialist). Industry jobs can be in small companies or big corporations, and can range from work as a private consultant who advises growers to a technical representative or researcher working for a chemical or seed company. Federal and state positions may include working for a regulatory agency or conducting research in a government lab.

5. How do you see your profession changing in the next five years? What role will technology play in those changes, and what skills will be required?

As food safety and security become an increasingly global issue, the need for agricultural scientists, including plant pathologists, will increase, but the focus of the work will be more international. Thus, the ability to communicate with and transfer technologies to other countries, especially those in the developing world, will be increasingly important.

6. What do you enjoy most about your job? What do you enjoy least about your job?

I most enjoy solving problems through careful observation, experiments, and analyses, as well as coming up with solutions to growers' problems and helping to improve plant disease management. I least enjoy the times I am unable to come up with solutions—at least not right away—but in the end, these challenges keep the job interesting.

7. Can you suggest a valuable "try this" for students considering a career in your profession?

High school students can look for opportunities at agricultural extension services, which are usually run by states. Undergraduate students at research universities should be able to find ample opportunities to work in a lab or assist with field work. Private industry offers internships. You could also get experience helping out on a farm for the summer.

SELECTED SCHOOLS

Many colleges and universities offer programs in agricultural science; a variety of them also have concentrations in food science. Some of the more prominent schools in this field are listed below.

Cornell University
Ithaca, New York 14850
Phone: (607) 254-4636
www.cornell.edu

Harvard University
Massachusetts Hall
Cambridge, Massachusetts 02138
Phone: (617) 495-1000
www.harvard.edu

Rutgers State University
96 Davidson Road
Piscataway Township, NJ 08854
Phone: (973) 353-1766
www.rutgers.edu

Tufts University
Medford, Massachusetts 02155
Phone: (617) 628-5000
www.tufts.edu

University of California, Davis
1 Shields Avenue
Davis, California 95616
Phone: (530) 752-1011
www.ucdavis.edu

University of Florida
201 Criser Hall
Gainesville, Florida 32611
Phone: (352) 392-3261
www.ufl.edu

University of Illinois, Urbana, Champaign
601 East. John Street
Champaign, Illinois 61820-5711
Phone: (217) 333-1000
www.illinois.edu

University of Massachusetts, Amherst
Amherst, MA 01002-01003
Phone: (413) 545-0111
www.umass.edu

University of Minnesota, Twin Cities
100 Church Street SE
Minneapolis, Minnesota 55455-0213
Phone: (612) 625-5000
www.umn.edu

University of Wisconsin, Madison
500 Lincoln Drive
Madison, Wisconsin 53708
Phone: (608) 263-2400
www.wisc.edu

MORE INFORMATION

**American Society for
Horticultural Science**
1018 Duke Street
Alexandria, VA 22314-2851
703.836.4606
www.ashs.org

**American Society of Agronomy
Career Development &
Placement Services**
5585 Guilford Road
Madison, WI 53711
608.273.8080
www.agronomy.org

**Council for Agricultural Science
and Technology**
4420 W. Lincoln Way
Ames, IA 50014-3447
515.292.2125
www.cast-science.org

Food and Drug Administration
10903 New Hampshire Avenue
Silver Springs, MD 20993
888.463.6332
www.fda.gov

**Institute of Food and
Agricultural Sciences**
P.O. Box 110180
Gainesville, FL 32611-0180
352.392.1971
www.ifas.ufl.edu

Institute of Food Technologists
525 W. Van Buren, Suite 1000
Chicago, IL 60607
312.782.8348
www.ift.org

**Soil and Water Conservation
Society**
945 SW Ankeny Road
Ankeny, IA 50021
515.289.2331
www.swcs.org

U.S. Department of Agriculture
Natural Resources Conservation
Service
14th and Independence Avenue SW
Washington, DC 20250
202.720.3210
www.nrcs.usda.gov

Animal Caretakers

Snapshot

Career Cluster(s): Agriculture, Food & Natural Resources, Hospitality & Tourism

Interests: Training and grooming animals, spending time outdoors, solving problems, communicating with people

Earnings (Median Pay): $22,230 per year; $10.69 per hour

Job Growth: Much faster than average

OVERVIEW

Sphere of Work

Animal caretakers tend to the needs of mammals, birds, fish, amphibians, and reptiles for various nonprofit organizations, research facilities, and private businesses, as well as for individuals. Animal caretaking encompasses many job titles and occupational specialties, including trainers, groomers, pet sitters, aquarists, zookeepers or animal keepers, veterinary assistants, and attendants in animal shelters, pet shops, and kennels.

Work Environment

Animal caretakers work in zoos, kennels, pet stores, shelters, animal hospitals, wildlife sanctuaries, horse stables, grooming salons, and animal laboratories. Pet sitters usually attend to animals in private residences. Some caretakers travel between client homes or with their animals to special shows. Although some caretakers are limited to working either outside or inside, most divide their time between indoor and outdoor locations. Flexible schedules are common and hours might include nights, evenings, weekends, and/or holiday shifts.

Profile

Working Conditions: Work both Indoors and Outdoors

Physical Strength: Medium to Heavy Work

Education Needs: On-the-Job Training, High School Diploma or G.E.D., Technical Education, Apprenticeship

Licensure/Certification: Usually Not Required

Physical Abilities Not Required: N/A

Opportunities For Experience: Apprenticeship, Volunteer Work, Part Time Work

Holland Interest Score*: RCS

* See Appendix A

Occupation Interest

Animal caretaker positions attract people who respect animals and understand their particular needs and abilities. In exchange for performing hard physical labor and sometimes unpleasant tasks, animal caretakers gain insight into the unique behavior of animals. They need to be patient and kind yet firm in their treatment of animals. Prospective animal caretakers should be good at following schedules and directions, reading animal behavior, solving problems, and communicating with people.

A Day in the Life—Duties and Responsibilities

The two most common responsibilities of animal caregivers are feeding animals and cleaning their living environments. They feed animals according to guidelines set by veterinarians or other professionals, or the animals' owners. Most animals are given pre-packaged, formulated food, although some may be fed live prey such as rodents, insects, or other small animals. Some baby mammals must be fed by a bottle or dropper. Before cleaning a cage, stall, aquarium, or other enclosure, the animal caretaker typically removes the animal and places it in another safe location. The habitat is then emptied of debris and sprayed, wiped, mopped, or scrubbed with a strong disinfectant

and/or detergent. After rinsing and drying, the caretaker applies a
fresh layer of bedding and/or replaces heat lamps, lights, toys, water
bottles, and other equipment. In addition to cages, animal caretakers
must clean carriers, dog runs, quarantine areas, medical treatment
areas, and other supplies and rooms that may become contaminated.

Bathing, grooming, exercising, and socializing are also typical
components of animal care. Caretakers may walk dogs, ride horses, or
observe mice scurrying through special mazes, which are often among
the greatest rewards of the work.

Some animal caretakers assist professional trainers or train animals
themselves for educational, entertainment, security, and medical
purposes. They also transport animals to shows, animal hospitals,
and other locations. Depending on training and work setting, animal
caretakers may perform health-care tasks, such as dressing wounds
and administering medications. They are also sometimes involved
with the death of animals or assist with euthanasia.

When not working directly with animals, animal caretakers often
keep records, maintain inventories of food and supplies, and greet
customers or give educational presentations.

Duties and Responsibilities

- Watering and feeding animals
- Washing and grooming animals
- Leading animals between living areas and other locations
- Exercising animals
- Administering prescribed medications/vitamins
- Assisting in the transport of animals
- Maintaining cleanliness of animal living spaces

OCCUPATION SPECIALTIES

Animal Keepers

Animal keepers feed, water, and clean the quarters of the birds and animals in zoos, circuses, and menageries. They prepare the food to be given to the animals and add vitamins and medication to the food.

Animal Trainers

Animal trainers train animals for riding, security, performance, obedience, or assisting people with disabilities. They familiarize animals with human voices and contact, and they teach animals to respond to commands.

Animal-Nursery Workers

Animal-nursery workers care for newborn and young animals in a zoo nursery and exhibit area. They prepare the liquid formula and other foods for the animals and standard diets for mothers and newborns according to the requirements of the species.

Kennel Attendants

Kennel attendants maintain dog kennels and assist trainers in teaching dogs to be obedient, guide the blind, hunt, track, or work as police dogs.

Pet Shop Attendants

Pet shop attendants show pets to customers, order and sell supplies, and keep sales records.

Pet Sitters

Pet sitters work with clients' pets in their homes, feeding, walking, and otherwise tending to them as requested by the client.

Stable Attendants

Stable attendants exercise animals regularly, polish saddles and bridles, and assist with horseshoeing. They may also harness, saddle, and unsaddle horses as well as rub them down after exercise periods.

Aquarists

Aquarists attend fish and other aquatic life in aquarium exhibits. They also take water samples for laboratory analysis and maintain records of numbers and kinds of fish.

WORK ENVIRONMENT

Physical Environment

Animals and their environments often come with strong odors or noises. Animal caretakers are at some risk for diseases, bites, scratches, or kicks from animals, and they can be exposed to harsh cleaning chemicals, germicides, and insecticides. The work may be physically demanding, requiring heavy lifting, standing for long periods, and regular bending and kneeling. Some caretakers might also find the work emotionally difficult at times.

Relevant Skills and Abilities

Interpersonal/Social Skills
- Being able to work independently
- Communicating with others

Organization & Management Skills
- Being reliable
- Following instructions
- Performing routine work

Work Environment Skills
- Working with animals

Human Environment

Many animal caretakers spend as much time working with humans as they do animals. Most report to a supervisor, director, or manager, and interact with volunteers and various staff members, such as veterinarians, research scientists, and professional groomers or trainers. Self-employed pet sitters interact with their clients and household staff. Caretakers who work in animal shelters and commercial settings also interact with the public. Animal trainers and attendants in zoos, public aquariums, and marine parks may stage live demonstrations for audiences.

Technological Environment

The level of technological sophistication varies with the type of facility. Some caretakers work in fully equipped offices with computerized feeding schedules and high-tech security systems. Many caretakers also use hand and power tools to maintain cages or other animal environments. Some animal caretakers drive wagons, trucks, vans, or cars to transport animals.

EDUCATION, TRAINING, AND ADVANCEMENT

High School/Secondary

A high school diploma or its equivalent is required for most jobs. A vocational course in animal science, usually offered through agricultural education programs, will provide a suitable foundation for some animal caretaker jobs; however, students interested in becoming a zookeeper, aquarist, or veterinary technician must follow a college-preparatory program. Important courses include biology, health, English, and speech communication. Volunteer or part-time work in an animal shelter, veterinary office, pet store, kennel, or farm, or pet sitting for friends and neighbors will provide the experience desired by many employers. Students should also consider 4-H and similar extracurricular opportunities that build familiarity with animals and their care.

Suggested High School Subjects

- Agricultural Education
- Biology
- English

Famous First

The first animal humane society in the United States was the American Society for the Prevention of Cruelty to Animals (ASPCA), founded in New York City in 1866. Its founder, Henry Bergh, had been a member of a U.S. diplomatic mission in St. Petersburg, Russia, where he witnessed carriage drivers beating their horses. Upon his return to America he organized the ASPCA, patterned after the Royal SPCA in London.

College/Postsecondary

Most animal caretakers are trained on the job. Continuing education courses in animal care, offered through community colleges, vocational schools, and various animal and veterinary organizations, provide additional skills and knowledge and might be necessary to attain certification for more advanced positions. Business courses will help those who intend to open a kennel or operate a professional pet-sitting business. A bachelor's degree in zoology or biology is usually the minimum requirement for professional zookeepers and public aquarium specialists, while an associate's degree is sometimes the minimum requirement for animal laboratory caretakers and veterinary technicians.

Related College Majors
- Agricultural Production & Management
- Animal Science
- Biology
- Environmental Science
- Fisheries Sciences & Management
- Zoology

Adult Job Seekers

Adults with the appropriate educational background and firsthand experience as pet owners, animal foster caretakers, or volunteers in pet shelters or rehabilitation centers may be qualified for many animal caretaker jobs. Pet sitting and grooming may offer the most flexible schedules. Interested landowners might be in a good position to establish a kennel or boarding stables. The necessary skills and knowledge for animal care can be learned from online courses, as well as evening or weekend continuing education courses. Qualified animal caretakers should apply directly to companies and organizations that have posted open positions.

New animal caretakers are often limited to cleaning cages and feeding animals but are given additional responsibilities after gaining experience. Animal caretakers can move into supervisory or management positions with additional experience or education.

Professional Certification and Licensure

There are no licenses required for animal caretakers, although the owners of kennels, laboratories, and rescue shelters are regulated. Professional certification is available from the National Association of Professional Pet Sitters (NAPPS), American Association for Laboratory Animal Science (AALAS), and other professional associations. Most certifications require completion of an exam, which in some cases includes a practical section.

Additional Requirements

A driver's license is required for many jobs. Animal caretakers also need to be in good health, with good eyesight and hearing. Familiarity with the Animal Welfare Act (AWA) is also beneficial.

Fun Fact

Veterinary technicians have a higher-than-average rate of injury on the job, and it's not hard to imagine why. Sick or injured animals can get a bit snippy during treatment, most often when being held, restrained, or cleaned. Vet techs are trained to identify aggressive behavior, which can help prevent injury.

Source: veterinary-technician-colleges.com

EARNINGS AND ADVANCEMENT

The median annual wage for animal trainers was $27,690 in May 2016. The median wage is the wage at which half the workers in an occupation earned more than that amount and half earned less. The lowest 10 percent earned less than $18,740, and the highest 10 percent earned more than $58,050.

The median annual wage for nonfarm animal caretakers was $21,990 in May 2016. The lowest 10 percent earned less than $17,550, and the highest 10 percent earned more than $35,860.

In May 2016, the median annual wages for animal trainers in the top industries in which they worked were as follows

Arts, entertainment, and recreation	$32,470
Retail trade	$21,800

In May 2016, the median annual wages for nonfarm animal caretakers in the top industries in which they worked were as follows:

Other personal services	$21,910
Social advocacy organizations	$21,230
Professional, scientific, and technical services	$21,220
Retail trade	$20,820

Animals may need care around the clock in facilities such as kennels, animal shelters, and stables that operate 24 hours a day. Caretakers often work irregular hours, including evenings, weekends, and holidays.

About 2 in 5 nonfarm animal caretakers worked part time in 2016.

Median annual wages, May 2016

Total, all occupations: $37,040

Animal trainers: $27,690

Personal care and service occupations: $22,710

Animal care and service workers: $22,230

Nonfarm animal caretakers: $21,990

Note: "All Occupations" includes all occupations in the U.S. Economy. Source: U.S. Bureau of Labor Statistics, Occupational Employment Statistics

EMPLOYMENT AND OUTLOOK

Overall employment of animal care and service workers is projected to grow 20 percent from 2016 to 2026, much faster than the average for all occupations.

Many people consider their pets to be a part of their family and are willing to pay more for pet care than pet owners have in the past. As more households include companion pets, employment of animal care and service workers in the pet services industry will continue to grow. Employment of animal care and service workers in kennels, grooming shops, and pet stores is projected to increase in order to keep up with the growing demand for animal care.

Overall job prospects should be good. The majority of job openings will result from the need to replace workers who leave the occupation.

Percent change in employment
Projected 2016-26

Occupational Title	Employment, 2016	Projected Employment, 2026	Change, 2016-26	
			Percent	Numeric
Animal care and service workers	296,400	355,100	20	58,700
Animal trainers	54,900	60,700	11	5,900
Nonfarm animal caretakers	241,500	294,400	22	52,800

Source: U.S. Bureau of Labor Statistics, Employment Projections program

Related Occupations
- Agricultural Workers
- Farmers, Ranchers, and Other Agricultural Managers
- Veterinarians
- Veterinary Assistants and Laboratory Animal Caretakers
- Veterinary Technologists and Technicians
- Zoologists and Wildlife Biologists

Conversation With . . .
LEXA ELWELL

Veterinary Assistant, 8 years
Tidewater Veterinary Hospital
Charlotte Hall, MD

1. What was your individual career path in terms of education/training, entry-level job, or other significant opportunity?

I didn't go to college but had jobs like waiting tables or being a receptionist. I stumbled across my vet hospital's ad eight years ago. I wasn't looking for a job in the animal field but I love dogs and cats and am the type who always wants to be around animals. Like everyone, I wanted to be a veterinarian when I was little. But I didn't have an interest in doing more school; I'm more of a hands-on person. I think this is what I'm meant to do in life. I wake up every day wondering what's going to happen. A veterinary assistant is someone who did not go to school to get a degree in the veterinary field and has to work under a doctor.

2. What are the most important skills and/or qualities for someone in your profession?

I work for six doctors and that gets demanding. You need to think fast, remember routine things, be organized, and be ready for what the day brings. We often have to work fast, especially in a crisis. Say a dog is not breathing. There's no time to prepare. You have to be on top of things.

3. What do you wish you had known going into this profession?

Since I'm not a licensed or certified veterinary technician, I have to do things like injections under the supervision of a doctor. Still, I wish I could do mathematics off the top of my head to figure out injection doses and those types of needs like the veterinarians can do.

4. Are there many job opportunities in your profession? In what specific areas?

It's hard for me to say, but from what I've seen people seem to stay in their veterinary assistant jobs for awhile. It really does take a special kind of person; you don't get paid a lot and you need to have a heart for the animals. If you have a love of animals,

I would suggest checking with vet hospitals in your area to explore the possible opportunities.

5. **How do you see your profession changing in the next five years? What role will technology play in those changes, and what skills will be required?**

There might be some new machines for diagnostic testing and they are always coming up with new ways to handle patient records. But this is a job where human care for the animals is not going to be replaced.

6. **What do you like most about your job? What do you like least about your job?**

Part of the job is that every day is different, and I like the adrenaline rush of an emergency. For example, we recently did a C-section for a dog, which is a pretty quick thing because you don't want the mom under anesthesia very long. The doctor does the surgery and usually a couple of us are assisting; the doctor hands each veterinary assistant a puppy and we get the placenta off, make sure it's breathing, and get the doctor involved if it's not. Another vet is around in case something additional needs to be done. We did one the other night. Unfortunately the dog had one puppy on its own that died but we ended up doing the C-section and she successfully birthed five more puppies.

My least favorite part of the job is when that dog, cat, or horse has been under our care for a long time—animals I have a relationship with—and we have to put them down. I also don't like being the person watching an animal as the owner drags his feet while the animal suffers, even though I know it's difficult to decide to let your animal go.

7. **Can you suggest a valuable "try this" for students considering a career in your profession?**

We have people come in and out of our clinic to shadow the doctors and staff. The biggest problem I notice they have—and not just the shadowers, but anyone new to the situation—is the first time they see an animal cut open. That's the test. If you can handle it, this job might be for you.

SELECTED SCHOOLS

Many agricultural, technical, and community colleges offer programs in animal science. Interested students are advised to consult with their school guidance counselor or to research area postsecondary schools and training programs. For those interested in pursuing a bachelor's degree, refer to the list of schools in the "Wildlife Biologist" chapter in the present volume.

MORE INFORMATION

American Association for Laboratory Animal Science (AALAS)
9190 Crestwyn Hills Drive
Memphis, TN 38125
901.754.8620
www.aalas.org

American Humane Association
63 Inverness Drive East
Englewood, CO 80112
800.227.4645
www.americanhumane.org

American Society for the Prevention of Cruelty to Animals (ASPCA)
424 East 92nd Street
New York, NY 10128-6804
212.876.7700
www.aspca.org

Association of Zoos and Aquariums
8403 Colesville Road, Suite 710
Silver Spring, MD 20910-3314
301.562.0777
www.aza.org

Humane Society of the United States
Companion Animals Division
2100 L Street, NW
Washington, DC 20037
202.452.1100
www.hsus.org

International Marine Animal Trainer's Association
1200 S. Lake Shore Drive
Chicago, IL 60605
312-692-3193
www.imata.org

National Association of Professional Pet Sitters (NAPPS)
15000 Commerce Parkway
Suite C
Mount Laurel, NJ 08054
856.439.0324
www.petsitters.org

Sally Driscoll/Editor

Botanists

Snapshot

Career Cluster(s): Agriculture, Food & Natural Resources, Science, Technology, Engineering & Mathematics

Interests: Plant life, plant biology, environmental studies, nature, working outdoors

Earnings (Median Pay): $61,180 per year, $33.31 per hour

Job Growth: As fast as average

OVERVIEW

Sphere of Work

Botanists are scientists who study and conduct basic and applied research on plants and plant characteristics, such as physiology and reproduction, as well as the environments in which plants grow, including soil, climate, and elevation. Some botanists specialize in the study of plant life processes or cultivate useful plants for food, while others focus on the structure of plants, species hierarchy, or how different plants react to adverse environmental conditions. Botanists are employed by universities,

government agencies, and private organizations. In addition to their research and study of plant life, botanists frequently share their knowledge with the general public at botanical gardens and other venues.

Work Environment

Botanists study plant life and the environment in which they grow. Much of the work that is performed is conducted in the field, over time, and often in remote locations. Field botanists are accustomed to taking long walks, hikes, or drives in order to view research specimens. Botanists also spend time in the laboratory, conducting experiments and analyzing data. Many botanists are university and college professors, working in offices at institutions of higher learning. Additionally, a large number of botanists work in public settings, such as botanical gardens, zoos, and museums.

Profile

Working Conditions: Work both Indoors and Outdoors
Physical Strength: Light Work
Education Needs: Bachelor's Degree, Master's Degree, Doctoral Degree
Licensure/Certification: Usually Not equired
Physical Abilities Not Required: No Heavy Labor
Opportunities For Experience: Internship
Holland Interest Score*: IRS

* See Appendix A

Occupation Interest

Botanists enjoy the study of plant species and how plants interact with their environments. Because of their knowledge of trees, algae, and many other forms of plant life, botanists are often consulted in the study of how pollution and other elements affect the air, ground, and water. Economic botanists research the effectiveness of certain plant species in fighting human hunger and disease, as well as supplementing a healthy diet. Botanists contribute to the understanding and stewardship of a wide range of important industries, such as agriculture, conservation, and forestry. First and foremost, botanists are individuals who love nature and the outdoors, and as such, they spend a great deal of time during their careers working outdoors, usually away from urban settings.

A Day in the Life—Duties and Responsibilities

Botanists conduct basic or applied research on trees, mosses, flowering plants, fungi, algae, and other types of plants. In basic research, inquiry is driven by curiosity; in applied research, study is geared toward testing a specific theory or advancing the development of a product. Applied research has a specific purpose.

In order to conduct their research, whether it is basic or applied, many botanists live in remote locations for long periods of time. During this time, they will take samples, study growth and distribution patterns, and take environmental readings. When they return to the laboratory or their base of operations, botanists will carefully study samples and data and write reports and scholarly papers to share their findings with the scientific community. Many botanists work for non-profit institutions such as universities and scientific foundations. To fund their research, they must spend time applying for grants, fellowships, and other private and public funding programs.

Many botanists are also employed by government agencies, such as the U.S. Department of Agriculture and the U.S. Department of the Interior. In these settings, botanists help the government gain a better understanding of current trends in environmental degradation, the impact of droughts and crop disease outbreaks, and other environmental incidents and trends.

A large number of botanists work in museums, botanical gardens, and zoological institutions. These botanists present scientific information about plant life to daily visitors, helping the general public to better understand the natural world. Botanists who are members of university faculties present this type of information to undergraduate and graduate students, conduct classes and seminars, and perform independent research.

Duties and Responsibilities

- Conducting research in the field and in laboratories and greenhouses
- Observing and analyzing plant specimens
- Examining environmental conditions, including soil, water, and air quality
- Understanding plant habitats and potential threats to those habitats
- Being knowledgeable about plant diseases and methods for managing them
- Publishing research papers and teaching students

OCCUPATION SPECIALTIES

Plant Pathologists

Plant pathologists conduct research into the nature and control of plant diseases and the decay of plant products.

Plant Scientists

Plant scientists work to improve crop yields and give advice to food and crop developers about techniques that could enhance production efforts. They develop ways to control pests and weeds safely and effectively.

Paleobotanists

Paleobotanists study fossilized remains of plants and animals found in geological formations to trace evolution and development of past life.

Mycologists

Mycologists study all types of fungi to discover those that are useful to medicine, agriculture, and industry.

WORK ENVIRONMENT

Physical Environment

Botanists conduct frequent research, examining species in forests, in farm country, and other locations. A great deal of time is also spent in the laboratory, studying samples and analyzing data. Additionally, botanists often work in classroom settings, museums, botanical gardens, and similar venues, where they present to students and the general public.

Relevant Skills and Abilities

Analytical Skills
- Analyzing specimens and data

Communication Skills
- Speaking and writing effectively

Interpersonal/Social Skills
- Being able to work independently and as a member of a team

Organization & Management Skills
- Organizing information or materials
- Paying attention to and handling details

Technical Skills
- Working with tools and equipment
- Working with your hands

Work Environment Skills
- Working outdoors

Human Environment

In the field, botanists work in teams with other scientists and students. In the laboratory, botanists interact with equipment technicians and other scientists. Government officials, farmers, and foresters, and the general public sometimes contact botanists with questions about local plant and environmental issues.

Technological Environment

Botanists use laboratory analytical equipment such as microscopes, spectrometers, and photometers. They use cameras and similar surveillance equipment to monitor plant life remotely and to document research. Computers and research-related software, such as word processing, spreadsheet, and presentation programs, are typically used to share research results and theories with other scientists.

EDUCATION, TRAINING, AND ADVANCEMENT

High School/Secondary

High school students interested in careers in botany should take classes in biology, chemistry, physics, and geography. Math skills are useful as well, including algebra, calculus, and geometry. Basic writing classes help future scientists learn how to write research papers, a skill they will need throughout their careers.

Suggested High School Subjects

- Algebra
- Biology
- Calculus
- Chemistry
- Earth Science
- English
- Geometry
- Physics
- Science
- Social Studies
- Trigonometry

Famous First

The first DNA bank for plant species was the Tropical Plant DNA Bank, started in 1999 as a joint project between the Fairchild Tropical Botanical Gardens of Coral Gables, Florida, and Florida International University. The bank collects, stores, analyzes, and shares DNA samples from tropical plants worldwide, including more than one thousand species of palm.

College/Postsecondary

Botanists need to obtain, at minimum, a bachelor's degree in botany, biology, or a related natural science. Some individuals supplement their scientific coursework with studies in other disciplines, such as engineering, environmental studies, and agriculture. Most botanists obtain a doctorate in botany, receiving training in plant taxonomy and physiology, as well as other specific subfields of botany. Doctoral work is usually followed by independent research (a post-doctoral position at a college or university).

Related College Majors
- Biology
- Botany
- Ecology/Environmental Science
- Forestry
- Wildlife & Wildlands Science & Management
- Zoology

Adult Job Seekers

No matter the phase of life an individual decides to pursue a career in botany, all botanists must follow the same academic path. For those with the appropriate academic credentials, they may apply directly to universities with open faculty positions. They may also apply to government agency openings, such as the Department of the Interior, or to private organizations posting openings. Furthermore, botanists may join professional botany organizations, such as the Botanical Society of America, where they network with peers and other scientific professionals. They may also find employment by connecting with fellow botany enthusiasts through related associations such as the Torrey Botanical Society.

Professional Certification and Licensure

Botanists seeking positions with government agencies may be required to obtain professional licenses and certification, such as a professional engineer's license or a certificate to operate specific research equipment. Consult credible professional associations within the field, and follow professional debate as to the relevancy and value of any certification program.

Additional Requirements

Botanists should be excellent critical thinkers, with an ability to analyze complex concepts and a strong interest in understanding the natural world. Botanists should also have an understanding of the government regulatory environment, as well as an appreciation of the industries affected by their work (such as agriculture and forestry). They should have strong verbal and written communication skills, and be comfortable with public speaking. Because botanists conduct frequent field research, they should be physically fit, as they may need to hike great distances in challenging weather and terrain to study certain species.

Fun Fact

Plants are amazing! A mature strawberry can have as many as 200 seeds, and is the only plant that bears its seeds on its exterior. An average pomengranate has around 1000 seeds.

Source: www.makemegenius.com

EARNINGS AND ADVANCEMENT

The median annual wage for foresters was $58,700 in May 2016. The lowest 10 percent earned less than $39,100, and the highest 10 percent earned more than $82,400.

In May 2016, the median annual wages for conservation scientists in the top industries in which they worked were as follows:

Federal government, excluding postal service	$73,380
Professional, scientific, and technical services	$66,120
Social advocacy organizations	$61,450
State government, excluding education and hospitals	$54,070
Local government, excluding education and hospitals	$49,700

In May 2016, the median annual wages for foresters in the top industries in which they worked were as follows:

Federal government, excluding postal service	$63,660
Local government, excluding education and hospitals	$55,820
State government, excluding education and hospitals	$53,310

Most conservation scientists and foresters work full time and have a standard work schedule.

Median annual wages, May 2016

Life scientists: $71,950

Conservation scientists: $61,810

Conservation scientists and foresters: $60,610

Foresters: $58,700

Total, all occupations: $37,040

Note: "All Occupations" includes all occupations in the U.S. Economy. Source: U.S. Bureau of Labor Statistics, Occupational Employment Statistics

EMPLOYMENT AND OUTLOOK

Employment of conservation scientists and foresters is projected to grow 6 percent from 2016 to 2026, about as fast as the average for all occupations.

Most employment growth is expected to be in state and local government-owned forest lands, particularly in the western United States. In recent years, the prevention and suppression of wildfires has become the primary concern for government agencies managing forests and rangelands. Governments are likely to hire more foresters as the number of forest fires increases and more people live on or near forest lands. Both the development of previously unused lands and changing weather conditions have contributed to increasingly devastating and costly fires.

In addition, continued demand for American timber and wood pellets is expected to drive employment growth for conservation scientists and foresters. Jobs in private forests are expected to grow alongside demand for timber and pellets.

The need to replace retiring workers should create opportunities for conservation scientists and foresters. Job prospects will likely be best for conservation scientists and foresters who have a strong understanding of Geographic Information System (GIS) technology, remote sensing, and other software tools.

Percent change in employment
Projected 2016-26

Life scientists: 10%

Total, all occupations: 7%

Conservation scientists: 7%

Conservation scientists and foresters: 6%

Foresters: 5%

Note: "All Occupations" includes all occupations in the U.S. Economy. Source: U.S. Bureau of Labor Statistics, Employment Projections program

Related Occupations
- Conservation scientists and foresters
- Conservation scientists
- Foresters

Conversation With . . .
CHRISTOPHER T. MARTINE

David Burpee Professor of Plant Genetics and Research
Bucknell University, 9 years
Botanist, 18 years

1. What was your individual career path in terms of education/training, entry-level job, or other significant opportunity?

As a child I spent a lot of time outdoors but I didn't really understand that was something I could do as a career until a couple of years into college. I went to Rutgers University and took two courses that really inspired me: dendrology, where we'd identify trees and shrubs, and field ecology, where we went into a different habitat each week. After college I worked for the New Jersey Forest Service and the Mercer County Soil Conservation District and most of what I did was teach kids outside. That really helped me to figure out I loved teaching about plants. Then I did my Master's, then my PhD, and that's when I went from being a person who appreciated nature to a person who wanted to discover new things about it, and that plants were the group of things I really wanted to spend my time working on. I realized how much of the world was right there, right beyond my understanding.

2. What are the most important skills and/or qualities for someone in your profession?

You need to possess a patience and a willingness to unplug and carefully watch things because that's what biological research requires. Also, having a passion and enthusiasm for your work is important.

3. What do you wish you had known going into this profession?

I wish I had realized there are many paths to the same career goal. It's OK to not follow the exact steps you think everybody else has had to follow. Eventually, I learned this lesson by living it.

4. Are there many job opportunities in your profession? In what specific areas?

Botanists, who understand crop development and agriculture, are in the lead in terms of figuring out how to feed more people worldwide. The planet is also facing a major biodiversity crisis and there is a need to figure out what species are out there, how they all help to maintain the global ecosystem, and how we can best conserve their habitats. The fact that plants are the backbone of most biological systems means there are lots of opportunities for botanists to make a contribution. This takes a certain level of training and a certain ability to see things, but that's perfectly within reach of most people – and then the options open up. There are botanists, like me, who choose to become professors and academic researchers, but there are many other options. Across the U.S., many agencies at the county, state and federal level are doing on-the-ground management of natural habitat, have a mission to protect landscapes, and employ lots of people with botany backgrounds. Non-governmental organizations like The Nature Conservancy are great starting points for internships and seasonal jobs that can help someone get their feet wet; they also permanently employ scores of botanists.

5. How do you see your profession changing in the next five years? What role will technology play in those changes, and what skills will be required?

My work involves genetics and DNA; that area of study is only going to become more important. Having a background in biochemistry and in lab science will help anyone develop a career in botany. That ability to do high tech lab research in addition to being a natural historian who understands how real organisms work, is a perfect combination for folks hoping to make a career as a botanist.

6. What do you enjoy most about your job? What do you enjoy least about your job?

I love what I do. That's good because as a botanist, I'm at work every day—even if I'm working in the garden, or going to the grocery store—and I am seeing plants and observing nature. As a professor of botany, I love teaching and I really like to work with young people. There's a certain level of enthusiasm young people bring to my job every day. I also really appreciate that I get to do biological and botanical research. In the last five or six years, I've been part of teams that discovered six new species. It never gets stale.

On the difficult side, academic research can be a high pressure environment, particularly early in your career. It takes five to eight years to get your PhD and one to three years to get a post-doc before you can become a professor. Then you're trying to get a professorship in a tight job market. You have to be willing to put in the time and work on your skill set. It's totally worth it if you get there but it's not easy and it can be high stakes once you do arrive because of a grueling tenure process and continuous pressure to write grants to attract research money. And you won't become filthy rich. Being a professor and being a botanist is not for somebody who wants to acquire great wealth. You make a good living and enjoy a wonderful lifestyle, but it's a job you do because it's what you want to do.

7. Can you suggest a valuable "try this" for students considering a career in your profession?

Start a garden. Put seeds in the ground, grow some plants, watch them, and see if you can gather a harvest from them. If you're not hooked by this, perhaps botany isn't for you.

I do a lot of field work in the Australian Outback. So when I go out to find the plants I'm looking for, I am in a tent, sometimes for weeks at a time. Have outside experiences and see if that's the sort of thing you would enjoy doing for your career.

I also do a lot of lab work, and for that, it makes sense to work in a lab. Attempt to do an independent study with your high school teacher. Generate a hypothesis, develop a good experiment, collect data, and then synthesize the data. You need to be able to do that in any science field.

SELECTED SCHOOLS

Most colleges and universities have bachelor's degree programs in biology, often with a specialization in plant biology. The student may also gain an initial grounding in the field at an agricultural, technical, or community college. For advanced positions, a doctoral degree is commonly obtained. Below are listed some of the more prominent graduate schools in this field.

Cornell University
Graduate School
Caldwell Hall
Ithaca, NY 14853
607.255.5820
www.gradschool.cornell.edu

Iowa State University
Enrollment Services Center
Ames, IA 50011
800.262.3810
admissions.iastate.edu

Michigan State University
479 W. Circle Drive, Room 110
East Lansing, MI 48824
517.353.3220
www.msu.edu

Penn State University
Plant Biology Program
101 Life Sciences Building
University Park, PA 16802
814.865.8165
bio.psu.edu/graduate-portal

Purdue University
Botany and Plant Biology
915 W. State Street
West Lafayette, IN 47907
765.494.4614
ag.purdue.edu/btny

University of Arizona
Graduate College
Administration 322, PO Box 2106
Tucson, AZ 85721
520.621.3471
grad.arizona.edu

University of California, Berkeley
Graduate Division
Sproul Hall, 3rd Floor
Berkeley, CA 94704
510.642.7405
grad.berkeley.edu

University of California, Davis
250 Mrak Hall
One Shields Avenue
Davis, CA 95616
530.752.0650
gradstudies.ucdavis.edu

University of Missouri
Office of Research and Graduate Studies
210 Jesse Hall
Columbia, MO 65211
gradstudies.missouri.edu

University of Wisconsin
Graduate School
217 Bascom Hall
500 Lincoln Drive
Madison, WI 53706
608.262.2433
grad.wisc.edu

MORE INFORMATION

American Bryological and Lichenological Society
P.O. Box 7065
Lawrence, KS 66044-8897
785.843.1234
www.abls.org

American Phytopathological Society
3340 Pilot Knob Road
St. Paul, MN 55121-2097
651.454.7250
www.apsnet.org

American Society of Plant Biologists
15501 Monona Drive
Rockville, MD 20855-2768
301.251.0560
www.aspb.org

American Society of Plant Taxonomists
University of Wyoming
Department of Botany
1000 E. University Avenue
Laramie, WY 82071
307.766.2556
www.aspt.org

Botanical Society of America
P.O. Box 299
St. Louis, MO 63166-0299
314.577.9566
www.botany.org

Ecological Society of America
1990 M Street, NW, Suite 700
Washington, DC 20006-3915
202.833.8773
www.esa.org

Torrey Botanical Society
P.O. Box 7065
Lawrence, KS 66044-8897
800.627.0326
www.torreybotanical.org

U.S. Botanic Garden
245 First Street SW
Washington, DC 20024
202.225.8333
www.usbg.gov

U.S. Department of Agriculture
1400 Independence Avenue SW
Washington, DC 20250
202.720.2791
www.usda.gov

Michael Auerbach/Editor

Bulldozer & Construction Equipment Operators

Snapshot

Career Cluster(s): Agriculture, Food & Natural Resources, Architecture & Construction

Interests: Managing heavy equipment, working outdoors, working as part of a team

Earnings (Median pay): $45,040 per year; $21.65 per hour

Job Growth: Faster than average

OVERVIEW

Sphere of Work

A bulldozer or construction equipment operator works in the construction industry, driving and operating a heavy-duty tractor used to level ground and move large amounts of soil, rocks, sand, and other materials. A bulldozer may also be used to demolish buildings or other structures. Construction equipment operators are responsible for cleaning and maintaining bulldozers to ensure that they work properly and must at times identify mechanical malfunctions and carry out repairs.

Work Environment

Construction equipment operators work in a large variety of outdoor environments, in all climates and weather conditions. They perform duties at commercial, industrial, residential, and roadside jobsites. When performing roadwork, a bulldozer operator may be required to work on the side of a highway. Construction equipment operators are typically exposed to a high level of noise from the machines themselves as well as the ongoing work and must take precautions to avoid hearing damage and ensure effective communication with other workers. Construction jobsites present a number of additional hazards, so safety measures must always be enforced.

Profile

Working Conditions: Work Outdoors
Physical Strength: Heavy Work
Education Needs: On-The-Job Training, High School Diploma or G.E.D., High School Diploma with Technical Education, Apprenticeship
Licensure/Certification: Usually Not Required
Opportunities For Experience: Apprenticeship, Military Service
Holland Interest Score*: REC

* See Appendix A

Occupation Interest

Work as a bulldozer operator encompasses many tasks, including hauling, leveling, and excavating. Those interested in this profession should be adaptable to the variety of challenging tasks and should enjoy working outdoors and with a team. They also must be able to focus consistently on the job, as bulldozers can be dangerous.

A Day in the Life—Duties and Responsibilities

Prior to beginning any construction or demolition work, a bulldozer operator must first inspect the bulldozer to make sure all of the components are functioning properly. These components include levers, pedals, and the hydraulics that operate the blade. The blade, the large metal plate at the front of the bulldozer, is used to move, haul, or level materials. Depending on the job, a bulldozer may be equipped with a shovel or digging scoop rather than a blade. The bulldozer operator must next go over the day's tasks with the rest of the construction crew. Bulldozers move a large quantity of material and greatly alter the landscape, so significant coordination is required by the entire crew to ensure that nothing is done out of turn or incorrectly.

The bulldozer operator controls the movement of the machine using pedals similar to those of a car. The blade or scooper mechanism is controlled using a lever, also known as a joystick. If a bulldozer is being used to level a surface, the operator will lower the blade to the surface and slowly drive forward. This flattens the surface. For digging jobs, an operator will maneuver the blade or scooper mechanism to dig up and transport the materials to a designated spot. While carrying out these tasks, the operator must consistently meet safety standards.

Duties and Responsibilities

- Moving levers and pushing pedals to move the tractor and manipulate the blade
- Reshaping and distributing earth to raise or lower the ground to grade specifications
- Estimating the depth of cuts by the feel of levers and the stalling action of the engine
- Repairing tractors and attachments

OCCUPATION SPECIALTIES

Scarifier Operators

Scarifier Operators strictly operate a bulldozer for the purpose of loosening soil.

Angledozer Operators

Angledozer Operators drive a bulldozer equipped with a special angled blade attached to the front.

Crawler-Tractor Operators

Crawler-Tractor Operators drive a tractor that is specially equipped to move over rough or muddy ground.

Fine-Grade-Bulldozer Operators

Fine-Grade-Bulldozer Operators grade land to close specification.

Scraper Operators

Scraper Operators operate bulldozers for the purpose of scraping surface clay to determine the existence and types of clay deposits or to gather clay into piles in preparation for its removal to brick-and-tile manufacturing plants.

WORK ENVIRONMENT

Physical Environment

Construction equipment operators most frequently work at construction sites, which can be in commercial, industrial, or residential zones, or along roadways. These sites are often very loud due to the heavy machinery being used and may present additional hazards based on the nature of the construction being carried out.

Relevant Skills and Abilities

Interpersonal/Social Skills
- Working as a member of a team

Technical Skills
- Working with machines, tools or other objects

Unclassified Skills
- Using set methods and standards in your work

Work Environment Skills
- Working outdoors

Human Environment

Because construction equipment operators must coordinate and collaborate with other workers on jobsites in order to complete their work successfully, strong communication skills are essential. Construction equipment operators are usually required to check in with site managers and contractors daily.

Technological Environment

In addition to bulldozers, a bulldozer operator may be required to operate other pieces of heavy machinery. This may include road graders and trench excavators. An operator will also handle light safety equipment such as reflector vests and hardhats.

EDUCATION, TRAINING, AND ADVANCEMENT

High School/Secondary

Most employers require construction equipment operators to have completed high school or an equivalent degree program. Prospective construction equipment operators will benefit from high school courses in subjects such as geology and machine repair.

Suggested High School Subjects
- Building Trades & Carpentry
- Computer Fundamentals
- Construction
- Industrial Arts
- Electricity

Famous First

The traditional design of the bulldozer is made up of two parts, the blade and the tracks. The blade was originally pulled behind mules and oxen in order to plow the land, but in the early 1900s, Benjamin Holt of Stockton, CA created the first continuously moving tracks for a tractor known as the Caterpillar. The first real bulldozer, however, was created in the 1920s by James Cummings of Morrowville, KS. Meanwhile, the tracks that Holt had developed were used to create the first military tank!

College/Postsecondary

A number of schools offer specialized vocational programs in the operation of construction equipment. These courses typically provide students with several weeks of hands-on training by qualified instructors. Students are also instructed in the basics of surveying, project layout, and safety and maintenance. Some of these courses allow students to earn operator credentials from the National Center for Construction Education and Research.

Completion of an operation course at a vocational school may greatly increase an operator's ability to secure a job in the industry. An individual considering enrolling in such a course should research the school's reputation and credibility and consult established workers in the construction industry in regard to the relevance of any particular course.

Adult Job Seekers

An adult seeking to transition to a career as a bulldozer operator will benefit greatly from prior experience operating construction equipment or other heavy machinery. Adults with no background in the construction industry should consider applying for a specialized program at a vocational school. Such programs can properly train applicants and provide them with an easier transition into the industry.

Professional Certification and Licensure

Many construction equipment operators learn the trade through a formal apprenticeship. These programs commonly last for three to four years. During each year of the program, an apprentice is required to complete at least 144 hours of technical instruction and 2,000 hours of on-the-job training. The technical instruction commonly takes place in a classroom environment and focuses on operating procedures for specific equipment, safety and first aid, and maintenance. Apprentices typically learn to operate a variety of machines in addition to bulldozers.

Once on the job, apprentices perform basic tasks and learn how to use and maintain construction equipment. As they progress, apprentices eventually become able to operate machinery with less supervision. Once the apprenticeship is complete, a bulldozer operator is considered a journeyman worker and may perform duties without any supervision.

Construction equipment operators may be required to hold a commercial driver's license (CDL) in order to transport a bulldozer to a jobsite. A CDL allows an operator to drive a semitruck, a vehicle commonly used to haul construction equipment. Employers may be more likely to hire an operator who can transport as well as drive a bulldozer. The requirements for a CDL differ from state to state. In addition, some states have specific licenses for bulldozer operators.

Additional Requirements

A strong knowledge of mechanics and an ability to handle physically demanding tasks are essential to a bulldozer operator. Problem-solving skills are especially important, as construction equipment operators must at times identify and repair mechanical malfunctions while on-site.

Fun Fact

The Komatsu D575A is the world's largest bulldozer with a 1,150 horsepower engine that can move up to 125 cubic yards of material in a single pass.
Source: http://www.totalequipmentonlinetraining.com/freebies/bulldozer_fun_facts.pdf

EARNINGS AND ADVANCEMENT

The median annual wage for construction equipment operators was $45,040 in May 2016. The median wage is the wage at which half the workers in an occupation earned more than that amount and half earned less. The lowest 10 percent earned less than $29,030, and the highest 10 percent earned more than $79,700.

Median annual wages for construction equipment operators in May 2016 were as follows:

Pile-driver operators	$55,070
Operating engineers and other construction equipment operators	$45,890
Paving, surfacing, and tamping equipment operators	$38,970

In May 2016, the median annual wages for construction equipment operators in the top industries in which they worked were as follows:

Construction of buildings	$49,510
Heavy and civil engineering construction	$48,450
Mining, quarrying, and oil and gas extraction	$45,340
Specialty trade contractors	$44,560
Local government, excluding education and hospitals	$40,720

The starting pay for apprentices is usually between 60 percent and 70 percent of what fully trained operators make. They receive pay increases as they learn to operate more complex equipment.

Median annual wages, May 2016

Construction equipment operators: $45,040

Construction trades workers: $42,310

Total, all occupations: $37,040

Note: "All Occupations" includes all occupations in the U.S. Economy. Source: U.S. Bureau of Labor Statistics, Occupational Employment Statistics

EMPLOYMENT AND OUTLOOK

Construction equipment operators held about 426,600 jobs in 2016. Employment in the detailed occupations that make up construction equipment operators was distributed as follows:

Operating engineers and other construction equipment operators	371,100
Paving, surfacing, and tamping equipment operators	51,900
Pile-driver operators	3,700

The largest employers of construction equipment operators were as follows:

Heavy and civil engineering construction	29%
Specialty trade contractors	28%
Local government, excluding education and hospitals	14%
Mining, quarrying, and oil and gas extraction	6%
Construction of buildings	5%

Construction equipment operators work in nearly every weather condition, although rain or extremely cold weather can stop some types of construction. Workers often get dirty, greasy, muddy, or dusty. Some operators work in remote locations on large construction projects, such as highways and dams, or in factories or mines.

Operating engineers and other construction equipment operators have a higher rate of injuries and illnesses than the national average. Slips, falls, and transportation incidents can generally be avoided by observing proper operating procedures and safety practices. Bulldozers, scrapers, and especially pile-drivers, are noisy and shake or jolt the operator, which may lead to repetitive stress injuries.

Construction equipment operators may have irregular schedules because work on construction projects must sometimes continue around the clock or be done late at night. The majority of construction equipment operators work full time.

Workers with the ability to operate multiple types of equipment should have the best job opportunities. In addition, employment opportunities should be best in metropolitan areas, where most large commercial and residential buildings are constructed, and in states that undertake large transportation-related projects. Because apprentices learn to operate a wider variety of machines than do other beginners, they usually have better job opportunities.

As with many other types of construction worker jobs, employment of construction equipment operators is sensitive to fluctuations of the economy. On the one hand, workers may experience periods of unemployment when the overall level of construction falls. On the other hand, some areas may need additional workers during peak periods of building activity.

Employment Trend, Projected 2016–22

Construction equipment operators: 12%

Construction trades workers: 11%

Total, all occupations: 7%

Note: "All Occupations" includes all occupations in the U.S. Economy. Source: U.S. Bureau of Labor Statistics, Occupational Employment Statistics

Related Occupations

The following are examples of types of construction equipment operators:

Operating Engineers and Other Construction Equipment Operators

Operating engineers and other construction equipment operators work with one or several types of power construction equipment. They may operate excavation and loading machines equipped with scoops, shovels, or buckets that dig sand, gravel, earth, or similar materials. In addition to operating bulldozers, they operate trench excavators, road graders, and similar equipment. Sometimes, they may drive and control industrial trucks or tractors equipped with forklifts or booms for lifting materials. They may also operate and maintain air compressors, pumps, and other power equipment at construction sites.

Paving and Surfacing Equipment Operators

Paving and surfacing equipment operators control the machines that spread and level asphalt or spread and smooth concrete for roadways or other structures.

Pile-driver Operators

Pile-driver operators use large machines mounted on skids, barges, or cranes to hammer piles into the ground. Piles are long, heavy beams of concrete, wood, or steel driven into the ground to support retaining walls, bridges, piers, or building foundations. Some pile-driver operators work on offshore oil rigs.

Conversation With . . .
CHRISTOPHER TREML

Director of Construction Training
International Union of Operating Engineers
Washington, DC
Heavy equipment operator, 28 years

1. What was your individual career path in terms of education/training, entry-level job, or other significant opportunity?

My father was training director for the apprentice program at Local 57 in Providence, Rhode Island, when I graduated from high school, so I applied to their three-year program. I trained in the classroom and had 6,000 on-the-job training hours because when you go through your apprenticeship program, you work for a contractor. I ended up working for that same contractor for almost twenty years. I ran all the equipment they had, such as bulldozers, cranes, backhoes, front-end loaders, bobcats, and asphalt paving equipment. I also repaired and maintained the equipment, which is part of an operating engineer's job.

During that time, I was hired by the union local to be a part-time instructor for their apprentice program, and then spent nine years as training director. Eventually I was offered a job at the international union in Washington, D.C. I travel to different locals and supply them with curricula, training materials, and pieces of equipment. I provide the instructors with what they need to run their training programs smoothly. From time to time, I get on different pieces of equipment to demonstrate; there are more than thirty different machines we're responsible for operating and maintaining.

2. What are the most important skills and/or qualities for someone in your profession?

You have to love the outdoors and be willing to do physical labor because this is not just about sitting in machines and pulling levers. You may have your knuckles scratched on a job or be accidentally burned with a torch. You have to have mechanical ability, a willingness to work long hours, and be physically fit. You need to take care of your body—wear hearing and eye protection, don't jump off machines, and pay attention to your doctor's appointments to maintain your health as you get older.

You have to be a people person, because you're going to be working with a crew of people who come with a lot of different attitudes and at the end of the day, you have to get the job done.

3. What do you wish you had known going into this profession?

I knew what I was getting into because I followed my father into this profession. But one thing I see a lot today is that many young people need to learn how to manage their finances. Maybe 90 percent of operating engineers go from contractor to contractor, getting laid off from one job and moving on to another. The work is definitely seasonal; by Thanksgiving, guys may be laid off until spring. You need to manage your money through the slow times.

4. Are there many job opportunities in your profession? In what specific areas?

Yes, jobs are available because people are retiring. Equipment is computer-based now, so it's easier for young people to come in and troubleshoot because they are computer savvy.

5. How do you see your profession changing in the next five years? What role will technology play in those changes, and what skills will be required?

There will always be a need for operators because at the end of the day, you need someone in the machine to go through the normal paces because you can't have a machine in the middle of a city digging around gas and electrical lines. That said, computers are highly involved. For example, in excavation you have GPS pulling grades off satellites and dictating how much dirt to pull off or pull in. A computer tells you how much a load weighs so you can set up a crane.

6. What do you enjoy most about your job? What do you enjoy least about your job?

I enjoy all the people I've met throughout my career and I still enjoy making friends or picking up new ideas. The most difficult part of the job probably is getting on a new piece of equipment you're unfamiliar with. You can't be afraid to ask questions.

7. Can you suggest a valuable "try this" for students considering a career in your profession?

Different groups hold summer camps for young people so they can learn about the different trades. You should try to spend a day with each trade if you can. As an example of what might happen, you might get on a piece of equipment with us and help dig a hole. The University of Rhode Island holds a Construction Academy; maybe a guidance counselor can help you find one near your home.

MORE INFORMATION

Associated Builders and Contractors
4250 N. Fairfax Drive, 9th Floor
Arlington, VA 22203
703.812.2000
www.abc.org

Associated General Contractors of America
Director, Construction Education Services
2300 Wilson Boulevard, Suite 400
Arlington, VA 22201
703.548.3118
www.agc.org

Building Trades Association
16th Street, NW
Washington, DC 20006
800.326.7800
www.buildingtrades.com

Industrial Truck Association
1750 K Street, NW, Suite 460
Washington, DC 20006
202.296.9880
www.indtrk.org

International Union of Operating Engineers
Director of Research and Education
1125 17th Street, NW
Washington, DC 20036
202.429.9100
www.iuoe.org

Laborers' International Union of North America
905 16th Street NW
Washington, DC 20006
212.737.8320
www.liuna.org

National Center for Construction Education and Research
13614 Progress Boulevard
Alachua, FL 32615
386.518.6500
www.nccer.org

United Construction Workers
3109 Martin Luther King Jr. Avenue SE
Washington, DC 20032
www.unitedconstructionworkers.co

Patrick Cooper/Editor

Cement Masons & Masonry Workers

Snapshot

Career Cluster(s): Architecture & Construction
Interests: Working with machinery, working with your hands
Earnings (Median pay): $39,180 per year; $18.84 per hour
Job Growth: Faster than average

OVERVIEW

Sphere of Work

Cement masons perform a large variety of construction tasks. They pour and smooth concrete and other cement mixtures to create and repair sidewalks, walkways, roads, and other surfaces. Cement masons work with engineers and construction workers to properly set the frames that hold concrete in place while it is drying. Reinforcing rebar or mesh wires are placed within these frames by cement masons to further strengthen the concrete. Once the concrete is poured, cement masons spread, level, and smooth the composite.

Work Environment

Cement masons work in a variety of environments, both indoors and outdoors and in all kinds of weather. Cement masons will often work within a construction site, but they can also perform jobs at commercial buildings and residential locations.

Depending on the job location, a cement mason could work in an environment that is dusty or muddy, so proper protective gear is recommended. Like all construction jobs, a cement mason's work environment has hazards to be aware of.

Profile

Working Conditions: Work both Indoors and Outdoors
Physical Strength: Medium Work, Heavy Work
Education Needs: On-The-Job Training, High School Diploma with Technical Education, Apprenticeship
Licensure/Certification: Usually Not Required
Opportunities For Experience: Apprenticeship, Military Service
Holland Interest Score*: RES

* See Appendix A

Occupation Interest

A cement mason's job covers a diverse range of construction tasks. This job attracts professionals who enjoy working with their hands outside of an office environment and can adapt to different work environments. Cement masons use a variety of tools to complete their jobs, so the ability to handle heavy and light machinery is recommended.

A Day in the Life—Duties and Responsibilities

After assessing a particular job, a cement mason will set the frames and reinforcing materials that hold the concrete in place. Concrete is made through a mixture of cement, sand, and water inside a concrete mixing machine. The frames need to be set at the proper pitch and depth and aligned correctly. Concrete is then poured into the frames. The concrete can be poured from a truck, by hand, or via a wheelbarrow. The cement mason needs to watch and make sure that the concrete is poured evenly in the correct places. Throughout the process, a cement mason must ensure the job is in compliance with certain laws, regulations, and standards.

While the concrete is still wet, a cement mason will spread, level, and smooth the concrete using a variety of hand tools, including rakes, shovels, trowels, and screeds. The edges of the concrete are smoothed and straightened with tools such as jointers and straightedges. After the concrete has dried, a cement mason will determine if the surface requires any hardening, sealing, or waterproofing compounds. A cement mason can also use colored powder to create a predetermined finish on the concrete.

If the cement mason is performing a repair job, different tools and tasks are required. In order to repair concrete that has already been set and dried, a cement mason will chip, grind, and remove areas using pneumatic chisels, power grinders, or a variety of hand tools.

Duties and Responsibilities

- Spreading concrete to specified depth and consistency
- Leveling and shaping surfaces of freshly poured concrete
- Finishing surfaces by wetting concrete and rubbing with abrasive stone
- Removing rough or defective spots from surfaces, patching holes with fresh concrete or epoxy compound
- Molding expansion joints and edges
- Operating machines to smooth concrete surfaces
- Coloring and texturing concrete to prescribed finish
- Mixing cement, using hoes or concrete mixing machines
- Setting forms

OCCUPATION SPECIALTIES

Step Finishers

Step Finishers are cement masons who specialize in finishing steps and stairways.

Maintenance Cement Masons

Maintenance Cement Masons break up and repair old concrete surfaces using pneumatic tools.

Cementers

Cementers may spread premixed cement over the deck, inner surfaces, joints, and crevices of ships.

Terrazzo Workers

Terrazzo Workers apply cement, sand, coloring materials and marble chips to floors, stairways and cabinet fixtures to create durable and decorative surfaces.

WORK ENVIRONMENT

Physical Environment

Construction sites are the most common environments that cement masons will work in, but they can also work in and around commercial and residential locations. While the job is being assessed and during the planning stages, a cement mason may work in an office environment with other construction workers and contractors.

Relevant Skills and Abilities

Organization & Management Skills
- Following instructions
- Meeting goals and deadlines

Organization & Management Skills
- Paying attention to and handling details
- Performing routine work
- Working quickly when necessary

Technical Skills
- Performing scientific, mathematical and technical work
- Working with data or numbers
- Working with machines, tools or other objects

Unclassified Skills
- Performing work that produces tangible results

Human Environment

Cement masons collaborate and interact with a variety of professionals in the construction business, including engineers, site managers, contractors, and other masons.

Technological Environment

Cement masons use a variety of technologies, ranging from power tools such as power drills and grinders to hand tools such as chisels and straightedges. They also have to wear a variety of safety gear, including helmets, gloves, and goggles.

EDUCATION, TRAINING, AND ADVANCEMENT

High School/Secondary

There are no specific education requirements to become a cement mason, but masons most commonly have a high-school diploma or the equivalent. Cement masons should be adept in a variety of subjects that may be taught in high school, including mathematics, mechanical drawing, and how to read blueprints.

Suggested High School Subjects
- Applied Math
- Blueprint Reading
- English
- Machining Technology
- Masonry

- Mechanical Drawing
- Metals Technology
- Shop Math
- Woodshop

Famous First

While cement was originally invented in England in the second half of the nineteenth century, American David Oliver Saylor of Allentown, PA, bettered the process in 1871. Even though his hydraulic cement received a patent, the prevailing idea was that English cement was better and continued to be brought to America on ballast ships because it was so heavy. In 1897, American cement usage outstripped European usage for the first time.

Postsecondary

Cement masons are usually not required to have a college degree, but it is a great help if they have a strong background in a variety of subjects. Since the job often requires the ability to read and modify blueprints, knowledge of mechanical drawing and mathematics is important. Many technical colleges offer appropriate courses for a cement mason.

Knowledge of administration and management is also helpful for a cement mason. Management courses can help a mason understand the strategic planning, resource allocation, and human resource aspects of the construction business. Many community colleges offer such courses.

Adult Job Seekers

Adults who are interested in becoming cement masons should first research forecasted job opportunities and annual income to make sure this position matches their needs. Being a cement mason requires a lot of communication and collaboration with others in the construction trade, so a potential mason should be very outgoing and possess great interpersonal and communication skills. A cement mason should be in excellent physical condition, as the job requires constant kneeling, bending over, and using power tools. Job seekers should also be mindful that a cement mason works in a large variety of environments that can be hazardous.

Professional Certification and Licensure

Cement masons will often be trained in a three-year apprenticeship under an experienced mason. Cement masons in training must receive 144 hours of technical instruction and 2,000 hours of paid training every year during their apprenticeship. Cement masons are instructed in a variety of construction basics, such as safety practices, first aid, and blueprint reading. Once cement masons complete their apprentice programs, they are considered to be journeymen, which will allow them to complete tasks without supervision.

Additional Requirements

Becoming a cement mason requires a lot of on-the-job training. Many cement masons begin their career as a laborer or helper on a construction site. This is when a lot of the basics of construction are learned. On-the-job training programs for cement masons are typically informal. Experienced cement masons and others in the construction trade will train new masons to use the tools, machines, and materials required of them. Training commonly begins with the use of tools and how to edge, joint, and modify wet concrete after it has been poured. Training will then progress to more complex tasks such as framing, reinforcing, and pouring.

After completing an apprenticeship, a cement mason can apply to join a local construction union. Once a cement mason has been accepted into a local union, he or she can contact the local union contractor or business agent to ask about joining the Laborers' International Union of North America (LIUNA), which is one of the largest unions in the United States. Joining any union requires proof of hours worked, such as pay stubs or W-2 tax forms. There are initiation fees to be paid while joining a union and yearly fees after the cement mason has become a member.

Fun Fact

The English quarried a natural deposit of cement rock in 1796, sold as Roman Cement. In 1874, a bricklayer created a powdered cement he named Portland Cement because its color was similar to quarried stone from the Isle of Portland.

Source: http://sciencewithkids.com/science-facts/facts-about-concrete.html

EARNINGS AND ADVANCEMENT

The median annual wage for masonry workers was $41,330 in May 2016. The median wage is the wage at which half the workers in an occupation earned more than that amount and half earned less. The lowest 10 percent earned less than $26,940, and the highest 10 percent earned more than $74,310.

Median annual wages for masonry workers in May 2016 were as follows:

Brickmasons and blockmasons	$49,250
Terrazzo workers and finishers	$40,930
Stonemasons	$39,780
Cement masons and concrete finishers	$39,180

In May 2016, the median annual wages for masonry workers in the top industries in which they worked were as follows:

Masonry contractors	$46,580
Construction of buildings	$44,190
Heavy and civil engineering construction	$40,970
Poured concrete foundation and structure contractors	$38,520

Although most masons work full time, some work more hours to meet construction deadlines. Masonry work is done mostly outdoors, so masons may have to stop work during inclement weather. Terrazzo masons may need to work at night when businesses are closed.

Median annual wages, May 2016

Construction trades workers: $42,310

Masonry workers: $41,330

Total, all occupations: $37,040

Note: "All Occupations" includes all occupations in the U.S. Economy. Source: U.S. Bureau of Labor Statistics, Occupational Employment Statistics

EMPLOYMENT AND OUTLOOK

Overall employment of masonry workers is projected to grow 12 percent from 2016 to 2026, faster than the average for all occupations. Although employment growth will vary by occupation, it will be driven by the level of construction needed to meet the demands of a growing population, including demands for more commercial, public, and civil construction projects such as new roads, bridges, and buildings.

Employment of cement masons and concrete finishers is projected to grow 13 percent from 2016 to 2026, faster than the average for all occupations. Cement masons will be needed to build and renovate highways, bridges, factories, and residential structures in order to meet the demands of a growing population and to make repairs to aging infrastructure.

Employment of brickmasons and block masons is projected to grow 11 percent from 2016 to 2026, faster than the average for all occupations. Population growth will result in the construction of more schools, hospitals, apartment buildings, and other structures, many of which are made of brick and block. In addition, masons will be needed to restore a growing number of other kinds of brick buildings. Although expensive, brick exteriors should remain popular, reflecting a preference for low-maintenance, durable exterior materials.

Employment of stonemasons is projected to grow 10 percent from 2016 to 2026, faster than the average for all occupations. Natural stone is both a durable and popular material. As incomes and the population continue to grow, more homeowners will prefer natural stone for its durability and aesthetic value.

Employment of terrazzo workers and finishers is projected to grow 12 percent from 2016 to 2026, faster than the average for all occupations. Terrazzo is a durable and attractive flooring option that is often used in schools, government buildings, and hospitals. The construction and renovation of such buildings will spur demand for these workers.

Overall job prospects for masons should be good as construction activity continues to grow to meet the demand for new buildings and roads. Workers with experience in construction should have the best opportunities.

As with many other construction workers, employment of masons is sensitive to the fluctuations of the economy. On the one hand, workers may experience periods of unemployment when the overall level of construction falls. On the other hand, during peak periods of building activity some areas may require additional number of these workers.

Employment Trend, Projected 2016–22

Masonry workers: 12%

Construction trades workers: 11%

Total, all occupations: 7%

Note: "All Occupations" includes all occupations in the U.S. Economy. Source: U.S. Bureau of Labor Statistics, Occupational Employment Statistics

Related Occupations

- Brickmasons and blockmasons
- Cement masons and concrete finishers
- Stonemasons
- Terrazzo workers and finishers

> # *Conversation With . . .*
> # MICHELLE WILSON
>
> Director of Concrete Technology
> Portland Cement Association, Skokie, Illinois
> Cement industry, 22 years

1. What was your individual career path in terms of education/training, entry-level job, or other significant opportunity?

Growing up, I wanted to be an architect and was obsessed with structures. I have a bachelor's degree in architectural engineering with an emphasis in structural engineering and concrete materials from the Milwaukee School of Engineering. One of my first structural engineering courses was in concrete design and I loved it. It was partly due to a great professor, as well as the subject. My professor did a hands-on demonstration about reinforced concrete. I was mesmerized by how different materials handle stress, and how the component materials of concrete and steel worked together.

After receiving my bachelor's degree, I continued researching concrete materials while taking graduate classes at University of Wisconsin-Milwaukee. I also worked full-time as a field inspector performing quality control and laboratory testing of concrete and other construction materials for STS Consultants in Milwaukee. While working at STS, I subcontracted with Construction Technology Laboratories (now CTLGroup) on a restoration project. That led to a full time position with CTL as an assistant engineer, troubleshooting concrete and inspecting repair projects all over North America. It was an exciting time in my career. My only regret was leaving graduate school without completing my master's degree.

In 1999, I was offered a position in the education and training department at the Portland Cement Association (PCA), educating members and other industry professionals through literature, e-learning, and in-house training. It was a big change from field work, so I was hesitant at first to accept, but it has been a perfect fit. My role has expanded into a job that blends university research with industry needs. It's essential that I keep up with trends, technologies, and other matters affecting the industry.

Now, as Director of Concrete Technology, in addition to teaching courses and writing about concrete technology, I help develop industry standards through committee involvement with the American Concrete Institute (ACI) and the American Society of Testing and Materials (ASTM).

2. **What are the most important skills and/or qualities for someone in your profession?**

You'll need math, chemistry, geology, problem-solving, and hands-on laboratory and testing skills.

You'll also need strong communication skills, enthusiasm for the materials, motivation, attention to detail, a good work ethic, time-management skills, and the ability to work as a team player.

3. **What do you wish you had known going into this profession?**

I wish, as a student, I had been more involved with professional associations such as the American Concrete Institute. I would have gained a much broader perspective of the jobs available in the concrete industry earlier in my career if I'd attended chapter meetings and conventions as a student. Mentors are available to students. Both PCA and ACI have education foundations that provide scholarships for students who study concrete-related research topics.

4. **Are there many job opportunities in your profession? In what specific areas?**

Yes, many. We have a high demand for a skilled labor force. Certifications in this area are often required, and very desirable, whether you're a driver working at a ready-mix plant, field laborer, or testing technician.

The cement industry employs many engineers—ceramics, chemical, civil, electrical, environmental, geological, materials, and mechanical; analytical, organic, and inorganic chemists; geologists; and computer scientists. In addition to people who can manage companies, we need researchers to develop new technologies. Educators, promoters, and technical sales and marketing are also needed.

5. **How do you see your profession changing in the next five years? What role will technology play in those changes, and what skills will be required?**

Concrete is a highly technical field that is ever-changing. Recent innovations include translucent, smog-eating, bendable, and self-consolidating concretes. Yes, you can throw some water in with cement and gravel and install a fencepost. But concrete used for commercial structures is very technical. There are minimum code requirements and science behind changing the mixture to meet the end performance, such as setting faster, gaining higher strengths, and resisting different types of weather.

6. What do you enjoy most about your job? What do you enjoy least about your job?

I love the subject matter. I still get excited when talking and writing about concrete. I also love the interaction and collaboration with leaders and experts in the industry. The relationships I have built with my colleagues over the past 20 years mean the most to me. On the downside, there can be long meetings and late nights reviewing reports and ballots.

7. Can you suggest a valuable "try this" for students considering a career in your profession?

Take a tour of a local ready-mix or cement plant and attend a chapter meeting of a concrete-related organization such as the American Concrete Institute. Volunteer for Habitat for Humanity. Take a class on geology.

MORE INFORMATION

ACI International
P.O. Box 9094
Farmington Hills, MI 48333
248.848.3700
www.aci-int.org

American Concrete Pavement Association
9450 Bryn Mawr, Suite 150
Rosemont, IL 60018
847.966.2272
www.pavement.com

Associated General Contractors of America
Director, Construction Education Services
2300 Wilson Boulevard, Suite 400
Arlington, VA 22201
703.548.3118
www.agc.org

Building Trades Association
16th Street, NW
Washington, DC 20006
800.326.7800
www.buildingtrades.com

International Masonry Institute
The James Brice House
42 East Street
Annapolis, MD 21401
410.280.1305
www.imiweb.org

International Union of Bricklayers and Allied Craftworkers
620 F Street NW
Washington, DC 20004
202.783.3788
www.bacweb.org

Laborers' International Union of North America
905 Sixteenth Street NW
Washington, DC 20006
212.737.8320
www.liuna.org

National Association of Home Builders
1201 15th Street, NW
Washington, DC 20005
800.368.5242
www.nahb.com

National Center for Construction Education and Research
13614 Progress Boulevard
Alachua, FL 32615
888.622.3720
www.nccer.org

National Concrete Masonry Association
13750 Sunrise Valley Drive
Herndon, VA 20171-4662
703.713.1900
www.ncma.org

National Terrazzo & Mosaic Association
P.O. Box 2605
Fredericksburg, TX 78624
800.323.9736
www.ntma.com

Operative Plasterers' & Cement Masons' Intl. Association
11720 Beltsville Drive, Suite 700
Beltsville, MD 20705
301.623.1000
www.opcmia.org

Portland Cement Association
5420 Old Orchard Road
Skokie, IL 60077
847.966.6200
www.cement.org

United Brotherhood of Carpenters
101 Constitution Avenue, NW
Washington, DC 20001
202.546.6206
www.carpenters.org

Patrick Cooper/Editor

Civil Engineers

Snapshot

Career Cluster(s): Architecture & Construction Manufacturing, Science, Technology, Engineering & Mathematics, Transportation, Distribution & Logistics

Interests: Research, innovation, construction, working with small details

Earnings (Median pay): $83,540 per year; $40.16 per hour

Job Growth: Faster than average

OVERVIEW

Sphere of Work

Civil engineers plan and oversee infrastructure construction projects such as bridges, dams, roads and highways, sewer systems, power plants, and buildings. They assess costs, durability of building materials, and the physical environments in which the project is being constructed. Civil engineers direct and help survey sites, analyze all blueprints, drawings, and photographs, test soil and other materials, and write and present important reports. They work for federal, state, and local governments as well as engineering and architectural firms. Most civil engineers specialize in a subfield such as

sanitation engineering, structural engineering, or transportation engineering.

Work Environment

Civil engineers work in government offices, architectural firms, engineering consultant groups, utility companies, and other office environments where meetings are conducted, plans are drafted, and reports are filed. Civil engineers also spend a great deal of time at project sites, which include building renovation and construction projects, active roadways and highways, along sewer and water lines, and other parts of a region's infrastructure. Many civil engineers spend the majority of their time on site. Although most civil engineers work a standard forty-hour workweek, they may work extra hours as deadlines approach or emergencies occur.

Profile

Working Conditions: Work both Indoors and Outdoors
Physical Strength: Light Work
Education Needs: Bachelor's Degree, Master's Degree, Doctoral Degree
Licensure/Certification: Required
Opportunities For Experience: Internship, Apprenticeship, Military Service, Part-Time Work
Holland Interest Score*: IRE

* See Appendix A

Occupation Interest

Civil engineering is essential to all developed communities— civil engineers help build roads, water and sewer systems, waste management units, and irrigation networks. As they are responsible for public safety, civil engineers must be attentive to detail, demonstrate sound judgment, work well under pressure, and adhere to a strict code of ethics. They also need to be innovative and have strong reasoning skills. The demand for civil engineers remains high, and the number of open jobs is expected to increase dramatically over the next decade. Civil engineering salaries are competitive, and civil engineers typically receive strong benefits.

A Day in the Life—Duties and Responsibilities

Civil engineers' daily responsibilities and duties vary based on their place of employment and specialty. A civil engineer employed by a city government may focus on only one or two major projects per year, while a civil engineer employed by a major architectural firm may be involved in a greater number of projects. Some civil engineers conduct thorough soil studies in addition to structural integrity and strength tests on building materials. Many civil engineers are also supervisors, overseeing construction crews and other engineers at work sites. Civil engineers occasionally act as consultants, providing technical advice and studies to the client as needed.

In general, civil engineers conduct studies and evaluations of existing engineering issues, such as traffic flow studies for roadway construction projects or flow rate analyses for water system upgrades. They prepare public reports, such as environmental impact assessments, bid proposals for contractors, and detailed descriptions of the proposed project site or sites. Civil engineers write feasibility studies in which they estimate the costs and quantities of building materials, equipment, and labor required for a given project. Using drafting tools and software, they create designs for new or improved infrastructure. During the construction phase, civil engineers visit and inspect work sites regularly, monitoring progress and ensuring compliance with government safety standards and the client's wishes. These inspections also entail testing the strength and integrity of the materials used as well as the environment in which they are being used.

Duties and Responsibilities

- Preparing plans and specifications
- Estimating costs and requirements of projects
- Testing materials to be used
- Determining solutions to problems
- Supervising construction and maintenance
- Inspecting existing or newly constructed projects and recommending repairs
- Performing technical research
- Determining the impact of construction on the environment

OCCUPATION SPECIALTIES

Transportation Engineers

Transportation Engineers design and prepare plans, estimates and specifications for the construction and operation of surface transportation projects. Transportation engineers may specialize in a particular phase of the work such as making surveys of roads, improving road signs or lighting, or directing and coordinating construction or maintenance activity.

Structural Engineers

Structural Engineers plan, design and oversee the erection of steel and other structural materials in buildings, bridges and other structures that require a stress analysis.

Hydraulic Engineers

Hydraulic Engineers design and direct the construction of power and other hydraulic engineering projects for the control and use of water.

Construction Engineers

Construction Engineers manage construction projects to ensure that they are built according to plan and completed on schedule.

Geotechnical Engineers

Geotechnical Engineers are concerned primarily with foundations and how structures interact with the earth (i.e., soil, rock).

WORK ENVIRONMENT

Physical Environment

Civil engineers work in office environments, where they conduct meetings with clients and government officials, prepare public reports, design systems and structures, and organize all documentation pertaining to projects. They also spend a great deal of time at project sites, conducting inspections and overseeing personnel. Some civil engineers also teach at colleges and universities.

Relevant Skills and Abilities

Communication Skills
- Speaking effectively
- Writing concisely

Organization & Management Skills
- Coordinating tasks
- Demonstrating leadership
- Managing people/groups
- Paying attention to and handling details

Research & Planning Skills
- Analyzing information
- Solving problems

Technical Skills
- Performing scientific, mathematical and technical work

Human Environment

Depending on their areas of specialty, civil engineers interact and collaborate with government officials, architects, construction crews, materials and equipment suppliers, business executives, and other engineers. Civil engineering professors also work with students, other professors, and school administrators.

Technological Environment

Civil engineers work with a wide range of technologies and tools during the course of their work. In the office, they use computer-aided design (CAD) and other design software, cartography software, project management systems and databases, and other analytical and scientific programs. At a project site, they use soil collection equipment, electronic distance-measuring devices, levels, compasses, pressure gauges, and scales.

EDUCATION, TRAINING, AND ADVANCEMENT

High School/Secondary

High school students should study physics, chemistry, and biology. Mathematics, including algebra, geometry, trigonometry, and calculus, are also essential courses. Furthermore, high school students should take computer science courses and hone their writing and public speaking skills through English and communications classes. Courses that help students understand blueprints and architecture, such as drafting and industrial arts, are also highly useful.

Suggested High School Subjects

- Algebra
- Applied Communication
- Applied Math
- Applied Physics
- Biology
- Blueprint Reading
- Calculus
- Chemistry
- College Preparatory
- Composition
- Computer Science
- Drafting
- Economics
- English
- Geometry
- Mathematics
- Mechanical Drawing
- Physics
- Science
- Trigonometry

Famous First

The first bridge with piers sunk in the open sea, thus forming the foundation for its towers, was the Golden Gate Bridge in San Francisco. It was the first bridge to be built across the outer mouth of a major ocean harbor—in this case, San Francisco Bay, opening out to the Pacific Ocean. Construction took from 1933 to 1937.

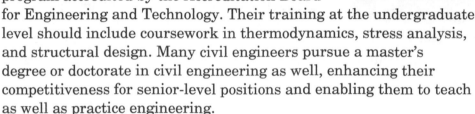

College/Postsecondary

Civil engineers must receive a bachelor's degree in civil engineering from an engineering program accredited by the Accreditation Board for Engineering and Technology. Their training at the undergraduate level should include coursework in thermodynamics, stress analysis, and structural design. Many civil engineers pursue a master's degree or doctorate in civil engineering as well, enhancing their competitiveness for senior-level positions and enabling them to teach as well as practice engineering.

Related College Majors
- Architectural Engineering
- Civil Engineering
- Civil Engineering/Civil Technology
- Engineering Design

Adult Job Seekers

Qualified civil engineers may apply directly to government agencies, architectural firms, and other employers with open positions. Many universities have placement programs that can help recent civil engineering graduates find work. Additionally, civil engineers may join and network through professional associations and societies, such as the American Society of Civil Engineers (ASCE).

Professional Certification and Licensure

Civil engineers who work with the public must be licensed as a Professional Engineer (PE) in the state or states in which they seek to practice. The licensure process includes a written examination, a specified amount of education, and at least four years of work experience. Continuing education is a common requirement for ongoing licensure.

Some professional civil engineering associations, like the American Society of Civil Engineers, the Academy of Geo-Professionals, and the American Academy of Water Resources Engineers, offer specialty certification programs as well. Leadership in Energy and Environmental Design (LEED) certification may be necessary for some project.

Additional Requirements

Civil engineers must be able to analyze and comprehend complex systems. In addition to acquiring a strong understanding of the engineering field and their area of specialty, civil engineers must be excellent communicators, as they often work with others in a team environment or in a supervisory capacity. Successful completion of a civil service exam may be required for employment by a government agency.

Fun Fact

Civil engineers do more that build roads and bridges . . . a civil engineer created the slippery part of a water slide by designing a pumping system to circulate the proper amount of water to the flume, along with the proper design to hold the rider's weight, the water, and the wind force!

Source: www.nspe.org/resources/media/resources/ten-fun-and-exciting-facts-about-engineering

EARNINGS AND ADVANCEMENT

The median annual wage for civil engineers was $83,540 in May 2016. The median wage is the wage at which half the workers in an occupation earned more than that amount and half earned less. The lowest 10 percent earned less than $53,470, and the highest 10 percent earned more than $132,880.

In May 2016, the median annual wages for civil engineers in the top industries in which they worked were as follows:

Federal government, excluding postal service	$92,320
Local government, excluding education and hospitals	$88,370
Engineering services	$82,710
State government, excluding education and hospitals	$80,200
Nonresidential building construction	$77,170

Civil engineers typically work full time, and about 3 in 10 worked more than 40 hours per week in 2016. Engineers who direct projects may need to work extra hours in order to monitor progress on projects, to ensure that designs meet requirements, and to guarantee that deadlines are met.

Applicants who gain experience by participating in a co-op program while in college will have the best opportunities. In addition, new standards known collectively as the Body of Knowledge are growing in importance within civil engineering, and this development is likely to result in a heightened need for a graduate education. Therefore those who enter the occupation with a graduate degree will likely have better prospects.

Median annual wages, May 2016

Engineers: $91,010

Civil engineers: $83,540

Total, all occupations: $37,040

Note: "All Occupations" includes all occupations in the U.S. Economy. Source: U.S. Bureau of Labor Statistics, Occupational Employment Statistics

EMPLOYMENT AND OUTLOOK

Employment of civil engineers is projected to grow 11 percent from 2016 to 2026, faster than the average for all occupations. As current U.S. infrastructure experiences growing obsolescence, civil engineers will be needed to manage projects to rebuild, repair, and upgrade bridges, roads, levees, dams, airports, buildings, and other structures.

A growing population likely means that new water systems will be required while, at the same time, aging, existing water systems must be maintained to reduce or eliminate leaks. In addition, more waste treatment plants will be needed to help clean the nation's waterways. Civil engineers will continue to play a key part in all of this work.

The work of civil engineers will be needed for renewable-energy projects. Thus, as these new projects gain approval, civil engineers will be further involved in overseeing the construction of structures such as wind farms and solar arrays.

Although state and local governments continue to face financial challenges and may have difficulty funding all projects, some delayed projects will have to be completed to build and maintain critical infrastructure, as well as to protect the public and the environment.

Employment Trend, Projected 2016–22

Civil engineers: 11%

Engineers: 8%

Total, all occupations: 7%

Note: "All Occupations" includes all occupations in the U.S. Economy. Source: U.S. Bureau of Labor Statistics, Occupational Employment Statistics

Related Occupations
Construction Engineers

Construction engineers manage construction projects, ensuring that they are scheduled and built in accordance with plans and specifications. These engineers typically are responsible for the design and safety of temporary structures used during construction. They may also oversee budgetary, time-management, and communications aspects of a project.

Geotechnical Engineers

Geotechnical engineers work to make sure that foundations for built objects ranging from streets and buildings to runways and dams, are solid. They focus on how structures built by civil engineers, such as buildings and tunnels, interact with the earth (including soil and rock). In addition, they design and plan for slopes, retaining walls, and tunnels.

Structural Engineers

Structural engineers design and assess major projects, such as buildings, bridges, or dams, to ensure their strength and durability.

Transportation Engineers

Transportation engineers plan, design, operate, and maintain everyday systems, such as streets and highways, but they also plan larger projects, such as airports, ship ports, mass transit systems, and harbors.

The work of civil engineers is closely related to the work of environmental engineers.

Conversation With . . .
JAMES W. BLAKE, P.E., P.L.S.

Owner, Blake Consulting Services, LLC
Civil Engineer, 35 years

1. What was your individual career path in terms of education/training, entry-level job, or other significant opportunity?

My father was a civil engineer, and although I wasn't quite sure what I wanted to do, I knew if I had that degree, I'd have options. I earned a B.S. in civil engineering from the University of Maryland, and considered becoming a pilot. Unfortunately, my vision wasn't good enough. So I went to work as a civil/structural engineer, then went right back to school and earned a B.S. in business and accounting because I was interested in management and the business of engineering. My first job was a lot of sitting at a desk and crunching numbers and I wanted more variety, so I moved into transportation and general civil engineering, which allowed me to interact with clients, politicians and a greater variety of projects. I got into management about eight to ten years out of college. My specialty is roadway design and construction management. A lot of what I do now is business development related and involves competing for and winning consulting contracts from federal, state, and local governmental agencies.

2. What are the most important skills and/or qualities for someone in your profession?

The ability to communicate technical ideas in plain language is critical. You also need to be organized, and to have the ability to analyze a complex problem quickly, break it down into its various parts and then come up with a practical and economical solution that serves the client's best interests.

3. What do you wish you had known going into this profession?

Construction and civil engineering can be cyclical, and it's very much tied to the economy. So that means my workload can be cyclical. The politics of winning work through public agencies is also more involved and complex than I'd imagined it to be. Someone who wants to win public sector work must be very visible and involved with a particular governmental agency and those who oversee it.

4. **Are there many job opportunities in your profession? In what specific areas?**

I'd say very many. Job opportunities are excellent in transportation, structural, civil, environmental and geotechnical engineering, as well as construction inspection. Civil engineering is a very broad and diverse field, and there are some great challenges and opportunities.

5. **How do you see your profession changing in the next five years? What role will technology play in those changes, and what skills will be required?**

Technical advances are being adapted to complete projects more efficiently and expeditiously. If you need to do a technical analysis of a building—for example, an unusually-shaped building or structure—software analysis and document production programs allow you to do a more elaborate analysis more quickly and cheaply. Aerial drones are being used for inspection work on tall buildings and bridges; you just fly your drone over the area you wish to observe and it takes video as well as pictures of the subject area. An engineer on the ground can then confirm that construction is in fact proceeding in accordance with the construction documents. GPS is relatively old news; it's being programmed into black boxes on earthwork machines so they automatically excavate and grade areas; the machine will then drive itself and make all the cuts and fills using GPS and lasers for elevations. Other construction-related uses for GPS have continued to become more common.

6. **What do you enjoy most about your job? What do you enjoy least about your job?**

I most enjoy the variety of projects and my ability to interact with various people who have different roles in the development and completion of a project. As with any industry, there are difficult people you have to deal with and that's probably the hardest part.

7. **Can you suggest a valuable "try this" for students considering a career in your profession?**

Find an engineering company and see if they sponsor a student mentor day. Some professional organizations do that, such as the American Society of Civil Engineers or the Society of American Military Engineers. You could also intern or work part-time. There are also many good books on the topic, as well as YouTube videos, of different types of construction projects.

SELECTED SCHOOLS

Most colleges and universities offer programs in engineering; a variety of them also have concentrations in civil engineering. Some of the more prominent schools in this field are listed below.

Carnegie Mellon University
5000 Forbes Ave
Pittsburgh, PA 15213
Phone: (412) 256-2000
http://www.cmu.edu

Cornell University
242 Carpenter Hall
Ithaca, NY 14850
Phone: (607) 254-4636
https://www.cornell.edu

Georgia Institute of Technology
225 North Avenue
Atlanta, GA 30332
Phone: (404) 894-2000
http://www.gatech.edu

Massachusetts Institute of Technology
77 Massachusetts Avenue
Room 1-206
Cambridge, MA 02139
Phone: (617) 253-1000
http://web.mit.edu

Purdue University, West Lafayette
701 W. Stadium Avenue
Suite 3000 ARMS
West Lafayette, IN 47907
Phone: (765) 494-4600
http://www.purdue.edu

Stanford University
Huang Engineering Center Suite 226
450 Serra Mall
Stanford, CA 94305-4121
Phone: (650) 723-2300
https://www.stanford.edu

University of California, Berkeley
320 McLaughlin Hall #1700
Berkeley, CA 94720-1700
Phone: (510) 642-6000
http://www.berkeley.edu/

University of Illinois, Urbana, Champaign
1398 West Green
Urbana, IL 061801
Phone: (217) 333-1000
http://illinois.edu

University of Michigan Ann Arbor
Robert H. Lurie Engineering Center
Ann Arbor, MI 48109
Phone: (734) 764-1817
https://www.umich.edu

University of Texas, Austin (Cockrell)
301 E. Dean Keeton St.
Stop C2100
Austin, TX 78712
Phone: (512) 471-1166
http://www.engr.utexas.edu

MORE INFORMATION

Academy of Geo-Professionals
1801 Alexander Bell Drive
Reston, VA 20191
703.295.6314
www.geoprofessionals.org

**Accreditation Board for
Engineering and Technology**
111 Market Place, Suite 1050
Baltimore, MD 21202-4012
410.347.7700
www.abet.org

**American Academy of Water
Resources Engineers**
1801 Alexander Bell Drive
Reston, VA 20191
703.295.6414
www.aawre.org

**American Society of Civil
Engineers**
1801 Alexander Bell Drive
Reston, VA 21091-4400
800.548.2723
www.asce.org

**National Action Council for
Minorities in Engineering**
440 Hamilton Avenue, Suite 302
White Plains, NY 10601-1813
914.539.4010
www.nacme.org

**National Council of Structural
Engineers Associations**
645 North Michigan Avenue, Suite
540
Chicago, IL 60611
312.649.4600
www.ncsea.com

**National Society of Black
Engineers**
205 Daingerfield Road
Alexandria, VA 22314
703.549.2207
www.nsbe.org

**National Society of Professional
Engineers**
1420 King Street
Alexandria, VA 22314-2794
703.684.2800
www.nspe.org

**Society of Hispanic Professional
Engineers**
13181 Crossroads Parkway North
Suite 450
City of Industry, CA 91746-3497
323.725.3970
www.shpe.org

Society of Women Engineers
203 N. La Salle Street, Suite 1675
Chicago, IL 60601
877.793.4636
www.swe.org

Technology Student Association
1914 Association Drive
Reston, VA 20191-1540
703.860.9000
www.tsaweb.org

Michael Auerbach/Editor

Construction & Building Inspectors

Snapshot

Career Cluster(s): Architecture & Construction, Government & Public Administration, Manufacturing

Interests: Engineering, physical science, architecture, civic planning

Earnings (Median pay): $58,480 per year; $28.12 per hour

Job Growth: As fast as average

OVERVIEW

Sphere of Work

Construction and building inspectors survey construction and remodeling sites to ensure the safety of the surrounding community, site workers, and future tenants. While building inspectors may also survey existing structures, construction inspectors focus primarily on new building sites. Many building inspectors are employed by local, state, and national governments. Construction inspectors are privately employed by contracting companies, engineering firms, and commercial developers.

Construction inspection is a multidisciplinary field that requires an extensive knowledge

of architecture and construction. In addition to possessing a sound knowledge of the effects of physical exposure on infrastructure, many contemporary building inspectors are also well versed in green engineering practices and energy-efficient building practices.

Work Environment

Building inspectors work primarily on construction sites. Depending on an inspector's specialty, such sites can range from large-scale civic engineering projects such as bridges, highways, and transportation hubs to smaller-scale projects such as residential work sites, antique home restorations, or new housing developments. Building inspectors must be comfortable working in potentially hazardous construction sites as well as with exposure to subterranean spaces, harsh natural elements, and high altitudes.

Profile

Working Conditions: Work both Indoors and Outdoors
Physical Strength: Light Work
Education Needs: On-The-Job Training, High School Diploma with Technical Education, Junior/Technical/Community College, Apprenticeship
Licensure/Certification: Required
Opportunities For Experience: Apprenticeship, Part-Time Work
Holland Interest Score*:RCS, REC

* See Appendix A

Occupation Interest

The field of building inspection often attracts those with backgrounds in engineering, physical science, architecture, and civic planning. Many inspectors arrive at the position after several years in the private construction industry, either as skilled laborers or as engineering consultants, project managers, or architects.

Construction is a multifaceted discipline that requires knowledge of an array of logistics and systematic infrastructure, including architecture, HVAC, plumbing, electrical circuitry, weatherproofing, load-bearing metrics, and aerodynamics. Inspectors must also be very well versed in local, state, and national building regulations.

A Day in the Life—Duties and Responsibilities

Much of the day-to-day responsibilities of building inspectors involve traveling to and inspecting construction sites. The scale, location, and breadth of site surveys will depend on the specialty of the inspector.

Civic building inspectors survey all new construction sites and renovation projects within their particular jurisdictions to ensure that the projects fall within the parameters of regional, state, and federal building codes.

Construction inspectors spend much of their noninspection time educating themselves about alterations to existing codes as well as new building codes, which are traditionally issued on an annual basis. In many cases, inspectors are required to attend conferences and seminars where new building codes or code-friendly building techniques are taught.

Civic inspectors possess the capacity to halt construction projects that are in violation of building codes. Reasons for a building inspector to shut down construction can range from the use of illegal materials to improper site waste management, hazardous work conditions, improper implementation of safety equipment, or repetition of a combination of such offenses. Construction projects that are halted by inspectors are required to reapply for building certificates and often must pass thorough inspections prior to being allowed to proceed. Building inspectors are often called upon to interpret construction laws and building codes for project managers eager to preempt a disruption of progress.

Duties and Responsibilities

- Inspecting buildings, dams, highways or bridges
- Inspecting wiring, fixtures, plumbing, sewer systems and fire sprinklers for safety
- Preparing reports concerning violations not corrected
- Interpreting blueprints and specifications
- Verifying levels, alignment and elevation of installations
- Reviewing requests for and issuing building permits

OCCUPATION SPECIALTIES

Electrical Inspectors

Electrical Inspectors check electrical installations to verify safety laws and ordinances.

Plumbing Inspectors

Plumbing Inspectors check plumbing installations for conformance to governmental codes, sanitation standards and construction specifications.

Construction Inspectors

Construction Inspectors examine and oversee the construction of bridges, dams, highways and other types of construction work to insure that procedures and materials comply with specifications.

Elevator Inspectors

Elevator Inspectors examine the safety of lifting and conveying devices such as elevators, escalators, ski lifts and amusement rides.

Mechanical Inspectors

Mechanical Inspectors examine the installation of kitchen appliances, heating and air conditioning equipment and gasoline tanks to insure that they comply with safety standards.

WORK ENVIRONMENT

Physical Environment

Building inspectors work primarily on job sites of varying scales and across all climates and weather conditions. Many environments require the use of safety equipment such as hard hats and safety goggles. Comfort with construction environments, including both underground sites and sites at high altitudes, is a necessity of the role.

Relevant Skills and Abilities

Communication Skills
- Speaking effectively
- Writing concisely

Interpersonal/Social Skills
- Cooperating with others
- Working as a member of a team

Organization & Management Skills
- Organizing information or materials
- Paying attention to and handling details

Technical Skills
- Performing scientific, mathematical and technical work

Human Environment

Construction and building inspectors must be effective interpersonal communicators who can explain complicated technical and legal parameters with relative ease. Conflict-resolution strategies and relationship-building techniques also benefit those in the profession.

Technological Environment

Construction inspectors must be well-versed in a variety of measurement systems and analytical tools measuring corrosion, exposure, and temperature. Advanced mathematic skills are also highly beneficial.

EDUCATION, TRAINING, AND ADVANCEMENT

High School/Secondary

High school students can best prepare to enter the field of building inspection by completing courses in algebra, calculus, geometry, industrial arts, trigonometry, chemistry, physics, and computer science. Coursework related to drafting and architecture can also be beneficial to those interested in the field. Exposure to the construction industry via summer employment, school internships, or administrative volunteer work can be especially beneficial to students who are interested in building inspection.

Suggested High School Subjects
- Applied Communication
- Applied Math
- Blueprint Reading
- Building Trades & Carpentry
- Drafting
- English
- Shop Math
- Woodshop

Famous First

Not until 1799 were there laws in place to ensure that buildings housing workers were safe to operate in. That year, Massachusetts made a law to create the Massachusetts Fire Insurance Company and created the first requirement for construction and building inspectors. Thenceforth, companies had to submit to an examination of their affairs and take an oath. Further, they had to be approved to continue to run their businesses.

College/Postsecondary

A postsecondary degree is not typically required but may be preferred by some employers. Construction and building inspectors often arrive at the profession after postsecondary study in related fields such as architecture, engineering, and civic planning. Beneficial postsecondary coursework can include surveys of building and home inspection, drafting, blueprint reading, construction safety, and inspection techniques and reporting methods.

Many aspiring building inspectors use their undergraduate years both to learn the fundamental aspects of construction engineering and to gain experience in the field through internships with private construction, engineering, or building inspection firms.

Related College Majors
- Architectural Engineering Technology
- Construction/Building Inspection
- Construction/Building Technology
- Electrical, Electronic & Communication Engineering Technology
- Electrician Training
- Heating, Air Conditioning & Refrigeration Mechanics & Repair
- Plumbing & Pipefitting

Adult Job Seekers

Adult job seekers can prepare for a career in building inspection by gaining sustained experience in the engineering field, particularly at the supervisory level. Leadership and managerial experience in construction management is also desirable. Many inspectors have several years of experience working as carpenters, systems engineers, or electricians. Sound collaborative and communication skills are also paramount for those seeking careers in the field. Candidates with multidisciplinary backgrounds in construction often have broadened opportunities.

Professional Certification and Licensure

Local, state, and national certification is required for all professional building inspectors. Most certificates and licenses are issued on an annual basis, so inspection professionals must stay up to date with developments in the field. Inspectors working in specialized fields of construction may also receive on-the-job training specific to a particular firm's needs.

Additional Requirements

Aspiring construction and building inspectors must be committed to mastering a broad array of constantly changing building codes and legal requirements. While the knowledge base of each inspector is grounded in basic construction principles, the ability to survey, interpret, and adapt to constantly changing regulations is just as important, as is the ability to convey complex technical concepts in an informative manner.

Fun Fact

The American Society of Home Inspectors reports these three deal-breakers for home buyers: a fixer-upper with too many problems; expensive repairs to large systems like a roof; and problems lurking inside the walls.

Source: http://www.homeinspector.org

EARNINGS AND ADVANCEMENT

The median annual wage for construction and building inspectors was $58,480 in May 2016. The median wage is the wage at which half the workers in an occupation earned more than that amount and half earned less. The lowest 10 percent earned less than $34,830, and the highest 10 percent earned more than $94,220.

In May 2016, the median annual wages for construction and building inspectors in the top industries in which they worked were as follows:

Engineering services	$60,300
Construction	$58,020
Local government, excluding education and hospitals	$57,910
State government, excluding education and hospitals	$54,450

Most inspectors work full time during regular business hours. However, some may work additional hours during periods of heavy construction activity. Also, if an accident occurs at a construction site, inspectors must respond immediately and may work additional hours to complete their report. Some inspectors—especially those who are self-employed—may have to work evenings and weekends. This is particularly true of home inspectors, who typically inspect homes during the day and write reports in the evening.

Median annual wages, May 2016

Construction and building inspectors: $58,480

Construction and extraction occupations: $43,610

Total, all occupations: $37,040

Note: "All Occupations" includes all occupations in the U.S. Economy. Source: U.S. Bureau of Labor Statistics, Occupational Employment Statistics

EMPLOYMENT AND OUTLOOK

Construction and building inspectors held about 105,100 jobs in 2016. The largest employers of construction and building inspectors were as follows:

Local government, excluding education and hospitals	39%
Engineering services	16%
Self-employed workers	8%
Construction	6%
State government, excluding education and hospitals	5%

Although construction and building inspectors spend most of their time inspecting worksites, they also spend time in a field office reviewing blueprints, writing reports, and scheduling inspections.

Some inspectors may have to climb ladders or crawl in tight spaces to complete their inspections.

Inspectors typically work alone. However, some inspectors may work as part of a team on large, complex projects, particularly because inspectors usually specialize in different areas of construction.

Most inspectors work full time during regular business hours. However, some may work additional hours during periods of heavy construction activity. Also, if an accident occurs at a construction site, inspectors must respond immediately and may work additional hours to complete their report. Some inspectors—especially those who are self-employed—may have to work evenings and weekends. This is particularly true of home inspectors, who typically inspect homes during the day and write reports in the evening.

Employment of construction and building inspectors is projected to grow 10 percent from 2016 to 2026, faster than the average for all occupations.

Public interest in safety and the desire to improve the quality of construction are factors that are expected to continue to create demand for inspectors. Employment growth for inspectors is expected to be strongest in government and in firms specializing in architectural, engineering, and related services.

Certified construction and building inspectors who can perform a variety of inspections should have the best job opportunities. Inspectors with construction-related work experience or training in engineering, architecture, construction technology, or related fields are also likely to have better job prospects.

Those who are self-employed, such as home inspectors, are more likely to be affected by economic downturns or fluctuations in the real estate market.

Employment Trend, Projected 2016–22

Construction and extraction occupations: 11%

Construction and building inspectors: 10%

Total, all occupations: 7%

Note: "All Occupations" includes all occupations in the U.S. Economy. Source: U.S. Bureau of Labor Statistics, Employment Projections program

Related Occupations

The following are examples of types of construction and building inspectors:

Building Inspectors

Building inspectors heck the structural quality and general safety of buildings. Some specialize further, inspecting only structural steel or reinforced-concrete structures, for example.

Coating Inspectors

Coating inspectors examine the exterior paint and coating on bridges, pipelines, and large holding tanks. Inspectors perform checks at various stages of the painting process to ensure proper coating.

Electrical Inspectors

Electrical inspectors examine the installed electrical systems to ensure they function properly and comply with electrical codes and standards. The inspectors visit worksites to inspect new and existing sound and security systems, wiring, lighting, motors, photovoltaic systems, and generating equipment. They also inspect the installed electrical wiring for HVACR systems and appliances.

Elevator Inspectors

Elevator inspectors examine lifting and conveying devices, such as elevators, escalators, moving sidewalks, lifts and hoists, inclined railways, ski lifts, and amusement rides. The inspections include both the mechanical and electrical control systems.

Home Inspectors

Home inspectors typically inspect newly built or previously owned homes, condominiums, townhomes, and other dwellings. Prospective home buyers often hire home inspectors to check and report on a home's structure and overall condition. Sometimes, homeowners hire a home inspector to evaluate their home's condition before placing it on the market.

In addition to examining structural quality, home inspectors examine all home systems and features, including the roof, exterior walls, attached garage or carport, foundation, interior walls, plumbing, electrical, and HVACR systems. They look for violations of building codes, but home inspectors do not have the power to enforce compliance with the codes.

Mechanical Inspectors

Mechanical inspectors examine the installation of HVACR systems and equipment to ensure that they are installed and function properly. They also may inspect commercial kitchen equipment, gas-fired appliances, and boilers. Mechanical inspectors should not be confused with quality control inspectors, who inspect goods at manufacturing plants.

Plan Examiners

Plan examiners determine whether the plans for a building or other structure comply with building codes. They also determine whether the structure is suited to the engineering and environmental demands of the building site.

Plumbing Inspectors

Plumbing inspectors examine the installation of systems that ensure the safety and health of drinking water, the sanitary disposal of waste, and the safety of industrial piping.

Public Works Inspectors

Public works inspectors ensure that the construction of federal, state, and local government water and sewer systems, highways, streets, bridges, and dams conforms to detailed contract specifications. Workers inspect excavation and fill operations, the placement of forms for concrete, concrete mixing and pouring, asphalt paving, and grading operations. Public works inspectors may specialize in highways, structural steel, reinforced concrete, or ditches. Others may specialize in dredging operations required for bridges, dams, or harbors.

Specification Inspectors

Specification inspectors ensure that construction work is performed according to design specifications. Specification inspectors represent the owner's interests, not those of the general public. Insurance companies and financial institutions also may use their services.

Some building inspectors are concerned with fire prevention safety. Fire inspectors and investigators ensure that buildings meet fire codes.

Conversation With . . .
AUDREY CLINE

Code Official
Town of Stratham Building/Codes Department
Stratham, New Hampshire
Building inspector, 10 years

1. What was your individual career path in terms of education/training, entry-level job, or other significant opportunity?

Like many (if not most) building inspectors, code enforcement officers, and code officials, I landed in this field as a mid-career change. I graduated from Boston University with a degree in business administration. A handful of years later, I developed an interest in architecture and attended the architectural engineering program at New Hampshire Technical Institute. After graduation, I worked as a self-employed residential designer. After a decade or so, the work began to feel mundane and I starting casting about for another situation where I could use my skills and training.

I "discovered" the field of building codes when I saw an ad in my local paper for an employment opportunity with the Town of Wolfeboro, N.H. As the town's building official, I managed the building department's processes, which included reviewing plans for compliance with the New Hampshire State Building Code and local zoning ordinances and collaborating with local fire officials for compliance with the New Hampshire State Fire Code. I enjoy the legal aspects of code administration and property rights. My favorite projects are redevelopment or so-called "infill" projects that rejuvenate older buildings and neighborhoods while bringing them up to code to meet structural strength and safety regulations.

2. What are the most important skills and/or qualities for someone in your profession?

It's important to realize that the decisions you make may have a significant effect on personal property rights. It's critical to develop an approach based on the desire to be part of the solution, while fulfilling your responsibility to the public health, safety, and welfare. This is not a career for the faint-of-heart. In the end, credibility is the goal. With credibility, even difficult decisions can be understood as being necessary and fair.

3. What do you wish you had known going into this profession?

There isn't anything I regret about making this career move. What I didn't know, and what was most surprising to me, is that public service is very different from working in the private sector. I had to re-evaluate my basic decision-making and judgment processes in order to accommodate the notion of the public good rather than the good of an individual, or indeed, my own preference.

4. Are there many job opportunities in your profession? In what specific areas?

In New Hampshire as well as many other states, the next five to ten years will see a major shortage of people entering this field. In response to the expected shortage, New Hampshire Technical Institute has begun a certificate program designed to attract people to the industry. The program can lead to immediate employment after six courses or can be the foundation for stepping into an associate's or bachelor's degree program in a related field like construction management or architecture/engineering.

While building inspectors and code officials typically work for a city or town, there are home inspection jobs in private industry. When people buy a home, the bank typically requires a home inspection that covers the condition of the home from the foundation to the roof: heating and a/c systems, plumbing and electrical systems, attic/insulation, ceiling, windows and floors. Home inspectors inspect these systems and write up a report for the buyer.

5. How do you see your profession changing in the next five years? What role will technology play in those changes, and what skills will be required?

Just as in fields like medicine and technology, there will be distinct sub-specialties. There will be a need for management personnel who have a thorough grasp of technical codes, as well as the education (such as a degree in public administration) to manage a municipal office. Most building offices are instituting electronic applications, plan review, and inspection protocols.

6. What do you enjoy most about your job? What do you enjoy least about your job?

As the town's building official, I am just as apt to be outside on a job site as in the plan review room or attending a policy committee meeting. I love the variety. Being a resource for builders and potentially saving a project from an expensive or time-consuming retrofit is very satisfying. It can be discouraging to see a project that has derailed because of lack of proper design, planning or implementation. But after ten years, I am still waiting to learn what I least like about my job!

7. Can you suggest a valuable "try this" for students considering a career in your profession?

I would urge interested students to contact the association of building officials in their state. If you're in New Hampshire or nearby, contact the New Hampshire Building Officials Association (www.nhboa.net). The association has the ability to set up a shadowing program and will reserve a seat for a curious student at one of our monthly training meetings. I'm sure other state organizations have similar programs.

MORE INFORMATION

International Association of Electrical Inspectors
P.O. Box 830848
Richardson, TX 75803-0848
972.235.1455
www.iaei.org

International City/County Management Association
Member Services Department
777 N. Capitol Street NE, Suite 500
Washington, DC 20002
202.289.4262
www.icma.org

International Code Council
500 New Jersey Avenue NW
6th Floor
Washington, DC 20001
888.422.7233
www.iccsafe.org

National Association of Commercial Building Inspectors and Thermographers
10599 E Betony Drive
Scottsdale, AZ 85255
480.308.4967
www.nacbi.org

National Association of Home Builders
1201 15th Street, NW
Washington, DC 20005
800.368.5242
www.nahb.com

National Center for Construction Education and Research
13614 Progress Boulevard
Alachua, FL 32615
888.622.3720
www.nccer.org

National Conference of States on Building Codes & Standards
505 Huntmar Park Drive, Suite 210
Herndon, VA 20170
703.437.0100
www.ncsbcs.org

National Institute of Building Inspectors
2 N Main Street, Suite 203
Medford, NJ 08055
www.nibi.com

John Pritchard/Editor

Environmental Engineers

Snapshot

Career Cluster(s): Agriculture, Food & Natural Resources, Manufacturing, Science, Technology, Engineering & Mathematics
Interests: Science, mathematics, environmental issues, research, data analysis
Earnings (Median Pay): $84,890
Employment & Outlook: Faster Than Average Growth Expected

OVERVIEW

Sphere of Work

Environmental engineers use the chemical, biological, and mechanical sciences to quantify, analyze, and mitigate pollution and other dangers to the natural environment. Environmental engineers design, implement, and supervise the operation of environmental systems used to address environmental pollution and health hazards and help mediate the environmental impact of human activities. On a typical day, an environmental engineer might investigate cases of pollution, write

environmental impact assessments, or provide technical expertise and advice on environmental cleanup projects to legislators, corporate managers, and other professionals. Environmental engineers usually specialize in one area of the field, such as water pollution or solid waste management.

Work Environment

Environmental engineers perform a great deal of their work in the field, visiting construction areas, pollution cleanup sites, reservoirs and water supply pipelines, forests, waste storage facilities and landfills, or any other area in which an environmental threat has been reported or suspected. Environmental engineers travel regularly to conduct research and investigations and, depending on the engineer's specific field, may have the opportunity to travel abroad for extended periods. Engineers working in the field risk exposure to toxic chemicals and pollutants and must observe safety guidelines when conducting their work. Other engineers work primarily indoors in engineering and industrial plants, laboratories, government agencies, or architectural firms. Environmental engineers usually work a regular forty-hour week, although they may work additional hours in the case of a professional emergency or when working under tight deadlines.

Profile

Interests: Data, Things
Working Conditions: Work Both Inside and Outside
Physical Strength: Light Work
Education Needs: Bachelor's Degree, Master's Degree, Doctoral Degree
Licensure/Certification: Required
Physical Abilities Not Require: Not Climb, Not Kneel
Opportunities For Experience: Internship
Holland Interest Score*: IRC

* See Appendix A

Occupation Interest

Environmental engineers are integral figures in the effort to protect the environment, natural resources, and wildlife from the threat of pollution and toxic substances and, as scientists, engineers rely on measurement and data (rather than political rhetoric or personal opinion) when they report on environmental issues. Data collected over the past thirty years demonstrating that human-mediated climate change has accelerated environmental degradation has increased demand for environmental engineers and prospective professionals should have a strong interest in environmental protection and remediation. Environmental engineers are an important resource in the growing effort to limit ecological damage and work in the cutting edge of green and renewable technology.

A Day in the Life—Duties and Responsibilities

Environmental engineers examine industrial and municipal sites to ensure compliance with environmental regulations as well as to estimate the efficiency and potential hazards of various types of environmental equipment. Engineers test emissions and waste to ensure that the environment is not exposed to excessive amounts of toxic pollution and help make recommendations to protect ecological areas and workers who are potentially exposed to pollutants. Environmental engineers also help design wastewater filtration, recycling, waste containment, air quality, and municipal water programs in cities and towns around the world, helping to balance the needs of the populace with the effort to limit pollution.

Environmental engineers also conduct research on the impact of industrial processes on the environment, and may study phenomena like acid rain, global climate change, air pollution, water quality, deforestation, loss of wildlife, and a variety of other environmental issues. In many cases, academic engineers write scholarly papers on various environmental issues, while others working in corporate or governmental fields may author environmental impact assessments and reports for corporate leaders or legislators to use in assessing various programs. Many environmental engineers help lawmakers and government officials craft environmental policies and regulations and conduct research on the effectiveness of such policies.

As with all true sciences, environmental engineering is a collaborative field and engineers frequently work with other scientists, legislators and community leaders, and corporate representatives when conducting their work. As environmental engineering is increasingly an essential part of development and construction projects, engineers are also involved with programs to expand housing and utilities, build roads and bridges, and a variety of other residential and commercial expansion projects. They may be asked to develop and maintain plans, obtain permits, and implement operating procedures to ensure that construction and engineering projects are handled safely and with limited environmental impact.

Duties and Responsibilities

- Designing and developing systems and equipment that comply with environmental standards
- Consulting with environmental scientists, hazardous waste technicians and other engineers and specialists
- Inspecting facilities to ensure observance with environmental regulations
- Educating organizations and government agencies on the necessary steps to clean up a contaminated site
- Creating and updating environmental investigation and recommendation reports
- Securing and maintaining necessary plans and permits for development of systems and equipment
- Overseeing the progress of environmental improvement programs

WORK ENVIRONMENT

Immediate Physical Environment

Environmental engineers conduct part of their work indoors, in office environments, and part of their work on-site at various facilities, projects, or environmental areas. When working in the field, engineers may be exposed to dirty, uncomfortable, or potentially hazardous conditions. The amount of time spent in the field varies depending on the engineer's specialization, employer, and field.

Human Environment

Environmental engineers interact with other professionals regularly, including government officials, environmentalists and environmental scientists, laboratory technicians, construction managers and

Transferable Skills and Abilities

Communication Skills
- Speaking effectively
- Writing concisely

Interpersonal/Social Skills
- Being able to work independently
- Working as a member of a team
- Having good judgment

Organization & Management Skills
- Initiating new ideas
- Paying attention to and handling details
- Managing time
- Promoting change
- Making decisions
- Meeting goals and deadlines
- Performing duties which change frequently

Research & Planning Skills
- Creating ideas
- Identifying problems
- Determining alternatives
- Identifying resources
- Solving problems
- Developing evaluation strategies
- Using logical reasoning

Technical Skills
- Performing scientific, mathematical and technical work
- Working with data or numbers

Unclassified Skills
- Using set methods and standards in your work

contractors, and architects. In many cases, engineers may be asked to speak at meetings or assemblies or may give reports to community or corporate leaders on various environmental issues.

Technological Environment

Environmental engineers use a wide range of tools and technologies in their work, including specialized measurement tools like air velocity and temperature monitors, spectrometers, and photometers. Engineers might also use a variety of hand and power tools when conducting work in the field. In the laboratory or office, environmental engineers use computers and other digital tools, including a variety computer modeling and design software, including computer-aided design (CAD) and photo-imaging software, to design plans and maps of sites or projects. Engineers also regularly utilize basic office programs and tools, like work processing, spreadsheet, and presentation software, as well as email and other digital communication programs.

EDUCATION, TRAINING, AND ADVANCEMENT

High School/Secondary

High school students interested in environmental engineering should study a wide range of natural sciences, such as biology, chemistry, physics, and earth sciences, as well as engineering and mathematics, including algebra, geometry, calculus, and trigonometry. Classes in social studies, political science, history, and other humanities can provide a deeper understanding of the intersection between public and environmental welfare and foreign language courses are helpful for those considering working overseas. Computer science and drafting classes are also highly beneficial and students should develop strong writing skills by taking English or composition classes.

Suggested High School Subjects
- Agricultural Education
- Algebra
- Applied Biology/Chemistry
- Applied Communication
- Applied Math
- Applied Physics
- Biology
- Blueprint Reading
- Calculus
- Chemistry
- College Preparatory
- Computer Science
- Drafting
- Earth Science
- English
- Forestry
- Geometry
- Humanities
- Mathematics
- Physical Science

- Physics
- Science
- Social Studies
- Trigonometry

Related Career Pathways/Majors

Agriculture, Food & Natural Resources Cluster
- Environmental Service Systems Pathway

Manufacturing Cluster
- Manufacturing Production Process Development Pathway

Science, Technology, Engineering & Mathematics Cluster
- Engineering & Technology Pathway

Postsecondary

Most environmental engineers earn postsecondary degrees in engineering, with a secondary specialization in environmental science. Engineers may improve their career prospects by obtaining advanced degrees in engineering with focus on an environmental field and many high-level environmental engineers obtain master's or doctorate level degrees in the field. At the post-graduate level, some universities offer environmental engineering programs or programs focusing specifically on a sub-field of environmental engineering, such as soil engineering or waste management.

Related College Majors
- Engineering, General
- Environmental & Pollution Control Technology
- Environmental Health
- Environmental Science/Studies
- Environmental/Environmental Health Engineering

Adult Job Seekers

Qualified environmental engineers may apply directly to firms and government agencies that have openings. Job fairs, Internet job boards, government employment web pages, and professional placement agencies may also be able to help qualified engineers find employment in their field. Additionally, prospective engineers may join professional organizations, such as the American Academy of Environmental Engineers, in order to network and potentially find new job opportunities.

Professional Certification and Licensure

In the United States, environmental engineers must obtain a Professional Engineer (PE) license from the state or states in which they work. This process entails passing a state examination as well as meeting educational and work experience requirements. Because the field of environmental engineering is broad, engineers may obtain training and certification in specialized fields offered through various engineering associations and organizations. Licensing and certification requirements for engineers working abroad vary according to national or regional laws and engineers planning on working abroad should research the legal requirements of working abroad before applying for open positions.

Additional Requirements

Engineering is a scientific field most suited to individuals who are inquisitive and enjoy investigation and solving problems. Environmental engineers must be attentive to detail, able to research and understand complex systems, and must be able to adhere to set procedures and scientific standards. Engineers should demonstrate strong research, writing, and analytical skills as well as the ability to use a wide range of technologies, including computer software and technical tools specific to their field. Federal government-employed environmental engineers must be U.S. citizens, and some must receive additional government security clearance as part of the hiring process.

EARNINGS AND ADVANCEMENT

In 2016, the median annual wage for environmental engineers in the United States was $84,890 per year, with those at the lowest ten percent earning less than $49,000, while the highest paid engineers might earn over $130,000. Pay for engineers working abroad may vary considerably according to their employer and the nature of their job. In many cases, environmental engineers receive paid vacations, holidays and sick days; life and health insurance; and retirement benefits through their employer. Advancing in the field may involve seeking employment in higher-paid or more prestigious positions or advancing within an organization to become a senior engineer or project manager in charge of a team of engineers and other technical personnel.

Median annual wages, May 2016

Engineers: $91,010

Environmental engineers: $84,890

Total, all occupations: $37,040

Note: "All Occupations" includes all occupations in the U.S. Economy. Source: U.S. Bureau of Labor Statistics, Occupational Employment Statistics

EMPLOYMENT AND OUTLOOK

The Bureau of Labor Statistics (BLS) estimates that the environmental engineering field will grow by more than 12 percent between 2014 and 2024, which is faster than the average of 6-7 percent predicted for all U.S. occupations. Growth in the industry has been driven by the evolving environmental consciousness of the global population as decades of research have demonstrated the increasingly destructive impact of human culture on the world's environment and natural resources. In an effort to limit environmental destruction, reduce the risk of pollution-related injury or illness, and to preserve remaining natural resources, more and more companies and governmental organizations make use of environmental engineers and this has created an increasing demand for trained professionals.

In addition, as environmental engineers are important to commercial and residential expansion, the rapid growth of the human population also serves to increase demand for environmental engineers around the world. While there are many domestic opportunities for trained engineers, there are also numerous opportunities for engineers willing to travel abroad to conduct environmental studies and help mediate the environmental impact of various programs and projects. Environmental threats like climate change and water pollution are worldwide issues and so engineers involved in research may need to travel internationally to collect data.

Related Occupations
- Agricultural Engineer
- Biological Scientist
- Chemical Engineer
- Chemist
- Energy Engineer
- Environmental Science Technician
- Forester & Conservation Scientist
- Hazardous Waste Manager
- Petroleum Engineer
- Water & Wastewater Engineer
- Wind Energy Engineer

Related Military Occupations
- Environmental Health & Safety Officer
- Environmental Health & Safety Specialist

Percent change in employment Projected 2016-26

Engineers: 8%

Environmental engineers: 8%

Total, all occupations: 7%

Note: "All Occupations" includes all occupations in the U.S. Economy. Source: U.S. Bureau of Labor Statistics, Employment Projections program

Conversation With . . .
JAN VERTEFEUILLE

Senior Director, World Wildlife Fund
Advocacy, 15 years

1. **What was your individual career path in terms of education/training, entry-level job, or other significant opportunity?**

I transitioned into international advocacy for conservation after working at newspapers and loving it. But after a decade, I started thinking about what else I could do with my strongest skills: researching, writing, delivering work on deadline, and drawing stories and information out of people.

I went to work for a nonprofit in D.C. called Environmental Media Services, which was run by a bunch of former reporters who educated journalists about environmental issues and worked to generate media coverage of issues like environmental health and genetically engineered food. I worked there for four years before learning of a communications job at World Wildlife Fund. Since my passion was wildlife, it seemed a great fit.

My job focuses on figuring out advocacy strategies to achieve a specific wildlife conservation goal, like trying to reduce illegal ivory sales in a particular country to reduce elephant poaching. We might launch a campaign that includes policy advocacy (i.e. lobbying), media outreach to raise public awareness, and direct public engagement, like asking citizens to pledge not to buy ivory or sign a petition to their government. Then we look at who might be influential with the decision-makers in that country. Would diplomatic pressure help? Would a celebrity or influential business leader take up the cause?

2. **What are the most important skills and/or qualities for someone in your profession?**

People think of advocacy as lobbying legislators and government officials to get a law passed, and that's part of it. But to be successful, you need to really understand the players you're trying to influence and what tactics will be successful and what ones might actually hurt your efforts.

Professional training and a degree is less important than innate skills, which can be cultivated and improved through practice: creativity, curiosity, strategic thinking, flexibility, persuasion and the ability to work with a cross-cultural team. And by that last one I mean the ability to really listen to members of your team from other cultures and draw out their ideas. During a brainstorming discussion, for instance, Americans tend to be forthright with their ideas and have no problem sharing ideas. Colleagues from other cultures may be more reluctant to speak up. I've learned the hard way that some people I work with find it very rude to tell me my idea is a bad one, even when they know it won't work, so I now ask a lot of questions and listen carefully to the answers. I then offer ideas in ways that can be rejected by someone without the fear of being rude.

3. What do you wish you had known before starting your career?

I wish I'd known how fulfilling international work is—I would have started sooner! I love working with people all over the world even though it means holding conference calls at crazy hours, so that team members in Asia and North America can talk to each other. I also wish Americans were better informed about issues outside the U.S. There is a whole big fascinating world full of people who are just as smart, well-educated, compassionate and creative, and they're working just as hard to protect the environment where they live and improve their quality of life. It seems obvious, but it's worth stating explicitly.

4. Are there many job opportunities overseas in your profession?

As the population hurtles close to 9 billion people on the planet, there will be a surge in need for people interested in advocating for change internationally, whether it's figuring out how to feed all those people while protecting the environment, mitigating climate change before our coasts are swamped, ensuring elephants and tigers continue to roam in the wild, or improving the way we build cities. Nonprofit organizations and governments in wealthy countries like the U.S. that have a long history of international charitable giving will be doing a lot of the hiring.

5. Will the need for professionals in your career change in the next five years? What role will technology play in those changes, and what skills will be required?

Advances in video conferencing and communication apps like Skype, Webex, Whatsapp and Line have provided huge benefits in being able to keep in touch with colleagues all over the world at all hours of the day. That has cut down on the need for some international travel. But there is really no substitute for face-to-face interaction with colleagues, so I think some international travel will always be a part of jobs like mine.

Social media and platforms like change.org, Avaaz, and other petition sites have increased opportunities to bring global attention to a problem. A great example is when WWF launched a campaign to press the president of Mexico to take more action to save the world's most endangered marine mammal, the tiny vaquita porpoise that's found only in Mexico's Gulf of California. We generated hundreds of thousands of emails to his office and launched a social media effort that Leo DiCaprio joined on Twitter. The president of Mexico, WWF, and DiCaprio started a public dialogue on Twitter about the vaquita and the president and DiCaprio ended up signing a formal agreement to work together to save this critically endangered species.

6. What do you enjoy most about your job? What do you enjoy least about your job?

I enjoy being part of a global organization with such a diverse number of issues to work on (endangered species, climate change, fresh water, forests and oceans) and with team members all over the world to learn from.

My least favorite part of the job is dealing with budgets. Funding and tracking spending is important, but not something I enjoy.

7. Can you suggest a valuable "try this" for students considering a career overseas in your profession?

Start by writing a letter to the editor of your local paper or emailing the appropriate decision-makers about an issue you care about (school funding, lack of bike lanes in town, not enough recycling in the parks). Be constructive (criticizing people immediately makes them less likely to listen to you) and consider the issue from their perspective so you can be persuasive, and propose a solution. Will it require a new rule, for instance, to stop selling plastic water bottles at park concessions? What can you suggest to make that feasible?

MORE INFORMATION

Air and Waste Management Association
1 Gateway Center, 3rd Floor
420 Fort Duquesne Boulevard
Pittsburgh, PA 15222-1435
800.270.3444
www.awma.org

American Academy of Environmental Engineers
130 Holiday Court, Suite 100
Annapolis, MD 21401
410.266.3311
info@aaee.net
www.aaee.net

Association of Environmental & Engineering Geologists
P.O. Box 460518
Denver, CO 80246
303.757.2926
www.aegweb.org

Institute of Professional Environmental Practice
600 Forbes Avenue
339 Fisher Hall
Pittsburgh, PA 15282
412.396.1703
www.ipep.org

Solid Waste Association of North America
1100 Wayne Avenue, Suite 700
Silver Spring, MD 20910
800.467.9262
www.swana.org

U.S. Army Corps of Engineers Research and Development Center
3909 Halls Ferry Road
Vicksburg, MS 39180-6199
866.373.2872
www.erdc.usace.army.mil

Michael Auerbacht/Editor

Farmers, Ranchers & Other Agricultural Managers

Snapshot

Career Cluster(s): Agriculture, Food & Natural Resources, Business, Management & Administration

Interests: Agriculture, business practices, being outside, working independently

Earnings (Median pay): $66,360 per year; $31.91 per hour

Job Growth: As fast as average

OVERVIEW

Sphere of Work

Farmers and farm managers, also called farm operators and agricultural managers, grow food for personal consumption and for wholesale and retail consumers. Farmers and farm managers oversee agricultural production and financial operations at farms, nurseries, ranches, and greenhouses. Farmers and farm managers grow crops, livestock, poultry, and aquatic animals. Although specific tasks vary by type of agricultural work, all farmers and farm managers are

responsible for ensuring the care of crops and animals from conception to market. Farmers often perform the hands-on labor of planting, cultivating, operating farm machinery, harvesting, and marketing and selling crops and animals. Farm managers hire, train, and supervise farm staff to complete these tasks.

Work Environment

Farmers, ranchers, and other agricultural managers typically work outdoors, but they may spend some time in offices.

Farmers, ranchers, and other agricultural managers typically work outdoors, but may spend some time in offices. They often do strenuous physical work.

Some farmers work primarily with crops and vegetables. Other farmers and ranchers handle livestock.

The work environment for farmers, ranchers, and other agricultural managers can be hazardous. Tractors, tools, and other farm machinery can cause serious injury, so workers must be alert on the job. They must operate equipment and handle chemicals properly to avoid accidents and safeguard the surrounding environment.

Most farmers, ranchers, and other agricultural managers work full time. Farm work can be seasonal, and the number of hours worked may change according to the season. Farmers and farm managers on crop farms usually work from sunrise to sunset during the planting and harvesting seasons. During the rest of the year, they plan the next season's crops, market their output, and repair and maintain machinery. About 1 in 3 worked more than 40 hours per week in 2016.

On livestock-producing farms and ranches, work goes on throughout the year. Animals must be fed and cared for every day.

On large farms, farmers and farm managers spend time meeting with farm supervisors. Managers who oversee several farms may divide their time between traveling to meet farmers and landowners and staying in their offices to plan farm operations.

Profile

Working Conditions: Work both Indoors and Outdoors

Physical Strength: Medium Work, Heavy Work

Education Needs: On-The-Job Training, High School Diploma with Technical Education, Junior/Technical/Community College, Apprenticeship, Bachelor's Degree

Licensure/Certification: Usually Not Required

Physical Abilities Not Required: N/A

Opportunities For Experience: Internship, Apprenticeship, Volunteer Work, Part Time Work

Holland Interest Score*: ESR, REI, RIE

* See Appendix A

Occupation Interest

Individuals attracted to the farming profession tend to be physically strong and detail-oriented people. Successful farmers and farm managers exhibit stamina, resilience, organizational abilities, integrity and ethics, independence, and effective time management. Business acumen and familiarity with computer technology is becoming increasingly advantageous. Farmers and farm managers should enjoy physical labor and have a strong background in agriculture and business.

A Day in the Life—Duties and Responsibilities

Farmers and farm managers perform different daily occupational duties and responsibilities depending on their specialization and work environment. They may specialize in the production of crops, beef, poultry, pork, dairy, or aquaculture.

On crop farms, farmers and farm managers oversee activities related to the planting, tending, and harvesting of crops. These tasks may include preparing soil and managing its nutrient levels, using natural or chemical methods to eliminate pests, irrigating and draining fields, weather forecasting, and storing fuels and chemicals. Crop farmers and farm managers promote and sell crops to distributors and food-processing companies, retail customers in farmers markets or farm stands, or shareholders in a community-supported agriculture (CSA) program.

Animal farmers and farm managers oversee meat production operations. They raise beef cattle, chickens, turkeys, ducks, game birds, goats, or pigs. Animal farmers and farm managers must ensure proper breeding and birthing and feeding, housing, transportation, and slaughtering. Those who work with beef cattle and pigs medicate and vaccinate the animals as needed. On poultry farms, they also manage the hatchery, establish egg or meat-bird production effort, adjust the lighting in poultry buildings to promote molting or egg laying, and match stock size to seasonal demand. All animal farmers and farm managers are responsible for promoting and selling meat products.

Dairy farmers and farm managers direct tasks related to the production, collection, and sale of milk. They must ensure the proper care for milk cows. These farmers and farm managers oversee the establishment of a feed storage system for corn silage, alfalfa, hay, cottonseed, and soybeans. They also supervise the construction and maintenance of a milking parlor, a milking and milk storage system, and a manure management system. Dairy farmers and farm managers promote, transport, and sell dairy products.

Aquaculture farmers and farm managers oversee aquaculture production tasks. They or their staff stock ponds or floating nets with eggs, shellfish, or juvenile fish, feed fish stock, and protect fish stock from predators and contamination. Like their meat and dairy counterparts, these farmers and farm managers are responsible for the promotion and sale of their products.

In addition, all farmers and farm managers are responsible for purchasing supplies, maintaining farm machinery, ensuring the cleanliness of farm facilities, and educating themselves about government regulations and business trends affecting their industry.

Duties and Responsibilities

- **Planning crops to be planted or livestock to be raised**
- **Preparing soil for planting**
- **Cultivating and irrigating crops**
- **Spraying crops with insecticides and fungicides**
- **Harvesting and marketing produce**
- **Tending and marketing livestock and poultry**
- **Handling business functions as needed to keep the operation running**

OCCUPATION SPECIALTIES

Individuals attracted to the farming profession tend to be physically strong and detail-oriented people. Successful farmers and farm managers exhibit stamina, resilience, organizational abilities, integrity and ethics, independence, and effective time management. Business acumen and familiarity with computer technology is becoming increasingly advantageous. Farmers and farm managers should enjoy physical labor and have a strong background in agriculture and business.

Farmers and Ranchers

Farmers and ranchers own and operate mainly family-owned farms. They also may lease land from a landowner and operate it as a working farm.

The size of the farm or range determines which tasks farmers and ranchers handle. Those who operate small farms or ranges may do all tasks, including harvesting and inspecting the land, growing crops, and raising animals. In addition, they keep records, service machinery, and maintain buildings.

By contrast, farmers and ranchers who operate larger farms generally have employees—including agricultural workers—who help with physical work. Some employees of large farms are in nonfarm occupations, working as truck drivers, sales representatives, bookkeepers, or information technology specialists.

Farmers and ranchers track technological improvements in animal breeding and seeds, choosing new products that might increase output. Many livestock and dairy farmers monitor and attend to the health of their herds, which may include assisting in births.

Agricultural Managers

Agricultural managers take care of the day-to-day operations of one or more farms, ranches, nurseries, timber tracts, greenhouses, and other agricultural establishments for corporations, farmers, and owners who do not live and work on their farm or ranch.

Agricultural managers usually do not participate in production activities themselves. Instead, they hire and supervise farm and livestock workers to do most daily production tasks.

Managers may determine budgets. They may decide how to store, transport, and sell crops. They may also oversee the proper maintenance of equipment and property.

The following are examples of types of farmers, ranchers, and other agricultural managers:

Crop farmers and managers are responsible for all steps of plant growth, which include planting, fertilizing, watering, and harvesting crops. These farmers can grow grain, fruits, vegetables, and other crops. After a harvest, they make sure that the crops are properly packaged and stored.

Livestock, dairy, and poultry farmers, ranchers, and managers feed and care for animals, such as cows or chickens, in order to harvest meat, milk, or eggs. They keep livestock and poultry in barns, pens, and other farm buildings. These workers may also oversee the breeding of animals in order to maintain the appropriate herd or flock size.

Nursery and greenhouse managers oversee the production of trees, shrubs, flowers, and plants (including turf) used for landscaping. In addition to applying pesticides and fertilizers to help plants grow, they are often responsible for keeping track of inventory and marketing activities.

Aquaculture farmers and managers raise fish and shellfish in ponds, floating net pens, raceways, and recirculating systems. They stock, feed, protect, and maintain aquatic life used for food and recreational fishing.

WORK ENVIRONMENT

Physical Environment

Farmers and farm managers work in farms, nurseries, ranches, and greenhouses. Farming tends to be very physical and require extensive hard labor, walking, lifting, and bending. Farmers and farm managers are at high risk for back strain, pesticide exposure, and machine accidents.

Human Environment

Farms, nurseries, ranches, and greenhouses tend to be remotely located and isolated. However, farmers and farm managers interact with farm workers, families, customers, landholders, bankers, veterinarians, and government inspectors. The amount of human interaction often depends on the scale and business model of the farm operation. Farm managers typically report to a farmer or corporation.

Technological Environment

In the course of their work, farmers and farm managers use farm machinery and equipment such as animal feeders, hay balers, mowers, trucks, irrigation systems, tractors, chain saws, and milking machines. In addition, farmers and farm managers use computers, Internet communication tools, accounting and farm management software, and spreadsheets to assist them with the business tasks of farming.

EDUCATION, TRAINING, AND ADVANCEMENT

High School/Secondary

High school-level study of agricultural science, biology, chemistry, and business can provide a strong foundation for work as a farmer or college-level study in the field. High school students interested in this career path may benefit from internships, apprenticeships, or part-time work with local farms that expose them to the diversity and challenges of farming responsibilities.

Suggested High School Subjects
- Agricultural Education
- Applied Biology/Chemistry
- Bookkeeping
- Business
- Economics
- English
- Forestry
- Mathematics

Famous First

The first tomatoes eaten by European descendants in America were from a batch grown in Virginia in 1745. Until that time, colonists thought tomatoes to be poisonous. It took a physician, John Siccary, to examine this red fruit of the nightshade plant and declare it edible to convince people of the tomato's worth. Later, Siccary's fellow Virginian Thomas Jefferson raised tomatoes on his plantation, Monticello (his hand drawn garden plans are shown here), and publicized their safety.

College/Postsecondary

Although a postsecondary degree is not strictly necessary for farm work, aspiring farmers or farm managers should pursue the associate's degree or bachelor's degree in agriculture, farm management, agronomy, and dairy science. Formal postsecondary studies afford students a better understanding of the work and industry and provide greater opportunities for advancement. Postsecondary students can gain work experience and potential advantage in their future job searches by securing internships or part-time employment with local farms.

Related College Majors
- Agricultural Business & Management
- Agricultural Production Workers & Managers
- Agricultural Supplies Retailing & Wholesaling
- Farm & Ranch Management
- Horticulture Science
- Horticulture Services Operations & Management
- International Agriculture
- Plant Sciences

Adult Job Seekers

Adults seeking employment as farmers or farm managers should have, at a minimum, a high school diploma or associate's degree. Some farm manager jobs require extensive experience, on-the-job training, and a bachelor's or master's degree. Those seeking farm manager positions should educate themselves about the educational and professional requirements of their prospective employers.

Adult job seekers may benefit from joining professional associations to help with networking and job searching. Professional farming and agricultural associations, such as the American Farm Bureau Federation, the American Society of Agronomy and the American Society of Farm Managers & Rural Appraisers, generally offer job-finding workshops and maintain lists and forums of available jobs.

Professional Certification and Licensure

Certification and licensure is not required for farmers but may be required of farm managers as a condition of employment, salary increase, or promotion. The Accredited Farm Manager (AFM) certification, offered by the American Society of Farm Managers and Rural Appraisers, is the leading option for voluntary farm manager certification. The Accredited Farm Manager certification requires a minimum of four years of farm management experience, a bachelor's degree in agricultural science, a sample farm management plan, and the successful completion of a national exam covering farm business, finances, and law.

Additional Requirements

Successful farmers and farm managers will be knowledgeable about the profession's requirements, responsibilities, and opportunities. The U.S. Environmental Protection Agency requires farmers and farm workers to be trained in agricultural pesticide safe practices. Operating licenses for farm vehicles may be required for some types of agricultural work.

Fun Fact

Could there be some good news down on the farm? Though the U.S. has seen a long-term trend of fewer farms, the decline of less than one percent between 2007 and 2012 was the third smallest decline since 1950, according to the 2012 Census of Agriculture. Crop sales increased 48 percent in the five years between the 2007 and 2012 censuses, and livestock sales increased 19 percent.

Source: http://www.agcensus.usda.gov/Publications/2012/Preliminary_Report/Highlights.pdf

EARNINGS AND ADVANCEMENT

The median annual wage for farmers, ranchers, and other agricultural managers was $66,360 in May 2016. The median wage is the wage at which half the workers in an occupation earned more than that amount and half earned less. The lowest 10 percent earned less than $35,020, and the highest 10 percent earned more than $126,070.

Incomes of farmers and ranchers vary from year to year because prices of farm products fluctuate with weather conditions and other factors. In addition to earning income from their farm business, farmers can receive government subsidies or other payments that add to their income and reduce some of the risks of farming.

Also, more farmers, especially operators of small farms, are relying more on off-farm sources of income, such as community-supported agriculture (CSA) programs.

Most farmers, ranchers, and other agricultural managers work full time. Farm work can be seasonal and the number of hours worked may change according to the season. Farmers and farm managers on crop farms usually work from sunrise to sunset during the planting and harvesting seasons. During the rest of the year, they plan the next season's crops, market their output, and repair and maintain machinery. About 1 in 3 worked more than 40 hours per week in 2016.

On livestock-producing farms and ranches, work goes on throughout the year. Animals must be fed and cared for every day.

Median annual wages, May 2016

Other management occupations: $87,420

Farmers, ranchers, and other agricultural managers: $66,360

Total, all occupations: $37,040

Note: "All Occupations" includes all occupations in the U.S. Economy. Source: U.S. Bureau of Labor Statistics, Occupational Employment Statistics

EMPLOYMENT AND OUTLOOK

Employment of farmers, ranchers, and other agricultural managers is projected to grow 7 percent from 2016 to 2026, about as fast as the average for all occupations. Owners of large tracts of land, who often do not live on the property they own, increasingly will seek the expertise of agricultural managers to run their farms and ranches as businesses.

Despite a projected decline in the number of acres being used for farming, output is expected to remain steady due to increasing crop yields. In addition, the demand for meats and dairy products should remain strong and result in higher livestock production.

Job prospects should be favorable. Some job opportunities will arise from retirements of older farmers, ranchers, and agricultural managers.

Some small-scale farmers may improve their job prospects by developing successful market niches that involve personalized, direct contact with their customers. Many are finding opportunities in organic food production. Others sell their output at farmers' markets that cater directly to urban and suburban consumers, allowing the farmers to capture a greater share of consumers' food dollars.

Farmers, ranchers, and other agricultural managers held about 1.0 million jobs in 2016. The largest employers of farmers, ranchers, and other agricultural managers were as follows.

Self-employed workers	73%
Crop production	16%
Animal production and aquaculture	10%

Employment Trend, Projected 2016–22

Other management occupations: 9%

Total, all occupations: 7%

Farmers, ranchers, and other agricultural managers: 7%

Note: "All Occupations" includes all occupations in the U.S. Economy. Source: U.S. Bureau of Labor Statistics, Employment Projections program

Related Occupations
Livestock Ranchers

Livestock ranchers breed and raise livestock such as beef cattle dairy cattle, goats, horses, sheep and swine to sell meat, dairy products, wool and hair.

Poultry Farmers

Poultry farmers raise chickens, turkeys or other fowl for meat or egg production.

Vegetable Farmers

Vegetable farmers plan and plant vegetables according to weather, type of soil and size and location of the farm.

Tree-Fruit-And-Nut Crop Farmers

Tree-fruit-and-nut crop farmers plant and cultivate fruit producing trees.

Nursery Managers

Nursery managers supervise plant nurseries which produce plants for sale to wholesale or retail customers.

Farm General Managers

Farm general managers operate farms for corporations, cooperatives or other owners.

Fish Farmers

Fish farmers spawn and raise fish for commercial purposes.

Horse Trainers

Horse trainers train horses for riding or harness.

Organic Farmers/Farm Managers

Organic farmers/farm managers grow crops, control pests and maintain soil health without the use, or the limited use, of synthetic fertilizers and pesticides.

Conversation With . . .
PETER JOHNSON

Farmer Owner Pete's Greens, Pete's Pastured Meats
Good Eats CSA, Craftsbury, Vermont
Farmer, 17 years

1. What was your individual career path in terms of education/training, entry-level job, or other significant opportunity?

I've always been involved in growing things. Even as a kid, I had a small pumpkin operation. I got a bachelor's degree in environmental studies from Middlebury College and after college, I got right back into farming. I returned to my parents' land in Greensboro (Vermont) and cleared ¾ of an acre to start my farm. For the first four years, Pete's Greens produced only salad greens. Then we began to diversify, which required land. I rented 10 acres from a friend, about six miles away. For five years, I looked for a farm to buy. I struck gold in 2003. It has 190 acres, a huge house and beautiful barn. Today Pete's Greens is a four-season organic vegetable farm. In the Northeast, 80 acres of vegetables is a lot, but on a national and international level, we're small.

The locavore movement has been huge for us. Our Good Eats CSA (Community Supported Agriculture) is probably the most profitable part of our business. People buy a share and we deliver food to sites where they pick it up. We had a healthy, strong business before we started the CSA, but it's helped us grow.

2. What are the most important skills and/or qualities for someone in your profession?

Endurance is probably the biggest one. For the kind of farm that I have, that relies on staying ahead of the curve. You have to have vision, be adaptable and be innovative. But that's different from what a lot of farming requires. For most farming, you have to have endurance, the ability to make good financial decisions, and be reliable and steady.

3. What do you wish you had known going into this profession?

I wish that I had been able to recognize the extremely low prices land was selling for and had been able to figure out a way to buy some of it, because not only was it cheap, but it was available. In our area, a new wave of agricultural ventures is driving up prices. I've been very much a part of that, and it's been incredible, but it's kind of hurting us now.

4. Are there many job opportunities in your profession? In what specific areas?

Oh yes, there are plenty of opportunities in farming for smart, capable, hardworking, common sense people. Unfortunately, a lot of young Americans don't really have those traits. I don't know a farm that isn't always looking for help. Once you get there, you can very quickly move up. It's a very quick, very clear path to get close to the top. And actually, right now in Vermont, we have a wave of folks with really nice vegetable farms who are thinking about retiring. A lot of them are working on succession plans that don't involve people who are related to them. I read that the average age of a farmer across the country is 57. Some of them have kids that love it, and some have kids that don't want anything to do with it.

5. How do you see your profession changing in the next five years? What role will technology play in those changes, and what skills will be required?

We're all using our smart phones more and more. I monitor my cooler temperatures with it. I communicate with my customers with it. I sell things with it. In the future, we'll probably be using more GPS technology for fertilizing, watering, things like that, which is already common on bigger farms.

The ability to communicate in real time has really changed things. It's amazing. I hardly ever go into the office or use my computer anymore. I can be sitting on the tractor doing business.

We can't afford some of the automated equipment that much bigger farms use, so I've been looking to China and India for niche products.

6. What do you enjoy most about your job? What do you enjoy least about your job?

What I enjoy most is having a problem with an important crop and, through research or intuition or some other means, coming up with a solution that leads to genuine success with the crop down the road. It's difficult, but it's very gratifying. You can't get it in a book—books can help, information can help you—but no one's situation is exactly like yours in terms of soil, temperature, pests. You have to spend time in the field.

What I enjoy least is people management. It's not my strong suit. It's a really big part of my job.

7. Can you suggest a valuable "try this" for students considering a career in your profession?

Go find a farm and get a summer job. Oftentimes, you know pretty quickly whether this is something you're going to enjoy or not.

SELECTED SCHOOLS

Many agricultural, technical, and community colleges offer programs related to farming and farm management. Interested students are advised to consult with their school guidance counselor or to research area postsecondary schools and training programs. For those interested in pursuing a bachelor's degree, a state land-grant college is often the best place to start.

MORE INFORMATION

American Farm Bureau Federation
600 Maryland Avenue, SW
Suite 1000
Washington, DC 20024
202.406.3600
www.fb.org

American Society of Agronomy
Career Development & Placement Services
5585 Guilford Road
Madison, WI 53711
608.273.8080
www.agronomy.org

American Society of Farm Managers & Rural Appraisers
950 South Cherry Street, Suite 508
Denver, CO 80246-2664
303.758.3513
www.asfmra.org

Center for Rural Affairs
145 Main Street
PO Box 136
Lyons, NE 68038
402.687.2100
www.cfra.org

National Agri-Marketing Association
11020 King Street, Suite 205
Overland Park, KS 66210
913.491.6500
www.nama.org

National FFA Organization (Future Farmers of America)
P.O. Box 68960
6060 FFA Drive
Indianapolis, IN 46268-0960
317.802.6060
www.ffa.org

National Institute of Food and Agriculture
800 9th Street SW
Washington, DC 20024
202.720.4423
www.csrees.usda.gov

National Sustainable Agriculture Information Service
P.O. Box 3838
Butte, MT 59702
www.attra.org

USDA Farm Service Agency
1400 Independence Avenue, SW
Washington, DC 20250
www.fsa.usda.gov

Simone Isadora Flynn/Editor

Firefighters

Snapshot

Career Cluster(s): Law, Public Safety & Security
Interests: Working in dangerous situations, helping others
Earnings (Median pay): $48,030 per year; $23.09 per hour
Job Growth: As fast as average

OVERVIEW

Sphere of Work

Firefighters are public safety workers who extinguish structure, forest, and other fires. They also administer first aid to accident victims and conduct search-and-rescue operations. Firefighters are also responsible for creating and implementing public fire prevention campaigns and promoting safe practices for the home and workplace. Additionally, firefighters often conduct building inspections, enforce building and fire codes, and investigate alleged violations of those rules.

Work Environment

Firefighters are based in fire stations, where they store equipment and trucks, located in all types of municipalities. These stations are well organized and maintained so that when a call comes in, all of the necessary equipment is close at hand and fully operational. When the station receives a call, firefighters enter highly dangerous work environments, including burning and destabilized buildings and accident scenes. At such sites, they must wear heavy suits, boots, and helmets and carry heavy equipment. Frequently, firefighters visit schools and other public locations to promote fire safety.

Profile

Working Conditions: Work both Indoors and Outdoors
Physical Strength: Heavy Work
Education Needs: On-The-Job Training, Technical/Community College, Apprenticeship
Licensure/Certification: Required
Physical Abilities Not Required: N/A
Opportunities For Experience: Apprenticeship, Military Service, Volunteer Work, Part-Time Work
Holland Interest Score*: RES

* See Appendix A

Occupation Interest

Firefighters perform a wide range of duties, all of which center around saving lives. Firefighters enter burning buildings and accident scenes, risking their own lives and safety for others. As first responders, they are trained to treat victims on the scene; their quick work can make the difference between life and death. The job of a firefighter is exciting and challenging, with dangerous situations occurring regularly. Firefighters typically have excellent job benefits, including full insurance and a strong retirement plan.

A Day in the Life—Duties and Responsibilities

Firefighters work in stations, where they organize and maintain trucks, hoses, rescue equipment, first aid kits, and outerwear so that crews can immediately depart when an alarm sounds. They also meet members of the public at the station, performing outreach activities such as installing child car seats and giving fire safety presentations. Fire stations are normally staffed around the clock by full-time firefighters whose shifts may last twenty-four hours or more. During their shifts, firefighters eat and sleep at the station when not performing training or maintenance duties.

When a call comes in, the dispatcher informs the firefighters of the address and nature of the emergency. The firefighters then suit up, gather the appropriate equipment, and take the necessary vehicles to the site. At the scene of a fire, firefighters work closely with their company mates. As a team, they coordinate various assignments, such as using hoses, breaking down walls, opening fire hydrants, operating rescue equipment, and administering first aid to victims. Upon returning to the station, firefighters complete reports on each incident and how the company responded. They restock supplies and make repairs to equipment as needed.

Some firefighters are also fire inspectors, who investigate suspicious fires and enforce fire safety codes. These individuals enter buildings and assess whether sprinklers, fire escapes, and smoke alarms are installed and operating properly and according to code. Many others teach fire safety and prevention at schools and other venues. Some firefighters have specialized training in emergencies that require different approaches, such as toxic chemical spills, forest fires, and boat fires.

Duties and Responsibilities

- Responding to fire alarms and other emergency calls
- Selecting appropriate equipment to direct water or chemicals onto fire
- Positioning and climbing ladders to gain access to upper levels of burning buildings
- Using axes to create openings in buildings for ventilation or entrance
- Rescuing victims
- Completing fire incident reports
- Providing public education on fire safety

OCCUPATION SPECIALTIES

Fire Inspectors and Investigators

Fire inspectors examine buildings to detect fire hazards and ensure that federal, state, and local fire codes are met. Fire investigators determine the origin and cause of fires and explosions.

Forest Firefighters

Forest firefighters use heavy equipment and water hoses to control forest fires. They also frequently create fire lines—a swathe of cut-down trees and dug-up grass in the path of a fire—to deprive a fire of fuel. Some forest firefighters, known as smoke jumpers, parachute from airplanes to reach otherwise inaccessible areas.

Hazmat Specialists

Hazmat specialists work in hazardous materials (hazmat) units and are specially trained to control, prevent, and clean up hazardous materials, such as oil spills and chemical accidents.

WORK ENVIRONMENT

Physical Environment

Firefighters work mostly in fire stations when they are not on a call. When a call comes in, they risk injury or death when putting out fires, rescuing and treating fire and traffic accident victims, and responding to other emergencies. Exposure to fire, smoke, hazardous materials, and structural collapse are a few of the dangers firefighters face.

Human Environment

The team dynamic is vitally important for firefighters; company members must work together extremely well. In addition to their fellows, firefighters must work with other emergency and public safety personnel, such as police, emergency medical technicians, and hospital staff. They must also work with the public, both victims and people seeking information.

Relevant Skills and Abilities

Communication Skills
- Speaking effectively

Interpersonal/Social Skills
- Being able to remain calm
- Providing support to others
- Working as a member of a team

Organization & Management Skills
- Coordinating tasks
- Following instructions
- Handling challenging situations
- Making decisions
- Meeting goals and deadlines
- Performing duties that change frequently

Technical Skills
- Operating machines and equipment
- Working with your hands

Technological Environment

Firefighters use a variety of rescue and fire equipment in addition to fire trucks and hoses, including fire extinguishers, oxygen tanks, and various hydraulic rescue tools for extricating victims from buildings and vehicles. Forest firefighters, meanwhile, use helicopters and all-terrain vehicles during the course of their work. Firefighters often use global positioning system (GPS) navigational aids and must be capable of using radio and computer systems as well.

EDUCATION, TRAINING, AND ADVANCEMENT

High School/Secondary

Aspiring firefighters are encouraged to take science and math courses in high school, which will help them to understand fires and emergency equipment. They should also study English and other subjects that build communication skills. Finally, physical education courses are essential to building the strength and endurance firefighters need.

Suggested High School Subjects

- Driver Training
- English
- First Aid Training
- Mathematics
- Physical Education
- Science

Famous First

The first all-female fire department was the Ashville, NY, Fire Department (located in the far western part of the state). In 1943 thirteen women replaced the department's male firefighters, most of whom were serving in the armed forces during World War II. The women worked without pay, operating a large fire pump and becoming proficient in rescue work and all of the other firefighting duties and responsibilities.

Postsecondary

Although it is not required, most firefighters take some courses at the postsecondary level. Many have associate's degrees in fire science or related disciplines from community and technical colleges or even four-year universities. Such degrees can help a firefighter become a fire specialist or gain a promotion.

Adult Job Seekers

Qualified firefighters should apply for jobs directly with municipal fire departments. The job market for firefighters is competitive, so applicants should send their resumes to many departments rather than simply their preferred location. While pursuing full-time jobs as firefighters, many individuals take positions as seasonal, part-time, or volunteer firefighters.

Professional Certification and Licensure

Prospective firefighters must take a physical and written civil service fire exam, which includes a drug test. Those individuals who score highest on this exam are invited to attend a fire academy, where they spend several weeks of intensive classroom and physical training before they enter the job market.

Additional Requirements

Firefighters must be physically fit, with great strength and stamina. They must also be at least eighteen years old. Upon completion of their training at the fire academy, firefighters must spend several years in apprenticeships. They must have extensive first aid training, be able to think quickly, and work in intense situations as part of a team.

Fun Fact

In reported home fires in which the smoke alarms were present but did not operate, almost half (46%) of the smoke alarms had missing or disconnected batteries. Nuisance alarms were the leading reason for disconnected smoke alarms.

Source: www.nfpa.org

EARNINGS AND ADVANCEMENT

The median annual wage for firefighters was $48,030 in May 2016. The median wage is the wage at which half the workers in an occupation earned more than that amount and half earned less. The lowest 10 percent earned less than $23,700, and the highest 10 percent earned more than $81,110.

In May 2016, the median annual wages for firefighters in the top industries in which they worked were as follows:

Federal government, excluding postal service	$49,520
Local government, excluding education and hospitals	$48,790
State government, excluding education and hospitals	$48,230
Administrative and support services	$29,130

Median annual wages, May 2016

Fire fighting and prevention workers: $48,290

Firefighters: $48,030

Total, all occupations: $37,040

Note: "All Occupations" includes all occupations in the U.S. Economy. Source: U.S. Bureau of Labor Statistics, Occupational Employment Statistics

EMPLOYMENT AND OUTLOOK

Firefighters held about 327,300 jobs in 2016. The largest employers of firefighters were as follows.

Local government, excluding education and hospitals	90%
Administrative and support services	4%
Federal government, excluding postal service	3%
State government, excluding education and hospitals	2%

These employment numbers exclude volunteer firefighters.

Volunteer firefighters share the same duties as paid firefighters and account for the majority of firefighters in many areas. According to the National Fire Protection Association, about two thirds of firefighters were volunteer firefighters in 2015.

When not on the scene of an emergency, firefighters work at fire stations, where they sleep, eat, work on equipment, and remain on call. When an alarm sounds, firefighters respond, regardless of the weather or time of day.

Firefighters have one of the highest rates of injuries and illnesses of all occupations. They often encounter dangerous situations, including collapsing floors and walls, traffic accidents, and overexposure to flames and smoke. As a result, workers must wear protective gear to help lower these risks. Often, the protective gear can be very heavy and hot.

Firefighters typically work long periods and varied hours. Overtime is common. Most firefighters work 24-hour shifts on duty and are off the following 48 or 72 hours. Some firefighters may work 10/14 shifts, which means 10 hours working and 14 hours off.

When combating forest and wildland fires, firefighters may work for extended periods. For example, wildland firefighters may have to stay for days or weeks when a wildland fire breaks out.

Employment Trend, Projected 2016–26

Total, all occupations: 7%

Fire fighting and prevention workers: 7%

Firefighters: 7%

Note: "All Occupations" includes all occupations in the U.S. Economy. Source: U.S. Bureau of Labor Statistics, Employment Projections program

Conversation With . . .
JOHN RHATIGAN

Retired Captain
Firefighter, 19 years

1. What was your individual career path in terms of education/training, entry-level job, or other significant opportunity?

I went to college at St. John's University and graduated with an accounting degree. While I was in school, I did some auditing work for Pathmark and Supermarkets General Corporation and I thought, "Geez, this isn't for me, life in a cubicle." So I took the firefighters exam while I was in college as a "just in case." When I graduated, I went into sales for the Shulton Company, selling Old Spice and Breck. I did very well with it. Right out of college, they gave me a company car, an expense account, all that good stuff. That lasted about five years. It got to a point where I just wanted to work with other people. I quit and worked with my dad in construction for about six months before I got on with the fire department.

2. What are the most important skills and/or qualities for someone in your profession?

You have to be physically fit, obviously. It requires strength and speed and agility. It can be mentally challenging. It requires a lot of people skills. As you move up the ladder, you'll need to deal with the firefighters working under you. Even a regular firefighter has to deal with the public, when you're out doing building inspections and fire inspections. Especially in Manhattan, where I worked, you have to dress well and present yourself well.

You have to be able to remain calm. It's really controlled chaos when you're in a fire. We run into buildings while other people are running out. It takes a certain type of person to do that. Most of the people who do this, they're like caregivers. They do a lot for other people. They're always shoveling snow for their neighbors or cutting their lawns.

3. What do you wish you had known going into this profession?

I wish I had known that once you retire, you can't get back on! I retired because I had to have back surgery as a result of a 9/11 injury. I was at a meeting of retirees today and we all miss it tremendously. It's a lot of camaraderie and laughing and joking and breaking people's chops every day.

4. Are there many job opportunities in your profession? In what specific areas?

The (NY) fire department is hiring. There are preferences for veterans, minorities and women. A lot of firefighters take a different path after they retire, working in fire science or getting certified as fire engineers, working in high rises and working on fire alarm systems. It can be very lucrative.

5. How do you see your profession changing in the next five years? What role will technology play in those changes, and what skills will be required?

Technology is changing the fire department just the way society is advancing. All information from building inspections is computerized now and you get a printout on your way to a fire. It's called the CIDS—Critical Information Dispatch System. It will tell you the type of construction, number of apartments per floor, if there are any handicapped people living there, all kinds of things.

There's thermal imaging cameras and better equipment, chin straps and better helmets. The firefighter's gear is much more protective, which can be good and bad because sometimes you're so protected that you might expose yourself to a dangerous situation like a backdraft, because you can't feel it.

6. What do you enjoy most about your job? What do you enjoy least?

It's easy to say now that what I enjoy most was just being with a common group of people. You come in together, work your shift, and go home safe. You could rely on each other. It was like one big family.

The worst is anytime a kid passes away in a fire. It's just horrible. That's the hardest part, whether it's a kid dying in a fire or a car accident. For me, that was the worst. And then there was the whole 9/11 thing, which is a whole other story. I had the day off and was painting my house when a guy called me. The towers had collapsed just before I got there. I told my son he should take the (qualifying) exam, but he said, "Why would anyone want to do that job, after everything that has happened?"

7. Can you suggest a valuable "try this" for students considering a career in your profession?

In smaller towns, you can be a volunteer firefighter. But I caution anyone thinking about that to be aware that the municipalities might not have very good life insurance policies on them. I tell everyone, even my own son, just take the test. You never know what can happen. I took it as a goof. But it's a great job. You can work 24-hour shifts, then have time for maybe bartending on the side. You can raise a family and be there to watch them grow.

SELECTED SCHOOLS

Training beyond high school is not necessarily expected of beginning firefighters. However, completing a fire science program at a community college or vocational school can prove beneficial. A tool for locating such schools and programs is available on the website of the U.S. Fire Administration (see below).

MORE INFORMATION

American Helicopter Services and Aerial Firefighting Association
3223 N. Tacoma Street
Arlington, VA 22213-1343
703.409.4355
www.ahsafa.org

Emergency Services Training Institute
Texas Engineering Extension Service
The Texas A&M University System
301 Tarrow Street
College Station, TX 77840-7896
877.833.9638
www.teex.com/esti

International Association of Fire Fighters
1750 New York Avenue, NW
Washington, DC 20006
202.737.8484
www.iaff.org

International Association of Women in Fire and Emergency Services
4025 Fair Ridge Drive
Fairfax, VA 22033
703.896.4858
www.i-women.org

International Fire Service Training Association
Fire Protection Publications
Oklahoma State University
930 N. Willis
Stillwater, OK 74078
800.654.4055
www.ifsta.org

National Fire Protection Association
Public Fire Protection Division
1 Batterymarch Park
Quincy, MA 02169-7471
617.770.3000
hr@nfpa.org
www.nfpa.org

National Volunteer Fire Council
7852 Walker Drive, Suite 450
Greenbelt, MD 20770
202.887.5700
www.nvfc.org

U.S. Fire Administration
16825 South Seton Avenue
Emmitsburg, MD 21727
301.447.1000
www.usfa.fema.gov

Michael Auerbachn/Editor

Fish & Game Wardens

Snapshot

Career Cluster(s): Agriculture, Food & Natural Resources, Law, Public Safety & Security, Manufacturing

Interests: Law enforcement, the environment, being outdoors

Earnings (Median pay): $52,714 per year

Job Growth: As fast as average

OVERVIEW

Sphere of Work

Fish and game wardens are responsible for the protection of wildlife and their habitats in parks, animal refuges, wildlife sanctuaries, and other protected public lands. They typically patrol these areas, enforcing state and federal laws regarding hunting, fishing, and other activities. This includes the enforcement of hunting and fishing quotas, boating laws and regulations, and otherwise working to ensure that protected wildlife and ecosystems remain safe. In many cases, fish and game wardens work with scientists and naturalists to monitor protected species. They also work with law enforcement officials regarding situations such as hunting accident investigations.

Because of their expertise, fish and game wardens are often called upon to share their knowledge with the media, schools, and other interested organizations. Public officials and scientists may also request their input on the creation of new hunting and fishing rules and other regulations.

Work Environment

A fish and game warden's workplace is the great outdoors. Most of their time is spent patrolling public roads, waterways, and coastlines using an assortment of vehicles and aircraft, ranging from helicopters, all-terrain vehicles (ATVs), and boats to bicycles and horses. Fish and game wardens face all types of weather conditions during the course of their daily responsibilities. They may face other issues as well, including forest fires, accidents and emergencies, and pollution. Upon their return to an office or station, wardens file reports, store confiscated weapons and items, and meet with scientists, law enforcement, and other relevant professionals.

Profile

Working Conditions: Work both Indoors and Outdoors
Physical Strength: Medium Work
Education Needs: Bachelor's Degree, Master's Degree
Licensure/Certification: Required
Physical Abilities Not Required: No Heavy Labor
Opportunities For Experience: Volunteer Work, Part-Time Work
Holland Interest Score*: RES

* See Appendix A

Occupation Interest

Individuals interested in becoming fish and game wardens tend to have a strong appreciation for the environment and the outdoors. Many have studied biology and the natural sciences in addition to having received some level of law enforcement training. Additionally, fish and game wardens are unconcerned with extreme weather or the dangers of the wilderness. Lastly, those interested in becoming a fish and game warden should have an interest in law enforcement, one of the most important aspects of a fish and game warden's job.

A Day in the Life—Duties and Responsibilities

Generally speaking, fish and game wardens are uniformed, armed law enforcement officials, assigned to enforce state and federal regulations and laws regarding hunting, fishing, and trapping on public lands or areas. This task includes patrolling a particular territory or jurisdiction, inspecting commercial fishing and hunting operations, serving warrants, making arrests, and seizing illegal equipment. Fish and game wardens are also involved in accident recovery, search-and-rescue operations, and investigations.

In addition to defending a natural environment from illegal activity and protecting the site's visitors, fish and game wardens are also invaluable to the efforts of scientists in monitoring the condition of wildlife and ecosystems. Wardens monitor food supplies, habitats, and the number of certain animals within the territory. They then report this information to scientists and other interested parties. Similarly, they track the number of hunters, fishermen, and others who enter the area in order to understand how effective existing regulations and laws are with regard to the habitats they oversee.

Furthermore, a fish and game warden is often invited to share his or her knowledge of how the current laws affect the many animals and natural resources of an ecosystem. Fish and game wardens frequently speak to schools, civic organizations, and other interested groups about the environment as well as the current rules and regulations of hunting and fishing.

Duties and Responsibilities

- Overseeing fish and game habitats and enforcing the laws that apply to them
- Collecting, compiling, and interpreting data
- Helping to establish methods of conservation
- Recommending rules and regulations to protect fish and wildlife
- Reporting the results of established programs
- Serving warrants and making arrests
- Preparing and presenting evidence in court
- Investigating hunting accidents
- Addressing schools and civic groups to educate and promote public relations
- Enlisting the aid of hunting and fishing groups
- Running lake and stream rehabilitation and game habitat improvement programs

WORK ENVIRONMENT

Relevant Skills and Abilities

Communication Skills
- Speaking and writing effectively

Interpersonal/Social Skills
- Cooperating with others
- Working both independently and as a member of a team

Organization & Management Skills
- Coordinating tasks
- Managing people/groups
- Paying attention to and handling details
- Performing duties that change frequently

Research & Planning Skills
- Analyzing information
- Developing evaluation strategies

Work Environment Skills
- Working outdoors

Physical Environment

The immediate environment in which fish and game wardens operate is the outdoors; some wardens work in the woods where hunting takes place, while others patrol the waters in a boat to investigate fishing activity. Natural elements can pose a risk to the individual's safety, including weather, terrain, and wildlife. Also presenting a danger are uncooperative visitors, criminals, accident scenes, and exposure to pollution.

Wardens also return to a central office or station to file paperwork, book criminals, and perform administrative duties. They are often called into meetings at other sites as well.

Human Environment

Fish and game wardens often work alone when out in the field. However, many work in teams, particularly during peak hunting and fishing seasons, when additional temporary or seasonal workers may be hired. Additionally, they coordinate with other professionals, such as police, fire officials, scientists, environmental engineers, and political leaders. Finally, they interact with visitors to the territory they patrol, ensuring their safety and compliance with state and federal regulations and laws.

Technological Environment

Fish and game wardens must be able to operate all-terrain vehicles, boats, and other modes of transportation. They should be knowledgeable on hunting weapons, fishing equipment, and other devices used by fishermen, trappers, and hunters. They also need to use global positioning systems, radios, computers, and other monitoring and communications tools.

EDUCATION, TRAINING, AND ADVANCEMENT

High School/Secondary

High school students who wish to become fish and game wardens are encouraged to study such subjects as agriculture, biology, chemistry, forestry, and other natural sciences. They may also seek summer employment with fish and game departments and government agencies.

Suggested High School Subjects
- Agricultural Science
- Algebra
- Applied Biology/Chemistry
- Applied Math
- Biology
- Chemistry
- College Preparatory
- English
- Forestry
- Geometry
- Physics

Famous First

The first full-time, paid game warden was William Alden Smith of Grand Rapids, Mich., who starting in 1887 earned $1,200 per year, plus expenses, to enforce laws regarding "the preservation of moose, wapiti [elk], deer, birds, and fish." Later that same year Wisconsin passed a similar law and hired four state game wardens.

College/Postsecondary

Most fish and game wardens receive a bachelor's degree, and many possess a master's degree as well. In college and graduate school, they may study geography, environmental science, law and government, biology, agriculture, and public safety.

Related College Majors
- Fisheries Management
- Natural Resources Law Enforcement & Protection
- Natural Resources Management & Policy
- Wildlife & Wildlands Management

Adult Job Seekers

Fish and game warden positions are typically federal or state jobs. Qualified adults who seek to become wardens can directly apply to government agencies or take civil service examinations. They may also consult college and professional placement services. They usually need to acquire additional training at a training academy, which familiarizes cadets with the job responsibilities as well as builds physical strength and endurance.

Professional Certification and Licensure

Most states require that aspiring fish and game wardens become familiar with fish and game policies. They must also receive formal training, which can last three to twelve months, and field training. Most prospective wardens are required to pass physical exams. Fish and game wardens are expected to be U.S. citizens with no criminal records.

Additional Requirements

Fish and game wardens must be physically fit. Because they interact directly with the public, they should have skills in interpersonal communication, conflict resolution, and customer service. They may join a national fish and game warden-related professional organization, such as the American Fisheries Society, or state game warden associations and networks.

Fun Fact

According to the National Park Service, more than half of forest rangers, aka park rangers, work east of the Mississippi River, and predominately work outside.

Source: www.ehow.com

EARNINGS AND ADVANCEMENT

Earnings depend on the employer as well as employee's education, experience, type of work performed and level of responsibility. Mean annual earnings of fish and game wardens were $54,760 in 2012. The lowest ten percent earned less than $34,360, and the highest ten percent earned more than $77,440. Fish and game wardens may be required to purchase some or all of their supplies, such as uniforms, waders, boots, cameras, and binoculars.

Fish and game wardens may receive paid vacations, holidays, and sick days; life and health insurance; and retirement benefits. These are usually paid by the employer.

EMPLOYMENT AND OUTLOOK

Fish and game wardens held about 7,000 jobs nationally in 2012. Employment is expected to grow slower than the average for all occupations through the year 2022, which means employment is projected to increase 3 percent to 9 percent. Because most employees work in government, they are fairly well-protected from negative changes in the job market.

Employment Trend, Projected 2012–22

Total, all occupations: 11%

Protective Service Occupations: 8%

Fish and Game Wardens: 5%

Note: "All Occupations" includes all occupations in the U.S. Economy. Source: U.S. Bureau of Labor Statistics, Employment Projections program

Related Occupations
- Customs Inspector
- Park Ranger

Conversation With . . . TIM KRAEMER

Natural Resources Police, 10 years
Park Service Ranger, 3 years

1. What was your individual career path in terms of education/training, entry-level job, or other significant opportunity?

I worked summers at Sandy Point State Park starting at age 14 in the food concession. When I was old enough to get a driver's license, I worked at the park's marina renting out motor boats. I did that for seven summers before becoming a seasonal technician doing maintenance projects. Later I became a welder, a plumber, and, for six years, a commercial waterman. In winters, I worked as a seasonal technician for another state park. Finally the park service offered me a full-time job as a ranger recruit. I went on to the police academy for six months, then went to Point Lookout State Park as a full-time ranger. We did law enforcement, conservation enforcement, plus programming, interpretation, and maintenance, which was a large part of the park ranger job.

At the time I became a Natural Resources Police Officer, the job was similar to a park ranger here in Maryland. That has since changed, and many of the assignments we had as rangers are now done by Natural Resources Police Officers, such as law and conservation enforcement. Also, we police officers are on waterways doing commercial seafood inspections and waterways enforcement. I'm on the Potomac River, the Patuxent River and the Chesapeake Bay. Natural Resources Police handle private lands and waterways.

All of those years in the private sector gave me a lot of good experience for the career I have now. For instance, when I check the watermen and the fisheries, I have a better grasp of how those guys work, and I know their gear.

2. What are the most important skills and/or qualities for someone in your profession?

A good work ethic, honesty, integrity, knowledge of fishing laws and hunting laws. You definitely need to be a self-starter. You have to want to be outside, on vessels, and know the mechanical workings of a vessel and fishing gear.

3. What do you wish you had known going into this profession?

I wish I was better with the academic part of it. I'm more of a hands-on learner.

4. Are there many job opportunities in your profession? In what specific areas?

In the last year or two, the state started hiring more Natural Resources Police Officers and they are constantly taking applications in every part of the state.

5. How do you see your profession changing in the next five years? What role will technology play in those changes, and what skills will be required?

We're already starting to see technology play a big role with the Natural Resources Police, with new programs and new report management systems. Officers are issued laptops now that are linked with the new Maritime Law Enforcement Information Network (MLEIN) that we just got trained on. It's a series of cameras and radar stations up and down the Chesapeake Bay that the Natural Resources Police use to track vessels or illegal activities.

In 2007 we had the introduction of new vessels with better outboard/inboard motors and more advanced high tech. The outboards are better, faster, more efficient, more reliable, and more comfortable for officers in harsh environments. They're rigged out for law enforcement use.

I don't ever see us getting away from low-tech completely; there's nothing more reliable than a pad of paper and a pen. Sometimes we're on foot in the middle of a field and you have to travel light and you have to travel fast. A pad of paper doesn't need to be recharged.

6. What do you enjoy most about your job? What do you enjoy least?

It's probably one of the best jobs around. The best part is being in on the water. I like running the boats, as well as the feeling you're making a difference and making sure there's something there tomorrow, such as when you enforce crabbing regulations. Or oysters, which are a big thing. We make sure the kids will have seafood out there to harvest one day. I love being in the state parks, talking to people, doing campground enforcement, and just being there for public information.

Natural resource law changes constantly, and keeping yourself updated on laws and regulations is very challenging. That is probably the hardest part of this job.

7. Can you suggest a valuable "try this" for students considering a career in your profession?

You've really got to want to be outside and talk to people. For people who like to hunt and fish and like fishing and game law, this is a great job. Be a volunteer or, if you're old enough, be a reserve officer.

SELECTED SCHOOLS

Programs in fisheries and wildlife management are available at many four-year colleges and universities. The student can also gain initial training at a community college. The website of the National Association of University Fisheries and Wildlife Programs (see below) provides a state-by-state listing of member institutions. Other programs besides those listed exist and should be considered as well. Interested students are advised to consult with a school guidance counselor.

MORE INFORMATION

American Fisheries Society
5410 Grosvenor Lane
Bethesda, MD 20814
301.897.8616
www.fisheries.org

Association of Fish & Wildlife Agencies
444 North Capitol Street NW
Suite 725
Washington, DC 20001
202.624.7890
fishwildlife.org

National Association of University Fisheries and Wildlife Programs
Virginia Tech
100 Cheatham Hall
Blacksburg, VA 24061
540.231.5573
naufwp.org

North American Wildlife Enforcement Officers Association
P.O. Box 22
Holidaysburg, PA 16648
naweoa.org

U.S. Fish and Wildlife Service
Department of the Interior
1849 C Street NW
Washington, DC 20240
800.344.9453
www.fws.gov

Wildlife Society
5410 Grosvenor Lane
Suite 200
Bethesda, MD 20814
301.897.9770
www.wildlife.org

Michael Auerbach/Editor

Fishers/Hunters/ Trappers

Snapshot

Career Cluster(s): Agriculture, Food & Natural Resources
Interests: Nature, animals, working outdoors
Earnings (Yearly Average): $29,280 per year; $14.08 per hour
Job Growth: As fast as average

OVERVIEW

Sphere of Work

Fishers, hunters, and trappers catch animals for human consumption as well as for industrial or scientific use. Individuals in these fields may work alone and often function as independent contractors, hunting or fishing in designated areas and delivering their products to clients. Other fishers, hunters, and trappers work in groups, and some individuals in these occupations are employed directly by agricultural corporations or government-run agencies.

Work Environment

The work environment for a fisher, hunter, or trapper varies widely depending on region and seasonal variations. In some areas, fishing, hunting, and trapping may be conducted year-round, while in other

areas, inclement weather, extreme temperatures, or animal migration patterns may lead to seasonal variations in the availability of work. Fishers, hunters, and trappers tend to work long hours during peak seasons and are at risk from environmental threats, including dangerous river or ocean conditions, inclement weather, and other potentially hazardous conditions.

Commercial fishing and hunting can be dangerous and can lead to workplace injuries or fatalities. Fishing and hunting workers often work under hazardous conditions. Transportation to a hospital or doctor is often not readily available for these workers because they can be out at sea or in a remote area.

Most fatalities that happen to fishers and related fishing workers are from drowning. The crew must guard against the danger of injury from malfunctioning fishing gear, entanglement in fishing nets and gear, slippery decks, ice formation, or large waves washing over the deck. Malfunctioning navigation and communication equipment and other factors may lead to collisions, shipwrecks, or other dangerous situations, such as vessels becoming caught in storms. For more information on injuries and fatalities of fishers and fishing related works, read the Beyond the Numbers article "Facts of the catch: occupational injuries, illnesses, and fatalities to fishing workers, 2003–2009."

Hunters and trappers have fewer injuries and fatalities than fishers, but hunting accidents can occur because of the weapons and traps they use. Hunters and trappers minimize injury by wearing the appropriate gear and following detailed safety procedures. Specific safety guidelines vary by state.

Fishing and hunting workers often endure long shifts and irregular work schedules. Commercial fishing trips may require workers to be away from their home port for several weeks or months.

Many fishers are seasonal workers, and those jobs are usually filled by students and by people from other occupations who are available for seasonal work, such as teachers. For example, employment of fishers in Alaska increases significantly during the summer months, which constitute the salmon season. During these times, fishers can expect to work long hours. Additionally, states may only allow hunters and trappers to hunt or trap during certain times of the year depending on the type of wild animals sought.

Profile

Working Conditions: Work Outdoors
Physical Strength: Medium to Heavy Work
Education Needs: On-The-Job Training, High School Diploma or G.E.D.
Licensure/Certification: Recommended
Physical Abilities Not Required: No Strenuous Labor
Opportunities For Experience: Apprenticeship, Part-Time Work
Holland Interest Score*: CRS, RCE, RCI

* See Appendix A

Occupation Interest

Those who make a living fishing, hunting, or trapping typically have significant experience with outdoor environments and knowledge of nature and animal behavior. Many individuals drawn to these occupations have been introduced to the field through family or friends, and many began learning the skills needed at a young age.

A Day in the Life—Duties and Responsibilities

A typical day for a fisher begins early in the morning with gathering the necessary equipment and supplies. The fisher then travels, either alone or with a fishing crew, to the location for that day's fishing. Ocean fishers may need to travel a significant distance to fertile fishing grounds, and traveling from one fishing site to another may represent a significant portion of the day for many professional fishers. Fishing may last for only a few hours or may take most of the day, depending on the type of quarry and the season. Following active fishing, most fishers must then process their catch for the day, which may involve scaling and gutting the fish or packaging it for transport to a processing facility.

Hunters also typically begin their day early in the morning by traveling to a predesignated hunting ground. Depending on the type of game, hunters may move through an area searching for potential quarry or may stay hidden in one location, using bait to attract prey. After an animal has been killed, the hunter must transport his or her quarry to a processing location. In many cases, hunters may also remove the pelt from an animal or may begin the processing by cutting the animal into pieces before selling it to prospective buyers.

Trappers use bait and traps to ensnare animals and birds. On a typical day, trappers must check their traps to see if any animals were captured and must set up new traps or reset existing ones in a number of different areas. Trappers must also collect and process any game collected during a day. In some cases, captured animals must be killed if they are still alive. These animals must then be transported to a location for processing.

Duties and Responsibilities

- Setting traps and nets to capture prey
- Working in a cooperative team of other people
- Using firearms, clubs and other devices to dispatch prey
- Processing or properly disposing of fish and animals
- Conducting research such as blood sampling, banding, and tracking migratory patterns

OCCUPATION SPECIALTIES

Net Fishers

Net fishers catch finned fish and shellfish using a variety of specially constructed nets, with or without the aid of a boat.

Pot Fishers

Pot Fishers catch crab, eel, and lobster using pots (cages with funnel-shaped net openings).

Line Fishers

Line fishers catch fish and other marine animals using line and hook. They may work alone or in crews of other fisherman.

Diving Fishers

Diving fishers gather and harvest marine life such as sponges, abalone, pearl oysters, and geoducks from the sea bottom. These fishers can use snorkel, scuba, or diving suit with an air line connected to the surface.

Spear Fishers

Spear fishers catch fish such as eel, salmon, and swordfish using a spear with a barbed tip.

Predatory Animal Hunters

Predatory animal hunters stalk, trap and kill for bounty predatory animals such a coyotes, wolves, and vermin.

Animal Trappers

Animal trappers capture animals for pelts, live sale, bounty, or for relocation to other areas.

Bird Trappers

Bird trappers capture live birds for brood stock, exhibition, extermination, identification or relocation.

WORK ENVIRONMENT

Physical Environment

Fishers, hunters, and trappers work outdoors, typically in environments that have sufficient ecological integrity to maintain large populations of wildlife. Many fishers, hunters, and trappers work in areas that are removed from human settlement, though they must be near enough to an area appropriate for storing and processing their quarry prior to sale.

Fishers, hunters, and trappers may utilize a processing plant to prepare game before selling it to their clients. In these environments, employees must cooperate to complete a variety of manual tasks in order to process raw animals into products ready for sale.

Relevant Skills and Abilities

Interpersonal/Social Skills
- Being able to work independently
- Being patient
- Working as a member of a team (SCANS Workplace Competency Interpersonal)

Organization & Management Skills
- Performing routine work

Unclassified Skills
- Being physically active

Work Environment Skills
- Traveling
- Working outdoors

Human Environment

Fishers who work on commercial fishing boats may be part of a crew that also includes an experienced captain or pilot, as well as a number of assistants and technicians who oversee the operation of the boat. Typically, on a fishing vessel, there is a rank of seniority among the crew, with each member being responsible for specific activities. Many commercial fishers begin working as deckhands, who are responsible for cleaning, basic maintenance, and supply activities aboard the boat. As a fisher advances in rank, his or her duties may include more time managing fish or setting nets and lines.

Technological Environment

While some fishing vessels may use complex technology, such as sonar to find fish or other types of sensors to enhance productivity, many in the fishing industry use equipment similar to that used for centuries to catch and process fish. Hunters and trappers also use equipment similar to what was used in the past.

EDUCATION, TRAINING, AND ADVANCEMENT

High School/Secondary

Many fishers, hunters, and trappers learn their occupations from parents or family members, and some begin as apprentices to professionals as teenagers or younger. While a high school education is not required for a career in professional fishing, hunting, or trapping, learning the basics of business communication and accounting can be beneficial for those looking to operate as private contractors.

Professional fishing, hunting, or trapping requires years of on-the-job training, and individuals in high school may want to enroll in classes offered by federal- or state-run wildlife organizations, which can provide training in how to find and handle wildlife. In addition, there are a variety of private fishing, hunting, and trapping instruction programs that will enroll high school students with the consent of a parent or guardian.

Suggested High School Subjects
- Agricultural Education
- Applied Biology/Chemistry
- Biology
- English
- First Aid Training
- Forestry
- Geography

- Physical Science
- Physics

Postsecondary

There are few postsecondary programs aimed at professional fishers, hunters, or trappers, and there are typically no postsecondary education requirements for those seeking to work in one of these professions. However, there are certain college-level courses that may aid fishers, hunters, and trappers in establishing their business or finding employment in the wildlife-management fields, such as degree programs in forestry and fisheries management.

Adult Job Seekers

Adults seeking employment as professional fishers, hunters, or trappers can attempt to apprentice with a professional in the field in order to receive on-the-job training. Though many professionals begin working at a young age, persons of all ages can become involves in the hunting and fishing industries.

Professional Certification and Licensure

In most areas, professionals must follow guidelines set by government agencies that manage wildlife populations. Professional fishers must learn about the guidelines for fishing in their area and must maintain a fishing license for commercial activities. Some professional fishing companies require that employees complete training in boat operation and safety, which may be offered through the United States Coast Guard or another government organization.

Hunters must be licensed to carry and use firearms, and many areas place restrictions on the types of weapons and ammunition that may be used for specific types of game. In addition, hunters typically need to renew and maintain valid licenses for hunting in specific areas and for hunting certain types of game during the year.

Additional Requirements

Fishing, hunting, or trapping can be hazardous and physically demanding, and those seeking to work as professionals should be capable of sustained physical labor and comfortable with confronting potential hazards on the job. Knowledge of and familiarity with the ecology and natural environment of an area can be helpful to those seeking to work in the field.

EARNINGS AND ADVANCEMENT

The median annual wage for fishing and hunting workers was $29,280 in May 2016. The median wage is the wage at which half the workers in an occupation earned more than that amount and half earned less. The lowest 10 percent earned less than $18,080, and the highest 10 percent earned more than $47,530.

Fishers are typically paid a percentage of the boat's overall catch, commonly referred to as a crew share. The more fish that are caught, the greater the crew share becomes. This can lead to unpredictable swings in pay from one season to another, as the overall catch can vary. More experienced crewmembers often receive a greater share compared to entry-level workers.

Trappers are typically paid per pelt, and the amount received can vary depending on the species and the quality of the fur. For example, trappers typically receive more for coyote pelts than for smaller species, such as muskrats.

Fishing and hunting workers endure strenuous outdoor work and long hours. Commercial fishing trips may require workers to be away from their home port for several weeks or months.

Many fishers are seasonal workers, and those jobs are usually filled by students and by people from other occupations who are available for seasonal work, such as teachers. For example, employment of fishers in Alaska increases significantly during the summer months, which constitute the salmon season. During these times, fishers can expect to work long hours. Additionally, states may only allow hunters and trappers to hunt or trap during certain times of the year.

Median annual wages, May 2016

Total, all occupations: $37,040

Fishing and hunting workers: $29,280

Farming, fishing, and forestry occupations: $23,510

Note: "All Occupations" includes all occupations in the U.S. Economy. Source: U.S. Bureau of Labor Statistics, Occupational Employment Statistics

EMPLOYMENT AND OUTLOOK

Employment of fishing and hunting workers is projected to grow 7 percent from 2016 to 2026, about as fast as the average for all occupations. Fishing and hunting workers depend on the ability of fish stocks and wild animals to reproduce and grow. The demand for seafood should increase, as it is widely seen as a healthy choice of protein.

Governmental efforts to replenish fish stocks have led to some species being regulated under fishing quotas or catch shares. These quotas dictate how many fish each fisher may catch and keep. Additional quotas or catch shares can typically be purchased, but they are often very expensive. The implementation of additional catch share programs may reduce demand for fishers. However, new programs must undergo several years of research and public review before being approved.

Animal pelts will continue be used to manufacture fur coats, hats, and gloves, which may increase demand for trappers. However, the majority of fur used in clothing comes from ranches or farms that breed, maintain, and harvest desirable species, such as mink.

Many job openings will result from the need to replace fishing and hunting workers who leave the occupation. Many workers leave because of the strenuous and hazardous nature of the job and the lack of a steady year-round income. The best prospects should be with large fishing operations and for seasonal employment.

Employment Trend, Projected 2016–26

Total, all occupations: 7%

Fishing and hunting workers: 7%

Farming, fishing, and forestry occupations: 0%

Note: "All Occupations" includes all occupations in the U.S. Economy. Source: U.S. Bureau of Labor Statistics, Employment Projections program

Related Occupations
- Fish & Game Warden
- Range Manager

Conversation With . . . MARK HOOS, Sr.

Captain of the fishing vessel *Marli*
Ocean City, Maryland
Boat captain, 15 years

1. What was your individual career path in terms of education/training, entry-level job, or other significant opportunity?

I grew up north of Baltimore and loved hunting, and fishing in the farm ponds and streams. For a year after high school, I worked at a Giant Food grocery store, but decided that wasn't for me. I wanted to be outdoors.

For three years, I was a crabber. After that, I had banked enough money to open a fishing tackle store and started running fishing charters. At that time, you did not need a U.S. Coast Guard captain's license.

From that point on, I worked as a fishing guide in the upper Chesapeake Bay, fished professionally in tournaments, and worked in the marine industry. I was speaking and doing seminars at fishing shows. I also ran a boat dealership and probably the largest tackle store in the state of Maryland, up until the mid-90s.

After I obtained my captain's license, I started freelancing in Ocean City, Maryland, aboard boats going offshore. I also ran Norman Creek Marina in the Baltimore corridor, so I was back and forth for six years until I finally moved to Ocean City.

I went full-bore into charter fishing in 2003 when I bought the *Marli*. Six years ago, I went through a divorce and sold the boat, but stayed as on captain. We've been the top boat since I started in 2004 and are blessed, but we've worked hard. We fish every day, April through October, weather permitting. In the winter, I do a lot of deer hunting or push snow.

I hold a 100-ton Near Coastal Master license, which is in demand and gives me options. But I may keep doing this.

2. What are the most important skills and/or qualities for someone in your profession?

You've got to be a people person because you're dealing with clients. You have to be in decent shape, because you're out in the heat or you're out in the cold. You have to love the outdoors.

Maritime captains have to pay attention to detail because there are crew and charter customers onboard. There's only one captain onboard, and he's responsible for everyone. Liability always goes back to the captain. You need to be hands-on.

You have to be able to hang in there because the economy controls everything. Charter fishing is a luxury business.

You need to be at the top of the game and catch fish so you'll be in demand.

You also need basic mathematical skills to calculate things like fuel burning and distance so you don't run out of fuel.

3. What do you wish you had known going into this profession?

You have a shelf life. I run every day, weather permitting, from mid-April to late October. It's a long day. You're on the boat at 4 a.m., off the boat at 6:30 or 7 p.m., and then you have reports you need to turn in, social media to post, or you may need to deal with a repair. Many nights we don't leave the boat until 11 or 11:30 p.m.

You can't do this forever. It's a young man's game.

4. Are there many job opportunities in your profession? In what specific areas?

There are many part-time jobs. To make a living full-time, if you're willing to travel, then yes. If you want to stay put, there are very few jobs based out of one port. You can go around the world on a 60-foot boat today, the electronics and engines and technology have gotten so good. So people are going to Jamaica, Aruba, South Africa … all over the place, and they need licensed captains. These are sport fishing boats chasing billfish. It's tough on a family, but it's great if you're single and want to spend winter in the tropics.

5. How do you see your profession changing in the next five years, what role will technology play in those changes, and what skills will be required?

Every year, we see more stringent rules; there's now mandatory drug testing, and they're trying to pay more attention to alcohol abuse. Enforcement is linked between the state and the Coast Guard. That will continue.

The distance that boats now travel has created more opportunity. Since Cuba opened up, you can fish the Cuban bank. People go fish off the coast of Africa. That will continue.

You need to be savvy with electronics to navigate the boat and find fish, and social media is an important marketing tool, particularly for younger clients.

6. **What do you most enjoy about your job? What do you least enjoy about your job?**

I like being on the water. You never know what you're going to see or catch. I've seen two great white sharks in my career and a lot of different whales. You also meet interesting people.

I least enjoy dealing with Mother Nature. That can be really tough if it's a bad day. I also don't like dealing with people who don't respect the boat. They charter the boat, so they think they can do whatever they want, but it doesn't work that way. Fortunately, we don't get many of those.

7. **Can you suggest a valuable "try this" for students considering a career in your profession?**

The best thing you could do is shadow for a day. Go to your local port and walk the dock. You're going to get a lot of nos, but you'll achieve some yeses. Boats can't take a paid hand out if they're not drug-tested.

MORE INFORMATION

American Fisheries Society
5410 Grosvenor Lane
Bethesda, MD 20814
301.897.8616
main@fisheries.org
www.fisheries.org

Marine Technology Society
5565 Sterrett Place, #108
Columbia, MD 21044
410.884.5330
membership@mtsociety.org
www.mtsociety.org

National Fisheries Institute
7918 Jones Branch Drive, Suite 700
McLean, VA 22102
703.524.8880
gthomas@nfi.org
www.aboutseafood.com

**National Marine Fisheries
Service**
1315 East West Highway
Silver Spring, MD 20910
www.nmfs.noaa.gov

**National Rifle Association of
America**
Hunter Services Department
11250 Waples Mill Road
Fairfax, VA 22030
800.672.3888
www.nra.org

Professional Anglers Association
P.O. Box 655
1102 Main Street
Benton, KY 42025
270.527.2030
www.fishpaa.com

U.S. Fish and Wildlife Service
1849 C Street NW
Washington, DC 20240
800.344.9453
www.fws.gov

Micah Issitt/Editor

Foresters & Conservation Scientists

Snapshot

Career Cluster(s): Agriculture, Food & Natural Resources, Manufacturing, Science, Technology, Engineering & Mathematics

Interests: Environmental issues, natural resources, working outdoors, solving problems

Earnings (Median pay): $60,610 per year; $29.14 per hour

Job Growth: As fast as average

OVERVIEW

Sphere of Work

Foresters and conservation scientists oversee the development, use, and management of forests, rangelands, recreational areas, and other natural sites. Foresters develop plans and policies for safeguarding against forest fires, tree disease outbreaks, and insect infestations. Conservation scientists help landowners make sustainable use of timber, water, and other natural resources.

Both foresters and conservation scientists often work for government agencies, managing and enforcing regulations that

pertain to sustainable development activities, such as controlled burns and land clearances, reforestation, and proper harvesting techniques. Foresters and conservation scientists often specialize in a particular subfield like wildlife management, soil science, procurement, or environmental law enforcement.

Work Environment

Foresters and conservation scientists typically work in a combination of outdoor, laboratory, and office settings. When doing outdoor fieldwork, they frequently hike deep into forests and other rural and underpopulated areas in order to conduct research, analyze trends, and assess environmental issues. In the laboratory, they study soil, plant, water, and other samples and collate data regarding long-term trends. In their offices, they write reports, conduct meetings, and coordinate with farmers, timber industry representatives, and government officials. Foresters and conservation scientists usually work a forty-hour week, although they may work erratic hours. When conducting fieldwork, they must outdoors (on many occasions by themselves) in all climates and conditions. During natural disasters such as forest fires, flooding, and other emergencies, foresters and conservation scientists work longer hours and spend most of their time outdoors.

Profile

Working Conditions: Work both Indoors and Outdoors
Physical Strength: Light to Medium Work
Education Needs: Bachelor's Degree, Master's Degree
Licensure/Certification: Required
Physical Abilities Not Required: No Heavy Labor
Opportunities For Experience: Apprenticeship, Volunteer Work, Part Time Work
Holland Interest Score*: RIE, RIS

* See Appendix A

Occupation Interest

Foresters and conservation scientists are key figures in the ongoing effort to promote sustainable development and protect ecosystems. They must balance using and harvesting wood, water, and other natural resources for economic purposes with protecting the environment. Because foresters and conservation scientists must resolve a wide range of environmental issues, the work performed by these individuals is rarely monotonous. Foresters and conservation scientists should enjoy spending a great deal of time outdoors in different areas of the forest or in open spaces.

A Day in the Life—Duties and Responsibilities

The responsibilities of foresters and conservation scientists vary based on individual area of expertise. For example, procurement foresters contact and gain permission from forest property owners to take inventory of the different types of timber standing within the territory, appraise the value of that inventory, and develop contracts for its procurement. Range conservation scientists, meanwhile, work with ranchers to determine the maximum number of cattle that can live in and feed off an area in a sustainable fashion.

Foresters negotiate the terms of a wide range of land use contracts and regulate how timber is cut and moved. They also supervise other forestry workers, direct fire suppression protocols, and analyze how development and tree removal affect tree growth rates and species durability. Conservation scientists, meanwhile, take soil samples to address soil erosion issues and provide counsel to farmers, ranchers, and landowners on how to engage in sustainable development and natural resource extraction. Conservation scientists also plan and implement plans for replanting trees and plants after development has taken place. In both cases, conservation scientists and foresters carefully study trends and resource quantities to ensure long-term use while minimizing the impact of such activities on the ecosystem in question.

Duties and Responsibilities

- Planning and directing projects for all aspects of forest management, including seeding and replanting forests
- Making maps of soil and vegetation of forest areas
- Researching methods of processing timber for various uses
- Directing or participating in the control of forest fires and conducting fire-prevention programs
- Planning campsites and recreational facilities
- Monitoring habitats for conformance to state and federal environmental protection regulations
- Negotiating land-use contracts with outside interests

OCCUPATION SPECIALTIES

Silviculturists

Silviculturists manage tree nurseries and thin forests. They also conduct research in forest propagation, life span of seeds and the effects of fire and animal grazing.

Range Managers

Range managers protect rangelands to maximize their use without damaging the environment.

Soil Conservationists

Soil conservationists assist farmers, ranchers, and others to conserve soil, water and related natural resources.

Forest Ecologists

Forest ecologists conduct research upon the various environmental factors affecting forests.

Urban Foresters

Urban foresters live and work in larger cities and manage urban trees. These workers are concerned with quality-of-life issues, including air quality, shade, and storm water runoff.

Conservation Education Foresters

Conservation education foresters train teachers and students about issues facing forest lands.

WORK ENVIRONMENT

Physical Environment

Foresters and conservation scientists spend some time working in offices and laboratories, where they analyze samples, collate data, write reports, and hold meetings. These environments are clean, well-lit, and organized. Foresters and conservation scientists also conduct fieldwork in farm country, open ranges, and forests, which are rugged, at times remote, and subject to a wide range of weather conditions.

Relevant Skills and Abilities

Communication Skills
- Speaking and writing effectively

Interpersonal/Social Skills
- Being able to work independently and as a member of a team

Organization & Management Skills
- Making decisions
- Paying attention to and handling details
- Performing duties which change frequently

Research & Planning Skills
- Developing evaluation strategies
- Using logical reasoning

Technical Skills
- Performing scientific, mathematical and technical work

Work Environment Skills
- Driving a vehicle
- Working outdoors
- Working with plants or animals

Human Environment

Foresters and conservation scientists work with a wide range of public and private employees, including ranchers, loggers, land owners, business executives, government regulators, political leaders, and emergency and public safety officials.

Technological Environment

Foresters and conservation scientists use analytical and data collection technologies. Foresters use clinometers, increment borers, and bark gauges to measure tree height and growth, as well as aerial and remote sensors to map areas of land use and undeveloped forests. Conservation scientists use water testing kits, soil spectrometers, and other equipment to analyze the impact of development on natural resources. Both foresters and conservation scientists must use basic office software, scientific databases, and mapping programs.

EDUCATION, TRAINING, AND ADVANCEMENT

High School/Secondary

High school students should take courses in biology, chemistry, and the natural sciences. Geometry, algebra, and trigonometry are essential mathematics courses for foresters and conservation scientists. Additional training in computer science and agriculture are also useful, as is an understanding of environmental laws and sustainable development issues, which may be obtained through social studies or history courses. Furthermore, English and communications courses build the writing skills that future foresters and conservation scientists need.

Suggested High School Subjects

- Agricultural Education
- Algebra
- Biology
- Chemistry
- College Preparatory
- Computer Science
- English
- Forestry
- Geometry
- Science
- Trigonometry

Famous First

The first great conservationist in the United States was John Muir, born in 1838 in Scotland. Muir came to America as a youth and spent many years traveling on foot as a naturalist. He founded the Sierra Club in 1892, and succeeded in gaining protection for Yosemite National Park in California along with other national parks and forests.

College/Postsecondary

Foresters and conservation scientists need a bachelor's degree, preferably in forestry, ecology, or environmental studies. A graduate degree can enhance a candidate's competitiveness and enable these individuals to attain senior-level research positions within these fields.

Related College Majors
- Agronomy & Crop Science
- Forest Harvesting & Production Technology
- Forestry
- Horticulture Services Operations & Management
- Natural Resources Conservation
- Plant Sciences
- Wildlife & Wildlands Manage

Adult Job Seekers

Qualified foresters and conservation scientists may apply directly to private logging and lumber companies, research and testing consultancies, and federal and state government agencies that have posted openings. The US Department of Agriculture, which includes the US Forest Service and the Natural Resource Conservation Service, lists job openings on its website. Foresters and conservation scientists may also join and network through professional organizations and nonprofit groups, such as the Society of American Forests or the Conservation Science Institute.

Professional Certification and Licensure

A few states require that foresters obtain licensure or certification, for which they may need to satisfactorily pass a written test. Foresters and conservation scientists seeking to specialize in a particular field may take certification courses from nonprofit organizations and professional associations. The certification process usually involves a combination of education and professional experience.

Additional Requirements

Foresters and conservation scientists must have a strong attention to detail and exceptional data collection and analytical skills. They should have strong communication skills, be physically fit, and be willing to stand outdoors all day, even through inclement weather.

EARNINGS AND ADVANCEMENT

The median annual wage for conservation scientists was $61,810 in May 2016. The median wage is the wage at which half the workers in an occupation earned more than that amount and half earned less. The lowest 10 percent earned less than $37,270, and the highest 10 percent earned more than $95,970.

The median annual wage for foresters was $58,700 in May 2016. The lowest 10 percent earned less than $39,100, and the highest 10 percent earned more than $82,400.

In May 2016, the median annual wages for conservation scientists in the top industries in which they worked were as follows:

Federal government, excluding postal service	$73,380
Professional, scientific, and technical services	$66,120
Social advocacy organizations	$61,450
State government, excluding education and hospitals	$54,070
Local government, excluding education and hospitals	$49,700

In May 2016, the median annual wages for foresters in the top industries in which they worked were as follows:

Federal government, excluding postal service	$63,660
Local government, excluding education and hospitals	$55,820
State government, excluding education and hospitals	$53,310

Most conservation scientists and foresters work full time and have a standard work schedule.

Many conservation scientists and foresters advance to take on managerial duties. They also may conduct research or work on policy issues, often after getting an advanced degree. Foresters in management usually leave fieldwork behind, spending more of their time in an office, working with teams to develop management plans and supervising others.

Soil conservationists usually begin working within one district and may advance to a state, regional, or national level. Soil conservationists also can transfer to occupations such as farm or ranch management advisor or land appraiser.

Median annual wages
May 2016

Life scientists: $71,950

Conservation scientists: $61,810

Conservation scientists and foresters: $60,610

Foresters: $58,700

Total, all occupations: $37,040

Note: "All Occupations" includes all occupations in the U.S. Economy. Source: U.S. Bureau of Labor Statistics, Occupational Employment Statistics

EMPLOYMENT AND OUTLOOK

Conservation scientists held about 22,300 jobs in 2016. The largest employers of conservation scientists were as follows:

Federal government, excluding postal service	32%
State government, excluding education and hospitals	22%
Local government, excluding education and hospitals	20%
Social advocacy organizations	12%
Professional, scientific, and technical services	5%

Foresters held about 12,300 jobs in 2016. The largest employers of foresters were as follows:

State government, excluding education and hospitals	25%
Support activities for agriculture and forestry	17%
Forestry and logging	13%
Federal government, excluding postal service	11%
Local government, excluding education and hospitals	11%

In the western and southwestern United States, conservation scientists and foresters usually work for the federal government because of the number of national parks in that part of the country. In the eastern United States, they often work for private landowners. Social advocacy organizations employ foresters and conservation scientists in working with lawmakers on behalf of sustainable land use and other issues facing forest land.

Conservation scientists and foresters typically work in offices, in laboratories, and outdoors, sometimes doing fieldwork in remote locations. When visiting or working near logging operations or wood yards, they wear a hardhat and other protective gear.

The work can be physically demanding. Some conservation scientists and foresters work outdoors in all types of weather. They may need to walk long distances through dense woods and underbrush to carry out their work. Insect bites, poisonous plants, and other natural hazards present some risk.

In an isolated location, a forester or conservation scientist may work alone, measuring tree densities and regeneration or performing other outdoor activities. Other foresters work closely with the public, educating them about the forest or the proper use of recreational sites.

Fire suppression activities are an important aspect of the duties of a forester or conservation scientist. Because those activities involve prevention as well as emergency responses, the work of a forester or conservation scientist has occasional risk.

Most conservation scientists and foresters work full time and have a standard work schedule.

Employment of conservation scientists and foresters is projected to grow 6 percent from 2016 to 2026, about as fast as the average for all occupations.

Most employment growth is expected to be in state and local government-owned forest lands, particularly in the western United States. In recent years, the prevention and suppression of wildfires has become the primary concern for government agencies managing forests and rangelands. Governments are likely to hire more foresters as the number of forest fires increases and more people live on or near forest lands. Both the development of previously unused lands and changing weather conditions have contributed to increasingly devastating and costly fires.

In addition, continued demand for American timber and wood pellets is expected to drive employment growth for conservation scientists and foresters. Jobs in private forests are expected to grow alongside demand for timber and pellets.

The need to replace retiring workers should create opportunities for conservation scientists and foresters. Job prospects will likely be best for conservation scientists and foresters who have a strong understanding of Geographic Information System (GIS) technology, remote sensing, and other software tools.

Employment Trend, Projected 2016–22

Life scientists: 10%

Total, all occupations: 7%

Conservation scientists: 7%

Conservation scientists and foresters: 6%

Foresters: 5%

Note: "All Occupations" includes all occupations in the U.S. Economy. Source: U.S. Bureau of Labor Statistics, Employment Projections program

Related Occupations

- Agricultural Engineer
- Agricultural Scientist
- Biological Scientist
- Botanist
- Environmental Engineer
- Farmer/Farm Manager
- Fish & Game Warden
- Forestry Worker
- Landscape Architect
- Park Ranger
- Range Manager
- Soil Scientist
- Water & Wastewater Engineer
- Wildlife Biologist

Conversation With . . .
BRIAN M. DEEB

Procurement Forester, 7 years
Weaber Lumber, Lebanon, PA

1.   What was your individual career path in terms of education/training, entry-level job, or other significant opportunity?

Originally, I wanted to be a marine biologist but realized I didn't want to be in school as long as that would take. Forestry is specialized biology, so I took a forestry course when I was at Penn State University, liked it, and received a four-year degree in Forest Science. I had interned with the Pennsylvania Dept. of Natural Resources for a summer. When I graduated, Weaber Lumber hired me as a forest tech, so I was in the field doing the physical work of cruising timber. My main job now is to secure raw material. I go out and talk with landowners; I am selling a service. I work on contracts and negotiate. Each landowner has a different objective for their woodlands, so my job is to evaluate the woodland to determine which management strategy best meets their objectives. Each property is different. I wouldn't advocate clear-cutting, for instance, for every tract but there's more biodiversity in a clearcut than an old growth forest and sometimes it's the way to go. We're in this for the long haul and want to preserve the resources.

Also, these jobs have big equipment with heavy trees coming down and sometimes things happen, like a truck takes out a neighbor's mailbox. Part of my job is to talk with the public and satisfy any concerns. I also deal with state and local regulations and obtain approvals and permits, as well as annual company audits for SFI, Sustainable Forestry Initiative Certification. Back when I was in college, I had a part-time job in retail sales, and that helped me learn to deal with people.

2. What are the most important skills and/or qualities for someone in your profession?

I work from home, so I need to be self-sufficient. You also need to have physical stamina. I climb to the top of a mountain in all sorts of weather to evaluate a stand of timber.

3. What do you wish you had known going into this profession?

I wish I'd know there would be as much public interaction. I got into forestry to go out in the woods. In procurement, I'm on the phone a lot. We also have to go to township and county meetings. I have to be able to express to a lot of different people what we're doing and why we're doing it. I wish I'd taken more public speaking classes in school.

4. Are there many job opportunities in your profession? In what specific areas?

Speaking broadly, foresters go into three sectors: government or research forestry, where your main objective is research; a private timber broker; or foresters who work for a sawmill as an industrial forester. This is a small profession—you may need to relocate—with an aging workforce. I graduated in '02 and am a member of the Society of American Foresters. Until recently, I was one of the youngest guys there. So I think in the next five-to-10 years, it could be a sector where there is a lot of turnover.

5. How do you see your profession changing in the next five years? What role will technology play in those changes, and what skills will be required?

GPS and GIS (geographic information systems) are getting bigger. You can draw pretty accurate maps with this technology.

Also, we're seeing more regulation. Counties and townships are putting in ordinances that make it harder to work. Plus, competing products are being made of materials other than wood; for example, composite decking has some wood product but it's mainly plastic and chemicals. In the future, a forester will need to work harder and negotiate more regulations.

6. What do you enjoy most about your job? What do you enjoy least about your job?

I like being independent; I make my own schedule. I like being outside.

What I like least is that you're not going to click with everyone you talk with. Sometimes I put a lot of work into a job and don't see a return. Sometimes it's hard not to take that personally.

7. Can you suggest a valuable "try this" for students considering a career in your profession?

Find a state property where you can hike, get off the trail and hike to the top of the mountain around rocks and downed trees. That will give you some idea of what you need to do physically.

Federal and state agencies offer seasonal work that will give you an idea of the skills you need to learn.

See if you can shadow a forester.

SELECTED SCHOOLS

Many state colleges and universities have bachelor's degree programs related to forestry and conservation. The student may also gain an initial grounding in the field at an agricultural, technical, or community college. For advanced positions, a master's or doctoral degree is usually obtained. Below are listed some of the more prominent schools in this field.

Clemson University
109 Drive
Clemson, SC 29634
864.656.3311
www.clemson.edu

Colorado State University
1062 Campus Delivery
Fort Collins, CO 80523
970.491.6909
www.colostate.edu

Michigan State University
220 Trowbridge Road
East Lansing, MI 48824
517.355.1855
www.msu.edu

North Carolina State University
203 Peele Hall, Box 7103
Raleigh, NC 27695
919.515.2434
www.ncsu.edu

Oregon State University
104 Kerr Admin Building
Corvallis, OR 97331
541.734.4411
oregonstate.edu

Pennsylvania State University
University Park
State College, PA 16801
814.865.4700
www.psu.edu

University of Georgia
210 South Jackson Street
Athens, GA 30602
706.542.8776
www.nau.edu

University of Washington
4000 15th Avenue NE
Box 352100
Seattle, WA 98195
206.543.2730
www.cfr.washington.edu

University of Wisconsin
702 W. Johnson Street
Suite 1101
Madison, WI 53715
608.262.3961
www.wisc.edu

Virginia Tech
925 Price Forks Road
Blacksburg, VA 24061
540.231.3242
www.vt.edu

MORE INFORMATION

American Forests
P.O. Box 2000
Washington, DC 20013
202.737.1944
www.americanforests.org

Forest Guild
2019 Galisto Street
Suite N7
Santa Fe, NM 87505
505.983.8992
www.forestguild.org

National Association of State Foresters
Hall of the States
444 N. Capitol Street NW
Suite 540
Washington, DC 20001
202.624.5415
www.stateforesters.org

Society for Range Management
10030 West 27th Avenue
Wheat Ridge, CO 80215-6601
303.986.3309
www.rangelands.org

Society of American Foresters
Career Information Department
5400 Grosvenor Lane
Bethesda, MD 20814-2198
301.897.8720
www.safnet.org

Soil and Water Conservation Society
945 SW Ankeny Road
Ankeny, IA 50021
515.289.2331
www.swcs.org

USDA Forest Service
1400 Independence Avenue SW
Washington, DC 20250-0002
800.832.1355
www.fs.fed.us

USDA Natural Resources Conservation Service
P.O. Box 2890
Washington, DC 20013
202.720.3210
www.nrcs.usda.gov/programs

Michael Auerbach/Editor

Gardeners & Groundskeepers

Snapshot

Career Cluster(s): Agriculture, Food & Natural Resources, Architecture & Construction

Interests: Environment, working outdoors, working with your hands

Earnings (Median pay): $26,830 per year; $12.90 per hour

Job Growth: Faster than average

OVERVIEW

Sphere of Work

As outdoor maintenance specialists, gardeners and groundskeepers usually perform similar tasks, such as pruning trees and shrubs, maintaining flowerbeds, and picking up litter. These titles are often interchangeable; however, some employers distinguish between their responsibilities. Groundskeepers tend to be responsible for the overall maintenance of a property, which means they might shovel snow, sweep tennis courts, clean swimming pools, or, if employed by an athletic organization, maintain synthetic turf. Gardeners might focus

strictly on caring for plants and maintaining a variety of different types of gardens, including above-ground gardens (e.g., patios and decks) with potted plants.

Work Environment

Gardeners and groundskeepers are employed in residential, government, commercial, and industrial settings, including college campuses, golf courses, apartment complexes, museums and public gardens, amusement parks, resorts, and cemeteries. They work alone, with assistants, or with a large crew. Many of these jobs are seasonal or part-time, with hours that depend on weather conditions.

Profile

Working Conditions: Work Outdoors
Physical Strength: Medium to Heavy Work
Education Needs: On-The-Job Training, High School Diploma Or G.E.D.
Licensure/Certification: Recommended
Physical Abilities Not Required: No Strenuous Labor
Opportunities For Experience: Apprenticeship, Part-Time Work
Holland Interest Score*: CRS, RCE, RCI

* See Appendix A

Occupation Interest

People who are interested in gardening and groundskeeping enjoy being outside and value a well-manicured environment. They are physically fit and able to handle many different responsibilities. Successful gardeners and groundskeepers have the ability to follow a schedule, solve problems, and attend to details as well as the larger landscape.

A Day in the Life—Duties and Responsibilities

The outdoor work performed by gardeners and groundskeepers usually depends greatly on the regional climate of their place of employment. Cold-weather tasks might involve shoveling snow and plowing parking lots, tending to plants in a privately owned greenhouse, and performing indoor jobs, such as sharpening and cleaning tools or building wooden trellises.

Springtime tends to be a busy time. During these months, groundskeepers commonly paint and repair outdoor furniture, edge sidewalks and flower beds, lay sod, clean fountains, and maintain lawns, including fertilizing, aerating, and mowing. Gardening responsibilities include weeding, raking debris from flowerbeds, pruning shrubs and trees, adding compost to soil, and planting bushes, trees, and flowers.

During hot periods, gardeners and groundskeepers usually give special attention to irrigation or watering systems. Weeding, mowing, deadheading flowers, transplanting plants, and applying fertilizer and insecticides occupy much of the time for many workers. Winter preparations may include raking leaves, putting away outdoor furniture, cleaning gardens, and additional weeding and pruning.

Gardeners and groundskeepers also handle a variety of paperwork, maintain inventories, purchase supplies and tools, and study gardening catalogues and manuals. Some employers may require additional tasks. Groundskeepers employed by cemeteries also dig graves and prepare for funerals. Those responsible for athletic stadiums also spray paint lines, names, and numbers on the turf in preparation for games.

Duties and Responsibilities

- Cutting lawns and pruning trees and shrubs
- Trimming and edging around walks, flower beds, and walls
- Raking and removing leaves and cleaning up litter
- Repairing concrete or asphalt walks and driveways
- Maintaining small equipment
- Planting, fertilizing, mulching, and watering flowers, grass, trees, and shrubs
- Hauling in dirt, rock, and other material to improve or alter the landscape

OCCUPATION SPECIALTIES

Arborists

Arborists, or tree service specialists, cut away dead or excess branches from trees or shrubs to clear utility lines, roads, and sidewalks. Although many workers strive to improve the appearance and health of trees and plants, some specialize in diagnosing and treating tree diseases. Others specialize in pruning, trimming, and shaping ornamental trees and shrubs. Tree trimmers and pruners use chain saws, chippers, and stump grinders while on the job. When trimming near power lines, they usually work on truck-mounted lifts and use power pruners.

Groundskeepers and Greenskeepers

Groundskeepers maintain existing grounds. They care for plants and trees, rake and mulch leaves, and clear snow from walkways. They also see to the proper upkeep of sidewalks, parking lots, groundskeeping equipment, fountains, fences, planters, and benches. A special type of groundskeeper known as a greenskeeper maintains golf courses.

Landscapers

Landscapers, or landscape specialists, create new outdoor spaces or upgrade existing ones by planting trees, flowers, and shrubs. They also trim, fertilize, mulch, and water plants. Some grade and install lawns or construct hardscapes such as walkways, patios, and decks. Others help install lighting or sprinkler systems. Landscaping workers are employed in a variety of residential and commercial settings, such as homes, apartment buildings, office buildings, shopping malls, and hotels and motels. Landscape laborers assist landscape specialists by moving soil, equipment, and materials, digging holes, and performing related duties.

Pesticide Application Specialists

Pesticide application specialists apply herbicides, fungicides, or insecticides on plants or the soil to prevent or control weeds, insects, and diseases. Those who work for chemical lawn or tree service firms are more specialized, inspecting lawns for problems and applying fertilizers, pesticides, and other chemicals to stimulate growth and prevent or control weeds, diseases, or insect infestation.

WORK ENVIRONMENT

Physical Environment

The work performed by gardeners and groundskeepers is physically demanding, as it involves much walking, bending, pushing, and heavy lifting. It is especially hard on the back, hands, and knees. The use of ladders and power tools puts workers at risk for injuries. Other occupational hazards are related to sun exposure, insects, pesticides, and herbicides. Gardeners and groundskeepers are also exposed to variable weather conditions throughout the year.

Relevant Skills and Abilities

Organization & Management Skills
- Following instructions
- Paying attention to and handling details
- Performing routine work

Technical Skills
- Working with machines, tools, or other objects

Other Skills
- Using set methods and standards in your work

Work Environment Skills
- Working outdoors
- Working with plants

Human Environment

Unless self-employed, a gardener or groundskeeper usually reports to a supervisor and may work closely with that person until he or she gains enough experience to work independently. Some gardeners and groundskeepers might supervise part-time or temporary workers. While some work alone, others interact regularly with horticulturalists, botanists, landscape architects, and other professionals.

Technological Environment

Gardeners and groundskeepers use many hand and power tools, including electric clippers, chain saws, and lawnmowers. They may drive riding mowers, golf carts, tractors, or trucks. Landscapers may use backhoes, borers, and other heavy equipment, while tree trimmers must be adept at maneuvering through the crowns of trees, either manually (rope and tackle) or by means of a basket crane ("cherry picker"). Most gardeners or groundskeepers use cell phones and may use two-way radios to communicate with coworkers.

Grounds maintenance workers have a higher rate of injuries and illnesses than the national average. Workers who use dangerous equipment, such as lawnmowers and chain saws, must wear protective clothing, eyewear, and earplugs. Those who apply chemicals such as pesticides or fertilizers must wear protective gear, including appropriate clothing, gloves, goggles, and sometimes respirators.

Tree trimmers and pruners, who often work at great heights, must always use fall protection gear in addition to wearing hardhats and eye protection for most activities.

EDUCATION, TRAINING, AND ADVANCEMENT

High School/Secondary

A high school diploma is usually sufficient for gardening and groundskeeping jobs; however, some employers require postsecondary training as well. A vocational program in agriculture, horticulture, or landscaping can prepare students for directly after high school, but might limit advancement possibilities. Courses of prime importance include botany, biology, chemistry, and earth sciences. Art courses may help future gardeners design pleasing flowerbeds. Students should also consider volunteer or part-time jobs in horticultural or agricultural businesses as well as participating in relevant extracurricular programs, such as 4-H clubs.

Suggested High School Subjects
- Agricultural Education
- Applied Biology/Chemistry
- Applied Math
- Building & Grounds Maintenance
- English
- Landscaping
- Mathematics
- Ornamental Horticulture

Famous First

The first Japanese cherry trees in North America were a gift to the United States from the people of Tokyo, Japan. The first shipment arrived in 1909 but had to be destroyed because of insect infestation. A second shipment was planted along the waterway in Potomac Park, Washington, DC, where they remain today and serve as an annual springtime tourist attraction.

Postsecondary

While gardeners and groundskeepers traditionally learn their skills on the job, a postsecondary certificate or an associate's or bachelor's degree can give job seekers an advantage, allow for more flexibility in job duties, and provide a foundation for future advancement. Relevant programs include landscaping, botany, horticulture, ecology, agriculture, and turfgrass science. Those who envision establishing their own businesses might want to consider a degree in business as well.

Related College Majors
- Horticulture Services Operations & Management

Adult Job Seekers

On-the-job training is typically available for those who wish to become gardeners or groundskeepers. Adults who have personal garden or property management experience or have worked in a nursery or related business will find professional gardening or groundskeeping to be a rewarding occupation and easy career transition. The long summer and weekend hours required may prove challenging for those who have personal responsibilities.

Advancement depends on experience and education. Advancement opportunities include supervisory positions, responsibility for larger or more complicated properties, or specializing in one particular area, such as turfgrass management or rose gardens.

Professional Certification and Licensure

There are no required licenses or certificates for most gardeners and groundskeepers. State licensure may be required for those who work with pesticides. Interested individuals should check the requirements of their home state.

Some colleges, professional associations, and trade schools offer their own voluntary certifications. The American Society for Horticultural Science (ASHS) certifies horticulturists, and the Professional Grounds Management Society (PGMS) offers the Certified Grounds Manager (CGM) and Certified Grounds Technician (CGT) certification programs. These certification programs require specified amounts of education or work experience or both as well as satisfactory completion of a written exam.

Additional Requirements

A driver's license and clean driving record is usually required. Some employees might have to pass drug tests and background checks. Those who intend to establish their own business must have strong business and marketing skills. As the wages in this occupation tend to be low, prospective gardeners and groundskeepers should appreciate and find satisfaction in the work itself.

EARNINGS AND ADVANCEMENT

Earnings depend on the geographic location of the employer and the particular job. Earnings are higher in urban areas than in small rural areas. Gardeners and groundskeepers are often employed on a part-time, seasonal basis. Mean annual earnings for gardeners and groundskeepers were $26,320 in 2016. The lowest ten percent earned less than $19,160, and the highest ten percent earned more than $41,070.

Gardeners and groundskeepers may receive paid vacations, holidays, and sick days; life and health insurance; and retirement benefits. These are usually paid by the employer.

States with the Highest Employment Level in this Occupation

State	Employment[1]	Employment per thousand jobs	Location quotient[9]	Hourly mean wage	Annual mean wage[2]
California	104,820	6.56	1.02	$15.11	$31,440
Florida	82,520	10.04	1.55	$12.13	$25,220
Texas	66,770	5.68	0.88	$12.89	$26,800
New York	46,440	5.10	0.79	$15.55	$32,340
Ohio	35,550	6.66	1.03	$12.76	$26,530

[1]Estimates for detailed occupations do not sum to the totals because the totals include occupations not shown separately. Estimates do not include self-employed workers.

[2] Annual wages have been calculated by multiplying the hourly mean wage by a "year-round, full-time" hours figure of 2,080 hours; for those occupations where there is not an hourly wage published, the annual wage has been directly calculated from the reported survey data.

[9] The location quotient is the ratio of the area concentration of occupational employment to the national average concentration. A location quotient greater than one indicates the occupation has a higher share of employment than average, and a location quotient less than one indicates the occupation is less prevalent in the area than average.

EMPLOYMENT AND OUTLOOK

Grounds maintenance workers held about 1.3 million jobs in 2016. Employment in the detailed occupations that make up grounds maintenance workers was distributed as follows:

Landscaping and groundskeeping workers	1,197,900
Tree trimmers and pruners	54,500
Pesticide handlers, sprayers, and applicators, vegetation	38,000
Grounds maintenance workers, all other	18,900

The largest employers of grounds maintenance workers were as follows:

Services to buildings and dwellings	44%
Self-employed workers	22%
Government	8%
Amusement, gambling, and recreation industries	7%
Educational services; state, local, and private	3%

Many grounds maintenance jobs are seasonal. Jobs are most common in the spring, summer, and fall, when planting, mowing, and trimming are most frequent. However, many also provide other seasonal services, such as snow removal and installation and removal of holiday décor.

Overall employment of grounds maintenance workers is projected to grow 10 percent from 2016 to 2026, faster than the average for all occupations. Employment growth will vary by specialty.

Employment of landscaping and groundskeeping workers—the largest specialty—is projected to grow 10 percent from 2016 to 2026, faster than the average for all occupations. More workers will be needed to keep up with increasing demand for lawn care and landscaping services from aging or busy homeowners and large institutions, such as universities and corporate campuses. The growing popularity of outdoor kitchen and living areas should also increase demand for the services these workers provide.

Employment of tree trimmers and pruners is projected to grow 11 percent from 2016 to 2026, faster than the average for all occupations. Many municipalities are planting more trees in urban areas, likely increasing the demand for these workers.

Overall job opportunities are expected to be very good. Job opportunities will stem from employment growth and from the need to replace workers who leave the occupation each year.

Job opportunities should be best in areas with temperate climates, where more landscaping services are required year round.

Employment Trend, Projected 2016–26

Grounds maintenance workers: 10%

Building and grounds cleaning and maintenance occupations: 9%

Total, all occupations: 7%

Note: "All Occupations" includes all occupations in the U.S. Economy. Source: U.S. Bureau of Labor Statistics, Employment Projections program

Conversation With . . .

NED CABE

Assistant Greenhouse Manager
Elizabethan Gardens, Manteo, NC
8 years in the industry

1. What was your individual career path in terms of education/training, entry-level job, or other significant opportunity?

I was a field engineer for Xerox for 33 years. When I retired from Xerox, I started volunteering at the Elizabethan Gardens. I did maintenance, pruning, anything that they needed. I found I loved the work, so I took the Master Gardener program run by North Carolina State University. It's a three-month program that meets once a week. After about a year of volunteering, I was hired to work here.

2. What are the most important skills and/or qualities for someone in your profession?

You have to love plants, first of all. But you also have to be able to visualize what a garden bed will look like once the flowers bloom. That way, you'll be able to create a planting design for an area and plant flowers that will bloom at different times of the year so you'll always have color. We continually have color year round. Another important quality is that you can't be scared of getting dirty. Most of all, you have to be someone who's interested in botany and in school. The first several weeks of the Master Gardener program is all about learning or refreshing your knowledge of botany.

3. What do you wish you had known going into this profession?

I wish I had known how much fun it is! It's something you really get into. I come from a family of farmers, but I left that field to become an engineer. But it gets in your blood and it's been great to get back to the basics.

4. Are there many job opportunities in your profession? In what specific areas?

There are quite a few job opportunities in this area of North Carolina. The only unfortunate part of them is they're mostly seasonal. However, at Elizabethan

Gardens, we tend the gardens year-round. There are a lot of things we do in the winter that you can't do in the summer when we have lots of tourists. In the winter we do things like pruning the trees and planting. We plant twice a year, winter annuals and summer annuals.

5. How do you see your profession changing in the next five years? What role will technology play in those changes, and what skills will be required?

We're going to continue to see new plants developed. The major seed companies that do plant research are constantly coming out with new types of plants, new colors, plants that will survive in different temperate zones. The seed companies patent these plants. When the new items come out, we can buy them and put them in the garden, but we can't propagate them to sell in our greenhouse until the patent expires.

6. What do you enjoy most about your job? What do you enjoy least?

Probably, what I most enjoy about my job is being out and bonding with nature because I spent most of my life in computer rooms looking out windows and wishing I could be outside. We're 100 yards or so from the [Roanoke] Sound, so when I'm outside and hear the waves lapping, it's just about the best. About the closest you can get to heaven is working at a garden.

What I enjoy least about my job is also being outside—when the weather is bad. When we get a nor'easter and the wind is whipping and its 28 degrees, that's not fun. We've had several hurricanes since I've been here. I don't enjoy cleaning up after hurricanes.

7. Can you suggest a valuable "try this" for students considering a career in your profession?

The best thing you can do is look for a community garden in the area where you live. They're always looking for volunteers. We get lots of kids here who volunteer and who do internships. Some find they're not suited for the job. Some find that this is what they want to do. If you can't get your hands dirty, you don't want to do this.

SELECTED SCHOOLS

It is generally not expected that gardeners and groundskeepers receive training beyond high school. However, obtaining college credits in horticulture or landscaping from a technical/community college program can prove beneficial, particularly for those interested in operating their own business or becoming managers. Experience in the trade continues to be one of the most important qualifications.

MORE INFORMATION

American Hort
2130 Stella Court
Columbus, OH 43215
614.487.1117
americanhort.org

**American Society for
Horticultural Science**
1018 Duke Street
Alexandria, VA 22314
703.836.4606
www.ashs.org

Garden Club of America
14 East 60th Street, 3rd Floor
New York, NY 10022
212.753.8287
www.gcamerica.org

National Garden Clubs, Inc.
4401 Magnolia Avenue
St. Louis, MO 63110
314.776.7574
ngcdev.org

**Professional Grounds
Management Society**
720 Light Street
Baltimore, MD 21230-3816
410.223.2861
www.pgms.org

Professional Landcare Network
950 Herndon Parkway
Suite 450
Herndon, VA 20170
703.736.9666
www.landcarenetwork.org

Tree Care Industry Association
135 Harvey Road
Suite 101
Londonderry, NH 03053
603.314.5386

Sally Driscoll/Editor

Geologists & Geophysicists

Snapshot

Career Cluster(s): Agriculture, Food & Natural Resources, Science, Technology, Engineering & Mathematics

Interests: Seismology, hydrology, earth science, helping others

Earnings (Median pay): $89,780 per year; $43.16 per hour

Job Growth: As fast as average

OVERVIEW

Sphere of Work

Geologists and geophysicists—also called geoscientists—study the composition, natural history, and other aspects of the earth. Geologists analyze rocks, plant and animal fossils, soil, minerals, and precious stones. They work for government agencies, oil and petroleum corporations, construction companies, universities, and museums. Geophysicists use physics, chemistry, mathematics, and geology to study the earth's magnetic fields, oceans, composition, seismic forces, and other elements. Most geologists

and geophysicists specialize in sub-fields such as mineralogy, hydrology, paleontology, seismology, and geochemistry. Geologists and geophysicists may be employed by organizations that intend to locate new oil deposits, predict earthquakes and volcano activity, or analyze environmental degradation.

Work Environment

Most geologists and geophysicists spend a significant portion of their time in the field conducting research. Fieldwork often involves traveling great distances into remote, rugged environments. Some geologists and geophysicists travel to foreign countries to pursue field research opportunities. Geologists and geophysicists must also work in all weather conditions. When performing field research, geologists and geophysicists typically work long and irregular hours. When not conducting fieldwork, geologists and geophysicists are at work in offices and laboratories, studying samples, writing papers, and analyzing and interpreting data.

Profile

Working Conditions: Work both Indoors and Outdoors

Physical Strength: Light Work, Medium Work

Education Needs: Master's Degree, Doctoral Degree

Licensure/Certification: Required

Physical Abilities Not Required: No Heavy Labor

Opportunities For Experience: Military Service, Part-Time Work

Holland Interest Score*: IRE, IRS

* See Appendix A

Occupation Interest

Geophysicists and geologists play an important role in protecting people from natural disasters – their work in seismology, hydrology, and other fields can help people avoid flood damage, prepare for seismic activity, or escape the impending eruption of a volcano. These geoscientists also help businesses, universities, and government agencies locate safe locations for construction, find dinosaur remains, and identify new areas in which to dig for oil, metals, or precious stones. The work performed by geophysicists and geologists changes frequently, and new research contributes to a growing body of knowledge about the history and characteristics of the earth. This occupation attracts inquisitive individuals with an interest in earth sciences and a desire to help others.

A Day in the Life—Duties and Responsibilities

The work performed by geologists and geophysicists varies based on their area of expertise. For example, some mineralogists prepare cross-sectional diagrams and geographic surveys of areas from which precious stones and metals may be located and extracted. Others set up and maintain seismic monitors in and around active volcanic areas. Some geophysicists and geologists spend a great deal of time in the laboratory, while others spend the vast majority of time in the field.

Most often, geologists and geophysicists plan and conduct geological surveys, field studies, and other technical analyses. They take small samples of stones, soil, and sediment, or use sensory equipment to sample magnetic waves, tremors, and subterranean water flows. Using these samples and data, geologists and geophysicists compile technical reports, academic papers, charts, maps, and policy recommendations. Geologists and geophysicists rely on computer modeling software, sensory data recorders, and other pieces of hardware and software to ensure that data is complete and organized. Scientists who study the compositions of rocks, minerals, and other resources must also conduct laboratory experiments using chemicals and other analytical tools.

Geologists and geophysicists employed by educational institutions may also need to write research proposals and grant applications in addition to performing their own research. Some geologists and geophysicists are also university professors, overseeing lectures and laboratory sections in addition to performing their own independent research.

Duties and Responsibilities

- Examining rocks, minerals, and fossil remains
- Determining and explaining the sequence of the earth's development
- Interpreting research data
- Recommending specific studies or actions
- Preparing reports and maps
- Managing and cleaning up toxic waste
- Exploring for natural resources (e.g., oil and natural gas)

OCCUPATION SPECIALTIES

Petroleum Geologists

Petroleum geologists study the earth's surface and subsurface to locate gas and oil deposits and help develop extraction processes.

Mineralogists

Mineralogists examine, analyze and classify minerals, gems and precious stones and study their occurrence and chemistry.

Paleontologists

Paleontologists study the fossilized remains of plants and animals to determine the development of past life and history of the earth.

Hydrologists

Hydrologists study the distribution and development of water in land areas and evaluate findings in reference to such problems as flood and drought, soil and water conservation and inland irrigation.

Oceanographers

Oceanographers study the physical aspects of oceans such as currents and their interaction with the atmosphere. They also study the ocean floor and its properties.

Seismologists

Seismologists interpret data from seismographs and other instruments to locate earthquakes and earthquake faults.

Stratigraphers

Stratigraphers study the distribution and arrangement of sedimentary rock layers by examining their contents.

WORK ENVIRONMENT

Physical Environment

Geologists and geophysicists spend much of their time in the field. Fieldwork is typically conducted in remote areas and may require long travel across rugged terrain to reach. These geoscientists must work outdoors in a wide range of climates and weather conditions. When not in the field, geologists and geophysicists work in offices and laboratories, which are clean, comfortable work environments.

Relevant Skills and Abilities

Analytical Skills
- Collecting and analyzing data

Communication Skills
- Editing written information
- Writing concisely

Interpersonal/Social Skills
- Cooperating with others
- Working as a member of a team

Organization & Management Skills
- Paying attention to and handling details

Research & Planning Skills
- Analyzing information
- Creating ideas
- Gathering information
- Solving problems

Technical Skills
- Applying the technology to a task
- Performing scientific, mathematical and technical work
- Working with machines, tools or other objects

Work Environment Skills
- Working outdoors

Human Environment

Depending on their area of specialty, geologists and geophysicists work with a number of different individuals. Among the people with whom they interact are engineers, other geoscientists, laboratory assistants, environmental scientists, oceanographers, chemists, geographers, business executives, and government officials.

Technological Environment

Geologists and geophysicists need to use a wide range of technology to complete their work. Geological compasses, electromagnetic instruments, water flow measurement instruments, soil core sampling tools, sonar, magnetic field measurement devices, geographic information systems software (GIS), global positioning systems (GPS), map creation systems, and scientific databases are only some of the tools and technologies used by individuals in this field.

EDUCATION, TRAINING, AND ADVANCEMENT

High School/Secondary

High school students should study chemistry, physics, environmental science, and other physical science courses. Math classes, such as algebra, geometry, and trigonometry, are essential in geology and geophysics. History, computer science, geography, English, foreign language, and photography courses can also be highly useful for future geologists and geophysicists.

Suggested High School Subjects
- Algebra
- Applied Math
- Chemistry
- College Preparatory
- Earth Science
- English
- Geography
- Geometry
- History
- Photography
- Physical Science
- Science
- Trigonometry

College/Postsecondary

Geologists and geophysicists generally need a master's degree in geology, paleontology, mineralogy, or a related geosciences subject for entry-level jobs. Those who wish to pursue a senior-level research position or employment at an educational institution will need to obtain a doctorate.

Famous First

The first woman geologist was Florence Bascom (1862-1945). Bascom was also the first woman to earn a PhD at Johns Hopkins University. She was appointed assistant geologist to the US Geological Survey in 1896. In addition to this work, she founded the geology department at Bryn Mawr College in Pennsylvania and edited the magazine American Geologist.

Related College Majors
- Geography
- Geological Engineering
- Geophysical Engineering
- Geophysics & Seismology
- Ocean Engineering
- Oceanography

Adult Job Seekers

Qualified geologists and geophysicists may apply directly to postings by government agencies and private business organizations. University geology departments may also have access to entry-level openings. Geoscience journals frequently post openings in this field, and professional geology and geophysics societies and associations create opportunities for job searching and networking.

Professional Certification and Licensure

Some states require geologists and geophysicists who work for government agencies to obtain state licensure. An examination and proof of academic and professional experience are typically required for these licenses. Geologists and geophysicists may choose to pursue voluntary certification in specialized areas of expertise.

Additional Requirements

Geologists and geophysicists should be physically fit, as they frequently work in remote and rugged areas and sometimes carry heavy equipment and samples. They should also have familiarity with computer systems, GIS, GPS, and other technologies. Strong communication and interpersonal skills, writing abilities, and a sense of teamwork are important for geologists and geophysicists, as are an inquisitive nature and the desire to spend time working outdoors.

Fun Fact

Landslides occur in all of the 50 states in the U.S. Washington, Oregon, and California's mountainous and coastal regions are the major areas where landslides occur. Eastern U.S. mountain and hill regions are also susceptible.

Source: http://geology.com/usgs/landslides

EARNINGS AND ADVANCEMENT

The median annual wage for geoscientists was $89,780 in May 2016. The median wage is the wage at which half the workers in an occupation earned more than that amount and half earned less. The lowest 10 percent earned less than $47,450, and the highest 10 percent earned more than $189,020.

In May 2016, the median annual wages for geoscientists in the top industries in which they worked were as follows:

Mining, quarrying, and oil and gas extraction	$124,180
Federal government, excluding postal service	$97,440
Architectural, engineering, and related services	$80,220
State government, excluding education and hospitals	$71,820
Colleges, universities, and professional schools; state, local, and private	$62,270

Most geoscientists work full time and may work additional or irregular hours when doing fieldwork. Geoscientists travel frequently to meet with clients and to conduct fieldwork.

(

Median annual wages, May 2016

Geoscientists, except hydrologists and geographers: $89,780

Physical scientists: $77,790

Total, all occupations: $37,040

Note: "All Occupations" includes all occupations in the U.S. Economy. Source: U.S. Bureau of Labor Statistics, Occupational Employment Statistics

EMPLOYMENT AND OUTLOOK

Geoscientists held about 32,000 jobs in 2016. The largest employers of geoscientists were as follows:

Architectural, engineering, and related services	26%
Mining, quarrying, and oil and gas extraction	24%
Federal government, excluding postal service	7%
State government, excluding education and hospitals	7%
Colleges, universities, and professional schools; state, local, and private	6%

About 3 out of 10 geoscientists were employed in Texas in 2016, because of the prominence of oil and gas activities in that state. Workers in natural resource extraction fields usually work as part of a team, with other scientists and engineers. For example, they may work closely with petroleum engineers to find and develop new sources of oil and natural gas.

Most geoscientists split their time between working in the field, in laboratories, and in offices. Fieldwork can take geoscientists to remote locations all over the world. For example, oceanographers may spend months at sea on a research ship, and petroleum geologists may spend long periods in remote areas while doing exploration activities. Extensive travel and long periods away from home can be physically and psychologically demanding. Having outdoor skills, such as camping and hiking skills, may be useful.

Most geoscientists work full time. They may work additional or irregular hours when doing fieldwork. Geoscientists travel frequently to meet with clients and to conduct fieldwork.

Employment of geoscientists is projected to grow 14 percent from 2016 to 2026, faster than the average for all occupations. The need for energy, environmental protection, and responsible land and resource management is projected to spur demand for geoscientists.

Many geoscientists work in oil and gas extraction and related engineering services and consulting firms. Demand for their services in these industries will be dependent on the demand for the exploration and development of oil and gas wells. New technologies, such as horizontal drilling and hydraulic fracturing, allow for the extraction of previously inaccessible oil and gas resources, and geoscientists will be needed to study the effects such technologies have on the surrounding areas.

Geoscientists will be involved in discovering and developing sites for alternative energies, such as geothermal energy and wind energy. For example, geothermal energy plants must be located near sufficient hot ground water, and one task for geoscientists would be evaluating if the site is suitable.

Related Occupations
- Geographer
- Metallurgical/Materials Engineer
- Mining & Geological Engineer
- Oceanographer
- Petroleum Engineer
- Surveyor & Cartographer

Related Military Occupations
- Oceanographer

Conversation With . . .
RON PYLES

Geotechnical Engineer
Principal Engineer, 15 Years
VP, Kim Engineering, Baltimore MD

1. What was your individual career path in terms of education/training, entry-level job, or other significant opportunity?

I first was exposed to construction, and went to a junior college in Upstate New York for construction management. Then I decided to go on to a four-year school where I took civil engineering. While there, I found the geotechnical discipline, which offered more of a challenge, and took as many courses in that area as I could. I went on to work for three years to make sure I was interested in geotech, and then I earned a Master's in Civil Engineering specializing in geology.

Being a geotechnical engineer is not being a geologist per se. My field merges geology and engineering, and I mostly deal with foundations that a specific building requires, or pilings, groundwater problems, retaining walls, and that sort of thing.

Geotechnical engineering, in my opinion, is more creative than other engineering disciplines. When you think of the different formations associated with the massive earth movements that formed some of this geology, it takes a lot of force. You need to know geology. For example, if a region is limestone, which creates sinkholes, you need to know that and recommend specific techniques to build within and/ or explore the karst terrain. If you're in an area where massive erosion occurred in past geologic times, and everything is consolidated because it's overburdened, then bearing capacities for foundations or walls can be much higher. Areas of Maryland, Washington, DC and Virginia, for example, have specific types of clays. These clays have specific characteristics, with high plasticity, and they may swell or shrink with moisture changes. You need to know that.

To specialize in geotechnical engineering, you should pursue advanced degrees. In geology that's not necessary, although it's always good to have an advanced degree.

2. What are the most important skills and/or qualities for someone in your profession?

Good writing skills are critical, because we produce reports that other engineers and developers read. You need good verbal communications skills with clients. It can be a high-risk business if you're not careful with your quality of work, so you need to be cognitive of legal aspects. Being organized is a plus. And, you need to be able to manage people if you are directing subordinates.

3. **What do you wish you had known going into this profession?**

In our work we deal with the substrate but once they build a foundation, they cover up the substrate. You can't stand there and appreciate your work.

4. **Are there many job opportunities in your profession? In what specific areas?**

There is very good demand relative to employment. Geotechnical engineering is good, and geologists interfacing with the geotechnical field have pretty good overall demand as well.

5. **How do you see your profession changing in the next five years, what role will technology play in those changes, and what skills will be required?**

Many of our theories have not changed a lot over the years. As technology has progressed we've obtained newer advanced equipment to assess the soils. An example would be the geophysical device that sends electrical waves to measure the resistance of those waves as they pass through the earth. We use that to find sinkholes and rock levels.

6. **What do you enjoy most about your job? What do you enjoy least about your job?**

Most enjoyable is exploring new areas from a geology viewpoint and soils aspect relative to proposed construction. Each site offers sort of a surprise because you don't know what's under the ground. You have the ability to assess and confirm the geology of the site, then look forward to the lab analysis.

This is a pretty demanding business, and there can be demanding turnaround. Unfortunately, sometimes clients can be hard to deal with.

7. **Can you suggest a valuable "try this" for students considering a career in your profession?**

Visit construction sites and field trips with a geologist or engineer. There are a lot of areas where you can get exposed to geologic formations; field trips are obviously an excellent way to get some exposure. Also, consider interning. Each summer my company has an intern program. We bring in 3-4 interns from colleges who are taking engineering and they can learn more about what we do.

SELECTED SCHOOLS

Most colleges and universities have bachelor's degree programs in geology or related subjects. The student may also gain an initial grounding in the field at an agricultural, technical, or community college. For advanced positions, a master's or doctoral degree is commonly obtained. Below are listed some of the more prominent graduate schools in this field.

California Institute of Technology
Division of Geological and Planetary Sciences
1200 East California Boulevard
Mail Code 170-25
Pasadena, CA 91125
626.395.6123
www.gps.caltech.edu

Massachusetts Institute of Technology
Earth, Atmospheric, and Planetary Sciences
77 Massachusetts Avenue
Cambridge, MA 02139
617.253.2127
eapsweb.mit.edu

Penn State University
Geosciences Department
503 Deike Building
University Park, PA 16802
814.867.4760
www.geosc.psu.edu

Stanford University
Geological and Environmental Sciences
450 Serra Mall, Building 320
Stanford, CA 94305
650.723.0847
pangea.stanford.edu/departments/ges

University of Arizona
Department of Geosciences
1040 E. 4th Street
Tucson, AZ 85721
520.621.6000
www.geo.arizona.edu

University of California, Berkeley
Earth and Planetary Science
307 McCone Hall
Berkeley, CA 94720
510.642.3993
eps.berkeley.edu

University of Colorado, Boulder
Department of Geological Sciences
UCB 359
Boulder, CO 80309
303.492.8141
www.colorado.edu/geolsci

University of Michigan, Ann Arbor
Earth and Environmental Sciences
2534 C.C. Little Building
1100 North University Avenue
Ann Arbor, MI 48109
734.763.1435
www.lsa.umich.edu/earth

University of Texas, Austin
Department of Geological Sciences
2275 Speedway Stop C9000
Austin, TX 78712
512.471.5172
www.jsg.utexas.edu/dgs

University of Wisconsin, Madison
Department of Geoscience
1215 West Dayton Street
Madison, WI 53706
608.262.8960
www.geoscience.wisc.edu

MORE INFORMATION

**American Association of
Petroleum Geologists**
P.O. Box 979
Tulsa, OK 74101-0979
800.364.2274
www.aapg.org

American Geosciences Institute
4220 King Street
Alexandria, VA 22302-1502
703.379.2480
www.americangeosciences.org

**Environmental and Engineering
Geophysical Society**
1720 South Bellaire, Suite 110
Denver, CO 80222-4303
303.531.7517
www.eegs.org

Geological Society of America
P.O. Box 9140
Boulder, CO 80301-9140
303.357.1000
www.geosociety.org

Paleontological Society
P.O. Box 9044
Boulder, CO 80301
855.357.1032
www.paleosoc.org

Seismological Society of America
201 Plaza Professional Building
El Cerrito, CA 94530
510.525.5474
www.seismosoc.org

**Society of Exploration
Geophysicists**
P.O. Box 702740
Tulsa, OK 74170-2740
918.497.5500
www.seg.org

United States Geological Survey
12201 Sunrise Valley Drive
Reston, VA 20192
703.648.5953
www.usgs.gov

Michael Auerbach/Editor

Insurance Claims Adjusters & Examiners

Snapshot

Career Cluster(s): Business, Management & Administration, Finance

Interests: Investigation, risk assessment, solving problems, helping others

Earnings (Median pay): $63,670 per year; $30.61 per hour

Job Growth: Little or no change

OVERVIEW

Sphere of Work

Insurance claims adjusters and examiners, also referred to as insurance claims investigators, insurance claims assessors, insurance claims analysts, and liability assessors, are responsible for investigating and settling claims that insurance policyholders have made to their insurance companies. Adjusters visit the scene of an accident, injury, or natural disaster and estimate the cost of the damage done. They write reports recommending whether the claim should be approved or not. Examiners are very similar

to adjusters, although in some companies they may follow up on adjusters' work by checking their reports for accuracy and to ensure that the adjuster has followed the insurance company's procedures properly. Adjusters and examiners may be independent agents or employed by insurance companies.

Work Environment

Insurance claims adjusters and examiners work in offices writing and evaluating claims reports as well as in the field investigating claims and inspecting damaged property. They visit claimants and insurance policyholders at their homes, accident scenes, hospitals and rehabilitation facilities, and automobile repair shops. Insurance claims adjusters and examiners may work a forty-hour week or in an on-call capacity responding to claims as they are made. They may be expected to work overtime during busy times or when responding to emergencies or natural disasters that affect many people at once. When investigating claims in the field, especially in the aftermath of an event like a tornado or a fire, insurance claims adjusters and examiners may be exposed to physical hazards.

Profile

Working Conditions: Work both Indoors and Outdoors
Physical Strength: Light Work
Education Needs: Junior/Technical/Community College, Bachelor's Degree
Licensure/Certification: Required
Opportunities For Experience: Internship, Part-Time Work
Holland Interest Score*: ESC

* See Appendix A

Occupation Interest

Individuals attracted to the insurance claims adjuster and examiner profession tend to be organized, diplomatic, and detail-oriented people who find satisfaction in resolving questions and helping people in times of need. Those individuals who excel as insurance claims adjusters and examiners exhibit traits such as responsibility, time management, composure under pressure, attention to detail, and a desire to help. Insurance claims adjusters and examiners should enjoy insurance work and have a background in investigation and risk assessment.

A Day in the Life—Duties and Responsibilities

The daily duties and responsibilities of insurance claims adjusters and examiners will vary with job specialty and employer. Areas of insurance claims specialization include claims adjusters, appraisers, examiners, and investigators. Insurance claims adjusters and examiners investigate and settle property damage, liability, and bodily injury claims. Insurance companies encourage insurance claims adjusters and examiners to settle claims without legal arbitration whenever possible.

When they receive claims, insurance claims adjusters and examiners may begin work by reviewing insurance policies to determine what type and amount of coverage applies to the claim. They may travel to the site of damaged property and confirm the cause and extent of the damage; they may interview people involved in the incident, including policyholders, witnesses, first responders (police, firemen, and paramedics), and physicians. They gather information and records related to the incident, such as police reports, and work with appraisers, colleagues, and relevant professionals, such as builders or auto mechanics, to determine the extent of the damage. Providing emotional and customer service support to customers is a very important aspect of processing claims, especially since customers may have experienced a personal loss or a significant loss of property due to the event. Claims adjusters and examiners may assist policyholders with various requests, and communicate with them about the process of investigating the claim. If a widespread natural disaster occurs, the adjuster may be sent to assist local residents with the filing of their claims before the evaluation process begins.

When the initial work is complete, insurance claims adjusters and examiners prepare the claim report and attempt to negotiate a monetary settlement with the policyholder. Most of the time this is successful, but if the claimant contests the company's decision regarding a claim, sometimes claims adjusters and examiners must initiate legal proceedings if an out-of-court settlement cannot be reached. The final claims report is submitted by the adjuster or examiner to supervisors at the insurance company. Examiners are also responsible for checking the accuracy of adjusters' reported findings and for confirming that adjusters followed correct procedures while investigating the claim or claims.

All insurance claims adjusters and examiners should stay up to date with regulatory and ethical issues and news in the insurance industry by reading insurance industry journals and participating in insurance industry associations.

Duties and Responsibilities

- Determining the amount of damage
- Determining if the claim is covered by the insurance policy
- Interviewing or corresponding with the person making the claim
- Inspecting property damage or loss
- Consulting police, fire and medical reports and records
- Preparing a detailed report of findings
- Recommending any legal action necessary
- Testifying in court on contested claims
- Preparing and maintaining files on clients' policies
- Making adjustments to existing policies, such as change in type or amount of coverage

WORK ENVIRONMENT

Physical Environment

Insurance claims adjusters and examiners work in office environments as well as in the field investigating claims and visiting damaged property and injured people. Insurance claims adjusters and examiners generally must be physically able to drive as well as walk over potentially rough terrain damaged by flood, winds, earthquakes, and fire.

Human Environment

Insurance claims adjusters and examiners interact with insurance policyholders, lawyers, doctors, automobile repair mechanics, business owners, and coworkers and supervisors. Insurance claims adjusters and examiners should be comfortable meeting with policyholders and industry professionals and show good judgment, objectivity, and tact when responding to policyholders.

Relevant Skills and Abilities

Communication Skills
- Persuading others
- Speaking effectively
- Writing concisely

Interpersonal/Social Skills
- Cooperating with others
- Working as a member of a team

Organization & Management Skills
- Making decisions

Research & Planning Skills
- Developing evaluation strategies

Technical Skills
- Performing scientific, mathematical and technical work

Technological Environment

Insurance claims adjusters and examiners use computers, telephones, tape measures, cameras, calculators, and the Internet communication tools, insurance business software programs, and spreadsheets to complete their work.

EDUCATION, TRAINING, AND ADVANCEMENT

High School/Secondary

High school students interested in pursuing a career as an insurance claims adjuster or examiner should prepare by building good study habits. High school–level study of sociology, bookkeeping, and mathematics will provide a strong foundation for work as an insurance claims adjuster and examiner or for college-level study in the field. High school students interested in this career path will benefit from seeking internships or part-time work with insurance businesses or investigators.

Suggested High School Subjects

- Applied Communication
- Bookkeeping
- Business
- Business Law
- Computer Science
- Economics
- English
- Keyboarding
- Mathematics
- Psychology
- Statistics

Famous First

The first title guaranty insurance company was the Real Estate Title Insurance and Trust Company, organized in Philadelphia on March 31, 1876. It offered security against errors in property titles. Prior to the creation of title insurance, buyers bore sole responsibility for ensuring the validity of land titles.

College/Postsecondary

Postsecondary students interested in becoming insurance claims adjusters and examiners should work toward an associate's or bachelor's degree in economics, finance, statistics, or accounting. Coursework in computer science, political science, and ethics may also prove useful in their future work. Postsecondary students can gain work experience and potential advantage in their future job searches by securing internships or part-time employment with local insurance businesses.

Related College Majors

- Banking & Financial Support Services
- Finance, General
- Insurance & Risk Management

Adult Job Seekers

Adults seeking insurance claims adjuster and examiner jobs have generally earned an associate's or bachelor's degree. Some insurance claims adjuster and examiner jobs require extensive experience and on-the-job training. Adult job seekers should educate themselves about the educational and professional requirements of the organizations where they seek employment. Adult job seekers will benefit from joining professional insurance associations as a means of professional networking. Professional insurance associations, such as the National Association of Professional Insurance Agents, the Independent Automotive Damage Appraisers Association, the Insurance Institute of America, and the National Association of Independent Insurance Adjusters, generally maintain job lists advertising open positions in the field.

Professional Certification and Licensure

Certification is not legally required for insurance claims adjusters and examiners but may be required as a condition of employment or promotion. Extensive options for voluntary insurance claims adjuster and examiner certification exist within the insurance industry. These voluntary credentials or designations have education, experience, testing, employer sponsorship, recertification, and continuing education requirements. Licensing requirements for insurance claims adjusters and examiners vary significantly by state. At least sixteen states require insurance claims adjusters to hold a license earned through satisfying an education requirement or passing an examination. Some states award licenses directly to insurance companies or businesses rather than individual insurance adjusters. Insurance claims adjusters and examiners should contact the agency that oversees insurance in their home state for specific licensing requirements.

Additional Requirements

Successful insurance claims adjusters and examiners adhere to strict codes of professional ethics. Professionals in this occupation have access to confidential information and can influence the financial futures of individuals and businesses. Membership in professional insurance associations is encouraged among all insurance claims adjusters and examiners as a means of building professional community.

Fun Fact

Hurricane Harvey, with an estimated $190 billion in damages, making it the costliest storm in U.S. history.
Source: https://www.usatoday.com/

EARNINGS AND ADVANCEMENT

The median annual wage for claims adjusters, examiners, and investigators was $63,680 in May 2016. The median wage is the wage at which half the workers in an occupation earned more than that amount and half earned less. The lowest 10 percent earned less than $37,540, and the highest 10 percent earned more than $95,760.

The median annual wage for insurance appraisers, auto damage was $63,510 in May 2016. The lowest 10 percent earned less than $42,740, and the highest 10 percent earned more than $95,000.

In May 2016, the median annual wages for claims adjusters, examiners, and investigators in the top industries in which they worked were as follows:

Government	$70,680
Direct insurance (except life, health, and medical) carriers	$63,580
Agencies, brokerages, and other insurance related activities	$61,160
Direct health and medical insurance carriers	$56,860
Administrative and support services	$44,000

In May 2016, the median annual wages for insurance appraisers, auto damage in the top industries in which they worked were as follows:

Direct insurance (except life, health, and medical) carriers	$64,100
Agencies, brokerages, and other insurance related activities	$63,410
Management of companies and enterprises	$61,290
Professional, scientific, and technical services	$56,320

Most claims adjusters, appraisers, examiners, and investigators work full time. However, their work schedules vary.

Adjusters often arrange their work schedules to accommodate evening and weekend appointments with clients. This requirement sometimes results in adjusters working irregular schedules, especially when they have a lot of claims to review.

Insurance investigators often work irregular schedules because of the need to conduct surveillance and contact people who are not available during normal business hours. Early morning, evening, and weekend work is common.

In contrast, auto damage appraisers typically work regular hours and rarely work on weekends

Median annual wages
May 2016

Business operations specialists: $65,260

Claims adjusters, examiners, and investigators: $63,680

Claims adjusters, appraisers, examiners, and investigators: $63,670

Insurance appraisers, auto damage: $63,510

Total, all occupations: $37,040

Note: "All Occupations" includes all occupations in the U.S. Economy. Source: U.S. Bureau of Labor Statistics, Occupational Employment Statistics

EMPLOYMENT AND OUTLOOK

Nationally, insurance claims adjusters and examiners held about 310,000 jobs in 2014. Employment is expected to grow slower than the average for all occupations through the year 2024, which means employment is projected to increase 1 percent to 6 percent. As long as more insurance policies are being sold to accommodate a rising population, there will be a need for these workers. In addition, a growing elderly population, higher healthcare premiums, and insurance companies' attempts to lower costs will create demand for insurance claims adjusters and examiners. Job openings will also result from the need to replace workers who transfer to other occupations or leave the labor force.

Employment Trend, Projected 2016–26

Business operations specialists: 9%

Total, all occupations: 7%

Insurance appraisers, auto damage: 5%

Claims adjusters, appraisers, examiners, and investigators: -1%

Claims adjusters, examiners, and investigators: -1%

Note: "All Occupations" includes all occupations in the U.S. Economy. Source: U.S. Bureau of Labor Statistics, Employment Projections program

Related Occupations
- Insurance Underwriter
- Personal Financial Advisor
- Real Estate Appraiser

Conversation With . . .
MARY ANNE MEDINA

Director of Business Development & Training
One Call Claims, Orlando, Florida
Insurance adjuster, 25-plus years

1. What was your individual career path in terms of education/training, entry-level job, or other significant opportunity?

After I graduated from college, I taught for a year. Several people in my family worked in claims. It was during a time when the industry was under pressure to hire women. I went to work for a large adjusting firm that had its own training facility, so I got a lot of training. It intrigued me to be able to move into a position with so many benefits and a company vehicle and room for promotions and the ability to learn many aspects of the industry: property claims, catastrophe claims, casualty, litigation. I eventually moved to upper management.

Prior to the job that I have now, I was vice president of Vale Training Solutions, which is a training facility for adjusters. My career path was to go out and experience everything in the field, then bring it back and train others. It came full circle.

2. What are the most important skills and/or qualities for someone in your profession?

I think communication is probably the priority. If you're a catastrophe adjuster, you're dealing with someone who's been devastated and lost their home. You need to be able to guide them through the process. Or if you're called to testify, you have to be able to communicate in a courtroom. You have to be able to communicate with different cultural groups. We constantly get calls for what we call "soft skills." The new people coming in aren't used to not sending that instant text and their writing skills to communicate and explain are not there.

And secondly, being organized. Being an adjuster, especially a catastrophe adjuster, can be very demanding— trying to see everyone and return every call and every email and get people back on their feet.

You have to genuinely like people. If you can't deal with confrontation, it's not for you. You have to be empathetic. It may seem like a mild fender bender to you, but to this grandma who's never had an accident in her life, it's major.

3. What do you wish you had known going into this profession?

I wish I had known how physically demanding the job can be. When it's 105 degrees and you're putting a 70-pound ladder up on a roof 10 times a day or you're going through a commercial building that's been burned and you can't breathe because there's soot in your nasal passages, it's tough. When you go to a catastrophe, you're hoping you can find a hotel room; there may be no water or power. And it's emotionally demanding. I've seen things that I'll never forget. I had a claim for a family in Miami where during the height of a storm—and of course, they blamed themselves, they didn't board the windows up—well, a piece of the window came through and hit their 9-year-old across the chest and he bled to death. Things like that really do impact you.

4. Are there many job opportunities in your profession? In what specific areas?

Yes. No matter what happens with the economy, there are still tornadoes and storms and car accidents and people falling down in grocery stores.

5. How do you see your profession changing in the next five years? What role will technology play in those changes, and what skills will be required?

Technology constantly changes and you have to keep up. Drones can fly over and take pictures for adjusting purposes. We already have satellite capability in areas where the roof is too steep or you can't get to the area. You can examine damage, get in your car, dial your cell phone and update a voice-activated diary: 'Went to Mrs. Jones home, she had 6 feet of water' and Mrs. Jones can log into her claim and see what's going on.

Everything is fast, fast, fast, but now customers are saying, "I got this estimate and I don't understand it." I really see a shift in realizing that fast is not always better, that you can't replace human contact.

6. What do you enjoy most about your job? What do you enjoy least about your job?

Meeting people and helping people. It's a tough industry. I've always looked at it as really helping people get their lives back together.

For a while, what I liked least was the travel. I was missing a lot of the joys of life: my kids, my husband. Catastrophe adjusters can be gone for long periods and you can't get that time back.

7. **Can you suggest a valuable "try this" for students considering a career in your profession?**

There are claims offices located pretty much everywhere. Go in and talk to an adjuster. There's so much out there that you can read, like Claims Magazine and Claims Management Magazine.

SELECTED SCHOOLS

Many colleges and universities, especially those with business schools, offer programs related to a career in insurance. The student can also gain initial training through enrollment at a technical or community college. Below are listed some of the more prominent institutions in this field.

Georgia State University
PO Box 3965
Atlanta, GA 30302
404.413.2000
www.gsu.edu

Florida State University
Tallahassee, FL 32306
850.644.2525
www.fsu.edu

New York University
70 Washington Square S
New York, NY 10012
212.998.1212
www.nyu.edu

St. Joseph's University
5600 City Hall
Philadelphia, PA 19131
610.660.1000
www.sju.edu

Temple University
1801 N. Broad Street
Philadelphia, PA 19122
215.204.7000
www.temple.edu

University of Georgia
Administration Building
Athens, GA 30602
706.542.3000
www.uga.edu

University of Illinois, Urbana, Champaign
601 E. John Street
Champaign, IL 61820
217.333.1000
illinois.edu

University of Pennsylvania
1 College Hall, Rm 100
Philadelphia, PA 19104
215.898.5000
www.upenn.edu

University of Texas, Austin
1 University Station
Austin, TX 78712
512.471.3434
www.utexas.edu

University of Wisconsin, Madison
500 Lincoln Drive
Madison, WI 53706
608.262.1234
www.wisc.edu

MORE INFORMATION

American College
270 S. Bryn Mawr Avenue
Bryn Mawr, PA 19010
888.263.7265
www.theamericancollege.edu

**Independent Insurance Agents
and Brokers of America**
127 S. Peyton Street
Alexandria, VA 22314
800.221.7917
www.iiaa.org

**Independent Automotive
Damage Appraisers Association**
P.O. Box 12291
Columbus, GA 31917–2291
800.369.4232
www.iada.org

Insurance Institute of America
720 Providence Road, Suite 100
Malvern, PA 19335-0716
800.644.2101
www.aicpcu.org

**National Association of
Independent Insurance
Adjusters**
P.O. Box 807
Geneva, IL 60134
630.208.5002
www.naiia.com

**National Association of
Insurance and Financial
Advisors**
2901 Telestar Court
Falls Church, VA 22042-1205
877.866.2432
www.naifa.org

**National Association of
Professional Insurance Agents**
400 N. Washington Street
Alexandria, VA 22314
703.836.9340
www.pianet.com

Landscape Architects

Snapshot

Career Cluster(s): Agriculture, Food & Natural Resources, Architecture & Construction

Interests: Science, environment, technology, design, communicating with others

Earnings (Median pay): $63,480 per year; $30.52 per hour

Job Growth: As fast as average

OVERVIEW

Sphere of Work

Landscape architects are designers of exterior space. Much of the work they do is both decorative and functional. They plan the surrounding landscape for new buildings, deciding where to place walkways, lawns, trees, gardens, retaining walls, fountains, reflecting pools, and other natural and manmade objects. They also design bike trails, golf courses, playgrounds, highway and waterfront beautification projects, and other public spaces. In addition to planning aesthetically pleasing environments, they prepare environmental impact statements, solve environmental

problems such as flooding or mudslides, and restore habitats back to their original condition.

Work Environment

Landscape architects work in government and in the private sector. Many landscape architects are self-employed or work in small architectural firms. They interact with clients, architects, urban planners, engineers, and other professionals involved in construction and development. They also often supervise the contractors and gardeners who carry out their landscaping plans. They frequently work long or odd hours to meet deadlines.

Profile

Working Conditions: Work both Indoors and Outdoors
Physical Strength: Light Work
Education Needs: Bachelor's Degree, Master's Degree
Licensure/Certification: Required
Physical Abilities Not Required: No Heavy Labor
Opportunities For Experience: Internship, Apprenticeship, Volunteer Work, Part-Time Work
Holland Interest Score*: AIR

* See Appendix A

Occupation Interest

Landscape architecture attracts people who value the harmony between humans and nature that can be achieved through thoughtful planning and manipulating the environment. They are imaginative, artistic problem-solvers who are solidly grounded in science and technology. They are both detail-oriented and able to envision large-scale projects. Successful landscape architects use their excellent communication skills to convey their design ideas to others.

A Day in the Life—Duties and Responsibilities

The duties and responsibilities of landscape architects are many and varied. Larger jobs usually involve carrying out a preliminary assessment, or feasibility study, performed in collaboration with the architect, engineers, and environmental scientists. At that time, the landscape architect might take photographs or a video of the area to be developed. He or she might also have to submit applications to government agencies for zoning permits and environmental approval.

After a site has been approved, the landscape architect studies the area's topographic features. The landscape architect then offers suggestions on how best to situate the project's buildings, walkways and roadways, and natural elements based on environmental factors such as sunlight and drainage. He or she then designs the landscape to complement the design of the building, harmonize with the surrounding environment, and accommodate the spatial needs of various stakeholders. Much of the design work is done with a computer-aided design (CAD) program, but it may also be sketched by hand. The landscape architect might also prepare a video simulation or build a 3-D model of the design. He or she then puts together a proposal that also includes a cost analysis, written reports, permits, and other materials.

On large projects, the approval process typically involves many meetings with the developer over the course of several months. During this time, the landscape architect might give several presentations to a board of shareholders or a government commission. He or she also submits construction designs to local building commissioners for approval.

Once approved, the landscape architect refines the drawings and details specific construction guidelines. After construction begins, he or she may return to the site to oversee the work.

Duties and Responsibilities

- **Preparing site plans, working drawings, specifications and cost estimates for land developments**
- **Presenting design sketches to clients and community interest groups**
- **Outlining in detail the methods of construction**
- **Drawing up a list of necessary materials**
- **Inspecting construction work in progress to make sure specifications are followed**
- **Conferring with clients, engineering personnel and architects on overall programs for project**
- **Compiling and analyzing data on site conditions such as geographic location, soil, vegetation and rock features, drainage and location of structures**

WORK ENVIRONMENT

Physical Environment

Landscape architects work in offices but also spend much time at job sites. Undeveloped sites may have safety issues such as uneven terrain, mud, or plant and animal pests, while those under construction may involve loud noise, fumes, chemicals, or other hazards.

Relevant Skills and Abilities

Communication Skills
- Expressing thoughts and ideas clearly
- Speaking and writing effectively

Creative/Artistic Skills
- Being skilled in art or design

Organization & Management Skills
- Making decisions
- Paying attention to and handling details

Research & Planning Skills
- Using logical reasoning

Technical Skills
- Performing technical work

Human Environment

Unless they are self-employed, landscape architects usually work in firms or departments with other architects, assistants, and staff, under supervision by the head architect or director. They may supervise drafters, surveyors, gardeners, and other employees or contractors. Their clients range from homeowners to residential and commercial developers to boards of directors.

Technological Environment

Landscape architects use computers equipped with CAD software, word processing, geographic information systems (GIS), and spreadsheets, among other programs. They might also use photo imaging, illustration, modeling, and other computer graphics or design software. In addition to conventional office equipment, they use large format copiers and a variety of drafting and art tools and supplies. They may also use surveying equipment.

EDUCATION, TRAINING, AND ADVANCEMENT

High School/Secondary

A well-rounded college preparatory program that emphasizes math, science, and courses that introduce CAD, such as mechanical drawing or drafting, will provide the best foundation for a career in landscape design. Especially relevant courses include geometry, trigonometry, environmental science, biology, geology, and botany. Speech communication and English courses help develop communication skills, while drawing, sculpture, photography, computer graphics, and other art courses encourage creativity. Part-time jobs in gardening, lawn care, or construction, or volunteering at a nature center or arboretum can provide valuable hands-on work experience.

Suggested High School Subjects

- Applied Biology/Chemistry
- Applied Math
- Arts
- Blueprint Reading
- Drafting
- English
- Landscaping
- Mathematics
- Mechanical Drawing
- Ornamental Horticulture
- Photography

Famous First

The first American landscape architect of note was Frederick Law Olmstead (1822-1903), designer of Central Park and Prospect Park in New York City as well as numerous other notable municipal parks, state parks, and college campuses. Olmsted was also active in the conservation movement, and during the Civil War he headed the US Sanitary Commission, which oversaw care of sick and wounded soldiers.

College/Postsecondary

A bachelor's degree in landscape architecture is the minimum requirement for licensing as a landscape architect; some employers require an advanced degree. The undergraduate degree in landscape architecture often takes five years and includes courses in surveying, CAD and modeling, ecology, horticulture, earth sciences, landscape planning, design, and construction, and management. Some programs require, or strongly suggest, an internship and offer hands-on opportunities as part of the curriculum.

Related College Majors
- Architectural Environmental Design
- Landscape Architecture

Adult Job Seekers

Adults with a background in horticulture, gardening, botany, geology, urban planning, or another related discipline would have an advantage when entering this career. Those with a bachelor's degree in a related field may be able to enroll directly in a three-year master's degree program, thus saving time and money. Qualified landscape architects should consider membership in professional associations, which often provide opportunities for networking, job-finding, and professional development.

Professional Certification and Licensure

All states license landscape architects. In most cases, candidates are required to have a bachelor's degree from a Landscape Architectural

Accreditation Board (LAAB) accredited program as well as one to four years of experience and a passing score on the Landscape Architect Registration Examination (LARE). Some states also administer their own test and have slightly different requirements for experience and education. Continuing education is a common requirement for license renewal. Interested individuals should check the requirements of their home state.

Additional Requirements

Landscape architects must be familiar with local zoning regulations and environmental codes. Those who wish to establish their own landscape design firms should have business skills and motivation as well as experience in the field.

Fun Fact

A tree shading an outdoor air conditioner unit can increase its efficiency by as much as ten percent.
Source: signatureconcretedesign.com

EARNINGS AND ADVANCEMENT

The median annual wage for landscape architects was $63,480 in May 2016. The median wage is the wage at which half the workers in an occupation earned more than that amount and half earned less. The lowest 10 percent earned less than $38,950, and the highest 10 percent earned more than $106,770.

In May 2016, the median annual wages for landscape architects in the top industries in which they worked were as follows:

Government	$83,800
Construction	$69,760
Architectural, engineering, and related services	$64,270
Landscaping services	$51,380

Median annual wages, May 2016

Architects, surveyors, and cartographers: $70,010

Landscape architects: $63,480

Total, all occupations: $37,040

Note: "All Occupations" includes all occupations in the U.S. Economy. Source: U.S. Bureau of Labor Statistics, Occupational Employment Statistics

EMPLOYMENT AND OUTLOOK

Landscape architects held about 24,700 jobs in 2016. The largest employers of landscape architects were as follows:

Architectural, engineering, and related services	53%
Self-employed workers	20%
Landscaping services	12%
Government	7%
Construction	2%

Landscape architects spend much of their time in offices, where they create plans and designs, prepare models and preliminary cost estimates, and meet with clients and workers involved in designing or planning a project. They spend the rest of their time at jobsites.

Employment of landscape architects is projected to grow 6 percent from 2016 to 2026, about as fast as the average for all occupations.

The need for planning and developing new and existing landscapes for commercial, industrial, and residential construction projects is expected to drive employment growth. In addition, environmental concerns and increased demand for sustainably designed buildings and open spaces should spur demand for the services of landscape architects. For example, landscape architects are involved in the design of green roofs, which are covered with vegetation and help reduce air and water pollution, as well as reduce the costs of heating and cooling a building.

Landscape architects are also expected to be needed to design plans to manage storm-water runoff in order to conserve water resources and avoid polluting waterways. This is especially useful in areas prone to drought.

Job opportunities are expected to be good. Familiarity with Geographic Information Systems (GIS) may improve employment prospects with some employers.

Employment Trend, Projected 2016–26

Total, all occupations: 7%

Architects, surveyors, and cartographers: 7%

Landscape architects: 6%

Note: "All Occupations" includes all occupations in the U.S. Economy. Source: U.S. Bureau of Labor Statistics, Employment Projections program

Conversation With . . .
SHAWN BALON, PLA, ASLA

Career Discovery and Diversity Manager
American Society of Landscape Architects (www.asla.org)
Washington, D.C.
Landscape Architect, 12 years

1. What was your individual career path in terms of education/training, entry-level job, or other significant opportunity?

I was planning to get a degree in art, but when I heard about landscape architecture at freshman orientation, I was hooked. I received a bachelor's in landscape architecture from Clemson University in South Carolina.

During college, I interned locally and did a semester-long study abroad program in Barcelona, Spain. We worked on an abandoned site where we figured out how to build atop a landfill. This was my first real landscape architecture experience in an urban setting.

After graduation, I worked for a large Fort Lauderdale, FL, firm. I did a lot of work in the U.S., as well as in Mexico, Latin American countries, and the Caribbean. I'd fly to Mexico and spend a few days walking the site and figuring out the existing trees, as well as streams, rivers, and the health of the existing vegetation. I spent a year in their Beijing office and got really interested in urban design. After six years, I moved to Austin to earn my master's of science in urban design from the University of Texas. While there, I worked at a local firm. Texas was a much drier climate than the subtropical and tropical landscapes I had worked on before. Depending on where you live, the climate can bring a whole new learning curve.

After graduating, I moved to Washington, D.C. and worked for a larger architecture firm, then moved on to a smaller landscape architecture firm focusing on projects in the city. I spent a lot of time out of the office, whether on site at a project or at meetings.

During this time, I volunteered with the American Society of Landscape Architects. I've always been interested in education and when an opportunity here arose, I took it. We work with landscape architects across the nation on the mission of landscape architecture and awareness of the built environment.

2. What are the most important skills and/or qualities for someone in your profession?

Analytical and research skills; analysis may include a scientific study of water or research of a community's history. Communication and collaboration skills are needed because landscape architects share ideas, orally and in writing, and collaborate with planners, architects, engineers, ecologists, artists, communities, construction managers, and other professionals through every phase of a project.

Creativity and visualization skills are needed to plan and design projects from parks to residences. You must be able to imagine how an outdoor space will look once completed and know how to represent the design to clients in two-dimensional and three-dimensional form. Technical skills allow landscape architects to translate concept drawings into computer drawings.

Problem-solving skills are needed because landscape architects must be able to provide solutions to challenges that arise during a project.

3. What do you wish you had known going into this profession?

I wish I had known the breadth of work available. Early on, I stressed over trying to figure out the perfect career path. Landscape architecture can take you on a variety of paths and as you grow in the profession, you will continue to figure out the path that is right for you.

4. Are there many job opportunities in your profession? In what specific areas?

The U.S. Department of Labor states that landscape architecture is expected to continue to grow over the next decade. A quick glance online at available jobs shows high demand around the United States. A degree in landscape architecture will allow you to work in a variety of practice types: private, public/institutional, academic, and non-profit organizations. National Parks offer a good opportunity to be outdoors all the time.

5. How do you see your profession changing in the next five years, what role will technology play in those changes, and what skills will be required?

As our cities and communities continue to grow and densify, it is vital for the profession to help alleviate negative impacts by enhancing outdoor spaces. Technology will continue to play a role in how landscape architects work on a daily basis through analysis, three-dimensional drawings, and communication. Right now, BIM Modeling (Building Information Modeling), for example, is one of many programs being used by built environment professionals.

6. What do you enjoy most about your job? What do you enjoy least about your job?

My favorite part is that every day is different. One day you may be in the office drawing concepts by hand or working on technical drawings on the computer and the next day you could be outdoors overseeing a construction site. My least favorite part involves overtime. Like many occupations, landscape architects work late some nights in order to complete a project on time. Luckily, the projects are usually fun, which makes it a little easier to stay at work.

7. Can you suggest a valuable "try this" for students considering a career in your profession?

The best way to fully understand a "day in the life" is to visit a landscape architect in your town. Volunteering at events such as river cleanups and garden clubs may give you an understanding of the environment in which some landscape architects work. And finally, taking courses in drawing, computer-aided drafting, and construction will help you decide if the profession is right for you.

SELECTED SCHOOLS

Many colleges and universities have bachelor's degree programs in art and architecture, design, and related subjects; some offer concentrations in landscape architecture. The student may also gain an initial grounding in the field at an agricultural, technical, or community college. For advanced positions, a master's is commonly obtained. Below are listed some of the more prominent schools in this field.

Cal Poly, Pomona
3801 W. Temple Avenue
Pomona, CA 91768
909.869.7659
www.csupomona.edu

Cornell University
410 Thurston Avenue
Ithaca, NY 14850
607.255.5241
www.cornell.edu

Kansas State University
119 Anderson Hall
Manhattan, KS 66506
785.532.6250
www.k-state.edu

Louisiana State University
1146 Pleasant Hall
Baton Rouge, LA 70803
225.578.1175
www.lsu.edu

Purdue University
445 Stadium Mall
West Lafayette, IN 47907
765.494.1776
www.purdue.edu

Ohio State University
281 West Lane Avenue
Columbus, OH 43210
614.292.3980
www.osu.edu

Texas A&M University
PO Box 30014
College Station, TX 77842
978.845.1060
www.tamu.edu

University of Georgia
Terrell Hall
210 South Jackson Street
Athens, GA 30602
706.542.8776
www.uga.edu

University of Pennsylvania
1 College Hall, Room 1
Philadelphia, PA 19104
215.898.7507
www.upenn.edu

Virginia Tech
925 Prices Forks Road
Blacksburg, VA 24061
540.231.6267
www.vt.edu

MORE INFORMATION

American Institute of Architects
1735 New York Avenue NW
Washington, DC 20006-5292
800.242.3837
www.aia.org

**American Nursery and
Landscape Association**
1000 Vermont Avenue NW, Suite 300
Washington, DC 20005
202.789.2900
www.anla.org

**American Society of Landscape
Architects**
636 Eye Street NW
Washington, DC 20001-3736
888.999.2752
www.asla.org

**Association of Collegiate Schools
of Architecture**
1735 New York Avenue, NW
Washington, DC 20006
202.785.2324
www.acsa-arch.org

**Council of Landscape
Architectural Registration
Boards**
3949 Pender Drive, Suite 120
Fairfax, VA 22030
571.432.0332
www.clarb.org

**Landscape Architecture
Foundation**
818 18th Street NW, Suite 810
Washington, DC 20006
202.331.7070
www.lafoundation.org

**Society of American Registered
Architects**
14 E. 38th Street
New York, NY 10016
888.385.7272
www.sara-national.org

Sally Driscoll/Editor

Marine Biologists

Snapshot

Career Cluster(s): Science, Technology, Engineering & Mathematics

Interests: Biology, Science, marine wildlife and habitats, animal behavior, oceanography, field study and research, marine conservation

Earnings (Median pay): $60,520 per year; $29.10 per hour

Job Growth: As fast as average

OVERVIEW

Sphere of Work

Marine biologists study the habitats of sea, animal, and plant life in saltwater environments. There are many specialties within marine biology, including those focused in the areas of conservation, fisheries management, animal behavior, microbiology, and more. Marine biologists work all over the world; the occupation is one of the most all-encompassing fields of oceanography. Marine biologists study a range of species—from sea turtles to sharks, as well as sponges, plankton, and microorganisms. Studies may concentrate on the behavior of species, the chemical makeup of

water, the ocean's geology, plants, and biological habitats such as coral reefs.

Often, potential marine biologists are interested in mammals. Research jobs in this specialty are extremely popular, and therefore, the field of marine biology is competitive. Most marine biologists will have completed field work in their chosen concentration, such as internships at aquariums or natural history museums, and perhaps even spent a semester at sea.

Work Environment

Marine biologists' workplaces vary, and include but aren't limited to laboratory environments, underwater expeditions, fishing boats, and aquariums. In any of these environments, strong communication skills are essential, as is an eye for detail. Marine biologists often work with other researchers or professionals from other disciplines, which requires that marine biologists have great task flexibility. For instance, in underwater expeditions, it is useful to be licensed in scuba diving, while observation, education, and public speaking may be essential skills in an aquarium or museum environment.

Profile

Working Conditions: Work both Indoors and Outdoors
Physical Strength: Light Work, Medium Work
Education Needs: Master's Degree, Doctoral Degree
Licensure/Certification: Required
Physical Abilities Not Required: No Heavy Labor
Opportunities For Experience: Military Service, Part-Time Work
Holland Interest Score*: IRE, IRS

* See Appendix A

Occupation Interest

Marine biologists not only have a strong background in science, but also a healthy respect for the scientific process and for new discovery. Marine biologists deal directly with marine life and they must collaborate with co-workers to achieve established research goals. This requires open-mindedness, a continual willingness to learn, and respect for all marine organisms.

A Day in the Life—Duties and Responsibilities

Since the oceans cover about 70 percent of the earth, study of this environment is wide-ranging. Research is a significant component of what a marine biologist does. Studying wildlife in natural environments may be a part of that—a marine biologist could be part of a research team on a boat studying animal behavior, or could be employed by the federal fisheries as an observer on a fishing boat, monitoring fish catches. Some marine biologists' research may take them to Arctic waters or to the tropics. Other researchers may work in a laboratory, studying the chemical composition of water in a certain area or mapping the DNA of ocean microorganisms.

Marine biologists often record their findings, write and present reports and scientific papers, provide analysis, and perform administrative tasks relevant to their place of employment. Often, the research focuses on collecting, examining, and analyzing preserved specimens for experiments. In museum, aquarium, or zoo settings, a marine biologist may be asked to perform public outreach functions or participate in fundraising.

For researchers in the field, the hours may vary widely, from long days during a particularly successful fishing trip to quieter days with less activity as a boat travels to offshore fishing grounds. Researchers in an academic or corporate laboratory might have a more reliable schedule of 40-plus hours a week.

Duties and Responsibilities

- Conducting scientific research into oceanic plants and animals
- Observing and recording living species in their natural habitats
- Studying interactions of plants and animals with their ocean environment and other species
- Examining organisms in the laboratory
- Interpreting data and writing reports
- Conducting environmental impact studies
- Exploring the commercial uses of saltwater plants and animal

OCCUPATION SPECIALTIES

Icthyologists

Icthyologists study wild fishes, such as sharks and tuna.

Cetologists

Cetologists study marine mammals, including whales and dolphins.

Aquaculturists

Aquaculturists use their knowledge of fish and breeding to raise fish, lobster, clams, oysters and shrimp on commercial farms.

WORK ENVIRONMENT

Physical Environment

Marine biologists work primarily in laboratories, on boats, at the seashore, underwater, and in aquariums and marine museums. Working on boats is stressful at times, as people aboard the ship share tight quarters yet enjoy little privacy. Depending on the location of a research facility, climate and access to research facilities can be a challenge for some scientists. Laboratory research positions are often in academic, clinical, or corporate settings. Most marine biologists work in locations close to or on oceans.

Human Environment

Sometimes marine biologists are away from home for weeks, working in harsh weather conditions. For this reason, they must be hardy, focused, and strong multitaskers. They are also required to be open-minded in their interactions with others, as they may live in cramped quarters for long periods of time with people from various walks of life. Those in academic fields must be open to a range of learning styles and levels of understanding. Effective communication and interpersonal skills are a necessity.

Relevant Skills and Abilities

Analytical Skills
- Collecting and analyzing data

Communication Skills
- Speaking and writing effectively

Interpersonal/Social Skills
- Being able to work independently
- Being patient

Research & Planning Skills
- Identifying a research problem
- Laying out a plan
- Solving problems

Unclassified Skills
- Being curious

Work Environment Skills
- Working in a laboratory setting
- Working outdoors

Technological Environment

The technological equipment available for marine biologists to use in their research varies according to the setting, research funding, and need. Those mapping the genome of microorganisms, for example, use complex laboratory equipment and computers; those working in a not-for-profit aquarium have more limited resources, and therefore have limited access to sophisticated laboratory or computer equipment. Marine biologists may work with oceanographic instruments to help them navigate their way through the experiments relating to oceans, fisheries, federal or state government agencies, and private research institutions. Researchers on ocean vessels may be expected to have some familiarity with the sailing or operation of a boat or ship as a member of the crew.

EDUCATION, TRAINING, AND ADVANCEMENT

High School/Secondary

High school students seeking a career in marine biology should build a solid foundation in the natural sciences, especially biology. Developing an understanding of and a respect for the scientific process is desirable. When ready to explore college options, students should research colleges that have a strong science department with up-to-date lab facilities, opportunities for relevant internships, and an affiliation with a research facility. High school students should make use of career guidance counselors, who can help to navigate through the choices that best meet future career goals. They might also avail themselves of extracurricular programs or activities that can enhance their familiarity with saltwater habitats.

Suggested High School Subjects

- Applied Biology/Chemistry
- Applied Math
- Biology
- Chemistry
- College Preparatory
- Computer Science
- English
- Physics

Famous First

The first marine biologist was the Greek philosopher Aristotle (384-322 BC).He described many forms of marine life and recognized that gills are the breathing apparatus of fish.

College/Postsecondary

Marine biologists need a bachelor's degree in either marine biology or a related subject, such as biology, botany, biochemistry, chemistry, ecology, microbiology, or zoology. Those with bachelor's degrees and postgraduate degrees can expect to find opportunities appropriate to their education and experience, as technicians, educators, or researchers with employers such as industrial and private-sector companies, marine stations, research foundations, zoos, aquariums, federal agencies, or not-for-profit environmental advocacy organizations.

Related College Majors
- Marine/Aquatic Biology

Adult Job Seekers

Over the long term, advancement in marine biology requires graduate-level training. Most graduate students begin their careers in aquariums or marine centers. Even though graduate-level students may start out by cleaning tanks and feeding animals, after gaining some experience and showing initiative they can move on to the level of a marine center curator position and beyond. Doctoral graduates often conduct independent research or teach at the college level.

Professional Certification and Licensure

There is no license requirement to become a marine biologist, but most organizations require at least an undergraduate degree to meet the qualifications of existing positions. A master's degree is required for independent research roles, and a doctorate degree qualifies marine biologists to conduct professional work in their field.

Additional Requirements

Those interested in a career in marine biology should seek out internships and opportunities to work on or near the ocean in order to gain experience that enhances their academic studies. Experience and comfort in and on the water is essential, and it is useful to obtain a scuba diving license. Marine biologists should have good people skills and the ability to tolerate a wide variety of environmental conditions, such as rough seas, extreme temperatures, and inclement weather.

Fun Fact

Over 30,000 known species of fish exist, and over 1000 fish species are threatened by extinction.

Source: http://www.sciencekids.co.nz/sciencefacts/animals/fish.html

EARNINGS AND ADVANCEMENT

The median annual wage for zoologists and wildlife biologists was $60,520 in May 2016. The median wage is the wage at which half the workers in an occupation earned more than that amount and half earned less. The lowest 10 percent earned less than $39,150, and the highest 10 percent earned more than $98,540.

In May 2016, the median annual wages for zoologists and wildlife biologists in the top industries in which they worked were as follows:

Federal government, excluding postal service	$75,040
Research and development in the physical, engineering, and life sciences	$65,160
Management, scientific, and technical consulting services	$62,090
State government, excluding education and hospitals	$54,230
Colleges, universities, and professional schools; state, local, and private	$52,720

Most zoologists and wildlife biologists work full time. They may work long or irregular hours, especially when doing fieldwork.

Median annual wages, May 2016

Life scientists: $71,950

Zoologists and wildlife biologists: $60,520

Total, all occupations: $37,040

Note: "All Occupations" includes all occupations in the U.S. Economy. Source: U.S. Bureau of Labor Statistics, Occupational Employment Statistics

EMPLOYMENT AND OUTLOOK

Employment of marine biologists is projected to grow 8 percent from 2016 to 2026, about as fast as the average for all occupations. More marine and wildlife biologists will be needed to study human and wildlife interactions as the human population grows and development impacts wildlife and their natural habitats. However, because most funding comes from governmental agencies, demand for zoologists and wildlife biologists will be limited by budgetary constraints.

As the human population grows and expands into new areas, it will expose marine wildlife to threats such as disease, invasive species, and habitat loss. Increased human activity can cause problems such as pollution and climate change, which endanger wildlife. Marine biologists will be needed to study and gain an understanding of the impact of these factors. Many states will continue to employ marine and wildlife biologists to manage marine populations for tourism purposes, such as fishing, sightseeing, and conservation. Changes in climate patterns can be detrimental to the migration habits of marine animals, and increased sea levels can destroy wetlands; therefore, marine and wildlife biologists will be needed to research, develop, and carry out wildlife management and conservation plans that combat these threats and protect our natural resources.

Marine biologists may face strong competition when looking for employment. Applicants with practical experience gained through internships, summer jobs, or volunteer work done before or shortly after graduation should have better chances at finding employment.

Employment Trend, Projected 2016–26

Life scientists: 10%

Zoologists and wildlife biologists: 8%

Total, all occupations: 7%

Note: "All Occupations" includes all occupations in the U.S. Economy. Source: U.S. Bureau of Labor Statistics, Employment Projections program

Conversation With . . .
DR. KARA DODGE

Postdoctoral Investigator
Woods Hole Oceanographic Institution
Falmouth, Massachusetts
Marine Biologist, 20 years

1. What was your individual career path in terms of education/training, entry-level job, or other significant opportunity?

In 1998, I completed a bachelor of arts degree in anthropology at Harvard University, where I focused on biological anthropology—human evolution, behavior and diversity. During this time, I spent a semester in the Caribbean immersed in hands-on marine science courses and research. I spent the year after graduation assisting on research projects throughout the Caribbean, gaining experience in field work and data analysis. I spent the next six years working for the government on research and policy topics related to fish, marine mammals and sea turtles, and spent several months at sea on ocean-going research vessels. All of these experiences prompted me to return to graduate school to earn a PhD in biological sciences, studying endangered leatherback sea turtles in the North Atlantic. I've continued this research in my current position as a Postdoctoral Investigator at Woods Hole Oceanographic Institution (WHOI) on Cape Cod.

2. What are the most important skills and/or qualities for someone in your profession?

Research science requires flexibility, problem-solving abilities, persistence, and the ability to work well with others, often in less-than-ideal field conditions. A good sense of humor helps too, as things often go wrong or in unexpected directions! From an academic standpoint, it is very important to hone your critical thinking and writing skills, and to become adept at computer programming and software for data analyses. An often forgotten, but important, skill is communication. Sharing your work with others through public speaking and the popular press will generate interest, understanding, and engagement.

3. What do you wish you had known going into this profession?

I wish I had known how critical computer programming skills would be for efficiently analyzing data. Every aspiring marine biologist interested in research should take a course in statistical computing and become proficient in at least one programming language. This will make you a much more productive biologist, and a more desirable job candidate.

4. Are there many job opportunities in your profession? In what specific areas?

It depends on your goals! There are a wide variety of marine biology job opportunities in policy, education, and research, working for the government, non-profit organizations, colleges and universities, or private industry. There tend to be fewer opportunities overall in academia, especially teaching positions (professorships) in higher education. Many research positions are grant-funded and offer less stability than salaried positions in education, government, and industry, such as working for a consulting company doing environmental impact assessments.

Jobs that are primarily outdoors are usually lower level or entry-level positions, at least in research—for instance, a field technician or technician/engineer/crew on a ship. As you move up the ladder, you spend more time writing grants, reports, manuscripts and doing data analysis or managing programs. Most research scientists do some field work every year, but that is often less than 50 percent of their time—and usually a lot less than that!

5. How do you see your profession changing in the next five years? What role will technology play in those changes, and what skills will be required?

Technology is definitely changing the way marine biologists do their jobs, especially when it comes to data collection in the field. Technological innovations in aerial and underwater drones, ocean gliders, biologgers (small recording devices that we attach to marine animals to learn about movements, behavior, and physiology habitat) and other data-collection tools result in data from new vantage points and in areas that were previously less accessible—or inaccessible. Data sets have the potential to become larger and more complex. The well-rounded marine biologist will need strong computer and analytical skills. An understanding of engineering and robotics would be a plus.

6. What do you enjoy most about your job? What do you enjoy least about your job?

I can say without hesitation that I love my job! The most exciting part of a research job is learning something new about your subject and sharing it with your peers and the public. Research scientists are motivated by those "aha!" moments. Working on endangered species, I also am driven by the potential impact of our findings in the conservation and recovery of imperiled species. Field work is one of the most challenging but best parts of this job. I have been fortunate to experience beautiful, remote places and observe amazing animals at sea. But field work can also be uncomfortable (biting mosquitoes and flies, sunburn, getting sea sick); exhausting (long days and nights with minimal sleep); and frustrating (equipment breaking, uncooperative animals, bad weather). While field or lab work is part of every research job, most of your time will be spent in front of your computer, analyzing data and writing papers.

7. Can you suggest a valuable "try this" for students considering a career in your profession?

Interning or volunteering for a marine science organization will provide invaluable experience (and references!) for job or graduate school applications. If you can, get involved in field work, whether volunteering for a cruise or assisting on day trips in a coastal field site. This will help you decide if marine biology is for you. Working with professionals in the field will also help you network and get a foot in the door. If there are specific topics that appeal to you, read up on those science papers and reach out to the experts. Take a class in computer programming or do a free online tutorial. Taking some initiative (and a few risks) will make you more successful on your path to becoming a marine biologist!

SELECTED SCHOOLS

Virtually all colleges and universities have bachelor's degree programs in biology; some have concentrations in wildlife biology or marine biology. The student may also gain an initial grounding in the field at an agricultural, technical, or community college. For advanced positions, a master's or doctoral degree is usually obtained. Below are listed some of the more prominent graduate schools in this field.

Boston University
Department of Biology
5 Cummington Mall
Boston, MA 02215
617.353.2432
www.bu.edu/biology

Duke University
Nicholas School of the Environment
Box 90328
Durham, NC 27708
919.613.8070
nicholas.duke.edu

Stanford University
Department of Biology
Gilbert Hall
Stanford, CA 94305
650.723.2413
biology.stanford.edu

Stony Brook University
School of Marine and Atmospheric
Sciences
Stony Brook, NY 11794
631.632.8700
www.somas.stonybrook.edu

University of California, San Diego
Scripps Institute of Oceanography
9500 Gilman Drive
La Jolla, CA 92093
858.534.3624
scripps.ucsd.edu

University of California, Santa Barbara
Ecology, Evolution, and Marine Biology
4314 Life Sciences Building
Santa Barbara, CA 93106
805.893.2974
www.eemb.ucsb.edu

University of Maine
School of Marine Sciences
5706 Aubert Hall, Room 360
Orono, ME 04469
207.581.4381
www.umaine.edu

University of Oregon
Oregon Institute of Marine Biology
63466 Boat Basin Road
PO Box 5389
Charleston, OR 97420
541.888.2581
oimb.uoregon.edu

University of Texas
Marine Science Institute
750 Channel View Drive
Port Aransas, TX78373
361.749.6711
utmsi.utexas.edu

University of Washington
Marine Biology Program
1122 NE Boat Street
116 Fisheries Sciences Building
Box 355020
Seattle, WA 98195
206.543.7426
depts..washington.edu/marbio

MORE INFORMATION

MarineBio
1995 Fairlee Drive
Encinitas, CA 92024
713.248.257
marinebio.org

Marine Biological Laboratory
7 MBL Street
Woods Hole, MA 02543
508.548.3705
www.mbl.edu

Marine Technology Society
5565 Sterrett Place, #108
Columbia, MD 21044
410.884.5330
www.mtsociety.org

National Aquarium Society (NAS)
Commerce Building, Room B-077
14th and Constitution Avenue NW
Washington, DC 20230
202.482.2825
www.nationalaquarium.org

National Association for Research in Science Teaching (NARST)
12100 Sunset Hills Road, Suite 130
Reston, VA 20190-3221
703.234.4138
www.narst.org

Nature Conservancy
4245 North Fairfax Drive, Suite 100
Arlington, VA 22203-1606
800.628.6860
nature.org

Oceanic Society
Fort Mason Quarters 35
San Francisco, CA 94123
800.326.7491
www.oceanicsociety.org

Susan Williams/Editor

Meteorologists

Snapshot

Career Cluster(s): Agriculture, Food & Natural Resources, Science, Technology, Engineering & Mathematics

Interests: Weather, climate patterns, science, atmospheric science, analyzing and interpreting data, research

Earnings (Median pay): $92,460 per year: $44.45 per hour

Job Growth: Faster Than Average

OVERVIEW

Sphere of Work

Meteorology is the scientific study of the earth's atmosphere and the natural forces that shape weather and climate patterns. Using atmospheric forecasting and research, meteorologists explain and forecast how the atmosphere affects the earth. Meteorologists in all specialties use instruments to record the short- and long-term effects of climate and variations in weather patterns. They use their skills and experience to produce and deliver forecasts and other weather-related information to the public via radio and television broadcasts, among other mediums. Meteorologists can also use their forecasting

skills to help city planners locate and design construction projects, such as airports and factories.

Work Environment

Meteorologists collaborate with other scientists and researchers in basic disciplines such as chemistry, physics, mathematics, oceanography, and hydrology. They can operate in any environment, from weather centers to field offices to ships at sea. The government is the largest employer of meteorologists in the United States; meteorologists work for government agencies such as the Department of Defense, Department of Energy, and Department of Agriculture, while many serve as civilians in the military. Broadcast meteorologists typically work for television and radio stations. Some meteorologists are self-employed and consult for large corporations.

Profile

Working Conditions: Work both Indoors and Outdoors
Physical Strength: Light Work
Education Needs: Bachelor's Degree, Master's Degree, Doctoral Degree
Licensure/Certification: Recommended
Physical Abilities Not Required: No Heavy Labor
Opportunities For Experience: Internship, Military Service
Holland Interest Score*: IRS

* See Appendix A

Occupation Interest

Many people are drawn to meteorology because they are keen to address the challenge of forecasting natural events throughout the world. As such, meteorologists should be interested in the world around them and want to understand the scientific principles that explain the patterns of atmospheric behavior. They must also be comfortable working with computer and satellite technology and other research instruments, and analyzing and interpreting data; forecasting is continually changing and improving, resulting in more accurate predictions over longer spans of time (such as five- or ten-day outlooks).

A Day in the Life—Duties and Responsibilities

Meteorologists must be able to direct, plan, and oversee the work of others, and be able to use reasoning and logic to come to conclusions about forecasting weather. In a typical day, they consult charts and graphs and apply mathematical concepts to help them perceive differences in paths between still or moving objects and picture three-dimensional objects from drawings or photos. Meteorologists base their decisions on measurable data as well as on personal judgment.

Meteorologists from around the world work together daily. They take atmospheric measurements several times a day from surface weather stations and on board ships at sea. They then analyze and interpret weather data that is generated and gathered by upper air stations and satellites, and through weather reports and radar, to prepare forecasts for the media and public. They use computer modeling and simulation to assist in creating these forecasts. Meteorologists also analyze charts and photos and data and information related to barometric pressure, temperature, humidity, and wind velocity. They issue storm warnings and advise pilots on atmospheric conditions such as turbulence, winds aloft, and cloud formations. They also provide relevant forecasts for sea transportation. Some meteorologists make tailored predictions for specific clients, such as city managers and agricultural stakeholders.

Duties and Responsibilities

- Analyzing and interpreting meteorological data gathered by surface and upper air stations, satellites and radar
- Studying and interpreting reports, maps, photographs and charts to make both long and short –term weather predictions
- Preparing weather forecasts for the media and other users
- Interpreting charts, maps and other data in relation to such areas as barometric pressure, temperature, humidity, wind velocity and areas of precipitation
- Conducting research for long-range forecasting
- Directing forecasting services at a weather station

WORK ENVIRONMENT

Physical Environment

Meteorologists work in a variety of physical locations. They can work in large field offices near airports or big cities, or they may operate from smaller sites in remote areas. Those in smaller, remote stations often work alone. Other meteorologists are on board ships, doing field work where visual weather observations are required. Some are located at television and radio stations. Meteorologists work primarily indoors. Weather support units at US military bases include global weather centers and command and control centers at sea.

Relevant Skills and Abilities

Analytical Skills
- Collecting and analyzing data

Communication Skills
- Speaking and writing effectively

Organization & Management Skills
- Making decisions
- Paying attention to and handling details

Research & Planning Skills
- Creating ideas
- Developing evaluation strategies
- Using logical reasoning

Technical Skills
- Performing scientific, mathematical and technical work

Human Environment

Weather stations and offices are located nationwide. Meteorologists work with a variety of other scientists in addition to lay people, such as broadcast journalists, who may simply report on the weather; meteorologists should therefore be aware of other peoples' roles and level of knowledge so that technology terms can be explained at the appropriate level. Strong communication skills are essential.

Technological Environment

Meteorologists use highly sophisticated tools to collect and analyze data. Radar systems, aircraft, satellites, and weather balloons gather information from the atmosphere. Computers are used to analyze the collected data and create simulations, models, and forecasts.

EDUCATION, TRAINING, AND ADVANCEMENT

High School/Secondary

Since the field of meteorology is highly scientific, the most prepared high school students will have taken calculus-level mathematics, chemistry, physics, earth sciences, and computer science. Mathematical proficiency is required in every aspect of physical science. It is also necessary to have a strong command of written and spoken English as well as other languages for following international developments.

Suggested High School Subjects

- Algebra
- Applied Math
- Chemistry
- College Preparatory
- Computer Science
- English
- Geography
- Geometry
- Mathematics
- Literature
- Physical Science
- Physics
- Science
- Statistics
- Trigonometry

Famous First

The first weather forecasting service to use the telephone was launched in New York City in 1938. Although newspaper forecasts and radio broadcasts were available at the time, the telephone provided on-demand reports through the city's Weather Bureau. A steel tape recorder developed by Bell Telephone and capable of responding to 30,000 inquiries per day was the central component of the system.

College/Postsecondary

Many universities offer a bachelor's degree in meteorology or atmospheric science. Meteorology is calculus-based, which means the academic coursework is designed to maximize its use. Recommended courses include physics, chemistry, geography, hydrology, oceanography, differential equations, linear algebra, numerical analysis, and computer science. Some university programs focus more on broad-based meteorological studies, others in more specialty areas. Undergraduate programs provide the foundation needed to move into specialties, such as agricultural meteorology. Those interested in pursuing a career in meteorology should consider applying for relevant internships.

While a bachelor's degree is the norm, the best jobs are available to those with graduate-level education. Advanced degrees are highly useful, and often required, for atmospheric research. Those with a master's degree are qualified to work as operational meteorologists for the government or in private-sector organizations. Alternatively, they may work as assistants to researchers, who have doctoral degrees. Those who wish to teach at the university level must have at least a master's degree.

Related College Majors
- Atmospheric Sciences & Meteorology
- Earth Science
- Oceanography

Adult Job Seekers

When it is not possible to attend a college or university, it is useful to consider joining US military branches, such as the US Air Force or US Navy, for training in observation and forecasting. For those returning to the workforce, internal apprenticeships, mentorships, internships, community work with a relevant government agency, and volunteering with meteorologists can be highly valuable for gaining experience in the field of meteorology. Federal agencies often provide some on-the-job training.

Meteorologists often start as weather forecasting trainees at weather centers or airports. As meteorologists become more experienced, they may turn to supervising research analysis as administrators and mentoring meteorological technicians. Experienced meteorologists can advance to senior management and supervisory positions.

Professional Certification and Licensure

Meteorologists are encouraged to acquire certification according to their job function. The American Meteorological Society (AMS) currently has two certification programs: the Certified Broadcast Meteorologist Program (CBM) and the Certified Consulting Meteorologist Program (CCM). Candidates for the CBM must complete an undergraduate degree in meteorology, an examination, and a work review to be certified. The CCM program requires a specified level of education, at least five years of experience in meteorology or a related field, and successful completion of an examination. Certification renewal depends on continuing education in the field. Consult credible professional associations within the field and follow professional debate as to the relevancy and value of any certification program.

Additional Requirements

Aspiring meteorologists must have a thorough understanding of calculus-based mathematical concepts, and they must always be willing to learn new methods of collecting, analyzing, interpreting, and delivering useful data. Broadcast meteorologists must also be willing to work long or flexible hours, which may include nights, weekends, and holidays, to meet forecast deadlines.

Fun Fact

The fastest a raindrop can fall is 18 mph. Between evaporation and falling as precipitation, a droplet of water may travel thousands of miles. A molecule of water will stay in earth's atmosphere an average of 10-12 days. One billion tons of rain falls on the earth every minute of each day.

Source: http://www.science-facts.com/quick-facts/amazing-weather-facts

EARNINGS AND ADVANCEMENT

The median annual wage for atmospheric scientists, including meteorologists was $92,460 in May 2016. The median wage is the wage at which half the workers in an occupation earned more than that amount and half earned less. The lowest 10 percent earned less than $51,480, and the highest 10 percent earned more than $140,830.

In May 2016, the median annual wages for atmospheric scientists, including meteorologists in the top industries in which they worked were as follows:

Federal government, excluding postal service	$101,320
Research and development in the physical, engineering, and life sciences	$99,210
Television broadcasting	$87,990
Colleges, universities, and professional schools; state	$82,440
Management, scientific, and technical consulting services	$69,860

Most atmospheric scientists work full time. Weather conditions can change quickly, so weather forecasters need to continuously monitor conditions. Many, especially entry-level staff at field stations, work rotating shifts to ensure staff coverage for all 24 hours in a day, and they may work on nights, weekends, and holidays. In addition, they

may work extended hours during severe weather, such as hurricanes.
About one-third worked more than 40 hours per week in 2016.
Other atmospheric scientists have a standard workweek, although
researchers may work nights and weekends on particular projects.

Median annual wages,
May 2016

**Atmospheric scientists, including
meteorologists:** $92,460

Physical scientists: $77,790

Total, all occupations: $37,040

Note: "All Occupations" includes all occupations in the U.S. Economy. Source: U.S. Bureau of Labor
Statistics, Occupational Employment Statistics

EMPLOYMENT AND OUTLOOK

Employment of atmospheric scientists, including meteorologists
is projected to grow 12 percent from 2016 to 2026, faster than the
average for all occupations.

New types of computer models have vastly improved the accuracy
of forecasts and allowed atmospheric scientists to tailor forecasts
to specific purposes. This should maintain, and perhaps increase,
the need for atmospheric scientists working in private industry as
businesses demand more specialized weather information.

Businesses increasingly rely on just-in-time delivery to avoid the
expenses incurred by traditional inventory management methods.
Severe weather can interrupt ground or air transportation and delay
inventory delivery. Businesses have begun to maintain forecasting
teams around the clock to advise delivery personnel, and this

availability helps them stay on schedule. In addition, severe weather patterns have become widely recognizable, and industries have become increasingly concerned about their impact, which will create demand for work in atmospheric science.

As utility companies continue to adopt wind and solar power, they must depend more heavily on weather forecasting to arrange for buying and selling power. This should lead to increased reliance on atmospheric scientists employed in firms in professional, scientific, and technical services to help utilities know when they can sell their excess power, and when they will need to buy.

Prospective atmospheric scientists should expect continued competition because the number of graduates from meteorology programs is expected to exceed the number of job openings requiring only a bachelor's degree. Workers with a graduate degree should have better prospects than those with a bachelor's degree only. Prospective atmospheric scientists with knowledge of advanced mathematics also will have better job prospects because of the highly quantitative nature of much of this occupation's work.

Competition may be strong for research positions at colleges and universities because of the limited number of positions available. In addition, hiring by federal agencies is subject to budget constraints. The best job prospects for meteorologists are expected to be in private industry.

The National Weather Service and the University Corporation for Atmospheric Research (UCAR) sponsor an online training program called COMET. Completing such coursework may help prospective atmospheric scientists to have better job prospects.

Employment Trend, Projected 2016–26

Atmospheric scientists, including meteorologists: 12%

Physical scientists: 10%

Total, all occupations: 7%

Note: "All Occupations" includes all occupations in the U.S. Economy. Source: U.S. Bureau of Labor Statistics, Employment Projections program

Conversation With . . .
DON SCHWENNEKER

TV Meteorologist, 20 years
WTVD-TV, Raleigh, NC

1. What was your individual career path in terms of education/training, entry-level job, or other significant opportunity?

I didn't get my job in the traditional way. I actually started in radio and TV production running cameras and shooting and editing video. I had always performed in choir and theatre and one day I was asked to audition for a part-time weather job. Once I started talking about the weather, I loved it! So I went back to school part-time while working full time and earned my meteorology certification from Mississippi State University. If someone wants to be an on-air meteorologist, they should go to college for Meteorology and while there, take classes in speech and broadcasting.

2. What are the most important skills and/or qualities for someone in your profession?

You have to be able to think on your feet and roll with change. Some days are slow and sunny, some days we have severe weather moving through our viewing area. It's never the same day twice (unless you work in Hawaii). Good math and science skills are also important when it comes to actually making the forecast. Computer skills are essential in making the graphics seen on TV.

3. What do you wish you had known going into this profession?

I thought I could stay in the same place and work for 30 years. I didn't think I would move as much as I have. If you start in smaller markets and want to make a living that will support a family, you have to keep moving to bigger cities to increase the pay. I don't regret it; I've lived in some amazing places!

4. Are there many job opportunities in your profession? In what specific areas?

In TV, the need for meteorologists is steady. But supply for meteorologists in general continues to exceed demand. According to the National Oceanic and Atmospheric

Administration, U.S. colleges and universities confer meteorology degrees on approximately 600-1000 students every year. One study suggested the need for new meteorologists is only half that. Most people who go into meteorology do so because of a love of all things weather, and not because of the paycheck.

5. How do you see your profession changing in the next five years, what role will technology play in those changes, and what skills will be required?

I think TV meteorology is shrinking. You can get a forecast from many different sources. I think our point of difference is severe weather. When you have a tornado bearing down on you, you don't want to rely on a computer for accurate weather information. That may change in 10-20 years, but for now, I think that is where we can still be relevant. As far as skills go, computer skills will continue to become more and more relevant. Knowing where to go online to get official and often complex meteorological data and how to work with it will be key.

6. What do you enjoy most about your job? What do you enjoy least about your job?

TV weather is anything but routine. I love that my job is different every day. Some days it's sunny and quiet, some days I'm chasing a storm. Some days I'm working on the weather computer all day, some days I get to go out and speak to 150 school kids. As far as my least favorite thing about my job, it has to be the hours. We work when most people are home watching TV. There aren't a lot of 8am-5pm jobs in TV meteorology.

7. Can you suggest a valuable "try this" for students considering a career in your profession?

Try making a Power Point of today's weather. On your first page, show some current temperatures. You can get those off your local National Weather Service page. On the second and third pages show some pictures of the weather, either ones you've taken, or one's you've borrowed off the internet. On the last page, make a forecast. Then practice talking about each of the pages. Once you are comfortable, give the forecast to a family member or friend and ask them what you can do better. Don't be afraid to hear criticism! If you are planning on working in a field where you speak to people, there's always a critic.

SELECTED SCHOOLS

Virtually all colleges and universities have bachelor's degree programs in biology; some have concentrations in wildlife biology or marine biology. The student may also gain an initial grounding in the field at an agricultural, technical, or community college. For advanced positions, a master's or doctoral degree is usually obtained. Below are listed some of the more prominent graduate schools in this field.

Colorado State University
Department of Atmospheric Science
200 West Lake Street
1371 Campus Delivery
Fort Collins, CO 80523
970.491.8682
www.atmos.colostate.edu

Cornell University
Earth and Atmospheric Sciences
Snee Hall
Ithaca, NY 14853
607.255.3474
www.eas.cornell.edu

Massachusetts Institute of Technology
Earth, Atmospheric, and Planetary Sciences
77 Massachusetts Avenue
Cambridge, MA 02139
617.253.2127
eapsweb.mit.edu

Penn State University
Department of Meteorology
503 Walker Building
University Park, PA 16802
814.865.0478
ploneprod.met.psu.edu

Texas A&M University
Department of Atmospheric Science
MS 3150
College Station, TX 77843
979.845.7688
atmo.tamu.edu

University of California, Los Angeles
Atmospheric and Oceanic Sciences
Los Angeles, CA 90095
310.825.1217
www.atmos.ucla.edu

University of Maryland, College Park
Atmospheric and Oceanic Science
College Park, MD 20742
301.405.5391
www.atmos.umd.edu

University of Miami
Rosenstiel School of Marine and Atmospheric Science
4600 Rickenbacker Causeway
Miami, FL 33149
305.421.4000
www.rsmas.miami.edu

University of Oklahoma
School of Meteorology
120 David Boren Boulevard
Suite 5900
Norman, OK 73072
405.325.6561
som.ou.edu

University of Washington
Department of Atmospheric Science
408 ATG Building
Box 351640
Seattle, WA 98195
206.543.4250
www.atmos.washington.edu

MORE INFORMATION

American Geosciences Institute
4220 King Street
Alexandria, VA 22302-1502
703.379.2480
www.americangeosciences.org

American Meteorological Society
45 Beacon Street
Boston, MA 02108-3693
617.227.2425
www.ametsoc.org

National Weather Association
228 W. Millbrook Road
Raleigh, NC 27609-4303
919.845.7121
www.nwas.org

**National Oceanographic and
Atmospheric Administration**
1401 Constitution Avenue, NW
Room 5128
Washington, DC 20230
www.noaa.gov

**University Corporation for
Atmospheric Research**
3090 Center Green Drive
PO Box 3000
Boulder, CO 80301

Susan Williams/Editor

Park Rangers

Snapshot

Career Cluster(s): Government & Public Administration, Hospitality & Tourism, Law, Public Safety & Security
Interests: Public safety, law enforcement, wildlife, natural resources, conservation, history
Earnings (Median pay): $58,329.54 per year
Job Growth: As fast as average

OVERVIEW

Sphere of Work

Park rangers are professionals who enforce laws, regulations, and rules in parks, historic sites, and other sites. In this capacity, rangers investigate illegal activity in the parks and patrol the areas using a variety of vehicles. Rangers also work to protect natural resources and wildlife at these sites. They teach the public about how to enjoy the parks in ways that minimize negative impacts to the region's wildlife and resources. Furthermore, park rangers act as public safety officers. As such, they hunt animals that pose a danger to the public, rescue endangered campers, and administer first aid as needed.

Park rangers often work with police, fire, and other personnel in addressing emergency situations and other special circumstances.

Work Environment

Park rangers generally work outdoors at parks, historical sites, recreation areas, and similar venues. Rangers often work in rugged, heavily forested environments and in all weather conditions. Many rangers spend days and even weeks stationed in remote locations within these areas. Because they typically serve as law enforcement officer as well as protectors of the area's wildlife and natural resources, they may face dangerous situations involving park visitors as well as animals and terrain. Park rangers also work in offices, where they perform managerial and administrative duties. Experienced park rangers can expect to perform more work indoors over time.

Profile

Working Conditions: Work both Indoors and Outdoors
Physical Strength: Medium Work
Education Needs: Bachelor's Degree
Licensure/Certification: Recommended
Opportunities For Experience: Apprenticeship, Volunteer Work, Part-Time Work
Holland Interest Score*: ESR

* See Appendix A

Occupation Interest

Park rangers play an important role in protecting parks, recreational areas, historical sites, and similar locations. Those who enjoy working outdoors in rugged natural environments may be drawn to the position of a park ranger, as these individuals spend the majority of their workdays in the field. In addition, park rangers tend to like working with people. They also have the responsibility of teaching others about these natural and historical locations and demonstrating conservation principles. Although the job of a park ranger is challenging and often dangerous, those who work in this field demonstrate a great deal of personal satisfaction in their work.

A Day in the Life—Duties and Responsibilities

The day-to-day responsibilities of a park ranger often vary greatly based on where he or she works. A ranger who works at a historical site focuses primarily on teaching others about the significance of the building or area, providing to the general public presentations on and tours of the venue, answering questions, and protecting displays from damage. Meanwhile, a ranger who works in a national park such as Yosemite or the Grand Canyon spends a great deal of time on patrol in the field. Patrol tasks may include monitoring and protecting against forest fires, performing campground safety checks, and taking scientific samples for analysis.

Although a ranger's job responsibilities vary based on the type of recreational venue at which he or she works, all rangers perform certain duties. A park ranger works closely with the public. He or she shares information about conservation and history. The park ranger acts as the park's law enforcement and public safety officer, maintaining security, ensuring that the site is protected and safe, patrolling the trails or hallways, arresting or ejecting unruly visitors, and spotting dangers like forest fires. A park ranger is seen as the steward of a park, protecting it and encouraging others to do so as well.

Duties and Responsibilities

- Enforcing park regulations
- Maintaining park grounds
- Assisting visitors
- Offering conservation and recreation activities
- Patrolling park areas to check for fires or dangerous situations

WORK ENVIRONMENT

Physical Environment

Park rangers work mostly outdoors at natural and historical sites. They may work in parks, national forests, seashores, mountain ranges, battlefields, capitol buildings, and wildlife preserves, often in extreme weather conditions, in locations throughout the country. They also occasionally work in office environments, where they coordinate with other rangers and conduct the administrative business of the site.

Relevant Skills and Abilities

Communication Skills
- Speaking effectively

Interpersonal/Social Skills
- Working both independently and as part of a team

Organization & Management Skills
- Performing duties that may change
- Performing routine work

Technical Skills
- Working with your hands

Other Skills
- Being physically active
- Working outdoors
- Working with plants or animal

Human Environment

Park rangers work with a wide range of individuals. These parties include park visitors, law enforcement and fire officers, elected and appointment government officials, and scientists. They may travel extensively from site to site throughout the country to work with different groups of rangers and the public.

Technological Environment

Park rangers must be able to use the tools they will need to patrol and operate in the recreational sites at which they work. In mountain areas, for example, they will need to know how to use ski and snow equipment. Other equipment includes radios, computer mapping equipment, binoculars, fire control devices, and, where necessary, weapons.

EDUCATION, TRAINING, AND ADVANCEMENT

High School/Secondary

High school students who seek to become park rangers are encouraged to take courses that focus on interpersonal skills, public safety, and surveillance. Such training includes English, geography, math, and the natural sciences (such as biology, chemistry, physics, and ecology). Students may also benefit from activities in which public speaking is emphasized, such as debate club and oral presentations in class.

Interested students should consider pursuing volunteer opportunities and part-time or seasonal work at parks or with environmental groups.

Suggested High School Subjects

- Agricultural Education
- Algebra
- American History
- Applied Biology/Chemistry
- Biology
- Business
- English
- First Aid Training
- Geography
- Geometry
- Psychology
- Sociology
- Speech

Famous First

The first national park was Yellowstone National Park, in Wyoming, authorized in 1872. The first park ranger, hired in 1880, was Harry Yount, a Civil War veteran and all-around mountain man who bore the nickname "Rocky Mountain Harry." In one of his annual reports Yount noted that it was impossible for one man to patrol the park, and so he urged the creation of a professional ranger force within the National Park Service. Today, that force consists of commissioned law enforcement Rangers along with Special Agents who conduct criminal investigations.

College/Postsecondary

Park rangers usually have a bachelor's degree in a related field, such as zoology, geology, forestry, criminal justice, social science, or botany. Park ranger jobs are highly competitive. Individuals with an advanced degree in these disciplines have an advantage in the application process.

Related College Majors
- Geography
- Law Enforcement/Police Science
- Natural Resources Law Enforcement & Protective Services
- Parks and Recreation Management
- Public History

Adult Job Seekers

Park ranger jobs are highly competitive. Some adults may gain access to such jobs by obtaining short seasonal positions or serving as park volunteers, which will give them exposure to the field. The National Park Service holds on-the-job training programs for rangers in Harper's Ferry, West Virginia, in Brunswick, Georgia, and at the Grand Canyon. Because these positions are usually government jobs, aspiring rangers should research and apply directly to these agencies through their websites and job boards.

Advancement in the field depends on the ranger's education level and the size of the site. Park rangers may advance to supervisory positions at large sites, transfer between sites, or specialize in one aspect of the position.

Professional Certification and Licensure

Most park ranger positions require passing a civil service exam. Park rangers may also need licenses or permits to operate the equipment and vehicles used on the job.

Professional certification may be helpful but is not typically required. The National Recreation and Park Association is responsible for conducting Certified Park and Recreation Professional (CPRP) certification. Candidates must have a bachelor's degree, meet experience requirements, and obtain a passing score on the written CPRP exam. Continuing education is required for certification renewal. Consult credible professional associations within the field and follow professional debate as to the relevancy and value of any certification program.

Additional Requirements

Park rangers should be physically fit, able to spend a great deal of time on their feet and in rugged terrain. They should also have excellent communication and public speaking skills. Experience in the geographic area in which they seek to become a ranger is also useful. Employers may require a prospective park ranger to be a US citizen and pass a background check.

Fun Fact

More than 280 million people visit U.S. National Parks each year.
Source: NPS

EARNINGS AND ADVANCEMENT

Park rangers may advance to district or park manager levels or site superintendents. Administrative positions at various levels of park headquarters are also another advancement possibility. Entry-level annual salaries for park rangers with the National Park Service were between $29,616 and $37,020 in 2016. Park rangers who worked in state and local parks received a higher salary, starting between $66,363 and $74,040 in 2016.

Park rangers may receive paid vacations, holidays, and sick days; life and health insurance; and retirement benefits. These are usually paid by the employer. In most Federal and State parks, park rangers are supplied housing on the park premises and senior park rangers are usually given a vehicle.

EMPLOYMENT AND OUTLOOK

Police and detectives, of which park rangers are a part, held about 807,000 jobs nationally in 2016. Employment is expected to grow slower than the average for all occupations through the year 2022, which means employment is projected to increase 3 percent to 9 percent. The number of job openings will still increase because the last wave of entry-level park rangers hired in the 1970s will be retiring. Competition in the National Park Service is stiff, with one-hundred qualified applicants for every one park ranger hired. Budgets of Federal and State government also limit the number of open positions.

Related Occupations
* Fish and game warden

Conversation With . . .
JESSICA CONLEY

Park Ranger, 9 years

1. What was your individual career path in terms of education/training, entry-level job, or other significant opportunity?

I first became interested in environmental education through internships and programs I did growing up in middle school and high school, such as through the Chesapeake Bay Foundation. I knew I wanted to be in the environmental ed field, I just wasn't sure how. I earned a B.A. in environmental science from Messiah College in Pennsylvania, and had a number of jobs—from research biologist to managing a fish farm – when I was trying to decide what I wanted to do with my career. Then I started a family and earned a Master's of Education from American Intercontinental University. While I was working on my master's, I took a seasonal position as a naturalist. I worked for one year as a naturalist, then was hired as a civilian park ranger.

2. What are the most important skills and/or qualities for someone in your profession?

First and foremost, being clearheaded and calm in the face of emergency and crisis. We can literally be showing a 5-year-old leaves and how a tree grows and get a call for a medical emergency like heatstroke, then an hour later be telling someone to put dog on a leash. You also need to be flexible. You can't predict what will happen: a tree coming down, someone getting lost, or someone walking in and wanting information. Finally, it's important to be well-spoken and to have public speaking skills. You're interfacing with the public every single day.

3. What do you wish you had known going into this profession?

I wish I had realized it's more a way of life than a job. I'm on call a lot, and willing to jump in and help my co-workers. That's been a big adjustment for my family; they have to be the family of a park ranger.

4. **Are there many job opportunities in your profession? In what specific areas?**

I see turnover with retirement, for one, so while there are always positions coming open, they tend to come in waves. Also, I don't think everyone in the field realizes they are cut out for this before they begin. They usually figure out very quickly if it doesn't work out. There's not a lot of middle ground – you either love this, or figure it out quickly and leave.

5. **How do you see your profession changing in the next five years? What role will technology play in those changes, and what skills will be required?**

We're continually challenged with the resources necessary to manage the various needs of the park including operations, maintenance and programming. We must be creative with the funds we are given. Regarding technology, I think it can help us deliver services at lower cost. For example, we are offering trail maps online. Or, through the Dept. of Natural Resources app, you can make a reservation or learn to learn what's going on at a park at any given moment. Technology's important to get the word out to our visitors and help us do our job more effectively.

6. **What do you enjoy most about your job? What do you enjoy least?**

I love the unpredictable aspect of it. I love that if it's a gorgeous day I get to be outside. I get to work in place that people come to play, and be in one of Maryland's most beautiful places. What I like least is a harder question to answer. My family would certainly like it if I made more money; we don't get into this for the pay at all. I think a lot of people would complain about that. I don't have a lot of challenges to say about job; I love my job.

7. **Can you suggest a valuable "try this" for students considering a career in your profession?**

I think the best thing for someone to try would be a seasonal position. That gives you such a good idea of what goes on day in and day out in a park. Also, we recruit heavily from the Maryland Conservation Corps; its part of Americorps, a national program, so anyone should be able to access the program.

SELECTED SCHOOLS

Programs in parks and recreation management are available at many four-year colleges and universities. The student may also gain initial training at a community college. A degree in police science is especially useful for those seeking to become certified law enforcement rangers. Interested students are advised to consult with a school guidance counselor.

MORE INFORMATION

Association of National Park Rangers
25958 Genesee Trail Road
PMB 222
Golden, CO 80401
www.anpr.org

National Recreation and Park Association
22377 Belmont Ridge Road
Ashburn, VA 20148-4501
800.626.6772
www.nrpa.org

Park Law Enforcement Association
4397 McCullough Street
Port Charlotte, FL 33948
www.myparkranger.org

U.S. Forest Service
1400 Independence Avenue, SW
Washington, DC 20250-0002
800.832.1355
www.fs.fed.us

Michael Shally-Jensen/Editor

Police Officers & Detectives

Snapshot

Career Cluster(s): Government & Public Administration, Law, Public Safety & Security

Interests: Public safety, law enforcement, criminal justice, security, psychology, sociology, investigation

Earnings (Median pay): $61,316 per year

Job Growth: As fast as average

OVERVIEW

Sphere of Work

Police officers and detectives enforce federal, state, and local laws. They investigate criminal activity, arrest suspects, interview witnesses, redirect the flow of traffic around accidents, construction and crime scenes, and intervene in public disturbances. Police patrol and monitor the streets and other designated areas. They are trained to use both non-lethal and lethal force in subduing criminals. Some police are uniformed, using patrol cars and other marked vehicles, while others are detectives and investigators, who wear plain clothes while on duty. The duties of police

officers and detectives vary based on the size of the department and the community in which they serve.

Work Environment

All police officers (including harbormasters) are based in police stations, where they interview witnesses and suspects, detain suspects, conduct investigations, and perform administrative duties. On patrol and at the scenes of criminal activity, police officers face considerable dangers and stresses. The psychological impact on police officers comes not only from confrontations with suspects but from the trauma of witnessing crime and accident scenes. Police generally work forty-to sixty-hour workweeks, sometimes longer. Since police work is needed twenty-four hours a day, shifts may encompass late nights and holidays. Police are often on their feet while on duty and work in all types of weather.

Profile

Working Conditions: Work both Indoors and Outdoors
Physical Strength: Medium Work
Education Needs: Technical/ Community College
Licensure/Certification: Required
Opportunities For Experience: Apprenticeship, Military Service, Volunteer Work, Part-Time Work
Holland Interest Score*: REI, SCE, SCR, SEC, SER

* See Appendix A

Occupation Interest

Police officers protect people from crime and rescue people from emergency situations, such as vehicular accidents, muggings, and assaults. The work is rarely dull or routine – many aspiring police officers are attracted to the adrenaline rush of chasing down a suspect or otherwise capturing dangerous individuals. Police officers and detectives are often considered heroes in their communities, particularly in the wake of high-profile incidents. The demand for police officers continues to grow, even during periods of recession. Although police officers receive average compensation despite the dangers and stresses of their work, they also receive excellent benefits, including life insurance, health insurance, and retirement plans.

A Day in the Life—Duties and Responsibilities

Police officers and harbormasters maintain order and enforce federal, state, and local laws. Officers patrol designated areas on foot, horseback, motorcycle, and bicycle as well as in squad cars, boats, and other vehicles. Police respond to emergency calls or otherwise intervene when they see criminal activity. They interview witnesses, detain people of interest and suspects, and record information about the incident. Police also stop motor vehicle drivers for speeding and other safety violations, investigate accident scenes to assess whether a crime has been committed, and obtain warrants to search homes, offices, cars, and other personal property.

Police duties also include protecting and educating citizens. Police officers serve as first responders in the event of an accident or other medical emergency. They administer first aid, protect victims by keeping crowds away, and enable emergency vehicles to arrive, care for victims, and transport them to the hospital in a timely fashion. Additionally, police must testify in civil and criminal court cases when called upon by prosecutors and other attorneys. Police officers also educate both children and adults about the dangers of drugs, stranger abductions, child and spousal abuse, identity theft, terrorism, and other criminal activities.

Police officers' and detectives' responsibilities vary based on the size of the police force and community in which they serve. Large, urban police forces may have police officers, plainclothes detectives, and police patrolmen assigned to specific units, such as narcotics or robbery. Officers at smaller departments may perform multiple duties.

Duties and Responsibilities

- Patrolling an assigned area or beat
- Preventing crime and making arrests
- Investigating accidents and administering first aid to victims
- Controlling traffic and issuing tickets
- Writing and filing a variety of activity reports daily
- Investigating crimes and questioning witnesses
- Examining the scene of a crime for clues and evidence
- Preparing assigned cases for court
- Testifying before a court or grand jury

OCCUPATION SPECIALTIES

Uniformed Police Officers

Uniformed police officers have general law enforcement duties. They wear uniforms that allow the public to easily recognize them as police officers. They have regular patrols and also respond to emergency and non-emergency calls. Some police officers work only on a specific type of crime, such as narcotics. Others, especially those working in large departments, may work in special units, such as horseback, motorcycle, canine corps, and special weapons and tactics (SWAT) teams. Typically, officers must work as patrol officers for a certain number of years before they are appointed to one of these units.

State Highway Patrol Officers

State highway patrol officers, or state troopers, patrol state highways within an assigned area, in vehicles equipped with two-way radios, to enforce motor vehicle and criminal laws. State police officers have authority to work anywhere in the state and are frequently called on to help other law enforcement agencies, especially those in rural areas or small towns.

Transit Police

Transit police patrol transit stations and railroad yards. They protect passengers and employees from crimes such as thefts and robberies. They remove trespassers from transit and railroad properties and check IDs of people who try to enter secure areas, to protect people and property.

Sheriffs and Deputy Sheriffs

Sheriffs and deputy sheriffs enforce the law on the county level. Sheriffs' departments tend to be relatively small. Sheriffs usually are elected by the public and do the same work as a local or county police chief. Some sheriffs' departments do the same work as officers in urban police departments. Others mainly operate the county jails and provide services in local courts. Police and sheriffs' deputies who provide security in city and county courts are sometimes called bailiffs.

Detectives and Criminal Investigators

Detectives and criminal investigators are uniformed or plainclothes investigators who gather facts and collect evidence for criminal cases. They conduct interviews, examine records, observe the activities of suspects, and participate in raids and arrests. Detectives usually specialize in investigating one type of crime, such as homicide or fraud. Detectives are typically assigned cases on a rotating basis and work on them until an arrest and trial are completed or until the case is dropped.

WORK ENVIRONMENT

Physical Environment

Police officers and detectives are based in police stations, which tend to be well-organized, busy environments governed by strict procedures. Much of police officers' work is performed in locations throughout the community, including private residences, offices and businesses, and public roadways.

Police and detective work can be physically demanding, stressful, and dangerous. Officers must be alert and ready to react throughout their entire shift. Officers regularly work at crime and accident scenes and encounter suffering and the results of violence. Although a career in law enforcement may be stressful, many officers find it rewarding to help members of their communities.

Some federal agencies, such as the Federal Bureau of Investigation and U.S. Secret Service, require extensive travel, often on short notice. These agents may relocate a number of times over the course of their careers. Some special agents, such as U.S. Border Patrol agents, may work outdoors in rugged terrain and in all kinds of weather.

Police and sheriff's patrol officers have one of the highest rates of injuries and illnesses of all occupations. They may face physical injuries during conflicts with criminals and other high-risk situations.

Relevant Skills and Abilities

Communication Skills
- Speaking effectively

Interpersonal/Social Skills
- Being able to remain calm
- Cooperating with others
- Having good judgment
- Working as a member of a team

Organization & Management Skills
- Coordinating tasks
- Demonstrating leadership
- Handling challenging situations
- Making decisions
- Managing people/groups

Research & Planning Skills
- Solving problems
- Using logical reasoning

Other Skills
- Developing skill in

Human Environment

Police officers and detectives interact with all members of the general public, including victims of crime and suspects. Additionally, they work with attorneys, judges, and other public safety officials, such as firefighters, emergency medical technicians, and federal law enforcement officers. Depending on their area of specialization, police work as members of a local police force, at a state highway patrol facility, or in any number of federal departments and bureaus of law enforcement, such as the Federal Bureau of Investigation (FBI) or the Bureau of Indian Affairs (BIA).

Technological Environment

Police use different types of technology when on patrol or performing investigative work versus in the station. In addition to weapons of lethal force (including handguns and shotguns) and non-lethal force (such as mace and Tasers), officers use laptop computers, radar guns, two-way radios, cellular and smart phones, and global positioning satellite systems (GPS). In the station, police officers use the Integrated Automated Fingerprint Identification System (AFIS), the National Crime Information Center (NCIC) database, ballistics information networks, photo-imaging and crime-mapping software, and basic office software systems.

EDUCATION, TRAINING, AND ADVANCEMENT

High School/Secondary

High school students are encouraged to take psychology, physical education, government, history, communications, speech, foreign languages, and social studies. Proficiency in a widely-used foreign language, such as Spanish or Chinese, can be a great advantage when applying for future jobs or pursuing career advancement.

Suggested High School Subjects

- Applied Communication
- Driver Training
- English
- First Aid Training
- Government
- History
- Physical Education
- Psychology
- Social Studies
- Sociology
- Speech

Famous First

The first state police were the Texas Rangers, authorized in 1835 when Texas was still a province of Mexico. (Texas was admitted to the Union in 1845.) The main task of the first three companies of Rangers was to protect the border. They took on wider law enforcement responsibilities when Texas became a state, and soon they were forever linked to the history of the Old West. Since 1935 they have officially been the Texas Ranger Division of the Texas Department of Public Safety, There is a museum dedicated to the Texas Rangers in Waco.

College/Postsecondary

Most police officers are expected to have some formal postsecondary education. Many attend junior and community colleges, receiving an associate's degree in law enforcement, security, or a related field. Many other police officers, including detectives, complete a bachelor's degree in law enforcement, criminal justice, and similar fields. Many departments, agencies, and states have programs that reimburse officers or pay for their tuition at these institutions.

Some police departments have cadet programs for people interested in a career in law enforcement who do not yet meet age requirements for becoming an officer. These cadets do clerical work and attend classes until they reach the minimum age requirement and can apply for a position with the regular force. Military or police experience may be considered beneficial for potential cadets.

Cadet candidates must be U.S. citizens, usually be at least 21 years old, have a driver's license, and meet specific physical qualifications. Applicants may have to pass physical exams of vision, hearing, strength, and agility, as well as written exams. Previous work or military experience is often seen as a plus. Candidates typically go through a series of interviews and may be asked to take lie detector and drug tests. A felony conviction may disqualify a candidate.

Fish and game wardens typically need a bachelor's degree; desirable fields of study include wildlife science, biology, or natural resources management.

Federal agencies such as the Federal Bureau of Investigation also typically require prospective detectives and investigators to have a bachelor's degree.

Related College Majors
- Criminology
- Law Enforcement/Police Science
- Security

Adult Job Seekers

Qualified adults must apply directly to the agency, state, or municipality in which they seek to become officers. They may also network with peers through nationwide law enforcement organizations, such as the Fraternal Order of Police.

Professional Certification and Licensure

Police officers and detectives are subject to criminal background checks and must pass written, verbal, and physical examinations. Applying for a police job requires U.S. citizenship and a valid driver's license.

Additional Requirements

Police officers and detectives must be physically fit and of at least average physical strength, able to pass a number of physical tests. Officers must pass periodic drug and/or polygraph tests, as well as undergo extensive background checks, as a condition of continued employment.

Officers and detectives should be comfortable interacting with and providing assistance to the general public. Since police frequently deal with job-related tension and with unruly, violent, or uncooperative individuals, prospective police officers should be psychologically well-balanced and even-tempered; it is considered both professionally and ethically important to avoid escalating the level of violent conflict.

Fun Fact

The first "police officers" were medieval knights; their "badges" were their coats of arms. Today, police officers wear badges above their left chest pocket, over the heart, because officers pledge to protect, and because the left arm was used by medieval knights to hold up their shield, protecting their hearts and allowing them to fight with their dominant hand.

Source: symbolarts.com

EARNINGS AND ADVANCEMENT

The median annual wage for police and detectives was $61,600 in May 2016. The median wage is the wage at which half the workers in an occupation earned more than that amount and half earned less. The lowest 10 percent earned less than $34,970, and the highest 10 percent earned more than $102,750.

Median annual wages for police and detectives in May 2016 were as follows:

Detectives and criminal investigators	$78,120
Transit and railroad police	$66,610
Police and sheriff's patrol officers	$59,680
Fish and game wardens	$51,730

In May 2016, the median annual wages for police and detectives in the top industries in which they worked were as follows:

Federal government	$82,860
State government, excluding education and hospitals	$62,970
Local government, excluding education and hospitals	$60,160
Educational services; state, local, and private	$50,360

Uniformed officers, detectives, agents, and wardens usually work full time. Paid overtime is common. Shift work is necessary because the public must be protected at all times.

Many agencies provide officers with an allowance for uniforms, as well as extensive benefits and the option to retire at an age that is younger than the typical retirement age. Some police departments offer additional pay for bilingual officers or those with college degrees.

Police officers usually become eligible for promotion after a probationary period. Promotions to corporal, sergeant, lieutenant, and captain usually are made according to scores on a written examination and on-the-job performance. In large departments, promotion may enable an officer to become a detective or to specialize in one type of police work, such as working with juveniles.

Median annual wages, May 2016

Police and detectives: $61,600

Law enforcement workers: $53,240

Total, all occupations: $37,040

Note: "All Occupations" includes all occupations in the U.S. Economy. Source: U.S. Bureau of Labor Statistics, Occupational Employment Statistics

EMPLOYMENT AND OUTLOOK

Employment of police and detectives is projected to grow 7 percent from 2016 to 2026, about as fast as the average for all occupations.

While a continued desire for public safety is expected to result in a need for more officers, demand for employment is expected to vary depending on location, driven largely by local and state budgets. Even with crime rates falling in recent years, demand for police services to maintain and improve public safety is expected to continue.

Job applicants may face competition because of relatively low rates of turnover. Applicants with a bachelor's degree and law enforcement or military experience, especially investigative experience, as well as those who speak more than one language, should have the best job opportunities.

Because the level of government spending determines the level of employment for police and detectives, the number of job opportunities can vary from year to year and from place to place.

Employment Trend, Projected 2016–26

Total, all occupations: 7%

Police and detectives: 7%

Law enforcement workers: 1%

Note: "All Occupations" includes all occupations in the U.S. Economy. Source: U.S. Bureau of Labor Statistics, Employment Projections program

Related Occupations
- Detectives and criminal investigators
- Fish and game wardens
- Transit and railroad police

Conversation With . . .
SHEILA LUCEY

Harbormaster
Town of Nantucket, Nantucket, Massachusetts
Harbormaster, 6 years

1. What was your individual career path in terms of education/training, entry-level job, or other significant opportunity?

After I graduated from high school, I enlisted in the U.S. Coast Guard and did 24 years. I was a boatswain mate, which means we drove boats. I was stationed at a lot of small boat stations and worked closely with harbormasters. During my last year in the Coast Guard, I was in charge of Coast Guard Station Brant Point on Nantucket, which is an island off the coast of Cape Cod. A job for assistant harbormaster became available, so I decided to retire from the Coast Guard and apply. I had that job for five years, and became harbormaster in 2012.

I grew up in South Boston, which overlooks Boston Harbor. I never spent time on boats until I went into the Coast Guard, but we used to go to the beach all the time. I wouldn't say I grew up "on the water," but I grew up close to the water.

2. What are the most important skills and/or qualities for someone in your profession?

You have to have good management skills and administrative skills. You need to have boat-handling skills. And you have to be able to work with all different types of people. You can run into a lot of conflict because there are so many different rules. You have local rules as far as moorings and the town pier and things like that. Then you get into boating and people trying to do dangerous things that you have to talk them out of it. There's basic enforcement of wake regulations and speed limits on the water. And nobody likes being told what to do, especially when they're out boating and trying to have a good time. Sometimes you've got to be the person that comes along and tells them they can't do what they want to do.

3. What do you wish you had known going into this profession?

I think the Coast Guard was a really good segue into being harbormaster. I had a lot of experience dealing with all the things I deal with now, but now it's on a smaller, local scale. I do wish I was a little bit better at the computer end of things. I can do anything I want with a boat, but I have a hard time sometimes with the computer.

4. Are there many job opportunities in your profession? In what specific areas?

For the most part, harbormasters work for municipalities and communities that are coastal communities, so you're limited by geography. In some places, like Alaska, people who are actually dock masters are called harbormasters. They work for private companies, such as boat basins. If you want to be a harbormaster, you could start in a private marina and work your way up. You could also start in safe boating education.

5. How do you see your profession changing in the next five years? What role will technology play in those changes, and what skills will be required?

Technology plays a huge, huge part. GPS has come into play. Boats have become very computerized. We handle 2,200 moorings and used to handwrite them on cards, but now we use computer programs to manage it.

6. What do you enjoy most about your job? What do you enjoy least about your job?

What I enjoy most about my job is that it's outside most of the time. We're active even in the winter because there are people still commercial fishing and commercial scalloping. Pretty much anything that happens on the water, we're relied upon. Obviously we rely heavily on the Coast Guard to take care of the big stuff, but we try to take care of anything inside the harbor so that they can save their assets to help people offshore.

I also enjoy working with people and the fact that there's something different every day. You never know what will happen. A few weeks ago, a sewer line failed and raw sewage was flowing into the harbor. Separate from that, we ended up having a little bit of a diesel sheen, so we had to set booms and take care of all that with the help of the fire department. I just really like that it's exciting.

What I enjoy least is that you can't make everybody happy and they let you know it quite a bit. There are days when it's blowing 60 and raining sideways or snowing sideways and you need to be outside helping somebody who just didn't pay attention to the warnings or didn't heed the warnings. That can be frustrating.

7. Can you suggest a valuable "try this" for students considering a career in your profession?

Apply with the local harbormaster. We always have a lot of staff on in the summer time. We have a dock staff, we run a pump-out program, and we hire high school kids and young college kids all the time. We go from a full-time staff of three to a full-time staff of 50 in the summer—that's including the lifeguards. But even the lifeguards here on Nantucket get to take a look at what the harbormaster does. If somebody's stuck in shallow water, we might need someone to go in and swim, and the lifeguards have such good First Aid training that we take them with us on the boats. We try to expose the kids to everything just in case there's an interest.

SELECTED SCHOOLS

Programs in criminal justice, police science, security and related fields are available in many colleges and universities. The student may also gain solid training at a community college—and in many police departments an associate's degree or completion of some college is all that is required to become a candidate for police academy or similar basic training. For those seeking to become detectives or criminal investigators a bachelor's degree is necessary. Interested students are advised to consult with their school guidance counselor.

MORE INFORMATION

Federal Law Enforcement Training Center
1131 Chapel Crossing Road
Glynco, GA 31524
912.267.2100
www.fletc.gov

International Association of Chiefs of Police
515 N. Washington Street
Alexandria, VA 22314
703.836.6767
www.theiacp.org

National Association of Police Organizations
317 S. Patrick Street
Alexandria, VA 22314
703.549.0775
www.napo.org

National Fraternal Order of Police
Atnip-Orms Center
701 Marriott Drive
Nashville, TN 37214
615.399.0900
www.fop.net

Michael Auerbach/Editor

Recreation Program Directors

Snapshot

Career Cluster(s): Education & Training, Hospitality & Tourism, Human Services

Interests: Physical education, recreational activities, planning events and programs, public safety, marketing, fundraising

Earnings (Median pay): $64,680 per year; $31.10 per hour

Job Growth: Much faster than average

OVERVIEW

Sphere of Work

Recreation program directors work for private institutions as well as municipalities, developing and coordinating recreation needs for residents and visitors, including children, seniors, and adults. Recreation program directors develop these recreation programs by assessing community or service audience recreation needs; hiring and evaluating recreation workers and additional staff; overseeing the safety and maintenance of grounds, equipment, and facilities; promoting the recreation program to the community; planning events; scheduling programs; keeping records on program happenings

and staff; and fundraising through direct solicitation and grant-writing. Recreation program directors manage both public and private recreation programs through a variety of host agencies or institutions such as schools, camps, resorts, public agencies, retirement facilities, and hospitals.

Work Environment

Recreation program directors spend their workdays overseeing recreation programs in a wide variety of indoor and outdoor settings, including schools, public recreation centers, private resorts, indoor childcare centers, playgrounds, sports fields, swimming pools, residential facilities, or day camps. A recreation program director's work environment may involve extremes of heat, cold, or noise. Given the diverse demands of the recreation profession, recreation program directors may need to work a combination of days, evenings, weekends, vacation, and summer hours to ensure program success.

Profile

Working Conditions: Work both Indoors and Outdoors
Physical Strength: Light Work
Education Needs:
Technical/Community College, Bachelor's Degree
Licensure/Certification:
Recommended
Physical Abilities Not Required: No Heavy Labor
Opportunities For Experience:
Internship, Military Service, Part-Time Work
Holland Interest Score*: ESA

* See Appendix A

Occupation Interest

Individuals drawn to the field tend to be charismatic, intelligent, and organized people who have the ability to quickly assess situations, utilize resources, and solve problems. Successful recreation program directors are responsible leaders who display effective time management skills, a strong sense of initiative, and a concern for individuals and society. Recreation program directors should enjoy physical activity and spending time with a wide range of people, including those with special needs and those from diverse cultural, social, and educational backgrounds.

A Day in the Life—Duties and Responsibilities

The daily occupational duties and responsibilities of recreation program directors will be determined by the individual's area of job specialization and work environment. Recreation program directors must be able to assess the recreational needs and abilities of individuals, groups, or the local community. Before their busy season, they typically spend time interviewing, hiring, and evaluating recreation workers and staff, including food service workers and maintenance crews. They spend a portion of each day supervising seasonal and full-time recreation workers, such as lifeguards, coaches, and activity leaders, and overseeing the safety, upkeep, and maintenance of grounds, equipment, and facilities. Recreation program directors promote the recreation program to the local community through flyers, websites, em-mails, and press releases. They also plan and schedule program events such as tournaments, nature studies, leagues, dances, team sports, and classes, and periodically brainstorm new ways to recruit volunteers for all aspects of the recreation program. Conducting program assessment and evaluation through surveys and feedback requests is one way in which recreation program directors can gain an understanding of the success of their programming.

Recreation program directors have many legal, financial, and administrative responsibilities, such as ensuring that their recreation program meets national requirements for safety and the Americans with Disabilities Act, planning the short-term and long-term recreation program budget, and conducting background checks on staff, volunteers, and contractors. Recreation directors are sometimes responsible for raising money for programming through grantwriting, fundraising, and donation requests. Part of the job involves keeping the recreation program in the public eye so that it will continue to attract patrons and contributions. The recreation program director may represent the recreation program at conferences and meetings, including local and national recreation society meetings, or meet periodically with institutional supervisors, such as parks and recreation department commissioners, facility owners, or other stakeholders.

All recreation program directors are responsible for accurate record keeping on program safety, accidents, and staff performance.

Duties and Responsibilities

- Developing and overseeing recreational programs
- Setting up schedules and activities
- Soliciting financial resources
- Coordinating human resources
- Directing specialized activities and events
- Publicizing and promoting programs to the community
- Maintaining facilities in good working order
- Ensuring safety of all patrons and staff
- Dealing with emergencies as necessary

WORK ENVIRONMENT

Physical Environment

The immediate physical environment of recreation program directors varies based on the program's focus and location. Recreation program directors spend their workdays coordinating activities in a wide variety of settings including schools, public recreation centers, indoor childcare centers, ice skating rinks, hospitals, playgrounds, sports fileds, pools, and aquatic centers, residential facilities, or day camps. Most recreation directors spend part of their work day outdoors, but the majority of their time is spent inside an office.

Human Environment

Recreation program directors work with a wide variety of people and should be comfortable meeting with colleagues, supervisors, program benefactors, staff, children, the elderly, people with physical disabilities, and families. Because they represent the program to the public and function in a supervisory or administrative role, they should enjoy meeting new people and spending much of their job managing others. Excellent communication skills are an advantage.

Relevant Skills and Abilities

Communication Skills
- Promoting an idea
- Speaking effectively

Interpersonal/Social Skills
- Asserting oneself
- Being sensitive to others
- Motivating others

Organization & Management Skills
- Coordinating tasks
- Demonstrating Leadership
- Managing people/group

Other Skills
- Being physically active

Technological Environment

Recreation program directors work with a wide variety of people and should be comfortable meeting with colleagues, supervisors, program benefactors, staff, children, the elderly, people with physical disabilities, and families. Because they represent the program to the public and function in a supervisory or administrative role, they should enjoy meeting new people and spending much of their job managing others. Excellent communication skills are an advantage.

EDUCATION, TRAINING, AND ADVANCEMENT

High School/Secondary

High school students interested in pursuing a career as a recreation program director should prepare themselves by developing good study habits. High school study of physical education, foreign language, public safety, sociology, psychology, and education will provide a strong foundation for work as a recreation program director or college-level work in the field. High school students interested in this career path will benefit from seeking part-time or seasonal work that exposes the students to diverse groups of people and recreational activities. They can also obtain certification in lifesaving techniques through their school or town.

Suggested High School Subjects
- Accounting
- Algebra
- Applied Communication

- Arts
- Business
- Business Law
- Business Math
- Crafts
- English
- Physical Education
- Social Studies

Famous First

The first summer camp for boys was Camp Comfort in Milford, Conn, established in 1861. It was founded by Frederick William Gunn, founder of The Gunnery prep school. The camp took 50 boys on a two-week camping trip. Today there are about 7,000 overnight camps and 5,000 day camps in the United States; together they serve over 10 million children.

College/Postsecondary

Postsecondary students interested in becoming recreation program directors should earn an associate's or bachelor's degree in recreation or physical education. A small number of colleges (accredited by the National Recreation and Park Association) offer the bachelor's of parks and recreation degree. Courses in physical education, education, public safety, business management, accounting, and foreign languages may also prove useful in future recreation work. Postsecondary students can gain work experience and potential advantage in their future job searches by securing internships or part-time employment in parks and recreation departments or private recreation programs.

Related College Majors
- Adapted Physical Education/Therapeutic Recreation
- Parks, Recreation & Leisure Facilities Management
- Parks, Recreation & Leisure Studies
- Physical Education Teaching & Coaching
- Sport & Fitness Administration/Management

Adult Job Seekers

Adults seeking employment as recreation program directors should have, at a minimum, an associate's or bachelor's degree in recreation or a related field and extensive program directing experience. Some recreation programs require their directors to hold a master's degree and second language proficiency. Adult job seekers should educate themselves about the educational and professional license requirements of their home states and the organizations where they seek employment, and may benefit from joining professional associations that offer help with networking and job searches. Professional recreation associations, such as the American Camping Association and the Society of State Directors of Health, Physical Education & Recreation, generally offer job-finding workshops and maintain lists and forums of available jobs.

Professional Certification and Licensure

Professional certification and licensure is not required of general recreation program directors. Directors of specialized recreation programs, such as swimming or parks and recreation, may be requited to earn specialized certification as a condition of employment. Lifeguard certification, pool operations certification, and CPR/First Aid certification is offered by the American Lifeguard Association and requires coursework and passing an examination. The National Recreation and Park Association ((NRPA) certificate is offered in therapeutic recreation, park management, outdoor recreation, industrial or commercial recreation, and camp management. It also requires a bachelor's degree or its equivalent in education and work experience, as well as passing a national examination. Ongoing professional education is required for continued certification in both lifesaving techniques and NRPA disciplines.

Additional Requirements

Successful recreation program directors will be knowledgeable about the profession's requirements, responsibilities, and opportunities. High levels of integrity and personal and professional ethics are required of recreation program directors, as professionals in this role interact with staff in subordinate roles and have access to personal information. Membership in professional recreation associations is encouraged among all recreation program directors as a means of building status within a professional community and networking.

In most states, the names of those people working in the field of recreation are almost always required to be submitted for a criminal record check. This includes employees, volunteers, and those delivering special programs.

EARNINGS AND ADVANCEMENT

The median annual wage for social and community service managers was $64,680 in May 2016. The median wage is the wage at which half the workers in an occupation earned more than that amount and half earned less. The lowest 10 percent earned less than $39,770, and the highest 10 percent earned more than $110,970.

In May 2016, the median annual wages for social and community service managers in the top industries in which they worked were as follows:

Local government, excluding education and hospitals	$79,680
Religious, grantmaking, civic, professional, and similar organizations	$66,170
Nursing and residential care facilities	$60,320
Individual and family services	$59,140
Community and vocational rehabilitation services	$58,270

The majority of social and community service managers work full time. They may work extended hours to meet deadlines or when preparing new programs; about 1 in 4 worked more than 40 hours per week in 2016.

Social and Community Service Managers

Median annual wages, May 2016

Other management occupations: $87,420

Social and community service managers: $64,680

Total, all occupations: $37,040

Note: "All Occupations" includes all occupations in the U.S. Economy. Source: U.S. Bureau of Labor Statistics, Occupational Employment Statistics

The median annual wage for recreation workers was $23,870 in May 2016. The median wage is the wage at which half the workers in an occupation earned more than that amount and half earned less. The lowest 10 percent earned less than $18,000, and the highest 10 percent earned more than $41,660.

In May 2016, the median annual wages for recreation workers in the top industries in which they worked were as follows:

Nursing and residential care facilities	$25,790
Social assistance	$24,050
Local government, excluding education and hospitals	$23,880
Religious, grantmaking, civic, professional, and similar organizations	$22,200

Many recreation workers, such as camp counselors or activity specialists, work weekends or part-time or irregular hours, or may be seasonally employed. Seasonal workers may work as few as 90 days or as long as 9 months during a season, depending on where they are employed and the type of activity they lead. For example, in areas of the United States that have warm winters, outdoor swimming pools may employ related recreation workers for a majority of the year. In other areas of the country, they may work only during the summer.

Recreation Workers

Median annual wages, May 2016

Total, all occupations: $37,040

Recreation workers: $23,870

Personal care and service occupations: $22,710

Note: "All Occupations" includes all occupations in the U.S. Economy. Source: U.S. Bureau of Labor Statistics, Occupational Employment Statistics

EMPLOYMENT AND OUTLOOK

Employment of social and community service managers is projected to grow 16 percent from 2016 to 2026, much faster than the average for all occupations.

Much of the job growth in this occupation is the result of an aging population. An increase in the number of older adults will result in a need for more social services, such as adult daycare and meal delivery, creating demand for social and community service managers. Employment of social and community service managers is expected to increase the most in industries serving the elderly, such as services for the elderly and persons with disabilities.

In addition, employment growth is projected as people continue to seek treatment for their addictions, and as illegal drug offenders are increasingly sent to treatment programs rather than to jail. As a result, managers who direct treatment programs will be needed.

Job prospects are expected to be good because of the continued expected demand for individual and family social services.

Employment of recreation workers is projected to grow 9 percent from 2016 to 2026, about as fast as the average for all occupations. As more emphasis is placed on the importance of lifelong well-being, more recreation workers will be needed to work with children and adults in a variety of settings.

Additional recreation workers are expected to be needed to work for fitness and recreational sports centers, youth centers, sports clubs, and other for- and not-for-profit organizations because some parks and recreation departments may seek to cut costs by contracting out the services of activity specialists.

In addition, as the baby-boom generation grows older, there will be more demand for recreation workers to work with older clients, especially in continuing care retirement communities and assisted living facilities for the elderly.

Job prospects will be best for those seeking part-time, seasonal, or temporary recreation jobs. Because workers in these jobs tend to be students or young people, they must be replaced when they leave for school or jobs in other occupations, thus creating many job openings.

Workers with higher levels of formal education related to recreation should have better prospects at getting year-round full-time positions. Volunteer experience, part-time work during school, and a summer job also are viewed favorably for both full- and part-time positions.

Social and Community Service Managers

Employment Trend, Projected 2016–26

Social and community service managers: 16%

Other management occupations: 9%

Total, all occupations: 7%

Note: "All Occupations" includes all occupations in the U.S. Economy. Source: U.S. Bureau of Labor Statistics, Employment Projections program

Recreation Workers

Employment Trend, Projected 2016–26

Personal care and service occupations: 18%

Recreation workers: 9%

Total, all occupations: 7%

Note: "All Occupations" includes all occupations in the U.S. Economy. Source: U.S. Bureau of Labor Statistics, Employment Projections program

Related Occupations
- Athletes and Sports Competitors
- Athletic Trainers
- Exercise Physiologists
- Fitness Trainers and Instructors
- Meeting, Convention, and Event Planners
- Recreational Therapists
- Rehabilitation Counselors
- School and Career Counselors
- Social Workers

SELECTED SCHOOLS

Many community colleges and four-year colleges and universities offer programs in physical education; a number of them also offer programs in parks and recreation management, arts and crafts management, and related fields. Interested students are advised to consult with a school guidance counselor.

MORE INFORMATION

American Academy for Park and Recreation Administration
P.O. Box 1040
Mahomet, IL 61853
217.586.3360
www.aapra.org

American Alliance for Health, Physical Education, Recreation & Dance
1900 Association Drive
Reston, VA 20192-1598
800.213.7193
www.aahperd.org

American Camping Association
5000 State Road 67 North
Martinsville, IN 46151
765.342.8456
www.acacamps.org

American Lifeguard Association
8300 Boone Boulevard, 5th Floor
Vienna, VA 22182
703.761.6750
www.americanlifeguard.com

Employee Services Management Association
P.O. Box 10517
Rockville, MD 20849
www.esmassn.org

National Council for Therapeutic Recreation Certification
7 Elmwood Drive
New City, NY 10956
845.639.1439
nctrc@NCTRC.org
www.nctrc.org

National Recreation and Park Association
22377 Belmont Ridge Road
Ashburn, VA 20148-4501
800.626.6772
www.nrpa.org

Society of State Directors of Health, Physical Educ. & Recreation
1900 Association Drive, Suite 100
Reston, VA 20191-1599
703.390.4599
www.thesociety.org

YMCA of the USA
101 N. Wacker Drive
Chicago, IL 60606
800.872.9622
www.ymca.net

Simone Isadora Flynn/Editor

Structural Metal Workers

Snapshot

Career Cluster(s): Building & Construction, Architecture & Construction, Manufacturing
Interests: Construction, engineering, architecture, physics, mathematics
Earnings (Yearly Average): $36,570
Job Growth: Average Growth Expected

OVERVIEW

Sphere of Work

Structural metal workers construct and install iron and steel structures that are utilized in construction, ship building, and other areas of heavy industry and architecture. The design and construction of structural metal forms is a highly specialized construction process that requires strict adherence to the unique design specifications, which vary from project to project. Structural metal installations are a crucial part of commercial buildings, as well as roads, dams, bridges, and other major infrastructure projects. Metal forms are extremely dangerous because of their size and weight, and their

installation requires extensive planning and communication to ensure the safety of the workers.

Work Environment

Structural metal workers traditionally work outdoors on large-scale construction sites. Structural metal forms are typically one of the first installments in the construction of large buildings and other structures. Metal workers utilize a wide range of heavy machinery, including trucks and large cranes to position the structures into place. Much of the work takes place at great heights and in all types of weather conditions. The work environment of structural metal workers also includes frequent exposure to potentially hazardous equipment such as shears, drill presses, and welding guns.

Profile

Working Conditions: Work Outdoors
Physical Strength: Heavy Work
Education Needs: On-The-Job Training, High School Diploma or G.E.D., High School Diploma with Technical Education, Apprenticeship
Licensure/Certification: Usually Not Requiredd
Opportunities For Experience: Apprenticeship, Military Service
Holland Interest Score*: REI

* See Appendix A

Occupation Interest

Structural metal work attracts professionals who enjoy intense physical activity, such as climbing, lifting, and balancing. Given the team-oriented nature of many of the tasks inherent to structural metal work, professionals in the field tend to be collaborative in nature. Metal workers are also analytical thinkers who thrive in environments where quality standards and safety measures is top priority.

A Day in the Life—Duties and Responsibilities

The construction, transport, and installation of structural metal support beams and joists is a complex and highly intricate process.

The architectural designs that call for structural metal reinforcement vary in scope and complexity. Structural metal works whose expertise lies in the conception of parts for structures will study blueprints and layout specifications in an attempt to create pieces that conform to design specifications, building codes, and budgetary constraints. This design phase requires professionals to be well versed in mathematics, engineering, and physics.

Once the design specifications are finalized, metal pieces are constructed in steel mills and inspected by engineers, who may make markings on individual pieces to indicate necessary adjustments prior to installation. Adjustments include cuts, adhesion of plates and pivots, and other structural changes.

The transport of structural metal pieces from foundries to the construction site can also pose a tremendous challenge for workers. The large size of structural metal elements often requires special ground transport via a flat-bed truck. Speed restrictions are often placed on oversized loads, which can require several days of transport depending on their distance from a particular construction site.

The installation of structural metal pieces is another intricate process, often requiring extensive collaboration and communication between workers on the ground and at great heights. Pieces are often temporarily fitted before welding to ensure compliance with design specifications. Many times, pieces must be removed and adjusted by workers on the ground prior to their permanent installation.

Duties and Responsibilities

- Setting up hoisting equipment
- Fastening steel parts to the cables of hoisting equipment
- Guiding steel parts with ropes
- Pulling, pushing or prying steel parts into approximate position while supported by hoisting devices
- Forcing steel parts into final position
- Positioning rivet holes in steel parts and driving drift pins through holes
- Checking the vertical and horizontal position of steel parts
- Bolting positioned steel parts to keep them in place until permanently riveted, bolted or welded
- Cutting and welding steel parts to make alterations

OCCUPATION SPECIALTIES

Structural Steel Workers

Structural steel workers raise, place and unite large beams, columns and other structural steel parts to form framework or complete structures.

Reinforcing Metal Workers

Reinforcing metal workers position and secure steel bars in concrete forms to reinforce concrete.

WORK ENVIRONMENT

Physical Environment

Structural metal workers primarily work at construction sites. Structural metal workers who specialize in engineering and architecture, however, often work in office settings. They may also work at foundries, steel mills, or other industrial sites where metal pieces are formed prior to their transport to a construction site.

Relevant Skills and Abilities

Organization & Management Skills
- Managing time
- Meeting goals and deadlines
- Paying attention to and handling details

Technical Skills
- Performing scientific, mathematical and technical work
- Working with machines, tools or other objects

Human Environment

Work with heavy-duty construction materials requires extensive collaboration skills in design, transport, and installation. Extensive communication helps to eliminate design flaws and ensures the structural integrity of projects upon completion, as well as the safety of the workers.

Technological Environment

Structural metal work requires the extensive use of tools and technology. While blow torches, punches, surface gauges, and shears are common tools in the field, a variety of software and digital technologies are also utilized, ranging from computer-aided design tools, spreadsheet software, and resource-planning programs.

EDUCATION, TRAINING, AND ADVANCEMENT

High School/Secondary

High school students can prepare for a career in structural metal work with courses in algebra, calculus, geometry, trigonometry, chemistry, physics, and introductory computer science. Drafting or industrial arts classes can also provide a foundation for a future career in construction design. English composition and scholastic sports help to equip students with the communication and leadership skills that are needed in collaborative professional arenas such as construction.

Pre-employment exposure to the construction industry, through internships or volunteerism, can also provide important insights into the basics of the industry.

Suggested High School Subjects
- Applied Physics
- Blueprint Reading
- English
- Mathematics
- Mechanical Drawing
- Metals Technology
- Shop Math
- Shop Mechanics
- Welding

Famous First

The first skyscraper was a ten-story-high building with a steel frame erected in Chicago, Ill. It was developed by the Home Insurance Company and designed by Major William Le Baron Jenney in 1884. The frame supported the entire weight of the building, allowing it to be built high. Previously, the walls themselves supported the weight of a building, thus limiting height.

Postsecondary

Postsecondary course work is not traditionally a prerequisite for employment as a structural metal worker, given that large amount of training, particularly for entry-level positions, is provided on the job. However, candidates interested in a career in the design, fabrication, and engineering aspects of structural metal work and heavy-duty construction will benefit tremendously from bachelor's and associate's degree programs in subjects ranging from civil engineering, construction management, technology, and civic planning.

Related College Majors
• Welding

Adult Job Seekers

Structural metal work is a feasible option for adult job seekers interested in transitioning careers, particularly those who have previous experience in trades or construction. Many structural metal firms undertake jobs at on a national level, which may require workers to travel for certain projects. While structural metal workers traditionally work normal business hours, certain projects may require extensive overtime and weekend work.

Professional Certification and Licensure

No specific licensure or certification is required for a career as a structural metal worker, though applicants with commercial licenses and welding certification typically have an employment advantage.

Additional Requirements

Professionals who work with structural metal fabrications and other heavy-duty construction elements are team-oriented individuals who possess a respect for the rules and regulations that protect workers and civilians during large construction projects.

Fun Fact

New York City boasts the world's largest collection of cast-iron architecture. Cheaper than brick or stone and easy to cast into decorative designs, it has been used for decorative or structural purposes in the early 19th century.

Source: http://www.castironnyc.org/history.htm

EARNINGS AND ADVANCEMENT

Earnings for structural metal workers fluctuate because work time can be affected by both bad weather and the loss of time between jobs. Median annual earnings of structural metal workers were $36,570 in 2014. The lowest ten percent earned less than $24,690, and the highest ten percent earned more than $55,040. Apprentices usually start at about sixty percent of the wages paid to experienced workers.

Structural metal workers may receive paid vacations, holidays, and sick days; life and health insurance; and retirement benefits. These are usually paid by the employer.

Metropolitan Areas with the Highest Employment Level in this Occupation

Metropolitan area	Employment	Employment per thousand jobs	Hourly mean wage
Houston-Sugar Land-Baytown, TX	3,450	1.21	$17.89
Los Angeles-Long Beach-Glendale, CA	2,160	0.53	$20.07
Wichita, KS	1,380	4.76	$22.17
Minneapolis-St. Paul-Bloomington, MN-WI	1,200	0.66	$18.87
Philadelphia, PA	1,180	0.64	$19.88
Chicago-Joliet-Naperville, IL	1,160	0.31	$18.81
Atlanta-Sandy Springs-Marietta, GA	1,000	0.42	$16.88
Kansas City, MO-KS	1,000	0.99	$23.48
Seattle-Bellevue-Everett, WA	890	0.60	$20.05
Portland-Vancouver-Hillsboro, OR-WA	870	0.83	$19.37

Source: Bureau of Labor Statistics

EMPLOYMENT AND OUTLOOK

There were approximately 79,000 structural metal workers employed nationally in 2012. Employment is expected to as fast as the average for all occupations through the year 2022, which means employment is projected to increase 9 percent to 13 percent. This is primarily due to the continued growth of industrial and commercial construction. In addition, job growth will occur as a result of the need to repair and maintain this country's increasing number of older buildings, factories, highways and bridges.

Employment Trend, Projected 2012–22

Construction trades workers: 22%

Structural metal workers: 11%

Total, all occupations: 11%

Note: "All Occupations" includes all occupations in the U.S. Economy. Source: U.S. Bureau of Labor Statistics, Employment Projections program

Related Occupations
- Metal/Plastic Working Machine Operator
- Sheet Metal Worker
- Welder

Related Military Occupations
- Construction Equipment Operator

Conversation With . . .
MIKE RELYIN

General Organizer, International Association of Bridge
Structural, Ornamental and Reinforcing Ironworkers
Washington, DC
Reinforcing Ironworker, 27 years

1. What was your individual career path in terms of education/training, entry-level job, or other significant opportunity?

After I graduated from high school, I worked as an auto mechanic for about two years and also worked on maintaining industrial equipment. These jobs taught me to work with my hands, as well as manage the maintenance side of things. I had family in the ironwork trade, so when I heard about the opportunity to become an apprentice through our local in Detroit, I knew it was a good one. I did a two-year apprenticeship, became a journeyman, and worked as a journeyman, foreman, and general foreman in the field. Then I got an opportunity to apply for an instructor's position at the apprenticeship program in Detroit and did that for two and a half years before I became the apprenticeship coordinator. I did that for about ten years, and then I was offered a position at union headquarters in Washington, D.C. in the apprenticeship and training department working to provide training materials, resources, and assistance to training centers across the US and Canada.

I spent my career in the field working in the reinforcing part of the industry, placing reinforced steel and post-tensioning cables for concrete construction. We build bridges, foundations, sewage treatment plants, factories, power plants...anything that's got concrete in it.

A typical workday involved unloading, handling, and placing reinforcing steel. This included the use of cranes to get the material close to where we were working. Much of the material is placed by hand, while cranes are sometimes used to hoist larger pieces or partially assembled sections into place. Reinforcing steel is fastened together using wire that is tied using pliers, and occasionally welded.

My job now has two major functions: assisting and providing resources to local unions to help them provide training, and providing training programs for the union apprenticeship programs. I do a lot of support, creating training materials and curricula for our different certification programs.

2. What are the most important skills and/or qualities for someone in your profession?

People who gravitate toward our industry need to like to work with their hands and be good at it. You'll be working outside, so there is weather to deal with and it's physically very demanding. You need a good basic math background because you'll work with drawings and blueprints.

You need to pace yourself for the long haul and work smarter and take care of yourself because this work does wear and tear on the body.

3. What do you wish you had known going into this profession?

Ironwork's very rewarding, and for the most part I knew what I was getting into. I get to work with some great people and you build a great camaraderie because you rely on them and trust them. You create something. And you do neat stuff like working on a 30-story building, or being 100 feet in the ground, or working with cranes with 200-foot booms.

4. Are there many job opportunities in your profession? In what specific areas?

Job opportunities vary with the economy. Things have been getting better over the last year or two. All facets of ironwork need workers.

5. How do you see your profession changing in the next five years? What role will technology play in those changes, and what skills will be required?

One of the biggest things is safety and specialty certification for work such as welding. This continues to change; owners and certain contractors are adding their own training and certification requirements. Also, general foremen need more computer skills. Blueprints aren't always rolled out; sometimes guys are given iPads and use CAD or BIM software.

6. What do you enjoy most about your job? What do you enjoy least about your job?

What I like most in the field is that the fact you're always going to different projects. You meet new people and you solve problems every day. In my job now, I enjoy the fact that what we're doing has a positive influence at the local level and in how workers benefit.

What I like least in the field are the cold days, and being laid off can be trying at times. In my job now, I least like that on top of having many large projects going at once, things are always popping up that need immediate attention; it is easy to get frustrated and burned out from the workload.

7. Can you suggest a valuable "try this" for students considering a career in your profession?

Take a vocational class in welding or any of the building trades. That will give you a flavor of what the work is like, although most classes are geared toward residential construction, which is quite a bit different than the commercial and industrial side of the industry. Other vocational classes may also help a person decide if a hands-on physical career is for them, even though they may not be quite as demanding as working in the construction industry.

MORE INFORMATION

Associated General Contractors of America
Director, Construction Education Services
2300 Wilson Boulevard, Suite 400
Arlington, VA 22201
703.548.3118
www.agc.org

International Association of Bridge, Structural, Ornamental, and Reinforcing Iron Workers
1750 New York Avenue NW
Suite 400
Washington, DC 20006
202.383.4800
www.ironworkers.org

National Association of Home Builders
1201 15th Street, NW
Washington, DC 20005
800.368.5242
www.nahb.com

National Association of Reinforcing Steel Contractors
P.O. Box 280
Fairfax, VA 22030
703.591.1870
www.narsc.com

National Center for Construction Education and Research
13614 Progress Boulevard
Alachua, FL 32615
888.622.3720
www.nccer.org

NEA
The Association of Union Constructors
1501 Lee Highway, Suite 202
Arlington, VA 22209-1109
703.524.3336
www.nea-online.org

United Steelworkers of America
Five Gateway Center
Pittsburgh, PA 15222
412.562.2400
www.usw.org

John Pritchard/Editor

Travel Agents

Snapshot

Career Cluster(s): Hospitality & Tourism, Transportation, Distribution & Logistics

Interests: Travel, Event Planning, Tourism

Earnings (Yearly Average): $36,460

Employment & Outlook: Decline Expected

OVERVIEW

Sphere of Work

Travel agents are customer service experts who specialize in travel and vacation planning and scheduling and offer their services to prospective travelers, helping them with the logistics of vacation or business trips, whether domestic or international. While many different types of travelers once utilized the services of travel agents to organize their trips, web-based tools and direct airline-to-customer tools have reduced the need for professional travel agents,

though travel agent expertise is still utilized for certain types of travel. Travel agents help to book airfare or other forms of travel, organize lodging, help travelers obtain certificates needed to travel to certain destinations, and work with customers to organize travel plans that meet certain budgetary needs. Some travel agents form partnerships with certain resorts or hospitality companies, receiving payment for leading customers towards services offered by certain companies.

Work Environment

Travel agents typically work in clean, comfortable, and well-lit offices. Self-employed travel agents often work out of home offices. Most work alone or among a small staff of administrative personnel and/or other travel agents. It is customary for travel agents to work at least forty hours per week; however, many work overtime, especially during peak travel seasons. Travel agents may spend most of a typical day behind a desk, coordinating and negotiating with airlines, cruise lines, hotels, and tourism companies via phone and Internet. Being a travel agent is also highly interactive and travel agents spend much of their time working directly with their clients to schedule trips or to handle logistical issues that arise during a scheduled travel package.

Profile

Interests: Data, People
Working Conditions: Work Inside
Physical Strength: Light Work
Education Needs: Junior/ Technical/Community College
Licensure/Certification: Required
Physical Abilities Not Require: Not Climb, Not Kneel
Opportunities For Experience: Military Service, Part Time Work
Holland Interest Score*: ECS

* See Appendix A

Occupation Interest

The travel industry is often demanding and challenging. Successful transactions frequently rely on speed, effective communication, and in-depth knowledge of national and international destinations. Prospective travel agents should enjoy working with people, even when this becomes a challenge, and should be comfortable working with and communicating with people from a variety of backgrounds and cultures. Since people tend to hold idealized views of vacation trips, customer expectations are often difficult to fulfill. When unforeseen events occur, travel agents are sometimes blamed for a customer's poor travel experiences and a travel agent must therefore be able to calmly and diplomatically address complains and issues that arise. Travel agents are typically expected to have detailed knowledge about a variety of national and international travel locations, recommending lodging, food, and tourist destinations to their customers as well as providing cultural information that might affect travelers.

A Day in the Life—Duties and Responsibilities

Travel agents spend most of the workday at a desk, on the phone, and on the computer and often function as liaisons between travelers and travel or hospitality companies. Travel agents may also spend part of a typically day consulting with travelers about desired destinations, availability, budget restrictions, and any special travel requirements they might have in addition to conducting introductory meetings with customers considering utilizing a travel agency for an upcoming trip. Travel agents also provide customers with information regarding national and international regulations, including travel advisories, money exchange rates, and required documentation like passports and visas. For long-term or high-profile clients, some travel agents make themselves available on an "on-call" basis to deal with any travel-related issues that arise during a client's trip.

In some cases, travel agents may travel to specific destinations to research the quality of a travel experience themselves, which further bolsters their credibility with clients. Many travel agents specialize in a specific geographic area or region, demographic group, or cultural preference and specialization has become more common and increasingly advantageous due competition for travel agent positions and clients. Travel agents specializing in arranging international travel will benefit from specific linguistic and cultural knowledge about their specialty area. For instance, travel agents who specialize in booking travel in Latin America will benefit from a knowledge of Spanish and from specific experience with the resorts, tourist destination, and other specifics of travel within that region.

Duties and Responsibilities

- **Collecting payment for tickets and tour packages**
- **Promoting, advertising and selling travel services**
- **Advising on travel sites and weather conditions**
- **Arranging hotel reservations, car rentals, tours and recreation**
- **Informing clients on customs, regulations, passports, medical certificates and currency exchange rates**
- **Using computers for fares and schedules**
- **Visiting hotels and travel attractions for evaluations**

OCCUPATION SPECIALTIES

Government Travel Clerks

Government Travel Clerks plan itineraries and schedule travel accommodations for government personnel and relatives.

Automotive Club Travel Counselors

Automotive Club Travel Counselors plan trips for members, providing maps and brochures.

Reservation Clerks

Reservation Clerks make travel and hotel accommodations for guests and employees of businesses.

Hotel Travel Clerks

Hotel Travel Clerks provide travel information and arrange accommodations for tourists.

WORK ENVIRONMENT

Transferable Skills and Abilities

Communication Skills
- Persuading others
- Speaking effectively
- Writing concisely

Interpersonal/Social Skills
- Being able to work independently
- Cooperating with others
- Working as a member of a team

Organization & Management Skills
- Paying attention to and handling details
- Selling ideas or products

Technical Skills
- Using technology to process information
- Working with data or numbers
- Working with machines, tools or other objects

Work Environment Skills
- Traveling

Immediate Physical Environment

Most travel agents work in an office or out of their own homes and may conduct much of their work via telephone or email. In many cases, a travel agent may want to have access to a location where potential customers can meet in person to discuss a travel itinerary.

Human Environment

Travel agents constantly communicate with clients and customer service personnel over the phone, in person, and through e-mail. In some cases, travel agents may need to cope with difficult individuals and interactions and must be able to maintain an outwardly pleasant attitude and an accommodating demeanor at all times. In larger offices, travel agents interact with other office personnel, administrators, and other travel agents.

Technological Environment

Travel agents use basic office equipment to help them complete their daily tasks. They routinely use phones, fax machines, calculators, and digital communication tools. In addition, travel agents should be proficient with scheduling and spreadsheet software and must learn to use a variety of web-based software systems used to book various types of accommodation, hospitality, and travel. Travel agents should also be highly proficient at reading and understanding maps as they often help customers navigate in unfamiliar areas and should know how to use web and software based map programs.

EDUCATION, TRAINING, AND ADVANCEMENT

High School/Secondary

High school students who wish to become travel agents should enroll in academic courses that emphasize business, communications, geography, foreign languages, world history, and social studies. Students should also participate in extracurricular clubs and student groups that focus on travel and tourism or that sharpen skills with customer service and/or social interaction. It is also helpful for students to travel as much as possible, even to local or regional attractions, in order to develop a sense of how to evaluate and critique locations and exhibitions. Students can gain valuable research experience by investigating online travel sources, deals, itineraries, and popular tourist attractions across the globe.

Suggested High School Subjects
- Applied Communication
- Bookkeeping
- Business & Computer Technology
- Business Math
- College Preparatory
- Computer Science
- English
- Foreign Languages
- Geography
- History
- Mathematics
- Science
- Social Studies
- Speech

Related Career Pathways/Majors

Hospitality & Tourism Cluster
- Travel & Tourism Pathway

Transportation, Distribution & Logistics Cluster
- Sales & Service Pathway

Postsecondary

After graduating from high school, most prospective travel agents find it helpful to enroll in full- or part-time travel agent programs offered through vocational schools, public adult education programs, local community colleges, and distance learning programs. Travel agent programs provide students with a solid understanding of sales and marketing, ticketing and reservations, tour planning and development, and world geography, as well as introducing helpful software typically used in the industry. A small number of colleges and universities offer bachelor's and master's degrees travel and tourism and individuals looking for an employment advantage should consider enrolling in a higher degree program.

Related College Majors
- Tourism & Travel Services Marketing Operations
- Travel-Tourism Management

Adult Job Seekers

Though a postsecondary degree is not considered a requirement for prospective travel agents, many employers give hiring preference to those jobseekers with demonstrated experience in the field of travel and tourism. In addition, those who have personal travel experience and proven knowledge of a specific geographic region or foreign country are likely to have an easier time finding employment. Prospective travel agents can participate in mentorships with local travel agencies and some travel agents begin their careers as reservation clerks or agent assistants with local travel agencies.

Professional Certification and Licensure

Experienced travel agents who have worked in larger offices and wish to start their own businesses might need professional accreditation through a known travel organization, like the Airlines Reporting Corporation and the International Airlines Travel Agency Network.

Various cruise lines, and railways might also accredit certain travel agents or agencies. In order to receive approval, a travel agent's business must be financially viable and must employ at least one experienced manager or travel agent. Accreditation is meant to ensure quality in the industry and thus assure customers that the agent working with them is a professional in his or her field.

Additional Requirements

As more and more travel information becomes available via online sources, agents must continually add to their existing knowledge of cultures, destinations, lodging, procedures, government regulations, and attractions. They must possess impeccable research and computer skills, and they must also be able to effectively relay updated and new information to clients as it becomes available. As travelers more regularly arrange their own trips, travel agents must adapt to fill specific niches within the broader tourism and hospitality industry. To accomplish this, some travel agents specialize in organizing large group or business travel packages while others attempt to attract clients by offering specialize knowledge of a certain region, nation, or type of travel.

Fun Fact

The travel industry is one of the world's largest, contributing $7.6 trillion to the global economy in 2016. Worldwide, 1.24 billion international tourists were estimated to have arrived at their destinations that year.

Source: statista.com

EARNINGS AND ADVANCEMENT

In the United States, travel agents earn an average annual salary of $36,460, with a range of between $20,000 and 60,000. Higher wages can be found in prestigious travel agencies or by working directly with businesses to help organize conferences and business travel packages.

Travel agents usually receive paid vacations, holidays, and sick days; life and health insurance; and retirement benefits. These are usually paid by the employer. Self-employed agents must provide these benefits for themselves. In some companies, travel agents may also benefit from reduced cost for travel and lodging.

EMPLOYMENT AND OUTLOOK

According to the Bureau of Labor Statistics (BLS), the travel agent industry is expected to decline by approximately 12 percent between 2014 and 2024. A combination of factors, most notably the ease of booking travel and other activities through online travel companies, has contributed to the decline of the industry. Due to the overall decline in the industry, competition is expected to be significant for remaining positions. As web-booking services have emerged, the travel agent industry has begun to evolve with agencies and independent agents increasingly specializing in certain types of travel or in helping customers with complex travel arrangement that may involve multiple locations and layovers, various types of lodging and transportation, or specialized needs.

Related Occupations
- Reservation and Ticket Agent

Related Military Occupations
- Transportation Specialist

Conversation With . . .
KATE HOWE

Ski Instructor / Trainer / Examiner
Owner, katehowe.com
Aspen-based, teaches around the globe
11 years in profession

1. What was your individual career path in terms of education/training, entry-level job, or other significant opportunity ?

I was an athlete as a kid, a figure skater who learned to earn time with coaches by proving I was worth it. I developed an understanding of skill acquisition and the psychology of performing under pressure.

I went on to college at the Art Center College of Design in Pasadena, CA, but left to open a rock climbing gym with my husband. We ran that for five years, then moved to Montana.

I became a ski instructor almost by accident, when I took my 5-year-old son to a local ski area for a lesson. The supervisor offered me a job working with kids. I had told him I was a figure skating coach—and lousy skier—and he said, "We need people who can teach; we will teach you to ski."

That was 11 years ago. I started as an entry level instructor, making $7.25 an hour at Bridger Bowl Ski Area. I admired instructors who could take private guests to the top of Bridger Ridge (double black difficulty)—they earned more and had fun skiing difficult terrain.

I decided that if I wanted to get good quickly, I should train as if I were trying out for the Professional Ski Instructors of America (PSIA) National Alpine Team. I took advantage of my employer's in-house training with a talented instructor, an alumnus of the national team. I also read every book and watched every video I could about technique, and attended the PSIA National Academy to be trained by current team members.

In two years, I passed all three levels of certification by the PSIA and was recruited to teach on Aspen Mountain in Colorado. I am now an Examiner for PSIA. This means I give certification exams to ski instructors. I'm also a trainer at Aspen Snowmass.

I have a full calendar of private clients who ski with me for three to 25 days. My company, KH Global Ski Adventures, takes clients adventure/back country skiing all over the globe, from Japan to British Columbia to Switzerland … wherever they want to go.

I made my own career path and sought out the coaching and opportunities I needed. Starting a new, expensive career with two kids under 5 was scary.

2. What are the most important skills and/or qualities for someone in your profession, particularly if working overseas?

You need to manage guest relations and to always improve so you can better serve your guests. As a teacher, everything you do must be in service to your students' improvement and ability. Guest-centered teaching creates trust, and your guests will return.

You have to have the ability to be coached. You must be able to be critiqued and criticized without taking it personally. You can practice this skill in high school. It's about getting as good as you can at everything they put in front of you. Always move your goal ahead so that when you cross one line, you're already training for the next goal.

When working overseas, make friends with everyone. Overcome your fear of the unknown by saying yes as often as you can. Help others out. When I'm at an unfamiliar ski area, if someone has fallen or has trouble with their skis, I offer help. Be humble and grateful and cultivate friendships and doors will open for you. Because of this philosophy, I was the first woman and the seventh person to go heli skiing on the island of Hokkaido, Japan, invited by a tour operator I had made friends with by helping clear breakfast dishes.

3. What do you wish you had known before deciding to work abroad?

Plan for visas, which can be difficult. Always hire a local guide. You don't have to know the language to succeed. Google Maps can get you around a new country without a hitch. Figure out a way to fly business class so that you are rested and ready to work.

4. Are there many job opportunities overseas in your profession? In what specific geographic areas?

There's as much work as you want. To access it, put yourself in a position where people want to hire you. Skiing in China is booming right now.

5. Will the willingness of professionals to travel and live overseas need to change in the next five years? What role will technology play, and what skills will be required?

All instructors dream of traveling overseas with a private client for heli skiing, the pinnacle of our profession. I don't see that changing, but I do see the snow changing. Climate change is a real threat. There is less powder. Seasons are shorter. To stay relevant in the travel ski industry, you must seek the snow, and find clients who are willing to travel to find it.

6. What do you enjoy most about your job? What do you enjoy least about your job?

Skiing deep powder out of a helicopter off the top of an un-skied peak is the most incredible sensation I have ever experienced, topped only by watching a guest I have trained do the same. The next best piece is traveling, making friends, experiencing new things and embracing the scary, stressful chaos of being somewhere you don't understand.

The worst is being cold and getting frostbitten feet. And being exhausted from giving my all 24/7 from the moment I leave my house until the day I return. I usually sleep for two or three days when I get back from a trip.

7. Can you suggest a valuable "try this" for students considering a career overseas in your profession?

Go to Rookie Academy in New Zealand to get certified as a Level 2 instructor. Practice being coachable, ego-less, humble, and hard working. Apply to ski schools in Japan and China, where a lot of ski schools are just opening. They hire lower level instructors.

MORE INFORMATION

Airlines Reporting Corporation
3000 Wilson Boulevard, Suite 300
Arlington, VA 22201-3862
703.816.8000
www.arccorp.com

American Society of Travel Agents
1101 King Street, Suite 200
Alexandria, VA 22314
703.739.2782
askasta@astahq.com
www.asta.org

International Airlines Travel Agency Network
703 Waterford Way, Suite 600
Miami, FL 33126
877.734.2826
www.iatan.org

National Association of Career Travel Agents
1101 King Street, Suite 200
Alexandria, VA 22314
877.226.2282
www.nacta.com

Specialty Travel Agents Association
12381 Fenton Road
Fenton, MI 48430
810.629.2386
www.specialtytravelagents.com

The Travel Institute
148 Linden Street, Suite 305
Wellesley, MA 02482
800.542.4282
tech@thetravelinstitute.com
www.thetravelinstitute.com

Briana Nadeau/Editor

Wildlife Biologists

Snapshot

Career Cluster(s): Agriculture, Food & Natural Resources, Science, Technology, Engineering & Mathematics
Interests: Biology, Life Sciences, Environment, Conservation, Animal Behavior, Advocacy, Agriculture
Earnings (Median pay): $60,520 per year; $29.10 per hour
Job Growth: As fast as average

OVERVIEW

Sphere of Work

Wildlife biologists are scientists who study the origins, physiology, behavior, life cycles, and habitats of animals. Wildlife biologists conduct research on various aspects of animal species, including diseases, nutrition, genetics, and territory. Through their studies, these scientists work to protect animals' natural habitats. As a result, wildlife biologists are also called upon to provide recommendations on the protection of animal habitats.

Work Environment

Wildlife biologists may conduct their research in the field, often in remote locations, but they also have considerable contact with many different people. Environmental companies and consulting groups are increasingly seeking out wildlife biologists in their efforts to comply with government regulations. Other major companies, such as lumber businesses, chemical manufacturers, and ranchers, employ wildlife biologists for similar reasons. Many zoos and nature centers also hire wildlife biologists to provide better information about the species under their care.

Fieldwork can require zoologists and wildlife biologists to travel to remote locations anywhere in the world. For example, cetologists studying whale populations may spend months at sea on a research ship. Other zoologists and wildlife biologists may spend significant amounts of time in deserts or remote mountainous and woodland regions. The ability to travel and study nature firsthand is often viewed as a benefit of working in these occupations, but few modern amenities may be available to those who travel in remote areas.

Profile

Working Conditions: Work both Indoors and Outdoors
Physical Strength: Light Work
Education Needs: Bachelor's Degree, Master's Degree
Licensure/Certification: Usually Not Required
Physical Abilities Not Required: N/A
Opportunities For Experience: Internship, Volunteer Work
Holland Interest Score*: IRS

* See Appendix A

Occupation Interest

The field of wildlife biology attracts individuals who are interested in studying animals and concerned with their conservation. They enjoy working in remote locations to study their subjects' behavior and then reporting it to their superiors and/or the public at large. However, they also work in the public eye, offering their expertise to businesses, government agencies, and other groups to protect animal habitats from natural and man-made dangers. Wildlife biologists are analytical, attentive to detail, and well-organized.

Fieldwork can be physically demanding, and zoologists and wildlife biologists work in both warm and cold climates and in all types of weather. For example, ornithologists who study penguins in

Antarctica may need to spend significant amounts of time in cold weather and on ships, which may cause seasickness. In all environments, working as a zoologist or wildlife biologist can be emotionally demanding because interpersonal contact may be limited.

A Day in the Life—Duties and Responsibilities

A wildlife biologist spends much of his or her career in the field, studying animal species and their habitats. The biologist surveys the species' numbers, studies their behavior, examines their genetic profiles and life cycles, and observes their relationships with other animals. Wildlife biologists also examine disease outbreaks as well as the impacts of pollution and human activity and development on wildlife and their habitats. Additionally, wildlife biologists may work in a laboratory or other controlled environment, conducting behavioral experiments on live animals. Based on their field and laboratory research, they write research papers and conduct studies to create greater awareness of specific species.

In addition to their scholarly research, wildlife biologists may work as experts for zoos and nature conservancies, for both profit and non-profit businesses and organizations, and for the government. They represent a wide range of industries, from logging to commercial fishing. In this capacity, wildlife biologists use their scholarly expertise and research to provide recommendations to these entities or industries. Such advice can help these organizations understand how the presence of wildlife in a habitat will have an impact on the organization's activities or how the organization's expansion (or human activity in general) into that habitat will affect wildlife and their habitats. The biologists speak to groups on their findings, assist in filing environmental compliance reports, and help organizations or local agencies adjust their policies to protect these habitats if necessary.

Duties and Responsibilities

- Observing animals in their natural environments
- Working in laboratories
- Collecting data and writing reports and research papers
- Advising officials on public land use regulations

WORK ENVIRONMENT

Physical Environment

Wildlife biologists often work in the field, studying animals in their natural habitat. Such locations can leave the biologists vulnerable to animal attacks, injuries from traversing remote terrain, or extreme weather conditions. Biologists also conduct their work in animal-oriented parks and institutions, such as wildlife sanctuaries and zoos. Other biologists work in a laboratory and office setting, conducting controlled experiments and writing reports and scholarly articles.

Relevant Skills and Abilities

Analytical Skills
- Collecting and analyzing data

Communication Skills
- Speaking and writing effectively

Interpersonal/Social Skills
- Being able to work independently
- Being patient

Research & Planning Skills
- Identifying a research problem
- Laying out a plan
- Solving problems

Unclassified Skills
- Being curious

Work Environment Skills
- Working in a laboratory setting
- Working outdoors

Human Environment

Although wildlife biologists conduct a great deal of field research, they have considerable contact with other people. As experts in their particular fields, they frequently present their findings and recommendations to their immediate supervisors, employers, and peers and to the general public. Wildlife biologists also often work in teams with fellow biologists and other research scientists as they conduct research and experiments.

Technological Environment

Wildlife biologists employ many kinds of technology during the course of their research, from water samplers, specimen containers, and fishing nets, to satellite-based technology and computer hardware. They should also be proficient with analytical tools such as microscopes. When compiling data, wildlife biologists use computer software to create models and maps, manage databases, and author research papers. Additionally, they may rely on off-road vehicles, boats, and other modes of transportation while working in the field.

EDUCATION, TRAINING, AND ADVANCEMENT

High School/Secondary

High school students who are interested in becoming wildlife biologists are encouraged to study such scientific areas as biology, chemistry, mathematics, geography, and earth science. Additionally, they will benefit from studying computer science, statistics, and even communications, which will help them later compile data and present their findings to others.

Suggested High School Subjects

- Algebra
- Applied Biology/Chemistry
- Biology
- Calculus
- Chemistry
- Computer Science
- Earth Science
- English
- Forestry
- Geography
- Geometry
- Physics
- Science
- Statistics

Famous First

The first wildlife biologist to achieve popular recognition was Jane Goodall, who began studying chimpanzees in Gombe National Park, Tanzania, in 1960. She observed the animals in the wild, and wrote *In the Shadow of Man* (1971). Since then she has written numerous other books and founded a number of organizations focused on conservation and animal welfare.

College/Postsecondary

Wildlife biologists obtain a bachelor's degree in a related field, such as biology, ecology, or environmental science. Most organizations and agencies require that candidates obtain a master's degree and prefer individuals with a doctorate in a related field. Additionally, they expect that candidates have considerable training in specific fields, such as ornithology, animal ecology, population dynamics, or zoology. Students interested in becoming wildlife biologists should consider pursuing volunteer and internship positions at their academic institutions.

Related College Majors
- Botany
- Ecology
- Environmental Health
- Environmental Science/Studies
- Forestry, General
- Human & Animal Physiology
- Marine/Aquatic Biology
- Wildlife & Wildlands Management
- Zoology, General

Adult Job Seekers

One of the most effective ways for adults to obtain a career in wildlife biology is through the school at which they are receiving their master's and doctorate degrees. During the course of their schoolwork they may join research projects and participate in internship programs that can give them exposure to other biologists. Additionally, candidates may find networking opportunities by joining nonprofit organizations such as the Ecological Society of America, National Wildlife Federation, the Nature Conservancy, or the Worldwide Fund for Nature.

Professional Certification and Licensure

Most organizations require completion of a master's and doctorate degrees as a qualification for a wildlife biologist position. Some employers, such as the United States Geological Survey, only hire candidates for certain higher-level positions if they were in the highest third of their graduating class. Wildlife research biologists should have certification or licensure for the vehicles they are using in the field, such as a boating or driver's license.

Professional certification as a Certified Wildlife Biologist (CWB) or Associate Wildlife Biologist (AWB) is optional. Consult credible professional associations within the field and follow professional debate as to the relevancy and value of any certification program.

Additional Requirements

In addition to exceptional training in the natural sciences, a wildlife biologist must demonstrate strong communication skills. These attributes are useful in presenting data and recommendations to the organizations for which they work. Wildlife biologists should also be capable researchers, able to compile and organize a great deal of information and data:

Fun Fact

Elephants have a specific alarm call that means "human" and horses use facial expressions to communicate with each other.

Source: https://www.mnn.com/earth-matters

EARNINGS AND ADVANCEMENT

The median annual wage for zoologists and wildlife biologists was $60,520 in May 2016. The median wage is the wage at which half the workers in an occupation earned more than that amount and half earned less. The lowest 10 percent earned less than $39,150, and the highest 10 percent earned more than $98,540.

In May 2016, the median annual wages for zoologists and wildlife biologists in the top industries in which they worked were as follows:

Federal government, excluding postal service	$75,040
Research and development in the physical, engineering, and life sciences	$65,160
Management, scientific, and technical consulting services	$62,090
State government, excluding education and hospitals	$54,230
Colleges, universities, and professional schools; state, local, and private	$52,720

Most zoologists and wildlife biologists work full time. They may work long or irregular hours, especially when doing fieldwork.

Zoologists and wildlife biologists typically receive greater responsibility and independence in their work as they gain experience. More education also can lead to greater responsibility. Zoologists and wildlife biologists with a Ph.D. usually lead independent research and control the direction and content of projects. In addition, they may be responsible for finding much of their own funding.

Median annual wages, May 2016

Life scientists: $71,950

Zoologists and wildlife biologists: $60,520

Total, all occupations: $37,040

Note: "All Occupations" includes all occupations in the U.S. Economy. Source: U.S. Bureau of Labor Statistics, Occupational Employment Statistics

EMPLOYMENT AND OUTLOOK

Employment of zoologists and wildlife biologists is projected to grow 8 percent from 2016 to 2026, about as fast as the average for all occupations. More zoologists and wildlife biologists will be needed to study human and wildlife interactions as the human population grows and development impacts wildlife and their natural habitats. However, because most funding comes from governmental agencies, demand for zoologists and wildlife biologists will be limited by budgetary constraints.

As the human population grows and expands into new areas, it will expose wildlife to threats such as disease, invasive species, and habitat loss. Increased human activity can cause problems such as pollution and climate change, which endanger wildlife. Zoologists and wildlife biologists will be needed to study and gain an understanding of the impact of these factors. Many states will continue to employ zoologists and wildlife biologists to manage animal populations for tourism purposes, such as hunting game, sightseeing, and conservation. Changes in climate patterns can be detrimental to the migration habits of animals, and increased sea levels can destroy wetlands; therefore, zoologists and wildlife biologists will be needed to research, develop, and carry out wildlife management and conservation plans that combat these threats and protect our natural resources.

Zoologists and wildlife biologists may face strong competition when looking for employment. Applicants with practical experience gained through internships, summer jobs, or volunteer work done before or shortly after graduation should have better chances at finding employment.

Employment Trend
Projected 2016–22

Life scientists: 10%

Zoologists and wildlife biologists: 8%

Total, all occupations: 7%

Note: "All Occupations" includes all occupations in the U.S. Economy. Source: U.S. Bureau of Labor Statistics, Employment Projections program

Conversation With . . .
ANDY TIMMINS

New Hampshire Fish and Game Department
Bear Biologist, 12 years

1. What was your individual career path in terms of education/training, entry-level job, or other significant opportunity?

Growing up, I had an interest in the outdoors—I did a lot of hunting and fishing—but I didn't for a minute think it would be my career choice. In college, I was exposed to wildlife management and earned a BS in that field. I started working as a wildlife technician for the Fish and Game Department. After a few years, I saw I needed more education to advance in the field. Fortunately, my department paid for me to go to graduate school and earn an MS in wildlife management.

In grad school, I did my research on wild turkeys and I hoped to become the state's turkey biologist. But the bear position was the only open job when I got out. I had never had any exposure to bears before so it was in some ways an odd step to take. But I love it and wouldn't leave even if the turkey biologist position opened up.

I do a variety of things. I estimate population sizes, set population objectives and supervise, coordinate and participate in a fair amount of bear research. I'm most focused on nuisance behavior and mitigating bear-human conflict. The latter is a daily task from May through September. I'm the only bear biologist for the state but I have regional biologists that I can call on for assistance and I work with some folks with USDA Wildlife Services.

2. What are the most important skills and/or qualities for someone in your profession?

It's important to be true to your values toward the wildlife, especially in bear management, because I feel the species continues to be persecuted in many ways. It's important to force human responsibility in regards to conflict management, and not cave to pressure to remove bears (by trap or gun). I don't believe you can trap or shoot your way out of a bear problem. You have to educate the public about managing things that attract bears and force them to try to change their behaviors.

You also need a strong work ethic and a willingness to work long hours. You need a thick skin, especially in summer when you deal with people who are not particularly pleased with the agency or the bear. You have to let them vent and have to let some of that roll off your back. You have to remember you're probably hearing from the vocal minority and that there is a greater public out there that appreciates what you do but you may not hear from them.

3. What do you wish you had known going into this profession?

I wish I'd been a little more prepared for the political side of things and knew that at times science and the best information are not going to drive decision-making. Over the years, I've learned to pick my battles and let the small things roll off my back so I can be more effective with the big issues regarding bear management.

4. Are there many job opportunities in your profession? In what specific areas?

Yes and no. I think most kids in school now have probably heard that it's a competitive profession and there aren't a lot of openings. Actually, I've been amazed at the number of openings that have come along over the years. I'm convinced that if you have a strong work ethic, are dedicated, and are flexible enough to move around, you'll find opportunities.

5. How do you see your profession changing in the next five years, what role will technology play in those changes, and what skills will be required?

There will always be a need for boots on the ground and people in the field but technology will play more of a role. Students should be comfortable with computers and programming and using GIS. That would be a big advantage. A lot of us in the field right now aren't overly computer savvy.

6. What do you like most about your job? What do you like least about your job?

I most like feeling I'm having a positive impact on the state's wildlife resources, particularly bears. I like to think I have encouraged some segment of society to have more appreciation and tolerance for bears. I also appreciate interacting with members of the public, including both hunters and non-hunters, who have an appreciation for wildlife. It feels really good to connect with those types of people rather than the greedy person who always wants more out of the resource or the person who can't tolerate any kind of wildlife on their front lawn.

7. **Can you suggest a valuable "try this" for students considering a career in your profession?**

Volunteer. Get your name out there. Try to get as involved as you can so you can set yourself apart from the pack. And understand that first impressions mean everything. If you show up but don't pay attention and have no initiative, that's going to stick in people's minds. Work hard, be enthusiastic, and impress people with strong initiative.

SELECTED SCHOOLS

Most colleges and universities have bachelor's degree programs in animal biology, zoology, or other subjects related to wildlife biology. The student may also gain an initial grounding in the field at an agricultural, technical, or community college. For advanced positions, a master's or doctoral degree is usually obtained. Below are listed some of the more prominent schools in this field.

Brigham Young University
Plant & Wildlife Sciences
Life Sciences Building
Provo, UT 84602
801.422.2760
pws.byu.edu

Colorado State University
Fish, Wildlife, and Conservation
Biology
109D Wagar Building
1474 Campus Delivery
Fort Collins, CO 80523
970.491.5020
warnercnr.colostate.edu/fwcb-home

Michigan State University
Department of Fisheries and Wildlife
480 Wilson Road, Room 13
East Lansing, MI 48824
517.355.4478
www.fw.msu.edu

Texas A&M University
Department Wildlife and Fisheries
Science
TAMU 2258
College Station, TX 77843
979.845.5777
wfsc.tamy.edu

University of Arizona
Natural Resources and the
Environment
Biological Sciences East, Room 325
1311 East 4th Street
Tucson, AZ 85721
520.621.7255
snre.arizona.edu

University of Florida
Wildlife Ecology and Conservation
110 Newins-Zeigler Hall
PO Box 110430
Gainseville, FL 32611
352.846.0643
www.wec.ufl.edu

University of Maryland
Wildlife Ecology
Center for Environmental Science
PO Box 775
Cambridge, MD 21613
410.228.9250
www.umces.edu

University of Minnesota
Fisheries, Wildlife, and Conservation
Biology
135 Skok Hall
203 Upper Buford Circle
St. Paul, MN 55108
612.625.5299
Fwcb.cfans.umn.edu

University of Missouri
Fisheries and Wildlife Sciences
302 Anheuser-Busch Natural
Sciences Building
Columbia, MO 65211
573.882.3436
www.snr.missouri.edu/fw

University of Tennessee
Forestry, Wildlife, and Fisheries
274 Ellington Plant Science Building
Knoxville, TN 37996
865.974.7987
fwf.ag.utk.edu

MORE INFORMATION

Ecological Society of America
1990 M Street, NW, Suite 700
Washington, DC 20006-3915
202.833.8773
www.esa.org

The Wildlife Society
5410 Grosvenor Lane, Suite 200
Bethesda, MD 20814-2144
301.897.9770
joomla.wildlife.org

National Wildlife Federation
11100 Wildlife Center Drive
Reston, VA 20190-5362
800.822.9919
www.nwf.org

**World Wildlife Fund/Worldwide
Fund for Nature**
1250 24th Street NW
P.O. Box 97180
Washington, DC 20090-7180
202.293.4800
www.worldwildlife.org

Nature Conservancy
4245 North Fairfax Drive, Suite 100
Arlington, VA 22203-1606
800.628.6860
nature.org

Michael Auerbach/Editor

What Are Your Career Interests?

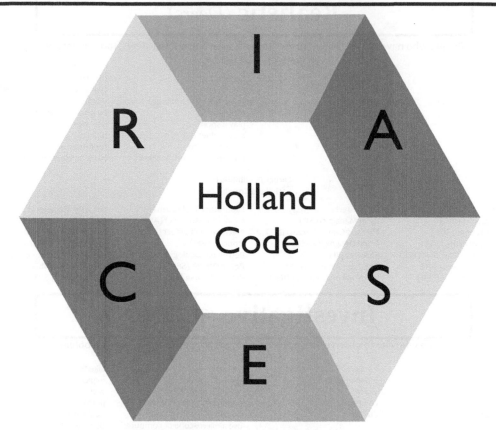

This is based on Dr. John Holland's theory that people and work environments can be loosely classified into six different groups. Each of the letters above corresponds to one of the six groups described in the following pages.

Different people's personalities may find different environments more to their liking. While you may have some interests in and similarities to several of the six groups, you may be attracted primarily to two or three of the areas. These two or three letters are your "Holland Code." For example, with a code of "RES" you would most resemble the Realistic type, somewhat less resemble the Enterprising type, and resemble the Social type even less. The types that are not in your code are the types you resemble least of all.

Most people, and most jobs, are best represented by some combination of two or three of the Holland interest areas. In addition, most people are most satisfied if there is some degree of fit between their personality and their work environment.

The rest of the pages in this booklet further explain each type and provide some examples of career possibilities, areas of study at MU, and co-curricular activities for each code. To take a more in-depth look at your Holland Code, take a self-assessment such as the SDS, Discover, or a card sort at the MU Career Center with a Career Specialist.

Realistic *(Doers)*

People who have athletic ability, prefer to work with objects, machines, tools, plants or animals, or to be outdoors.

Are you?		Can you?	Like to?
practical	independent	fix electrical things	tinker with machines/vehicles
straightforward/frank	ambitious	solve electrical problems	work outdoors
mechanically inclined	systematic	pitch a tent	be physically active
stable		play a sport	use your hands
concrete		read a blueprint	build things
reserved		plant a garden	tend/train animals
self-controlled		operate tools and machine	work on electronic equipment

**Career Possibilities
(Holland Code):**

Air Traffic Controller (SER)	Dental Technician (REI)	Laboratory Technician (RIE)	Property Manager (ESR)
Archaeologist (IRE)	Farm Manager (ESR)	Landscape Architect (AIR)	Recreation Manager (SER)
Athletic Trainer (SRE)	Fish and Game Warden (RES)	Mechanical Engineer (RIS)	Service Manager (ERS)
Cartographer (IRE)	Floral Designer (RAE)	Optician (REI)	Software Technician (RCI)
Commercial Airline Pilot (RIE)	Forester (RIS)	Petroleum Geologist (RIE)	Ultrasound Technologist (RSI)
Commercial Drafter (IRE)	Geodetic Surveyor (IRE)	Police Officer (SER)	Vocational Rehabilitation
Corrections Officer (SER)	Industrial Arts Teacher (IER)	Practical Nurse (SER)	Consultant (ESR)

Investigative *(Thinkers)*

People who like to observe, learn, investigate, analyze, evaluate, or solve problems.

Are you?		Can you?	Like to?
inquisitive	intellectually self-confident	think abstractly	explore a variety of ideas
analytical	Independent	solve math problems	work independently
scientific	logical	understand scientific theories	perform lab experiments
observant/precise	complex	do complex calculations	deal with abstractions
scholarly	Curious	use a microscope or computer	do research
cautious		interpret formulas	be challenged

**Career Possibilities
(Holland Code):**

Actuary (ISE)	Chemical Engineer (IRE)	Geologist (IRE)	Physician, General Practice (ISE)
Agronomist (IRS)	Chemist (IRE)	Horticulturist (IRS)	Psychologist (IES)
Anesthesiologist (IRS)	Computer Systems Analyst (IER)	Mathematician (IER)	Research Analyst (IRC)
Anthropologist (IRE)	Dentist (ISR)	Medical Technologist (ISA)	Statistician (IRE)
Archaeologist (IRE)	Ecologist (IRE)	Meteorologist (IRS)	Surgeon (IRA)
Biochemist (IRS)	Economist (IAS)	Nurse Practitioner (ISA)	Technical Writer (IRS)
Biologist (ISR)	Electrical Engineer (IRE)	Pharmacist (IES)	Veterinarian (IRS)

Artistic *(Creators)*

People who have artistic, innovating, or intuitional abilities and like to work in unstructured situations using their imagination and creativity.

Are you?		Can you?	Like to?
creative	original	sketch, draw, paint	attend concerts, theatre, art
imaginative	introspective	play a musical instrument	exhibits
innovative	impulsive	write stories, poetry, music	read fiction, plays, and poetry
unconventional	sensitive	sing, act, dance	work on crafts
emotional	courageous	design fashions or interiors	take photography
independent	complicated		express yourself creatively
Expressive	idealistic		deal with ambiguous ideas
	nonconforming		

**Career Possibilities
(Holland Code):**

Actor (AES)	Copy Writer (ASI)	Interior Designer (AES)	Medical Illustrator (AIE)
Advertising Art Director (AES)	Dance Instructor (AER)	Intelligence Research Specialist	Museum Curator (AES)
Advertising Manager (ASE)	Drama Coach (ASE)	(AEI)	Music Teacher (ASI)
Architect (AIR)	English Teacher (ASE)	Journalist/Reporter (ASE)	Photographer (AES)
Art Teacher (ASE)	Entertainer/Performer (AES)	Landscape Architect (AIR)	Writer (ASI)
Artist (ASI)	Fashion Illustrator (ASR)	Librarian (SAI)	Graphic Designer (AES)

Social *(Helpers)*

People who like to work with people to enlighten, inform, help, train, or cure them, or are skilled with words.

Are you?		Can you?	Like to?
friendly	cooperative	teach/train others	work in groups
helpful	generous	express yourself clearly	help people with problems
idealistic	responsible	lead a group discussion	do volunteer work
insightful	forgiving	mediate disputes	work with young people
outgoing	patient	plan and supervise an activity	serve others
understanding	kind	cooperate well with others	

**Career Possibilities
(Holland Code):**

City Manager (SEC)	Historian (SEI)	Park Naturalist (SEI)	Teacher (SAE)
Clinical Dietitian (SIE)	Hospital Administrator (SER)	Physical Therapist (SIE)	Social Worker (SEA)
College/University Faculty (SEI)	Psychologist (SEI)	Police Officer (SER)	Speech Pathologist (SAI)
Community Org. Director	Insurance Claims Examiner	Probation and Parole Officer	Vocational-Rehab. Counselor
(SEA)	(SIE)	(SEC)	(SEC)
Consumer Affairs Director	Librarian (SAI)	Real Estate Appraiser (SCE)	Volunteer Services Director
(SER)Counselor/Therapist	Medical Assistant (SCR)	Recreation Director (SER)	(SEC)
(SAE)	Minister/Priest/Rabbi (SAI)	Registered Nurse (SIA)	
	Paralegal (SCE)		

Enterprising *(Persuaders)*

People who like to work with people, influencing, persuading, leading or managing for organizational goals or economic gain.

Are you?		Can you?	Like to?
self-confident	ambitious	initiate projects	make decisions
assertive	agreeable	convince people to do things	be elected to office
persuasive	talkative	your way	start your own business
energetic	extroverted	sell things	campaign politically
adventurous	spontaneous	give talks or speeches	meet important people
popular	optimistic	organize activities	have power or status
		lead a group	
		persuade others	

**Career Possibilities
(Holland Code):**

Advertising Executive (ESA)	Credit Analyst (EAS)	Foreign Service Officer (ESA)	Politician (ESA)
Advertising Sales Rep (ESR)	Customer Service Manager	Funeral Director (ESR)	Public Relations Rep (EAS)
Banker/Financial Planner (ESR)	(ESA)	Insurance Manager (ESC)	Retail Store Manager (ESR)
Branch Manager (ESA)	Education & Training Manager	Interpreter (ESA)	Sales Manager (ESA)
Business Manager (ESC)	(EIS)	Lawyer/Attorney (ESA)	Sales Representative (ERS)
Buyer (ESA)	Emergency Medical Technician	Lobbyist (ESA)	Social Service Director (ESA)
Chamber of Commerce Exec	(ESI)	Office Manager (ESR)	Stockbroker (ESI)
(ESA)	Entrepreneur (ESA)	Personnel Recruiter (ESR)	Tax Accountant (ECS)

Conventional *(Organizers)*

People who like to work with data, have clerical or numerical ability, carry out tasks in detail, or follow through on others' instructions.

Are you?		Can you?	Like to?
well-organized	practical	work well within a system	follow clearly defined
accurate	thrifty	do a lot of paper work in a short	procedures
numerically inclined	systematic	time	use data processing equipment
methodical	structured	keep accurate records	work with numbers
conscientious	polite	use a computer terminal	type or take shorthand
efficient	ambitious	write effective business letters	be responsible for details
conforming	obedient		collect or organize things
	persistent		

**Career Possibilities
(Holland Code):**

Abstractor (CSI)	Claims Adjuster (SEC)	Elementary School Teacher	Medical Records Technician
Accountant (CSE)	Computer Operator (CSR)	(SEC)	(CSE)
Administrative Assistant (ESC)	Congressional-District Aide (CES)	Financial Analyst (CSI)	Museum Registrar (CSE)
Budget Analyst (CER)	Cost Accountant (CES)	Insurance Manager (ESC)	Paralegal (SCE)
Business Manager (ESC)	Court Reporter (CSE)	Insurance Underwriter (CSE)	Safety Inspector (RCS)
Business Programmer (CRI)	Credit Manager (ESC)	Internal Auditor (ICR)	Tax Accountant (ECS)
Business Teacher (CSE)	Customs Inspector (CEI)	Kindergarten Teacher (ESC)	Tax Consultant (CES)
Catalog Librarian (CSE)	Editorial Assistant (CSI)		Travel Agent (ECS)

BIBLIOGRAPHY

Building and Construction

Allen, Edward, and Joseph Iano. *Fundamentals of Building Construction: Materials and Methods*. 6th ed., Wiley, 2014.

Ching, Francis D.K. *Building Construction Illustrated*. 5th ed., Wiley, 2014.

Feirer, Mark, and John Louis Feirer. *Carpentry & Building Construction*. McGraw-Hill Education, 2015.

Gopi, Satheesh. *Basic Civil Engineering*. Dorling Kindersley (India) Pvt. Ltd., 2010.

Jackson, Barbara J. *Construction Management Jumpstart*. 2nd ed., Wiley Technology Pub., 2010.

Kicklighter, Clois E., and Timothy L. Andera. *Modern Masonry: Brick, Block, Stone*. The Goodheart-Willcox Company, Inc., 2016.

Mahoney, William D. *Construction Inspection Manual*. BNI Building News, 2008.

NCCR. *Heavy Equipment Operations: Level 1: Trainee Guide*. Pearson Prentice Hall, 2012.

Oles, Thomas, et al. *Go with Me: 50 Steps to Landscape Thinking*. Amsterdam Academy of Architecture, 2014.

Rogers, Leon. *Basic Construction Management: the Superintendent's Job*. 5th ed., BuilderBooks, 2009.

Taylor, Gil L. *Construction Codes and Inspection Handbook*. McGraw-Hill, 2006.

Thompson, Ian H. *Landscape Architecture: a Very Short Introduction*. Oxford University Press, 2014.

Environment, Forestry, and Meteorology

Ahrens, C. Donald, and Robert Henson. *Meteorology Today an Introduction to Weather, Climate, and the Environment*. 11th ed., Cengage Learning, 2016.

Bolen, Eric G., and William Laughlin Robinson. *Wildlife Ecology and Management*. 5th ed., Pearson Education, Inc., 2003.

Fryxell, John M., et al. *Wildlife Ecology, Conservation, and Management*. 3rd ed., John Wiley & Sons Inc, 2014.

Grebner, Donald L., et al. *Introduction to Forestry and Natural Resources*. Elsevier, 2013.

Kareiva, Peter. *Conservation Science: Balancing the Needs of People and Nature*. 2nd ed., W H Freeman, 2017.

Smith, Zachary A. *Environmental Policy Paradox*. 7th Ed., Routledge, 2018.

Farming and Agriculture

Holechek, Jerry L., et al. *Range Management: Principles and Practices*. 6th ed.,
    Prentice Hall, 2011.
Echaore-McDavid, Susan, and Richard A. McDavid. *Career Opportunities in
    Agriculture, Food, and Natural Resources*. Facts On File, 2011.
Hodge, Geoff. *Practical Botany for Gardeners: over 3,000 Botanical Terms Explained
    and Explored*. The University of Chicago Press, 2013.
Walters, Charles. *Eco-Farm: an Acres U.S.A. Primer*. Acres U.S.A., 2003.

Park Rangers and Firefighters

Callan, Steven T. *Badges, Bears, and Eagles: the True-Life Adventures of a California
    Fish and Game Warden*. Coffeetown Press, 2013.
Farabee, Charles R. *National Park Ranger: an American Icon*. Roberts Rinehart
    Publishers, 2003.
Ford, John. *Suddenly, the Cider Didn't Taste so Good*. Islandport Press, 2012.
Giesler. *Fire & Life Safety Educator Navigate 2 Advantage Access: Principles and
    Practice*. Jones & Bartlett Learning, 2016.
Lankford, Andrea. *Ranger Confidential: Living, Working, and Dying in the National
    Parks*. FalconGuides, 2010.
Lee, Bob H., et al. *Backcountry Lawman: True Stories from a Florida Game Warden*.
    University Press of Florida, 2015.
Shapiro, Larry. *Fighting Fire: Trucks, Tools, and Tactics*. MBI Pub. Co. and
    Motorbooks, 2008.

INDEX

A

AALAS 28, 35

Academy of Geo-Professionals 89, 96

Accounting 324

Accreditation Board for Engineering and Technology 88, 96

Accredited Farm Manager 137

ACI International 80

Adapted Physical Education 325

Advocacy 124, 360

AFIS 309

AFM 137

Agricultural and Food Science Technicians 15

Agricultural and food scientists 1, 2, 3, 5, 6, 11, 12, 14, 15

Agricultural Business & Management 136

Agricultural Education 8, 26, 119, 135, 178, 192, 210, 297

Agricultural Engineer 123, 199

Agricultural Managers 15, 32, 128, 132

Agricultural Mechanization 8

Agricultural Production & Management 27

Agricultural Production Workers & Managers 136

Agricultural Science 1, 20, 165

Agricultural Scientist 199

Agricultural Supplies Retailing & Wholesaling 136

Agricultural Workers 32

Agriculture 1, 2, 10, 12, 16, 20, 21, 36, 38, 51, 52, 114, 120, 128, 136, 137, 142, 146, 161, 172, 187, 193, 204, 218, 248, 278, 279, 360

Agronomy 1, 10, 11, 20, 136, 145, 193

AIR 249

Air and Waste Management Association 127

Airlines Reporting Corporation 353, 359

Algebra 8, 41, 87, 119, 165, 192, 223, 282, 297, 324, 364

American Academy for Park and Recreation Administration 332

American Academy of Environmental Engineers 120, 127

American Academy of Water Resources Engineers 89, 96

American Alliance for Health, Physical Education, Recreation & Dance 332

American Association for Laboratory Animal Science 28, 35

American Association of Petroleum Geologists 232

American Bryological and Lichenological Society 51

American Camping Association 326, 332

American Concrete Pavement Association 80

American Farm Bureau Federation 136, 145

American Fisheries Society 167, 171, 186

American Helicopter Services and Aerial Firefighting Association 159

American History 297

americanhort 217

American Humane Association 35

American Institute of Architects 261

American Lifeguard Association 326, 332

American Meteorological Society 284, 292

American Nursery and Landscape Association 261

American Phytopathological Society 51

American Registry of Professional Animal Scientists 11

American Society for Horticultural Science 20, 211, 217

American Society for the Prevention of Cruelty to Animals 27, 35

American Society of Agronomy 10, 11, 20, 136, 145

American Society of Civil Engineers 88, 89, 94, 96

American Society of Farm Managers & Rural Appraisers 136, 145

American Society of Home Inspectors 104

American Society of Landscape Architects 257, 261

American Society of Plant Biologists 51
American Society of Plant Taxonomists 51
American Society of Travel Agents 359
AMS 284
Angledozer Operators 54
Animal Behavior 360
Animal care 30, 31
Animal caretakers 21, 22, 25, 28
animal foster caretakers 27
Animal keepers 24
animal laboratory caretakers 27
Animal-nursery workers 24
Animal Science 27, 28, 35
Animal scientists 4, 13, 14, 15
Animal trainers 24, 26, 30, 31
Animal Trappers 176
Animal Welfare Act 28
Applied Biology 8, 119, 135, 165, 178, 210,
    252, 267, 297, 364
Applied Communication 87, 102, 119, 238,
    310, 324, 352
Applied Math 8, 70, 87, 102, 119, 165, 210,
    223, 252, 267, 282
Applied Physics 87, 119, 338
Apprenticeship 22, 53, 67, 83, 98, 130, 148,
    174, 188, 205, 249, 294, 305, 335
Aquaculture farmers 131, 133
Aquaculturists 265
Aquarists 25
Aquatic Biology 268, 365
Arborists 207
Architects 248, 255, 256, 257, 261
Architectural Engineering 88, 103
Architectural Environmental Design 253
Architecture 52, 66, 82, 97, 204, 248, 253, 261,
    334
ARPAS 11
Arts 29, 56, 252, 325
ASCE 88
ASHS 211
ASPCA 27, 35
Associated Builders and Contractors 65
Associated General Contractors of America
    65, 80, 346
associate's degree 27, 136, 311, 319, 339
Associate Wildlife Biologist 366
Association of Collegiate Schools of
    Architecture 261

Association of Environmental & Engineering
    Geologists 127
Association of Fish & Wildlife Agencies 171
Association of National Park Rangers 303
Association of Union Constructors 346
Association of Zoos and Aquariums 35
Athletes 331
Athletic Trainers 331
Atmospheric Science 291, 292
Atmospheric Scientists 285, 286, 287
Atnip-Orms Center 319
Automotive Club Travel Counselors 350
AWA 28
AWB 366

B

Banking 238
BIA 309
biochemistry 7, 9, 48, 267
Biochemists 15
Biological Sciences 373
Biological Scientist 123, 199
Biological Technicians 15
Biology 1, 8, 26, 27, 41, 42, 50, 87, 119, 135,
    165, 178, 192, 210, 252, 262, 267, 268, 275,
    276, 297, 360, 364, 365, 373
Biophysicists 15
biotechnology specialists 3
Bird Trappers 176
blockmasons 73, 76
Blueprint Reading 70, 87, 102, 119, 252, 338
Bookkeeping 135, 238, 352
Boston University 110, 275
Botanical Society of America 42, 51
Botanist 47, 199
Botany 42, 50, 51, 365
Brickmasons 73, 76
Brigham Young University 373
Bryn Mawr College 224
Building & Grounds Maintenance 210
Building inspectors 98, 99, 101, 107
Building Trades Association 65, 80
bulldozer operator 53, 54, 56, 57, 58
bulldozer or construction equipment operator
    52
Bureau of Indian Affairs 309
Business Law 238, 325

Business Math 325, 352
Business operations specialists 241, 242

C

CAD 86, 118, 250, 251, 252, 253, 344
Calculus 41, 87, 119, 364
California Institute of Technology 231
Cal Poly 260
Career Development & Placement Services 20, 145
Carnegie Mellon University 95
Carpentry 56, 102
Cartographer 228
CBM 284
CCM 284
Cementers 69
Cement masons 66, 67, 70, 71, 72, 73, 74, 76
Center for Environmental Science 373
Center for Rural Affairs 145
Certified Broadcast Meteorologist Program 284
Certified Consulting Meteorologist Program 284
Certified Grounds Manager 211
Certified Grounds Technician 211
Certified Park and Recreation Professional 298
Certified Wildlife Biologist 366
Cetologists 265
CGM 211
CGT 211
Chemical Engineer 123
Chemical Technicians 15
Chemist 123
Chemistry 1, 8, 41, 87, 119, 135, 165, 178, 192, 210, 223, 252, 267, 282, 297, 364
Civil Engineering 88, 229
Civil engineers 82, 83, 84, 86, 88, 89, 90, 91, 92
Civil Technology 88
Claims adjusters, examiners, and investigators 241, 242
Clemson University 202, 257
Coating inspectors 108
College Preparatory 8, 87, 119, 165, 192, 223, 267, 282, 352
Colorado State University 202, 291, 373

COMET 287
Commercial fishing 173, 180
Community College 98, 130, 148, 234, 305, 321, 348
community-supported agriculture 130, 138
Composition 87
computer-aided design 86, 118, 250, 338
Computer Science 87, 119, 192, 238, 267, 282, 352, 364
Computer Technology 352
concrete finishers 73, 74, 76
Conservation 15, 20, 45, 46, 47, 123, 187, 189, 190, 191, 193, 196, 197, 198, 203, 302, 360, 373
Conservation Biology 373
Conservation education foresters 190
Conservation Science Institute 193
Conservation Scientist 123
Construction and building inspectors 97, 101, 103, 105, 106, 107
Construction and extraction occupations 105, 107
Construction/Building Inspection 103
Construction/Building Technology 103
Construction Education Services 65, 80, 346
Construction Engineers 85, 92
Construction Equipment Operator 342
Construction Inspectors 100
Construction trades workers 60, 62, 74, 75, 342
Cornell University 19, 50, 95, 260, 291
Council for Agricultural Science and Technology 20
Council of Landscape Architectural Registration Boards 261
CPRP 298
Crafts 325
Crawler-Tractor Operators 55
criminal investigators 308, 313, 315, 319
Criminology 311
Crop farmers 130, 133
Crop Science 10, 193
CRS 174, 205
CSA 130, 138, 142
customer service experts 347
Customs Inspector 168
CWB 366

D

Dairy farmers 131
Dairy Science 10
deputy sheriffs 307
Detectives 304, 308, 313, 315
Diving Fishers 176
doctorate degree 268
Drafting 87, 102, 119, 252, 338
Driver Training 152, 310
Duke University 275
DVM 6, 8, 10

E

Earth Science 41, 119, 223, 283, 364
Ecology 42, 275, 365, 373
Economic botanists 37
Economics 87, 135, 238
ECS 348
Electrical, Electronic & Communication
    Engineering Technology 103
Electrical Inspectors 100, 108, 113
Electrician Training 103
Elevator Inspectors 100, 108
Emergency Services Training Institute 159
Employee Services Management Association
    332
Energy Engineer 123
Engineering Design 88
Engineering, General 120
Engineering & Technology Pathway 120
Engineers 62, 63, 65, 82, 85, 88, 89, 90, 91, 92,
    94, 96, 114, 115, 116, 118, 120, 121, 122,
    123, 127
Entomology 10
Environmental and Engineering Geophysical
    Society 232
Environmental Engineer 199
Environmental Health 120, 123, 365
Environmental Health Engineering 120
Environmental Health & Safety Officer 123
Environmental Health & Safety Specialist
    123
Environmental & Pollution Control
    Technology 120
Environmental Science 1, 27, 42, 120, 123,
    365, 373

Environmental Science Technician 123
Environmental Scientists and Specialists 15
Environmental Service Systems Pathway 120
environmental studies 36, 41, 123, 142, 193
esa 51, 374
ESA 321
ESC 234
ESR 130, 294
Evolution 275
Exercise Physiologists 331

F

Farmers 15, 32, 128, 129, 130, 132, 134, 138,
    139, 140, 141, 145
Farm general managers 141
Farm Manager 137, 199
farm operators 128
Farm & Ranch Management 136
Farm Service Agency 146
FBI 309
Federal Bureau of Investigation 308, 309, 311
Federal Law Enforcement Training Center
    319
Finance, General 238
Financial Support Services 238
Fine-Grade-Bulldozer Operators 55
Firefighters 147, 148, 150, 151, 153, 154, 155,
    156
Fire fighting and prevention workers 154, 156
Fire inspectors 109, 150
Fire Protection Publications 159
First Aid Training 152, 178, 297, 310
Fisheries Management 166
Fisheries Science 373
Fishers 172, 173, 175, 176, 177, 180
Fish farmers 141
Fish & Game Warden 182, 199
Fishing and hunting workers 173, 180, 181,
    182
Fitness Trainers and Instructors 331
Florida International University 41
Florida State University 246
Food and Drug Administration 20
food chemistry 7, 9
food engineering 7, 9
food microbiology 7, 9
Food Science 1, 15

food scientist 7, 9

Food scientists and technologists 4, 13, 14, 15

Foods & Nutrition Science 10

Foods & Nutrition Studies, General 10

Foreign Languages 352

Forest ecologists 190

Foresters 15, 45, 46, 187, 188, 189, 190, 191, 193, 194, 195, 196, 198, 201, 203

Forest firefighters 150, 151

Forest Guild 203

Forest Harvesting & Production Technology 193

forest rangers 167

Forestry, General 365

Forestry Worker 199

Forest Service 47, 193, 203, 303

Future Farmers of America 145

G

Garden Club of America 217

Gardeners 204, 205, 206, 208, 209, 212

G.E.D. 22, 53, 174, 205, 335

Geographer 228

Geographic Information System 46, 198

Geography 178, 223, 224, 282, 297, 298, 352, 364

Geological Engineering 224

Geological Sciences 231, 232

Geological Society of America 232

Geologists 127, 218, 219, 220, 221, 222, 224, 225, 232

geology 56, 78, 79, 218, 223, 224, 225, 229, 230, 231, 252, 253, 263, 297

Geometry 41, 87, 119, 165, 192, 223, 282, 297, 364

Geophysical Engineering 224

Geophysicists 218, 219, 232

Geophysics 224

Georgia Institute of Technology 95

Georgia State University 246

Geoscientists 226, 227, 228

Geotechnical Engineers 85, 92

GIS 46, 198, 201, 222, 225, 251, 256, 371

global positioning system 151

Government Travel Clerks 350

GPS 64, 94, 143, 151, 201, 222, 225, 309, 317

greenskeeper 207

Groundskeepers 204, 206, 207

Grounds maintenance workers 209, 213, 214

H

Harvard University 19, 272

Hazardous Waste Manager 123

Hazmat specialists 150

Heating, Air Conditioning & Refrigeration Mechanics & Repair 103

History 223, 297, 298, 310, 352

Home inspectors 108, 111

Horse trainers 141

Horticulture Science 10, 136

Horticulture Services Operations & Management 136, 193, 210

horticulturists 211

Hospitality 21, 293, 320, 347, 353

Hotel Travel Clerks 350

Human & Animal Physiology 365

Humane Society of the United States 35

Humanities 119

Human Services 320

hunters 163, 165, 172, 173, 174, 176, 177, 178, 179, 180, 371

Hunter Services Department 186

HVAC 98

HVACR systems 108

Hydraulic Engineers 85

Hydrologists 221

hydrology 218, 219, 279, 283

I

Icthyologists 265

IFT 11

Independent Automotive Damage Appraisers Association 239, 247

Independent Insurance Agents and Brokers of America 247

Industrial Truck Association 65

Institute of Food and Agricultural Sciences 20

Institute of Food Technologists 11, 20

Institute of Professional Environmental Practice 127

Insurance appraisers 241, 242

Insurance claims adjusters and examiners 233, 234, 235, 236, 237, 239 insurance claims analysts 233

insurance claims assessors 233

insurance claims investigators 233

Insurance Institute of America 239, 247

Insurance & Risk Management 238

Insurance Underwriter 242

Integrated Automated Fingerprint
Identification System 309

International Agriculture 10, 136

International Airlines Travel Agency Network
353, 359

International Association of Bridge,
Structural, Ornamental, and Reinforcing
Iron Workers 346

International Association of Chiefs of Police
319

International Association of Electrical
Inspectors 113

International Association of Fire Fighters 159

International Association of Women in Fire
and Emergency Services 159

International City/County Management
Association 113

International Code Council 113

International Fire Service Training
Association 159

International Marine Animal Trainer's
Association 35

International Masonry Institute 80

International Union of Bricklayers and Allied
Craftworkers 80

International Union of Operating Engineers
63, 65

Internship 2, 37, 83, 115, 130, 234, 249, 279,
321, 361

Iowa State University 50

IRC 115

IRE 83, 219, 263

IRS 2, 37, 219, 263, 279, 361

J

Johns Hopkins University 224

K

Kansas State University 260

Kennel attendants 24

Keyboarding 238

L

LAAB 254

Laboratory Animal Caretakers 32

laboratory assistants 222

Laborers' International Union of North
America 65, 72, 80

Landscape Architect 199, 254, 257

Landscape Architectural Accreditation Board
253

Landscape Architecture 253, 261

Landscape Architecture Foundation 261

Landscape laborers 207

Landscapers 207, 209

landscape specialists 207

Landscaping workers 207

LARE 254

Law 147, 161, 166, 170, 238, 253, 293, 298,
303, 304, 311, 314, 315, 319, 325

Law Enforcement 166, 170, 298, 303, 311, 319

Law enforcement workers 314, 315

Leadership in Energy and Environmental
Design 89

LEED 89

liability assessors 233

Life Sciences 50, 275, 360, 373

Life scientists 12, 15, 45, 46, 196, 198, 269,
271, 368, 369

Line Fishers 176

Literature 282

LIUNA 72

Livestock ranchers 140

Logistics 82, 347, 353

Louisiana State University 260

M

Machining Technology 70

Maintenance Cement Masons 69

Manufacturing Production Process
Development Pathway 120

MarineBio 277

Marine Biological Laboratory 277

Marine Biologist 272

Marine Biology 275, 276

marine conservation 262

Marine Science Institute 276

Marine Technology Society 186, 277

Masonry 66, 70, 73, 74, 75, 80

Masonry workers 74, 75

Massachusetts Institute of Technology 95, 231, 291

Mathematics 1, 36, 82, 87, 114, 119, 120, 135, 152, 187, 210, 218, 238, 252, 262, 278, 282, 338, 352, 360

Mechanical Drawing 71, 87, 252, 338

Mechanical Inspectors 100, 108

Meeting, Convention, and Event Planners 331

Metallurgical/Materials Engineer 228

Metal/Plastic Working Machine Operator 342

Metals Technology 71, 338

Meteorologists 278, 279, 280, 281, 284

Meteorology 278, 283, 289, 291, 292

Michigan State University 50, 202, 373

microbiology 7, 9, 16, 262, 267

Mineralogists 221

Mining & Geological Engineer 228

Mycologists 39

N

NAPPS 28, 35

NARST 277

NAS 277

National Action Council for Minorities in Engineering 96

National Agri-Marketing Association 145

National Aquarium Society 277

National Association for Research in Science Teaching 277

National Association of Career Travel Agents 359

National Association of Commercial Building Inspectors and Thermographers 113

National Association of Home Builders 80, 113, 346

National Association of Independent Insurance Adjusters 239, 247

National Association of Insurance and Financial Advisors 247

National Association of Police Organizations 319

National Association of Professional Insurance Agents 239, 247

National Association of Professional Pet Sitters 28, 35

National Association of Reinforcing Steel Contractors 346

National Association of State Foresters 203

National Association of University Fisheries and Wildlife Programs 171

National Center for Construction Education and Research 57, 65, 80, 113, 346

National Concrete Masonry Association 80

National Conference of States on Building Codes & Standards 113

National Council for Therapeutic Recreation Certification 332

National Council of Structural Engineers Associations 96

National Crime Information Center 309

National FFA Organization 145

National Fire Protection Association 155, 159

National Fisheries Institute 186

National Fraternal Order of Police 319

National Garden Clubs, Inc. 217

National Institute of Building Inspectors 113

National Institute of Food and Agriculture 146

National Institutes of Health 2, 12

National Marine Fisheries Service 186

National Oceanographic and Atmospheric Administration 292

National Park Service 167, 297, 298, 299, 300

National Recreation and Park Association 298, 303, 325, 326

National Rifle Association of America 186

National Society of Black Engineers 96

National Society of Professional Engineers 96

National Sustainable Agriculture Information Service 146

National Terrazzo & Mosaic Association 81

National Volunteer Fire Council 160

National Weather Association 292

National Weather Service 287, 290

National Wildlife Federation 366, 374

Natural Resources Conservation Service 20, 203

Natural Resources Law Enforcement & Protective Services 298

Natural Resources Management & Policy 166

natural sciences 8, 119, 162, 165, 192, 266, 296, 366
Nature Conservancy 48, 277, 366, 374
NCIC 309
NEA 346
Net Fishers 175
New York University 246
Nicholas School of the Environment 275
NIH 2, 12
North American Wildlife Enforcement Officers Association 171
North Carolina State University 202, 215
NRPA 326
Nursery and greenhouse managers 133
Nursery managers 141

O

Ocean Engineering 224
Ocean fishers 174
Oceanic Sciences 291
Oceanic Society 277
Oceanographer 228
Oceanography 224, 275, 283
Ohio State University 260
Oklahoma State University 159
Operating engineers 59, 60, 61, 62
Operative Plasterers' & Cement Masons' Intl. Association 81
Oregon Institute of Marine Biology 275
Oregon State University 202
Organic farmers 141
Ornamental Horticulture 210, 252
outdoor maintenance specialists 204

P

Paleobotanists 39
Paleontological Society 232
Paleontologists 221
Park Law Enforcement Association 303
Park Ranger 168, 199, 301
Parks and Recreation Management 298
Parks, Recreation & Leisure Facilities Management 325
Parks, Recreation & Leisure Studies 325
Paving and surfacing equipment operators 62
Penn State University 50, 200, 231, 291

Personal care and service occupations 30, 329, 331
Personal Financial Advisor 242
Pesticide application specialists 208
Petroleum Engineer 123, 228
Petroleum geologists 221
Pet shop attendants 24
Pet sitters 22, 24
PGMS 211
Photography 223, 252
Physical Education 152, 310, 325, 326, 332
Physical Education Teaching & Coaching 325
Physical Science 119, 179, 223, 282
Physical scientists 226, 286, 288
Physics 8, 41, 87, 119, 120, 165, 179, 267, 282, 338, 364
physiology 7, 9, 36, 41, 273, 360
Pile-driver operators 59, 60, 62
Pipefitting 103
Planetary Sciences 231, 291
Plan examiners 109
Plant Biology 50, 231, 291
plant conservation 7, 9
Plant pathologists 39
plant pathology 7, 9, 16, 17
plant physiology 7, 9
Plant Sciences, General 10
Plant scientists 5, 39
Plumbing Inspectors 100, 109
Police officers 304, 305, 306, 308, 309, 312, 313
Police Science 298, 311
Portland Cement Association 77, 81
postsecondary degree 103, 136
Pot Fishers 175
Poultry farmers 140
Poultry Science 10
Predatory Animal Hunters 176
Professional Anglers Association 186
Professional Grounds Management Society 211, 217
Professional Landcare Network 217
Psychology 238, 297, 310
Public Administration 97, 293, 304
public aquarium specialists 27
Public History 298
Public Safety 147, 161, 293, 304, 310
public safety officials 191, 309

public safety workers 147
Public works inspectors 109
Purdue University 50, 95, 260

R

railroad police 313, 315
Ranchers 15, 32, 128, 132, 140
Range Manager 182, 199
RCE 174, 205
RCI 174, 205
RCS 22, 98
Real Estate Appraiser 242
REC 53, 98
Recreational Therapists 331
Recreation program directors 320, 321, 322,
    323, 324
Recreation workers 329, 331
Rehabilitation Counselors 331
REI 130, 305, 335
Reinforcing metal workers 337
RES 67, 148, 162
RIS 188
Robert H. Lurie Engineering Center 95
Rosenstiel School of Marine and Atmospheric
    Science 291
Rutgers State University 19

S

Sales & Service Pathway 353
sanitation engineering 83
Scarifier Operators 54
SCE 305
School and Career Counselors 331
School of Marine Sciences 275
School of Meteorology 292
SCR 305
Scraper Operators 55
Scripps Institute of Oceanography 275
SEC 305
Security 147, 161, 293, 304, 311
Seismological Society of America 232
Seismologists 221
Seismology 218, 224
SER 305
Sheet Metal Worker 342
Sheriffs 307

Shop Math 71, 102, 338
Shop Mechanics 338
Silviculturists 190
Social and community service managers 328,
    330
Social Studies 41, 120, 310, 325, 352
Social Workers 331
Society for Range Management 203
Society of American Foresters 201, 203
Society of American Registered Architects 261
Society of Exploration Geophysicists 232
Society of Hispanic Professional Engineers 96
Society of State Directors of Health, Physical
    Educ. & Recreation 333
Society of Women Engineers 96
Sociology 297, 310
Soil and plant scientists 13, 14, 15
Soil and Water Conservation Society 20, 203
soil chemistry 7, 9
Soil conservationists 190, 195
Soil Sciences 10
Soil Science Society of America 10, 11
Soil Scientist 199
soil spectrometers 191
Solid Waste Association of North America 127
Spear Fishers 176
Specialty Travel Agents Association 359
Specification inspectors 109
Speech 252, 297, 310, 352
Sport & Fitness Administration/Management
    325
Sports Competitors 331
SSSA 11
Stable attendants 25
Stanford University 95, 231, 275
State highway patrol officers 307
state troopers 307
Step Finishers 69
St. Joseph's University 246
Stonemasons 73, 76
Stony Brook University 275
Stratigraphers 221
structural engineering 77, 83
Structural Engineers 85, 92, 96
Structural metal workers 334, 335, 337, 340,
    342
Structural steel workers 337
SWAT 307

T

Technical Education 22, 53, 67, 98, 130, 335
Technology 1, 10, 20, 36, 70, 71, 77, 82, 88, 95, 96, 103, 114, 120, 158, 186, 187, 193, 218, 231, 244, 258, 262, 273, 277, 278, 291, 302, 317, 338, 352, 360
Technology Student Association 96
Temple University 246
Terrazzo masons 74
Terrazzo Workers 69
Texas A&M University 159, 260, 291, 373
Texas Engineering Extension Service 159
Texas Rangers 310
Therapeutic Recreation 325, 332
Torrey Botanical Society 42, 51
Tourism 21, 293, 320, 347, 353
Transit police 307
transportation engineering 83
Transportation Engineers 85, 92
Transportation Specialist 355
trappers 165, 172, 173, 174, 175, 176, 177, 178, 179, 180, 182
Travel agents 347, 348, 349, 351, 355
Travel Institute 359
Travel Services Marketing Operations 353
Travel-Tourism Management 353
Travel & Tourism Pathway 353
Tree Care Industry Association 217
Tree-fruit-and-nut crop farmers 140
tree service specialists 207
Trigonometry 41, 87, 120, 192, 223, 282
Tufts University 19

U

UCAR 287
Uniformed police officers 307
United Brotherhood of Carpenters 81
United Construction Workers 65
United States Coast Guard 179
United Steelworkers of America 346
University Corporation for Atmospheric Research 287, 292
University of Arizona 16, 50, 231, 373
University of California 16, 19, 50, 95, 231, 275, 291
University of Colorado 231

University of Florida 19, 373
University of Georgia 202, 246, 260
University of Illinois 19, 95, 246
University of Maine 275
University of Massachusetts 19
University of Miami 291
University of Michigan 95, 231
University of Minnesota 19, 373
University of Missouri 50, 374
University of Oklahoma 292
University of Oregon 275
University of Pennsylvania 246, 260
University of Tennessee 374
University of Texas 95, 232, 246, 257, 276
University of Washington 202, 276, 292
University of Wisconsin 19, 50, 77, 202, 232, 246
University of Wyoming 51
Urban foresters 190
U.S. Army Corps of Engineers Research and Development Center 127
U.S. Botanic Garden 51
USDA 2, 12, 146, 203, 370
U.S. Department of Agriculture 16, 20, 38, 51
U.S. Environmental Protection Agency 137
U.S. Fire Administration 159, 160
U.S. Fish and Wildlife Service 171, 186
U.S. Forest Service 303
US Geological Survey 224

V

Vegetable Farmers 140
veterinarian 8, 10, 33
Veterinary Assistants 32
veterinary medicine 6, 8, 10
veterinary technicians 27
Veterinary Technologists 32
Virginia Tech 16, 171, 202, 260
vocational program 209
volunteer firefighters 153, 155
Volunteer Work 22, 130, 148, 162, 188, 249, 294, 305, 361

W

Water & Wastewater Engineer 123, 199
welder 169

welding 335, 336, 339, 344, 345
Wildlife Biologist 35, 199, 366
wildlife biology 275, 291, 361, 365, 373
Wildlife Ecology 373
Wildlife Sciences 373, 374
Wildlife Society 171, 374
Wildlife & Wildlands Management 166, 365
Wildlife & Wildlands Science 42
Wind Energy Engineer 123
Woodshop 71, 102
Worldwide Fund for Nature 366, 374

World Wildlife Fund 124, 374

Y

YMCA of the USA 333

Z

zookeepers 21, 27
Zoology, General 10, 365

MÄRCHEN
DER BRÜDER GRIMM

MÄRCHEN
DER BRÜDER GRIMM
BILDER VON NIKOLAUS HEIDELBACH

BELTZ & GELBERG

Die Brüder Grimm:
Jacob Grimm, geboren 4. 1. 1785 in Hanau, gestorben 20. 9. 1863 in Berlin;
Wilhelm Grimm, geboren 24. 2. 1786 in Hanau, gestorben 16. 12. 1859 in Berlin.
Die Auswahl der Märchen für diese Ausgabe
erfolgte meistenteils auf der Grundlage der zweiten, verbesserten Auflage von 1819
und teils auf der Grundlage der vollständigen, dritten Auflage von 1837
sowie den Auflagen von 1840, 1843 und 1850; einige Texte wurden der Erstauflage von 1812 entnommen.
Alle Texte wurden neu durchgesehen und heutiger Rechtschreibung behutsam angepaßt.
Redaktion Hermann Klippel, Korrektur Maria Rosken.
Die Auswahl der Märchen besorgte Nikolaus Heidelbach.

2. Auflage, 21.–40. Tausend, 1995
© 1995 Beltz Verlag, Weinheim und Basel
Programm Beltz & Gelberg, Weinheim
Alle Rechte vorbehalten
Einband und Ausstattung von Nikolaus Heidelbach
Gesamtherstellung Druckhaus Beltz, 69494 Hemsbach
Printed in Germany
ISBN 3 407 79684 6

In den alten Zeiten, wo das Wünschen noch geholfen hat …

6 *Des Schneiders Daumerling Wanderschaft*

Des Schneiders Daumerling Wanderschaft

Ein Schneider hatte einen Sohn, der war klein geraten und nicht größer als ein Daumen, darum hieß er der Daumerling. Er hatte aber Courage im Leibe und sagte zu seinem Vater: »Vater, ich soll und muß in die Welt hinaus.« – »Recht, mein Sohn«, sprach der Alte, nahm eine Stopfnadel und machte am Licht einen Knoten von Siegellack daran: »Da hast du auch einen Degen mit auf den Weg.« Nun wollte das Schneiderlein noch einmal mitessen, ging in die Küche, um zu sehen, was die Frau Mutter zu guter Letzt gekocht hätte. Es war aber eben angerichtet, und die Schüssel stand auf dem Herd. Da sprach es: »Nun, was essen wir heute?« – »Sieh selbst zu«, sagte die Mutter. Da sprang es auf den Herd und guckte in die Schüssel, weil es aber den Hals zu weit hineinstreckte, faßte es der Dampf von der Speise und trieb es zum Schornstein hinaus, bis es endlich wieder herabsank.

So kam das Schneiderlein in die Welt hinein, zog umher und ging bei einem Meister in die Arbeit, da war ihm aber das Essen nicht gut genug. »Frau Meisterin, wenn Sie uns kein besser Essen gibt«, sagte der Daumerling, »geh ich fort und schreib morgen früh mit Kreide an Ihre Haustüre: ›Kartoffel zuviel, Fleisch zuwenig, adies, Herr Kartoffelkönig!‹« – »Was willst du wohl, du Hüpferling«, sagte die Meisterin, ward bös, ergriff einen Lappen und wollte losschlagen. Mein Schneiderlein aber kroch behende unter den Fingerhut, guckte unten hervor und streckte der Frau Meisterin die Zunge heraus. Sie hob schnell den Fingerhut auf und wollte ihn packen, aber der Daumerling hüpfte in die Lappen, und wie die Meisterin die Lappen auseinander warf und ihn suchte, machte er sich in den Tischritz. »He, he! Frau Meisterin«, rief er und steckte den Kopf in die Höhe, und wenn sie zuschlagen wollte, sprang er immer in die Schublade hinunter. Endlich aber erwischte sie ihn doch und jagte ihn zum Haus hinaus.

Das Schneiderlein wanderte und kam in einen großen Wald, da begegnete ihm ein Haufen Räuber, die hatten vor, des Königs Schatz zu stehlen. Als sie das Schneiderlein sahen, dachten sie, so einer kann uns viel nützen. »Heda«, rief einer, »du gewaltiger Kerl, willst du mit zur Schatzkammer gehen, du kannst dich hineinschleichen und das Geld herauswerfen.« Der Daumling besann sich, endlich sagte er ja und ging mit zu der Schatzkammer. Da besah er die Türe oben und unten, ob kein Ritzen darin wäre, glücklicherweise fand er einen und wollte gleich einsteigen, aber die eine Schildwache sprach zur andern: »Was kriecht da für eine garstige Spinne? Die will ich tot treten.« – »Ei, laß doch das arme Tier gehen«, sagte die andere, »es hat dir ja nichts getan.« Nun kam der Daumerling durch den Ritz glücklich in die Schatzkammer, machte das Fenster, unter welchem die Räuber standen, auf und warf ihnen einen Taler nach dem andern hinaus. Als das Schneiderlein in der besten Arbeit war, hörte es den König kommen, der seine Schatzkammer besehen wollte, und es mußte sich einstweilen verkriechen. Der König merkte, daß viel harte Taler fehlten, konnte aber nicht begreifen, wer es sollte gestohlen haben, da die Schlösser in gutem Stand waren und alles wohl verwahrt schien. Da ging er wieder fort und sprach zu den zwei Wachen: »Habt acht, es ist einer hinter dem Geld!« Als der Daumerling nun seine Arbeit von neuem anfing, hörten sie das Geld drinnen sich regen und klingeln: klipp, klapp, klipp, klapp, sprangen geschwind hinein und wollten den Dieb greifen. Aber das Schneiderlein, das sie kommen hörte, war noch geschwinder, sprang in eine Ecke und deckte einen Taler über sich, so daß nichts von ihm zu sehen war, neckte die Wachen und rief: »Hier bin ich!« Die Wachen liefen dahin, wie sie aber ankamen, war es schon in eine andere Ecke unter einen Taler gehüpft und rief: »He! Hier bin ich!« Die Wachen sprangen eilends zurück, es war aber längst in einer dritten Ecke und rief: »He! Hier bin ich!« Und so hatte es sie zu Narren und trieb sie so lange in der Schatzkammer herum, bis sie müd waren und davongingen. Nun warf es die Taler nach und nach alle hinaus, und den letzten schnellte es mit aller Macht, hüpfte dann selber noch behendiglich darauf und flog damit durchs Fenster hinab. Die Räuber machten ihm große Lobsprüche: »Du großer Held«, sagten sie, »willst du unser Hauptmann werden?« Es bedankte sich aber und sagte, es müßte erst die Welt sehen. Sie teilten nun die Beute, das Schneiderlein aber wollte nur einen Kreuzer, weil es nicht mehr tragen konnte.

Darauf schnallte es seinen Degen wieder um den Leib, sagte den Räubern guten Tag und nahm den Weg zwischen die Beine. Bei etlichen Meistern ging es in Arbeit, endlich aber, weil's mit dem Handwerk nicht recht fort wollte, verdingte es sich als Hausknecht in einem Gasthof. Die Mägde aber konnten es nicht leiden, denn es sah alles, was sie heimlich taten, ohne daß sie es sehen konnten, und gab es bei der Herrschaft an, was sie sich von den Tellern weggenommen und aus dem Keller für sich mitgebracht hatten. Da sprachen sie: »Wart, wir wollen dir's auch einmal eintränken«, und verabredeten untereinander, ihm einen Schabernack anzutun. Als die eine nun im Garten mähte und den Daumling da herumspringen und an den Kräutern hinauf- und hinabkriechen sah, mähte sie ihn mit dem Gras schnell zusammen, band alles in ein großes Tuch und warf es daheim den Kühen vor. Nun war eine große schwarze darunter, die verschluckte ihn mit, ohne ihm weh zu tun; da unten gefiel's ihm aber schlecht, denn es war ganz finster und brannte da kein Licht. Als die Kuh gemolken wurde, da rief er:

>Strip, strap, stroll,
  ist der Eimer bald voll?«

Aber über dem Melken wurde er nicht verstanden. Hernach trat der Hausherr in den Stall und sprach: »Morgen soll die Kuh da geschlachtet werden.« Da ward dem Daumerling angst, daß er laut rief: »Ich bin ja hier!« Der Herr hörte ihn wohl, wußte aber nicht, wo die Stimme herkam, und sprach: »Wo bist du?« – »Ei, in der schwarzen«, antwortete er, aber der Herr verstand nicht, was das heißen sollte, und ging fort. Am andern Morgen wurde die Kuh geschlachtet, glücklicherweise traf bei dem Zerhacken und Zerlegen den Daumling kein Hieb, aber er geriet unter das Wurstfleisch. Wie nun der Metzger herbeitrat und seine Arbeit anfing, schrie er aus Leibeskräften: »Hackt nicht zu tief! Hackt nicht zu tief! Ich stecke ja drunter!« Vor dem Lärmen aber hörte das kein Mensch, da hatte der arme Daumling nun seine Not, aber Not macht Beine, und da sprang er so behend zwischen den Hackmessern durch, daß ihn keins anrührte und er mit heiler Haut davonkam. Aber entspringen konnte er auch nicht, es war keine andere Auskunft, er mußte sich mit den Speckbrocken in eine Blutwurst hinunter stopfen lassen. Da war das Quartier etwas eng, und dazu ward er noch in den Schornstein zum Räuchern aufgehängt, wo ihm Zeit und Weile gewaltig lang wurde. Endlich im Winter wurde er heruntergeholt, weil die Wurst einem Gast sollte vorgesetzt werden. Als sie nun die Frau Wirtin in Scheiben schnitt, nahm er sich in acht, daß er den Kopf nicht zu weit vorstreckte, damit ihm etwa der Hals nicht mit abgeschnitten würde, endlich ersah er seinen Vorteil, machte sich Luft und sprang heraus.

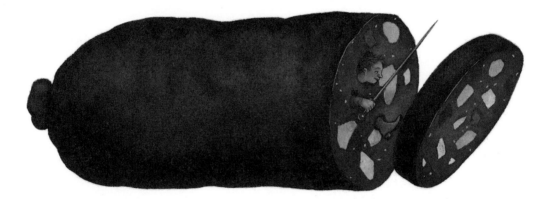

In dem Hause aber, wo es ihm so übel ergangen war, wollte das Schneiderlein nicht länger bleiben, sondern es begab sich gleich wieder auf die Wanderung. Aber als es durch ein Feld ging, kam es einem Fuchs in den Weg, der schnappte es in Gedanken auf. »Ei, Herr Fuchs«, rief's Schneiderlein, »ich bin's ja, der in Euerm Hals steckt, laßt mich wieder frei.« – »Du hast recht«, antwortete der Fuchs, »an dir hab ich doch soviel als nichts; versprichst du mir die Hühner in deines Vaters Hof, so will ich dich loslassen.« – »Von Herzen gern«, antwortete der Daumling, »die Hühner sollst du alle haben; das gelobe ich dir.« Da ließ ihn der Fuchs wieder los und trug ihn selber heim. Als der Vater sein Söhnlein wieder sah, gab er dem Fuchs gern die Hühner. »Dafür bring ich dir auch ein schön Stück Geld mit«, sprach der Daumling zu seinem Vater und reichte ihm den Kreuzer, den er auf seiner Wanderschaft erworben hatte.

   »Warum hat aber der Fuchs die armen Piephühner zu fressen kriegt?« – »Du Narr, deinem Vater wird ja sein Kind lieber sein als die Hühner auf dem Hof.«   1819

Der undankbare Sohn

Es saß einmal ein Mann mit seiner Frau vor der Haustür, und sie hatten ein gebraten Huhn vor sich stehen und wollten das zusammen verzehren. Da sah der Mann, wie sein alter Vater daherkam. Geschwind nahm er das Huhn und versteckte es, weil er ihm nichts davon gönnte. Der Alte kam, tat einen Trunk und ging fort. Nun wollte der Sohn das gebratene Huhn wieder auf den Tisch tragen, aber als er danach griff, war es eine große Kröte geworden, die sprang ihm ins Angesicht und saß da und ging nicht wieder weg, und wenn sie jemand wegtun wollte, sah sie ihn giftig an, als wollt' sie ihm ins Angesicht springen, so daß keiner sie anzurühren getraute. Und die Kröte mußte der undankbare Sohn alle Tage füttern, sonst fraß sie ihm aus seinem Angesicht, und also ging er in der Welt hin und her.

1819

Schneeweißchen und Rosenrot

Eine arme Witwe, die lebte einsam in einem Hüttchen, und vor dem Hüttchen war ein Garten, darin standen zwei Rosenbäumchen, davon trug das eine weiße, das andere rote Rosen; und sie hatte zwei Kinder, die glichen den beiden Rosenbäumchen, und das eine hieß Schneeweißchen, das andere Rosenrot. Sie waren aber so fromm und gut, so arbeitsam und unverdrossen, als je zwei Kinder auf der Welt gewesen sind. Schneeweißchen war nur stiller und sanfter als Rosenrot. Rosenrot sprang lieber in den Wiesen und Feldern umher, suchte Blumen und fing Sommervögel. Schneeweißchen aber saß daheim bei der Mutter, half ihr im Hauswesen oder las ihr vor, wenn nichts zu tun war. Die beiden Kinder hatten einander so lieb, daß sie sich immer an den Händen faßten, sooft sie zusammen ausgingen, und wenn Schneeweißchen sagte: »Wir wollen uns nicht verlassen«, so antwortete Rosenrot: »So lange wir leben nicht«, und die Mutter setzte hinzu: »Was das eine hat, soll's mit dem andern teilen.«

Oft liefen sie im Walde allein umher und sammelten rote Beeren, aber kein Tier tat ihnen etwas zuleid, sondern sie kamen vertraulich herbei; das Häschen fraß ein Kohlblatt aus ihren Händen; das Reh graste an ihrer Seite; der Hirsch sprang ganz lustig vorbei; die Vögel blieben auf den Ästen sitzen und sangen, was sie wußten. Kein Unfall traf sie. Wenn sie sich im Walde verspätet hatten und die Nacht sie überfiel, so legten sie sich nebeneinander auf das Moos und schliefen, bis der Morgen kam, und die Mutter wußte das und hatte ihretwegen keine Sorge. Einmal, als sie im Walde übernachtet hatten und das Morgenrot sie aufweckte, da sahen sie ein schönes Kind in einem weißen glänzenden Kleidchen neben ihrem Lager sitzen. Es stand auf und blickte sie ganz freundlich an, sprach aber nichts und ging in den Wald hinein. Und als sie sich umsahen, so hatten sie ganz nahe bei einem Abgrunde geschlafen und wären gewiß hinein gefallen, wenn sie in der Dunkelheit noch ein paar Schritte weiter gegangen wären. Die Mutter aber sagte ihnen, das müßte der Engel gewesen sein, der gute Kinder bewache.

Schneeweißchen und Rosenrot hielten das Hüttchen der Mutter so reinlich, daß es eine Freude war hineinzuschauen. Im Sommer besorgte Rosenrot das Haus und stellte der Mutter jeden Morgen, ehe sie aufwachte, einen Blumenstrauß vors Bett, darin war von jedem Bäumchen eine Rose. Im Winter zündete Schneeweißchen das Feuer an und hing den Kessel an den Feuerhaken, und der Kessel war von Messing, glänzte aber wie Gold, so rein war er gescheuert. Abends, wenn die Flocken fielen, sagte die Mutter: »Geh, Schneeweißchen, und schieb den Riegel vor«, und dann setzten sie sich an den Herd, und die Mutter nahm die Brille und las aus einem großen Buch vor, und die beiden Mädchen hörten zu, saßen und spannen. Neben ihnen lag ein Lämmchen auf dem Boden, und hinter ihnen auf einer Stange saß ein weißes Täubchen und hatte seinen Kopf unter den Flügel gesteckt.

Eines Abends, als sie so vertraulich beisammen saßen, klopfte jemand an die Türe, als wollte er eingelassen sein. Die Mutter sprach: »Geschwind, Rosenrot, mach auf, es wird ein Wanderer sein, der Obdach sucht.« Rosenrot ging und schob den Riegel weg, aber statt daß ein Mensch gekommen wäre, streckte ein Bär seinen dicken schwarzen Kopf zur Türe herein. Rosenrot schrie laut und sprang zurück; das Lämmchen blökte, das Täubchen flatterte auf, und Schneeweißchen versteckte sich hinter der Mutter Bett. Der Bär aber fing an zu sprechen und sagte: »Fürchtet euch nicht, ich tue euch nichts zuleid, ich bin halb erfroren und will mich nur ein wenig bei euch wärmen.« – »Ei, du armer Bär«, sprach die Mutter, »leg dich ans Feuer und gib nur acht, daß dir dein Pelz nicht brennt.« Dann rief sie: »Schneeweißchen, Rosenrot, kommt hervor, der Bär tut euch nichts, er meint's ehrlich.« Da kamen sie beide heran, und nach und nach näherten sich auch das Lämmchen und Täubchen und hatten keine Furcht mehr. Der Bär sprach: »Ihr Kinder, klopft mir den Schnee ein wenig aus dem Pelzwerk«, und sie holten den Besen und kehrten dem Bär das Fell rein, er aber streckte sich ans Feuer und brummte ganz vergnügt und behaglich. Nicht lange, so wurden sie ganz vertraut und trieben Mutwillen mit dem unbeholfenen Gast, zausten ihm das Fell mit den Händen, setzten ihre Füßchen auf seinen Rücken und rollten ihn hin und her oder nahmen eine Haselrute und schlugen auf ihn los, und wenn er brummte, so lachten sie. Der Bär ließ sich's aber gerne gefallen, nur wenn sie's gar zu arg machten, rief er:

>»Laßt mich am Leben, ihr Kinder:
>Schneeweißchen, Rosenrot,
>schlägst dir den Freier tot.«

Als Schlafenszeit war und die andern zu Bett gingen, sagte die Mutter zu dem Bär: »Du kannst in Gottes Namen da am Herde liegen bleiben, so bist du vor der Kälte und dem bösen Wetter geschützt.« Als der Tag graute, ließen ihn die beiden Kinder hinaus, und er trabte über den Schnee in den Wald hinein. Von nun an kam der Bär jeden Abend zu der bestimmten Stunde, legte sich an den Herd und erlaubte den Kindern, Kurzweil mit ihm zu treiben, soviel sie wollten; und sie waren so gewöhnt an ihn, daß die Türe nicht eher zugeriegelt wurde, als bis der schwarze Gesell angelangt war.

Als das Frühjahr herangekommen und draußen alles grün war, sagte der Bär eines Morgens zu Schneeweißchen: »Nun muß ich fort und darf den ganzen Sommer nicht wiederkommen.« – »Wo gehst du denn hin, lieber Bär?« fragte Schneeweißchen. »Ich muß in den Wald und meine Schätze vor den bösen Zwergen hüten. Im Winter, wenn die Erde hart gefroren ist, müssen sie wohl unten bleiben und können sich nicht durcharbeiten, aber jetzt, wenn die Sonne die Erde

aufgetaut und erwärmt hat, da brechen sie durch, steigen herauf, suchen und stehlen; und was einmal in ihren Händen ist und in ihren Höhlen liegt, das kommt so leicht nicht wieder an des Tages Licht.« Schneeweißchen war ganz traurig über den Abschied und riegelte ihm die Türe auf, und als der Bär sich hinausdrängte, blieb er an dem Türhaken hängen, und ein Stück seiner Haut riß auf, und da war es Schneeweißchen, als hätte es Gold durchschimmern gesehen. Aber es war seiner Sache nicht gewiß, weil der Bär eilig fort lief und bald hinter den Bäumen verschwunden war.

Nach einiger Zeit schickte die Mutter die Kinder in den Wald, Reisig zu sammeln. Da fanden sie draußen einen großen Baum, der lag gefällt auf dem Boden, und an dem Stamm sprang zwischen dem Gras etwas auf und ab, sie konnten aber nicht unterscheiden, was es war. Als sie näher kamen, sahen sie einen Zwerg mit einem alten verwelkten Gesicht und einem ellenlangen schneeweißen Bart. Das Ende des Bartes war in eine Spalte des Baums eingeklemmt, und der Kleine sprang hin und her wie ein Hündchen an einem Seil und wußte nicht, wie er sich helfen sollte. Er glotzte die Mädchen mit seinen roten, feurigen Augen an und schrie: »Was steht ihr da! Könnt ihr nicht herbeigehen und mir Beistand leisten?« – »Was hast du angefangen, kleines Männchen?« fragte Rosenrot. »Dumme, neugierige Gans«, antwortete der Zwerg, »den Baum habe ich mir spalten wollen, um kleines Holz in der Küche zu haben; bei den dicken Klötzen verbrennt gleich das bißchen Speise, das unsereiner braucht, der nicht soviel hinunterschlingt wie ihr grobes Volk. Ich hatte einen Keil hineingetrieben, und es wäre alles nach Wunsch gegangen, aber das verwünschte Holz war zu glatt und sprang unversehens heraus, und der Baum fuhr so geschwind zusammen, daß ich meinen schönen weißen Bart nicht mehr herausziehen konnte; nun steckt er drin, und ich kann nicht fort. Da lachen die albernen glatten Milchgesichter! Pfui, was seid ihr garstig!« Die Kinder gaben sich alle Mühe, aber sie konnten den Bart nicht herausziehen, er steckte zu fest. »Ich will laufen und Leute herbeiholen«, sagte Rosenrot. »Wahnsinnige Schafsköpfe«, schnarrte der Zwerg, »wer wird gleich Leute herbeirufen, ihr seid mir schon um zwei zuviel; fällt euch nichts Besseres ein?« – »Sei nur nicht ungeduldig«, sagte Schneeweißchen, »ich will schon Rat schaffen«, und holte sein Scherchen aus der Tasche und schnitt das Ende des Bartes ab. Sobald der Zwerg sich frei fühlte, griff er nach einem Sack, der zwischen den Wurzeln des Baums steckte und mit Gold gefüllt war, hob ihn heraus und brummte vor sich hin: »Ungehobeltes Volk, schneidet mir ein Stück von meinem stolzen Bart ab! Lohn's euch der Kuckuck!« Damit schwang er seinen Sack auf den Rücken und ging fort, ohne die Kinder nur noch einmal anzusehen.

Einige Zeit danach wollten Schneeweißchen und Rosenrot ein Gericht Fische angeln. Als sie auf den Bach zugingen, sahen sie, daß etwas wie eine große Heuschrecke nach dem Wasser zu hüpfte, als wollte es hinein springen. Sie liefen heran und erkannten den Zwerg. »Wo willst du hin?« sagte Rosenrot. »Du willst doch nicht ins Wasser?« – »Solch ein Narr bin ich nicht«, schrie der Zwerg. »Seht ihr nicht, der verwünschte Fisch will mich hinein ziehen?« Der Kleine hatte da gesessen und geangelt, und unglücklicherweise hatte der Wind seinen Bart mit der Angelschnur verflochten. Als gleich darauf ein großer Fisch anbiß, fehlten dem Zwerg die Kräfte, ihn herauszuziehen. Der Fisch behielt die Oberhand und riß den Zwerg zu sich hin. Zwar hielt er sich an allen Halmen und Binsen, aber das half nicht viel, er mußte den Bewegungen des Fisches folgen und war in beständiger Gefahr, ins Wasser gezogen zu werden. Die Mädchen kamen zu rechter Zeit, hielten ihn fest und versuchten, den Bart von der Schnur loszumachen, aber vergebens, Bart und Schnur waren fest ineinander verwirrt. Es blieb nichts übrig, als das Scherchen hervorzuholen und den Bart abzuschneiden; dabei ging ein kleiner Teil desselben verloren. Als der Zwerg das sah, schrie er sie an: »Ist das Manier, ihr Kröten, einem das Gesicht zu schänden! Nicht genug, daß ihr mir den Bart unten gestutzt habt, jetzt schneidet ihr mir den besten Teil davon ab. Ich darf mich vor den Meinigen gar nicht sehen lassen. Daß ihr laufen müßtet und die Schuhsohlen verloren hättet!« Dann holte er einen Sack Perlen, der im Schilf lag, und ohne ein Wort weiter zu sagen, schleppte er ihn fort und verschwand hinter einem Stein.

Es trug sich zu, daß bald hernach die Mutter die beiden Mädchen nach der Stadt schickte, Zwirn, Nadeln, Schnüre und Bänder einzukaufen. Der Weg führte sie über eine Heide, auf der hier und da mächtige Felsenstücke zerstreut lagen, da sahen sie einen großen Vogel in der Luft schweben, der langsam über ihnen kreiste, sich immer tiefer herabsenkte und endlich nicht weit bei einem Felsen niederstieß. Gleich darauf hörten sie einen durchdringenden, jämmerlichen

Schrei. Sie liefen herzu und sahen mit Schrecken, daß der Adler ihren alten Bekannten, den Zwerg, gepackt hatte und ihn forttragen wollte. Die mitleidigen Kinder hielten gleich das Männchen fest und zerrten sich so lange mit dem Adler herum, bis er seine Beute fahren ließ. Als der Zwerg sich von dem ersten Schrecken erholt hatte, sprach er: »Konntet ihr nicht säuberlicher mit mir umgehen? Gerissen habt ihr an meinem dünnen Röckchen, daß es überall zerfetzt und durchlöchert ist, unbeholfenes und täppisches Gesindel, das ihr seid!« Dann nahm er einen Sack mit Edelsteinen und schlüpfte wieder unter den Felsen in seine Höhle. Die Mädchen waren an seinen Undank schon gewöhnt, setzten ihren Weg fort und verrichteten ihr Geschäft in der Stadt.

Als sie beim Heimweg wieder auf die Heide kamen, überraschten sie den Zwerg, der auf einem reinlichen Plätzchen seinen Sack mit Edelsteinen ausgeschüttet und nicht gedacht hatte, daß so spät noch jemand daherkommen würde. Die Abendsonne schien über die glänzenden Steine, und sie schimmerten und leuchteten so prächtig in allen Farben, daß die Kinder stehen blieben und sie betrachteten. »Was steht ihr da und habt Maulaffen feil!« schrie der Zwerg, und sein aschgraues Gesicht ward zinnoberrot vor Zorn. Er wollte mit seinen Scheltworten fortfahren, als sich ein lautes Brummen hören ließ und ein schwarzer Bär aus dem Walde herbeitrabte. Erschrocken sprang der Zwerg auf, aber er konnte nicht mehr zu seinem Schlupfwinkel gelangen, der Bär war schon in seiner Nähe. Da rief er in Herzensangst: »Lieber Herr Bär, verschont mich, ich will Euch alle meine Schätze geben, seht, die schönen Edelsteine, die da liegen. Schenkt mir das Leben, was habt Ihr an mir kleinem schmächtigen Kerl? Ihr spürt mich nicht zwischen den Zähnen. Da, die beiden gottlosen Mädchen packt, das sind für Euch zarte Bissen, fett wie junge Wachteln, die freßt in Gottes Namen!« Der Bär kümmerte sich um seine Worte nicht, gab dem boshaften Geschöpf einen einzigen Schlag mit der Tatze, und es regte sich nicht mehr.

Die Mädchen waren fortgesprungen, aber der Bär rief ihnen nach: »Schneeweißchen, Rosenrot, fürchtet euch nicht, wartet, ich will mit euch gehen.« Da erkannten sie seine Stimme und blieben stehen, und als der Bär bei ihnen war, fiel plötzlich die Bärenhaut ab, und er stand da als ein schöner Mann und war ganz in Gold gekleidet. Er sagte: »Ich bin eines Königs Sohn und war von dem gottlosen Zwerg, der mir meine Schätze gestohlen hatte, verwünscht, als ein wilder Bär in dem Walde zu laufen, bis ich durch seinen Tod erlöst würde. Jetzt hat er seine wohlverdiente Strafe empfangen.«

Schneeweißchen wurde mit ihm und Rosenrot mit seinem Bruder vermählt, und sie teilten die großen Schätze miteinander, die der Zwerg in seiner Höhle zusammengetragen hatte. Die alte Mutter lebte noch lange Jahre ganz glücklich bei ihren Kindern. Die zwei Rosenbäumchen aber nahm sie mit, und sie standen vor ihrem Fenster und trugen jedes Jahr die schönsten Rosen, weiß und rot.

1837

Der Froschkönig
oder Der eiserne Heinrich

Es war einmal eine Königstochter, die wußte nicht, was sie anfangen sollte vor langer Weile. Da nahm sie eine goldene Kugel, womit sie schon oft gespielt hatte, und ging hinaus in den Wald. Mitten in dem Wald aber war ein reiner, kühler Brunnen, dabei setzte sie sich nieder, warf die Kugel in die Höhe, fing sie wieder, und das war ihr so ein Spielwerk. Es geschah aber, als die Kugel einmal recht hoch geflogen war und die Königstochter schon den Arm in die Höhe hielt und die Fingerchen streckte, um sie zu fangen, daß sie neben vorbei auf die Erde schlug und geradezu ins Wasser hinein rollte.

Erschrocken sah ihr die Königstochter nach; aber die Kugel sank hinab, und der Brunnen war so tief, daß kein Grund zu erkennen war. Als sie nun ganz verschwand, da fing das Mädchen gar jämmerlich an zu weinen und rief: »Ach! Meine goldene Kugel! Hätte ich sie wieder, ich wollte alles darum hingeben: meine Kleider, meine Edelsteine, meine Perlen, ja meine goldene Krone noch dazu.« Wie es das gesagt hatte, tauchte ein Frosch mit seinem dicken Kopf aus dem Wasser heraus und sprach: »Königstochter, was jammerst du so erbärmlich?« – »Ach«, sagte sie, »du garstiger Frosch, was kannst du mir helfen! Meine goldne Kugel ist mir da in den Brunnen gefallen.« Der Frosch sprach weiter: »Deine Kleider, deine Edelsteine, deine Perlen, ja deine goldne Krone, die mag ich nicht; aber wenn du mich willst zu deinem Freund und Gesellen annehmen, soll ich an deinem Tischlein sitzen zu deiner rechten Seite, von deinem goldenen Tellerlein mit dir essen, aus deinem Becherlein trinken und in deinem Bettlein schlafen, so will ich dir deine Kugel wieder herauf holen.« Die Königstochter dachte in ihrem Herzen: Was der einfältige Frosch wohl schwätzt! Ein Frosch ist keines Menschen Gesell und muß im Wasser bei seinesgleichen bleiben, vielleicht aber kann er mir die Kugel herauf holen; und sprach zu ihm: »Ja meinetwegen, schaff mir nur erst meine goldene Kugel, es soll dir alles versprochen sein.«

Als sie das gesagt hatte, tauchte der Frosch seinen Kopf wieder unter das Wasser, sank hinab, und über ein Weilchen kam er wieder in die Höhe gerudert, hatte die Kugel im Maul und warf sie heraus ins Gras. Da freute sich das Königskind, wie es wieder sein Spielwerk in den Händen hielt. Der Frosch rief: »Nun warte, Königstochter, und nimm mich mit«, aber das war in den Wind gesprochen, sie hörte nicht darauf, lief mit ihrer Goldkugel nach Haus und dachte gar nicht wieder an den Frosch.

Am andern Tag, als sie mit dem König und allen Hofleuten an der Tafel saß und von ihrem goldnen Tellerlein aß, kam – plitsch, platsch! plitsch, platsch! – etwas die Marmortreppe heraufgekrochen, und als es oben war, klopfte es an der Tür und rief: »Königstochter, jüngste, mach mir auf!« Sie lief und wollte sehen, wer draußen wär, als sie aber die Tür aufmachte, so saß der Frosch davor. Da warf sie die Türe hastig zu und setzte sich ganz erschrocken wieder an den Tisch. Der König sah, daß ihr das Herz gewaltig klopfte, und sprach: »Ei, was fürchtest du dich, steht etwa ein Riese vor der Tür und will dich holen?« – »Ach nein«, sprach das Kind, »es ist kein Riese, sondern ein garstiger Frosch, der hat mir gestern im Wald meine goldne Kugel aus dem Wasser geholt, dafür versprach ich ihm, er sollte mein Geselle werden, ich dachte aber nimmermehr, daß er aus seinem Wasser heraus könnte, nun ist er draußen und will zu mir herein.« Indem klopfte es zum zweitenmal und rief draußen:

> »Königstochter, jüngste,
> mach mir auf!
> Weißt du nicht, was gestern
> du zu mir gesagt
> bei dem kühlen Brunnenwasser?
> Königstochter, jüngste,
> mach mir auf!«

Da sagte der König: »Hast du's versprochen, mußt du's auch halten, geh und mach ihm auf.« Sie ging und öffnete die Türe, da hüpfte der Frosch herein, ihr immer auf dem Fuße nach, bis zu ihrem Stuhl. Da saß er und rief: »Heb mich herauf zu dir!« Sie wollte nicht, bis es der König befahl. Als der Frosch nun oben auf einem Stuhl neben ihr saß, sprach er: »Nun schieb dein goldenes Tellerlein näher, damit wir zusammen essen.« Voll Verdruß tat sie auch das, und der Frosch ließ sich's wohl schmecken, aber ihr blieb jedes Bißlein im Hals. Dann sprach er: »Nun hab ich mich satt gegessen und bin müd, trag mich hinauf in dein Kämmerlein und mach dein seiden Bettlein zurecht, da wollen wir uns schlafen legen.« Da fing die Königstochter an zu weinen, gar bitterlich, und fürchtete sich vor dem kalten Frosch, den sie sich nicht getraute anzurühren und der nun in ihrem schönen, reinen Bettlein schlafen sollte. Der König aber blickte sie zornig an und sprach: »Was du versprochen hast, sollst du auch halten, und der Frosch ist dein Geselle.« Da half nichts mehr, sie mochte wollen oder nicht, sie mußte den Frosch mitnehmen. Sie war aber in ihrem Herzen bitterböse, packte ihn mit zwei Fingern und trug ihn hinauf, und als sie im Bett lag, statt ihn hineinzuheben, warf sie ihn aus allen Kräften an die Wand: »Nun wirst du Ruhe haben, du garstiger Frosch!«

Was aber herunter fiel, war nicht ein toter Frosch, sondern ein lebendiger, junger Königssohn mit schönen und freundlichen Augen. Der war nun von Recht und mit ihres Vaters Wille ihr lieber Geselle und Gemahl. Da schliefen sie nun vergnügt zusammen ein, und am andern Morgen, als die Sonne sie aufweckte, kam ein Wagen herangefahren mit acht weißen Pferden bespannt, die waren mit Fe-

dern geschmückt und gingen in goldenen Ketten, und hinten stand der Diener des jungen Königs, das war der treue Heinrich. Der treue Heinrich hatte sich so betrübt, als sein Herr in einen Frosch verwandelt worden war, daß er drei eiserne Bande hatte müssen um sein Herz legen lassen, damit es ihm nicht vor Weh und Traurigkeit zerspränge. Der Wagen sollte den jungen König in sein Reich abholen; der treue Heinrich hob beide hinein und stellte sich wieder hinten auf, voller Freude über die Erlösung. Und als sie ein Stück Wegs gefahren waren, hörte der Königssohn hinter sich, daß es krachte, als wär etwas zerbrochen. Da drehte er sich um und rief:

»Heinrich, der Wagen bricht!«
»Nein, Herr, der Wagen nicht,
es ist ein Band von meinem Herzen,
das da lag in großen Schmerzen,
als Ihr in dem Brunnen saßt,
als Ihr eine Fretsche (Frosch) was't (wart).«

Noch einmal und noch einmal krachte es auf dem Weg, und der Königssohn meinte immer, der Wagen bräche, und es waren doch nur die Bande, die vom Herzen des treuen Heinrich absprangen, weil sein Herr wieder erlöst und glücklich war.

1819

Der Zaunkönig und der Bär

Zur Sommerszeit gingen einmal der Bär und der Wolf im Wald spazieren, da hörte der Bär so schönen Gesang von einem Vogel und sprach: »Bruder Wolf, was ist das für ein Vogel, der so schön singt?« – »Das ist der König der Vögel«, sagte der Wolf, »vor dem müssen wir uns neigen«; es war aber der Zaunkönig. »Wenn das ist«, sagte der Bär, »möcht ich auch gern seinen königlichen Palast sehen, komm und führ mich hin.« – »Das geht nicht so, wie du meinst«, sprach der Wolf, »du mußt warten, bis die Frau Königin kommt.«

Bald darauf kam die Frau Königin und hatte Futter im Schnabel und der Herr König auch und wollten ihre Jungen ätzen. Der Bär wäre gern nun gleich hintendrein gegangen, aber der Wolf hielt ihn am Ärmel und sagte: »Nein, du mußt warten, bis Herr und Frau Königin wieder fort sind.« Also nahmen sie das Loch in acht, wo das Nest stand, und gingen wieder ab. Der Bär aber hatte keine Ruhe, wollte den königlichen Palast sehen und ging nach einer kurzen Weile wieder vor. Da waren König und Königin wieder ausgeflogen, er guckte hinein und sah fünf

oder sechs Junge, die lagen darin. »Ist das der königliche Palast?« sagte der Bär. »Das ist ein elender Palast! Ihr seid auch keine Königskinder, ihr seid unehrliche Kinder!« Wie das die jungen Zaunkönige hörten, wurden sie gewaltig bös und schrien: »Nein, das sind wir nicht, unsere Eltern sind ehrliche Leute, Bär, das soll ausgemacht werden mit dir.« Dem Bär und dem Wolf ward angst, sie kehrten um und setzten sich in ihre Löcher. Die jungen Zaunkönige aber schrien und lärmten fort, und als ihre Eltern wieder Futter brachten, sagten sie: »Wir essen kein Fliegenbeinchen, und sollten wir verhungern, bis ihr erst ausmacht, ob wir ehrliche Kinder sind oder nicht, denn der Bär ist da gewesen und hat uns gescholten.«

Da sagte der alte König: »Seid nur ruhig, das soll ausgemacht werden.« Flog darauf mit der Frau Königin dem Bären vor seine Höhle und rief hinein: »Brummbär, du hast meine Kinder gescholten, das soll dir übel bekommen, das wollen wir in einem blutigen Krieg ausmachen.« Also war dem Bären der Krieg angekündigt und ward alles vierfüßige Getier berufen: Ochs, Esel, Rind, Hirsch, Reh und was die Erde sonst alles trägt. Der Zaunkönig aber berief alles, was in der Luft fliegt, nicht allein die Vögel groß und klein, auch die Mücken, Hornissen, Bienen und Fliegen mußten herbei.

Als nun die Zeit kam, wo der Krieg angehen sollte, da schickte der Zaunkönig Kundschafter aus, wer der kommandierende General des Feindes wär. Die Mücke war die listigste von allen, schwärmte im Wald, wo der Feind sich versammelte, und setzte sich endlich unter ein Blatt auf den Baum, wo die Parole ausgegeben wurde. Da stand der Bär, rief den Fuchs vor sich und sprach: »Fuchs, du bist der schlauste unter allem Getier, du sollst General sein und uns anführen; was für Zeichen wollen wir verabreden?« Da sprach der Fuchs: »Ich hab einen schönen, langen, bauschigen Schwanz, der sieht aus fast wie ein roter Federbusch, wenn ich den in die Höhe halte, so geht die Sache gut, und ihr müßt drauf los marschieren, laß ich ihn aber herunterhängen, so fangt an und lauft.« Als die Mücke das gehört hatte, flog sie wieder heim und verriet dem Zaunkönig alles haarklein.

Als der Tag anbrach, wo die Schlacht sollte geliefert werden, hu! da kam das vierfüßige Getier dahergerannt mit Gebraus, daß die Erde zitterte; Zaunkönig mit seiner Armee kam auch durch die Luft daher, die schnurrte, schrie und schwärmte, daß einem angst wurde; und gingen sie da von beiden Seiten an einander. Der Zaunkönig aber schickte die Hornisse hinab, sie sollte sich dem Fuchs unter den Schwanz setzen und aus Leibeskräften stechen. Wie nun der Fuchs den ersten Stich bekam, zuckte er, daß er das eine Bein aufhob, doch ertrug er's und ließ den Schwanz noch in der Höhe; beim zweiten mußt' er ihn einen Augenblick herunter lassen, beim dritten aber konnte er sich nicht mehr halten, schrie und nahm den Schwanz zwischen die Beine. Wie das die Tiere sahen, meinten sie, alles wär verloren, und fingen an zu laufen, jeder in seine Höhle, und hatten die Vögel die Schlacht gewonnen.

Da flogen der Herr König und die Frau Königin heim zu ihren Kindern und riefen: »Kinder, seid fröhlich, eßt und trinkt nach Herzenslust, wir haben den Krieg gewonnen.« Die jungen Zaunkönige aber sagten: »Noch essen wir nicht, der Bär soll erst vors Nest kommen und Abbitte tun und sagen, daß wir ehrliche Kinder sind.« Da flog der Zaunkönig vor das Loch des Bären und rief: »Brummbär, du sollst vor das Nest zu meinen Kindern gehen und Abbitte tun und sagen, daß sie ehrliche Kinder sind, sonst sollen dir die Rippen im Leib zertreten werden.« Da kroch der Bär in der größten Angst hin und tat Abbitte, und darauf setzten sich die jungen Zaunkönige zusammen, aßen und tranken und machten sich lustig bis in die späte Nacht hinein.

1819

Die drei Männlein im Walde

Es war ein Mann, dem starb seine Frau, und eine Frau, der starb ihr Mann; und der Mann hatte eine Tochter, und die Frau hatte auch eine Tochter. Die Mädchen waren miteinander bekannt und gingen zusammen spazieren und kamen hernach zu der Frau ins Haus. Da sprach sie zu des Mannes Tochter: »Hör, sag deinem Vater, ich wollt' ihn heiraten, dann sollst du jeden Morgen dich in Milch waschen und Wein trinken, meine Tochter aber soll sich in Wasser waschen und Wasser trinken.« Das Mädchen ging nach Haus und erzählte seinem Vater, was die Frau gesprochen hatte. Der Mann sprach: »Was soll ich tun? Das Heiraten ist eine Freude und ist auch eine Qual!« Endlich zog er seinen Stiefel aus und sagte: »Nimm diesen Stiefel, der hat in der Sohle ein Loch, geh damit auf den Boden, häng ihn an den großen Nagel und gieß dann Wasser hinein. Hält er das Wasser, so will ich wieder eine Frau nehmen, läuft's aber durch, so will ich nicht.« Das Mädchen tat, wie ihm geheißen war; aber das Wasser zog das Loch zusammen, und der Stiefel ward voll bis obenhin. Nun meldete es seinem Vater, wie's ausgefallen war;

er stieg selbst hinauf, und als er sah, daß es seine Richtigkeit hatte, ging er zu der Witwe und freite sie, und die Hochzeit ward gehalten.

Am andern Morgen, als die beiden Mädchen sich aufmachten, da stand vor des Mannes Tochter Milch zum Waschen und Wein zum Trinken, vor der Frau Tochter aber stand Wasser zum Waschen und Wasser zum Trinken. Am zweiten Morgen stand Wasser zum Waschen und Wasser zum Trinken so gut vor des Mannes Tochter als vor der Frau Tochter. Und am dritten Morgen stand Wasser zum Waschen und Wasser zum Trinken vor des Mannes Tochter und Milch zum Waschen und Wein zum Trinken vor der Frau Tochter, und dabei blieb's. Die Frau ward ihrer Stieftochter spinnefeind und wußte nicht, wie sie es ihr von einem Tag zum andern schlimmer machen sollte. Auch war sie neidisch, weil ihre Stieftochter schön und lieblich, ihre rechte Tochter aber häßlich und widerlich war.

Einmal im Winter, als es steinhart gefroren hatte und Berg und Tal vollgeschneit lag, machte die Frau ein Kleid von Papier, rief dann das Mädchen und sprach: »Da, zieh das Kleid an und geh in den Wald und hol mir ein Körbchen voll Erdbeeren, ich habe Lust danach.« – »Ei, du lieber Gott«, sagte das Mädchen, »im Winter wachsen ja keine Erdbeeren, die Erde ist gefroren, und der Schnee hat auch alles zugedeckt. Wie soll ich in dem Papierkleide gehen? Es ist draußen so kalt, daß einem der Atem friert, da weht ja der Wind hindurch, und die Dornen reißen mir's vom Leib.« – »Willst du mir noch widersprechen?« sagte die Stiefmutter. »Mach, daß du fortkommst, und laß dich nicht eher wieder sehen, als bis du das Körbchen voll Erdbeeren hast.« Dann gab sie ihm noch ein Stückchen hartes Brot und sprach: »Davon kannst du für den Tag essen«, und dachte, draußen wird's erfrieren und verhungern und mir nimmermehr wieder vor die Augen kommen.

Nun war das Mädchen gehorsam, tat das Papierkleid an und ging mit dem Körbchen hinaus. Da war nichts als Schnee die Weite und Breite und kein grünes Hälmchen zu merken. Als es in den Wald kam, sah es ein kleines Häuschen, daraus guckten drei kleine Haule-Männerchen, denen wünschte es die Tageszeit und klopfte an der Türe. Sie riefen »herein«, und es ging in die Stube und setzte sich auf die Bank am Ofen, da wollte es sich wärmen und sein Frühstück essen. Die Haule-Männerchen sprachen: »Gib uns auch etwas davon.« – »Gern«, sprach es, teilte sein Stückchen Brot entzwei und gab ihnen die Hälfte. Sie sprachen: »Was willst du zur Winterzeit in deinem Kleidchen hier im Wald?« – »Ach«, antwortete es, »ich soll ein Körbchen voll Erdbeeren suchen und darf nicht eher nach Haus kommen, als wenn ich es mitbringe.« Als es nun sein Brot gegessen, gaben sie ihm einen Besen und sprachen: »Damit kehre an der Hintertüre den Schnee weg.« Wie es aber draußen war, sprachen die drei Männerchen untereinander: »Was sollen wir ihm schenken, weil es so artig und gut ist und sein Brot mit uns geteilt hat?« Da sagte der erste: »Ich schenke ihm, daß es jeden Tag schöner wird.« Der zweite sprach: »Ich schenk ihm, daß die Goldstücke ihm aus dem Mund fallen, sooft es ein

Die drei Männlein im Walde 25

Wort spricht.« Der dritte sprach: »Ich schenk ihm, daß ein König kommt und es zu seiner Gemahlin macht.«

Das Mädchen aber kehrte mit dem Besen der Haule-Männerchen den Schnee hinter dem kleinen Haus weg und fand darunter alles rot von schönen, reifen Erdbeeren. Da raffte es in seiner Freude sein Körbchen voll, dankte den kleinen Männern, nahm Abschied von ihnen und lief nach Haus und wollte es der Stiefmutter bringen. Und wie es eintrat und »guten Abend« sagte, fiel schon ein Goldstück ihm aus dem Mund. Darauf erzählte es, was ihm im Walde begegnet war, aber bei jedem Wort, das es sprach, fielen ihm die Goldstücke aus dem Mund, so daß bald das ganze Haus reich wurde. Die Stiefschwester aber wurde neidisch darüber und lag der Mutter beständig an, daß sie es auch in den Wald schicken möchte, die wollte aber nicht und sprach: »Nein, mein lieb Töchterchen, es ist zu kalt, du könntest mir erfrieren«, weil es sie aber stets plagte und ihr keine Ruhe ließ, gab sie endlich ihren Willen, nähte ihm aber vorher einen prächtigen Pelzrock, den es anziehen mußte, und gab ihm Butterbrot und Kuchen mit auf den Weg.

Das Mädchen ging in den Wald und gerade nach dem kleinen Häuschen. Die drei kleinen Haule-Männer guckten wieder, aber es grüßte sie nicht, ging ohne weiteres zur Stube hinein, setzte sich an den Ofen und fing an, sein Butterbrot und seinen Kuchen zu essen. »Gib uns doch davon«, riefen die Kleinen, aber es antwortete: »Das schickt mir selber nicht, wie sollt' ich andern noch davon abgeben!«

Wie es nun fertig war mit dem Essen, sprachen sie: »Da hast du einen Besen, kehr uns vor der Hintertür rein.« – »Ei, kehrt euch selber«, antwortete es, »ich bin eure Magd nicht.« Wie es sah, daß sie ihm nichts schenken wollten, ging es zur Türe hinaus. Da sprachen die kleinen Männer untereinander: »Was sollen wir ihm schenken, weil es so unartig ist und ein böses neidisches Herz hat, das niemand etwas gönnt?« Der erste sprach: »Ich schenk ihm, daß es jeden Tag häßlicher wird.« Der zweite sprach: »Ich schenk ihm, daß ihm bei jedem Wort, das es spricht, eine Kröte aus dem Mund springt.« Der dritte sprach: »Ich schenk ihm, daß es eines unglücklichen Todes stirbt.« Das Mädchen suchte draußen nach Erdbeeren, als es aber keine fand, ging es verdrießlich nach Haus. Und wie es den Mund auftat und seiner Mutter erzählen wollte, was ihm im Walde begegnet war, da sprang ihm bei jedem Wort eine Kröte aus dem Mund, so daß alle einen Abscheu vor ihm bekamen.

Nun ärgerte sich die Stiefmutter noch viel mehr und dachte nur darauf, wie sie der Tochter des Mannes alles Herzeleid antun wollte, die doch alle Tage an Schönheit zunahm. Endlich nahm sie einen Kessel, setzte ihn zum Feuer und sott Garn darin. Als es gesotten war, gab sie es dem armen Mädchen und eine Axt dazu, damit sollte es auf den gefrorenen Fluß gehen, ein Eisloch hauen und das Garn schlittern. Nun war es gehorsam, ging hin und haute ein Loch, und mitten im Hauen kam ein prächtiger Wagen hergefahren, worin der König saß. Der hielt still und fragte: »Mein Kind, was machst du da?« – »Ich bin ein armes Mädchen und schlittere Garn.« Da wurde der König mitleidig, und als er sah, wie es so gar schön war, sprach er: »Willst du mit mir fahren?« – »Ach ja, von Herzen gern«, antwortete es, denn es war froh, daß es der Mutter und Schwester aus den Augen kommen sollte.

Also stieg es in den Wagen und fuhr mit dem König fort, und als sie auf sein Schloß gekommen waren, ward die Hochzeit mit großer Pracht gefeiert, wie es die kleinen Männlein dem Mädchen geschenkt hatten. Über ein Jahr gebar die junge Königin einen Sohn, und als die Stiefmutter, die gehört hatte, was für ein Glück ihm zuteil geworden, das vernahm, so kam sie mit ihrer Tochter gegangen und tat, als wollten sie einen Besuch machen. Als aber der König einmal hinausgegangen und sonst niemand zugegen war, packte das böse Weib sie am Kopf und ihre Tochter an den Füßen, hoben sie aus dem Bett und warfen sie zum Fenster hinaus in den vorbeifließenden Strom. Dann nahm sie ihre häßliche Tochter, legte sie ins Bett und deckte sie bis über den Kopf zu. Als der König wieder zurückkam und mit seiner Frau sprechen wollte, rief die Alte: »Still, still! Jetzt geht das nicht, sie liegt in großem Schweiß, ihr müßt sie heute ruhen lassen.« Der König dachte nichts Böses dabei und kam erst den andern Morgen wieder, und wie er mit seiner Frau sprach und sie ihm antworten mußte, sprang bei jedem Wort eine Kröte hervor, während sonst ein Goldstück herausgefallen war. Da fragte er, was das wäre, aber die Alte sprach, das hätte sie von dem großen Schweiß gekriegt und würde sich schon wieder verlieren. In der Nacht aber sah der Küchenjunge, wie eine Ente durch die Gosse geschwommen kam, und sprach:

>»König, was machst du?
>Schläfst du oder wachst du?«

Und als er keine Antwort gab, sprach sie:

>»Was machen meine Gäste?«

Da antwortete der Küchenjunge:

>»Sie schlafen feste.«

Fragte sie weiter:

>»Was macht mein Kindelein?«

Antwortete er:

>»Es schläft in der Wiege fein.«

Da ging sie in der Königin Gestalt hinauf, gab ihm zu trinken, schüttelte ihm sein Bettchen, deckte es zu und schwamm als Ente wieder durch die Gosse fort. So kam sie zwei Nächte, in der dritten sprach sie zu dem Küchenjungen: »Geh und sage dem König, daß er das Schwert nimmt und auf der Schwelle dreimal schwingt über mir.« Da lief der Küchenjunge und sagte es dem König, der kam mit seinem Schwert und schwang's dreimal über dem Geist, und beim drittenmal stand seine Gemahlin vor ihm, frisch, lebendig und gesund, wie sie vorher gewesen war.

Nun war der König in großer Freude und hielt die Königin in einer Kammer verborgen bis auf den Sonntag, wo das Kind getauft werden sollte. Und als es getauft war, sprach er: »Was gehört einem Menschen, der den andern aus dem Bett trägt und ins Wasser wirft?« – »Ei«, antwortete die Alte, »daß sie in ein Faß gesteckt wird, das mit Nägeln ausgeschlagen ist, und den Berg hinab ins Wasser gerollt.« Da ließ der König ein solches Faß holen und die Alte mit ihrer Tochter hineinstecken, dann ward der Boden zugehämmert und das Faß bergab gekullert, bis es in den Fluß rollte.

1819

Das kluge Gretel

Es war eine Köchin, die hieß Gretel, die trug Schuhe mit roten Absätzen, und wenn sie damit ausging, so drehte sie sich hin und her, war ganz fröhlich und dachte: du bist doch ein schönes Mädel. Und wenn sie nach Haus kam, so trank sie aus Fröhlichkeit einen Schluck Wein, und weil der Wein auch Lust zum Essen macht, so versuchte sie das Beste, was sie kochte, so lang, bis sie satt war, und sprach: »Die Köchin muß wissen, wie's Essen schmeckt.«

Es trug sich zu, daß der Herr einmal zu ihr sagte: »Gretel, heut abend kommt ein Gast, richt mir zwei Hühner fein wohl zu.« – »Will's schon machen, Herr«, antwortete das Gretel. Nun stach's die Hühner ab, brühte sie, rupfte sie, steckte sie an den Spieß und brachte sie, wie's gegen den Abend ging, zum Feuer, damit sie braten sollten. Die Hühner fingen an braun und gar zu werden, aber der Gast war noch nicht gekommen. Da rief Gretel dem Herrn: »Kommt der Gast nicht, muß ich die Hühner vom Feuer tun, ist aber Jammer und Schade, wenn sie nicht bald gegessen werden, wo sie am besten im Saft sind.« Sprach der Herr: »Ei, so will ich selbst laufen und den Gast holen.« Als der Herr den Rücken gekehrt hatte, legte das Gretel den Spieß mit den Hühnern beiseite und dachte: »So lange da beim Feuer stehen macht schwitzen und durstig, wer weiß, wann die kommen, derweil spring ich in den Keller und tu einen Schluck.« Lief hinab, setzte einen Krug an: »Gott gesegne's dir, Gretel«, und tat einen guten Zug. »Der Wein hängt aneinander«, sprach's zu sich, »und ist nicht gut davon abbrechen.« Nun ging es wieder hinauf, stellte die Hühner wieder übers Feuer, strich sie mit Butter und trieb den Spieß lustig herum. Weil aber der Braten so gut roch, dachte es: »Es könnte etwas

fehlen, versucht muß er werden!«, schleckte mit dem Finger und sprach: »Ei, was sind die Hühner so gut! Ist ja Sünd und Schand, daß man sie nicht gleich ißt!« Lief zum Fenster, ob der Herr mit dem Gast noch nicht käm, aber es sah niemand, stellte sich wieder zu den Hühnern, dachte: der eine Flügel verbrennt, besser ist's, ich eß ihn weg. Also schnitt es ihn ab und aß ihn, und er schmeckte ihm, und wie es fertig war, dachte es, der andere muß auch herab, sonst merkt der Herr, daß was fehlt. Wie die zwei Flügel verzehrt waren, ging es wieder und schaute nach dem Herrn und sah ihn nicht. »Ei«, fiel ihm ein, »wer weiß, sie kommen wohl gar nicht und sind wo eingekehrt.« Da sprach's: »Hei, Gretel! Sei guter Dinge, das eine ist doch angegriffen, tu noch einen frischen Trunk und iß es vollends dazu, wenn's all ist, hast du Ruh! Warum soll auch die Gottesgabe umkommen?« Also lief es noch einmal in den Keller, tat einen ehrbaren Trunk und aß das eine Huhn in aller Freudigkeit auf. Wie es drunten war und der Herr noch immer nicht kam, sah es das andere Huhn an und sprach: »Wo das eine ist, muß auch das andere sein, die zwei gehören zusammen, was dem einen recht ist, das ist dem andern billig, ich glaube, wenn ich noch einen Trunk tue, so sollte mir's nicht schaden.« Also tat es noch einen frischen Trunk und ließ das zweite Huhn wieder zum andern laufen.

Wie es so am besten aß, kam der Herr dahergegangen und rief: »Nun, eil dich, Gretel, der Gast kommt gleich nach.« – »Ja, Herr, will's schon zurichten«, antwortete Gretel. Der Herr sah indessen, ob der Tisch wohl gedeckt war, nahm das große Messer, womit er die Hühner zerschneiden wollte, und wetzte es auf dem Gang. Indem kam der Gast, klopfte sittlich und höflich an der Haustüre; Gretel lief und schaute, wer da war, und als es den Gast sah, hielt es den Finger an den Mund und sprach: »Still! still! macht geschwind, daß Ihr wieder fort kommt, denn wenn Euch mein Herr erwischt, so seid Ihr unglücklich; er hat Euch zwar zum Nachtessen eingeladen, aber er hat nichts anders im Sinn, als Euch die beiden Ohren abzuschneiden. Hört nur, wie er das Messer dazu wetzt.« Der Gast hörte das Wetzen und eilte, was er konnte, wieder die Stiegen hinab. Das Gretel war nicht faul, lief schreiend zu dem Herrn und sprach: »Da habt Ihr einen schönen Gast eingeladen!« – »Ei, warum, Gretel, was hast du?« – »Ja«, sagte es, »der hat mir beide Hühner, die ich eben auftragen wollte, von der Schüssel genommen und ist damit fortgelaufen.« – »Das ist feine Weise!« sprach der Herr und war ihm leid um die schönen Hühner: »Wenn er mir dann wenigstens das eine gelassen hätte, damit mir was zu essen geblieben wäre.« Rief ihm zu, er sollt' bleiben, aber der Gast tat, als hörte er es nicht; darum lief er ihm nach, das Messer noch immer in der Hand, und schrie: »Nur eins! nur eins«, und meinte, der Gast sollte ihm nur ein Huhn lassen und nicht alle beide nehmen, dieser aber meinte nicht anders, als er sollte eins von seinen Ohren hergeben, und lief, als wenn Feuer unter ihm brenne, damit er sie beide heimbrächte.

1819

Das tapfere Schneiderlein

An einem Sommermorgen saß ein Schneiderlein auf seinem Tisch am Fenster und nähte. Nun kam eine Bauersfrau die Straße daher und rief: »Gut Mus feil! Gut Mus feil!« Das klang dem Schneiderlein lieblich in die Ohren, es streckte sein zartes Häuptlein zum Fenster hinaus und rief: »Nur hier herauf, liebe Frau, hier wird sie ihre Ware los.« Als die Frau hinaufkam, mußte sie ihren ganzen Korb auspacken; das Männlein besah alle Töpfe, endlich kaufte es nur ein Viertelpfund, daß die Frau ganz ärgerlich und brummig fortging. »Nun, das soll mir Gott gesegnen«, sprach das Schneiderlein, »und soll mir Kraft und Stärke geben!« Holte das Brot, schnitt sich ein Stück über den ganzen Laib und strich das Mus darauf. »Du wirst gut schmecken«, sprach es, »aber ich will erst den Wams fertig machen, eh' ich anbeiße«, legte es neben sich, nähte und machte vor Freude immer größere Stiche. Indes ging der Geruch von dem Mus auf an die Wand, zu den Fliegen, also daß sie in großer Menge herabkamen und sich darauf niederließen. Da aber das Schneiderlein zuweilen nach dem Musbrot sich umsah, entdeckte es die fremden Gäste. »Ei«, sprach es, »wer hat euch eingeladen«, und jagte sie fort. Die Fliegen aber verstanden kein Deutsch und ließen sich nicht abweisen, und nicht lange, so kamen sie mit noch größerer Gesellschaft wieder. Da lief dem Schneiderlein die Laus über die Leber: es langte aus seiner Hölle einen großen Tuchlappen, und: »Wart, ich will's euch geben«, schlug es drauf. Danach zog es ab und zählte, da lagen sieben vor ihm tot und streckten die Beine. »Bist du so ein Kerl!« sprach es in Herzens-Verwunderung. »Das soll die Stadt erfahren.« Und in einer Hast schnitt es sich einen Gürtel, nähte ihn und stickte mit großen Buchstaben darauf: »Sieben auf einen Streich!« – »Ei was, Stadt!« sprach es weiter. »Die ganze Welt soll's erfahren!«, und sein Herz wackelte ihm vor Freude wie ein Lämmerschwänzchen.

Nun band es seinen Gürtel um den Leib und suchte im Haus herum, ob nichts da wäre, das es mitnehmen könnte, denn es wollte hinaus in die Welt. Es war aber nichts zu finden als ein alter Käs, den steckte es ein. Vor dem Tor fing's durch gut Glück noch einen Vogel, der mußte zu dem Käs in die Tasche. Nun nahm's den Weg zwischen die Beine und stieg einen hohen Berg hinauf; wie es oben ankam, saß da ein großer Riese auf der Spitze. »Gelt, Kamerad«, sprach es zu ihm, »du sitzest da und schaust in die Welt? Ich bin willens, mich auch hinein zu begeben; hast du Lust, mitzugehen?« Der Riese sah es an und sprach: »Du bist ein miserabler Kerl!« – »Das wär was«, sagte das Schneiderlein, knöpfte seinen Rock auf und zeigte dem Riesen seinen Gürtel und sprach: »Da hast du's schriftlich, was ich für ein Mann bin.« Der Riese las: »Sieben auf einen Streich!«, meinte, das wären Menschen gewesen, die er erschlagen hätte, und kriegte vor dem Schneiderlein doch ein wenig Respekt. Erst aber wollte er es prüfen. Da nahm er einen Stein in seine Faust und drückte ihn zusammen, daß das Wasser heraustropfte. »Das tu mir nach«, sprach er zu ihm, »wenn du stark sein willst.« – »Ist's weiter nichts«, sprach das Schneiderlein, »das kann ich auch«, griff in die Tasche, holte den faulen Käs und drückte ihn, daß der Saft herauslief. »Gelt«, sprach es, »das war ein bißchen besser?« Der Riese wußte nicht, was er sagen sollte, und konnt's gar nicht von dem Männlein glauben. Da hob er einen Stein auf und warf ihn so hoch, daß er kaum noch zu sehen war. »Du Erpelmännchen, das tu mir nach«, sprach er. »Gleich«, sagte es, »dein Wurf war gut, aber der Stein hat doch wieder zur Erde müssen herabfallen; ich will dir einen werfen, der soll gar nicht wieder herabkommen.« Darauf griff es in die Tasche, nahm den Vogel und warf ihn in die Luft, und der Vogel, froh, daß er frei geworden, stieg auf und flog fort. »Nun, Kamerad, wie gefällt dir das?« sprach es zum Riesen. »Werfen kannst du«, sprach der Riese, »aber nun wollen wir auch sehen, ob du etwas Ordentliches tragen kannst.« Darauf führte er es zu einem schweren und mächtigen Eichbaum, der da gefällt lag: »Den wollen wir zusammen aus dem Wald tragen.« – »So nimm du unten das dicke Ende auf deine Schulter«, sprach das Männlein, »ich will dann die Äste mit all ihrem Gezweig aufheben und tragen, das ist doch schwerer.« Der Riese hob den Stamm und legte ihn auf die Schulter, das Schneiderlein, statt zu heben, setzte sich hinten auf einen Ast, und der Riese mußte den ganzen Baum und es dazu allein tragen. Auch machte es sich dahinten ganz lustig und pfiff allerlei Liederchen, als wär das Baumtragen ein Kinderspiel. Der Riese, nachdem er ein Stück Wegs mit der großen Last gegangen war, konnt' es nicht länger aushalten und sprach: »Hör, ich muß den Baum fallen lassen.« Das Schneiderlein sprang behend herab, faßte den Baum mit beiden Armen, daß es aussah, als trüg es, und sprach zum Riesen: »Bist ein so großer Kerl und kannst den Baum nicht tragen!«

Nun gingen sie weiter und kamen an einem Kirschbaum vorbei, da faßte der Riese die Krone, wo die zeitigsten Früchte hingen, und gab sie dem Schneiderlein in die Hand, damit es auch äße. Das Schneiderlein aber war zu schwach, konnte der Stärke des Baums nicht widerstehen und ward mit in die Höhe geschnellt. »Was ist das?« sprach der Riese. »Kannst du die schwache Gerte nicht halten!« – »Das wär was«, antwortete es, »für einen dazu, der sieben mit einem Streich getroffen! Weißt du, was es ist? Da unten schießen die Jäger ins Gebüsch, darum bin ich über den Baum herüber gesprungen, das tu mir einmal nach.« Der Riese wollte auch über den Baum springen, konnte aber nicht, denn er sprang immer in die Äste und verwickelte sich darin; also daß das Schneiderlein auch hier die Oberhand behielt. »Nun, so komm mit in unsere Höhle und übernachte bei uns«, sprach der Riese, und das Schneiderlein war willig und folgte ihm. Da gab ihm der Riese ein Bett, worin es sich ausruhen sollte. Das Schneiderlein aber legte sich nicht hinein, sondern kroch in eine Ecke. Als es nun Mitternacht war, kam der Riese mit einem Stab Eisen und schlug das Bett, worin er meinte, daß das Schneiderlein schlief, mit einem Schlag ganz durch und dachte, nun ist's aus mit dem Grashüpfer, der wird

sich nicht weiter sehen lassen. Am andern Tag gingen die Riesen in den Wald und hatten das tote Schneiderlein ganz vergessen, da kam's auf einmal lustig und keck hergeschritten. Die Riesen erschraken, fürchteten, es schlüg sie alle tot, und liefen in einer Hast fort.

Nun ging das Schneiderlein allein weiter, immer seinem spitzigen Näschen nach, bis es in eines Königs Hof kam. Und weil es müd war, legte es sich in das Gras und schlief ein. Während es da lag, kamen des Königs Leute, betrachteten es von allen Seiten und lasen auf dem Gürtel: »Sieben auf einen Streich!« – »Ach«, sprachen sie, »was will der große Kriegsheld hier mitten in Friedenszeit, das ist gewiß ein mächtiger Herr.« Sie meldeten es dem König und sprachen zu ihm: Das wär, wenn Krieg ausbrechen sollte, ein gar wichtiger und nützlicher Mann, den dürft er nicht fortlassen. Dem König gefiel der Rat, und er schickte einen hin, der mußte dem Schneiderlein, als es ausgeschlafen hatte, Dienste anbieten. »Ja«, antwortete es, »eben darum bin ich hergekommen, um dem König Dienste zu leisten.« Also ward es wohl empfangen und ihm eine besondere Wohnung gegeben.

Die Kriegsleut aber waren dem Schneiderlein aufgesessen und wünschten, es wär beim Teufel. »Was soll draus werden«, sprachen sie untereinander, »wenn wir Zank mit ihm kriegen und er haut zu, so fallen auf jeden Streich sieben. Da kann unsereiner nicht bestehen!« Also faßten sie einen Entschluß, gingen allesamt zum König, baten um Abschied und sprachen: »Wir sind nicht gemacht, neben einem solchen starken Mann auszuhalten.« Der König war traurig, daß er um des einen willen alle seine Diener verlieren sollte, wär ihn gern losgewesen und wollte, daß ihn seine Augen nie gesehen hätten. Doch getraute er sich nicht, ihm den Abschied zu geben, weil er sich fürchtete, er möchte ihn samt seinem Volk totschlagen und sich hernach auf den Thron setzen. Er sann lange hin und her, endlich fand er einen Rat, schickte zu dem Schneiderlein und ließ ihm sagen, weil er nun wohl wüßte, was für ein gewaltiger Kriegsheld er wäre, so wollte er ihm ein Anerbieten machen. In einem Walde seines Landes hätte er zwei Riesen, die täten großen Schaden mit Rauben, Morden, Sengen und Brennen, denen niemand nah kommen dürfe, er möge bewaffnet sein, wie er wollte. Wenn er die tötete, so wollte er ihm seine Tochter zur Gemahlin und das halbe Königreich zur Ehesteuer geben; auch sollten ihm hundert Reiter zur Hilfe mitziehen. Das wär so was für einen Mann, wie du bist, sprach das Schneiderlein in seinem Sinn, die schöne Königstochter und ein halbes Reich, das ist nicht bitter. »O ja«, gab es zur Antwort, »die Riesen will ich schon abtun, und die hundert Reiter brauch ich nicht einmal, wer sieben auf einen Streich trifft, braucht sich vor zweien nicht zu fürchen.«

Nun zog es hinaus zu dem Wald. Als es ankam, sprach es zu den Reitern: »Bleibt nur außen, ich will schon allein mit den Riesen fertig werden«, trat hinein und ließ seine Äuglein nach ihnen hin und her gehen. Endlich fand es sie beide unter einem Baum schlafend und schnarchend, daß sich die Äste auf- und abbogen. »Gewonnen Spiel!« sprach das Schneiderlein, las seine Taschen voll Steine und stieg über den Riesen auf den Baum hinauf. Nun fing es an und warf dem einen Riesen einen Stein nach dem andern auf die Brust, bis er zornig aufwachte, seinen Gesellen anstieß und sprach: »Ei, was schlägst du mich?« – »Du träumst«, sagte der andere, »ich schlag dich nicht.« Sie wollten wieder einschlafen, da warf das Schneiderlein dem zweiten einen Stein auf die Brust; der fuhr auf und sprach: »Was hast du vor, was wirfst du mich?« – »Ich werf dich nicht«, sprach der erste. So zankten sie eine Weil, doch weil sie müd waren, ließen sie es gut sein, und die Augen fielen ihnen zu. Jetzt fing das Schneiderlein wiederum sein Spiel oben an, suchte den dicksten Stein und warf den ersten Riesen damit, so stark es konnte, auf die Brust. Da schrie dieser: »Das ist mir zu arg!«, sprang wie ein Unsinniger auf und schlug seinen Gesellen; der ließ sich das nicht gefallen und gab ihm gleiche Münze zurück. Da gerieten sie in Wut, rissen Bäume aus, schlugen aufeinander los und schlugen sich endlich tot. »Es ist nur gut«, sprach das Schneiderlein, »daß sie nicht meinen Baum ausgerissen haben, sonst hätte ich einen garstigen Sprung tun müssen.« Darauf stieg es lustig hinunter, zog sein Schwert und hieb mit aller Bequemlichkeit jedem ein paar Wunden in die Brust und ging dann hinaus zu den Reitern. »Drin liegen zwei Riesen«, sprach es, »ich habe ihnen beiden den Garaus gemacht, dazu gehört aber einer, der sieben auf einen Streich schlägt, denn sie haben in der Todesangst noch Bäume ausgerissen.« – »Habt Ihr gar keine Wunde?« fragten die Reiter. »Das hat gute Wege«, sprach das Schneiderlein, »sie haben mir kein Haar gekrümmt.«

Die Reiter wollten's nicht glauben und ritten in den Wald hinein, da fanden sie die Riesen in ihrem Blut und die ausgerissenen Bäume rings herum liegen. Sie verwunderten sich, erschraken aber noch mehr vor dem Schneiderlein und zweifelten nicht, daß es sie all umbrächte, wo es ihnen feind würde. Sie ritten nun heim und erzählten dem König die Tat; das Schneiderlein kam auch und sprach: »Nun wollte ich mir die Königstochter mit dem halben Reich ausgebeten haben.« Den König aber reute seine Verheißung, und er dachte aufs neue, wie er des Kriegshelden könnte loswerden, dem er seine Tochter zu geben nicht gesinnt war. Da sprach er zu ihm: Im Walde laufe noch ein Einhorn, das großen Schaden schon angerichtet an Tieren und Menschen, das solle er erst fangen, wenn er seine Tochter haben wolle. Nun, das Schneiderlein war's zufrieden, nahm ein Stricklein, ging zum Wald und hieß die, welche ihm zugeordnet waren, außen warten, er wollte das Einhorn schon allein festhalten. Es trat in den Wald, ging auf und ab und suchte das Einhorn. Indem kam es dahergesprungen, gerade auf das Schneiderlein zu, und wollte es aufspießen. »Sachte, sachte«, sprach es, blieb stehen, wartete, bis das Tier nahe war, und sprang dann gar behendiglich hinter den nebenstehenden Baum. Das Einhorn, das im vollen Laufe sich nicht wenden konnte, rannte gegen den Baum und rannte sein Horn so fest hinein, daß es dasselbe mit aller Kraft nicht wieder herausziehen konnte; und also war es gefangen. Nun kam das Schneiderlein hinter dem Baum hervor, tat ihm das Stricklein um den Hals und führte das Tier hinaus zu seinen Gesellen und danach vor den König, den er wieder um das Versprochene bat. Der König erschrak, sann aber eine neue List aus und sprach zu ihm, eh' die Hochzeit könnte gehalten werden, müßte er ihm erst ein Wildschwein, das im Wald lief, fangen; seine Jäger sollten ihm Beistand leisten. »Gern«, sprach das Schneiderlein, »das ist das geringste.« Also ging es wiederum in den Wald, ließ die Jäger außen, die waren's wohl zufrieden, denn das Schwein hatte sie oft so empfangen, daß sie ihm nicht nachzustellen begehrten. Das Schwein, als es das Männlein erblickte, lief mit schäumendem Mund und wetzenden Zähnen auf es zu und wollt's zur Erde werfen. Das Schneiderlein stand aber neben einer Kapelle, sprang hinein und oben zum Fenster gar leicht wieder hinaus. Das Schwein folgte ihm nach, alsbald sprang das Schneiderlein wieder hervor, schlug die Türe zu und hatte nun das Gewild darin gefangen, das zu dem Fenster in die Höhe nicht springen konnte. Es rief die Jäger herbei, damit sie's sähen, dann ging es zurück zum König und sprach: »Die Sau hab ich gefangen und die Königstochter damit auch.« Ob der König über die Nachricht traurig oder lustig war, ist leicht zu denken, er wußte sich aber nicht zu helfen, mußte sein Versprechen halten und dem Schneiderlein seine Tochter geben. Dennoch glaubte er, es wär ein großer Kriegsheld. Hätt' er gewußt, daß es ein Schneiderlein war, er hätte ihm lieber einen Strick gegeben. Die Hochzeit ward also mit großer Pracht und kleiner Freude gehalten und aus einem Schneider ein König gemacht.

Nach einigen Tagen hörte nachts die junge Königin, wie das Schneiderlein träumte und sprach: »Junge, mach mir ein Wams und flick mir die Hosen, oder ich will dir die Elle über die Ohren schlagen!« Da merkte sie, in welcher Gasse ihr junger Herr Gemahl geboren war, und am Morgen klagte sie es dem König und bat ihn, ihr von dem Mann zu helfen, der nur ein Schneider wäre. Der König tröstete sie und sprach: »Laß morgen deine Kammer offen, dann sollen einige Diener davor stehen und, wann er schläft, eingehen und ihn überwältigen.« Das war der Frau recht. Es hatte aber des Königs Waffenträger alles mit angehört, und weil er dem jungen Herrn gewogen und hold war, lief er hin und erzählte ihm alles. Das Schneiderlein war guten Muts und sprach: »Dem Ding will ich wohl steuern.« Abends legte es sich zu gewöhnlicher Zeit mit seiner Frau zu Bett und tat bald, als schlief es, da stand sie auf und öffnete die Tür und legte sich wieder. Nun hob es an, gleich als im Schlafe, mit heller Stimme zu reden: »Jung, mach mir das Wams und flick mir die Hosen, oder ich will dir die Elle über die Ohren schlagen! Ich hab sieben auf einen Streich geschlagen, ich hab zwei Riesen getötet, ein Einhorn und eine wilde Sau gefangen und sollte die vor der Kammer fürchten!« Als die draußen die Worte hörten, flohen sie, als wären tausend Teufel hinter ihnen, und keiner wollt sich an das Schneiderlein wagen. Also war es und blieb sein Lebtag ein König.   1819

Die drei Schlangenblätter

Es war einmal ein armer Mann, der hatte einen einzigen Sohn, er konnte ihn aber nicht mehr ernähren. Da sprach der Sohn: »Lieber Vater, es geht Euch so kümmerlich, Ihr könnt mir das Brot nicht mehr geben, ich will fort und sehen, wie ich mir durch die Welt helfe.« Da gab ihm der Vater seinen Segen und nahm mit großer Trauer Abschied, der Sohn aber ward Soldat und zog mit ins Feld. Als er vor den Feind kam, da ging's scharf her und regnete blaue Bohnen, daß seine Kameraden von allen Seiten niederstürzten. Endlich fiel auch ihr Anführer, da wollten die übrigen fliehen, aber der Jüngling trat heraus, sprach ihnen Mut ein und rief: »Unser Vaterland wollen wir nicht lassen!« Da folgten sie ihm, und er drang ein und schlug den Feind. Weil die Nachricht zum König kam, daß dieser allein die Schlacht gewonnen hätte, erhob er ihn, machte ihn zu einem mächtigen und angesehenen Mann und gab ihm große Schätze.

Dieser König hatte eine schöne, aber wunderliche Tochter, die einen seltsamen Schwur getan. Wer nämlich ihr Herr und Gemahl werden wolle, müsse versprechen, sie nicht zu überleben, also daß, wenn sie zuerst stürbe, er sich lebendig mit ihr müsse begraben lassen; dagegen wollte sie ein gleiches tun, wenn er zuerst stürbe. Dieser Schwur aber hatte alle Freier abgeschreckt, weil ein jeder sich fürchtete, lebendig ins Grab gehen zu müssen. Nun sah der Jüngling, als einer der ersten an des Königs Hof, die schöne Tochter und ward von ihrer Schönheit ganz eingenommen, daß er endlich bei dem alten König um sie anhielt. Da antwortete der König: »Wer meine Tochter heiratet, muß sich nicht fürchten, lebendig in das Grab zu gehen«, und erzählte ihm, was sie für einen Schwur getan. Aber seine Liebe war so groß, daß er das Versprechen tat und an die Gefahr nicht dachte, und da ward ihre Hochzeit mit großer Freude gefeiert.

Nun lebten sie eine Zeitlang glücklich und vergnügt miteinander, da geschah es, daß die junge Königin krank ward und kein Arzt ihr helfen konnte, also daß sie starb. Und als sie tot da lag, fiel ihm mit Schrecken ein, was er versprochen hatte, daß er sich lebendig mit ihr wolle begraben lassen, und der alte König ließ alle Tore mit Wachen besetzen, damit er nicht entfliehen sollte, und sprach, nun müßte er halten, was er gelobt hätte. Als der Tag kam, wo die Leiche in das königliche Gewölbe beigesetzt wurde, da ward er mit hinab geführt und dann das Tor verriegelt und verschlossen. Neben dem Sarg stand ein Tisch, darauf ein Licht, vier Laibe Brot und vier Flaschen Wein, wenn das zu Ende ging, mußte er verschmachten.

Nun saß er da bei dem Sarg voll Schmerz und Trauer und aß jeden Tag nur ein Bißlein Brot, trank nur einen Schluck Wein und sah doch, wie der Tod immer näher rückte. Da geschah es, daß er einmal aus der Ecke des Gewölbes eine

Schlange hervorkriechen sah, die sich der Leiche näherte. Und weil er dachte, sie käme, um die Leiche zu verletzen, zog er sein Schwert und sprach: »So lang ich lebe, sollst du sie nicht anrühren«, und hieb die Schlange in drei Stücke. Über eine Weile sah er, wie eine zweite Schlange aus der Ecke herauskroch, doch als sie die andere da tot und zerstückt liegen fand, kroch sie eilig zurück, kam aber bald wieder und hatte drei Blätter im Munde. Dann nahm sie die drei Stücke von der Schlange, legte sie zusammen, wie sich's gehörte, und tat auf jede Wunde eins von den Blättern. Alsbald fügte sich das Getrennte aneinander, und die Schlange regte sich, war lebendig, und beide eilten fort; die Blätter aber blieben auf der Erde liegen. Der Mann hatte alles mit angesehen und dachte: »Welche wunderbare Kraft muß in den Blättern stecken! Haben sie die Schlange wieder lebendig gemacht, so helfen sie vielleicht auch einem Menschen.« Da hob er sie auf und legte eins davon auf den Mund der Toten und auf jedes Auge eins. Alsbald bewegte sich das Blut in ihrem Leib und stieg in das bleiche Angesicht, daß es sich wieder rötete. Da zog sie Atem, schlug die Augen auf und öffnete den Mund und sprach: »Ach Gott! Wo bin ich?« – »Du bist bei mir, liebe Frau«, antwortete er und gab ihr etwas Wein und Brot, um sie zu stärken, und erzählte ihr dann alles, wie es gekommen und er sie wieder ins Leben erweckt. Da stand sie fröhlich auf, und sie klopften an der Türe; so laut, daß es die Wachen hörten und dem Könige meldeten. Der König kam selbst und öffnete die Türe; da standen beide frisch und gesund, und er führte sie hinauf und freute sich mit ihnen, daß nun alle Not überstanden war. Die drei Schlangenblätter aber, die der junge König mitgenommen, gab er einem treuen Diener und sprach: »Verwahr sie sorgfältig und trag sie zu jeder Zeit bei dir, wer weiß, ob sie uns noch helfen können.«

Es war aber, als ob der Frau, seit sie ihr Mann wieder ins Leben erweckt, das Herz sich ganz verändert und umgekehrt hätte. Und als nach einiger Zeit eine Fahrt nach seinem alten Vater geschehen sollte und sie aufs Meer kamen, vergaß sie gänzlich seine große Liebe und Treue, und es erwuchs in ihr eine böse Neigung zu dem Schiffer. Und als der junge König einmal da lag und schlief, ging ihre Bosheit so weit, daß sie zu dem Schiffer sprach: »Komm und hilf mir, wir wollen ihn ins Wasser werfen und zurückfahren, dann will ich sagen, er wär gestorben, und du wärst würdig, mein Mann zu werden und die Krone meines Vaters zu erben.« Da faßte sie ihn am Kopf und der Fischer an den Füßen und warfen ihn über Bord, daß er im Meer ertrinken mußte. Nun wäre der Frau ihr Anschlag gelungen, wenn nicht der treue Diener alles mit angesehen hätte, der machte heimlich ein kleines Schifflein von dem großen los und fuhr der Leiche nach und fischte sie wieder auf. Darauf nahm er die drei Schlangenblätter und legte sie ihm auf Augen und Mund, davon ward er alsbald wieder lebendig.

Nun sprach er zu dem Diener: »Wir wollen rudern Tag und Nacht, damit wir früher bei dem alten König anlangen.« Der König aber, als er sie wieder sah, verwunderte sich und sprach: »Was ist euch begegnet?« Da erzählte ihm der junge König alles, und der alte sprach: »Ich kann's nicht glauben, daß meine Tochter so schlecht soll gehandelt haben«, und hieß sie beide in eine verborgene Kammer gehen, da sollten sie sich vor jedermann heimlich halten. Bald darauf landete die Frau mit dem großen Schiff und kam vor ihren Vater mit ganz betrübtem Gesicht. Sprach er: »Meine Tochter, warum kommst du allein, wo ist dein Mann?« – »Ach«, antwortete sie, wie in großer Trauer, »er ist plötzlich auf dem Meer krank geworden und gestorben; dieser gute Schiffer hat mir beigestanden und weiß, wie alles zugegangen ist.« Da öffnete der König die Kammer und hieß die beiden herausgehen, und als sie ihren Mann erblickte, war sie wie vom Donner gerührt und sank auf die Knie und rief um Gnade. Der König aber sprach: »Da ist keine Gnade, er hat für dich sterben wollen, und du hast ihn im Schlaf umgebracht, du sollst deinen verdienten Lohn haben.« Da ward sie mit dem Schiffer in ein löcheriges Schiff gesetzt und ins Meer hinausgetrieben.

1819

Die sechs Schwäne

Es jagte einmal ein König in einem großen Wald und jagte einem Wild so eifrig nach, daß niemand von seinen Leuten ihm nachfolgen konnte. Zuletzt verirrte er sich und fand keinen Ausgang. Da sah er etwas auf sich zukommen, das ging wie eine alte Frau gebückt und mit wackelndem Kopf und war eine Hexe. Der König redete sie an und sprach: »Zeigt mir doch den Weg durch den Wald.« – »O ja, Herr König«, antwortete sie, »wenn Ihr meine Tochter heiraten und zur Frau Königin machen wollt, dann soll's geschehen, sonst aber nicht, und Ihr müßt hier bleiben und Hungers sterben, denn Ihr kommt nimmermehr ohne mich aus dem Wald.«

Der König, dem sein Leben lieb war, sagte in der Angst ja, und darauf führte ihn die Alte zu dem Mädchen. Es war sehr schön, aber der König hatte es doch nicht lieb und konnte es nicht ohne heimliches Grausen ansehen. Die Hexe brachte sie beide auf den Weg nach des Königs Schloß, und als sie da angelangt waren, mußte er Wort halten und sie zu seiner Gemahlin nehmen.

Der König aber war schon einmal verheiratet gewesen und hatte von der ersten Frau sechs Buben und ein Mädchen und liebte die Kinder über alles auf der Welt. Weil er nun fürchtete, die Stiefmutter könnte ihnen ein Leid antun, so brachte er sie in ein einsames Schloß, das mitten in einem Walde stand. Der Weg dahin war so schwer zu finden, daß er ihn selbst nicht gefunden hätte, wenn ihm nicht von einer weisen Frau ein Knäuel Garn wäre geschenkt worden, das sich, wenn er es vor sich hin auf die Erde warf, von selbst loswickelte und ihm den Weg zeigte. Der König ging oft hinaus zu seinen lieben Kindern, daß es endlich die Königin merkte, neugierig ward und wissen wollte, was er so oft allein in dem Wald zu schaffen habe.

Nun gewann sie die Diener, und diese verrieten ihr das Geheimnis.

Das erste, was sie tat, war, daß sie sich durch List das Knäuel verschaffte, und als sie es hatte, machte sie sieben kleine Hemdchen und ging damit hinaus. Das Knäuel zeigte ihr den Weg, und als die sechs Knaben jemand kommen sahen, meinten sie, es wäre ihr Vater, und sprangen voll Freude heran. Da warf sie über jeden eins von den Hemdchen, und alsbald, wie das ihren Leib berührt hatte, verwandelten sie sich in Schwäne, stiegen auf in die Luft und flogen davon. Sie glaubte nun die Stiefkinder loszusein, weil das Mädchen nicht mitgelaufen war und sie nichts von ihm wußte, und ging wieder heim. Andern Tags kam der König, da fand er niemand als das Mädchen, das erzählte ihm, daß es aus seinem Fensterlein gesehen, wie seine lieben Brüder als Schwäne fortgeflogen wären, und zeigte ihm die Federn, die sie in den Hof hatten fallen lassen und die es aufgelesen. Der König trauerte, dachte aber nicht, daß die Königin die böse Tat vollbracht hätte, und weil er fürchtete, das Mädchen würde ihm auch geraubt, wollte er es mit

fortnehmen. Aber es hatte Angst vor der Stiefmutter und bat, daß es nur noch diese Nacht im Waldschloß bleiben dürfte.

Als aber die Nacht kam, da entfloh es und ging geradezu in den Wald hinein. Es ging die ganze Nacht und auch den andern Tag in einem fort, bis es vor Müdigkeit nicht weiter konnte. Da sah es eine Wildhütte, stieg hinauf und fand eine Stube mit sechs kleinen Betten, aber es getraute nicht, sich in eins hinein zu legen, sondern legte sich unter eins auf die Erde und wollte die Nacht da zubringen. Als aber die Sonne bald untergehen wollte, hörte es ein Rauschen und sah, daß sechs Schwäne zum Fenster herein geflogen kamen. Sie setzten sich auf den Boden und bliesen einander an und bliesen sich alle Federn ab, und da streifte sich ihre Schwanenhaut herunter wie ein Hemd. Da sah sie das Mädchen an und sah, daß es ihre Brüder waren, freute sich und kroch unter dem Bett hervor. Die Brüder, als sie ihr Schwesterchen erblickten, freuten sich auch, waren aber zugleich traurig und sprachen: »Hier kann deines Bleibens nicht sein, das ist eine Herberge für Räuber, die vom Raub heimkommen; wenn sie dich fänden, würden sie dich ermorden.« Da sprach sie: »Könnt ihr mich denn nicht schützen?« – »Nein«, antworteten sie, »denn wir können nur eine Viertelstunde lang jeden Abend unsere Schwanenhaut uns abblasen und haben in der Zeit unsere menschliche Gestalt, hernach werden wir wieder verwandelt.« – »Kann ich euch aber nicht erlösen?« sprach das Mädchen. »Ach nein«, antworteten sie, »das kannst du nicht, denn es ist zu schwer: sechs Jahre lang darfst du nicht sprechen und nicht lachen und mußt in der Zeit sechs Hemdlein aus Sternenblumen für uns zusammennähen, sprichst du ein einziges Wort, so ist alle Arbeit verloren.« Und als die Brüder das gesprochen, war die Viertelstunde herum, und sie wurden wieder in Schwäne verwandelt.

Das Mädchen aber sprach in seinem Herzen: »Ich will meine Brüder erlösen, und sollt' es mein Tod sein.« Und am andern Morgen sammelte es sich Sternblumen, setzte sich damit auf einen hohen Baum und fing an zu nähen. Reden konnte es mit niemand, und lachen wollte es nicht, es saß da und sah nur auf seine Arbeit. Als es schon lange Zeit da zugebracht, geschah es, daß einmal der König dieses Landes in dem Wald jagte und seine Jäger zu dem Baum kamen, auf welchem das Mädchen saß und nähte. Sie riefen: »Wer bist du? Komm herab zu uns.« Aber es gab keine Antwort und schüttelte nur mit dem Kopf. Als sie von neuem riefen, wollte es sie mit Geschenken befriedigen und warf ihnen seine goldne Halskette herab. Und, weil sie nicht abließen, auch noch seinen Gürtel, als auch dies nichts half, seine Strumpfbänder, endlich alles, was es entbehren konnte, so daß es nichts mehr als sein Hemdlein behielt. Die Jäger waren aber damit nicht zufrieden, stiegen auf den Baum, hoben das Mädchen herab und brachten es vor den König. Der König fragte es auch: »Wer bist du? Und wie bist du dahin gekommen?« und fragte es in allen Sprachen, die er wußte. Aber es antwortete nicht und blieb stumm wie ein Fisch; doch weil es so schön war, daß er meinte, niemals jemand Schöneres gesehen zu haben, ward sein Herz gerührt von großer Liebe. Er wickelte es in seinen Mantel, nahm es vor sich aufs Pferd und brachte es in sein Schloß. Da ließ er ihm reiche Kleider antun, daß es strahlte wie der helle Tag, aber es war kein Wort aus ihm zu bringen. Doch setzte er es bei Tisch an seine Seite und ward von seinen Mienen und seiner Sittsamkeit so bewegt, daß er sprach: »Diese begehre ich zu heiraten und keine andere auf der Welt«, und vermählte sich nach einigen Tagen mit ihr.

Nun hatte der König eine böse Mutter, die war unzufrieden mit dieser Heirat, sprach schlecht von der Königin und sagte: »Wer weiß, wo die stumme Dirne her ist, die ist eines Königs nicht würdig.« Über ein Jahr, als die Königin das erste Kind zur Welt brachte, nahm es die Alte weg und bestrich ihm den Mund mit Blut. Dann ging sie zum König und klagte sie als eine Menschenfresserin an. Der König aber aus großer Liebe wollte es nicht glauben und litt nicht, daß ihr ein Leid angetan wurde. Sie aber saß beständig und nähte an den Hemden und achtete auf nichts anderes. Das nächstemal, als die Königin wieder einen schönen Knaben gebar, da übte die falsche Schwiegermutter denselben Betrug aus, aber der König konnte sich nicht entschließen, ihren Reden Glauben beizumessen, und sprach: »Sie ist stumm und kann sich nicht verteidigen, sonst würde ihre Unschuld an den Tag kommen.« Als aber zum drittenmal die Alte das neugeborne Kind raubte und die Königin anklagte, die kein Wort zu ihrer Verteidigung sprach, da konnte der König die Gesetze nicht länger abwenden, und sie ward verurteilt, durch Feuer vom Leben zum Tod gebracht zu werden.

Als der Tag herankam, wo das Urteil sollte vollzogen werden, da war auch gerade der letzte Tag von den sechs Jahren, in denen sie nicht sprechen und nicht lachen durfte, um ihre lieben Brüder aus des Zaubers Macht zu befreien. Die sechs Hemden waren fertig geworden, nur daß an dem letzten der linke Ärmel fehlte. Wie sie nun zum Scheiterhaufen geführt wurde, nahm sie die sechs Hemden mit sich, und als sie oben stand und das Feuer eben sollte angezündet werden, schaute sie aufwärts und sah sechs Schwäne durch die Luft her ziehen. Da regte sich ihr Herz in Freuden, und sie sprach zu sich: »Ach Gott, nun soll die schwere Zeit herum sein!« Die Schwäne rauschten bald über ihr und senkten sich herab, daß sie die Hemden überwerfen konnte, und wie sie davon berührt waren, fielen die Schwanenhäute ab, und ihre Brüder standen leibhaftig, frisch und schön vor ihr; nur dem sechsten fehlte der linke Arm, und er hatte dafür einen Schwanenflügel an dem Rücken. Sie herzten sich und küßten sich, und die Königin ging darauf zum König, der ganz bestürzt war, und sprach: »Liebster Gemahl, nun ist mir die Sprache wiedergegeben, ich bin unschuldig angeklagt worden«, und erzählte ihm, wie die alte Schwiegermutter so schändlich sie verleumdet und daß sie die drei jungen Söhne verborgen halte. Da wurden sie zu großer Freude des Königs herbeigeholt, die Alte aber wurde zur Strafe auf den Scheiterhaufen gebunden und zu Asche verbrannt. Der König und die Königin mit ihren sechs Brüdern lebten lange Jahre in Glück und Frieden.   1819

Der wunderliche Spielmann

Es war einmal ein wunderlicher Spielmann, der ging durch einen Wald mutterselig allein. Da sprach er zu sich selber: »Mir wird hier Zeit und Weile lang, ich muß einen guten Gesellen herbeiholen«, nahm seine Geige vom Rücken und fiedelte eins, daß es durch die Bäume schallte. Nicht lange, so kam ein Wolf dahergegangen. »Ach, ein Wolf kommt!« sagte der Spielmann; aber der Wolf schritt näher und sprach zu ihm: »Ei, du lieber Spielmann; was fiedelst du so schön! Das möcht ich auch lernen.« – »Das ist bald gelernt«, sagte der Spielmann, »wenn du alles tun willst, was ich dich heiße.« – »Ja«, antwortete der Wolf, »ich will dir gehorchen wie der Schüler seinem Meister.« Nun gingen sie ein Stück Weg zusammen und kamen an einen alten Eichbaum, der innen ganz hohl und in der Mitte durchgerissen war. »Siehst du«, sprach der Spielmann, »willst du fiedeln lernen, so leg die Vorderpfoten in diese Spalte.« Der Wolf tat's, aber der Spielmann hob schnell einen Stein auf und schlug ihm die beiden Pfoten mit einem Schlag fest, daß er wie ein Gefangener liegen bleiben mußte. »Nun warte da so lange, bis ich wiederkomme«, sagte der Spielmann und ging weiter.

Über eine Weile sprach er zu sich selber: »Mir wird die Zeit lang, ich muß einen andern Gesellen holen«, nahm seine Geige und fiedelte wieder in den Wald hinein. Alsbald kam ein Fuchs dahergewandelt.

»Ach, ein Fuchs kommt!« rief der Spielmann. Der Fuchs sprach aber zu ihm: »Ei, du lieber Spielmann, was fiedelst du schön! Das möcht ich auch lernen.« – »Das ist bald gelernt«, sprach der Spielmann, »wenn du alles tun willst, was ich dich heiße.« – »Ja«, antwortete der Fuchs, »ich will dir gehorchen wie der Schüler seinem Meister.« Nun gingen sie ein Stück Weg zusammen, bis sie zu einem engen Fußweg kamen, auf dessen beiden Seiten hohe Sträucher standen. Da hielt der Spielmann still, bog von der einen Seite einen Haselnußstamm zur Erde herab und hielt das Ende mit seinem Fuß fest, dann bog er auch einen von der andern Seite herab und sprach: »Nun, Füchslein, komm, wenn du was lernen willst, und reich mir deine linke Vorderpfote.« Der Fuchs tat's, und der Spielmann band sie ihm an den linken Stamm. »Füchslein, nun reich mir die rechte.« Es geschah, und der Spielmann band sie ihm an den rechten Stamm. Dann ließ er los, und die Bäumchen fuhren in die Höhe und schnellten das Füchslein hinauf, daß es in der Luft schwebte und zappelte. »Nun warte da, bis ich wiederkomme«, sagte der Spielmann und ging weiter.

Bald aber sprach er wiederum zu sich: »Die Zeit wird mir lang, ich muß mir einen Gesellen holen«, nahm die Geige und fiedelte, daß es eine Art hatte. Da kam ein Häslein dahergelaufen. »Ach, ein Hase kommt!« rief der Spielmann. Aber das Tier sprach zu ihm: »Ei, du lieber Spielmann, was fiedelst du so schön, das möcht ich auch lernen.« – »Das ist bald gelernt«, sprach der Spielmann, »wenn du alles tun willst, was ich dich heiße.« – »Ja«, antwortete das Häslein, »ich will dir gehorchen wie der Schüler seinem Meister.« Nun gingen sie ein Stück Wegs zusammen, bis sie zu einer lichten Stelle im Wald kamen, darauf ein Espenbäumchen stand. Der Spielmann band dem Häslein einen langen Bindfaden um den weichen Hals, das andere Ende knüpfte er an den Stamm des Bäumchens und sprach darauf: »Häslein, munter! Spring mir zwanzigmal um den Baum herum.« Das Häslein

tat's, und wie's zwanzigmal herumgelaufen war, so hatte sich der Bindfaden zwanzigmal um den Stamm gewickelt, und das Häschen war ganz fest und gefangen und mochte ziehen und zerren, wie es wollte, es schnitt sich nur den Faden in den Hals. »Nun warte da, bis ich wiederkomme«, sprach der Spielmann und ging fort.

Der Wolf aber hatte derweil gerückt, gezogen, an dem Stein gebissen und so lange gearbeitet, bis er die Pfoten wieder aus der Spalte brachte und frei wurde. Zornig rief er: »Ich muß dem Spielmann nach und muß ihn zerreißen!« Als ihn der Fuchs daherlaufen sah, rief er: »Ach, Bruder Wolf, mach mich frei, der Spielmann hat mich betrogen.« Da kam der Wolf und zog die Stämme herab und biß die Schnüre entzwei, und beide liefen darauf dem Spielmann nach. Als sie das Häslein kommen sah, rief es um Hilfe; wie sie seine Stimme hörten, gingen sie hin und machten es los; dann suchten sie alle drei ihren Feind.

Der Spielmann aber hatte auf seinem Weg mit der Fiedel sich wieder einen Gesellen herbeigespielt, denn ein armer Holzhauer, zu dem der Klang gedrungen war, konnte sich nicht helfen, mußte seine Arbeit verlassen und war mit dem Beil unter dem Arm gekommen, ihm zuzuhören. Der Spielmann war freundlich, weil er nun einen Menschen gefunden hatte, und dachte nicht, ihm ein Leids anzutun, ja, er blieb stehen und spielte ihm das Schönste und Lieblichste vor, daß jenem das Herz aufging vor Freude. Wie der Holzhauer so stand und horchte, sah er die drei Tiere, den Wolf, den Fuchs und das Häslein, herankommen und merkte wohl, daß sie Böses vorhatten. Da erhob er seine blinkende Axt und stellte sich vor den Spielmann, als wollt' er sagen: »Dem darf niemand etwas tun, so lang ich die Axt schwingen kann!« Und als die Tiere das sahen, ward ihnen so angst, daß sie in den Wald zurückliefen. Der Spielmann aber spielte dem armen Mann noch eins zum Dank und zog dann weiter. 1819

Rumpelstilzchen

Es war einmal ein Müller, der war arm, aber er hatte eine schöne Tochter. Nun traf es sich, daß er mit dem König zu sprechen kam und zu ihm sagte: »Ich habe eine Tochter, die kann Stroh zu Gold spinnen.« Dem König, der das Gold lieb hatte, gefiel die Kunst gar wohl, und er befahl, die Müllerstochter sollte alsbald vor ihn gebracht werden. Dann führte er sie in eine Kammer, die ganz voll Stroh war, gab ihr Rad und Haspel und sprach: »Wenn du diese Nacht durch bis morgen früh dieses Stroh nicht zu Gold versponnen hast, so mußt du sterben.« Darauf ward die Kammer verschlossen, und sie blieb allein darin.

Da saß nun die arme Müllerstochter und wußte um ihr Leben keinen Rat, denn sie verstand gar nichts davon, wie das Stroh zu Gold zu spinnen war, und ihre Angst ward immer größer, daß sie zu weinen anfing. Da ging auf einmal die Türe auf und trat ein kleines Männchen herein und sprach: »Guten Abend, Jungfer Müllerin, warum weint Sie so sehr?« – »Ach!« antwortete das Mädchen, »ich soll Stroh zu Gold spinnen und verstehe es nicht.« Sprach das Männchen: »Was gibst du mir, wenn ich dir's spinne?« – »Mein Halsband«, sagte das Mädchen. Das Männchen nahm das Halsband, setzte sich vor das Rädchen, und schnurr! schnurr! schnurr! dreimal gezogen, war die Spule voll. Dann steckte es eine andere auf, und schnurr! schnurr! schnurr! dreimal gezogen, war auch die zweite voll, und so ging's fort bis zum Morgen, da war alles Stroh versponnen und alle Spulen voll Gold. Als der König kam und nachsah, da erstaunte er und freute sich, aber sein Herz wurde nur noch begieriger, und er ließ die Müllerstochter in eine andere Kammer voll Stroh bringen, die noch viel größer war, und befahl ihr, das auch in einer Nacht zu spinnen, wenn ihr das Leben lieb wäre. Das Mädchen wußte sich nicht zu helfen und weinte, da ging abermals die Türe auf, und das kleine Männchen kam und sprach: »Was gibst du mir, wenn ich dir das Stroh zu Gold spinne?« – »Meinen Ring von der Hand«, antwortete das Mädchen. Das Männchen nahm den Ring und fing wieder an zu schnurren mit dem Rade und hatte bis zum Morgen alles Stroh zu glänzendem Gold gesponnen. Der König freute sich über die Maßen bei dem Anblick des Goldes, war aber noch nicht satt, sondern ließ die Müllerstochter in eine noch größere Kammer voll Stroh bringen und sprach: »Die mußt du noch in dieser Nacht verspinnen, wenn dir das gelingt, sollst du meine Gemahlin werden«; denn, dachte er, eine reichere Frau kannst du auf der Welt nicht haben. Als das Mädchen allein war, kam das Männlein zum drittenmal wieder und sprach: »Was gibst du mir, wenn ich dir auch diesmal das Stroh spinne?« – »Ich habe nichts mehr«, antwortete das Mädchen. »So versprich mir, wenn du Königin wirst, dein erstes Kind.« Wer weiß, wie das noch geht, dachte die Müllerstochter und wußte sich auch in der Not nicht anders zu helfen, so daß sie es dem Männchen versprach, und das Männchen spann noch einmal das Stroh zu Gold. Und als am Morgen der König kam und alles fand, wie er gewünscht hatte, so hielt er Hochzeit mit ihr, und die schöne Müllerstochter ward eine Königin.

Über ein Jahr brachte sie ein schönes Kind zur Welt und dachte gar nicht mehr an das Männchen, da trat es in ihre Kammer und forderte, was ihm versprochen war. Die Königin erschrak und bot dem Männchen alle Reichtümer des Königreichs an, wenn es ihr das Kind lassen wollte, aber das Männchen sprach: »Nein, etwas Lebendes ist mir lieber als alle Schätze der Welt.« Da fing die Königin so an zu jammern und zu weinen, daß es das Männchen doch dauerte, und es sprach: »Drei Tage will ich dir Zeit lassen, wenn du bis dahin meinen Namen weißt, so sollst du dein Kind behalten.«

Nun dachte die Königin die ganze Nacht über an alle Namen, die sie jemals gehört hatte, und schickte einen Boten aus über Land, der sollte sich erkundigen weit und breit nach neuen Namen. Als am andern Tag das Männchen kam, fing sie mit Caspar, Melchior und Balzer an und sagte alle, die sie wußte, nach der Reihe her, aber bei jedem sprach das Männlein: »So heiß ich nicht.« Den zweiten Tag ließ sie herumfragen bei allen Leuten und legte dem Männlein alle die ungewöhnlichsten und seltsamsten vor, als: Rippenbiest, Hammelswade, Schnürbein, aber es blieb wieder dabei: »So heiß ich nicht.« Den dritten Tag kam der Bote wieder zurück und erzählte: »Neue Namen habe ich keinen einzigen finden können, aber wie ich an einen hohen Berg um die Waldecke kam, wo Fuchs und Has sich gute Nacht sagen, so sah ich da ein kleines Haus, und vor dem Haus brannte ein Feuer, und um das Feuer sprang ein gar zu lächerliches Männchen, hüpfte auf einem Bein und schrie:

> ›Heute back ich, morgen brau ich,
> übermorgen hol ich der Frau Königin ihr Kind;
> ach, wie gut ist, daß niemand weiß,
> daß ich Rumpelstilzchen heiß!‹«

Wie die Königin das hörte, war sie ganz froh, und als bald das Männlein kam und sprach: »Nun, Frau Königin, wie heiß ich?«, da fragte sie erst: »Heißest du Cunz?« – »Nein.« – »Heißest du Heinz?« – »Nein.« –

»Heißt du etwa Rumpelstilzchen?«

»Das hat dir der Teufel gesagt! Das hat dir der Teufel gesagt!« schrie das Männlein und stieß mit dem rechten Fuß vor Zorn so tief in die Erde, daß es bis an den Leib hineinfuhr, dann packte es in seiner Wut den linken Fuß mit beiden Händen und riß sich mitten entzwei.

1819

Die kluge Else

Es war ein Mann, der hatte eine Tochter, die hieß die kluge Else. Als sie nun erwachsen war, sprach der Vater: »Wir wollen sie heiraten lassen.« – »Ja«, sagte die Mutter, »wenn nur einer käme, der sie haben wollte.« Endlich kam von weit her einer, der hieß Hans und hielt um sie an, unter der Bedingung, daß die kluge Else auch recht gescheit wäre. »Oh«, sprach der Vater, »die hat Zwirn im Kopf«, und die Mutter sagte: »Ach, die sieht den Wind auf der Gasse laufen und hört die Fliegen husten.« – »Ja«, sprach der Hans, »wenn sie nicht recht gescheit ist, so nehm ich sie nicht.« Als sie nun zu Tisch saßen und gegessen hatten, sprach die Mutter: »Else, geh in den Keller und hol Bier.« Da nahm die Else den Krug von der Wand, ging in den Keller und klappte unterwegs brav mit dem Deckel, damit ihr die Zeit ja nicht lang würde. Als sie unten war, holte sie ein Stühlchen und stellte es vors Faß, damit sie sich nicht zu bücken brauchte und ihrem Rücken etwa nicht weh täte und unverhofften Schaden nähme. Dann tat sie die Kanne vor sich und drehte den Hahn auf, und während der Zeit, da das Bier hinein lief, wollte sie doch ihre Augen nicht müßig lassen und sah oben an die Wand hinauf und erblickte nach vielem Hin- und Herschauen eine Kreuzhacke gerade über sich, welche die Maurer da aus Versehen hatten stecken lassen. Da fing die kluge Else an zu weinen und sprach: »Wenn ich den Hans kriege, und wir kriegen ein Kind, und das ist groß, und wir schicken das Kind in den Keller, daß es hier soll Bier zapfen, so fällt ihm die Kreuzhacke auf den Kopf und schlägt's tot!«

Da blieb sie sitzen und weinte aus Jammer über das bevorstehende Unglück. Die oben saßen, warteten auf den Trunk, aber die kluge Else kam immer nicht. Da sprach die Frau zur Magd: »Geh doch hinunter in den Keller und sieh, wo die Else bleibt.« Die Magd ging und fand sie vor dem Faß sitzend und laut schreiend. »Else, was weinst du?« fragte die Magd. »Ach«, antwortete sie, »soll ich nicht weinen! Wenn ich den Hans kriege, und wir kriegen ein Kind, und das ist groß und soll hier Trinken zapfen, so fällt ihm vielleicht die Kreuzhacke auf den Kopf und schlägt's tot.« Da sprach die Magd: »Was haben wir für eine kluge Else!«, setzte sich zu ihr und fing auch an, über das Unglück zu weinen. Über eine Weile, als die Magd nicht wiederkam und die droben durstig nach dem Trank waren, sprach der Mann zum Knecht: »Geh hinunter in den Keller und sieh, wo die Else und die Magd bleibt.« Der Knecht ging hinab, da saß die kluge Else und die Magd und weinten beide zusammen, da fragte er: »Was weint ihr denn?« – »Ach«, sprach die Else, »soll ich nicht weinen! Wenn ich den Hans kriege, und wir kriegen ein Kind, und das ist groß und soll hier Trinken zapfen, so fällt ihm die Kreuzhacke auf den Kopf und schlägt's tot.« Da sprach der Knecht: »Was haben wir für eine kluge Else!«, setzte sich zu ihr und fing auch an, laut zu heulen. Oben warteten sie auf den Knecht, als

er aber immer nicht kam, sprach der Mann zur Frau: »Geh doch hinunter in den Keller und sieh, wo die Else bleibt.« Die Frau ging hinab und fand alle drei in Wehklagen und fragte nach der Ursache, da erzählte ihr die Else auch, daß ihr zukünftiges Kind wohl würde von der Kreuzhacke totgeschlagen werden, wenn es erst groß wäre und Bier zapfen sollte und die Kreuzhacke fiele herab. Da sprach die Mutter gleichfalls: »Ach, was haben wir für eine kluge Else!«, setzte sich hin und weinte mit. Der Mann oben wartete auch ein Weilchen, als aber seine Frau nicht wieder kam und sein Durst immer stärker ward, sprach er: »Ich muß nur selber in den Keller gehn und sehen, wo die Else bleibt.« Als er aber in den Keller kam und alle da beieinander saßen und weinten und er die Ursache hörte, daß das Kind der Else schuld wäre, das sie vielleicht einmal zur Welt brächte, und von der Kreuzhacke könnte totgeschlagen werden, wenn es gerade zur Zeit, wo sie herab fiele, darunter säße, Bier zu zapfen, da rief er: »Was für eine kluge Else!«, setzte sich hin und weinte auch mit. Der Bräutigam blieb lange oben allein. Da niemand wiederkommen wollte, dachte er, sie werden unten auf dich warten, du mußt auch hingehen und sehen, was sie vorhaben. Als er hinab kam, saßen da fünfe und schrien und jammerten ganz erbärmlich, einer immer besser als der andere. »Ei, was für ein Unglück ist denn geschehen?« fragte er. »Ach, lieber Hans«, sprach die Else, »wenn wir einander heiraten und haben ein Kind, und es ist groß, und wir schicken's vielleicht hierher, Trinken zu zapfen, da kann ihm ja die Kreuzhacke, die da oben ist stecken geblieben, wenn sie herabfallen sollte, den Kopf zerschlagen, daß es liegen bleibt: sollen wir da nicht weinen?« – »Nun«, sprach Hans, »mehr Verstand ist nicht nötig; weil du so eine kluge Else bist, so will ich dich haben«, packte sie bei der Hand und nahm sie mit hinauf und hielt Hochzeit mit ihr.

Als sie der Hans eine Weil hatte, sprach er: »Frau, ich will ausgehen, arbeiten und uns Geld verdienen, geh du ins Feld und schneid das Korn, daß wir Brot haben.« – »Ja, mein lieber Hans, das will ich tun.« Nachdem der Hans fort war, kochte sie sich einen guten Brei und nahm ihn mit ins Feld. Als sie vor den Acker kam, sprach sie zu sich selbst: »Was tu ich? Schneid ich eher oder eß ich eher? Hei! Ich will erst essen!« Nun aß sie ihren Topf mit Brei aus, und als sie dick satt war, sprach sie wieder: »Was tu ich? Schneid ich eher oder schlaf ich eher? Hei! Ich will erst schlafen!« Da legte sie sich ins Korn und schlief ein. Der Hans war längst zu Haus, aber die Else wollte nicht kommen, da sprach er: »Was hab ich für eine kluge Else, die ist so fleißig, daß sie nicht einmal nach Haus kommt und ißt.« Als sie aber noch immer ausblieb und es Abend ward, ging der Hans hinaus und wollte sehen, was sie geschnitten hätte, aber es war nichts geschnitten, sondern sie lag im Korn und schlief. Da eilte Hans geschwind heim und holte ein Vogelgarn mit kleinen Schellen und hängte es um sie herum, und sie schlief noch immer fort. Dann lief er heim, setzte sich auf seinen Stuhl und schloß die Haustüre zu. Endlich erwachte die kluge Else, wie es schon ganz dunkel war, und als sie aufstand, rappelte es um sie herum bei jedem Schritt, den sie tat. Da erschrak sie und ward irre, ob sie auch wirklich die kluge Else wäre, und sprach: »Bin ich's oder bin ich's nicht?« Sie wußte aber nicht, was sie darauf antworten sollte, und stand eine Zeitlang zweifelhaft, endlich dachte sie: »Ich will nach Haus gehen und fragen, ob ich's bin oder nicht, die werden's ja wissen.« Da lief sie vor ihre Haustüre, die war verschlossen, also klopfte sie an das Fenster und rief: »Hans, ist die Else drinnen?« – »Ja«, antwortete der Hans, »sie ist drinnen.« Da war sie erschrocken und sprach: »Ach Gott! dann bin ich's nicht!« und ging vor eine andere Tür, aber als die Leute das Klingeln der Schellen hörten, wollten sie nicht aufmachen, und so ging's ihr überall, da lief sie fort zum Dorf hinaus.

1819

Die sieben Raben

Ein Mann hatte sieben Söhne und immer noch kein Töchterchen, sosehr er's auch wünschte. Endlich gab ihm seine Frau wieder gute Hoffnung zu einem Kinde, und wie's zur Welt kam, war's ein Mädchen. Ob es gleich gar schön war, so war's doch auch schmächtig und klein und sollte wegen seiner Schwachheit die Nottaufe haben. Da schickte der Vater einen der Knaben eilends zur Quelle, Taufwasser zu holen, aber die andern sechs liefen mit. Jeder wollte aber der erste beim Schöpfen sein, und darüber fiel ihnen der Krug in den Brunnen; da standen sie verlegen und wußten nicht, was sie tun sollten, und keiner getraute sich heim. Dem Vater ward unter der Weile angst, das Mädchen müßte ungetauft sterben, und wußte gar nicht, warum die Jungen so lange ausblieben. »Gewiß«, sprach er, »haben sie's wieder über ein Spiel vergessen!« Und als sie immer nicht kamen, fluchte er im Ärger: »Ich wollte, daß die Jungen alle zu Raben würden!« Kaum war das Wort ausgeredet, so hörte er ein Geschwirr über seinem Haupt in der Luft, blickte auf und sah sieben kohlschwarze Raben auf und davon fliegen.

Die Eltern konnten die Verwünschung nicht mehr zurücknehmen, und so traurig sie über den Verlust ihrer sieben Söhne waren, trösteten sie sich einigermaßen durch ihr liebes Töchterchen, das bald zu Kräften kam und mit jedem Tag schöner ward. Es wußte lange Zeit nicht einmal, daß es Geschwister gehabt, denn die Eltern hüteten sich, ihrer vor ihm zu erwähnen, bis es eines Tags von ungefähr die Leute von sich sprechen hörte: ja, sie wäre wohl schön, aber doch eigentlich schuld, daß ihre sieben Brüder durch sie unglücklich geworden. Da wurde sie tief betrübt, ging zu Vater und Mutter und fragte, ob sie denn Brüder gehabt und wo sie hingeraten wären? Nun durften die Eltern das Geheimnis nicht länger verschweigen, sagten jedoch, es sei so des Himmels Verhängnis und ihre Geburt nur der unschuldige

Anlaß gewesen. Allein, das Mädchen machte sich täglich ein Gewissen daraus und glaubte sich fest verbunden, ihre Geschwister zu erlösen, und hatte nicht Ruhe und Rast, bis sie sich heimlich aufmachte und in die weite Welt ging, ihre Brüder irgendwo aufzuspüren und, es koste, was da wolle, zu befreien. Sie nahm nichts mit sich als ein Ringlein von ihren Eltern, einen Laib Brot für den Hunger, ein Krüglein Wasser für den Durst und ein Stühlchen für die Müdigkeit.

Nun ging es immer zu, weit, weit bis an der Welt Ende. Da kam es zur Sonne, aber die war gar zu heiß und fürchterlich und fraß die kleinen Kinder; eilig lief es weg und hin zu dem Mond, aber der war gar zu kalt und auch grausig und bös, und als er das Kind merkte, sprach er: »Ich rieche, rieche Menschenfleisch!« Da machte es sich geschwind fort und kam zu den Sternen, die waren ihm freundlich und gut, und jeder saß auf seinem besondern Stühlchen. Der Morgenstern aber stand auf, gab ihm ein Hinkelbeinchen und sprach: »Wenn du das Beinchen nicht hast, kannst du nicht den Glasberg aufschließen, und in dem Glasberg da sind deine Brüder.«

Das Mädchen nahm das Beinchen, wickelte es wohl in ein Tüchlein und ging wieder fort, so lange, bis es an den Glasberg kam, dessen Tor verschlossen war. Nun wollte es das Beinchen holen, aber wie es das Tüchelchen aufmachte, so war es leer, und es hatte das Geschenk der guten Sterne verloren. Was sollte es nun anfangen, seine Brüder wollte es erretten und hatte keinen Schlüssel zum Glasberg? Das gute Schwesterchen nahm ein Messer, schnitt sich sein kleines Fingerchen ab, steckte es in das Tor und schloß glücklich auf. Als es hineingetreten war, kam ihm ein Zwerglein entgegen und sprach: »Mein Kind, was suchst du?« – »Ich suche meine Brüder, die sieben Raben«, antwortete es. Der Zwerg sprach: »Die Herren Raben sind nicht zu Haus, aber willst du hier so lang warten, bis sie kommen, so tritt ein.« Darauf brachte das Zwerglein die Speise der Raben getragen auf sieben Tellerchen und in sieben Becherchen, und von jedem Tellerchen aß das Schwesterchen ein Bröckchen, und aus jedem Becher trank es ein Schlückchen; in das letzte Becherchen aber ließ es das Ringlein fallen, das es mitgenommen.

Auf einmal hörte es in der Luft ein Geschwirr und ein Geweh, da sprach das Zwerglein: »Jetzt kommen die Herren Raben heimgeflogen!« Da kamen sie, wollten essen und trinken und suchten ihre Tellerchen und Becherchen, da sprach einer nach dem andern: »Wer hat von meinem Tellerchen gegessen? Wer hat aus meinem Becherchen getrunken? Das ist eines Menschen Mund gewesen!« Und wie der siebente auf den Grund kam, fiel ihm das Ringlein entgegen, da sah er ihn an und erkannte, daß er von Vater und Mutter war, und sprach: »Gott geb, unser Schwesterlein wär da, so wären wir erlöst!« Wie das das Mädchen hörte, das hinter der Türe stand und lauschte, so trat es hervor, und da bekamen alle die Raben ihre menschliche Gestalt wieder. Und sie herzten und küßten einander und zogen fröhlich heim.

1819

Der faule Heinz

Heinz war faul, und obgleich er weiter nichts zu tun hatte, als seine Ziege täglich auf die Weide zu treiben, so seufzte er dennoch, wenn er nach vollbrachtem Tagewerk abends nach Hause kam, und sprach: »Es ist in Wahrheit eine schwere Last und ein mühseliges Geschäft, so eine Ziege jahraus, jahrein bis in den späten Herbst ins Feld zu treiben. Und wenn man sich noch dabei hinlegen und schlafen könnte! Aber nein, da muß man die Augen aufhaben, damit sie die jungen Bäume nicht beschädigt, durch die Hecke in einen Garten dringt oder gar davon läuft. Wie soll da einer zur Ruhe kommen und seines Lebens froh werden!« Er setzte sich, sammelte seine Gedanken und überlegte, wie er sich von dieser Bürde frei machen könnte. Lange war alles Nachsinnen vergeblich, plötzlich fiel's ihm wie Schuppen von den Augen. »Ich weiß, was ich tue«, rief er aus, »ich heirate die dicke Trine; die hat auch eine Ziege und kann meine mit austreiben, so brauche ich mich nicht länger zu quälen.«

Heinz erhob sich also, setzte seine müden Glieder in Bewegung, ging quer über die Straße, denn weiter war der Weg nicht zu den Eltern der dicken Trine, und hielt um ihre arbeitsame und tugendreiche Tochter an. Die Eltern besannen sich nicht lange und willigten ein. Nun ward die dicke Trine Heinzens Frau und trieb die beiden Ziegen aus, und Heinz hatte gute Tage, so daß er sich von keiner andern Arbeit zu erholen brauchte als von seiner eigenen Faulheit. Nur dann und wann ging er mit hinaus und sagte: »Es geschieht bloß, damit mir die Ruhe hernach desto besser schmeckt; man verliert sonst alles Gefühl dafür.«

Aber die dicke Trine war auch faul. »Lieber Heinz«, sprach sie eines Tages, »warum sollen wir uns das Leben ohne Not sauer machen und unsere beste Jugendzeit verkümmern? Ist es nicht besser, wir geben die beiden Ziegen, die jeden Morgen einen mit ihrem Meckern im besten Schlaf stören, unserm Nachbar, und der gibt uns einen Bienenstock dafür? Den Bienenstock stellen wir an einen sonnigen Platz hinter das Haus und bekümmern uns weiter nicht darum. Die Bienen brauchen nicht gehütet und nicht ins Feld getrieben zu werden; sie fliegen aus, finden den Weg nach Haus von selbst wieder und sammeln Honig, ohne daß es uns die geringste Mühe macht.« – »Du hast wie eine verständige Frau gesprochen«, antwortete Heinz, »deinen Vorschlag wollen wir ohne Zaudern ausführen; außerdem schmeckt und nährt der Honig besser als die Ziegenmilch und läßt sich auch länger aufbewahren.«

Der Nachbar gab für die beiden Ziegen gerne einen Bienenstock. Die Bienen flogen unermüdlich vom frühen Morgen bis zum späten Abend aus und ein und füllten den Stock mit dem schönsten Honig, so daß Heinz im Herbst einen ganzen Krug voll herausnehmen konnte.

Sie stellten den Krug auf ein Brett, das oben an der Wand in ihrer Schlafkammer befestigt war, und weil sie fürchteten, er könnte ihnen gestohlen werden oder die Mäuse könnten darüber geraten, so holte Trine einen starken Haselstock herbei und legte ihn neben ihr Bett, damit sie ihn, ohne unnötigerweise aufzustehen, mit der Hand erreichen und die ungebetenen Gäste von dem Bette aus verjagen könnte.

Der faule Heinz verließ das Bett nicht gerne vor Mittag. »Wer früh aufsteht«, sprach er, »sein Gut verzehrt.« Eines Morgens, als er so am hellen Tag noch in den Federn lag und von dem langen Schlaf ausruhte, sprach er zu seiner Frau: »Die Weiber lieben die Süßigkeit, und du naschst von dem Honig, es ist besser, ehe er von dir allein ausgegessen wird, daß wir dafür eine Gans mit einem jungen Gänslein erhandeln.« — »Aber nicht eher«, erwiderte Trine, »als bis wir ein Kind haben, das sie hütet. Soll ich mich etwa mit den jungen Gänsen plagen und meine Kräfte unnötigerweise dabei zusetzen?« — »Meinst du«, sagte Heinz, »der Junge werde Gänse hüten? Heutzutage gehorchen die Kinder nicht mehr; sie tun nach ihrem eigenen Willen, weil sie sich klüger dünken als die Eltern, gerade wie jener Knecht, der die Kuh suchen sollte und drei Amseln nachjagte.« — »Oh«, antwortete Trine, »dem soll es schlecht bekommen, wenn er nicht tut, was ich sage.

Einen Stock will ich nehmen und mit ungezählten Schlägen ihm die Haut gerben. Siehst du, Heinz«, rief sie in ihrem Eifer und faßte den Stock, mit dem sie die Mäuse verjagen wollte, »siehst du, so will ich auf ihn losschlagen.« Sie holte aus, traf aber unglücklicherweise den Honigkrug über dem Bette. Der Krug sprang wider die Wand und fiel in Scherben herab, und der schöne Honig floß auf den Boden. »Da liegt nun die Gans mit dem jungen Gänslein«, sagte Heinz, »und braucht nicht gehütet zu werden. Aber ein Glück ist es, daß mir der Krug nicht auf den Kopf gefallen ist. Wir haben alle Ursache, mit unserm Schicksal zufrieden zu sein.« Und da er in einer Scherbe noch etwas Honig bemerkte, so langte er danach und sprach ganz vergnügt: »Das Restchen, Frau, wollen wir uns noch schmecken lassen, und dann nach dem gehabten Schrecken ein wenig ausruhen, was tut's, wenn wir etwas später als gewöhnlich aufstehen, der Tag ist doch noch lang genug.«

1837

Die zwölf Jäger

Es war einmal ein Königssohn, der hatte eine Braut und hatte sie sehr lieb. Als er nun bei ihr saß und ganz vergnügt war, da kam die Nachricht, daß sein Vater todkrank läge und ihn noch vor seinem Ende zu sehen verlangte. Da sprach er zu seiner Liebsten: »Ich muß nun fort und muß dich verlassen, da geb ich dir einen Ring zu meinem Andenken. Wenn ich König bin, komm ich wieder und hol dich heim.« Da ritt er fort, und als er bei seinem Vater anlangte, so war dieser sterbenskrank und dem Tode nah. Er sprach aber zu ihm: »Liebster Sohn, ich habe dich vor meinem Ende noch einmal sehen wollen, versprich mir, nach meinem Willen dich zu verheiraten«, und nannte ihm eine gewisse Königstochter, die sollte seine Gemahlin werden. Der Sohn war so betrübt, daß er sich gar nicht bedachte, sondern sprach: »Ja, lieber Vater, was Ihr Wille ist, soll geschehen«, und darauf schloß der König die Augen und starb.

Als nun der Sohn zum König ausgerufen und die Trauerzeit verflossen war, mußte er das Versprechen halten, das er seinem Vater gegeben hatte, und ließ um die Königstochter werben, und sie wurde ihm auch zugesagt. Da hörte das seine erste Braut und grämte sich über die Untreue so sehr, daß sie fast verging. Da sprach ihr Vater zu ihr: »Liebstes Kind, warum bist du so traurig? Was du wünschest, das soll doch geschehen.« Sie bedachte sich einen Augenblick, dann sprach sie: »Lieber Vater, ich wünsche mir elf Mädchen, von Angesicht, Gestalt und Wuchs mir völlig gleich.« Sprach der König: »Wenn's möglich ist, soll's erfüllt werden«, und ließ in seinem ganzen Reich so lange suchen, bis elf Jungfrauen gefunden waren, seiner Tochter von Angesicht, Gestalt und Wuchs völlig gleich.

Als sie zu der Königstochter kamen, ließ diese zwölf Jägerkleider machen, eins wie das andere, und die elf Jungfrauen mußten die Jägerkleider anziehen, und sie selber zog das zwölfte an. Und darauf nahm sie Abschied von ihrem Vater und ritt mit ihnen fort, und ritt an den Hof ihres ehemaligen Bräutigams, den sie so sehr liebte. Da fragte sie an, ob er Jäger brauche, und ob er sie alle zusammen nicht in seinen Dienst nehmen wollte. Der König sah sie an und erkannte sie nicht; weil es aber so schöne Leute waren, sprach er, ja, er wollte sie gerne nehmen, und da waren sie die zwölf Jäger des Königs.

Der König aber hatte einen Löwen, das war ein wunderliches Tier, denn er wußte alles Verborgene und Heimliche. Es trug sich zu, daß er eines Abends zum König sprach: »Du meinst, du hättest da zwölf Jäger?« – »Ja«, sagte der König, »zwölf Jäger sind's.« Sprach der Löwe weiter: »Du irrst dich, das sind zwölf Mädchen.« Antwortete der König: »Das ist nimmermehr wahr, wie willst du mir das beweisen?« – »Oh, laß nur Erbsen in dein Vorzimmer streuen«, antwortete der Löwe, »da wirst du's gleich sehen. Männer haben einen festen Tritt, wenn die darüber hingehen, regt sich keine, aber Mädchen, die trippeln und trappeln und schlurfeln, und die Erbsen rollen.« Dem König gefiel der Rat wohl, und er ließ die Erbsen streuen.

Es war aber ein Diener des Königs, der war den Jägern gut, und wie er hörte, daß sie sollten auf die Probe gestellt werden, ging er hin und erzählte ihnen alles wieder und sprach: »Der Löwe will dem König weismachen, ihr wärt Mädchen.« Da dankte ihm die Königstochter und sprach hernach zu ihren Jungfrauen: »Tut euch Gewalt an und tretet fest auf die Erbsen.« Als nun der König am andern Morgen die zwölf Jäger zu sich rufen ließ, und sie kamen ins Vorzimmer, wo die Erbsen lagen, so traten sie so fest darauf und hatten einen so sichern starken Gang, daß auch nicht eine rollte oder sich bewegte. Da gingen sie wieder fort, und der König sprach zum Löwen: »Du hast mich belogen, sie gehen ja wie Männer.« Antwortete der Löwe: »Sie haben's gewußt, daß sie sollten auf die Probe gestellt werden, und haben sich Gewalt angetan. Laß nur einmal zwölf Spinnräder ins Vorzimmer bringen, so werden sie herzukommen und werden sich daran freuen, und das tut kein Mann.« Dem König gefiel der Rat, und er ließ die Spinnräder ins Vorzimmer stellen.

Der Diener aber, der's redlich mit den Jägern meinte, ging hin und entdeckte ihnen den Anschlag. Da sprach die Königstochter, als sie allein waren, zu ihren elf Mädchen: »Tut euch Gewalt an und blickt nicht einmal nach den Spinnrädern.« Wie nun der König am andern Morgen seine zwölf Jäger rufen ließ, so kamen sie durch das Vorzimmer und sahen die Spinnräder gar nicht an. Da sprach der König wiederum zum Löwen: »Du hast mich belogen, es sind Männer, denn sie haben die Spinnräder nicht angesehen.« Der Löwe antwortete: »Sie haben's gewußt, daß sie sollten auf die Probe gestellt werden, und haben sich Gewalt angetan.« Sprach der König: »Ich glaube dir nun nicht mehr.«

Die zwölf Jäger aber folgten dem König beständig zur Jagd, und er hatte sie je länger, je lieber. Nun geschah es, daß, als sie einmal auf der Jagd waren, die Nachricht kam, die Braut des Königs wäre im Anzug. Wie die rechte Braut das hörte, tat ihr's so weh, daß es ihr fast das Herz abstieß und sie ohnmächtig auf die Erde fiel. Der König meinte, seinem lieben Jäger sei etwas begegnet, lief herzu und wollte ihm helfen und zog ihm den Handschuh aus. Und da erblickte er den Ring, den er seiner rechten Braut gegeben, und wie er ihr recht ins Gesicht sah, erkannte er sie. Da ward sein Herz so gerührt, daß er sie küßte, und als sie die Augen aufschlug, sprach er: »Du bist mein, und ich bin dein, und kein Mensch auf der Welt kann das ändern.« Zu der andern Braut aber schickte er einen Boten und ließ sie bitten, in ihr Reich zurückzukehren, denn er habe schon eine Gemahlin, und wer einen alten Schlüssel wiedergefunden habe, brauche den neuen nicht. Darauf ward die Hochzeit gefeiert, und der Löwe kam wieder in Gnade, weil er doch die Wahrheit gesagt hatte.

1819

Der Riese und der Schneider

Einem Schneider, der ein großer Prahler war, aber ein schlechter Zahler, kam es in den Sinn, ein wenig auszugehen und sich in dem Wald umzuschauen. Sobald er nur konnte, verließ er seine Werkstatt,

> wanderte seinen Weg,
> über Brücke und Steg,
> bald da, bald dort,
> immer fort und fort.

Als er nun draußen war, erblickte er in der blauen Ferne einen steilen Berg und dahinter einen himmelhohen Turm, der aus einem wilden und finstern Wald hervorragte. »Potz Blitz!« rief der Schneider. »Was ist das?« Und weil ihn die Neugierde gewaltig stach, so ging er frisch darauf los. Was sperrte er aber Maul und Augen auf, als er in die Nähe kam, denn der Turm hatte Beine, sprang in einem Satz über den steilen Berg und stand als ein großmächtiger Riese vor dem Schneider. »Was willst du hier, du winziges Fliegenbein«, rief er mit einer Stimme, als wenn's von allen Seiten donnerte. Der Schneider wisperte: »Ich will mich umschauen, ob ich mein Stückchen Brot in dem Wald verdienen kann.« – »Wenn's um die Zeit ist«, sagte der Riese, »so kannst du ja bei mir im Dienst eintreten.« – »Wenn's sein muß, warum das nicht? Was krieg ich aber für einen Lohn?« – »Was du für einen Lohn kriegst?« sagte der Riese. »Das sollst du hören. Jährlich dreihundertundfünfundsechzig Tage, und wenn's ein Schaltjahr ist, noch einen obendrein. Ist dir das recht?« – »Meinetwegen«, antwortete der Schneider und dachte in seinem Sinn: Man muß sich strecken nach seiner Decke. Ich such mich bald wieder loszumachen.

Darauf sprach der Riese zu ihm: »Geh, kleiner Halunke, und hol mir einen Krug Wasser.« – »Warum nicht lieber gleich den Brunnen mitsamt der Quelle?« fragte der Prahlhans und ging mit dem Krug zu dem Wasser. »Was, den Brunnen mitsamt der Quelle?« brummte der Riese, der ein bißchen tölpisch und albern war, in den Bart hinein und fing an, sich zu fürchten: Der Kerl kann mehr als Äpfel braten, der hat einen Alraun im Leib. Sei auf deiner Hut, alter Hans, das ist kein Diener für dich. Als der Schneider das Wasser gebracht hatte, befahl ihm der Riese, in dem Wald ein paar Scheite Holz zu hauen und heimzutragen. »Warum nicht lieber den ganzen Wald mit einem Streich,

> den ganzen Wald,
> mit jung und alt,

mit allem, was er hat,
knorzig und glatt?«

fragte das Schneiderlein und ging, das Holz zu hauen.

»Was, den ganzen Wald,
mit jung und alt,
mit allem, was er hat,
knorzig und glatt?

Und den Brunnen mitsamt der Quelle?« brummte der leichtgläubige Riese in den Bart und fürchtete sich noch mehr: Der Kerl kann mehr als Äpfel braten, der hat einen Alraun im Leib. Sei auf deiner Hut, alter Hans, das ist kein Diener für dich. Wie der Schneider das Holz gebracht hatte, befahl ihm der Riese, zwei oder drei wilde Schweine zum Abendessen zu schießen. »Warum nicht lieber gleich tausend auf einen Schuß, und die alle hierher?« fragte der hoffärtige Schneider. »Was«, rief der Hasenfuß von einem Riesen und war heftig erschrocken. »Laß es nur für heute gut sein und lege dich schlafen.«

Der Riese fürchtete sich so gewaltig, daß er die ganze Nacht kein Auge zutun konnte und hin und her dachte, wie er's anfangen sollte, um sich den verwünschten Hexenmeister von Diener je eher, je lieber vom Hals zu schaffen. Kommt Zeit, kommt Rat. Am andern Morgen gingen der Riese und der Schneider zu einem Sumpf, um den ringsherum eine Menge Weidenbäume standen. Da sprach der Riese: »Hör einmal, Schneider, setz dich auf eine von den Weidenruten, ich möchte um mein Leben gern sehen, ob du imstand bist, sie herabzubiegen.« Husch, saß das Schneiderlein oben, hielt den Atem an und machte sich schwer, so schwer, daß sich die Gerte niederbog. Als er aber wieder Atem schöpfen mußte, da schnellte sie ihn, weil er zum Unglück kein Bügeleisen in die Tasche gesteckt hatte, zur großen Freude des Riesen so weit in die Höhe, daß man ihn gar nicht mehr sehen konnte. Wenn er nicht wieder heruntergefallen ist, so wird er wohl noch oben in der Luft herumschweben.

1843

Die Boten des Todes

Vor alten Zeiten wanderte einmal ein Riese auf der großen Landstraße, da sprang ihm plötzlich ein unbekannter Mann entgegen und rief: »Halt! Keinen Schritt weiter!« – »Was«, sprach der Riese, »du Wicht, den ich zwischen den Fingern zerdrücken kann, du willst mir den Weg vertreten? Wer bist du, daß du so keck reden darfst?« – »Ich bin der Tod«, erwiderte der andere, »mir widersteht niemand, und auch du mußt meinen Befehlen gehorchen.« Der Riese aber weigerte sich und fing an, mit dem Tode zu ringen. Es war ein langer, heftiger Kampf; zuletzt behielt der Riese die Oberhand und schlug den Tod mit seiner Faust nieder, daß er neben einem Stein zusammensank. Der Riese ging seiner Wege, und der Tod lag da besiegt und war so kraftlos, daß er sich nicht wieder erheben konnte. »Was soll daraus werden«, sprach er, »wenn ich da in der Ecke liegenbleibe? Es stirbt niemand mehr auf der Welt, und sie wird so mit Menschen angefüllt werden, daß sie nicht mehr Platz haben, nebeneinander zu stehen.«

Indem kam ein junger Mensch des Wegs, frisch und gesund, sang ein Lied und warf seine Augen hin und her. Als er den halb Ohnmächtigen erblickte, ging er mitleidig heran, richtete ihn auf, flößte ihm aus seiner Flasche einen stärkenden Trank ein und wartete, bis er wieder zu Kräften kam. »Weißt du auch«, fragte der Fremde, indem er sich aufrichtete, »wer ich bin und wem du wieder auf die Beine geholfen hast?« – »Nein«, antwortete der Jüngling, »ich kenne dich nicht.« – »Ich bin der Tod«, sprach er, »ich verschone niemand und kann auch mit dir keine Ausnahme machen. Damit du aber siehst, daß ich dankbar bin, so verspreche ich dir, daß ich dich nicht unversehens überfalle, sondern dir erst meine Boten senden will, bevor ich komme und dich abhole.« – »Wohlan«, sprach der Jüngling, »immer ein Gewinn, daß ich weiß, wann du kommst, und so lange wenigstens sicher vor dir bin.« Dann zog er weiter, war lustig und guter Dinge und lebte in den Tag hinein. Allein, Jugend und Gesundheit hielten nicht lange aus, bald kamen Krankheiten und Schmerzen, die ihn bei Tag plagten und ihm nachts die Ruhe wegnahmen. »Sterben werde ich nicht«, sprach er zu sich selbst, »denn der Tod sendet erst seine Boten, ich wollte nur, die bösen Tage der Krankheit wären erst vorüber.«

Sobald er sich gesund fühlte, fing er wieder an, in Freuden zu leben. Da klopfte ihn eines Tages jemand auf die Schulter. Er blickte sich um, und der Tod stand hinter ihm und sprach: »Folge mir, die Stunde deines Abschieds von der Welt ist gekommen.« – »Wie«, antwortete der Mensch, »willst du dein Wort brechen? Hast du mir nicht versprochen, daß du mir, bevor du selbst kämest, deine Boten senden wolltest? Ich habe keinen gesehen.« – »Schweig«, erwiderte der Tod, »habe ich dir nicht einen Boten über den andern geschickt? Kam nicht das Fieber, stieß dich an,

rüttelte dich und warf dich nieder? Hat der Schwindel dir nicht den Kopf betäubt? Zwickte dich nicht die Gicht in allen Gliedern? Brauste dir's nicht in den Ohren? Nagte nicht der Zahnschmerz in deinen Backen? Ward dir's nicht dunkel vor den Augen? Über das alles, hat nicht mein leiblicher Bruder, der Schlaf, dich jeden Abend an mich erinnert? Lagst du nicht in der Nacht, als wärst du schon gestorben?« Der Mensch wußte nichts zu erwidern, ergab sich in sein Geschick und ging mit dem Tode fort.

1840

Der Räuberbräutigam

Es war einmal ein Müller, der hatte eine schöne Tochter. Als sie nun herangewachsen war, dachte er, wenn ein ordentlicher Freier kommt und um sie anhält, so will ich sie ihm geben, damit sie versorgt wird. Es trug sich zu, daß einer kam, der sehr reich schien, und da der Vater nichts an ihm auszusetzen wußte, so versprach er ihm seine Tochter; das Mädchen aber hatte ihn nicht recht lieb, wie eine Braut ihren Bräutigam lieb haben soll, und fühlte ein Grauen in seinem Herzen, sooft es ihn ansah oder an ihn dachte. Er sprach zu ihr: »Warum besuchst du mich nicht, da du meine Braut bist?« – »Ich weiß nicht, wo Euer Haus ist«, sagte das Mädchen. »Draußen ist's, im grünen dunkeln Wald«, antwortete der Bräutigam. Da suchte es Ausreden und sprach: »Ich kann den Weg dahin nicht finden.« Der Bräutigam aber sagte: »Bis Sonntag mußt du hinaus zu mir kommen, dazu hab ich schon Gäste eingeladen, und damit du den Weg durch den Wald findest, so will ich dir Asche streuen.«

Als es nun Sonntag war und das Mädchen fortgehen sollte, ward ihm so angst, und es steckte sich beide Taschen voll Erbsen und Linsen. Es kam zu dem Wald, da fand es die Asche gestreut und ging auf dem Weg fort, aber rechts und links warf es bei jedem Schritt ein paar Erbsen und Linsen auf die Erde. Nun ging es fast den ganzen Tag, bis es zu einem Haus kam, das mitten im dunkelsten Walde stand. Es sah niemand darin, und es war alles still, aber auf einmal rief eine Stimme:

> »Kehr um, kehr um, du junge Braut,
> du bist in einem Mörderhaus!«

Wie es sich umsah, war's ein Vogel, der da in einem Bauer saß und der noch einmal rief:

> »Kehr um, kehr um, du junge Braut,
> du bist in einem Mörderhaus.«

Nun ging die schöne Braut weiter aus einer Stube in die andere und durchs ganze Haus, aber es war alles leer, und keine Menschenseele war zu finden. Endlich kam sie auch in den Keller, da saß eine steinalte Frau. »Könnt Ihr mir nicht sagen«, sprach das Mädchen, »ob mein Bräutigam hier wohnt.« – »Ach, du liebes Kind«, antwortete die alte Frau, »du bist in eine Mördergrube gekommen; deine Hochzeit soll mit dem Tod sein, der Räuber will dich ums Leben bringen. Siehst du, da hab ich einen großen Kessel mit Wasser aufsetzen müssen, wenn sie dich haben, zerhacken sie dich und kochen dich darin und wollen dich dann essen. Wenn ich dich nicht rette, so bist du verloren!«

Darauf versteckte sie das Mädchen hinter ein großes Faß und sprach: »Reg dich und beweg dich nicht, sonst ist's um dich geschehen. Wenn die Räuber schlafen, so wollen wir entfliehen, ich habe auch schon längst fortgewollt.« Kaum war das geschehen, so kamen die Räuber heim und führten eine andere Jungfrau mit, waren trunken und hörten nicht ihr Schreien und Jammern. Sie gaben ihr Wein zu trinken, drei Gläser, ein Glas weißen Wein, ein Glas roten und ein Glas gelben, davon zersprang ihr das Herz. Darauf rissen sie ihr die feinen Kleider ab, legten sie auf einen Tisch und zerhackten ihren schönen Leib in Stücke und streuten Salz darüber. Da ward der Braut hinter dem Faß angst, als müßte sie nun auch sterben. Und einer sah, daß an dem kleinen Finger der Gemordeten ein goldener Ring war, und weil er sich nicht gut abziehen ließ, nahm er ein Beil und hieb den Finger ab, aber der Finger sprang in die Höhe und fiel hinter das Faß, der Braut gerade in den Schoß. Der Räuber nahm ein Licht und suchte danach, konnte ihn aber nicht finden, da sprach ein anderer: »Hast du auch schon hinter dem großen Faß gesucht?« – »Ei«, rief die alte Frau, »kommt und eßt und laßt das Suchen bis morgen, der Finger läuft euch nicht fort.«

Da ließen die Räuber vom Suchen ab, gingen und aßen und tranken, die Alte aber tröpfelte ihnen einen Schlaftrunk in den Wein, daß sie sich bald in den Keller hinlegten, schliefen und schnarchten. Als die Braut das hörte, trat sie hinter dem Faß hervor und mußte über die Schlafenden hinwegschreiten, die da reihenweis lagen, und hatte große Angst, sie möchte einen aufwecken. Aber Gott half ihr, daß sie glücklich durchkam, und die Alte stieg mit ihr hinauf, und sie machten sich aus der Mördergrube hinaus. Die gestreute Asche war fortgeweht, aber die Erbsen und Linsen hatten gekeimt und waren aufgegangen und zeigten ihnen beim Mondschein den Weg. Da gingen sie die ganze Nacht, bis sie morgens in der Mühle ankamen. Das Mädchen aber erzählte seinem Vater alles, wie es sich zugetragen hatte.

Als nun der Tag kam, wo die Hochzeit sollte gehalten werden, erschien der Bräutigam, der Müller aber ließ alle seine Verwandte und Bekannte einladen. Wie sie bei Tische saßen, ward einem jedem aufgegeben, etwas zu erzählen. Da sprach der Bräutigam zur Braut: »Nun, mein Herz, weißt du nichts? Erzähl uns auch etwas.« Sie antwortete: »So will ich einen Traum erzählen. Ich ging durch einen

Wald und kam an ein Haus, da war keine Menschenseele darin, aber ein Vogel im Bauer rief zweimal:

> ›Kehr um, kehr um, du junge Braut,
> du bist in einem Mörderhaus!‹

Mein Schatz, das träumte mir nur. – Da ging ich durch alle Stuben, die waren alle leer, bis ich in den Keller kam, wo eine steinalte Frau saß. Ich sprach: ›Wohnt mein Bräutigam hier?‹ Sie aber antwortete: ›Ach! du liebes Kind, du bist in eine Mördergrube gekommen, der Bräutigam will dich zerhacken und töten und will dich dann kochen und essen.‹ – Mein Schatz, das träumte mir nur. – Aber sie versteckte mich hinter ein großes Faß, und kaum war das geschehen, so kamen die Räuber heim und schleppten eine Jungfrau mit sich, der gaben sie dreierlei Wein zu trinken: weißen, roten und gelben, davon zersprang ihr das Herz. – Mein Schatz, das träumte mir nur. – Darauf zogen sie ihr die feinen Kleider ab und zerhackten auf einem Tisch ihren schönen Leib in Stücke und bestreuten sie mit Salz. – Mein Schatz, das träumte mir nur. – Und einer von den Räubern sah, daß an dem Goldfinger noch ein Ring steckte, und weil er schwer abzuziehen war, nahm er ein Beil und hieb ihn ab, aber der Finger sprang in die Höhe und sprang hinter das große Faß und fiel mir gerade in den Schoß, und da ist der Finger mit dem Ring!« Bei diesen Worten zog sie ihn hervor und zeigte ihn den Anwesenden.

Der Räuber, als er das sah und hörte, wurde vor Schrecken kreideweiß und wollte entfliehen, aber die Gäste hielten ihn fest und überlieferten ihn dem Gericht. Da ward er und die ganze Bande für ihre Schandtaten gerichtet. 1819

Tischchen deck dich,
Goldesel und Knüppel aus dem Sack

Es war ein Schneider, der hatte drei Söhne und nur eine Ziege, die alle zusammen mit ihrer Milch ernähren mußte. »Dafür soll sie auch ihr gutes Futter haben«, sagte der Schneider, »und jeden Tag auf die Weide geführt werden.« Nun mußten sie die Söhne nach der Reihe hinausführen. Der älteste brachte sie auf den Kirchhof, wo schöne Kräuter standen, und ließ sie da herum springen und fressen. Abends, als er mit ihr heim wollte, sprach er: »Ziege, bist du satt?« Die Ziege antwortete:

> »Ich bin so satt,
> ich mag kein Blatt: meh! meh!«

»So komm nach Haus«, sprach der Junge, faßte sie am Strickchen und führte sie heim in den Stall und band sie fest. »Nun«, sagte der alte Schneider, »hat die Ziege ihr Futter?« – »Oh«, sprach der Sohn, »die ist so satt, sie mag kein Blatt.« Der Vater wollte aber selbst nachsehen, ging in den Stall und fragte: »Ziege, bist du auch satt?« Da antwortete das Tier:

> »Wovon sollt ich satt sein?
> Ich sprang nur über Gräbelein
> und fand kein einzig Blättelein: meh! meh!«

Der Schneider ward zornig, lief hinauf und sprach zu dem Jungen: »Ei, du Lügner, was hast du meine Ziege hungern lassen?«, nahm seinen Stock von der Wand und jagte ihn hinaus. Am andern Tag war die Reihe am zweiten, der führte die Ziege auch unter lauter gute Kräuter, die fraß sie alle rein ab. Abends, als er heim wollte, sprach er: »Ziege, bist du satt?« Die Ziege antwortete:

> »Ich bin so satt,
> ich mag kein Blatt: meh! meh!«

»So komm nach Haus«, sprach der Junge, zog sie heim und band sie fest. »Nun«, fragte der alte Schneider, »hat die Ziege ihr Futter?« – »Oh«, antwortete der Sohn, »die ist so satt, sie mag kein Blatt.« Der alte Schneider aber wollte selbst nachsehen, ging hinab und fragte: »Ziege, bist du auch satt?« Das Tier antwortete:

> »Wovon sollt ich satt sein?
> Ich sprang nur über Gräbelein
> und fand kein einzig Blättelein: meh! meh!«

Tischchen deck dich, Goldesel und Knüppel aus dem Sack 73

»Ei, der Bösewicht!« schrie der Schneider. »So ein frommes Tier hungern zu lassen!« Lief hinauf, nahm den Stock und schlug den Jungen zur Haustüre hinaus. Die Reihe kam an den dritten, der wollte sich vorsehen und suchte der Ziege das saftigste Futter von der Welt aus. Abends, als er heim wollte, fragte er: »Ziege, bist du auch satt?« Sie antwortete:

>»Ich bin so satt,
>ich mag kein Blatt: meh! meh!«

»So komm nach Haus«, sagte der Junge und führte sie in den Stall und band sie an. »Nun«, sagte der Vater, »hat die Ziege endlich ihr Futter?« – »Oh«, sprach der Sohn, »die ist so satt, sie mag kein Blatt.« Der alte Schneider aber wollte nicht trauen, ging hinab und fragte: »Ziege, bist du auch satt?« Das boshafte Tier sprach:

>»Wie sollt ich satt sein?
>Ich sprang nur über Gräbelein
>und fand kein einzig Blättelein: meh! meh!«

»Wart, du Lügenbrut!« rief der Schneider im größten Zorn. »Willst du mich zum Narren haben!« Sprang mit einem roten Gesicht hinauf nach seinem Stock und jagte auch den jüngsten Sohn fort.

Nun war er mit seiner Ziege ganz allein. Am andern Morgen sprach er zu ihr: »Komm, liebes Tierlein, ich will dich zur Weide führen«, nahm es am Strick und brachte es an grüne Hecken und unter Schafrippe und was die Ziegen sonst gern haben und ließ sie weiden bis zum Abend.

Da sprach er: »Ziege, bist du satt?« Sie antwortete:

>»Ich bin so satt,
>ich mag kein Blatt: meh! meh!«

»So komm nach Haus«, sprach der Schneider, brachte sie in den Stall und band sie fest. »Nun bist du doch einmal satt!« sprach er beim Fortgehen; die Ziege aber machte es ihm nicht besser und rief:

>»Wie sollt ich satt sein?
>Ich sprang nur über Gräbelein
>und fand kein einzig Blättelein: meh! meh!«

Als der Schneider das hörte, stutzte er und sah wohl, daß er seine drei Kinder unschuldig verstoßen hatte. »Wart«, rief er, »du gottloses, undankbares Geschöpf, du sollst dich nicht mehr unter ehrlichen Menschen sehen lassen!«, sprang hinauf, holte sein Bartmesser, seifte der Ziege den Kopf ein und schor ihn so glatt wie seine flache Hand; darauf nahm er die Peitsche und jagte sie hinaus.

Nun war der Schneider traurig, daß er so ganz allein sein Leben zubringen mußte, und hätte gern seine Söhne wieder zu sich genommen, aber niemand wußte, wo sie hingeraten waren. Der älteste war aber zu einem Schreiner in die Lehre gegangen, lernte fleißig und unverdrossen, und als seine Zeit herum war, daß er wandern sollte, gab ihm der Meister ein Tischchen, das sah gar nicht sonderlich aus und war von ganz gewöhnlichem Holz, aber wenn man's hinstellte und sprach: »Tischchen, deck dich!«, ja, da war's auf einmal mit einem saubern Tüchlein bedeckt, und stand da ein Teller mit Messer und Gabel und auf Schüsseln Gesottenes und Gebratenes, so viel nur Platz hatte, und ein groß Glas mit rotem Wein leuchtete, daß einem das Herz lachte. Nun dachte der junge Gesell, du hast genug für dein Lebtag, zog guter Dinge in der Welt umher und bekümmerte sich gar nicht darum, ob ein Wirtshaus gut oder schlecht war, und hatte er Lust, so kehrte er gar nicht ein, sondern im Feld, im Wald oder auf einer Wiese, wo er war, nahm er sein Tischchen vom Rücken, stellte es vor sich und sprach: »Deck dich!« So war alles da, was sein Herz begehrte. Endlich dachte er, du mußt doch deinen Vater wieder sehen, der wird dich mit dem Tischchen gern aufnehmen. Es trug sich zu, daß er auf dem Heimweg abends in ein Wirtshaus kam, darin viel Gäste saßen, die hießen ihn willkommen und sprachen, so er was haben wollte, sollte er sich zu ihnen setzen. »Nein«, antwortete der Schreiner, »ich will euch die paar Bissen nicht von dem Mund wegnehmen, lieber sollt ihr meine Gäste sein.« Sie meinten, er triebe seinen Spaß, aber er stellte sein hölzernes Tischlein mitten in die Stube und sprach: »Tischchen, deck dich!« Da war's alsbald mit Speisen besetzt, die der Wirt gar nicht hätte herbeischaffen können und wovon der Geruch den Gästen gar lieblich in die Nase stieg. »Ei, ist's so gemeint«, sprachen sie, »so wollen wir zulangen«, rückten heran, zogen ihre Messer und ließen sich's wohlschmecken, denn wenn eine Schüssel abgenommen war, stellte sich eine andere von selbst an den leeren Platz.

So waren sie mit dem Gesellen guter Dinge, der Wirt aber stand in einer Ecke und sah zu und wußte nicht, was er davon denken sollte, sprach aber für sich: »So einen Koch könnte ich bei der Wirtschaft wohl brauchen.«

Als es spät ward, legten sich die Gäste nacheinander schlafen, und der junge Gesell war auch zu Bett gegangen und hatte sein Wünschtischchen in eine Ecke gestellt. Um Mitternacht aber machte sich der Wirt auf, denn die Gedanken ließen ihm keine Ruhe, ging in seine Rumpelkammer, holte ein altes Tischchen, das gerade so aussah wie das Tischchen deck dich, stellte das in die Ecke und vertauschte es mit dem guten. Am andern Morgen zahlte der Geselle das Schlafgeld, nahm sein Tischchen aus der Ecke mit, dachte gar nicht, daß er ein falsches hätte, und ging seiner Wege. Zu Mittag kam er bei seinem Vater an, der freute sich von Herzen, als er ihn wiedersah, und sprach: »Nun, mein Sohn, was hast du gelernt?«

– »Vater«, antwortete er, »ich bin ein Schreiner geworden.« – »Was hast du von der Wanderschaft mitgebracht?« sagte der Alte. »Vater, das Beste, was ich mitgebracht habe, ist das Tischchen da.« Der Schneider sah es an und sah, daß es ein altes, schlechtes Tischchen war, aber der Sohn sprach: »Vater, es ist ein Tischchen deck dich; wenn ich das hinstelle und sag ihm, es solle sich decken, so stehen die schönsten Gerichte darauf und ein Wein dabei, der das Herz erfreut; ladet nur alle Verwandten ein, damit sie sich erquicken und erlaben können, denn das Tischchen macht sie alle satt.«

Als nun alle Verwandten beisammen waren, stellte der Geselle sein Tischchen mitten in die Stube und sprach: »Tischchen, deck dich!«, aber es ließ sich nichts sehen, und es blieb so leer wie ein anderer Tisch auch, der die Sprache nicht versteht. Da sah der Sohn wohl, daß er ihm gestohlen war, schämte sich, daß er wie ein Lügner da stand, und die Verwandten gingen ungetrunken und ungegessen wieder heim. Der Vater aber mußte fort schneidern und der Sohn bei einem Meister in die Arbeit gehen.

Der zweite Sohn war zu einem Müller gekommen und hatte bei ihm gelernt. Als er nun seine Jahre herum hatte, sprach der Müller: »Weil du dich so wohl gehalten hast, so schenk ich dir einen Esel, der zieht aber nicht und trägt auch keine Säcke!« – »Wozu ist er dann nütze?« fragte der junge Geselle. »Der speit Gold«, antwortete der Müller, »wenn du ihn auf ein Tuch stellst und sprichst: ›Bricklebrit‹, so speit dir das gute Tier Goldstücke aus, hinten und vorn.« – »Das ist eine schöne Sache«, sprach der Geselle, dankte seinem Meister und zog in die Welt. Wo er hinkam, war ihm das Beste gut genug, und je teurer, je lieber, denn er konnt's bezahlen. Als er sich nun ein wenig in der Welt umgesehen, dachte er, du mußt doch sehen, was dein Vater macht, mit dem Esel wird er dich gern aufnehmen.

Nun trug sich's zu, daß er in dasselbe Wirtshaus kam, wo sein Bruder auch gewesen war. Der Wirt wollte ihm seinen Esel abnehmen, aber er sprach: »Nein, meinen Grauschimmel, den führ ich selbst in den Stall und bind ihn fest, denn ich muß wissen, wo er steht.« Darauf fragte er den Wirt, was zu haben wäre, und hieß ihn das Beste auftischen.

Der Wirt machte Augen und dachte: einer, der seinen Esel selbst anbindet, der hat auch nicht viel zu verzehren; als aber der Geselle in die Tasche griff und ihm zwei Goldstücke gab, um dafür einzukaufen, so lief er und suchte das Beste, das er auftreiben konnte. Nach der Mahlzeit sprach der Geselle: »Was bin ich dafür schuldig?« – »Noch ein paar Goldstücke«, antwortete der Wirt. Der Gast griff in die Tasche, aber sein Gold war gerade zu Ende. Da nahm er das Tischtuch und ging damit hinaus. Der Wirt wußte nicht, was das bedeuten sollte, schlich ihm nach und sah, wie er in den Stall ging, und schaute durch ein Astloch in der Türe. Da breitete der Gesell das Tuch unter den Esel und rief: »Bricklebrit!« Alsbald fing das Eselein an, Gold zu speien von hinten und vorn, daß es ordentlich auf das Tuch niederregnete. »Ei der Tausend!« sprach der Wirt. »So ein Geldbeutel, der ist nicht übel!« Als der Geselle seine Zeche bezahlt hatte, legte er sich schlafen, der Wirt aber schlich in der Nacht herab, band einen andern Esel an die Stelle und führte das Goldeselein in einen andern Stall. Morgens zog der Geselle fort, meinte, er hätte seinen Esel, und hatte einen andern. Zu Mittag kam er bei seinem Vater an, der freute sich, als er ihn sah, und sprach: »Mein Sohn, was bist du geworden?« – »Ein Müller, lieber Vater«, antwortete er. – »Nun, was hast du von der Wanderschaft mitgebracht?« – »Vater, einen Esel.« Sprach der Vater: »Esel gibt's hier auch, wenn's weiter nichts ist.« – »Ja«, sprach der Sohn, »es ist aber ein Goldeselein. Sag ich zu ihm: Bricklebrit, so speit es Gold ein ganzes Tuch voll. Laßt nur alle Verwandten rufen, ich will sie reich machen.« Da wurden alle Verwandten gerufen, und als sie beisammen waren, sprach der Müller: »Macht ein wenig Platz«, und breitete das beste Tuch auf die Erde, das im Haus war, und dann ging er und zog seinen Esel herein und stellte ihn darauf. Als er nun rief: »Bricklebrit!« und meinte, die Goldstücke sollten in der Stube herumspringen, zeigte sich's, daß der Esel nichts davon verstand, denn nicht jeder Esel bringt es soweit. Da machte er ein lang Gesicht und sah, daß er betrogen war. Die Verwandten aber gingen so arm heim, als sie gekommen waren, und er mußte sich wieder bei einem Müller verdingen.

Der dritte Bruder war zu einem Drechsler in die Lehre gegangen und mußte am längsten lernen. Seine Brüder aber schrieben ihm, wie es ihnen ergangen wäre und wie sie der Wirt noch am letzten Abend um ihre schönen Wunschdinge gebracht hätte. Als der Drechsler nun wandern wollte, sprach sein Meister zu ihm: »Weil du dich so wohl gehalten, so schenk ich dir da einen Sack, darin liegt ein Knüppel.« – »Den Sack kann ich wohl umhängen«, sprach der Geselle, »aber was soll ich den Knüppel drin tragen?« – »Das will ich dir sagen«, sprach der Meister, »hat dir jemand ein Leid angetan, ruf nur: ›Knüppel aus dem Sack!‹, so springt dir der Knüppel heraus unter die Leute und tanzt ihnen so lustig auf dem Rücken herum, daß sie acht Tage danach ruhen müssen und sich nicht regen können; und eher läßt er nicht ab, als bis du zu ihm sagst: ›Knüppel in den Sack!‹« Da dankte ihm der Geselle, hing den Sack um, und wenn ihm jemand zu nahe kam und auf den Leib wollte, so sprach er: »Knüppel aus dem Sack!« Da sprang der Knüppel aus dem Sack und klopfte einem nach dem andern den Rock oder Wams auf dem Rücken aus und wartete gar nicht, bis er ihn erst auszog, und das ging so geschwind, daß, eh' sich's einer versah, die Reihe schon an ihm war.

Nun kam der Drechsler auch eines Abends in das Wirtshaus, wo seine Brüder bestohlen waren. Er legte seinen Ranzen vor sich auf den Tisch und erzählte von köstlichen Dingen, die auf der Welt manchmal gefunden würden, als ein Tischchen deck dich, einen Goldesel, das wär aber noch alles nichts gegen den Schatz, den er erlangt habe und da in seinem Sack mit sich führe. Der Wirt spitzte die Ohren und dachte: Was mag das sein? Aller guten Dinge sind drei, das sollte ich billig auch noch haben. Der Gast streckte sich danach auf die Bank und legte den

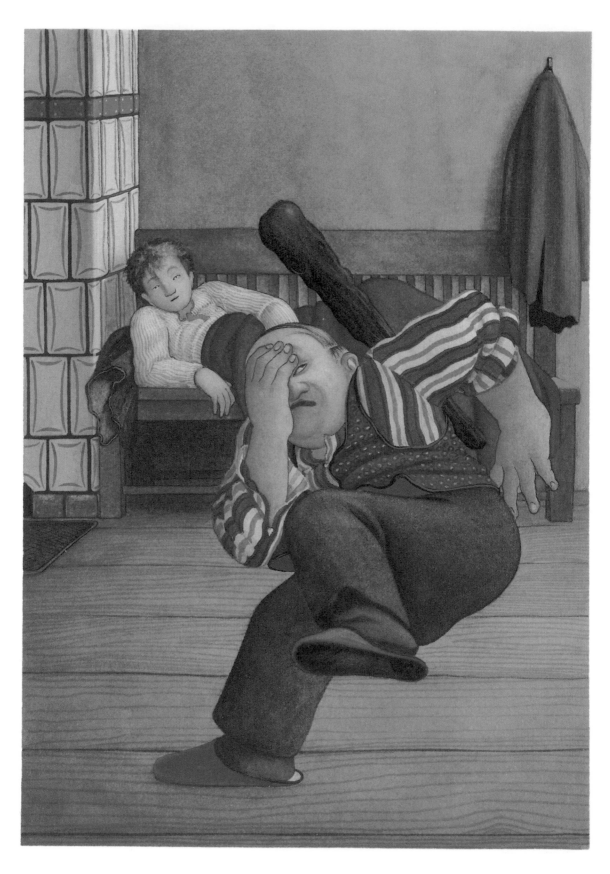

78 *Tischchen deck dich, Goldesel und Knüppel aus dem Sack*

Sack als Kissen unter den Kopf. Als der Wirt nun meinte, er schliefe fest, und sonst niemand in der Stube war, ging er herbei und fing an, den Sack vorsichtig zu rücken und daran zu ziehen, ob er ihn vielleicht hervorlangen und einen andern unterlegen könnte. Der Drechsler aber hatte schon lange auf ihn gewartet. Wie nun der Wirt eben einen herzhaften Ruck tun wollte, rief jener: »Knüppel aus dem Sack!« Alsbald fuhr das Knüppelchen heraus, dem Wirt auf den Leib, und rieb ihm die Nähte, daß es eine Art hatte. Der Wirt fing an, jämmerlich zu schreien, und je lauter er schrie, desto besser schlug es ihm den Takt dazu auf dem Rücken, bis er endlich zur Erde fiel. Sprach der Drechsler: »Willst du jetzt das Tischchen deck dich und den Goldesel wieder heraus geben? Oder der Tanz geht von neuem an.« – »Ach nein«, sprach der Wirt, »ich geb alles gern heraus, laß nur den kleinen Teufel wieder in den Sack kriechen.« Sprach der Geselle: »Diesmal soll's geschehen, aber hüt dich vor Schaden!« Dann sprach er: »Knüppel in den Sack!« und ließ ihn ruhen.

Nun zog der Drechsler am andern Morgen mit dem Tischchen deck dich und dem Goldesel heim zu seinem Vater. Der freute sich, als er ihn sah, und sprach: »Nun, was hast du gelernt?« – »Vater, ich bin ein Drechsler geworden.« – »Ein schönes Handwerk; was hast du aber von der Wanderschaft mitgebracht?« – »Vater, einen Knüppel in dem Sack.« »Ein Knüppel, das ist was Rechtes!« – »Ja, aber sag ich: Knüppel aus dem Sack!, so springt er heraus und tanzt mit dem, der mir nicht gut ist, und damit hab ich das Tischchen deck dich und den Goldesel wieder gewonnen. Laßt nur meine Brüder und alle Verwandten kommen, ich will sie reich machen und speisen und tränken.« Als sie nun alle beisammen waren, deckte er ein Tuch auf, holte den Esel und sprach: »Lieber Bruder, nun sprich mit ihm.« Da rief der Müller: »Bricklebrit!« Ei, da sprangen die Goldstücke, daß es klang, und hörten nicht eher auf, als bis die Leute alle ihre Taschen angefüllt hatten. Dann holte der Drechsler das Tischchen und sprach: »Lieber Bruder, nun sprich zu ihm.« Da rief der Schreiner: »Tischchen, deck dich!« Alsbald war es gedeckt und vollauf besetzt, nun wurden die Verwandten gespeist und getränkt und gingen vergnügt nach Haus. Der Schneider aber mit seinen Söhnen lebte von nun an in Glück und Freude.

Wo ist aber die Ziege hingekommen, die schuld war, daß die drei Schneiderssöhne fortgejagt worden? Die lief in eine Fuchshöhle; als nun der Fuchs heim kam und in sein Haus schaute, da funkelten ihm aus der Dunkelheit ein paar große Augen entgegen, er erschrak und lief wieder zurück. Der Bär begegnete ihm und sah, daß der Fuchs ganz verstört war. Da sprach er: »Bruder Fuchs, was machst du für ein Gesicht?« – »Ach«, antwortete der Rote, »ein grimmig Tier sitzt in meiner Höhle und hat mich mit feurigen Augen angeglotzt!« – »Das will ich dir schon heraustreiben«, sprach der Bär, ging mit ihm zur Höhle und schaute hinein, als er aber die feurigen Augen sah, kam die Furcht auch über ihn, daß er gleichfalls auszog und vor dem Feind nicht Stich halten wollte. Es begegnete ihm aber die

Biene, die merkte, daß er nicht ganz in seiner Lustigkeit war, und sprach: »Bär, was machst du ein verdrießlich Gesicht?« – »Ja, es sitzt dir auch ein grimmig Tier mit ein paar Glotzaugen in des roten Bruders Haus, das hinauszujagen sind wir zu schwach.« Die Biene sprach: »Ich bin ein armes, schwaches Ding, das ihr nicht im Wege anseht, aber ich will doch sehen, ob ich euch helfen kann.« Darauf flog sie zu der Fuchshöhle, setzte sich der Ziege auf den glatten, geschorenen Kopf und stach sie so gewaltig, daß sie aufsprang, meh! meh! schrie und wie toll in die Welt hineinlief, und weiß niemand auf diese Stunde, wo sie hingelaufen ist.   1819

Der Wolf und die sieben jungen Geißlein

Eine Geiß hatte sieben junge Geißlein, die sie recht mütterlich liebte und sorgfältig vor dem Wolf hütete. Eines Tags, als sie ausgehen mußte, Futter zu holen, rief sie alle zusammen und sagte: »Liebe Kinder, ich muß ausgehen und Futter holen, hütet euch vor dem Wolf und laßt ihn nicht herein; gebt auch acht, denn er verstellt sich oft, aber an seiner rauhen Stimme und an seinen schwarzen Pfoten könnt ihr ihn erkennen; ist er erst einmal im Hause, so frißt er euch alle mit Haut und Haar.« Nicht lange darauf, als sie weggegangen war, kam auch schon der Wolf vor die Haustüre und rief mit seiner rauhen Stimme: »Liebe Kinder, macht mir auf, ich bin eure Mutter und hab euch schöne Sachen mitgebracht.« Die sieben Geißerchen aber sprachen: »Unsere Mutter bist du nicht, die hat eine feine, liebliche Stimme, deine Stimme aber ist rauh, du bist der Wolf, und wir machen dir nicht auf.« Der Wolf aber besann sich auf eine List, ging fort zu einem Krämer und kaufte sich ein groß Stück Kreide, die aß er und machte seine Stimme fein damit. Danach ging er wieder zu der sieben Geißlein Haustüre und rief mit feiner Stimme: »Liebe Kinder, laßt mich ein, ich bin eure Mutter, jedes von euch soll etwas haben.« Er hatte aber seine Pfote in das Fenster gelegt, das sahen die sieben Geißerchen und sprachen: »Unsere Mutter bist du nicht, die hat keinen schwarzen Fuß wie du; du bist der Wolf, und wir machen dir nicht auf.« Der Wolf ging fort zu einem Bäcker und sprach: »Bäcker, bestreich mir meine Pfote mit frischem Teig«, und als das getan war, ging er zum Müller und sprach: »Müller, streu mir fein weißes Mehl auf meine Pfote.« Der Müller wollte nicht. »Wenn du es nicht tust«, sprach der Wolf, »so freß ich dich.« Da tat es der Müller aus Furcht.

Nun ging der Wolf wieder vor der sieben Geißerchen Haustüre und sagte: »Liebe Kinder, laßt mich ein, ich bin eure Mutter, jedes von euch soll etwas geschenkt kriegen.« Die sieben Geißerchen wollten erst die Pfote sehen, und wie sie sahen, daß sie schneeweiß war, und weil sie den Wolf so fein sprechen hörten,

glaubten sie, es wäre ihre Mutter, und machten die Türe auf, und der Wolf kam herein. Wie sie aber sahen, wer es war, wie erschraken sie da und versteckten sich geschwind, so gut es ging, das eine unter den Tisch, das zweite ins Bett, das dritte in den Ofen, das vierte in die Küche, das fünfte in den Schrank, das sechste unter eine große Schüssel, das siebente in die Wanduhr. Aber der Wolf fand sie alle und verschluckte sie, außer das jüngste in der Wanduhr, das blieb am Leben. Darauf, als er seine Lust gebüßt, ging er fort.

Bald darauf kam die Mutter nach Haus. Die Haustüre stand offen, Tisch, Stuhl und Bänke waren umgeworfen, die Schüsseln in der Küche zerbrochen, die Decke und die Kissen aus dem Bett gezogen: was für ein Jammer! Der Wolf war da gewesen und hatte ihre lieben Kinder gefressen. »Ach, meine sieben Geißerchen sind tot!« rief sie in ihrer Traurigkeit. Da sprang das jüngste aus der Wanduhr und sagte: »Eins lebt noch, liebe Mutter«, und erzählte ihr, wie das Unglück gekommen war.

Der Wolf aber, nachdem er sich also wohlgetan, satt und müd war, hatte sich auf eine grüne Wiese in den Sonnenschein gelegt und war in einen tiefen Schlaf gefallen. Die alte Geiß aber war klug und listig, dachte hin und her; sind denn meine Kindlein nicht zu retten? Endlich sagte sie ganz vergnügt zu dem jüngsten Geißlein: »Nimm Zwirn, Nadel und Schere und folg mir nach.« Nun gingen die beiden hinaus und fanden den Wolf schnarchend auf der Wiese liegen. »Da liegt der garstige Wolf«, sagte die Mutter und betrachtete ihn von allen Seiten, »nachdem er zum Vieruhrbrot meine sechs Kindlein hinuntergefressen hat. Gib mir einmal die Schere her! Ach! Wenn sie noch lebendig in seinem Leibe wären!« Damit schnitt sie ihm den Bauch auf, und die sechs Geißerchen, die er in der Gier und Hast ganz verschluckt hatte, sprangen unversehrt heraus. Ach, was herzten sie ihre Mutter und waren froh, daß sie aus dem dunkeln Gefängnis befreit waren. Sie aber hieß sie hingehen und große und schwere Wackersteine herbeitragen, damit mußten sie dem Wolf den Leib füllen, und sie nähte ihn wieder zu. Dann liefen sie alle fort und versteckten sich hinter einer Hecke.

Als der Wolf ausgeschlafen hatte, so fühlt' er es so schwer im Leib und sprach: »Es rumpelt und pumpelt mir im Leib herum! Es rumpelt und pumpelt mir im Leib herum! Was ist das? Ich hab nur sechs Geißerchen gegessen.« Er dachte, ein frischer Trunk wird mir schon helfen, machte sich auf und suchte einen Brunnen; aber wie er sich darüber bückte, konnte er sich vor der Schwere der Steine nicht mehr halten und stürzte ins Wasser und ertrank. Wie das die sieben Geißerchen sahen, kamen sie herzu gelaufen und tanzten vor Freude um den Brunnen. 1819

Einäuglein, Zweiäuglein und Dreiäuglein

Es war eine Frau, die hatte drei Töchter, davon hieß die älteste Einäuglein, weil sie nur ein einziges Auge mitten auf der Stirne hatte, und die mittlere Zweiäuglein, weil sie zwei Augen hatte wie andere Menschen, und die jüngste Dreiäuglein, weil sie drei Augen hatte, und das dritte stand bei ihr gleichfalls mitten auf der Stirne. Darum aber, daß Zweiäuglein nicht anders aussah als andere Menschenkinder, konnten es die Schwestern und die Mutter nicht leiden, und sie sprachen zu ihm: »Du siehst mit deinen zwei Augen nicht besser aus als das gemeine Volk, du gehörst nicht zu uns.« Und stießen es herum und warfen ihm schlechte, alte Kleider hin

und gaben ihm nicht mehr zu essen, als was sie übrig ließen, und taten ihm Herzeleid an, wo sie nur konnten.

Es trug sich zu, daß Zweiäuglein hinaus ins Feld gehen und die Ziege hüten mußte und noch ganz hungrig war, weil ihm seine Schwestern so wenig zu essen gegeben hatten. Da setzte es sich an einen Rain und fing an zu weinen und so zu weinen, daß zwei Bächlein aus seinen Augen herabflossen. Und wie es einmal aufsah, stand eine Frau neben ihm, die fragte: »Zweiäuglein, was weinst du?« Zweiäuglein antwortete: »Soll ich nicht weinen! Weil ich zwei Augen habe wie andere Menschen, so können mich meine Schwestern und meine Mutter nicht leiden, stoßen mich herum, werfen mir alte, schlechte Kleider hin und geben mir nur zu essen, was sie übrig lassen. Heute haben sie mir fast gar nichts gegeben, daß ich noch ganz hungrig bin.« Sprach die weise Frau: »Zweiäuglein, trockne dir dein Angesicht, ich will dir etwas sagen, daß du nicht mehr hungern sollst. Sprich nur zu deiner Ziege:

>Zicklein, meck!
Tischlein deck!<,

so wird ein sauber gedecktes Tischlein vor dir stehen und das schönste Essen darauf, daß du essen kannst, soviel du Lust hast. Und wenn du satt bist und das Tischlein nicht mehr brauchst, so sprich nur:

>Zicklein, meck!
Tischlein weg!<,

so wird's vor deinen Augen wieder verschwinden.« Darauf ging die weise Frau fort. Zweiäuglein aber dachte: Ich muß gleich einmal versuchen, ob es wahr ist, was sie gesagt hat, denn mich hungert gar zu sehr, und sprach:

»Zicklein, meck!
Tischlein deck!«

Und kaum hatte es die Worte ausgesprochen, so stand da ein Tischlein mit einem weißen Tüchlein gedeckt, darauf ein Teller mit Messer und Gabel und Löffel, und die schönsten Speisen standen rund herum und waren noch warm, als wären sie eben aus der Küche gekommen. Da sagte Zweiäuglein das kürzeste Gebet her, das es wußte: »Herr Gott, sei unser Gast zu aller Zeit. Amen!« und langte zu und ließ sich's wohl schmecken. Und als es satt war, sprach es, wie die weise Frau es geheißen hatte:

»Zicklein, meck!
Tischlein weg!«

Alsbald war das Tischlein und alles darauf wieder verschwunden. Das ist ein

schöner Haushalt, dachte Zweiäuglein, und war ganz vergnügt und guter Dinge. Abends trieb es seine Ziege heim und rührte das irdene Schüsselchen mit Essen, das ihm die Schwestern hingestellt hatten, gar nicht an, und am andern Tag zog es wieder mit seiner Ziege hinaus und ließ auch die paar Brocken, die ihm gereicht wurden, liegen. Das erstemal und das zweitemal achteten es die Schwestern nicht. Wie es aber jedesmal geschah, merkten sie auf und sprachen: »Es ist nicht richtig mit dem Zweiäuglein, das läßt jedesmal das Essen stehen und hat doch sonst alles aufgezehrt, was wir ihm gegeben, das muß andere Wege gefunden haben.« Damit sie aber hinter die Wahrheit kämen, sollte Einäuglein mitgehen, wenn Zweiäuglein auf die Weide ging, und sollte achthaben, was es da vorhätte, und ob ihm jemand etwa Essen und Trinken brächte.

Als nun Zweiäuglein die Ziege wieder hinaustrieb, trat Einäuglein zu ihm und sprach: »Ich will mitgehen und sehen, daß die Ziege auch recht gehütet und ins Futter getrieben wird.« Aber Zweiäuglein merkte, was Einäuglein im Sinne hatte, und trieb die Ziege hinaus in hohes Gras und sprach: »Komm, Einäuglein, wir wollen uns hinsetzen, ich will dir was vorsingen.« Einäuglein setzte sich hin und war von dem ungewohnten Weg und von der Sonnenhitze müd, und Zweiäuglein sang immer:

»Einäuglein, wachst du?
Einäuglein, schläfst du?«

Da tat Einäuglein das eine Auge zu und schlief ein. Und als Zweiäuglein sah, daß Einäuglein fest schlief und nichts verraten konnte, sprach es:

»Zicklein, meck!
Tischlein deck!«

und setzte sich an sein Tischlein und aß und trank, bis es satt war, dann rief es wieder:

»Zicklein, meck!
Tischlein weg!«

Und es verschwand alles, und Zweiäuglein weckte nun das Einäuglein und sprach: »Ei, Einäuglein, du willst hüten und schläfst dabei ein, derweil hätte die Ziege in alle Welt laufen können! Komm, wir wollen nach Haus gehen.« Da gingen sie nach Haus, und Zweiäuglein ließ wieder sein Schüsselchen unangerührt stehen, und Einäuglein konnte der Mutter nicht sagen, warum es nicht essen wollte, und sprach: »Ich war draußen eingeschlafen.«

Am andern Tag sprach die Mutter zu Dreiäuglein: »Geh du mit hinaus und hab acht, ob Zweiäuglein draußen ißt und ob ihm jemand Essen und Trinken bringt, denn essen und trinken muß es doch.« Da trat Dreiäuglein zum Zweiäuglein und sprach: »Ich will mitgehen und sehen, ob auch die Ziege recht gehütet und ins Futter getrieben wird.« Aber Zweiäuglein merkte, was Dreiäuglein im Sinne hatte, und trieb die Ziege hinaus ins hohe Gras und sprach: »Wir wollen uns dahin setzen, Dreiäuglein, ich will dir was vorsingen.«

Dreiäuglein setzte sich und war müd von dem Weg und der Sonnenhitze, und Zweiäuglein hub wieder das vorige Liedlein an und sang:

»Dreiäuglein, wachst du?«

Aber statt daß es nun singen mußte:

»Dreiäuglein, schläfst du?«,

sang es aus Unbedachtsamkeit:

»Zweiäuglein, schläfst du?«,
und sang immer:

»Dreiäuglein, wachst du?
Zweiäuglein, schläfst du?«

Da fielen dem Dreiäuglein seine zwei Augen zu und schliefen, aber das dritte, das von dem Sprüchlein nicht angeredet wurde, schlief nicht ein, doch Dreiäuglein tat es zu, aber aus List, gleich als schlief' es auch damit, doch blinzelte es und konnte alles gar wohl sehen. Und als Zweiäuglein meinte, Dreiäuglein schlafe fest, sagte es sein Sprüchlein:

>»Zicklein, meck!
>Tischlein deck!«

Aß und trank nach Herzenslust und hieß dann das Tischlein wieder fortgehen:

>»Zicklein meck!
>Tischlein weg!«,

und Dreiäuglein hatte alles mit angesehen. Da kam Zweiäuglein zu ihm und weckte es und sprach: »Ei, Dreiäuglein, bist du eingeschlafen! Du kannst gut hüten! Komm, wir wollen heim gehen.« Und als sie nach Haus kamen, aß Zweiäuglein wieder nicht, und Dreiäuglein sprach zur Mutter: »Ich weiß nun, warum das hochmütige Ding nicht ißt; wenn sie draußen zur Ziege spricht:

>›Zicklein, meck!
>Tischlein deck!‹,

so steht ein Tischlein vor ihr, das ist mit dem besten Essen besetzt, viel besser, als wir's hier haben; und wenn sie satt ist, so spricht sie:

>›Zicklein, meck!
>Tischlein weg!‹,

und alles ist wieder verschwunden. Ich hab es genau mit angesehen; zwei Augen hatte sie mir mit einem Sprüchlein eingeschläfert, aber das eine auf der Stirne, das war zum Glück wach geblieben.«

Da rief die Mutter zornig: »Willst du's besser haben als wir! Die Lust soll dir vergehen!« Und holte ein Schlachtmesser und stieß es der Ziege ins Herz, daß sie tot hinfiel.

Als Zweiäuglein das sah, ging es voll Trauer hinaus und setzte sich wieder auf den Feldrain und weinte seine bitteren Tränen. Da stand auf einmal die weise Frau wieder neben ihm und sprach: »Zweiäuglein, was weinst du?« – »Soll ich nicht weinen«, antwortete es, »die Ziege, die mir jeden Tag auf Euer Sprüchlein den Tisch so schön deckte, ist mir von meiner Mutter totgestochen; nun muß ich wieder Hunger und Kummer leiden.« Die weise Frau sprach: »Zweiäuglein, ich will dir einen guten Rat geben, bitt deine Schwestern, daß sie dir die Eingeweide von der geschlachteten Ziege geben, und vergrab's vor der Haustüre, so wird's dein Glück sein.«

Da verschwand sie, und Zweiäuglein ging heim und sprach zu den Schwestern: »Liebe Schwestern, gebt mir doch etwas von meiner Ziege, ich verlange nichts Gutes, gebt mir nur die Eingeweide.« Da lachten sie und sprachen: »Das können wir dir wohl geben, wenn du weiter nichts willst.« Und Zweiäuglein nahm die Eingeweide und vergrub sie abends in aller Stille nach dem Rat der weisen Frau vor der Haustüre.

Am andern Morgen, als sie insgesamt erwachten und vor die Haustüre traten, stand da ein wunderbarer, prächtiger Baum, der hatte Blätter von Silber, und Früchte von Gold hingen dazwischen, daß wohl nichts Schöneres und Köstlicheres auf der Welt zu sehen war. Sie wußten aber nicht, wie der Baum auf einmal in der Nacht gewachsen war, nur Zweiäuglein merkte es, daß er aus den Eingeweiden der Ziege aufgesproßt war, denn er stand gerade da, wo es sie begraben hatte. Da sprach die Mutter zu Einäuglein: »Steig hinauf, mein Kind, und brich uns die Früchte von dem Baume ab.« Einäuglein stieg hinauf, aber wie es einen von den goldenen Äpfeln greifen wollte, so fuhr ihm der Zweig aus den Händen, und das geschah jedesmal, so daß es keinen einzigen Apfel brechen konnte, es mochte sich anstellen, wie es wollte. Da sprach die Mutter: »Dreiäuglein, steig du hinauf, du kannst mit deinen drei Augen besser um dich schauen als Einäuglein.« Einäuglein rutschte herunter, und Dreiäuglein stieg hinauf, aber Dreiäuglein war nicht geschickter und mochte schauen, wie es wollte, die goldenen Äpfel wichen immer zurück.

Endlich ward die Mutter ungeduldig und stieg selbst hinauf, konnte aber sowenig wie Einäuglein und Dreiäuglein die Frucht fassen und griff nur immer in die leere Luft hinein. Da sprach Zweiäuglein: »Ich will mich einmal hinaufmachen, vielleicht gelingt mir's eher.« Die Schwestern riefen zwar: »Du mit deinen zwei Augen, was willst du wohl!«, aber Zweiäuglein stieg hinauf, und die goldenen Äpfel zogen sich nicht vor ihm zurück, sondern es war ordentlich, als eilten sie seinen Händen entgegen, also daß es einen nach dem andern abpflücken konnte und eine ganze Schürze voll mit herunter brachte. Die Mutter nahm sie ihm ab, und statt daß sie, Einäuglein und Dreiäuglein, dafür das arme Zweiäuglein hätten besser behandeln sollen, so wurden sie nur neidisch, daß es allein die Früchte holen konnte, und gingen noch härter mit ihm um.

Es trug sich zu, daß, als sie einmal beisammen an dem Baum standen, ein junger Ritter daherkam. »Geschwind, Zweiäuglein«, riefen die zwei Schwestern, »kriech unter, daß wir uns deiner nicht schämen müssen«, und stießen das arme Zweiäuglein mit Gewalt unter ein leeres Faß, das neben dem Baum stand, und stopften die goldenen Äpfel, die es gebrochen, auch darunter. Als nun der Ritter näher kam, war es ein schöner Herr, der bewunderte den prächtigen Baum von Gold und Silber und sprach zu den beiden Schwestern: »Wem gehört dieser schöne Baum? Wer mir einen Zweig davon gäbe, könnte dafür verlangen, was er wollte.« Da antworteten Einäuglein und Dreiäuglein, der Baum gehöre ihnen, und sie wollten ihm einen Zweig wohl abbrechen. Sie gaben sich auch beide große Mühe, aber sie waren es nicht im Stand, denn die Zweige und die Früchte wichen jedesmal vor ihnen zurück. Da sprach der Ritter: »Das ist ja wunderlich, daß der Baum euch zugehören soll und ihr doch nicht Macht habt, etwas davon abzubrechen!« Sie blieben dabei, der Baum wäre ihr Eigentum; indem sie aber so sprachen, rollte Zweiäuglein unter dem Fasse ein paar goldene Äpfel heraus, so daß sie zu Füßen des Ritters liefen, denn es war bös, daß Einäuglein und Dreiäuglein nicht die Wahrheit sprachen. Wie der Ritter die Äpfel sah, da erstaunte er und fragte, wo sie herkämen; Einäuglein und Dreiäuglein antworteten, sie hätten noch eine Schwester, die dürfe sich aber nicht sehen lassen, weil sie nur zwei Augen habe wie andere gemeine Menschen. Der Ritter aber wollte sie sehen und rief: »Zweiäuglein, komm hervor.« Da kam Zweiäuglein ganz getrost unter dem Faß hervor, und der Ritter war verwundert über seine große Schönheit und sprach: »Gewiß, Zweiäuglein, kannst du mir einen Zweig von dem Baum abbrechen.« – »Ja«, antwortete Zweiäuglein, »das will ich wohl können, denn der Baum gehört mir«, und stieg hinauf und brach mit leichter Mühe einen Zweig mit seinen silbernen Blättern und goldenen Früchten ab und gab ihn dem Ritter. Da sprach der Ritter: »Zweiäuglein, was soll ich dir dafür geben?« – »Ach«, antwortete Zweiäuglein, »ich leide an Hunger und Durst, Kummer und Not vom Morgen bis zum Abend. Wenn Ihr mich mitnehmen und erlösen wollt, so wär ich glücklich.« Da hob der Ritter das Zweiäuglein auf sein Pferd und brachte es heim auf sein väterliches Schloß, dort gab er ihm schöne Kleider, Essen und Trinken nach Herzenslust, und weil er es so lieb hatte, ließ er sich mit ihm einsegnen und ward die Hochzeit in großer Freude gehalten.

Wie nun Zweiäuglein so von dem schönen Rittersmann fortgeführt wurde, da waren die zwei Schwestern recht neidisch über sein Glück. »Nun, der wunderbare Baum bleibt uns«, dachten sie, »können wir auch keine Früchte davon brechen, so wird doch jedermann davor stehen bleiben, zu uns kommen und ihn rühmen. Wer weiß, was uns noch für ein Glück blüht.« Aber am andern Morgen war der Baum verschwunden und ihre Hoffnung dahin; und wie Zweiäuglein zu seinem Kämmerlein hinaussah, so stand er zu seiner großen Freude davor und war ihm also nachgegangen.

Zweiäuglein lebte lange Zeit vergnügt, da kamen einmal zwei arme Frauen auf ihr Schloß und baten um ein Almosen. Da sah ihnen Zweiäuglein ins Gesicht und erkannte ihre Schwestern Einäuglein und Dreiäuglein, die so in Armut geraten waren, daß sie umherziehen und vor den Türen ihr Brot suchen mußten. Zweiäuglein aber hieß sie willkommen und tat ihnen Gutes und pflegte sie, also daß die beiden von Herzen bereuten, was sie ihrer Schwester in der Jugend Böses angetan hatten.

1819

Die drei Federn

Es war einmal ein König, der hatte drei Söhne, davon waren zwei klug und gescheit, aber der dritte sprach nicht viel, war einfältig und wurde der Dummling genannt. Als der König nun alt wurde, daß er an sein Ende dachte, wußte er nicht, welcher von seinen Söhnen nach ihm das Reich erben sollte. Da sprach er zu ihnen: »Ziehet aus, und wer mir den feinsten Teppich bringt, der soll nach meinem Tod König sein.« Und damit es keinen Streit unter ihnen gab, führte er sie vor sein Schloß, blies drei Federn in die Luft und sprach: »Wie die fliegen, so sollt ihr ziehen.« Die eine Feder flog nach Osten, die andere nach Westen, die dritte flog aber geradaus und flog nicht weit, sondern fiel zur Erde. Nun ging der eine Bruder rechts, der andere ging links, und sie lachten den Dummling aus, der da bei der dritten Feder auf der Erde bleiben mußte.

Der Dummling setzte sich nieder und war traurig, da sah er auf einmal neben der Feder eine Türe in der Erde. Er machte sie auf, stieg eine Treppe hinab und kam vor eine andere Türe und klopfte an, da rief's inwendig:

> »Jungfer grün und klein,
> Hutzelbein!
> Hutzelbeins Hündchen,
> Hutzel hin und her,
> laß geschwind sehen, wer draußen wär.«

Nun tat sich die Türe auf, und er sah eine große, dicke Itsche (Kröte) sitzen, und rings um sie eine Menge kleiner Itschen. Die dicke Itsche fragte, was sein Begehren wäre? Antwortete er: »Ich hätte gern den schönsten und feinsten Teppich.« Da rief sie eine junge und sprach:

> »Jungfer grün und klein,
> Hutzelbein!
> Hutzelbeins Hündchen,
> Hutzel hin und her,
> bring mir die große Schachtel her!«

Die Itsche holte die Schachtel, und die dicke machte sie auf und gab dem Dummling einen Teppich daraus, so schön und so fein, wie oben auf der Erde keiner gewebt werden konnte. Da dankte er ihr und ging wieder fort.

Die beiden andern aber hatten ihren jüngsten Bruder für so albern gehalten, daß sie glaubten, er würde nicht das mindeste gegen sie aufbringen können. »Was

sollen wir uns mit Suchen groß Mühe geben!« sprachen sie und nahmen dem ersten, besten Schäfersweib, das ihnen begegnete, die groben Tücher vom Leib und trugen sie dem König hin. Da kam der Dummling auch und brachte seinen schönen Teppich, und als der König den sah, erstaunte er und sprach: »Das Reich gehört dem jüngsten.« Aber die zwei andern ließen dem König keine Ruh und sprachen, es wäre nicht möglich, daß der Dummling König würde, und baten ihn, er möchte noch eine Bedingung machen. Da sagte der Vater: »Der soll das Reich erben, der mir den schönsten Ring bringt«, und führte die drei Brüder hinaus und blies drei Federn in die Luft, denen sie nachgehen sollten. Die zwei ältesten zogen wieder nach Osten und Westen, und für den Dummling flog die Feder geradeaus und fiel neben der Erdtüre nieder. Da stieg er wieder hinab zu der dicken Itsche und sagte ihr, daß er den schönsten Ring brauche. Sie ließ sich ihre große Schachtel holen und gab ihm daraus einen Ring so schön, wie ihn kein Goldschmied auf der Erde machen konnte. Die zwei ältesten hatten über den Dummling gelacht, daß der einen goldenen Ring suchen wollte, gaben sich gar keine Mühe, sondern schlugen den ersten, besten Wagenringen die Nägel aus und brachten sie dem König. Als dieser dagegen den schönen Ring des Dummlings sah, sprach er: »Ihm gehört das Reich.« Aber die zwei ältesten quälten den König so lang, bis er noch eine dritte Bedingung machte und den Ausspruch tat, der solle das Reich haben, der die schönste Frau heimbrächte. Die drei Federn blies er auch wieder in die Luft, und sie flogen wie die vorigen Male. Da ging der Dummling zum drittenmal hinab zu der dicken Itsche und sprach: »Ich soll die schönste Frau heimbringen.« — »Ei«, antwortete die Itsche, »die schönste Frau! Nun, die sollst du haben.« Und gab ihm eine gelbe Rübe, mit sechs Mäuschen bespannt. Da dachte der Dummling ganz traurig: »Was soll ich damit anfangen?« Die Itsche aber sprach: »Nun setz eine von meinen kleinen Itschen hinein.« Da griff er auf Geratewohl eine aus dem Kreis und setzte sie auf die gelbe Rübe, aber kaum rührte sie daran, so ward sie zu einem wunderschönen Fräulein, die Rübe zur Kutsche und die sechs Mäuschen zu Pferden. Da stiegen sie in die Kutsche, und er küßte sie und brachte sie zu dem König. Seine Brüder kamen auch, die hatten den Dummling so verachtet, daß sie die ersten, besten Bauernweiber genommen und heimgeführt hatten. Da sprach der König: »Dem jüngsten gehört das Reich nach meinem Tod!« Aber die zwei ältesten lärmten von neuem, sprachen, wir können's nicht zugeben, und verlangten, der sollte den Vorzug haben, dessen Frau durch einen Ring springen könne, der in dem Saal mitten hing, und dachten, die Bauernweiber können das wohl, die sind stark genug, aber das zarte Fräulein springt sich tot. Endlich willigte der König ein. Da sprangen die zwei Bauernweiber, sprangen auch durch, waren aber so plump, daß sie fielen und ihre groben Arme und Beine entzwei brachen. Darauf sprang das schöne Fräulein, das der Dummling mitgebracht hatte, und sprang ganz leicht durch den Ring und gewann ihm das Reich. Und als der König starb, erhielt er die Krone und hat lange in Weisheit geherrscht.

1819

Märchen von der Unke

Ein Kind saß vor der Haustüre auf der Erde und hatte sein Schüsselchen mit Milch und Weckbrocken neben sich und aß. Da kam eine Unke gekrochen und senkte ihr Köpfchen in die Schüssel und aß mit. Am andern Tag kam sie wieder, und so eine Zeitlang jeden Tag. Das Kind ließ sich das gefallen, wie es aber sah, daß die Unke immerfort bloß die Milch trank und die Brocken liegen ließ, nahm es sein Löffelchen, schlug ihr ein bißchen auf den Kopf und sagte: »Ding, iß auch Brocken!« Das Kind war seit der Zeit schön und groß geworden, seine Mutter aber stand gerade hinter ihm und sah die Unke, da lief sie herbei und schlug sie tot; von dem Augenblick an ward das Kind mager und ist endlich gestorben.

1819

Die Nixe im Teich

Es war einmal ein Müller, der führte mit seiner Frau ein vergnügtes Leben. Sie hatten Geld und Gut, und ihr Wohlstand nahm von Jahr zu Jahr noch zu. Aber Unglück kommt über Nacht. Wie ihr Reichtum gewachsen war, so schwand er von Jahr zu Jahr wieder hin, und zuletzt konnte der Müller kaum noch die Mühle, in der er saß, sein Eigentum nennen. Er war voll Kummer, und wenn er sich nach der Arbeit des Tags niederlegte, so fand er keine Ruhe, sondern wälzte sich voll Sorgen in seinem Bett. Eines Morgens stand er schon vor Tagesanbruch auf, ging hinaus ins Freie und dachte, es sollte ihm leichter ums Herz werden. Als er über dem Mühldamm dahinschritt, brach eben der erste Sonnenstrahl hervor, und er hörte in dem Weiher etwas rauschen. Er wendete sich um und erblickte ein schönes Weib, das sich langsam aus dem Wasser erhob. Ihre langen Haare, die sie über den Schultern mit ihren zarten Händen gefaßt hatte, flossen an beiden Seiten herab und bedeckten ihren weißen Leib. Er sah wohl, daß es die Nixe des Teichs war, und wußte vor Furcht nicht, ob er davongehen oder stehenbleiben sollte. Aber die Nixe ließ ihre sanfte Stimme hören, nannte ihn beim Namen und fragte, warum er so traurig wäre. Der Müller war anfangs verstummt, als er sie aber so freundlich sprechen hörte, faßte er sich ein Herz und erzählte ihr, daß er sonst in Glück und Reichtum gelebt hätte, aber jetzt so arm wäre, daß er sich nicht zu raten wüßte. »Sei ruhig«, antwortete die Nixe, »ich will dich reicher und glücklicher machen, als du je gewesen bist, nur mußt du mir versprechen, daß du mir geben willst, was eben in deinem Hause jung geworden ist.« – »Was kann das anders sein«, dachte der Müller, »als ein junger Hund oder ein junges Kätzchen?« Und er sagte ihr zu, was sie verlangte.

Die Nixe stieg wieder in das Wasser hinab, und er eilte getröstet und guten Mutes nach seiner Mühle. Noch hatte er sie nicht erreicht, da trat die Magd aus der Haustüre und rief ihm zu, er solle sich freuen, seine Frau hätte ihm einen kleinen Knaben geboren. Der Müller stand wie vom Blitz gerührt. Er sah wohl, daß die tückische Nixe das gewußt und ihn betrogen hatte. Mit gesenktem Haupt trat er zu dem Bett seiner Frau, und als sie ihn fragte: »Warum freust du dich nicht über den schönen Knaben?«, so erzählte er ihr, was ihm begegnet war und was für ein Versprechen er der Nixe gegeben hatte. »Was hilft mir Glück und Reichtum«, fügte er hinzu, »wenn ich mein Kind verlieren soll? Aber was kann ich tun?« Auch die Verwandten, die herbeigekommen waren, Glück zu wünschen, wußten keinen Rat.

Indessen kehrte das Glück in das Haus des Müllers wieder ein. Was er unternahm, gelang. Es war, als ob Kisten und Kasten von selbst sich füllten und das Geld im Schrank über Nacht sich mehrte. Es dauerte nicht lange, so war sein Reichtum

größer als je zuvor. Aber er konnte sich nicht ungestört darüber freuen. Die Zusage, die er der Nixe getan hatte, quälte sein Herz. Sooft er an dem Teich vorbeikam, fürchtete er, sie möchte auftauchen und ihn an seine Schuld mahnen. Den Knaben selbst ließ er nicht in die Nähe des Wassers: »Hüte dich«, sagte er zu ihm, »wenn du das Wasser berührst, so kommt eine Hand heraus, hascht dich und zieht dich hinab.« Doch als Jahr auf Jahr verging und die Nixe sich nicht wieder zeigte, so fing der Müller an, sich zu beruhigen.

Der Knabe wuchs zum Jüngling heran und kam bei einem Jäger in die Lehre. Als er ausgelernt hatte und ein tüchtiger Jäger geworden war, nahm ihn der Herr des Dorfes in seine Dienste. In dem Dorf war ein schönes und treues Mädchen, das gefiel dem Jäger, und als sein Herr das bemerkte, schenkte er ihm ein kleines Haus. Die beiden hielten Hochzeit, lebten ruhig und glücklich und liebten sich von Herzen.

Einstmals verfolgte der Jäger ein Reh. Als das Tier aus dem Wald in das freie Feld ausbog, setzte er ihm nach und streckte es endlich mit einem Schuß nieder. Er bemerkte nicht, daß er sich in der Nähe des gefährlichen Weihers befand, und ging, nachdem er das Tier ausgeweidet hatte, zu dem Wasser, um seine mit Blut befleckten Hände zu waschen. Kaum aber hatte er sie hineingetaucht, als die Nixe emporstieg, lachend mit ihren nassen Armen ihn umschlang und so schnell hinabzog, daß die Wellen über ihm zusammenschlugen.

Als es Abend war und der Jäger nicht nach Haus kam, geriet seine Frau in Angst. Sie ging aus, ihn zu suchen, und da er ihr oft erzählt hatte, daß er sich vor den Nachstellungen der Nixe in acht nehmen müßte und nicht in die Nähe des Weihers sich wagen dürfte, so ahnte sie schon, was geschehen war. Sie eilte zu dem Wasser, und als sie am Ufer seine Jägertasche liegen fand, da konnte sie nicht länger an dem Unglück zweifeln. Wehklagend und händeringend rief sie ihren Liebsten mit Namen, aber vergeblich; sie eilte hinüber auf die andere Seite des Weihers und rief ihn aufs neue; sie schalt die Nixe mit harten Worten, aber keine Antwort erfolgte. Der Spiegel des Wassers blieb ruhig, nur das halbe Gesicht des Mondes blickte unbeweglich zu ihr herauf.

Die arme Frau verließ den Teich nicht. Mit schnellen Schritten, ohne Rast und Ruhe, umkreiste sie ihn immer von neuem, manchmal still, manchmal einen heftigen Schrei ausstoßend, manchmal in leisem Wimmern. Endlich waren ihre Kräfte zu Ende, sie sank zur Erde nieder und verfiel in einen tiefen Schlaf. Bald überkam sie ein Traum.

Sie stieg zwischen großen Felsblöcken angstvoll aufwärts; Dornen und Ranken hakten sich an ihre Füße, der Regen schlug ihr ins Gesicht, und der Wind zauste ihr langes Haar. Als sie die Anhöhe erreicht hatte, bot sich ein ganz anderer Anblick dar. Der Himmel war blau, die Luft mild, der Boden senkte sich sanft hinab, und auf einer grünen, bunt beblümten Wiese stand eine reinliche Hütte. Sie ging darauf zu und öffnete die Türe, da saß eine Alte mit weißen Haaren, die ihr freundlich winkte. In dem Augenblick erwachte die arme Frau. Der Tag war schon angebrochen, und sie entschloß sich gleich, dem Traum Folge zu leisten. Sie stieg mühsam den Berg hinauf, und es war alles so, wie sie es in der Nacht gesehen hatte. Die Alte empfing sie freundlich und zeigte ihr einen Stuhl, auf den sie sich setzen sollte. »Du mußt ein Unglück erlebt haben«, sagte sie, »weil du meine einsame Hütte aufsuchst.«

Die Frau erzählte ihr unter Tränen, was ihr begegnet war.

»Tröste dich«, sagte die Alte, »ich will dir helfen: Da hast du einen goldenen Kamm. Harre, bis der Vollmond aufgestiegen ist, dann geh zu dem Weiher, setze dich am Rand nieder und strähle dein langes schwarzes Haar mit diesem Kamm. Wenn du aber fertig bist, so lege ihn am Ufer nieder, und du wirst sehen, was geschieht.«

Die Frau kehrte zurück, aber die Zeit bis zum Vollmond verstrich ihr langsam. Endlich erschien die leuchtende Scheibe am Himmel, da ging sie hinaus an den Weiher, setzte sich nieder und kämmte ihre langen schwarzen Haare mit dem goldenen Kamm, und als sie fertig war, legte sie ihn an den Rand des Wassers nieder. Nicht lange, so brauste es aus der Tiefe, eine Welle erhob sich, rollte an das Ufer und führte den Kamm mit sich fort. Es dauerte nicht länger, als der Kamm nötig hatte, auf den Grund zu sinken, so teilte sich der Wasserspiegel, und der Kopf des Jägers stieg in die Höhe. Er sprach nicht, schaute aber seine Frau mit traurigen Blicken an. In demselben Augenblick kam eine zweite Welle herangerauscht und bedeckte das Haupt des Mannes.

Alles war verschwunden, der Weiher lag so ruhig wie zuvor, und nur das Gesicht des Vollmondes glänzte darauf.

Trostlos kehrte die Frau zurück, doch der Traum zeigte ihr die Hütte der Alten. Abermals machte sie sich am nächsten Morgen auf den Weg und klagte der weisen Frau ihr Leid. Die Alte gab ihr eine goldene Flöte und sprach: »Harre, bis der Vollmond wiederkommt, dann nimm diese Flöte, setze dich an das Ufer, blas ein schönes Lied darauf, und wenn du damit fertig bist, so lege sie auf den Sand; du wirst sehen, was geschieht.«

Die Frau tat, wie die Alte gesagt hatte. Kaum lag die Flöte auf dem Sand, so brauste es aus der Tiefe. Eine Welle erhob sich, zog heran und führte die Flöte mit sich fort. Bald darauf teilte sich das Wasser, und nicht bloß der Kopf, auch der Mann bis zur Hälfte des Leibes stieg hervor. Er breitete voll Verlangen seine Arme nach ihr aus, aber eine zweite Welle rauschte heran, bedeckte ihn und zog ihn wieder hinab.

»Ach, was hilft es mir«, sagte die Unglückliche, »daß ich meinen Liebsten nur erblicke, um ihn wieder zu verlieren.« Der Gram erfüllte aufs neue ihr Herz, aber der Traum führte sie zum drittenmal in das Haus der Alten. Sie machte sich auf den Weg, und die weise Frau gab ihr ein goldenes Spinnrad, tröstete sie und sprach: »Es ist noch nicht alles vollbracht. Harre, bis der Vollmond kommt, dann

nimm das Spinnrad, setze dich an das Ufer und spinn die Spule voll, und wenn du fertig bist, so stelle das Spinnrad nahe an das Wasser, und du wirst sehen, was geschieht.«

Die Frau befolgte alles genau. Sobald der Vollmond sich zeigte, trug sie das goldene Spinnrad an das Ufer und spann emsig, bis der Flachs zu Ende und die Spule mit dem Faden ganz angefüllt war. Kaum aber stand das Rad am Ufer, so brauste es noch heftiger als sonst in der Tiefe des Wassers, eine mächtige Welle eilte herbei und trug das Rad mit sich fort. Alsbald stieg mit einem Wasserstrahl der Kopf und der ganze Leib des Mannes in die Höhe. Schnell sprang er ans Ufer, faßte seine Frau an der Hand und entfloh. Aber kaum hatten sie sich eine kleine Strecke entfernt, so erhob sich mit entsetzlichem Brausen der ganze Weiher und strömte mit reißender Gewalt in das weite Feld hinein. Schon sahen die Fliehenden ihren Tod vor Augen, da rief die Frau in ihrer Angst die Hilfe der Alten an, und in dem Augenblick waren sie verwandelt, sie in eine Kröte, er in einen Frosch. Die Flut, die sie erreicht hatte, konnte sie nicht töten, aber sie riß sie beide voneinander und führte sie weit weg.

Als das Wasser sich verlaufen hatte und beide wieder den trocknen Boden berührten, so kam ihre menschliche Gestalt zurück. Aber keiner wußte, wo das andere geblieben war; sie befanden sich unter fremden Menschen, die ihre Heimat nicht kannten. Hohe Berge und tiefe Täler lagen zwischen ihnen. Um sich das Leben zu erhalten, mußten beide die Schafe hüten. Sie trieben lange Jahre ihre Herden durch Feld und Wald und waren voll Trauer und Sehnsucht.

Als wieder einmal der Frühling aus der Erde hervorgebrochen war, zogen beide an einem Tag mit ihren Herden aus, und der Zufall wollte, daß sie einander entgegenzogen. Er erblickte an einem fernen Bergesabhang eine Herde und trieb seine Schafe nach der Gegend hin. Sie kamen in einem Tal zusammen, aber sie erkannten sich nicht, doch freuten sie sich, daß sie nicht mehr so einsam waren. Von nun an trieben sie jeden Tag ihre Herde nebeneinander; sie sprachen nicht viel, aber sie fühlten sich getröstet. Eines Abends, als der Vollmond am Himmel schien und die Schafe schon ruhten, holte der Schäfer die Flöte aus seiner Tasche und blies ein schönes, aber trauriges Lied. Als er fertig war, bemerkte er, daß die Schäferin bitterlich weinte. »Warum weinst du?« fragte er. »Ach«, antwortete sie, »so schien auch der Vollmond, als ich zum letztenmal dieses Lied auf der Flöte blies und das Haupt meines Liebsten aus dem Wasser hervorkam.« Er sah sie an, und es war ihm, als fiele eine Decke von den Augen, er erkannte seine liebste Frau; und als sie ihn anschaute und der Mond auf sein Gesicht schien, erkannte sie ihn auch. Sie umarmten und küßten sich, und ob sie glückselig waren, braucht keiner zu fragen.

1843

Hans im Glück

Hans hatte sieben Jahre bei seinem Herrn gedient, da sprach er zu ihm: »Herr, meine Zeit ist herum, nun wollte ich gern wieder heim zu meiner Mutter, gebt mir meinen Lohn.« Der Herr antwortete: »Du hast mir treu und ehrlich gedient, wie der Dienst, so soll der Lohn sein«; und gab ihm ein Stück Gold, das so groß als Hansens Kopf war. Hans zog sein Tüchlein, wickelte den Klumpen hinein, setzte ihn auf die Schulter und machte sich auf den Weg nach Haus. Wie er so dahinging und immer ein Bein vor das andere setzte, kam ihm ein Reiter in die Augen, der frisch und fröhlich auf einem muntern Pferd vorbeitrabte. »Ach«, sprach Hans ganz laut, »was das Reiten ein schönes Ding ist, da sitzt einer wie auf einem Stuhl, stößt sich an keinen Stein, spart die Schuh und kommt fort, er weiß nicht wie!« Der Reiter, der das gehört hatte, rief ihm zu: »Ei, Hans, warum läufst du auch zu Fuß?« – »Ach, da muß ich den Klumpen heimtragen, es ist zwar Gold, aber ich kann den

Kopf dabei nicht gerad halten, und es drückt mir auf die Schulter.« — »Weißt du was«, sagte der Reiter und hielt an, »wir wollen tauschen, ich geb dir mein Pferd, und du gibst mir deinen Klumpen.« — »Von Herzen gern«, sprach Hans, »aber ich sag Euch, Ihr müßt Euch damit schleppen.« Der Reiter stieg ab, nahm das Gold und half dem Hans hinauf, gab ihm die Zügel fest in die Hände und sprach: »Wenn's nun recht geschwind soll gehen, so mußt du mit der Zunge schnalzen und hopp, hopp! rufen.«

Hans war seelenfroh, als er auf dem Pferd saß und so frank und frei dahin ritt. Über ein Weilchen fiel ihm ein, es sollte noch schneller gehen, und er fing an, mit der Zunge zu schnalzen und hopp, hopp! zu rufen. Das Pferd setzte sich in starken Trab, und ehe sich's Hans versah, war er abgeworfen und lag in einem Graben, der die Äcker von der Landstraße trennte. Das Pferd wär auch durchgegangen, wenn es nicht ein Bauer aufgehalten hätte, der des Weges kam und eine Kuh vor sich trieb. Hans suchte seine Glieder zusammen und machte sich wieder auf die Beine.

Er war aber verdrießlich und sprach zu dem Bauer: »Es ist ein schlechter Spaß, das Reiten, dazu, wenn man auf so eine Mähre gerät wie diese, die stößt und einen herabwirft, daß man den Hals brechen kann; ich setze mich nie und nimmermehr wieder auf. Da lob ich mir Eure Kuh, da kann einer mit Gemächlichkeit hinterher gehen und hat obendrein seine Milch, Butter und Käse jeden Tag gewiß. Was gäbe ich drum, wenn ich so eine Kuh hätte!« — »Nun«, sprach der Bauer, »geschieht Euch so ein großer Gefallen, so will ich Euch wohl die Kuh für das Pferd vertauschen.« Hans willigte mit tausend Freuden ein; der Bauer schwang sich aufs Pferd und ritt eilig davon.

Hans trieb nun seine Kuh ruhig vor sich her und bedachte den glücklichen Handel. »Hab ich nur ein Stück Brot, und daran wird mir's doch nicht fehlen, so kann ich, sooft mir's beliebt, Butter und Käse dazu essen; hab ich Durst, so melk ich meine Kuh und trinke Milch: Herz, was verlangst du mehr?« Als er zu einem Wirtshaus kam, machte er halt, aß in der großen Freude alles, was er bei sich hatte, sein Mittags- und Abendbrot, rein auf, und ließ sich für seine letzten paar Heller ein halbes Glas Bier einschenken. Dann trieb er seine Kuh weiter, immer nach dem Dorfe seiner Mutter zu. Die Hitze wurde aber drückender, je näher der Mittag kam, und Hans befand sich in einer Heide, die wohl noch eine Stunde dauerte. Da ward es ihm ganz heiß, so daß ihm vor Durst die Zunge am Gaumen klebte. Dem Ding ist zu helfen, dachte Hans, jetzt will ich meine Kuh melken und mich an der Milch laben. Er band sie an einen dürren Baum und stellte seine Ledermütze unter, aber so sehr er sich auch abmühte, es kam kein Tropfen Milch zum Vorschein. Weil er sich aber ungeschickt dabei anstellte, so gab ihm das ungeduldige Tier endlich mit einem der Hinterfüße einen solchen Schlag vor den Kopf, daß er zu Boden taumelte und eine Zeitlang sich gar nicht besinnen konnte, wo er war. Glücklicherweise kam gerade ein Metzger des Weges, der auf einem Schubkarren ein junges Schwein liegen hatte. »Was sind das für Streiche?« rief er und half dem guten Hans auf. Hans erzählte, was vorgefallen war. Der Metzger reichte ihm seine Flasche und sprach: »Da trinkt einmal und erholt Euch; die Kuh will Euch wohl keine Milch geben, das ist ein altes Tier, das höchstens noch zum Ziehen taugt oder zum Schlachten.« – »Ei, ei«, sprach Hans und strich sich die Haare über den Kopf, »wer hätte das gedacht! Es ist freilich gut, wenn man so ein Tier ins Haus abschlachten kann, was gibt's für Fleisch! Aber ich mache mir aus dem Kuhfleisch nicht viel, es ist mir nicht saftig genug. Ja, wer so ein junges Schwein hätte, das schmeckt anders, dabei noch die Würste!« – »Hört, Hans«, sprach da der Metzger, »Euch zulieb will ich tauschen und will Euch das Schwein für die Kuh lassen.« – »Gott lohn Euch Eure Freundschaft«, sprach Hans, übergab ihm die Kuh und ließ sich das Schweinchen vom Karren losmachen und den Strick, woran es gebunden war, in die Hand geben.

Hans zog weiter und überdachte, wie ihm doch alles nach Wunsch ginge; begegnete ihm je eine Verdrießlichkeit, so würde sie doch gleich wieder gut gemacht. Es gesellte sich danach ein Bursch zu ihm, der trug eine schöne, weiße Gans unter dem Arm. Sie boten einander die Zeit, und Hans fing an, ihm von seinem Glück zu erzählen, und wie er immer so vorteilhaft getauscht hätte.

Der Bursche sagte, daß er die Gans zu einem Kindtaufsschmaus bringe: »Hebt einmal«, fuhr er fort und packte sie bei den Flügeln, »wie sie schwer ist, sie ist aber auch acht Wochen lang genudelt worden. Wer in den Braten beißt, muß sich das Fett von beiden Seiten abwischen.« – »Ja«, sprach Hans und wog sie mit der einen Hand, »die hat ihr Gewicht, aber mein Schwein ist auch keine Sau.«

Indessen sah sich der Bursch nach allen Seiten ganz bedenklich um, schüttelte auch wohl mit dem Kopf. »Hört«, fing er darauf an, »mit Eurem Schwein mag's nicht ganz richtig sein. In dem Dorf, durch das ich gekommen bin, ist eben dem Schulzen eins aus dem Stall gestohlen worden. Ich fürchte, ich fürchte, Ihr habt's da in der Hand, es wäre ein schlimmer Handel, wenn sie Euch damit fänden, das geringste ist, daß Ihr ins finstere Loch gesteckt werdet.« Dem guten Hans ward bang: »Ach Gott«, sprach er, »helft mir aus der Not, Ihr wißt hier herum besser Bescheid, nehmt mein Schwein da und laßt mir Eure Gans.« – »Ich muß schon etwas aufs Spiel setzen«, antwortete der Bursche, »aber ich will doch nicht schuld sein, daß Ihr ins Unglück geratet.« Er nahm also das Seil in die Hand und trieb das Schwein schnell auf einem Seitenweg fort; der gute Hans aber ging, seiner Sorgen entledigt, mit der Gans unter dem Arm seiner Heimat zu. »Wenn ich's recht überlege«, sprach er mit sich selbst, »habe ich noch Vorteil bei dem Tausch, erstlich den guten Braten, hernach die Menge von Fett, die herausträufeln wird, das gibt Gänsfettbrot auf ein Vierteljahr, und endlich die schönen weißen Federn, die laß ich mir in mein Kopfkissen stopfen, und darauf will ich wohl ungewiegt einschlafen. Was wird meine Mutter eine Freude haben!«

Als er durch das letzte Dorf gekommen war, stand da ein Scherenschleifer mit seinem Karren und sang zu seiner schnurrenden Arbeit:

»Ich schleife die Schere und drehe geschwind
und hänge mein Mäntelchen nach dem Wind!«

Hans blieb stehen und sah ihm zu; endlich redete er ihn an und sprach: »Euch geht's auch wohl, weil Ihr so lustig bei Eurem Schleifen seid.« – »Ja«, antwortete der Scherenschleifer, »das Handwerk hat einen güldenen Boden. Ein rechter Schleifer ist ein Mann, der, sooft er in die Tasche greift, auch Geld darin findet. Aber wo habt Ihr die schöne Gans gekauft?« – »Die hab ich nicht gekauft, sondern für mein Schwein eingetauscht.« – »Und das Schwein?« – »Das hab ich für eine Kuh gekriegt.« – »Und die Kuh?« – »Die hab ich für ein Pferd bekommen.« – »Und das Pferd?« – »Dafür hab ich einen Klumpen Gold, so groß als mein Kopf, gegeben.« – »Und das Gold?« – »Ei, das war mein Lohn für sieben Jahre Dienst.« – »Ihr habt Euch jederzeit zu helfen gewußt«, sprach der Schleifer, »könnt Ihr's nun dahin bringen, daß Ihr das Geld in der Tasche springen hört, wenn Ihr aufsteht, so habt Ihr Euer Glück gemacht.« – »Wie soll ich das anfangen?« sprach Hans. »Ihr müßt ein Schleifer werden wie ich, dazu gehört eigentlich nichts als ein Wetzstein, das andere findet sich schon von selbst. Da hab ich einen, der ist ein wenig schadhaft, dafür sollt Ihr mir aber auch weiter nichts als Eure Gans geben, wollt Ihr das?« – »Wie könnt Ihr noch fragen«, antwortete Hans, »ich werde ja zum glücklichsten Menschen auf Erden, hab ich Geld, sooft ich in die Tasche greife, was brauche ich da zu sorgen!« und reichte ihm die Gans hin. »Nun«, sprach der Schleifer und hob einen schweren, gewöhnlichen Feldstein, der neben ihm lag, auf, »da habt Ihr auch noch einen tüchtigen Stein dazu, auf dem sich's gut schlagen läßt und Ihr Eure alten Nägel gerade klopfen könnt. Nehmt ihn und hebt ihn ordentlich auf.«

Hans lud den Stein auf und ging mit vergnügtem Herzen weiter, seine Augen leuchteten vor Freude, und er sprach für sich: »Ich muß in einer Glückshaut geboren sein. Alles, was ich wünsche, trifft mir ein, wie einem Sonntagskind.« Indessen, weil er seit Tagesanbruch auf den Beinen gewesen, begann er müd zu werden; auch plagte ihn der Hunger, da er allen Vorrat auf einmal in der Freude über die erhandelte Kuh aufgezehrt hatte. Er konnte endlich nur mit Mühe weitergehen und mußte jeden Augenblick halt machen, dabei drückten ihn die Steine ganz erbärmlich. Da konnte er sich des Gedankens nicht erwehren, wie gut es wäre, wenn er sie gerade jetzt nicht zu tragen brauchte. Wie eine Schnecke kam er zu einem Feldbrunnen geschlichen, da wollte er ruhen und sich mit einem frischen Trunk laben; damit er aber die Steine im Niedersitzen nicht beschädigte, legte er sie bedächtig neben sich auf den Rand des Brunnens. Darauf drehte er sich um und wollte sich zum Trinken bücken, da versah er's, stieß ein klein wenig an, und

beide Steine plumpsten hinab. Hans, als er sie mit seinen Augen in die Tiefe hatte
versinken sehen, sprang vor Freuden auf, kniete dann nieder und dankte Gott mit
Tränen in den Augen, daß er ihm auch diese Gnade erwiesen und auf eine so gute
Art von den Steinen befreit, das sei das einzige, was ihm noch zu seinem Glück
gefehlt. »So glücklich wie ich«, rief er aus, »gibt es keinen Menschen unter der
Sonne.« Mit leichtem Herzen und frei von aller Last sprang er nun, bis er daheim
bei seiner Mutter war.

1819

Der Teufel mit den drei goldenen Haaren

Es war eine arme Frau, die gebar ein Söhnlein, das hatte eine Glückshaut um, wie es zur Welt kam. Da ward ihm geweissagt, daß es im vierzehnten Jahr die Königstochter zur Frau haben würde. Es geschah aber, daß der König unerkannt nach wenigen Tagen durch das Dorf kam und fragte, was es Neues gäbe? »Es«, antworteten die Leute, »es ist ein Kind mit einer Glückshaut geboren worden, das soll des Königs Tochter im vierzehnten Jahr zur Frau haben.« Dem König gefiel das nicht, ging zu den armen Eltern und fragte, ob sie ihm das Kind nicht verkaufen wollten. »Nein«, sprachen sie; doch weil ihnen der fremde Mann so zusetzte und schweres Gold bot, sie aber kein Brot zu essen hatten, so willigten sie endlich ein und dachten, es ist ein Glückskind, dem kann's doch nicht fehlen.

Der König nahm das Kind, legte es in eine Schachtel und ritt dann mit ihm fort; als er aber zu einem tiefen Wasser kam, warf er es hinein und dachte, nun wird es nicht der Mann meiner Tochter werden. Die Schachtel schwamm fort, und durch Gottes Gnade geschah es, daß kein Tröpfchen Wasser hineinkam. Sie schwamm fort, bis zwei Meilen von des Königs Hauptstadt, da blieb sie bei einer Mühle an dem Wehr hängen. Ein Mahlbursche sah die Schachtel, nahm einen großen Haken und zog sie herbei, und weil sie so schwer war, meinte er, es läge Geld darin, aber als er sie aufmachte, lag ein kleiner, schöner Junge darin und frisch und lebendig. Die Müllersleute hatten keine Kinder, waren froh über das Gefundene und sprachen: »Gott hat es uns beschert.« Also pflegten sie es wohl und zogen es in allen Tugenden groß.

Als etwa dreizehn Jahre herum waren, kam der König zufällig in die Mühle und fragte die Müllersleute, ob das ihr Sohn wäre? »Nein«, antworteten sie, »der Mahlbursch hat ihn gefunden in einer Schachtel, die ans Wehr geschwommen ist.« – »Wie lang ist das schon geschehen?« fragte der König weiter. – »Vor etwa dreizehn Jahren.« – »Das ist ja recht schön«, sprach der König, »mein, kann mir der Junge nicht einen Brief an die Königin forttragen? Es wär mir ein großer Gefallen, und ich will ihm zwei Goldstücke dafür geben.« – »Wie der Herr König gebietet«, sprach der Müller. Der König aber, der wohl merkte, daß es das Glückskind war, schrieb einen Brief an die Königin, darin stand: »Sobald dieser Knabe mit dem Schreiben angelangt ist, soll er getötet und begraben werden, und alles soll geschehen sein, eh' ich komme.«

Mit diesem Brief ging der Knabe fort, verirrte sich aber und kam abends in einen großen Wald. Wie es ganz dunkel war, sah er darin ein Licht, auf das er zuging und das ihn zu einem kleinen Häuschen führte. Es war niemand darin als eine alte Frau, die erschrak, als sie ihn hereintreten sah, und sprach: »Wo kommst du her und wo willst du hin?« – »Zu der Frau Königin, der soll ich einen Brief bringen, ich habe mich verirrt und wollte gern hier übernachten.« — »Du armer Junge«, sprach die Frau, »du bist hier in ein Räuberhaus geraten, wenn sie heimkommen, bringen sie dich um.« — »Ich bin so müd, daß ich nicht weiter kann«, antwortete er, legte den Brief auf den Tisch, dann streckte er sich auf eine Bank und schlief ein. Als die Räuber kamen und ihn sahen, fragten sie, was das für ein fremder Knabe wäre? »Aus Barmherzigkeit hab ich ihn geherbergt«, sprach die Alte, »er soll der Königin einen Brief bringen und hat sich verirrt.« Die Räuber nahmen den Brief, brachen ihn auf und lasen darin, daß der Knabe solle ermordet werden. Da zerriß ihn der Anführer und schrieb einen andern, darin stand, sobald der Knabe käm, sollt' er mit der Königstochter vermählt werden. Sie ließen den Knaben schlafen bis zum andern Morgen, da gaben sie ihm den Brief und zeigten ihm den rechten Weg, auf dem er zur Königin gelangte. Als sie den Brief gelesen, ließ sie gleich die Hochzeit anstellen, und weil das Glückskind schön war, nahm ihn das Königsfräulein gern zum Mann, und sie lebten vergnügt miteinander.

Nach einiger Zeit kam der König wieder nach Haus, und als er sah, daß die Weissagung erfüllt und das Glückskind mit seiner Tochter verheiratet war, erschrak er und sprach: »Wie ist das zugegangen? Was hab ich in dem Brief geschrieben?« — »Lieber Mann«, sagte die Königin, »hier ist dein Brief, lies selber, was darin steht.« Der König las und sah wohl, daß der Brief vertauscht war, und fragte den Jüngling, wie es mit dem Schreiben, das er ihm anvertraut, zugegangen wäre? »Ich weiß von nichts«, antwortete er, »es müßte in der Nacht geschehen sein, als ich geschlafen habe.« Der König aber war zornig und sprach: »Nein, so soll es nicht gehen. Wer meine Tochter will haben, muß mir aus der Hölle drei goldne Haare von des Teufels Haupt holen; bringst du mir die, so sollst du meine Tochter behalten.« — »Die will ich schon holen«, sprach das Glückskind, nahm Abschied von seiner Frau und zog fort.

Nun kam er vor eine große Stadt, da fragte ihn der Wächter vor dem Tor, was er für ein Gewerbe verstehe und was er wisse? »Ich weiß alles«, gab er zur Antwort. »So kannst du uns einen Gefallen tun und sagen, warum unser Marktbrunnen, der sonst Wein quoll, jetzt nicht einmal Wasser quillt; wir wollen dir zwei Esel mit Gold dafür geben.« — »Recht gern«, antwortete er, »wenn ich wiederkomme.« Da ging er weiter und kam vor eine andere Stadt, deren Wächter fragte auch: »Was für ein Gewerbe verstehst du und was weißt du?« — »Ich weiß alles«, antwortete er. »So kannst du uns einen Gefallen tun und sagen, warum ein Baum, der sonst goldne Äpfel trug, jetzt nicht einmal Blätter hervortreibt?« — »Recht gern«, antwortete er, »wenn ich wiederkomme.« Da ging er weiter und kam an ein großes Wasser, über das er hinüber mußte. Der Schiffmann fragte ihn: »Was für ein Gewerbe verstehst du und was weißt du?« — »Ich weiß alles«, antwortete er. »So kannst du mir einen Gefallen tun«, sprach der Schiffmann, »und mir sagen, warum ich ewig fahren muß und nicht abgelöst werde? Ich will dir's vergüten.« — »Recht gern«, antwortete er, »wenn ich wiederkomme.«

Als er nun über das Wasser gefahren war, kam er in die Hölle, da sah's schwarz und rußig aus. Der Teufel war aber nicht zu Haus, nur seine Großmutter, die saß in einem breiten Sorgenstuhl. »Was willst du?« sprach sie. »Drei goldene Haare von des Teufels Kopf«, antwortete er, »sonst kann ich meine Frau nicht behalten.« – »Du jammerst mich«, antwortete sie, »wenn der Teufel kommt, so bringt er dich ums Leben, doch will ich sehen, was ich für dich tun kann.« Da verwandelte sie ihn in eine Ameise und sprach: »Kriech in meine Rockfalten, da bist du sicher.« – »Ja«, sagte er, »ich möcht auch gern wissen, warum ein Brunnen, der sonst Wein quoll, nicht mehr Wasser quillt, warum ein Baum, der sonst goldne Äpfel trug, nicht einmal Laub treibt, und warum ein Schiffmann immer fahren muß und nicht abgelöst wird.« – »Das sind drei schwere Fragen«, sprach sie, »aber sei still und hab acht, was der Teufel spricht, wenn ich ihm die drei goldenen Haare ausziehe.«

Danach nicht lange, als es Abend ward, kam der Teufel nach Haus. Er roch hin und her und sprach: »Ich rieche, rieche Menschenfleisch, es ist nicht rein!« Dann suchte er und guckte sich um, aber umsonst. Die Großmutter schalt und sprach: »Wirf mir nicht alles umeinander, ich habe eben erst gekehrt: sitz und iß dein Abendbrot, du hast immer Menschenfleisch in der Nase.« Nun aß und trank der Teufel, und hernach legte er der Großmutter seinen Kopf in den Schoß und sagte, er wäre müd, sie sollte ihn ein wenig lausen. Bald schlummerte er ein, blies und schnarchte; da faßte sie ein goldenes Haar und riß es aus und legte es neben sich. »Au weh«, rief der Teufel, »was ist das?« – »Ich hatte einen schweren Traum«, sprach die Großmutter, »da hab ich dir in die Haare gefaßt.« – »Was träumte dir denn?« – »Mir träumte, ein Marktbrunnen, der sonst Wein quoll, wäre versiegt und wollte nicht einmal Wasser quellen; was ist wohl schuld?« – »Ha, wenn sie's wüßten!« antwortete der Teufel. »Es sitzt eine Kröte unter einem Stein im Brunnen, die müssen sie töten, dann wird er schon wieder anfangen zu fließen.« Nun lauste ihn die Großmutter wieder, bis er einschlief und schnarchte, daß die Fenster zitterten, da riß sie ihm das zweite Haar aus. »Hu! Was machst du?« schrie der Teufel zornig. »Sei nicht bös«, sprach sie, »ich hab's im Traum getan.« – »Was träumte dir denn?« – »Mir träumte, in einem Königreich ständ ein Obstbaum, der hatte sonst goldne Äpfel getragen und wollte jetzt nicht einmal Laub treiben: was ist wohl schuld?« – »Ha, wenn sie's wüßten!« antwortete der Teufel. »An der Wurzel nagt eine Maus, wenn sie die töten, wird er schon wieder Goldäpfel tragen; nagt sie noch weiter, so verdorrt er. Aber laß mich mit deinen Träumen in Ruh, und wenn du mich noch einmal weckst, so kriegst du eine Ohrfeige.« Sie lauste ihn wieder, bis er einschlief und schnarchte; dann faßte sie auch das dritte goldne Haar und riß es aus. Der Teufel fuhr in die Höhe und wollte übel wirtschaften, aber sie besänftigte ihn und sprach: »Das sind böse Träume!« – »Was träumte dir denn?« – »Mir träumte von einem Schiffmann, der fuhr immer hin und her und wurde gar nicht abgelöst: was ist wohl schuld?« – »He! Der Dummbart!« antwortete der Teufel. »Wenn einer kommt und will überfahren, muß er ihm die Stange in die

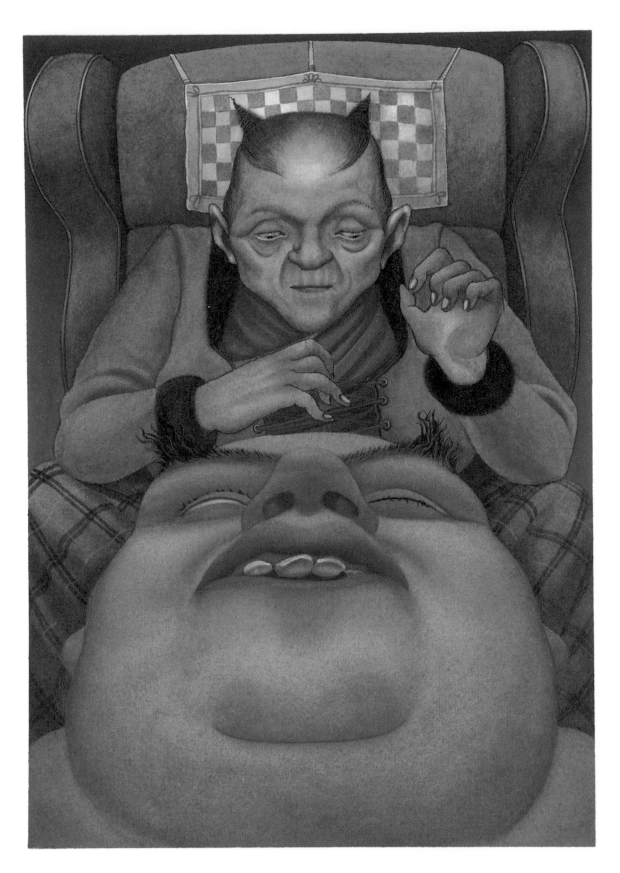

Hand geben, dann muß der fahren, und er ist frei. Aber laus mich, daß ich wieder einschlafe.« Nun ließ sie ihn schlafen, bis es Tag ward, da zog der Teufel fort. Als sie sicher war, holte sie die Ameise wieder aus der Rockfalte und machte ihn zu dem Menschen, der er gewesen war. Dann gab sie ihm die drei goldenen Haare und sprach: »Hast du auch alles gehört und verstanden, was der Teufel gesagt hat?« – »Ja«, antwortete er, »ich will's auch wohl behalten.« – »So ist dir geholfen«, sprach sie, »nun zieh deiner Wege.«

Also bedankte sich das Glückskind bei des Teufels Großmutter und verließ die Hölle. Als er zu dem Schiffmann kam, der ihn wieder überfahren mußte, wollte dieser die versprochene Antwort haben. »Fahr mich nur erst hinüber«, sagte er, »dann will ich dir's sagen.« Und wie er aus dem Schiff gestiegen war, gab er ihm des Teufels Rat: »Wenn einer wieder kommt, der will übergefahren sein, so gib ihm die Stange in die Hand und lauf davon.«

Da ging er weiter und kam zu der Stadt, worin der unfruchtbare Baum stand und wo der Wächter auch Antwort haben wollte. Da sagte er ihm, wie er vom Teufel gehört hatte: »Tötet die Maus, die an seiner Wurzel nagt, so wird er wieder goldne Äpfel tragen.« Da bedankte er sich und gab ihm zwei Esel mit Gold beladen, die mußten ihm nachfolgen.

Nun kam er auch zuletzt wieder zu der Stadt, deren Brunnen versiegt war, da wollte der Wächter auch die Antwort haben. Da sprach er, wie der Teufel gesprochen: »Es sitzt eine Kröte unter einem Brunnenstein, die sucht und tötet, so wird er wieder Wein geben.« Er dankte ihm und gab ihm auch zwei Esel mit Gold beladen.

Nun langte das Glückskind daheim bei seiner Frau an, die sich herzlich freute, als sie ihn wiedersah, und hörte, wie wohl ihm alles gelungen war. Dem König gab er die drei goldenen Haare des Teufels, so daß er nichts mehr gegen ihn einwenden konnte; und als dieser gar die vier Esel mit dem Golde sah, ward er ganz vergnügt und sprach: »Ei, du lieber Schwiegersohn, wo ist das viele Gold her? Das sind gewaltige Schätze!« – »Bei einem Wasser«, antwortete das Glückskind, »hab ich's kriegt, und da ist es noch zu haben.« – »Kann ich mir davon auch holen?« sprach der König und war ganz begierig. »Soviel Ihr wollt«, antwortete er, »es ist ein Schiffmann auf dem Wasser, von dem laßt Euch überfahren, drüben liegt das Gold wie Sand am Ufer.« Da eilte der alte König hin, und wie er an das Wasser kam, winkte er dem Schiffmann, der nahm ihn auf, wie er aber drüben aussteigen wollte, gab ihm der Schiffmann die Ruderstange in die Hand und sprang davon. Nun mußte der Alte fahren zur Strafe für seine Sünden. – »Fährt er wohl noch?« – »Was denn? Es wird ihm niemand die Stange abgenommen haben!«

1819

Der Eisenhans

Es war einmal ein König, der hatte einen großen Wald bei seinem Schloß, darin lief Wild aller Art herum. Zu einer Zeit schickte er einen Jäger hinaus, der sollte ein Reh schießen, aber er kam nicht wieder. »Vielleicht ist ihm ein Unglück zugestoßen«, sagte der König und schickte den folgenden Tag zwei andere Jäger hinaus, die sollten ihn aufsuchen, aber die blieben auch weg. Da ließ er am dritten Tag alle seine Jäger kommen und sprach: »Streift durch den ganzen Wald und laßt nicht ab, bis ihr sie alle drei gefunden habt.«

Aber auch von diesen kam keiner wieder heim, und von der Meute Hunde, die sie mitgenommen hatten, ließ sich keiner wieder sehen. Von der Zeit an wollte sich niemand mehr in den Wald wagen, und er lag da in tiefer Stille und Einsamkeit, und man sah nur zuweilen einen Adler oder Habicht darüber hinfliegen. Das dauerte viele Jahre, da meldete sich ein fremder Jäger bei dem König, suchte eine Versorgung und erbot sich, in den gefährlichen Wald zu gehen. Der König aber wollte seine Einwilligung nicht geben und sprach: »Es ist nicht geheuer darin. Ich fürchte, es geht dir nicht besser als den andern, und du kommst nicht wieder

heraus.« Der Jäger antwortete: »Herr, ich will's auf meine Gefahr wagen. Von Furcht weiß ich nichts.«

Der Jäger begab sich also mit seinem Hund in den Wald. Es dauerte nicht lange, so geriet der Hund einem Wild auf die Fährte und wollte hinter ihm her; kaum aber war er ein paar Schritte gelaufen, so stand er vor einem tiefen Pfuhl, konnte nicht weiter, und ein nackter Arm streckte sich aus dem Wasser, packte ihn und zog ihn hinab. Als der Jäger das sah, ging er zurück und holte drei Männer, die mußten mit Eimern kommen und das Wasser ausschöpfen. Als sie auf den Grund sehen konnten, so lag da ein wilder Mann, der braun am Leib war wie rostiges Eisen und dem die Haare über das Gesicht bis zu den Knien herabhingen. Sie banden ihn mit Stricken und führten ihn fort in das Schloß. Da war große Verwunderung über den wilden Mann, der König aber ließ ihn in einen eisernen Käfig auf seinen Hof setzen und verbot bei Lebensstrafe, die Türe des Käfigs zu öffnen, und die Königin mußte den Schlüssel selbst in Verwahrung nehmen. Von nun an konnte ein jeder wieder mit Sicherheit in den Wald gehen.

Der König hatte einen Sohn von acht Jahren, der spielte einmal auf dem Hof, und bei dem Spiel fiel ihm sein goldener Ball in den Käfig. Der Knabe lief hin und sprach: »Gib mir meinen Ball heraus.« – »Nicht eher«, antwortete der Mann, »als bis du mir die Türe aufgemacht hast.« – »Nein«, sagte der Knabe, »das tue ich nicht, das hat der König verboten«, und lief fort. Am andern Tag kam er wieder und forderte seinen Ball. Der wilde Mann sagte: »Öffne meine Türe«, aber der Knabe wollte nicht. Am dritten Tag war der König auf die Jagd geritten, da kam der Knabe nochmals und sagte: »Wenn ich auch wollte, ich kann die Türe nicht öffnen, ich habe den Schlüssel nicht.« Da sprach der wilde Mann: »Er liegt unter dem Kopfkissen deiner Mutter, da kannst du ihn holen.« Der Knabe, der seinen Ball wiederhaben wollte, schlug alle Bedenken in den Wind und brachte den Schlüssel herbei. Die Türe ging schwer auf, und der Knabe klemmte sich den Finger. Als sie offen war, trat der wilde Mann heraus, gab ihm den goldenen Ball und eilte hinweg. Dem Knaben war angst geworden, er schrie und rief ihm nach: »Ach, wilder Mann, geh nicht fort, sonst bekomme ich Schläge.« Der wilde Mann kehrte um, hob ihn auf, setzte ihn auf seinen Nacken und ging mit schnellen Schritten in den Wald hinein. Als der König heimkam, bemerkte er den leeren Käfig und fragte die Königin, wie das zugegangen wäre. Sie wußte nichts davon, suchte den Schlüssel, aber er war weg. Sie rief den Knaben, aber niemand antwortete. Der König schickte Leute aus, die ihn auf dem Feld suchen sollten, aber sie fanden ihn nicht. Da konnte er leicht erraten, was geschehen war, und es herrschte große Trauer an dem königlichen Hof.

Als der wilde Mann wieder in dem finstern Wald angelangt war, setzte er den Knaben von den Schultern herab und sprach zu ihm: »Vater und Mutter siehst du nicht wieder, aber ich will dich bei mir behalten, denn du hast mich befreit, und ich habe Mitleid mit dir. Wenn du alles tust, was ich dir sage, so sollst du's gut haben.

Schätze und Gold habe ich genug und mehr als jemand in der Welt.« Er machte dem Knaben ein Lager von Moos, auf dem er einschlief, und am andern Morgen führte ihn der Mann zu einem Brunnen und sprach: »Siehst du, der Goldbrunnen ist hell und klar wie Kristall. Du sollst dabei sitzen und achthaben, daß nichts hineinfällt, sonst ist er verunehrt. Jeden Abend komme ich und sehe, ob du mein Gebot befolgt hast.«

Der Knabe setzte sich an den Rand des Brunnens, er sah, wie manchmal ein goldner Fisch, manchmal eine goldene Schlange sich darin zeigte, und hatte acht, daß nichts hineinfiel. Als er so saß, schmerzte ihn einmal der Finger so heftig, daß er ihn unwillkürlich in das Wasser steckte. Er zog ihn schnell wieder heraus, sah aber, daß er ganz vergoldet war, und wie große Mühe er sich gab, das Gold wieder abzuwischen, es war alles vergeblich. Abends kam der Eisenhans zurück, sah den Knaben an und sprach: »Was ist mit dem Brunnen geschehen?« – »Nichts, nichts«, antwortete er und hielt den Finger auf den Rücken, daß er ihn nicht sehen sollte. Aber der Mann sagte: »Du hast den Finger in das Wasser getaucht. Diesmal mag's hingehen, aber hüte dich, daß du nicht wieder etwas hineinfallen läßt.«

Am frühsten Morgen saß er schon bei dem Brunnen und bewachte ihn. Der Finger tat ihm wieder weh, und er fuhr damit über seinen Kopf, da fiel unglücklicherweise ein Haar herab in den Brunnen. Er nahm es schnell heraus, aber es war schon ganz vergoldet. Der Eisenhans kam und wußte schon, was geschehen war. »Du hast ein Haar in den Brunnen fallen lassen«, sagte er, »ich will dir's noch einmal nachsehen, aber wenn's zum drittenmal geschieht, so ist der Brunnen entehrt, und du kannst nicht länger bei mir bleiben.« Am dritten Tag saß der Knabe am Brunnen und bewegte den Finger nicht, wenn er ihm noch so weh tat. Aber die Zeit ward ihm lang, und er betrachtete sein Angesicht, das auf dem Wasserspiegel stand. Und als er sich dabei immer mehr beugte und sich recht in die Augen sehen wollte, so fielen ihm seine langen Haare von den Schultern herab in das Wasser. Er richtete sich schnell in die Höhe, aber das ganze Haupthaar war schon vergoldet und glänzte wie die Sonne. Ihr könnt euch denken, wie der arme Knabe erschrak. Er nahm sein Taschentuch und band es um den Kopf, damit es der Mann nicht sehen sollte. Als er kam, wußte er schon alles und sprach: »Binde das Tuch auf.« Da quollen die goldenen Haare hervor, und der Knabe mochte sich entschuldigen, wie er wollte, es half ihm nichts. »Du hast die Probe nicht bestanden und kannst nicht länger hierbleiben. Geh hinaus in die Welt, da wirst du erfahren, wie die Armut tut. Aber weil du kein böses Herz hast und ich's gut mit dir meine, so will ich dir eins erlauben: Wenn du in Not gerätst, so geh zu dem Wald und rufe ›Eisenhans‹, dann will ich kommen und dir helfen. Meine Macht ist groß, größer als du denkst, und Gold und Silber habe ich im Überfluß.«

Da verließ der Königssohn den Wald und ging über gebahnte und ungebahnte Wege immerzu, bis er zuletzt in eine große Stadt kam. Er suchte da Arbeit, aber er konnte keine finden und hatte auch nichts erlernt, womit er sich hätte forthelfen können. Endlich ging er in das Schloß und fragte, ob sie ihn behalten wollten. Die Hofleute wußten nicht, wozu sie ihn brauchen sollten, aber sie hatten Wohlgefallen an ihm und hießen ihn bleiben. Zuletzt nahm ihn der Koch in Dienst und sagte, er könnte Holz und Wasser tragen und die Asche zusammenkehren. Einmal, als gerade kein anderer zur Hand war, hieß ihn der Koch die Speisen zur königlichen Tafel tragen. Da er aber seine goldenen Haare nicht wollte sehen lassen, so behielt er sein Hütchen auf. Dem König war so etwas noch nicht vorgekommen, und er sprach: »Wenn du zur königlichen Tafel kommst, mußt du deinen Hut abziehen.« – »Ach Herr«, antwortete er, »ich kann nicht, ich habe einen bösen Grind auf dem Kopf.« Da ließ der König den Koch herbeirufen, schalt ihn und fragte, wie er einen solchen Jungen hätte in seinen Dienst nehmen können; er sollte ihn gleich fort-jagen. Der Koch aber hatte Mitleid mit ihm und vertauschte ihn mit dem Gärtnerjungen.

Nun mußte der Junge im Garten pflanzen und begießen, hacken und graben und Wind und böses Wetter über sich ergehen lassen. Einmal im Sommer, als er allein im Garten arbeitete, war der Tag so heiß, daß er sein Hütchen abnahm und die Luft ihn kühlen sollte. Wie die Sonne auf das Haar schien, glitzte und blitzte es, daß die Strahlen in das Schlafzimmer der Königstochter fielen und sie aufsprang, um zu sehen, was das wäre. Da erblickte sie den Jungen und rief ihn an: »Junge, bring mir einen Blumenstrauß!« Er setzte in aller Eile sein Hütchen auf, brach wilde Feldblumen ab und band sie zusammen. Als er damit die Treppe hinaufstieg, begegnete ihm der Gärtner und sprach: »Wie kannst du der Königstochter einen Strauß von schlechten Blumen bringen? Geschwind, hole andere und suche die schönsten und seltensten aus.« – »Ach nein«, antwortete der Junge, »die wilden riechen kräftiger und werden ihr besser gefallen.« Als er in ihr Zimmer kam, sprach die Königstochter: »Nimm dein Hütchen ab, es ziemt sich nicht, daß du es vor mir aufbehältst.« Er antwortete wieder: »Ich darf nicht, ich habe einen grin-digen Kopf.« Sie griff aber nach dem Hütchen und zog es ab, da rollten seine goldenen Haare auf die Schultern herab, daß es prächtig anzusehen war. Er wollte fortspringen, aber sie hielt ihn am Arm und gab ihm eine Handvoll Dukaten. Er ging damit fort, achtete aber des Goldes nicht, sondern er brachte es dem Gärtner und sprach: »Ich schenke es deinen Kindern, die können damit spielen.« Den andern Tag rief ihm die Königstochter abermals zu, er sollte ihr einen Strauß Feldblumen bringen, und als er damit eintrat, grapste sie gleich nach seinem Hütchen und wollte es ihm wegnehmen, aber er hielt es mit beiden Händen fest. Sie gab ihm wieder eine Handvoll Dukaten, aber er wollte sie nicht behalten und gab sie dem Gärtner zum Spielwerk für seine Kinder. Den dritten Tag ging's nicht anders, sie konnte ihm sein Hütchen nicht wegnehmen, und er wollte ihr Gold nicht.

Nicht lange danach ward das Land mit Krieg überzogen. Der König sammelte sein Volk und wußte nicht, ob er dem Feind, der übermächtig war und ein großes Heer hatte, Widerstand leisten könnte. Da sagte der Gärtnerjunge: »Ich bin her-angewachsen und will mit in den Krieg ziehen, gebt mir nur ein Pferd.« Die andern lachten und sprachen: »Wenn wir fort sind, so suche dir eins: wir wollen dir eins im Stall zurücklassen.« Als sie ausgezogen waren, ging er in den Stall und zog das Pferd heraus; es war an einem Fuß lahm und hickelte hunkepuus, hunkepuus. Dennoch setzte er sich auf und ritt fort nach dem dunkeln Wald. Als er an den Rand desselben gekommen war, rief er dreimal »Eisenhans« so laut, daß es durch die Bäume schallte. Gleich darauf erschien der wilde Mann und sprach: »Was verlangst du?« – »Ich verlange ein starkes Roß, denn ich will in den Krieg ziehen.« – »Das sollst du haben und noch mehr, als du verlangst.« Dann ging der wilde

Mann in den Wald zurück, und es dauerte nicht lange, so kam ein Stallknecht aus dem Wald und führte ein Roß herbei, das schnaubte aus den Nüstern und war kaum zu bändigen. Und hinterher folgte eine große Schar Kriegsvolk, ganz in Eisen gerüstet, und ihre Schwerter blitzten in der Sonne. Der Jüngling übergab dem Stallknecht sein dreibeiniges Pferd, bestieg das andere und ritt vor der Schar her. Als er sich dem Schlachtfeld näherte, war schon ein großer Teil von des Königs Leuten gefallen, und es fehlte nicht viel, so mußten die übrigen weichen. Da jagte der Jüngling mit seiner eisernen Schar heran, fuhr wie ein Wetter über die Feinde und schlug alles nieder, was sich ihm widersetzte. Sie wollten fliehen, aber der Jüngling saß ihnen auf dem Nacken und ließ nicht ab, bis kein Mann mehr übrig war.

Statt aber zu dem König zurückzukehren, führte er seine Schar auf Umwegen wieder zu dem Wald und rief den Eisenhans heraus. »Was verlangst du?« fragte der wilde Mann. »Nimm dein Roß und deine Schar zurück und gib mir mein dreibeiniges Pferd wieder.« Es geschah alles, was er verlangte, und er ritt auf seinem dreibeinigen Pferd heim. Als der König wieder in sein Schloß kam, ging ihm seine Tochter entgegen und wünschte ihm Glück zu seinem Sieg. »Ich bin es nicht, der den Sieg davongetragen hat«, sprach er, »sondern ein fremder Ritter, der mir mit seiner Schar zu Hilfe kam.« Die Tochter wollte wissen, wer der fremde Ritter wäre, aber der König wußte es nicht und sagte: »Er hat die Feinde verfolgt, und ich habe ihn nicht wiedergesehen.« Sie erkundigte sich bei dem Gärtner nach seinem Jungen; der lachte aber und sprach: »Eben ist er auf seinem dreibeinigen Pferd heimgekommen, und die andern haben gespottet und gerufen: ›Da kommt unser Hunkepuus wieder an.‹ Sie fragten auch: ›Hinter welcher Hecke hast du derweil gelegen und geschlafen?‹ Er sprach aber: ›Ich habe das Beste getan, und ohne mich wäre es schlecht gegangen.‹ Da ward er noch mehr ausgelacht.«

Der König sprach zu seiner Tochter: »Ich will ein großes Fest ansagen lassen, das drei Tage währen soll, und du sollst einen goldenen Apfel werfen: vielleicht kommt der Unbekannte herbei.« Als das Fest verkündigt war, ging der Jüngling hinaus zu dem Wald und rief den Eisenhans. »Was verlangst du?« fragte er. »Daß ich den goldenen Apfel der Königstochter fange.«—»Es ist so gut, als hättest du ihn schon«, sagte Eisenhans, »du sollst auch eine rote Rüstung dazu haben und auf einem stolzen Fuchs reiten.« Als der Tag kam, sprengte der Jüngling heran, stellte sich unter die Ritter und ward von niemand erkannt. Die Königstochter trat hervor und warf den Rittern einen goldenen Apfel zu, aber keiner fing ihn als er allein, aber sobald er ihn hatte, jagte er davon. Am zweiten Tag hatte ihn Eisenhans als weißen Ritter ausgerüstet und ihm einen Schimmel gegeben. Abermals fing er allein den Apfel, verweilte aber keinen Augenblick, sondern jagte damit fort. Der König ward bös und sprach: »Das ist nicht erlaubt, er muß vor mir erscheinen und seinen Namen nennen.« Er gab den Befehl, wenn der Ritter, der den Apfel gefangen habe, sich wieder davonmachte, so sollte man ihm nachsetzen, und wenn er nicht gutwillig zurückkehrte, auf ihn hauen und stechen. Am dritten Tag erhielt er vom Eisenhans eine schwarze Rüstung und einen Rappen und fing auch wieder den Apfel. Als er aber damit fortjagte, verfolgten ihn die Leute des Königs, und einer kam ihm so nahe, daß er mit der Spitze des Schwerts ihm das Bein verwundete. Er entkam ihnen jedoch, aber sein Pferd sprang so gewaltig, daß der Helm ihm vom Kopf fiel, und sie konnten sehen, daß er goldene Haare hatte. Sie ritten zurück und meldeten dem König alles.

Am andern Tag fragte die Königstochter den Gärtner nach seinem Jungen. »Er arbeitet im Garten; der wunderliche Kauz ist auch bei dem Fest gewesen und erst gestern abend wiedergekommen; er hat auch meinen Kindern drei goldene Äpfel gezeigt, die er gewonnen hat.« Der König ließ ihn vor sich fordern, und er erschien und hatte wieder sein Hütchen auf dem Kopf. Aber die Königstochter ging auf ihn zu und nahm es ihm ab, und da fielen seine goldenen Haare über die Schultern, und er war so schön, daß alle erstaunten. »Bist du der Ritter gewesen, der jeden Tag zu dem Fest gekommen ist, immer in einer andern Farbe, und der die drei goldenen Äpfel gefangen hat?« fragte der König. »Ja«, antwortete er, »und da sind die Äpfel«, holte sie aus seiner Tasche und reichte sie dem König. »Wenn Ihr noch mehr Beweise verlangt, so könnt Ihr die Wunde sehen, die mir Eure Leute geschlagen haben, als sie mich verfolgten. Aber ich bin auch der Ritter, der Euch zum Sieg über die Feinde geholfen hat.« – »Wenn du solche Taten verrichten kannst, so bist du kein Gärtnerjunge, sage mir, wer ist dein Vater?« – »Mein Vater ist ein mächtiger König, und Gold habe ich die Fülle und soviel ich nur verlange.« – »Ich sehe wohl«, sprach der König, »ich bin dir Dank schuldig, kann ich dir etwas zu Gefallen tun?« – »Ja«, antwortete er, »das könnt Ihr wohl, gebt mir Eure Tochter zur Frau.« Da lachte die Jungfrau und sprach: »Der macht keine Umstände, aber ich habe schon an seinen goldenen Haaren gesehen, daß er kein Gärtnerjunge ist«, ging dann hin und küßte ihn. Zur Vermählung kamen sein Vater und seine Mutter und waren in großer Freude, denn sie hatten schon alle Hoffnung aufgegeben, ihren lieben Sohn wiederzusehen. Und als sie an der Hochzeitstafel saßen, da schwieg auf einmal die Musik, die Türen gingen auf, und ein stolzer König trat herein mit großem Gefolge. Er ging auf den Jüngling zu, umarmte ihn und sprach: »Ich bin der Eisenhans und war in einen wilden Mann verwünscht, aber du hast mich erlöst. Alle Schätze, die ich besitze, die sollen dein Eigentum sein.«   1850

Der Geist im Glas

Es war einmal ein armer Holzhacker, der arbeitete vom Morgen bis in die späte Nacht. Als er sich endlich etwas Geld zusammengespart hatte, sprach er zu seinem Jungen: »Du bist mein einziges Kind, ich will das Geld, das ich mit saurem Schweiß erworben, zu deinem Unterricht anwenden; wenn du etwas Rechtschaffenes lernst, so kannst du mich im Alter ernähren, wenn ich einst daheim sitzen muß und meine Glieder steif geworden sind.«

Da ging der Junge auf eine Hohe Schule und lernte fleißig, so daß ihn seine Lehrer rühmten, und blieb eine Zeit lang dort; als er ein paar Schulen durchgelernt hatte, aber noch nicht in allem vollkommen war, so war das bißchen Armut, das der Vater erworben, drauf gegangen, und er mußte wieder zu ihm heimkehren. »Ach«, sprach der Vater betrübt, »ich kann dir nichts mehr geben und kann in der teuern Zeit auch keinen Heller mehr verdienen als das tägliche Brot.« – »Lieber Vater«, antwortete der Sohn, »macht Euch darüber keine Gedanken, wenn's Gottes Wille also ist, so wird's zu meinem Besten ausschlagen; ich will mich schon drein schicken: ich bleibe bei Euch und gehe mit hinaus in den Wald, um etwas am Malterholz (am Zuhauen und Aufrichten) zu verdienen.« – »Ja, mein Sohn«, sagte der Vater, »das soll dir beschwerlich ankommen, du bist an harte Arbeit nicht gewöhnt, du hältst das nicht aus; ich habe auch nur eine Axt und kein Geld übrig, um noch eine zu kaufen.« – »Geht nur zum Nachbar«, antwortete der Sohn, »der leiht Euch seine Axt so lange, bis ich mir selbst eine verdient habe.«

Da ging der Vater zum Nachbar und borgte eine Axt, und am andern Morgen, wie der Tag anbrach, gingen sie miteinander hinaus in den Wald. Der Sohn half dem Vater und war ganz munter und frisch dabei. Als nun die Sonne über ihnen stand, sprach der Vater: »Wir wollen rasten und Mittag halten, hernach geht's noch einmal so gut.« Der Sohn nahm sein Brot in die Hand und sprach: »Ruht Euch nur aus, Vater, ich bin nicht müd, ich will in dem Wald ein wenig auf- und abgehen und Vogelnester suchen.« – »O du Geck!« sprach der Vater. »Was willst du da herumlaufen, hernach bist du müd und kannst den Arm nicht mehr aufheben; bleib hier und setz dich zu mir.«

Der Sohn aber ging in den Wald, aß sein Brot ganz fröhlich und sah in die grünen Zweige hinein, ob er etwa ein Nest entdeckte. So ging er hin und her, bis er endlich zu einer großen, gefährlichen Eiche kam, die gewiß schon viele Hundert Jahre da gestanden und die keine fünf Menschen umspannt hätten. Er blieb stehen und sah sie an und dachte, es muß doch mancher Vogel sein Nest hineingebaut haben! Da war ihm auf einmal, als hörte er eine Stimme. Er horchte danach und vernahm, wie es mit so einem recht dumpfen Ton rief: »Laß mich heraus! Laß mich heraus!« Er sah sich ringsum, konnte aber nichts entdecken, auch war es ihm, als ob die Stimme unten aus der Erde käme; da rief er: »Wo bist du?« Die Stimme antwortete: »Da unten stecke ich, bei der Eichwurzel! Laß mich heraus! Laß mich heraus!« Der Schüler fing an, unter dem Baum aufzuräumen und bei den Wurzeln zu suchen, bis er endlich in einer kleinen Höhlung eine Glasflasche entdeckte. Er hob sie in die Höh und hielt sie gegen das Licht, da sah er ein Ding, gleich einem Frosch gestaltet, das sprang darin auf und nieder. »Laß mich heraus! Laß mich heraus!« rief's von neuem, und der Schüler, der an nichts Böses dachte, nahm den Pfropfen von der Flasche ab. Alsbald stieg ein Geist heraus und fing an zu wachsen und nahm in jedem Augenblick so gewaltig zu, daß er bald als ein entsetzlicher Kerl und wie der halbe Baum so groß vor dem Schüler stand. »Weißt du«, rief er mit einer fürchterlichen Stimme, »was dein Lohn dafür ist, daß du mich herausgelassen hast?« – »Nein«, antwortete der Schüler ohne Furcht, »wie soll ich das wissen!« – »So will ich dir's sagen«, rief der Geist, »den Hals muß ich dir dafür brechen!« – »Das hättest du mir früher sagen sollen«, antwortete der Schüler, »so hätte ich dich stecken lassen; mein Kopf aber soll vor dir wohl feststehen, da müssen mehr Leute gefragt werden.« – »Mehr Leute hin, mehr Leute her! Deinen verdienten Lohn, den sollst du haben! Denkst du, ich wär aus Gnade da so lange Zeit eingeschlossen worden, nein, es war zu meiner Strafe; ich bin der großmächtige Merkurius. Wer mich losläßt, dem muß ich den Hals brechen.« – »Sachte«, antwortete der Schüler, »so geschwind geht das nicht, erst muß ich auch wissen, daß du wirklich in der kleinen Flasche gesessen und du der rechte Geist bist; kannst du auch wieder hinein, so will ich's glauben, und dann magst du mit mir anfangen, was du willst.« – »Oh«, sprach der Geist hochmütig, »das ist mir ein Geringes«, und zog sich zusammen und machte sich so dünn und klein, wie er anfangs gewesen, also daß er durch dieselbe Öffnung und den Hals der Flasche wieder hineinkroch. Kaum aber war er darin, so drückte der Schüler den abgezogenen Pfropfen wieder auf und warf die Flasche unter die Eichwurzeln an ihren alten Platz, und der Geist war betrogen.

Nun wollte der Schüler zu seinem Vater zurückgehen, aber der Geist rief ganz kläglich und sprach: »Ach! laß mich doch heraus! Laß mich doch heraus!« – »Nein«, antwortete der Schüler, »zum zweitenmal nicht wieder; wer mir einmal nach dem Leben gestrebt hat, den laß ich nicht los, wenn ich ihn wieder gefangen habe.« – »Mach mich frei«, rief der Geist, »so will ich dir so viel geben, daß du dein

Lebtag genug hast.« – »Nein«, antwortete der Schüler, »du betrügst mich wie das erstemal.« – »Du verscherzest dein Glück«, sprach der Geist, »ich will dir nichts tun, sondern dich reichlich belohnen.«

Der Schüler dachte, ich will's wagen, vielleicht hält er Wort, und anhaben soll er mir doch nichts. Da nahm er den Pfropfen ab, und der Geist stieg wie das vorige Mal heraus, dehnte sich auseinander und ward gewaltig groß. Da reichte er dem Schüler einen kleinen Lappen, ganz wie ein Pflaster, und sprach: »Wenn du mit dem einen Ende eine Wunde bestreichst, so heilt sie, und wenn du mit dem anderen Stahl und Eisen bestreichst, so wird es in Silber verwandelt sein.« – »Das muß ich erst versuchen«, sprach der Schüler, ging an einen Baum und ritzte die Rinde mit seiner Axt und bestrich sie mit dem einen Ende des Pflasters, alsbald schloß sie sich wieder zusammen und war geheilt. »Nun, es hat seine Richtigkeit«, sprach er zum Geist, »jetzt können wir uns trennen.« Der Geist dankte ihm für seine Erlösung, und der Schüler dankte dem Geist für sein Geschenk und ging zurück zu seinem Vater.

»Wo bist du herumgelaufen?« sprach der Vater. »Und hast die Arbeit vergessen; ich hab's ja gleich gesagt, daß du nichts tun würdest.« – »Gebt Euch zufrieden, Vater, ich will's nachholen.« – »Ja, nachholen«, sprach der Vater zornig, »das hat keine Art.« – »Habt acht, Vater, den Baum da will ich gleich einhauen, daß er umkrachen soll.« Da nahm er sein Pflaster, bestrich die Axt damit und tat einen gewaltigen Hieb, aber das Eisen war in Silber verwandelt, und die Schärfe legte sich ganz um. »Ei, Vater, seht einmal, was habt Ihr mir für eine schlechte Axt gegeben, die ist ganz schief geworden!« Da erschrak der Vater und sprach: »Ach, was hast du gemacht! Nun muß ich die Axt bezahlen und weiß nicht, womit; das ist der Nutzen, den ich von deiner Arbeit habe.« – »Werdet nicht bös«, antwortete der Sohn, »die Axt will ich schon bezahlen.« – »O du Dummbart«, rief der Vater, »wovon willst du sie bezahlen? Du hast nichts, als was ich dir gebe; das sind Studentenkniffe, die dir im Kopf stecken, vom Holzhacken hast du keinen Verstand.«

Über ein Weilchen sprach der Schüler: »Vater, ich kann doch nichts mehr arbeiten, wir wollen lieber Feierabend machen.« – »Ei was«, antwortete er, »meinst du, ich wollte auch die Hände in den Schoß legen wie du? Ich muß noch schaffen, du kannst dich heim packen.« – »Vater, ich bin zum erstenmal hier in dem Wald, ich weiß den Weg nicht allein, geht nur mit mir.« Weil sich der Zorn gelegt hatte, so ließ er sich endlich bereden und ging mit ihm heim. Da sprach er zum Sohn: »Geh und verkauf die verschändete Axt und sieh zu, was du dafür kriegst; das übrige muß ich verdienen, um sie zu bezahlen.« Der Sohn nahm die Axt und trug sie in die Stadt zu einem Goldschmied, der probierte sie, legte sie auf die Waage und sprach: »Sie ist vierhundert Taler wert, soviel hab ich nicht bar.« Der Schüler sprach: »Gebt mir, was Ihr habt, das übrige will ich Euch borgen.« Der Goldschmied gab ihm dreihundert Taler und blieb einhundert noch schuldig. Darauf ging der Schüler heim und sprach: »Vater, ich habe Geld, geht und fragt, was der Nachbar für die Axt haben will.« – »Das weiß ich schon«, antwortete der Alte, »einen Taler sechs Groschen.« – »So gebt ihm zwei Taler zwölf Groschen, das ist das Doppelte und ist genug; seht Ihr, ich habe Geld im Überfluß«; und gab dem Vater einhundert Taler und sprach: »Es soll Euch niemals fehlen, lebt nach Eurer Bequemlichkeit.« – »Mein Gott«, sprach der Alte, »wie bist du zu dem Reichtum gekommen?« – Da erzählte er ihm, wie alles zugegangen wäre, und wie er im Wald im Vertrauen auf sein Glück einen so reichen Fang getan. Mit dem übrigen Geld aber zog er wieder hin auf die Hohe Schule und lernte weiter, und weil er mit seinem Pflaster alle Wunden heilen konnte, ward er der berühmteste Doktor auf der ganzen Welt.

1819

Herr Korbes

Es war einmal ein Hühnchen und ein Hähnchen, die wollten zusammen eine Reise machen. Da baute das Hähnchen einen schönen Wagen, der vier rote Räder hatte, und spannte vier Mäuschen davor. Das Hühnchen setzte sich mit dem Hähnchen auf, und sie fuhren miteinander fort. Nicht lange, so begegnete ihnen eine Katze, die sprach: »Wo wollt ihr hin?« Hähnchen antwortete:

> »Als hinaus
> nach des Herrn Korbes seinem Haus.«

»Nehmt mich mit«, sprach die Katze. Hähnchen antwortete: »Recht gerne, setz dich hinten auf, daß du vorne nicht herabfällst.

> Nehmt euch wohl in acht,
> daß ihr meine roten Räderchen nicht schmutzig macht.
> Ihr Räderchen, schweift,
> ihr Mäuschen, pfeift,
> als hinaus
> nach des Herrn Korbes seinem Haus.«

Danach kam ein Mühlstein, dann ein Ei, dann eine Ente, dann eine Stecknadel und zuletzt eine Nähnadel, die setzten sich auch alle auf den Wagen und fuhren mit. Wie sie aber zu des Herrn Korbes' Haus kamen, so war der Herr Korbes nicht da. Die Mäuschen fuhren den Wagen in die Scheune, das Hühnchen flog mit dem Hähnchen auf eine Stange, die Katze setzte sich in den Kamin, die Ente in den

Brunnen, das Ei wickelte sich ins Handtuch, die Stecknadel steckte sich ins Stuhl-
kissen, die Nähnadel aufs Bett ins Kopfkissen, und der Mühlstein legte sich über
die Türe. Da kam der Herr Korbes nach Haus, ging zum Kamin und wollte Feuer
anmachen, da warf ihm die Katze das Gesicht voll Asche. Er lief geschwind in die
Küche und wollte sich abwaschen, da spritzte ihm die Ente Wasser ins Gesicht. Er
wollte sich an dem Handtuch abtrocknen, aber das Ei rollte ihm entgegen, zerbrach und klebte ihm die Augen zu. Er wollte sich ausruhen und setzte sich auf den
Stuhl, da stach ihn die Stecknadel. Er wurde ganz verdrießlich und warf sich aufs
Bett. Wie er aber den Kopf aufs Kissen niederlegte, stach ihn die Nähnadel, so daß
er aufschrie und ganz außer sich fortlaufen wollte. Wie er aber an die Haustüre
kam, sprang der Mühlstein herunter und schlug ihn tot. 1837

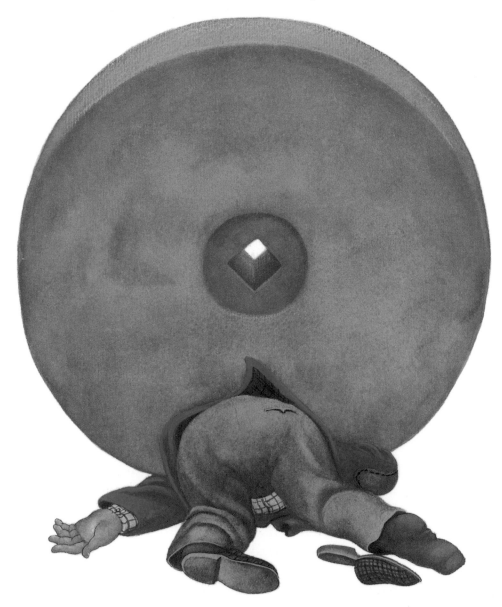

Die weiße und die schwarze Braut

Eine Frau ging mit ihrer Tochter und Stieftochter über Feld, Futter zu schneiden. Da kam der liebe Gott als ein armer Mann zu ihnen gegangen und fragte: »Wo führt der Weg ins Dorf?« – »Ei«, sprach die Mutter, »sucht ihn selber«, und die Tochter setzte noch hinzu: »Habt Ihr Sorge, daß Ihr ihn nicht findet, so bringt Euch einen Wegweiser mit.« Die Stieftochter aber sprach: »Armer Mann, ich will dich führen, komm mit mir.« Da erzürnte der liebe Gott über die Mutter und Tochter, wendete ihnen den Rücken zu und verwünschte sie, daß sie sollten schwarz werden wie die Nacht und häßlich wie die Sünde. Der armen Stieftochter aber ward Gott gnädig und ging mit ihr, und als sie nah am Dorf waren, sprach er einen Segen über sie und sagte: »Wähl dir drei Sachen aus, die will ich dir gewähren.« Da sprach das Mädchen: »Ich möchte gern schön werden wie die Sonne«, alsbald wurde sie weiß und schön wie der Tag. »Dann möchte ich einen Geldbeutel haben, der nie leer würde«; den gab ihr der liebe Gott auch, sprach aber: »Vergiß das Beste nicht, meine Tochter!« Sagte sie: »Ich wünsche mir zum dritten das ewige Himmelreich nach meinem Tode.« Das wurde ihr auch zugesagt, und also schied der liebe Gott von ihr.

Wie nun die Stiefmutter mit ihrer Tochter nach Hause kam und sah, daß sie beide kohlschwarz und häßlich waren, die Stieftochter aber weiß und schön, ward sie ihr im Herzen noch böser und hatte nur im Sinn, wie sie ihr ein Leid antun könnte. Die Stieftochter aber hatte einen Bruder namens Reginer, den liebte sie sehr und erzählte ihm alles, was geschehen war. Nun sprach der Reginer einmal zu ihr: »Liebe Schwester, ich will dich abmalen, damit ich dich beständig vor Augen sehe, denn meine Liebe zu dir ist so groß, daß ich dich immer in Gedanken habe.« Da antwortete sie: »Aber laß niemand das Bild sehen.« Er malte nun seine Schwester ab und hing das Bild in seiner Stube auf, in des Königs Schloß, bei dem er Kutscher war, und alle Tage blieb er davor stehen und dankte Gott für das Glück seiner lieben Schwester.

Nun war aber gerade dem König, bei dem er diente, seine Gemahlin verstorben, welche so schön gewesen war, daß man keine finden konnte, die ihr gliche, und der König war darüber in tiefer Trauer. Die Hofdiener sahen es indessen dem Kutscher ab, wie er täglich vor dem schönen Bilde stand, mißgönnten es ihm und meldeten es dem König. Da ließ dieser das Bild vor sich bringen und sah, daß es in allem seiner verstorbenen Frau glich, nur noch schöner war, so daß er sich sterblich hinein verliebte und den Kutscher fragte, wen das Bild vorstellte? Als der Kutscher gesagt hatte, daß es seine Schwester wäre, entschloß sich der König, keine andere als diese zur Gemahlin zu nehmen, gab ihm Wagen und Pferde und prächtige Goldkleider und schickte ihn fort, seine erwählte Braut abzuholen.

Wie Reginer mit der Botschaft ankam, freute sich seine Schwester, allein die Schwarze ärgerte sich über alle Maßen vor großer Eifersucht und sprach zu ihrer Mutter: »Was helfen nun all Eure Künste, da Ihr mir kein solches Glück verschaffen könnt.« Da sagte die Alte: »Sei still, ich will dir's schon zuwenden«, und durch ihre Hexenkünste trübte sie dem Kutscher die Augen, daß er halb blind war, und der Weißen verstopfte sie die Ohren, daß sie schwer hörte. Darauf stiegen sie in den Wagen, erst die Braut in den herrlichen königlichen Kleidern, dann die Stiefmutter mit ihrer Tochter, und Reginer saß auf dem Bock, um zu fahren. Wie sie eine Weile gereist waren, rief unterwegs der Kutscher:

>»Deck dich zu, mein Schwesterlein,
>daß Regen dich nicht näßt,
>daß Wind dich nicht bestäubt,
>daß du fein schön zum König kommst!«

Die Braut fragte: »Was sagt mein lieber Bruder?« – »Ach«, sprach die Alte, »er hat gesagt, du solltest dein gülden Kleid ausziehen und es deiner Schwester geben.« Da zog sie's aus und tat's der Schwarzen an, die gab ihr dafür einen schlechten grauen Kittel. So fuhren sie weiter, über ein Weilchen rief der Bruder abermals:

>»Deck dich zu, mein Schwesterlein,
>daß Regen dich nicht näßt,
>daß Wind dich nicht bestäubt
>und du fein schön zum König kommst!«

Die Braut fragte: »Was sagt mein lieber Bruder?« – »Ach«, sprach die Alte, »er hat gesagt, du solltest deine güldene Haube abtun und deiner Schwester geben.« Da tat sie die Haube ab und der Schwarzen auf und saß im bloßen Haar. So fuhren sie weiter. Wiederum über ein Weilchen rief der Bruder:

>»Deck dich zu, mein Schwesterlein,
>daß Regen dich nicht näßt,
>daß Wind dich nicht bestäubt
>und du fein schön zum König kommst!«

Die Braut fragte: »Was sagt mein lieber Bruder?« – »Ach«, sprach die Alte, »er hat gesagt, du möchtest einmal aus dem Wagen sehen.« Sie fuhren aber gerade über ein tiefes Wasser. Wie nun die Braut aufstand und aus dem Fenster sah, da stießen sie die beiden andern hinaus, daß sie gerad ins Wasser fiel. Sie versank auch, aber in demselben Augenblick stieg eine schneeweiße Ente hervor und schwamm den Fluß hinab. Der Bruder hatte gar nichts davon gemerkt und fuhr den Wagen

weiter, bis sie an den Hof kamen, da brachte er dem König die Schwarze als seine Schwester, und meinte auch, sie wär's, weil es ihm trüb vor den Augen war und er doch die Goldkleider schimmern sah. Der König, wie er die grundlose Häßlichkeit an seiner vermeinten Braut erblickte, ward sehr bös und befahl, den Kutscher in eine Grube zu werfen, die voll Ottern- und Schlangengezücht war. Die alte Hexe aber wußte den König doch so zu bestricken und ihm die Augen zu verblenden, daß er sie und ihre Tochter behielt und zu sich nahm, bis daß sie ihm ganz leidlich vorkam und er sich wirklich mit ihr verheiratete.

Einmal abends saß die schwarze Braut dem König auf dem Schoß, da kam eine weiße Ente zum Gossenstein in die Küche geschwommen und sagte zum Küchenjungen:

> »Jüngelchen, mach Feuer an,
> daß ich meine Federn wärmen kann!«

Das tat der Küchenjunge und machte ihr ein Feuer auf dem Herd, da kam die Ente und setzte sich daneben, schüttelte sich und strich sich die Federn mit dem Schnabel zurecht. Während sie so saß und sich wohltat, fragte sie:

> »Was macht mein Bruder Reginer?«

Der Küchenjunge antwortete:

>Liegt tief bei Ottern und Schlangen.«

Fragte sie:

>Was macht die schwarze Hex im Haus?«

Der Küchenjunge antwortete:

>Die sitzt warm in Königs Arm.«

Sagte die Ente:

>Daß Gott erbarm!«

und schwamm den Gossenstein hinaus.

Den folgenden Abend kam sie wieder und tat dieselben Fragen und den dritten Abend noch einmal. Da konnte es der Küchenjunge nicht länger übers Herz bringen und sagte dem König alles. Der König aber ging den andern Abend hin, und wie die Ente den Kopf durch den Gossenstein hereinstreckte, nahm er sein Schwert und hieb ihr den Hals durch, da wurde sie auf einmal zum schönsten Mädchen und glich genau dem Bild, das der Bruder von ihr gemacht hatte. Der König aber war voll Freuden, und weil sie ganz naß dastand, ließ er ihr köstliche Kleider bringen. Als sie die angetan hatte, erzählte sie ihm, wie sie in den Fluß war hinabgeworfen worden, und die erste Bitte, die sie tat, war, daß ihr Bruder aus der Schlangenhöhle herausgeholt würde, welches auch gleich geschah.

Aber der König ging in die Kammer, wo die alte Hexe saß, und fragte: >Was verdient die, welche das und das tut?«, indem er den ganzen Hergang erzählte. Da war sie verblendet, merkte nichts und sprach: >Die verdient, daß man sie nackt auszieht und in ein Faß mit Nägeln legt und vor das Faß ein Pferd spannt und das Pferd in alle Welt schickt.« Alles das geschah nun an ihr und ihrer schwarzen Tochter, der König heiratete die schöne Braut und belohnte den treuen Bruder, indem er ihn zu einem reichen und angesehenen Mann machte.   1819

Die sieben Schwaben

Einmal waren sieben Schwaben beisammen; der erste war der Herr Schulz, der zweite der Jackli, der dritte der Marli, der vierte der Jergli, der fünfte der Michal, der sechste der Hans, der siebente der Veitli; die hatten sich alle sieben vorgenommen, die Welt zu durchziehen, Abenteuer zu suchen und große Taten zu vollbringen. Damit sie aber auch mit bewaffneter Hand und sicher gingen, sahen sie's für gut an, daß sie sich zwar nur einen einzigen, aber recht starken und langen Spieß machen ließen.

Diesen Spieß faßten sie alle sieben zusammen an, vorne ging der kühnste und männlichste, das mußte der Herr Schulz sein, und dann folgten die andern nach der Reihe, und der Veitli war der letzte.

Nun geschah es, daß, als sie im Heumonat eines Tags einen weiten Weg gegangen, auch noch ein gut Stück bis in das Dorf hatten, wo sie über Nacht bleiben mußten, in der Dämmerung auf einer Wiese ein großer Roßkäfer oder eine Hornisse nicht weit von ihnen hinter einer Staude vorbeiflog und feindlich brummelte. Der Herr Schulz erschrak, daß er fast den Spieß hätte fallen lassen und ihm der Angstschweiß am ganzen Leibe ausbrach. »Horcht, horcht!« rief er seinen Gesellen. »Gott! Ich höre eine Trommel!« Der Jackli, der hinter ihm den Spieß hielt und dem ich weiß nicht was für ein Geruch in die Nase kam, sprach: »Etwas ist ohne Zweifel vorhanden, denn ich schmeck das Pulver und den Zündstrick!« Bei diesen Worten hub der Herr Schulz an, die Flucht zu ergreifen, und sprang im Hui über einen Zaun, weil er aber gerade auf die Zinken eines Rechen sprang, der vom Heumachen da liegen geblieben war, so fuhr ihm der Stiel ins Gesicht und gab ihm einen ungewaschenen Schlag. »O wei! O wei!« schrie der Herr Schulz. »Nimm mich gefangen, ich ergeb mich! Ich ergeb mich!« Die andern sechs hüpften auch alle einer über den andern herzu und schrien: »Gibst du dich, so geb ich mich auch! Gibst du dich, so geb ich mich auch!« Endlich, wie kein Feind da war, der sie binden und fortführen wollte, merkten sie, daß sie betrogen waren, und damit die Geschichte nicht unter die Leute käme und sie nicht damit genarrt und gespottet würden, schworen sie untereinander, so lang davon still zu schweigen, bis einer das Maul auftät.

Hierauf zogen sie weiter. Die zweite Gefährlichkeit, die sie erlebten, kann aber mit der ersten nicht verglichen werden; denn nach etlichen Tagen trug sie ihr Weg durch ein Brachfeld, da saß ein Has in der Sonne und schlief, streckte die Ohren in die Höhe und hatte die großen, gläsernen Augen starr aufstehen. Da erschraken sie bei dem Anblick des grausamen und wilden Tieres insgesamt und hielten Rat, was zu tun, das am wenigsten gefährlich wäre. Denn wenn sie fliehen wollten, war zu besorgen, das Ungeheuer setzte ihnen nach und verschläng sie alle mit Haut und Haar. Also sprachen sie: »Wir müssen einen großen und gefährlichen Kampf wagen! Frisch gewagt ist halb gewonnen!«, faßten alle sieben den Spieß an, der Herr Schulz vorne und der Veitli hinten. Der Herr Schulz wollte den Spieß noch immer anhalten, der Veitli aber war hinten ganz mutig geworden, wollte losbrechen und rief:

> »Stoß zu in aller Schwabe Name!
> Sonst wünsch i, daß ihr mögt erlahme!«

Aber der Hans wußt' ihn zu treffen und sprach:

> »Beim Element, du hascht gut schwätze,
> bischt stets der letscht beim Drachehetze!«

Der Michal rief:

> »Es wird nit fehle um ei Haar,
> so ischt es wohl der Teufel gar!«

Drauf kam an den Jergli die Reih, der sprach:

> »Ischt er es nit, so ischt's sei Mutter
> oder des Teufels Stiefbruder!«

Der Marli hatte einen guten Gedanken und sagte zum Veitli:

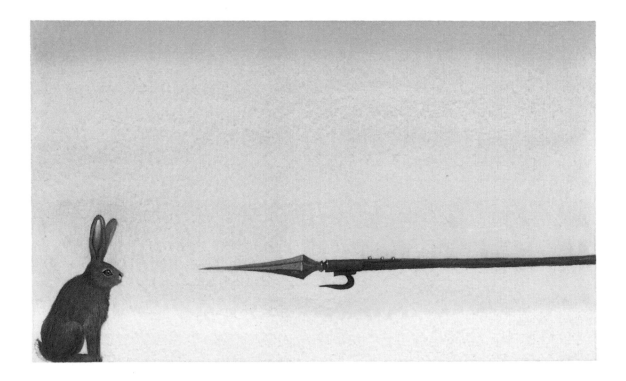

»Gang, Veitli, gang, gang du voran,
i will dahinte vor di stahn!«

Der Veitli hörte aber nicht drauf, und der Jackli sagte:

»Der Schulz, der muß der erschte sei,
denn ihm gebührt die Ehr allei!«

Da nahm sich der Herr Schulz ein Herz und sprach gravitätisch:

»So zieht denn herzhaft in den Streit,
hieran erkennt man tapfre Leut!«

Und da gingen sie insgesamt auf den Drachen los, der Herr Schulz segnete sich und rief Gott um Beistand an; wie aber das alles nicht helfen wollte und er dem Feind immer näher kam, schrie er in großer Angst: »Hau! Hurlehau! Hau! Hauhau!« Davon erwachte der Has, erschrak und sprang eilig davon. Als ihn der Herr Schulz so feldflüchtig sah, rief er voll Freude:

»Potz, Veitli, lueg, lueg, was ischt das?
Das Ungehüer ischt a Has!«

Der Schwabenbund suchte aber weiter Abenteuer und kam an die Mosel, ein moosiges, stilles und tiefes Wasser, darüber nicht viel Brücken sind, sondern man an mehreren Orten sich muß in Schiffen überfahren lassen. Weil die sieben Schwaben dessen unberichtet waren, riefen sie einem Mann, der jenseits des Wassers seine Arbeit vollbrachte, zu, wie man doch hinüber kommen könnte? Der Mann verstand wegen der Weite, auch wegen ihrer Sprache nicht, was sie wollten, und fragte auf sein Trierisch: »Wat? Wat?« Da meinte der Herr Schulz, er spräche nicht anders als: »Wate, wate durchs Wasser« und hub an, weil er der Vorderste war, sich auf den Weg zu machen und in die Mosel hineinzugehen. Nicht lang, so versank er in den Schlamm und in die antreibenden, tiefen Wellen. Seinen Hut aber jagte der Wind hinüber an das jenseitige Ufer, und ein Frosch setzte sich dabei und quakte wat, wat, wat! Die sechs andern hörten das drüben und sprachen: »Unser Gesell, der Herr Schulz, ruft uns. Kann er hinüber waten, warum wir nicht auch?« Sprangen darum eilig alle zusammen in das Wasser und ertranken, also daß ein Frosch allein ihrer sechse ums Leben brachte und niemand von dem Schwabenbund wieder nach Haus kam.

1819

Der starke Hans

Es waren einmal ein Mann und eine Frau, die hatten nur ein einziges Kind und lebten in einem abseits gelegenen Tale ganz allein. Es trug sich zu, daß die Mutter einmal ins Holz ging, Tannenreiser zu lesen, und den kleinen Hans, der erst zwei Jahr alt war, mitnahm. Da es gerade in der Frühlingszeit war und das Kind seine Freude an den bunten Blumen hatte, so ging sie immer weiter mit ihm in den Wald hinein. Plötzlich sprangen aus dem Gebüsch zwei Räuber hervor, packten die Mutter und das Kind und führten sie tief in den schwarzen Wald, wo jahraus, jahrein kein Mensch hinkam. Die arme Frau bat die Räuber inständig, sie mit ihrem Kinde freizulassen, aber das Herz der Räuber war von Stein. Sie hörten nicht auf ihr Bitten und Flehen und trieben sie mit Gewalt an, weiterzugehen. Nachdem sie etwa zwei Stunden durch Stauden und Dörner sich hatten durcharbeiten müssen, kamen sie zu einem Felsen, wo eine Türe war, an welche die Räuber klopften und die sich alsbald öffnete. Sie mußten durch einen langen dunklen Gang und kamen endlich in eine große Höhle, die von einem Feuer, das auf dem Herd brannte, erleuchtet war. An der Wand hingen Schwerter, Säbel und andere Mordgewehre, die in dem Lichte blinkten, und in der Mitte stand ein schwarzer Tisch, an dem vier andere Räuber saßen und spielten, und obenan saß der Hauptmann. Dieser kam, als er die Frau sah, heran, redete sie an und sagte, sie sollte nur ruhig und ohne Angst sein, sie täten ihr nichts zuleid, aber sie müßte das Hauswesen besorgen, und wenn sie alles in Ordnung hielte, so sollte sie es nicht schlimm bei ihnen haben. Darauf gaben sie ihr etwas zu essen und zeigten ihr ein Bett, wo sie mit ihrem Kinde schlafen könnte.

Die Frau blieb viele Jahre bei den Räubern, und Hans ward groß und stark. Die Mutter erzählte ihm Geschichten und lehrte ihn in einem alten Ritterbuch, das sie in der Höhle fand, lesen. Als Hans neun Jahr alt war, machte er sich aus einem Tannenast einen starken Knüttel und versteckte ihn hinter das Bett; dann ging er zu seiner Mutter und sprach: »Liebe Mutter, sage mir jetzt einmal, wer mein Vater ist, ich will und muß es wissen.« Die Mutter schwieg still und wollte es ihm nicht sagen, damit er nicht das Heimweh bekäme, und die gottlosen Räuber hätten den Hans doch nicht fortgelassen. Aber es hätte ihr fast das Herz zersprengt, daß Hans nicht sollte zu seinem Vater kommen. In der Nacht, als die Räuber von ihrem Raubzug heimkamen, holte Hans seinen Knüttel hervor, stellte sich vor den Hauptmann und sagte: »Jetzt will ich wissen, wer mein Vater ist, und wenn du mir's

nicht gleich sagst, so schlag ich dich nieder.« Da lachte der Hauptmann und gab dem Hans eine Ohrfeige, daß er unter den Tisch kugelte. Hans machte sich wieder auf, schwieg und dachte: »Ich will noch ein Jahr warten und es dann noch einmal versuchen, vielleicht geht's besser.«

Als das Jahr herum war, holte er seinen Knüttel wieder hervor, wischte den Staub ab, betrachtete ihn und sprach: »Es ist ein tüchtiger, wackerer Knüttel.« Nachts kamen die Räuber heim, tranken Wein, einen Krug nach dem andern, und fingen an, die Köpfe zu hängen. Da holte der Hans seinen Knüttel herbei, stellte sich wieder vor den Hauptmann und fragte ihn, wer sein Vater wäre. Der Hauptmann gab ihm abermals eine so kräftige Ohrfeige, daß Hans unter den Tisch rollte, aber es dauerte nicht lange, so war er wieder oben und schlug mit seinem Knüttel auf den Hauptmann und die Räuber, daß sie Arme und Beine nicht mehr regen konnten. Die Mutter stand in einer Ecke und sah voll Verwunderung über seine Tapferkeit und Stärke zu, und als Hans mit seiner Arbeit fertig war, ging er zu seiner Mutter und sagte: »Jetzt ist mir's Ernst gewesen, aber jetzt muß ich auch wissen, wer mein Vater ist.« – »Lieber Hans«, antwortete die Mutter, »komm, wir wollen gehen und ihn suchen, bis wir ihn finden.« Sie nahm dem Hauptmann den Schlüssel zu der Eingangstüre ab, aber Hans holte einen großen Mehlsack, packte Gold, Silber und was er sonst noch für schöne Sachen fand, zusammen, bis er voll war, und nahm ihn dann auf den Rücken.

Sie verließen die Höhle, aber was tat Hans die Augen auf, als er aus der Finsternis heraus in das Tageslicht kam und den grünen Wald, Gras, Blumen und Vögel und die Morgensonne am Himmel erblickte. Er stand da und staunte alles an, als wenn er nicht recht gescheit wäre. Die Mutter suchte den Weg nach Haus, und als sie ein paar Stunden gegangen waren, so kamen sie glücklich in ihr einsames Tal und zu ihrem Häuschen. Der Vater saß unter der Türe und weinte vor Freude, als er seine Frau erkannte und hörte, daß Hans sein Sohn war, die er beide längst für tot gehalten hatte. Aber Hans, obgleich erst zwölf Jahr alt, war doch einen Kopf größer als sein Vater. Sie gingen zusammen in das Stübchen, aber kaum hatte Hans seinen Sack auf die Ofenbank gestellt, so fing das ganze Haus an zu krachen, die Bank brach ein und dann auch der Fußboden, und der schwere Sack sank in den Keller hinab. »Gott behüte uns«, rief der Vater, »was ist das? Jetzt hast du unser Häuschen zerbrochen.« – »Laßt Euch keine grauen Haare darüber wachsen, lieber Vater«, antwortete Hans, »da in dem Sack steckt mehr, als für ein neues Haus nötig ist.« Der Vater und Hans fingen auch gleich an, ein neues Haus zu bauen, Vieh zu erhandeln und Land zu kaufen und zu wirtschaften. Hans ackerte die Felder, und wenn er hinter dem Pflug ging und ihn in die Erde hinein schob, so hatten die Stiere fast nicht nötig zu ziehen. Den nächsten Frühling sagte Hans: »Vater, behaltet alles Geld und laßt mir einen zentnerschweren Spazierstab machen, damit ich in die Fremde gehen kann.«

Als er den verlangten Stab hatte, verließ er seines Vaters Haus, zog fort und kam in einen tiefen und finstern Wald. Da hörte er etwas knistern und knastern und schaute um sich und sah eine Tanne, die von unten bis oben wie ein Seil gewunden ward; und wie er die Augen in die Höhe richtete, so erblickte er einen großen Kerl, der den Baum gepackt hatte und ihn wie eine Weidenrute umdrehte. »He!« rief Hans. »Was machst du da droben?« Der Kerl antwortete: »Ich habe gestern Reisigbündel zusammengetragen und will mir jetzt ein Seil dazu drehen.« – »Das laß ich mir gefallen«, dachte Hans, »der hat noch Kräfte«, und rief ihm zu: »Laß du das gut sein und komm mit mir.« Der Kerl kletterte von oben herab und war einen ganzen Kopf größer als Hans, und der war doch auch nicht klein. »Du heißest jetzt Tannendreher«, sagte Hans zu ihm. Sie gingen darauf weiter und hörten etwas klopfen und hämmern, so stark, daß bei jedem Schlag der Erdboden zitterte. Bald darauf kamen sie zu einem mächtigen Felsen, vor dem stand ein Riese und schlug mit der Faust große Stücke davon ab. Als Hans fragte, was er da treibe, antwortete er: »Wenn ich nachts schlafen will, so kommen Bären, Wölfe und anderes Ungetier der Art, die schnuppern und schnuffeln an mir herum und lassen mich nicht schlafen, da will ich mir ein Haus bauen und mich hinein legen, damit ich Ruhe habe.« – »Ei, jawohl«, dachte Hans, »den kannst du auch noch brauchen«, und sprach zu ihm: »Laß das gut sein und geh mit mir, du sollst der Felsenklipperer heißen.« Er willigte ein, und sie strichen alle drei durch den Wald hin, und wo sie hinkamen, da wurden die wilden Tiere aufgeschreckt und liefen vor ihnen weg. Abends kamen sie in ein altes, verlassenes Schloß, stiegen hinauf und legten sich in den Saal schlafen. Am andern Morgen ging Hans hinab in den Garten, der war ganz verwildert und stand voll Dörner und Gebüsch. Und wie er so herumging, sprang ein Wildschwein auf ihn los, er aber gab ihm mit seinem Stab einen Schlag, daß es gleich niederfiel. Dann nahm er es auf die Schulter und brachte es hinauf; da steckten sie es an einen Spieß und machten sich einen Braten zurecht und waren guter Dinge. Nun verabredeten sie, daß jeden Tag, der Reihe nach, zwei auf die Jagd gehen sollten und einer daheim bleiben und kochen, für jeden neun Pfund Fleisch. Den ersten Tag blieb der Tannendreher daheim, und Hans und der Felsenklipperer gingen auf die Jagd. Als der Tannendreher beim Kochen beschäftigt war, kam ein kleines, altes, zusammengeschrumpeltes Männchen zu ihm auf das Schloß und forderte Fleisch. »Pack dich, Duckmäuser«, antwortete er, »du brauchst kein Fleisch.« Aber wie verwunderte sich der Tannendreher, als das kleine unscheinbare Männlein an ihm hinaufsprang und mit den Fäusten so auf ihn losschlug, daß er sich nicht wehren konnte, zur Erde fiel und nach Atem schnappte. Und das Männlein ging nicht eher fort, als bis es seinen Zorn völlig an ihm ausgelassen hatte. Als die zwei andern von der Jagd heimkamen, sagte ihnen der Tannendreher nichts von dem alten Männchen und den Schlägen, die er bekommen hatte, und dachte: Wenn sie daheim bleiben, so können sie's auch einmal mit dem kleinen Ungeheuer versuchen, und der bloße Gedanke machte ihm schon Vergnügen. Den folgenden Tag blieb der Felsenklipperer daheim, und dem ging es gerade so wie dem Tannendreher, und er ward von dem Männlein übel zugerichtet, weil er ihm kein Fleisch hatte geben wollen. Als die andern abends nach Haus kamen, sah es ihm der Tannendreher wohl an, was er erfahren hatte, aber beide schwiegen still und dachten: Der Hans muß auch von der Suppe kosten. Der Hans, der den nächsten Tag daheim bleiben mußte, tat seine Arbeit in der Küche, wie sich's gebührte, und als er oben stand und den Kessel abschaumte, kam das Männchen und forderte ohne weiteres ein Stück Fleisch. Da dachte Hans: Er ist ein armer Wicht, ich will ihm von meinem Anteil geben, damit die andern nicht zu kurz kommen, und reichte ihm ein Stück Fleisch. Als es der Zwerg verzehrt hatte, verlangte er nochmals Fleisch, und der gutmütige Hans gab es ihm und sagte, da wäre noch ein schönes Stück, damit sollte er zufrieden sein. Der Zwerg forderte aber zum drittenmal. »Du wirst unverschämt«, sagte Hans und gab ihm nichts. Da wollte der boshafte Zwerg an ihm hinaufspringen und ihn wie den Tannendreher und Felsenklipperer behandeln, aber er kam an den Unrechten. Hans gab ihm, ohne sich anzustrengen, ein paar Hiebe, daß er die Schloßtreppe hinabsprang; dann wollte er ihm nachlaufen, fiel aber, so lang er war, über ihn hin. Als Hans sich wieder aufgerichtet hatte, war ihm der Zwerg voraus. Hans eilte ihm nach und in den Wald hinein und sah, wie er in eine Felsenhöhle schlüpfte. Hans merkte sich die Stelle und ging heim.

Die beiden andern, als sie nach Haus kamen, wunderten sich, daß Hans so wohlauf war. Er erzählte ihnen, was sich zugetragen hatte, und da verschwiegen sie nicht länger, wie es ihnen ergangen war. Hans lachte und sagte: »Es ist euch ganz recht, warum seid ihr so geizig mit eurem Fleisch gewesen; aber es ist eine Schande, ihr seid so groß, und habt euch von dem Zwerg Schläge geben lassen.« Sie nahmen darauf Korb und Seil und gingen alle drei zu der Felsenhöhle, in welche der Zwerg geschlüpft war, und ließen den Hans mit seinem Stab im Korb hinab. Als Hans auf dem Grund angelangt war, fand er eine Türe, und als er sie öffnete, saß da eine bildschöne Jungfrau, nein, so schön, daß es nicht zu sagen ist, und neben ihr saß der Zwerg und grinste den Hans an wie eine Meerkatze. Sie aber war mit Ketten gebunden und blickte ihn so traurig an, daß Hans großes Mitleid empfand und dachte, du mußt sie aus der Gewalt des bösen Zwerges erlösen, und gab ihm einen Streich mit seinem Stab, daß er tot niedersank. Alsbald fielen die Ketten von der Jungfrau ab, und Hans war wie verzückt über ihre Schönheit. Sie erzählte ihm, sie wäre eine Königstochter, die ein wilder Graf aus ihrer Heimat geraubt und hier in den Felsen eingesperrt hätte, weil sie nichts von ihm hätte wissen wollen; den Zwerg aber hätte der Graf zum Wächter gegeben, und er hätte ihr Leid und Drangsal genug angetan. Drauf setzte Hans die Jungfrau in den Korb und ließ sie hinaufziehen. Der Korb kam wieder herab, aber Hans traute den beiden Gesellen nicht und dachte: Sie haben sich schon falsch gezeigt und dir nichts von dem Zwerg gesagt, wer weiß, was sie gegen dich im Schild führen. Da legte er seinen Stab in den Korb, und das war sein Glück, denn

als der Korb halb in der Höhe war, ließen sie ihn fallen, und hätte Hans wirklich darin gesessen, so wäre er tot gewesen.

Aber nun wußte er nicht, wie er sich aus der Tiefe heraushelfen sollte, und wie er hin und her dachte, er fand keinen Rat. »Es ist doch traurig«, sagte er, »daß du da unten verschmachten sollst.« Und als er so auf und ab ging, kam er wieder zu dem Kämmerchen, wo die Jungfrau gesessen hatte, und sah, daß der Zwerg einen Ring am Finger hatte, der glänzte und schimmerte. Da zog er ihn ab und steckte ihn an, und als er ihn an dem Finger umdrehte, so hörte er plötzlich etwas über seinem Kopf rauschen. Er blickte in die Höhe und sah da Luftgeister schweben, die sagten, er wäre ihr Herr, und fragten, was sein Begehren wäre. Hans war anfangs ganz verstummt, dann aber sagte er, sie sollten ihn hinauftragen. Augenblicklich gehorchten sie, und es war nicht anders, als flöge er hinauf. Als er aber oben war, so war niemand mehr da, und als er in das Schloß ging, fand er auch dort niemand. Der Tannendreher und der Felsenklipperer waren fortgeeilt und hatten die schöne Jungfrau mitgeführt. Aber Hans drehte den Ring, da kamen die Luftgeister, und sagten ihm, die zwei wären auf dem Meer. Da lief Hans und lief in einem fort, bis er zu dem Meeresstrand kam, da erblickte er weit, weit auf dem Wasser ein Schiffchen, in welchem seine treulosen Gefährten saßen. Und in heftigem Zorn sprang er, ohne sich zu besinnen, mitsamt seinem Stab ins Wasser und fing an zu schwimmen, aber der zentnerschwere Stab zog ihn so tief hinab, daß er fast ertrunken wäre. Da drehte er noch zu rechter Zeit den Ring, alsbald kamen die Luftgeister und trugen ihn so schnell wie der Blitz in das Schiffchen. Da schwang er seinen Stab und gab den bösen Gesellen den verdienten Lohn und warf sie hinab ins Wasser. Dann aber ruderte er mit der schönen Jungfrau, die in den größten Ängsten gewesen war und die er zum zweiten Male befreit hatte, heim zu ihrem Vater und ihrer Mutter und ward mit ihr verheiratet, und alle haben sich gewaltig gefreut.

1837

Der Trommler

Eines Abends ging ein junger Trommler ganz allein auf dem Feld und kam an einen See, da sah er an dem Ufer drei Stückchen weiße Leinewand liegen. »Was für feines Leinen«, sprach er und steckte eines davon in die Tasche. Er ging heim, dachte nicht weiter an seinen Fund und legte sich zu Bett. Als er eben einschlafen wollte, war es ihm, als nenne jemand seinen Namen. Er horchte und vernahm eine leise Stimme, die ihm zurief: »Trommler, Trommler, wach auf.« Er konnte, da es finstere Nacht war, niemand sehen, aber es kam ihm vor, als schwebe eine Gestalt vor seinem Bett auf und ab. »Was willst du?« fragte er. »Gib mir mein Hemdchen zurück«, antwortete die Stimme, »das du mir gestern abend am See weggenommen hast.« – »Du sollst es wieder haben«, sprach der Trommler, »wenn du mir sagst, wer du bist.« – »Ach«, erwiderte die Stimme, »ich bin die Tochter eines mächtigen Königs, aber ich bin in die Gewalt einer Hexe geraten und bin auf den Glasberg gebannt. Jeden Tag muß ich mit meinen zwei Schwestern im See baden, aber ohne mein Hemdchen kann ich nicht wieder fortfliegen. Meine Schwestern haben sich fortgemacht, ich aber habe zurückbleiben müssen. Ich bitte dich, gib mir mein Hemdchen wieder.« – »Sei ruhig, armes Kind«, sprach der Trommler, »ich will dir's gerne zurückgeben.« Er holte es aus seiner Tasche und reichte es ihr in der Dunkelheit hin. Sie erfaßte es hastig und wollte damit fort. »Weile einen Augenblick«, sagte er, »vielleicht kann ich dir helfen.« – »Helfen kannst du mir nur, wenn du auf den Glasberg steigst und mich aus der Gewalt der Hexe befreist. Aber zu dem Glasberg kommst du nicht, und wenn du auch ganz nahe daran wärst, so kannst du nicht hinauf.« – »Was ich will, das kann ich«, sagte der Trommler, »ich habe Mitleid mit dir, und ich fürchte mich vor nichts. Aber ich weiß den Weg nicht, der nach dem Glasberge führt.« – »Der Weg geht durch den großen Wald, in dem die Menschenfresser hausen«, antwortete sie, »mehr darf ich dir nicht sagen.« Darauf hörte er, wie sie fortschwirrte.

Bei Anbruch des Tags machte sich der Trommler auf, hing seine Trommel um und ging ohne Furcht geradezu in den Wald hinein. Als er ein Weilchen gegangen war und keinen Riesen erblickte, so dachte er: Ich muß die Langschläfer aufwekken, hing die Trommel vor und schlug einen Wirbel, daß die Vögel aus den Bäumen mit Geschrei aufflogen. Nicht lange, so erhob sich auch ein Riese in die Höhe, der im Gras gelegen und geschlafen hatte, und war so groß wie eine Tanne. »Du Wicht«, rief er ihm zu, »was trommelst du hier und weckst mich aus dem besten Schlaf?« – »Ich trommle«, antwortete er, »weil viele Tausende hinter mir herkommen, damit sie den Weg wissen.« – »Was wollen die hier in meinem Wald?« fragte der Riese. »Sie wollen dir den Garaus machen und den Wald von einem Ungetüm, wie du bist, säubern.« – »Oho«, sagte der Riese, »ich trete euch wie

Ameisen tot.« – »Meinst du, du könntest gegen sie etwas ausrichten?« sprach der Trommler. »Wenn du dich bückst, um einen zu packen, so springt er fort und versteckt sich; wie du dich aber niederlegst und schläfst, so kommen sie aus allen Gebüschen herbei und kriechen an dir hinauf. Jeder hat einen Hammer von Stahl am Gürtel stecken, damit schlagen sie dir den Schädel ein.« Der Riese ward verdrießlich und dachte: Wenn ich mich mit dem listigen Volk befasse, so könnte es doch zu meinem Schaden ausschlagen. Wölfen und Bären drücke ich die Gurgel zusammen, aber vor den Erdwürmern kann ich mich nicht schützen. »Hör, kleiner Kerl«, sprach er, »zieh wieder ab, ich verspreche dir, daß ich dich und deine Gesellen in Zukunft in Ruhe lassen will, und hast du noch einen Wunsch, so sag's mir, ich will dir wohl etwas zu Gefallen tun.« – »Du hast lange Beine«, sprach der Trommler, »und kannst schneller laufen als ich. Trag mich zum Glasberge, so will ich den Meinigen ein Zeichen zum Rückzug geben, und sie sollen dich diesmal in Ruhe lassen.« – »Komm her, Wurm«, sprach der Riese, »setz dich auf meine Schulter, ich will dich tragen, wohin du verlangst.«

Der Riese hob ihn hinauf, und der Trommler fing oben an, nach Herzenslust auf der Trommel zu wirbeln. Der Riese dachte: Das wird das Zeichen sein, daß das andere Volk zurückgehen soll. Nach einer Weile stand ein zweiter Riese am Weg, der nahm den Trommler dem ersten ab und steckte ihn in sein Knopfloch. Der Trommler faßte den Knopf, der wie eine Schüssel groß war, hielt sich daran und schaute ganz lustig umher. Dann kamen sie zu einem dritten, der nahm ihn aus dem Knopfloch und setzte ihn auf den Rand seines Hutes; da ging der Trommler oben auf und ab und sah über die Bäume hinaus, und als er in blauer Ferne einen Berg erblickte, so dachte er: Das ist gewiß der Glasberg, und er war es auch. Der Riese tat nur noch ein paar Schritte, so waren sie an dem Fuß des Bergs angelangt, wo ihn der Riese absetzte. Der Trommler verlangte, er solle ihn auch auf die Spitze des Glasberges tragen, aber der Riese schüttelte den Kopf, brummte etwas in den Bart und ging in den Wald zurück.

Nun stand der arme Trommler vor dem Berg, der so hoch war, als wenn drei Berge aufeinandergesetzt wären, und dabei so glatt wie ein Spiegel, und wußte keinen Rat, um hinaufzukommen. Er fing an zu klettern, aber vergeblich, er rutschte immer wieder herab. Wer jetzt ein Vogel wäre, dachte er, aber was half das Wünschen, es wuchsen ihm keine Flügel. Indem er so stand und sich nicht zu helfen wußte, erblickte er nicht weit von sich zwei Männer, die heftig miteinander stritten. Er ging auf sie zu und sah, daß sie wegen eines Sattels uneins waren, der vor ihnen auf der Erde lag und den jeder von ihnen haben wollte. »Was seid ihr für Narren«, sprach er, »zankt euch um einen Sattel und habt kein Pferd dazu.« – »Der Sattel ist wert, daß man darum streitet«, antwortete der eine von den Männern, »wer darauf sitzt und wünscht sich irgendwohin, und wär's ans Ende der Welt, der ist im Augenblick angelangt, wie er den Wunsch ausgesprochen hat. Der Sattel gehört uns gemeinschaftlich, die Reihe, darauf zu reiten, ist an mir, aber der

andere will es nicht zulassen.« – »Den Streit will ich bald austragen«, sagte der Trommler, ging eine Strecke weit und steckte einen weißen Stab in die Erde. Dann kam er zurück und sprach: »Jetzt lauft nach dem Ziel! Wer zuerst dort ist, der reitet zuerst.« Beide setzten sich in Trab, aber kaum waren sie ein paar Schritte weg, so schwang sich der Trommler auf den Sattel, wünschte sich auf den Glasberg, und ehe man die Hand umdrehte, war er dort. Auf dem Berg oben war eine Ebene, da stand ein altes steinernes Haus, und vor dem Haus lag ein großer Fischteich, dahinter aber ein finsterer Wald. Menschen und Tiere sah er nicht, es war alles still, nur der Wind raschelte in den Bäumen, und die Wolken zogen ganz nah über seinem Haupt weg. Er trat an die Türe und klopfte an. Als er zum drittenmal geklopft hatte, öffnete eine Alte mit braunem Gesicht und roten Augen die Türe. Sie hatte eine Brille auf ihrer langen Nase und sah ihn scharf an, dann fragte sie, was sein Begehren wäre. »Einlaß, Kost und Nachtlager«, antwortete der Trommler. »Das sollst du haben«, sagte die Alte, »wenn du dafür drei Arbeiten verrichten willst.« – »Warum nicht?« antwortete er. »Ich scheue keine Arbeit, und wenn sie noch so schwer ist.« Die Alte ließ ihn ein, gab ihm Essen und abends ein gutes Bett.

Am Morgen, als er ausgeschlafen hatte, nahm die Alte einen Fingerhut von ihrem dürren Finger, reichte ihn dem Trommler hin und sagte: »Jetzt geh an die Arbeit und schöpfe den Teich draußen mit diesem Fingerhut aus; aber ehe es Nacht wird, mußt du fertig sein, und alle Fische, die in dem Wasser sind, müssen nach ihrer Art und Größe ausgesucht und nebeneinandergelegt sein.« – »Das ist eine seltsame Arbeit«, sagte der Trommler, ging aber zu dem Teich und fing an zu schöpfen. Er schöpfte den ganzen Morgen, aber was kann man mit einem Fingerhut bei einem großen Wasser ausrichten, und wenn man tausend Jahre schöpft? Als es Mittag war, dachte er: Es ist alles umsonst und ist einerlei, ob ich arbeite oder nicht, hielt ein und setzte sich nieder. Da kam ein Mädchen aus dem Haus gegangen, stellte ihm ein Körbchen mit Essen hin und sprach: »Du sitzest da so traurig, was fehlt dir?« Er blickte es an und sah, daß es wunderschön war. »Ach«, sagte er, »ich kann die erste Arbeit nicht vollbringen, wie wird es mit den andern werden? Ich bin ausgegangen, eine Königstochter zu suchen, die hier wohnen soll, aber ich habe sie nicht gefunden; ich will weitergehen.« – »Bleib hier«, sagte das Mädchen, »ich will dir aus deiner Not helfen. Du bist müde, lege deinen Kopf in meinen Schoß und schlaf. Wenn du wieder aufwachst, so ist die Arbeit getan.« Der Trommler ließ sich das nicht zweimal sagen. Sobald ihm die Augen zufielen, drehte sie einen Wunschring und sprach: »Wasser herauf, Fische heraus.« Alsbald stieg das Wasser wie ein weißer Nebel in die Höhe und zog mit den andern Wolken fort, und die Fische schnalzten, sprangen ans Ufer und legten sich nebeneinander, jeder nach seiner Größe und Art. Als der Trommler erwachte, sah er mit Erstaunen, daß alles vollbracht war. Aber das Mädchen sprach: »Einer von den Fischen liegt nicht bei seinesgleichen, sondern ganz allein.

Wenn die Alte heute abend kommt und sieht, daß alles geschehen ist, was sie verlangt hat, so wird sie fragen: ›Was soll dieser Fisch allein?‹ Dann wirf ihr den Fisch ins Angesicht und sprich: ›Der soll für dich sein, alte Hexe.‹« Abends kam die Alte, und als sie die Frage getan hatte, so warf er ihr den Fisch ins Gesicht. Sie stellte sich, als merkte sie es nicht, und schwieg still, aber sie blickte ihn mit boshaften Augen an. Am andern Morgen sprach sie: »Gestern hast du es zu leicht gehabt, ich muß dir schwerere Arbeit geben. Heute mußt du den ganzen Wald umhauen, das Holz in Scheite spalten und in Klaftern legen, und am Abend muß alles fertig sein.«

Sie gab ihm eine Axt, einen Schläger und zwei Keile. Aber die Axt war von Blei, der Schläger und die Keile waren von Blech. Als er anfing zu hauen, legte sich die Axt um, und Schläger und Keile drückten sich zusammen. Er wußte sich nicht zu helfen, aber mittags kam das Mädchen wieder mit dem Essen und tröstete ihn. »Lege deinen Kopf in meinen Schoß«, sagte sie, »und schlaf. Wenn du aufwachst, so ist die Arbeit getan.« Sie drehte ihren Wunschring, in dem Augenblick sank der ganze Wald mit Krachen zusammen, das Holz spaltete sich von selbst und legte sich in Klaftern zusammen. Es war, als ob unsichtbare Riesen die Arbeit vollbrächten. Als er aufwachte, sagte das Mädchen: »Siehst du, das Holz ist geklaftert und gelegt. Nur ein einziger Ast ist übrig, aber wenn die Alte heute abend kommt und fragt, was der Ast solle, so gib ihr damit einen Schlag und sprich: ›Der soll für dich sein, du Hexe.‹« Die Alte kam. »Siehst du«, sprach sie, »wie leicht die Arbeit war. Aber für wen liegt der Ast noch da?« – »Für dich, du Hexe«, antwortete er und gab ihr einen Schlag damit. Aber sie tat, als fühlte sie es nicht, lachte höhnisch und sprach: »Morgen früh sollst du alles Holz auf einen Haufen legen, es anzünden und verbrennen.«

Er stand mit Anbruch des Tages auf und fing an, das Holz herbeizuholen, aber wie kann ein einziger Mensch einen ganzen Wald zusammentragen? Die Arbeit rückte nicht fort. Doch das Mädchen verließ ihn nicht in der Not: Es brachte ihm mittags seine Speise, und als er gegessen hatte, legte er seinen Kopf in den Schoß und schlief ein. Bei seinem Erwachen brannte der ganze Holzstoß in einer ungeheuern Flamme, die ihre Zungen bis in den Himmel ausstreckte. »Hör mich an«, sprach das Mädchen, »wenn die Hexe kommt, wird sie dir allerlei auftragen. Tust du ohne Furcht, was sie verlangt, so kann sie dir nichts anhaben; fürchtest du dich aber, so packt dich das Feuer und verzehrt dich. Zuletzt, wenn du alles getan hast, so packe sie mit beiden Händen und wirf sie mitten in die Glut.«

Das Mädchen ging fort, und die Alte kam herangeschlichen. »Hu! mich friert«, sagte sie, »aber das ist ein Feuer, das brennt, das wärmt mir die alten Knochen, da wird mir wohl. Aber dort liegt ein Klotz, der will nicht brennen, den hol mir heraus. Hast du das noch getan, so bist du frei und kannst ziehen, wohin du willst. Nur munter hinein.« Der Trommler besann sich nicht lange, sprang mitten in die Flammen, aber sie taten ihm nichts, nicht einmal die Haare konnten sie ihm versengen. Er trug den Klotz heraus und legte ihn hin. Kaum aber hatte das Holz die Erde berührt, so verwandelte es sich, und das schöne Mädchen stand vor ihm, das ihm in der Not geholfen hatte; und an den seidenen goldglänzenden Kleidern, die es anhatte, merkte er wohl, daß es die Königstochter war. Aber die Alte lachte giftig und sprach: »Du meinst, du hättest sie, aber du hast sie noch nicht.« Eben wollte sie auf das Mädchen losgehen und es fortziehen, da packte er die Alte mit beiden Händen, hob sie in die Höhe und warf sie den Flammen in den Rachen, die über ihr zusammenschlugen.

Die Königstochter blickte darauf den Trommler an, und als sie sah, daß er ein schöner Jüngling war, und bedachte, daß er sein Leben darangesetzt hatte, um sie zu erlösen, so reichte sie ihm die Hand und sprach: »Du hast alles für mich gewagt, aber ich will auch für dich alles tun. Versprichst du mir deine Treue, so sollst du mein Gemahl werden. An Reichtümern fehlt es uns nicht, wir haben genug an dem, was die Hexe hier zusammengetragen hat.« Sie führte ihn in das Haus, da standen Kisten und Kasten, die mit ihren Schätzen angefüllt waren. Sie ließen Gold und Silber liegen und nahmen nur die Edelsteine. Sie wollte nicht länger auf dem Glasberg bleiben, da sprach er zu ihr: »Setze dich zu mir auf meinen Sattel, so fliegen wir hinab wie Vögel.« — »Der alte Sattel gefällt mir nicht«, sagte sie, »ich brauche nur an meinem Wunschring zu drehen, so sind wir zu Haus.« — »Wohlan«, antwortete der Trommler, »so wünsch uns vor das Stadttor.« Im Nu waren sie dort, der Trommler aber sprach: »Ich will erst zu meinen Eltern gehen und ihnen Nachricht geben, harre mein hier auf dem Feld, ich will bald zurück sein.« — »Ach«, sagte die Königstochter, »ich bitte dich, nimm dich in acht, küsse deine Eltern bei deiner Ankunft nicht auf die rechte Wange, denn sonst wirst du alles vergessen, und ich bleibe hier allein und verlassen auf dem Feld zurück.« — »Wie kann ich dich vergessen?« sagte er und versprach ihr in die Hand, recht bald wiederzukommen.

Als er in sein väterliches Haus trat, wußte niemand, wer er war, so hatte er sich verändert, denn die drei Tage, die er auf dem Glasberg zugebracht hatte, waren drei lange Jahre gewesen. Da gab er sich zu erkennen, und seine Eltern fielen ihm vor Freude um den Hals, und er war so bewegt in seinem Herzen, daß er sie auf beide Wangen küßte und an die Worte des Mädchens nicht dachte. Wie er ihnen aber den Kuß auf die rechte Wange gegeben hatte, verschwand ihm jeder Gedanke an die Königstochter. Er leerte seine Taschen aus und legte Händevoll der größten Edelsteine auf den Tisch. Die Eltern wußten gar nicht, was sie mit dem Reichtum anfangen sollten. Da baute der Vater ein prächtiges Schloß, von Gärten, Wäldern und Wiesen umgeben, als wenn ein Fürst darin wohnen sollte. Und als es fertig war, sagte die Mutter: »Ich habe ein Mädchen für dich ausgesucht, in drei Tagen soll die Hochzeit sein.«

Der Sohn war mit allem zufrieden, was die Eltern wollten.

Die arme Königstochter hatte lange vor der Stadt gestanden und auf die

Rückkehr des Jünglings gewartet. Als es Abend ward, sprach sie: »Gewiß hat er seine Eltern auf die rechte Wange geküßt und hat mich vergessen.« Ihr Herz war voll Trauer, sie wünschte sich in ein einsames Waldhäuschen und wollte nicht wieder an den Hof ihres Vaters zurück. Jeden Abend ging sie in die Stadt und ging an seinem Haus vorüber. Er sah sie manchmal, aber er kannte sie nicht mehr. Endlich hörte sie, wie die Leute sagten: »Morgen wird seine Hochzeit gefeiert.« Da sprach sie: »Ich will versuchen, ob ich sein Herz wiedergewinne.« Als der erste Hochzeitstag gefeiert ward, da drehte sie ihren Wunschring und sprach: »Ein Kleid, so glänzend wie die Sonne.« Alsbald lag das Kleid vor ihr und war so glänzend, als wenn es aus lauter Sonnenstrahlen gewebt wäre. Als alle Gäste sich versammelt hatten, trat sie in den Saal. Jedermann wunderte sich über das schöne Kleid, am meisten die Braut, und da schöne Kleider ihre größte Lust waren, so ging sie zu der Fremden und fragte, ob sie es ihr verkaufen wollte. »Für Geld nicht«, antwortete sie, »aber wenn ich die erste Nacht vor der Türe verweilen darf, wo der Bräutigam schläft, so will ich es hingeben.« Die Braut konnte ihr Verlangen nicht bezwingen und willigte ein, aber sie mischte dem Bräutigam einen Schlaftrunk in seinen Nachtwein, wovon er in tiefen Schlaf verfiel. Als nun alles still geworden war, so kauerte sich die Königstochter vor die Türe der Schlafkammer, öffnete sie ein wenig und rief hinein:

> »Trommler, Trommler, hör mich an,
> hast du mich denn ganz vergessen?
> Hast du auf dem Glasberg nicht bei mir gesessen?
> Habe ich vor der Hexe nicht bewahrt dein Leben?
> Hast du mir auf Treue nicht die Hand gegeben?
> Trommler, Trommler, hör mich an.«

Aber es war alles vergeblich, der Trommler wachte nicht auf, und als der Morgen anbrach, mußte die Königstochter unverrichteter Dinge wieder fortgehen. Am zweiten Abend drehte sie ihren Wunschring und sprach: »Ein Kleid, so silbern wie der Mond.« Als sie mit dem Kleid, das so zart war wie der Mondschein, bei dem Fest erschien, erregte sie wieder das Verlangen der Braut und gab es ihr für die Erlaubnis, auch die zweite Nacht vor der Türe der Schlafkammer zubringen zu dürfen. Da rief sie in nächtlicher Stille:

> »Trommler, Trommler, hör mich an,
> hast du mich denn ganz vergessen?
> Hast du auf dem Glasberg nicht bei mir gesessen?
> Habe ich vor der Hexe nicht bewahrt dein Leben?
> Hast du mir auf Treue nicht die Hand gegeben?
> Trommler, Trommler, hör mich an.«

Aber der Trommler, von dem Schlaftrunk betäubt, war nicht zu erwecken. Traurig ging sie den Morgen wieder zurück in ihr Waldhaus. Aber die Leute im Haus hatten die Klage des fremden Mädchens gehört und erzählten dem Bräutigam davon. Sie sagten ihm auch, daß es ihm nicht möglich gewesen wäre, etwas davon zu vernehmen, weil sie ihm einen Schlaftrunk in den Wein geschüttet hätten. Am dritten Abend drehte die Königstochter den Wunschring und sprach: »Ein Kleid, flimmernd wie Sterne.« Als sie sich darin auf dem Fest zeigte, war die Braut über die Pracht des Kleides, das die andern weit übertraf, ganz außer sich und sprach: »Ich soll und muß es haben.« Das Mädchen gab es wie die andern für die Erlaubnis, die Nacht vor der Türe des Bräutigams zuzubringen. Der Bräutigam aber trank den Wein nicht, der ihm vor dem Schlafengehen gereicht wurde, sondern goß ihn hinter das Bett. Und als alles im Haus still geworden war, so hörte er eine sanfte Stimme, die ihn anrief:

>»Trommler, Trommler, hör mich an,
> hast du mich denn ganz vergessen?
> Hast du auf dem Glasberg nicht bei mir gesessen?
> Habe ich vor der Hexe nicht bewahrt dein Leben?
> Hast du mir auf Treue nicht die Hand gegeben?
> Trommler, Trommler, hör mich an.«

Plötzlich kam ihm das Gedächtnis wieder. »Ach«, rief er, »wie habe ich so treulos handeln können, aber der Kuß, den ich meinen Eltern in der Freude meines Herzens auf die rechte Wange gegeben habe, der ist schuld daran, der hat mich betäubt.«

Er sprang auf, nahm die Königstochter bei der Hand und führte sie zu dem Bett seiner Eltern. »Das ist meine rechte Braut«, sprach er, »wenn ich die andere heirate, so tue ich großes Unrecht.« Die Eltern, als sie hörten, wie alles sich zugetragen hatte, willigten ein. Da wurden die Lichter im Saal wieder angezündet, Pauken und Trompeten herbeigeholt, die Freunde und Verwandten eingeladen, wiederzukommen, und die wahre Hochzeit ward mit großer Freude gefeiert. Die erste Braut behielt die schönen Kleider zur Entschädigung und gab sich zufrieden.

1843

Der Okerlo

Eine Königin setzte ihr Kind in einer goldenen Wiege aufs Meer und ließ es fortschwimmen; es ging aber nicht unter, sondern schwamm zu einer Insel, da wohnten lauter Menschenfresser.

Wie nun so die Wiege geschwommen kam, stand gerade die Frau des Menschenfressers am Ufer, und als sie das Kind sah, welches ein wunderschönes Mädchen war, beschloß sie, es großzuziehen für ihren Sohn, der sollte es einmal zur Frau haben. Doch hatte sie große Not damit, daß sie es sorgfältig vor ihrem Mann, dem alten Okerlo, versteckte, denn hätte er es zu Gesicht bekommen, so wäre es mit Haut und Haar aufgefressen worden.

Als nun das Mädchen groß geworden war, sollte es mit dem jungen Okerlo verheiratet werden, es mochte ihn aber gar nicht leiden und weinte den ganzen Tag. Wie es so einmal am Ufer saß, da kam ein junger, schöner Prinz geschwommen, der gefiel ihm, und es gefiel ihm auch, und sie versprachen sich miteinander; indem aber kam die alte Menschenfresserin, die wurde gewaltig bös, daß sie den Prinzen bei der Braut ihres Sohnes fand, und kriegte ihn gleich zu packen: »Wart nun, du sollst zu meines Sohnes Hochzeit gebraten werden!«

Der junge Prinz, das Mädchen und die drei Kinder des Okerlo schliefen aber alle in einer Stube zusammen. Wie es nun Nacht wurde, kriegte der alte Okerlo Lust nach Menschenfleisch und sagte: »Frau, ich habe nicht Lust, bis zur Hochzeit zu warten, gib mir den Prinzen nur gleich her!« Das Mädchen aber hörte alles durch die Wand, stand geschwind auf, nahm dem einen Kind des Okerlo die goldene Krone ab, die es auf dem Haupte trug, und setzte sie dem Prinzen auf. Die alte Menschenfresserin kam gegangen, und weil es dunkel war, so fühlte sie an den Häuptern, und das, welches keine Krone trug, brachte sie dem Mann, der es augenblicklich aufaß. Indessen wurde dem Mädchen himmelangst, es dachte: »Bricht der Tag an, so kommt alles heraus, und es wird uns schlimm gehen.« Da stand es heimlich auf und holte einen Meilenstiefel, eine Wünschelrute und einen Kuchen mit einer Bohne, die auf alles Antwort gab.

Nun ging sie mit dem Prinzen fort, sie hatte den Meilenstiefel an, und mit jedem Schritt machten sie eine Meile. Zuweilen frugen sie die Bohne:

»Bohne, bist du auch da?«

»Ja«, sagte die Bohne, »da bin ich, eilt euch aber, denn die alte Menschenfresserin kommt nach im andern Meilenstiefel, der dort geblieben ist!« Da nahm das Mädchen die Wünschelrute und verwandelte sich in einen Schwan, den Prinzen in einen Teich, worauf der Schwan schwimmt. Die Menschenfresserin kam und

lockte den Schwan ans Ufer, allein, es gelang ihr nicht, und verdrießlich ging sie heim. Das Mädchen und der Prinz setzten ihren Weg fort.

»Bohne, bist du da?«

»Ja«, sprach die Bohne, »hier bin ich, aber die alte Frau kommt schon wieder, der Menschenfresser hat ihr gesagt, warum sie sich habe anführen lassen.« Da nahm das Mädchen den Stab und verwandelte sich und den Prinzen in eine Staubwolke, wodurch die Frau Okerlo nicht dringen kann, also kehrte sie unverrichteter Sache wieder um, und die andern setzten ihren Weg fort.

»Bohne, bist du da?«

»Ja, hier bin ich, aber ich sehe die Frau Okerlo noch einmal kommen, und gewaltige Schritte macht sie.« Das Mädchen nahm zum drittenmal den Wünschelstab und verwandelte sich in einen Rosenstock und den Prinzen in eine Biene. Da kam die alte Menschenfresserin, erkannte sie in dieser Verwandlung nicht und ging wieder heim.

Allein, nun konnten die zwei ihre menschliche Gestalt nicht wieder annehmen, weil das Mädchen das letztemal in der Angst den Zauberstab zu weit weggeworfen; sie waren aber schon so weit gegangen, daß der Rosenstock in einem Garten stand, der gehörte der Mutter des Mädchens. Die Biene saß auf der Rose, und wer sie abbrechen wollte, den stach sie mit ihrem Stachel. Einmal geschah es, daß die Königin selber in den Garten ging und die schöne Blume sah, worüber sie sich so verwunderte, daß sie sie abbrechen wollte. Aber Bienchen kam und stach sie so stark in die Hand, daß sie die Rose mußte fahren lassen, doch hatte sie schon ein wenig eingerissen. Da sah sie, daß Blut aus dem Stengel quoll, ließ eine Fee kommen, damit sie die Blume entzauberte. Da erkannte die Königin ihre Tochter wieder und war von Herzen froh und vergnügt. Es wurde aber eine große Hochzeit angestellt, eine Menge Gäste gebeten, die kamen in prächtigen Kleidern, tausend Lichter flimmerten im Saal, und es wurde gespielt und getanzt bis zum hellen Tag.

»Bist du auch auf der Hochzeit gewesen?« – »Jawohl, bin drauf gewesen:
Mein Kopfputz war von Butter, da kam ich in die Sonne,
und er ist mir abgeschmolzen;
mein Kleid war von Spinnweb, da kam ich durch
Dornen, die rissen es mir ab;
meine Pantoffel waren von Glas, da trat ich auf einen
Stein, da sprangen sie entzwei.«

1812

Dornröschen

Vor Zeiten waren ein König und eine Königin, die sprachen jeden Tag: »Ach, wenn wir doch ein Kind hätten!«, und kriegten immer keins. Da trug sich zu, als die Königin einmal im Bade saß, daß ein Frosch aus dem Wasser ans Land kroch und zu ihr sprach: »Dein Wunsch wird erfüllt werden, und du wirst eine Tochter zur Welt bringen.« Was der Frosch vorausgesagt hatte, das geschah, und die Königin

gebar ein Mädchen, das war so schön, daß der König vor Freude sich nicht zu lassen wußte und ein großes Fest anstellte. Er lud nicht bloß seine Verwandte, Freunde und Bekannte, sondern auch die weisen Frauen dazu ein, damit sie dem Kind hold und gewogen würden. Es waren ihrer dreizehn in seinem Reiche, weil er aber nur zwölf goldene Teller hatte, von welchen sie essen sollten, konnte er eine nicht einladen. Die geladen waren, kamen, und als das Fest vorbei war, beschenkten sie das Kind mit ihren Wundergaben: die eine mit Tugend, die andere mit Schönheit, die dritte mit Reichtum, und so mit allem, was Herrliches auf der Welt ist. Als elfe ihre Wünsche eben getan hatten, kam die dreizehnte herein, die nicht eingeladen war und sich dafür rächen wollte. Sie rief: »Die Königstochter soll sich in ihrem fünfzehnten Jahr an einer Spindel stechen und tot hinfallen.« Da trat die zwölfte hervor, die noch einen Wunsch übrig hatte. Zwar konnte sie den bösen Ausspruch nicht aufheben, aber sie konnte ihn doch mildern, und sprach: »Es soll aber kein Tod sein, sondern ein hundertjähriger tiefer Schlaf, in welchen die Königstochter fällt.«

Der König, der sein liebes Kind vor dem Unglück gerne bewahren wollte, ließ den Befehl ausgeben, daß alle Spindeln im ganzen Königreiche sollten abgeschafft werden. An dem Mädchen aber wurden die Gaben der weisen Frauen sämtlich erfüllt, denn es war so schön, sittsam, freundlich und verständig, daß es jedermann, der es ansah, lieb haben mußte. Es geschah, daß an dem Tage, wo es gerade fünfzehn Jahre alt ward, der König und die Königin nicht zu Haus waren und das Mädchen ganz allein im Schloß zurückblieb. Da ging es aller Orten herum, besah Stuben und Kammern, wie es Lust hatte, und kam endlich auch an einen alten Turm. Es stieg eine enge Treppe hinauf und gelangte zu einer kleinen Türe. In dem Schloß steckte ein verrosteter Schlüssel, und als es umdrehte, sprang die Türe auf, und saß da in einem kleinen Stübchen eine alte Frau und spann emsig ihren Flachs. »Ei du altes Mütterchen«, sprach die Königstochter, »was machst du da?« – »Ich spinne«, sagte die Alte und nickte mit dem Kopf. »Wie das Ding so lustig herumspringt!« sprach das Mädchen, nahm die Spindel und wollte auch spinnen. Kaum hatte sie aber die Spindel angerührt, so ging der Zauberspruch in Erfüllung, und sie stach sich damit.

In dem Augenblick aber, wo sie den Stich empfand, fiel sie auch nieder in einen tiefen Schlaf. Und der König und die Königin, die eben zurückgekommen waren, fingen an, mit dem ganzen Hofstaat einzuschlafen. Da schliefen auch die Pferde im Stall ein, die Hunde im Hofe, die Tauben auf dem Dach, die Fliegen an der Wand, ja, das Feuer, das auf dem Herde flackerte, ward still und schlief ein, und der Braten hörte auf zu brutzeln, und der Koch, der den Küchenjungen, weil er etwas versehen hatte, in den Haaren ziehen wollte, ließ ihn los und schlief, und alles was lebendigen Atem hatte, ward still und schlief.

Rings um das Schloß aber begann eine Dornenhecke zu wachsen, die jedes Jahr höher ward und endlich das ganze Schloß umzog und drüber hinaus wuchs, daß gar nichts mehr, selbst nicht die Fahnen auf den Dächern, zu sehen war. Es ging aber die Sage in dem Land von dem schönen schlafenden Dornröschen, denn so wurde die Königstochter genannt, also daß von Zeit zu Zeit Königssöhne kamen und durch die Hecke in das Schloß dringen wollten. Es war ihnen aber nicht möglich, denn die Äste hielten sich, als hätten sie Hände, zusammen, und die Jünglinge blieben in den Dornen hängen und starben jämmerlich.

Nach langen, langen Jahren kam wieder ein Königssohn durch das Land, dem erzählte ein alter Mann von der Dornenhecke, es sollte ein Schloß dahinter stehen,

in welchem eine wunderschöne Königstochter, Dornröschen genannt, schliefe, und mit ihr schliefe der ganze Hofstaat. Er erzählte auch, daß er von seinem Großvater gehört, wie viele Königssöhne schon versucht hätten, durch die Dornenhecke zu dringen, aber darin hängengeblieben und eines traurigen Todes gestorben wären. Da sprach der Jüngling: »Das soll mich nicht abschrecken, ich will hindurch und das schöne Dornröschen sehen.« Der Alte mochte ihm abraten, wie er wollte, er hörte gar nicht darauf.

Nun waren aber gerade an dem Tag, wo der Königssohn kam, die hundert Jahre verflossen. Und als er sich der Dornenhecke näherte, waren es lauter große schöne Blumen, die taten sich von selbst auseinander, daß er unbeschädigt hindurch ging. Und hinter ihm taten sie sich wieder als eine Hecke zusammen. Er kam ins Schloß, da lagen im Hof die Pferde und scheckigen Jagdhunde und schliefen, auf dem Dach saßen die Tauben und hatten das Köpfchen unter den Flügel gesteckt. Und als er ins Haus kam, schliefen die Fliegen an der Wand, der Koch in der Küche hielt noch die Hand, als wollte er den Jungen anpacken, und die Magd saß vor dem schwarzen Huhn, das sollte gerupft werden. Da ging er weiter und sah im Saale den ganzen Hofstaat liegen und schlafen, und oben bei dem Thron lag der König und die Königin. Da ging er noch weiter, und alles war so still, daß einer seinen Atem hören konnte, und endlich kam er zu dem Turm und öffnete die Türe zu der kleinen Stube, in welcher Dornröschen schlief. Da lag es und war so schön, daß er die Augen nicht abwenden konnte, und er bückte sich und gab ihm einen Kuß. Wie er es mit dem Kuß berührt hatte, schlug Dornröschen die Augen auf, erwachte und blickte ihn ganz freundlich an. Da gingen sie zusammen herab, und der König erwachte und die Königin und der ganze Hofstaat und sahen einander mit großen Augen an. Und die Pferde im Hof standen auf und rüttelten sich; die Jagdhunde sprangen und wedelten; die Tauben auf dem Dach zogen das Köpfchen unterm Flügel hervor, sahen umher und flogen ins Feld; die Fliegen an den Wänden krochen weiter; das Feuer in der Küche erhob sich, flackerte und kochte das Essen; und der Braten brutzelte fort; und der Koch gab dem Jungen eine Ohrfeige, daß er schrie; und die Magd rupfte das Huhn fertig. Und da wurde die Hochzeit des Königssohns mit dem Dornröschen in aller Pracht gefeiert, und sie lebten vergnügt bis an ihr Ende.

1837

Die Wichtelmänner

1. Von einem Schuster, dem sie die Arbeit gemacht

Es war ein Schuster ohne seine Schuld allmählich so arm geworden, daß ihm endlich nichts mehr übrigblieb als Leder zu einem einzigen Paar Schuhe. Nun schnitt er das abends zu, um es morgens in die Arbeit zu nehmen, und weil er ein gutes Gewissen hatte, legte er sich darauf ruhig zu Bett, befahl sich Gott und schlief ein. Morgens, nachdem er sein Gebet verrichtet hatte und sich zur Arbeit setzen wollte, so standen die beiden Schuhe ganz fertig auf seinem Tisch. Er wußte nicht, was er vor Verwunderung sagen sollte. Als er sie näher betrachtete, waren sie so sauber gearbeitet, daß kein Stich daran falsch war, als sollt' es ein Meisterstück sein. Auch trat denselben Tag schon ein Käufer ein, und dem gefielen die Schuhe so gut, daß er mehr als gewöhnlich dafür bezahlte und der Schuster von dem Geld Leder zu zwei Paar Schuhen erhandeln konnte. Abends schnitt er die zu und wollte morgens frisch an die Arbeit gehen, aber er brauchte es nicht, denn als er aufstand, waren sie schon fertig, und es blieben auch nicht Käufer aus, die ihm so viel Geld gaben, daß er zu vier Paar Schuhen das Leder kaufen konnte. Die schnitt er abends wieder zu und fand sie am Morgen fertig, und so ging's immer fort: Was er abends zuschnitt, das war am Morgen verarbeitet, also daß er bald wieder zu einem wohlhabenden Mann ward mit ehrlichem Auskommen. Nun geschah es, daß eines Abends kurz vor Weihnachten, nachdem der Mann wieder zugeschnitten hatte, er vor Schlafengehen zu seiner Frau sprach: »Wie wär's, wenn wir diese Nacht aufblieben, um zu sehen, wer uns solche hilfreiche Hand leiste?« Die Frau war's zufrieden und steckte ein Licht an, darauf verbargen sie sich in den Stubenecken hinter den Kleidern, die da aufgehängt waren, und gaben acht. Als es Mitternacht war, da kamen zwei kleine, niedliche, nackte Männlein, setzten sich vor des Schusters Tisch, nahmen alle zugeschnittene Arbeit zu sich und fingen an mit ihren Fingerlein so behend und schnell zu stechen, nähen, klopfen, daß der Schuster vor

Verwunderung die Augen nicht abwenden konnte. Sie ließen nicht nach, bis alles zu Ende gebracht war und fertig auf dem Tisch stand, und das war lange vor Tag, und dann sprangen sie schnell fort.

Am andern Morgen sprach die Frau: »Die kleinen Männer haben uns reich gemacht, dafür müßten wir dankbar sein. Sie dauern mich, daß sie so herumlaufen und nichts am Leib haben und frieren. Weißt du was? Ich will Hemdlein, Rock, Wams und Höslein für sie nähen, auch jedem ein Paar Strümpfe stricken; mach du jedem ein Paar Schühlein dazu.« Der Mann war es wohl zufrieden. Abends, wie sie alles zusammen hatten, legten sie es statt der zugeschnittenen Arbeit auf den Tisch und versteckten sich dann, weil sie sehen wollten, wie sich die Männlein dabei anstellen würden. Um Mitternacht kamen sie beide gelaufen und wollten arbeiten, als sie aber die Kleider liegen sahen, bezeigten sie große Freude. Mit der größten Geschwindigkeit zogen sie sie an, strichen die schönen Kleider am Leib und sangen:

> »Sind wir nicht Knaben, glatt und fein?
> Was sollen wir länger Schuster sein!«

Dann hüpften, sprangen und tanzten sie, tanzten zur Türe hinaus und blieben von nun an aus, dem Schuster aber ging es sein Lebtag wohl.

2. Von einer Frau, der sie das Kind vertauscht haben

Einer Mutter war ihr Kind von den Wichtelmännern aus der Wiege geholt und ein Wechselbalg mit dickem Kopf und starren Augen hineingelegt, der nichts als trinken und essen wollte. In ihrer Not ging sie zu ihrer Nachbarin und fragte sie um Rat. Die sagte, sie solle den Wechselbalg in die Küche tragen, auf den Herd setzen, Feuer anmachen und in zwei Eierschalen Wasser kochen, das bringe den Wechselbalg zum Lachen, und wenn er lache, dann sei es aus mit ihm. Die Frau tut alles; wie sie die Eierschalen mit Wasser übers Feuer setzt, spricht der Klotz-kopf:

> »Nun bin ich so alt
> wie der Westerwald
> und hab nicht gesehen,
> daß jemand in Schalen kocht!«

und muß darüber lachen. Und wie er lacht, kommt auf einmal eine Menge von Wichtelmännerchen, die bringen das rechte Kind, setzen es auf den Herd und nehmen ihren Gesellen wieder mit fort.

1819

Die goldene Gans

Es war ein Mann, der hatte drei Söhne, davon hieß der jüngste der Dummling und wurde verachtet und verspottet und bei jeder Gelegenheit zurückgesetzt. Es geschah, daß der älteste in den Wald gehen wollte, Holz hauen, und eh' er ging, gab ihm noch seine Mutter einen schönen, feinen Eierkuchen und eine Flasche Wein mit, damit er nicht Hunger und Durst litt. Als er in den Wald kam, begegnete ihm ein altes graues Männlein, das bot ihm einen guten Tag und sprach: »Gib mir doch ein Stück von deinem Kuchen aus der Tasche und laß mich einen Schluck von deinem Wein trinken, ich bin so hungrig und durstig.« Der kluge Sohn aber antwortete: »Geb ich dir meinen Kuchen und meinen Wein, so hab ich selber nichts, pack dich deiner Wege!« und ging fort. Als er nun anfing einen Baum zu behauen, dauerte es nicht lange, so hieb er fehl, und die Axt fuhr ihm in den Arm, daß er mußte heimgehen und sich verbinden lassen. Das war aber von dem grauen Männchen gekommen.

Darauf ging der zweite Sohn in den Wald, und die Mutter gab ihm, wie dem ältesten, einen Eierkuchen und eine Flasche Wein. Dem begegnete gleichfalls das alte graue Männchen und hielt um ein Stückchen Kuchen und einen Trunk Wein an. Aber der zweite Sohn sprach auch ganz verständig: »Was ich dir gebe, das geht mir selber ab, pack dich deiner Wege!« und ging fort. Das Männchen ließ die Strafe nicht ausbleiben, und als er ein paar Hiebe am Baum getan, hieb er sich ins Bein, daß er mußte nach Haus getragen werden.

Da sagte der Dummling auch: »Vater, ich will hinausgehen und Holz hauen.« Antwortete der Vater: »Deine Brüder haben sich Schaden getan, laß du's gar bleiben, du verstehst nichts davon.« Der Dummling aber bat, daß er's erlauben möchte, da sagte er endlich: »Geh nur hin, durch Schaden wirst du klug werden.« Die Mutter aber gab ihm einen Kuchen, der war mit Wasser in der Asche gebacken, und eine Flasche saures Bier. Als er in den Wald kam, begegnete ihm gleichfalls das alte graue Männchen und grüßte ihn und sprach: »Gib mir ein Stück von deinem Kuchen und einen Trunk aus deiner Flasche, ich bin so hungrig und durstig.« Antwortete der Dummling: »Ich habe aber nur Aschenkuchen und saures Bier, wenn dir das recht ist, so wollen wir uns setzen und essen.« Da setzten sie sich, und als der Dummling seinen Aschenkuchen herausholte, so war's ein feiner Eierkuchen, und das saure Bier war ein guter Wein. Nun aßen und tranken sie, und danach sprach das Männlein: »Weil du ein gutes Herz hast und das Deine gern mitteilst, so will ich dir Glück bescheren. Dort steht ein alter Baum, den hau ab, so wirst du in den Wurzeln etwas finden.« Und darauf nahm es Abschied.

Der Dummling ging hin und hieb den Baum um, und wie er fiel, saß in den Wurzeln eine Gans, die hatte Federn von reinem Gold. Er hob sie heraus, nahm sie

mit sich und ging in ein Wirtshaus, da wollte er übernachten. Der Wirt hatte aber drei Töchter, die sahen die Gans, waren neugierig, was das für ein wunderlicher Vogel wäre, und hätten gar gern eine von seinen goldenen Federn gehabt. Endlich dachte die älteste: »Ich soll und muß eine Feder haben!«, wartete, bis der Dummling hinausgegangen war, und faßte die Gans beim Flügel, aber Finger und Hand blieben ihr daran festhängen. Bald danach kam die zweite und hatte keinen andern Gedanken, als sich eine Feder zu holen, ging heran, kaum aber hatte sie ihre Schwester angerührt, so blieb sie an ihr fest hängen. Endlich kam auch die dritte und wollte eine Feder, da schrien die andern: »Bleib weg! Ums Himmels willen, bleib weg!«, aber sie begriff nicht, warum, und dachte: Sind die dabei, so kann ich auch dabei sein, sprang herzu, aber wie sie ihre Schwester angerührt hatte, so blieb sie an ihr fest hängen. So mußten sie die Nacht bei der Gans zubringen.

Am andern Morgen nahm der Dummling die Gans in den Arm, ging fort und bekümmerte sich nicht um die drei Mädchen, die daran hingen. Die mußten immer hinter ihm drein laufen, links und rechts, wie's ihm in die Beine kam. Mitten auf dem Felde begegnete ihnen der Pfarrer, und als er den Aufzug sah, sprach er: »Ei, so schämt euch, ihr garstigen Mädchen, was lauft ihr dem jungen Bursch durchs Feld nach, schickt sich das?« Damit faßte er die jüngste an die Hand und wollte sie zurückziehen, wie er sie aber anrührte, blieb er gleichfalls hängen und mußte selber hinten drein laufen. Nicht lange, so kam der Küster und sah den Herrn Pfarrer drei Mädchen auf dem Fuß folgen, da verwunderte er sich und rief: »Ei! Herr Pfarrer! Wo hinaus so geschwind? Heut ist noch eine Kindtaufe!«, lief auf ihn zu und faßte ihn am Ärmel und blieb auch fest hängen. Wie die fünf so hintereinander her trabten, kamen zwei Bauern mit ihren Hacken vom Feld, da rief der Pfarrer ihnen zu, sie sollten sie doch los machen. Kaum aber hatten sie den Küster angerührt, so blieben sie hängen und waren ihrer nun sieben, die dem Dummling mit der Gans nachliefen.

Er kam darauf in eine Stadt, da herrschte ein König, der hatte eine Tochter, die war so ernsthaft, daß niemand sie zum Lachen bringen konnte. Darum hatte er ein Gesetz gegeben, wer sie könnte zu lachen machen, der sollte sie heiraten. Der Dummling, als er das hörte, ging mit seiner Gans und ihrem Anhang vor die Königstochter, und wie diese die sieben Menschen immer hintereinander herlaufen sah, fing sie überlaut an zu lachen und wollte gar nicht wieder aufhören. Da verlangte sie der Dummling zur Braut, aber der König machte allerlei Einwendungen und sagte, er müßte ihm erst einen Mann bringen, der einen Keller voll Wein austrinken könnte. Der Dummling dachte an das graue Männchen, das könnte ihm wohl helfen, ging hinaus in den Wald, und auf der Stelle, wo er den Baum abgehauen hatte, sah er einen Mann sitzen, der machte ein gar betrübtes Gesicht. Der Dummling fragte, was er sich so sehr zu Herzen nähme? »Ei!« antwortete er. »Ich bin so durstig und kann nicht genug zu trinken kriegen, ein Faß Wein hab ich zwar ausgeleert, aber was ist ein Tropfen auf einem heißen Stein?« – »Da kann ich dir helfen«, sagte der Dummling, »komm nur mit mir, du sollst satt haben.« Er führte ihn darauf in des Königs Keller, und der Mann machte sich über die großen Fässer, trank und trank, daß ihm die Hüften weh taten, und ehe ein Tag herum war, hatte er den ganzen Keller ausgetrunken. Der Dummling verlangte wieder seine Braut; der König aber ärgerte sich, daß ein schlechter Bursch, den jedermann einen Dummling nannte, seine Tochter davontragen sollte, und machte neue Bedingungen: Er müsse ihm erst einen Mann schaffen, der einen Berg voll Brot aufessen könnte. Der Dummling ging wieder in den Wald, da saß auf des Baumes Platz ein Mann, der schnürte sich den Leib mit einem Riemen zusammen, machte ein grämliches Gesicht und sagte: »Ich habe einen ganzen Backofen voll Raspelbrot gegessen, aber was hilft das bei meinem großen Hunger, ich spür nichts im Leib und muß mich nur zuschnüren, wenn ich nicht Hungers sterben soll.« Wie der Dummling das hörte, war er froh und sprach: »Steh auf und geh mit mir, du sollst dich satt essen.« Er führte ihn an den Hof des Königs, der hatte alles Mehl aus dem ganzen Reich zusammenfahren und einen ungeheuern Berg davon backen lassen; der Mann aber aus dem Wald stellte sich davor, fing an zu essen, und in einem Tag und einer Nacht war der ganze Berg verschwunden. Der Dummling forderte wieder seine Braut; der König aber suchte noch einmal Ausflucht und verlangte ein Schiff, das zu Land wie zu Wasser fahren könnte;

schaffe er aber das, dann solle er gleich die Königstochter haben. Der Dummling ging noch einmal in den Wald, da saß das alte graue Männchen, dem er seinen Kuchen gegeben, und sagte: »Ich hab für dich getrunken und gegessen, ich will dir auch das Schiff geben. Das alles tu ich, weil du barmherzig gegen mich gewesen bist.« Da gab er ihm das Schiff, das zu Land und zu Wasser fuhr, und als der König das sah, mußte er ihm seine Tochter geben. Da ward die Hochzeit gefeiert, und der Dummling erbte das Reich und lebte lange Zeit vergnügt mit seiner Gemahlin.

1819

Rapunzel

Es war einmal ein Mann und eine Frau, die hatten sich schon lange ein Kind gewünscht und nie eins bekommen, endlich aber ward die Frau guter Hoffnung. Diese Leute hatten in ihrem Hinterhause ein kleines Fenster, daraus konnten sie in den Garten einer Zauberin sehen, der voll Blumen und Kräuter stand, allerlei Art, keiner aber durfte wagen hineinzugehen. Eines Tages stand die Frau an diesem

Fenster und sah hinab, da erblickte sie wunderschöne Rapunzeln auf einem Beet und wurde lüstern danach und wußte doch, daß sie keine davon bekommen konnte, daß sie ganz abfiel und elend wurde.

Ihr Mann erschrak endlich und fragte nach der Ursache. »Ach, wenn ich keine von den Rapunzeln aus dem Garten hinter unserm Haus zu essen kriege, so muß ich sterben.«

Der Mann, welcher sie gar lieb hatte, dachte, es mag kosten, was es will, so willst du ihr doch welche schaffen, stieg eines Abends über die hohe Mauer und stach in aller Eile eine Hand voll Rapunzeln aus, die er seiner Frau brachte. Die Frau machte sich sogleich Salat daraus und aß sie in vollem Heißhunger auf. Sie hatten ihr aber so gut, so gut geschmeckt, daß sie den andern Tag noch dreimal soviel Lust bekam. Der Mann sah wohl, daß keine Ruh wäre, also stieg er noch einmal in den Garten, allein, er erschrak gewaltig, als die Zauberin darin stand und ihn heftig schalt, daß er es wage, in ihren Garten zu kommen und daraus zu stehlen. Er entschuldigte sich, so gut er konnte, mit dem Gelüsten seiner Frau, und wie gefährlich es sei, ihr jetzt etwas abzuschlagen, endlich sprach die Zauberin: »Ich will mich zufrieden geben und dir selbst gestatten, Rapunzeln mitzunehmen, soviel du willst, wofern du mir das Kind geben wirst, das deine Frau gebiert.«

In der Angst sagte der Mann alles zu, und als die Frau in Wochen kam, erschien die Zauberin sogleich, nannte das kleine Mädchen Rapunzel und nahm es mit sich fort.

Dieses Rapunzel wurde das schönste Kind unter der Sonne. Wie es aber zwölf Jahre alt war, so schloß es die Zauberin in einen hohen, hohen Turm, der hatte weder Tür noch Treppe, nur bloß ganz oben war ein kleines Fensterchen. Wenn nun die Zauberin hinein wollte, so stand sie unten und rief:

> »Rapunzel, Rapunzel!
> Laß mir dein Haar herunter.«

Rapunzel hatte aber prächtige lange Haare, fein wie gesponnen Gold, und wenn die Zauberin so rief, so band sie ihre Zöpfe los, wickelte sie oben um einen Fensterhaken, und dann fielen die Haare zwanzig Ellen tief hinunter, und die Zauberin stieg daran hinauf.

Eines Tages kam nun ein junger Königssohn durch den Wald, wo der Turm stand, sah das schöne Rapunzel oben am Fenster stehen und hörte sie mit so süßer Stimme singen, daß er sich ganz in sie verliebte. Da aber keine Türe im Turm war und keine Leiter so hoch reichen konnte, so geriet er in Verzweiflung; doch ging er alle Tage in den Wald hin, bis er einstmals die Zauberin kommen sah, die sprach:

> »Rapunzel, Rapunzel!
> Laß dein Haar herunter.«

Darauf sah er wohl, auf welcher Leiter man in den Turm kommen konnte. Er hatte sich aber die Worte wohl gemerkt, die man sprechen mußte, und des andern Tages, als es dunkel war, ging er an den Turm und sprach hinauf:

>>Rapunzel, Rapunzel,
laß dein Haar herunter!<<

Da ließ sie die Haare los, und wie sie unten waren, machte er sich daran fest und wurde hinaufgezogen.

Rapunzel erschrak nun anfangs, bald aber gefiel ihr der junge König so gut, daß sie mit ihm verabredete, er solle alle Tage kommen und hinaufgezogen werden. So lebten sie lustig und in Freuden eine geraume Zeit und hatten sich herzlich lieb, wie Mann und Frau. Die Zauberin aber kam nicht dahinter, bis eines Tages das Rapunzel anfing und zu ihr sagte: >>Sag Sie mir doch, Frau Gotel, Sie wird mir viel schwerer heraufzuziehen als der junge König.<< – >>Ach, du gottloses Kind<<, sprach die Zauberin, >>was muß ich von dir hören<<, und sie merkte gleich, daß sie betrogen wäre, und war ganz aufgebracht. Da nahm sie die schönen Haare Rapunzels, schlug sie ein paar Mal um ihre linke Hand, griff eine Schere mit der rechten, und ritsch, ritsch waren sie abgeschnitten. Darauf verwies sie Rapunzel in eine Wüstenei, wo es ihr sehr kümmerlich erging und sie nach Verlauf einiger Zeit Zwillinge, einen Knaben und ein Mädchen, gebar.

Denselben Tag aber, wo sie Rapunzel verstoßen hatte, machte die Zauberin abends die abgeschnittenen Haare oben am Haken fest, und als der Königssohn kam:

>>Rapunzel, Rapunzel,
laß dein Haar herunter!<<,

so ließ sie zwar die Haare nieder, allein, wie erstaunte er, als er statt seines geliebten Rapunzels die Zauberin fand. >>Weißt du was<<, sprach die erzürnte Zauberin, >>Rapunzel ist für dich Bösewicht auf immer verloren!<<

Da wurde der Königssohn ganz verzweifelt und stürzte sich gleich den Turm hinab; das Leben brachte er davon, aber die beiden Augen hatte er sich ausgefallen. Traurig irrte er im Wald umher, aß nichts als Gras und Wurzeln und tat nichts als weinen. Einige Jahre nachher geriet er in jene Wüstenei, wo Rapunzel kümmerlich mit ihren Kindern lebte; ihre Stimme deuchte ihm so bekannt, und in demselben Augenblick erkannte sie ihn auch und fiel ihm um den Hals. Zwei von ihren Tränen aber fielen in seine Augen, da wurden sie wieder klar, und er konnte damit sehen wie sonst.

1819

Von dem Fischer un siine Fru

Daar was mal eens een Fischer un siine Fru, de waanten tosamen in'n Pispott, dicht an de See – un de Fischer ging alle Dage hen un angelt, un ging he hen lange Tid.

Daar satt he eens an de See bi de Angel un sach in dat blanke Water, un he sach ümmer na de Angel – daar ging de Angel to Grun'n, deep unner, un as he se heruttreckt, so haalt he eenen groten Butt herut – de Butt sed to em: »Ick bidd di, datt du mi lewen lettst, ick bin keen rechte Butt, ick bin een verwünscht' Prins, sett mi wedder in dat Water un laat mi swemmen.« – »Nu«, sed de Mann, »du bruukst nich so veele Woord' to maken, eenen Butt, de spreken kan, hadd ick doch woll swemmen laten.« Daar sett't he en wedder in dat Water, un de Butt ging fuurts weg to Grun'n un leet eenen langen Stripen Bloot hinner sich.

De Mann averst ging to siine Fru in'n Pispott un vertellt eer, dat he eenen Butt fangen hadd, de hadd to em segt, he weer een verwünscht' Prins, daar hadd he em wedder swemmen laten. »Hest du di den nix wünscht?« sed de Fru. – »Nee!« sed de Mann, »watt sull ick mi wünschen?« – »Ach!« sed de Fru, »dat is doch övel, ümmer

in'n Pispott to wanen, dat is so stinkig un dreckig hier, ga du noch hen un wünsch uns ne lütte Hütt!«

Den Mann was dat nich so recht, doch ging he hen na de See, un as he hen kamm, so was de See gans geel un grön, da ging he an dat Water staan un sed:

> »Mandje! Mandje! Timpe Te!
> Buttje, Buttje in de See!
> Mine Fru, de Ilsebill,
> Will nich so, as ick wol will.«

Daar kam de Butt answemmen un sed: »Na, wat will se denn?« – »Ach!« sed de Mann, »ick hev di doch fangen hätt, nu sed mine Fru, ick hadd mi doch wat wünschen sullt, se mag nich meer in'n Pispott wanen, se wull geern ne Hütt hebben.« – »Ga man hen«, sed de Butt, »se is all daar in.«

Daar ging de Mann hen, und siine Fru stund in eene Hütt in de Döör un sed to em: »Kumm man herin; sü, nu is dat doch veel beter!« Und daar was eene Stuwe un Kamer un eene Köck daar in, un da achter was een lütte Gaarn mit allerhand Grönigkeiten un een Hoff, da weeren Höner und Aanten. »Ach«, sed de Mann, »nu willn wi vergnögt lewen.« – »Ja«, sed de Fru, »wi willn't versöken.«

So ging dat nu wol een acht oder veertein Daag, dar sed de Fru: »Mann! de Hütt wart mi to eng, de Hoff un Gaarn is to lütt, ick will in een grot steenern Slott wanen; ga hen tum Butt, he sall uns een Slott schaffen.« – »Ach, Fru«, sed de Mann, »de Butt hett uns eerst de Hütt gewen, ick mag nu nich all wedder kamen, den Butt mügt et verdreeten.« – »I watt«, sed de Fru, »he kann dat recht good un deet dat geern, ga du man hen!« Daar ging der Mann hen, un siin Hart was em so swar; as he averst bi de See kam, was dat Water gans vigelett un grag un dunkelblag, doch was't noch still, dar ging he staan un sed:

> »Mandje! Mandje! Timpe Te!
> Buttje, Buttje in de See!
> Mine Fru, de Ilsebill,
> Will nich so, as ick wol will.«

»Na, wat will se denn?« sed de Butt. – »Ach«, sed de Mann, ganz bedrövd, »mine Fru will in een steenern Slott wanen.« – »Ga man hen, se steit vör de Döör«, sed de Butt.

Daar ging de Mann hen, un siine Fru stund vör eenen groten Palast. »Sü, Mann«, sed se, »wat is dat nu schön!« Mit des gingen se tosamen herin, daar weeren so veel Bedeenters, un de Wände weeren all blank, un goldne Stööl un Dische weeren in de Stuw, un achter dat Slott was een Gaarn un Holt, woll eene halve Miil lang, daar in weren Hirsche, Reeh un Hasen un up den Hoff Köh- und Peerdställ. »Ach!« sed de Mann, »nu willn wi ook in dat schöne Slott bliwen un tofreden sin!« – »Dat willn wi uns bedenken«, sed de Fru, »un willn't beschlapen.« Mit des gingen se to Bed.

Den annern Morgen waakt de Fru up, dat was all Dag: da stödd se den Mann mit den Ellbagen in de Siid un sed: »Mann, stah up, wi möten König warden över all dat Land.« – »Ach! Fru«, sed de Mann, »wat wulln wi König warden, ick mag nich König siin.« – »Na, denn will ick König siin.« – »Ach! Fru«, sed de Mann, »wo kannst du König siin, de Butt mügt dat nich doon.« – »Mann«, sed de Fru, »ga stracks hen, ick möt König sin.«

Daar ging de Mann un was gans bedrövd, dat sin Fru König warden wull. Un as he an de See kamm, was se all gans swartgrag, un dat Water geert so van unnen up. Daar ging he staan un sed:

> »Mandje! Mandje! Timpe Te!
> Buttje, Buttje in de See!
> Mine Fru, de Ilsebill,
> Will nich so, as ick wol will.«

»Na, wat will se denn?« sed de Butt. – »Ach!« sed de Mann, »mine Fru will König warden.« – »Ga man hen, se is't all«, sed de Butt.

Daar ging de Mann hen, un as he na den Palast kamm, da weren daar so veele Soldaten un Pauken un Trumpeten, un siine Fru satt up eenen hogen Troon van Gold un Demant un had eene grote goldne Kroon up, un up beiden Siiden bi eer, daar stunden sös Jumfern, ümmer eene eenen Kops lüttjer als de annre. »Ach«, sed de Mann, »bist du nu König?« – »Ja«, sed se, »ick bin König.« Un as he eer so ne Wile anseen had, so sed he: »Ach, Fru! Wat lett dat schön, wenn du König bist, nu willn wi ook nix meer wünschen.« – »Nee, Mann«, sed se, »mi duurt dat all to lang, ick kan dat nich meer utholln, König bin ick, nu möt ick ook Kaiser warden!« – »Ach! Fru«, sed de Mann, »wat wullst du Kaiser warden?« – »Mann«, sed se, »ga tum Butt, ick wull Kaiser sin.« – »Ach! Fru«, sed de Mann, »Kaiser kann he nich maken, ick mag den Butt dat nich seggen.« – »Ick bin König«, sed de Fru, »un du bist min Mann, ga gliik hen!«

Daar ging de Mann weg, un as he so ging, dacht he: »Dit geit un geit nich good, Kaiser is to unverschamt, de Butt ward am Ende möde.« Mit des kamm he an de See, dat Water was gans swart un dick, un et ging so een Keekwind äver hen, dat dat sik so köret; daar ging he staan un sed:

> »Mandje! Mandje! Timpe Te!
> Buttje, Buttje in de See!
> Mine Fru, de Ilsebill,
> Will nich so, as ick wol will.«

»Na, wat will se denn?« sed de Butt. – »Ach«, sed he, »min Fru will Kaiser warden.«
– »Ga man hen«, sed de Butt, »se is't all.«

Daar ging de Mann hen, un as he daar kamm, so satt siine Fru up eenen seer
hogen Troon, de was van een Stück Gold, un had eene grote Kron up, de was wol
twee Ellen hoch, bi eer up de Siiden, dar stunnen de Trabanten, ümmer een lüttjer
as de anner, von den allergrötsten Risen bet to den lüttsten Dwark, de was man so
lang as miin lüttje Finger. Vor eer, dar stunnen so veele Fürsten un Graven, da ging
de Mann unner staan un sed: »Fru! bist du nu Kaiser?« – »Ja«, sed se, »ick bin
Kaiser.« – »Ach!« sed de Mann, un sach se so recht an. »Fru, wat lett dat schön,
wenn du Kaiser bist.« – »Mann«, sed se, »wat steist du daar, ick bin nu Kaiser, nu
will ick awerst ook Pabst warden.« – »Ach! Fru«, sed de Mann, »wat wist du Pabst
warden, Pabst is man eenmal in de Christenheit.« – »Mann«, sed se, »ick möt hüüt
noch Pabst warden.« – »Ne, Fru«, sed he, »to Pabst kan de Butt nich maken, dat geit
nich good.« – »Mann, wat Snak, kan he Kaiser maken, kan he ook Pabst maken, ga
fuurts hen!« Daar ging de Man hen, un em was gans flau, dee Knee un de Waden
slakkerten em, un buten ging de Wind, un dat Water was, as kaakt dat, de Schep
schoten in de Noot un dansten un sprungen up de Bülgen, doch was de Himmel in
de Midde noch so'n beeten blag, awerst an de Siiden, daar toog dat so recht rood
up, as een swaar Gewitter. Da ging he recht vörzufft staan un sed:

>»Mandje! Mandje! Timpe Te!
>Buttje, Buttje in de See!
>Mine Fru, de Ilsebill,
>Will nich so, as ick wol will.«

»Na, wat will se denn?« sed de Butt. – »Ach!« sed de Mann. »Min Fru will Pabst
warden.« – »Ga man hen«, sed de Butt, »se is't all.«

Daar ging he hen, und as he daar kamm, satt sine Fru up eenen Troon, de was
twee Miilen hoch, un had dree groote Kroonen up, un um eer, da was so veel van
geistlike Staat, un up de Siiden bi eer, daar stunnen twee Reegen Lichter, dat
grötste so dick un groot as de allergrötste Torm bet to dat allerlüttste Kökenlicht.
»Fru«, sed de Mann, un sach se so recht an, »bist du nu Pabst?« – »Ja«, sed se, »ick
bin Pabst!« – »Ach, Fru«, sed de Mann, »wat lett dat schön, wenn du Pabst bist; Fru,
nu wes tofreden, nu du Pabst bist, kannst du nix meer warden.« – »Dat will ick mi
bedenken«, sed de Fru, daar gingen se beede to Bed, awerst se was nich tofreden,
un de Girigkeit leet eer nich slapen, se dacht ümmer, wat se noch wol warden wull.
Mit des ging de Sünn up; ha, dacht se, as se se ut den Finster so herup kamen sach,
kann ick nich ook de Sünn upgaan laten? Daar wurde se recht so grimmig un stödd
eeren Mann an: »Mann, ga hen tum Butt, ick will warden as de lewe Gott!« De
Mann was noch meist im Slaap, awerst he verschrack sich so, dat he ut den Bed feel.
»Ach! Fru«, sed he, »ga in di un bliw Pabst.« – »Ne«, sed de Fru un reet sich dat

Liivken up, »ick bin nich ruhig un kan dat nich uthollen, wenn ick de Sünn un de Maan upgaan see, un kan se nich ook upgaan laten, ick möt warden as de lewe Gott!« – »Ach, Fru«, sed de Mann, »dat kan de Butt nich, Kaiser un Pabst kan he maken, awerst dat kan he nich.« – »Mann«, sed se un sach so recht gräsig ut, »ick will warden as de lewe Gott, ga gliik hen tum Butt.«

Dat fuur den Mann so dörch de Gleder, dat he bewt vör Angst; buten awer ging de Storm, dat alle Böme un Felsen umweigten, un de Himmel was gans swart, un dat dunnert un blitzt; daar sach man in de See so swarte hoge Bülgen as Barg' un hadden baben all eene witte Kroon van Schuum up, da sed he:

> »Mandje! Mandje! Timpe Te!
> Buttje, Buttje in de See!
> Mine Fru, de Ilsebill,
> Will nich so, as ick woll will.«

»Na, wat will se den?« sed de Butt. – »Ach!« sed he, »se will warden as de lewe Gott.« – »Ga man hen, se sitt all wedder in'n Pispott.« Daar sitten se noch hüt up dissen Dag.

1819

Vom Fundevogel

Es war einmal ein Förster, der ging in den Wald auf die Jagd, und wie er in den Wald kam, hörte er schreien, als ob's ein kleines Kind wäre, und ging dem Schreien nach, da sah er endlich einen hohen Baum, und oben darauf saß ein kleines Kind. Es war aber die Mutter mit dem Kinde unter dem Baum eingeschlafen, da hatte ein Raubvogel das Kind in ihrem Schoß gesehen, flog hinzu, nahm es mit seinem Schnabel weg und setzte es auf den hohen Baum.

Der Förster stieg hinauf, holte das Kind herunter und dachte: »Du willst das Kind mit nach Haus nehmen und mit deinem Lenchen zusammen aufziehen«, brachte es heim, und die zwei Kinder wuchsen so miteinander auf. Das aber, das auf dem Baum gefunden worden war und weil es ein Vogel weggetragen hatte, wurde Fundevogel geheißen. Fundevogel und Lenchen hatten sich so lieb, nein so lieb, daß, wenn eins das andere nicht sah, wurde es traurig.

Der Förster hatte aber eine alte Köchin, die nahm eines Abends zwei Eimer und fing an, Wasser zu schleppen, und ging nicht einmal, sondern viele Mal hinaus an den Brunnen. Lenchen sah es und sprach: »Hör einmal, alte Sanne, was trägst du denn so viel Wasser zu?« – »Wenn du's keinem Menschen wiedersagen willst, so will

ich dir's wohl sagen.« Da sagte Lenchen nein, sie wollte es keinem Menschen wiedersagen, so sprach die Köchin: »Morgen früh, wenn der Förster auf die Jagd ist, da koche ich das Wasser, und wenn's in dem Kessel siedet, werf ich den Fundevogel 'nein und will ihn darin kochen.«

Und des andern Morgens in aller Frühe stand der Förster auf und ging auf die Jagd, und als er weg war, lagen die Kinder noch im Bett, da sprach Lenchen zum Fundevogel: »Verläßt du mich nicht, so verlaß ich dich auch nicht!« So sprach der Fundevogel: »Nun und nimmermehr.« Da sprach Lenchen: »Ich will es dir nur sagen, die Sanne schleppte gestern abend so viel Eimer Wasser ins Haus, da fragte ich sie, warum sie das täte, so sagte sie: Wenn ich's keinem Menschen sagen wollte, so wollte sie es mir wohl sagen; sprach ich: ich wollte es gewiß keinem Menschen sagen, da sagte sie, morgen früh, wenn der Vater auf die Jagd wäre, wollte sie den Kessel voll Wasser sieden und dich hineinwerfen und kochen. Wir wollen aber geschwind aufstehen, uns anziehen und zusammen fortgehen.«

Also standen die beiden Kinder auf, zogen sich geschwind an und gingen fort. Wie nun das Wasser im Kessel kochte, ging die Köchin in die Schlafkammer und wollte den Fundevogel holen, um ihn hinein zu werfen. Aber als sie hineinkam und zu den Betten trat, waren die Kinder alle beide fort, da wurde ihr grausam angst, und sie sprach vor sich: »Was will ich nun sagen, wenn der Förster heim kommt und sieht, daß die Kinder weg sind. Geschwind hinten nach, daß wir sie wieder kriegen!«

Da schickte die Köchin drei Knechte nach, die sollten laufen und die Kinder einlangen. Die Kinder aber saßen vor dem Wald, und als sie die drei Knechte von weitem laufen sahen, sprach Lenchen zum Fundevogel: »Verläßt du mich nicht, so verlaß ich dich auch nicht!« So sprach Fundevogel: »Nun und nimmermehr!« Da sagte Lenchen: »Werde du zum Rosenstöckchen und ich zum Röschen drauf!« Wie nun die drei Knechte vor den Wald kamen, so war nichts da als ein Rosenstrauch und ein Röschen oben drauf, die Kinder aber nirgends. Da sprachen sie: »Hier ist nichts zu machen«, und gingen heim und sagten der Köchin, sie hätten nichts in der Welt gesehen als nur ein Rosenstöckchen mit einem Röschen oben drauf. Da schalt die alte Köchin: »Ihr Einfaltspinsel, ihr hättet das Rosenstöckchen sollen entzwei schneiden und das Röschen abbrechen und mit nach Haus bringen: geschwind und tut's!« Sie mußten also zum zweitenmal hinaus und suchen. Die Kinder sahen sie aber von weitem kommen, da sprach Lenchen: »Fundevogel, verläßt du mich nicht, verlaß ich dich auch nicht!« Fundevogel sagte: »Nun und nimmermehr.« Sprach Lenchen: »So werde du eine Kirche und ich die Krone darin!« Wie nun die drei Knechte dahin kamen, war nichts da als eine Kirche und eine Krone darin. Sie sprachen also zueinander: »Was sollen wir hier machen, laßt uns nach Hause gehen!« Wie sie nach Haus kamen, fragte die Köchin, ob sie nichts gefunden, so sagten sie nein, sie hätten nichts gefunden als eine Kirche, da wäre eine Krone darin gewesen. »Ihr Narren«, schalt die Köchin, »warum habt ihr nicht die Kirche zerbrochen und die Krone mit heimgebracht?« Nun machte sich die alte Köchin selbst auf die Beine und ging mit den drei Knechten den Kindern nach. Die Kinder sahen aber die drei Knechte von weitem kommen, und die Köchin wackelte hinten nach. Da sprach Lenchen: »Fundevogel, verläßt du mich nicht, so verlaß ich dich auch nicht.« Da sprach der Fundevogel: »Nun und nimmermehr!« Sprach Lenchen: »Werde du zum Teich und ich die Ente drauf!« Die Köchin aber kam herzu, und als sie den Teich sah, legte sie sich drüber hin und wollte ihn aussaufen. Aber die Ente kam schnell geschwommen, faßte sie mit ihrem Schnabel beim Kopf und zog sie ins Wasser hinein, da mußte die alte Hexe ertrinken. Da gingen die Kinder zusammen nach Haus und waren herzlich froh, und wenn sie nicht gestorben sind, leben sie noch.

1819

Das Waldhaus

Ein armer Holzhauer lebte mit seiner Frau und drei Töchtern in einer kleinen Hütte am Rande eines einsamen Waldes. Eines Morgens, als er wieder an seine Arbeit wollte, sagte er zu seiner Frau: »Laß mir mein Mittagsbrot von dem ältesten Mädchen hinaus in den Wald bringen, ich werde sonst nicht fertig. Und damit es sich nicht verirrt«, setzte er hinzu, »will ich einen Beutel mit Hirse mitnehmen und die Körner auf den Weg streuen.«

Als nun die Sonne mitten über dem Walde stand, machte sich das Mädchen mit einem Topf voll Suppe auf den Weg. Aber die Feld- und Waldsperlinge, die Lerchen und Finken, Amseln und Zeisige hatten die Hirse schon längst aufgepickt, und das Mädchen konnte die Spur nicht finden. Da ging es auf gut Glück immer fort, bis die Sonne sank und die Nacht einbrach. Die Bäume rauschten in der Dunkelheit, die Eulen schnarrten, und es fing an, ihm angst zu werden. Da erblickte es in der Ferne ein Licht, das zwischen den Bäumen blinkte. »Dort sollten wohl Leute wohnen«, dachte es, »die mich über Nacht behalten«, und ging auf das Licht zu. Nicht lange, so kam es an ein Haus, dessen Fenster erleuchtet waren. Es

klopfte an, und eine rauhe Stimme rief von innen »herein«. Das Mädchen trat auf die dunkle Diele und pochte an der Stubentür. »Nur herein«, rief die Stimme, und als es öffnete, saß da ein alter, eisgrauer Mann an dem Tisch, hatte das Gesicht auf die beiden Hände gestützt, und sein weißer Bart floß über den Tisch herab fast bis auf die Erde. Am Ofen aber lagen drei Tiere, ein Hühnchen, ein Hähnchen und eine buntgescheckte Kuh. Das Mädchen erzählte dem Alten sein Schicksal und bat um ein Nachtlager. Der Mann sprach:

»Schön Hühnchen,
schön Hähnchen,
und du, schöne bunte Kuh,
was sagst du dazu?«

»Duks!« antworteten die Tiere, und das mußte wohl heißen: »Wir sind es zufrieden.« Denn der Alte sprach weiter: »Hier ist Hülle und Fülle, geh hinaus an den Herd und koch uns ein Abendessen.« Das Mädchen fand in der Küche Überfluß an allem und kochte eine gute Speise, aber an die Tiere dachte es nicht. Es trug die volle Schüssel auf den Tisch, setzte sich zu dem grauen Mann, aß und stillte seinen Hunger. Als es satt war, sprach es: »Aber jetzt bin ich müde, wo ist ein Bett, in das ich mich legen und schlafen kann?« Die Tiere antworteten:

»Du hast mit ihm gegessen,
du hast mit ihm getrunken,
du hast an uns gar nicht gedacht,
nun sieh auch, wo du bleibst die Nacht.«

Da sprach der Alte: »Steig nur die Treppe hinauf, so wirst du eine Kammer mit zwei Betten finden, schüttle sie auf und decke sie mit weißem Linnen, so will ich auch kommen und mich schlafen legen.« Das Mädchen stieg hinauf, und als es die Betten geschüttelt und frisch gedeckt hatte, legte es sich in das eine, ohne weiter auf den Alten zu warten. Nach einiger Zeit aber kam der graue Mann, beleuchtete das Mädchen mit dem Licht und schüttelte mit dem Kopf. Als er sah, daß es fest eingeschlafen war, öffnete er eine Falltüre und ließ es in den Keller sinken.

Der Holzhauer kam am späten Abend nach Haus und machte seiner Frau Vorwürfe, daß sie ihn den ganzen Tag habe hungern lassen. »Ich habe keine Schuld«, antwortete sie, »das Mädchen ist mit dem Mittagsessen hinausgegangen, es muß sich verirrt haben. Morgen wird es schon wiederkommen.« Vor Tag aber stand der Holzhauer auf, wollte in den Wald und verlangte, die zweite Tochter sollte ihm diesmal das Essen bringen. »Ich will einen Beutel mit Linsen mitnehmen«, sagte er, »die Körner sind größer als Hirse, das Mädchen wird sie besser sehen und kann den Weg nicht verfehlen.« Zur Mittagszeit trug auch das Mädchen die Speise hinaus, aber die Linsen waren verschwunden. Die Waldvögel hatten sie, wie am vorigen Tag, aufgepickt und keine übriggelassen. Das Mädchen irrte im Walde umher, bis es Nacht ward, da kam es ebenfalls zu dem Haus des Alten, ward hereingerufen und bat um Speise und Nachtlager. Der Mann mit dem weißen Barte fragte wieder die Tiere:

>Schön Hühnchen,
schön Hähnchen,
und du, schöne bunte Kuh,
was sagst du dazu?«

Die Tiere antworteten abermals »duks«, und es geschah alles wie am vorigen Tag. Das Mädchen kochte eine gute Speise, aß und trank mit dem Alten und kümmerte sich nicht um die Tiere. Und als es sich nach seinem Nachtlager erkundigte, antworteten sie:

>Du hast mit ihm gegessen,
du hast mit ihm getrunken,
du hast an uns gar nicht gedacht,
nun sieh auch, wo du bleibst die Nacht.«

Als es eingeschlafen war, kam der Alte, betrachtete es mit Kopfschütteln und ließ es in den Keller hinab.

Am dritten Morgen sprach der Holzhacker zu seiner Frau: »Schicke mir heute unser jüngstes Kind mit dem Essen hinaus, das ist immer gut und gehorsam gewesen, das wird auf dem rechten Weg bleiben und nicht wie seine Schwestern, die wilden Hummeln, herumschwärmen.« Die Mutter wollte nicht und sprach: »Soll ich mein liebstes Kind auch noch verlieren?« – »Sei ohne Sorge«, antwortete er, »das Mädchen verirrt sich nicht, es ist zu klug und verständig; zum Überfluß will ich Erbsen mitnehmen und ausstreuen, die sind noch größer als Linsen und werden ihm den Weg zeigen.« Aber als das Mädchen mit dem Korb am Arm hinauskam, so hatten die Waldtauben die Erbsen schon im Kropf, und es wußte nicht, wohin es sich wenden sollte. Es war voll Sorgen und dachte beständig daran, wie der arme Vater hungern und die gute Mutter jammern würde, wenn es ausbliebe. Endlich, als es finster ward, erblickte es das Lichtchen und kam an das Waldhaus. Es bat ganz freundlich, sie möchten es über Nacht beherbergen, und der Mann mit dem weißen Bart fragte wieder seine Tiere:

>Schön Hühnchen,
schön Hähnchen,
und du, schöne bunte Kuh,
was sagst du dazu?«

»Duks«, sagten sie. Da trat das Mädchen an den Ofen, wo die Tiere lagen, und liebkoste Hühnchen und Hähnchen, indem es mit der Hand über die glatten Federn hinstrich, und die bunte Kuh kraulte es zwischen den Hörnern. Und als es auf Geheiß des Alten eine gute Suppe bereitet hatte und die Schüssel auf dem Tisch stand, so sprach es: »Soll ich mich sättigen und die guten Tiere sollen nichts haben? Draußen ist die Hülle und Fülle, erst will ich für sie sorgen.« Da ging es, holte Gerste und streute sie dem Hühnchen und Hähnchen vor und brachte der Kuh wohlriechendes Heu, einen ganzen Arm voll. »Laßt's euch schmecken, ihr lieben Tiere«, sagte es, »und wenn ihr durstig seid, sollt ihr auch einen frischen Trunk haben.« Dann trug es einen Eimer voll Wasser herein, und Hühnchen und Hähnchen sprangen auf den Rand, steckten den Schnabel hinein und hielten den Kopf dann in die Höhe, wie die Vögel trinken, und die bunte Kuh tat auch einen herzhaften Zug. Als die Tiere gefüttert waren, setzte sich das Mädchen zu dem Alten an den Tisch und aß, was er ihm übriggelassen hatte. Nicht lange, so fingen Hühnchen und Hähnchen an, das Köpfchen zwischen die Flügel zu stecken, und die bunte Kuh blinzelte mit den Augen. Da sprach das Mädchen: »Sollen wir uns nicht zur Ruhe begeben?

> Schön Hühnchen,
> schön Hähnchen,
> und du, schöne bunte Kuh,
> was sagst du dazu?«

Die Tiere antworteten:

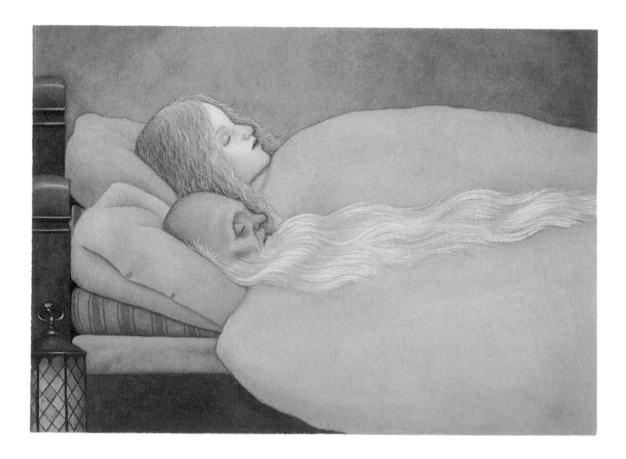

>»Duks, du hast mit uns gegessen,
du hast mit uns getrunken,
du hast uns alle wohl bedacht,
wir wünschen dir eine gute Nacht.«

Da ging das Mädchen die Treppe hinauf, schüttelte die Federkissen und deckte frisches Linnen auf, und als es fertig war, kam der Alte und legte sich in das eine Bett, und sein weißer Bart reichte ihm bis an die Füße. Das Mädchen legte sich in das andere, tat sein Gebet und schlief ein.

Es schlief ruhig bis Mitternacht, da ward es so unruhig in dem Hause, daß das Mädchen erwachte. Da fing es an, in den Ecken zu knittern und zu knattern, und die Türe sprang auf und schlug an die Wand; die Balken dröhnten, als wenn sie aus ihren Fugen gerissen würden, und es war, als wenn die Treppe herabstürzte, und endlich krachte es, als wenn das ganze Dach zusammenfiele. Da es aber wieder still ward und dem Mädchen nichts zuleid geschah, so blieb es ruhig liegen und schlief wieder ein. Als es aber am Morgen bei hellem Sonnenschein aufwachte, was er blickten seine Augen? Es lag in einem großen Saal, und ringsumher glänzte alles in königlicher Pracht. An den Wänden wuchsen auf grünseidenem Grund goldene Blumen in die Höhe, das Bett war von Elfenbein und die Decke darauf von rotem Samt, und auf einem Stuhl daneben stand ein Paar mit Perlen gestickte Pantoffel. Das Mädchen glaubte, es wäre ein Traum, aber es traten drei reichgekleidete Diener herein und fragten, was es zu befehlen hätte. »Geht nur«, antwortete das Mädchen, »ich will gleich aufstehen und dem Alten eine Suppe kochen und dann auch schön Hühnchen, schön Hähnchen und die schöne bunte Kuh füttern.« Es dachte, der Alte wäre schon aufgestanden, und sah sich nach seinem Bett um, aber er lag nicht darin, sondern ein fremder Mann. Und als es ihn betrachtete und sah, daß er jung und schön war, erwachte er, richtete sich auf und sprach: »Ich bin ein Königssohn und war von einer bösen Hexe verwünscht worden, als ein alter, eisgrauer Mann in dem Wald zu leben. Niemand durfte um mich sein als meine drei Diener in der Gestalt eines Hühnchens, eines Hähnchens und einer bunten Kuh. Und nicht eher sollte die Verwünschung aufhören, als bis ein Mädchen zu uns käme, so gut von Herzen, daß es nicht gegen die Menschen allein, sondern auch gegen die Tiere sich liebreich bezeigte, und das bist du gewesen, und heute um Mitternacht sind wir durch dich erlöst, und das alte Waldhaus ist wieder in meinen königlichen Palast verwandelt worden.«

Und als sie aufgestanden waren, sagte der Königssohn den drei Dienern, sie sollten hinfahren und Vater und Mutter des Mädchens zur Hochzeitsfeier herbeiholen. »Aber wo sind meine zwei Schwestern?« fragte das Mädchen. »Die habe ich in den Keller gesperrt, und morgen sollen sie in den Wald geführt werden und sollen bei einem Köhler so lange als Mägde dienen, bis sie sich gebessert haben und auch die armen Tiere nicht hungern lassen.«

1840

Aschenputtel

Einem reichen Mann wurde seine Frau krank, und als sie fühlte, daß ihr Ende herankam, rief sie ihr einziges Töchterlein zu sich ans Bett und sprach: »Bleib fromm und gut, so wird dir der liebe Gott immer beistehen, und ich will vom Himmel herab auf dich blicken und um dich sein.« Darauf tat sie die Augen zu und verschied. Das Mädchen ging jeden Tag hinaus auf ihr Grab und weinte und blieb fromm und gut. Der Schnee aber deckte ein weißes Tüchlein auf das Grab, und als die Sonne es wieder herabgezogen hatte, nahm sich der Mann eine andere Frau.

Die Frau hatte zwei Töchter, die sie mit ins Haus brachte und die schön und weiß von Angesicht waren, aber garstig und schwarz von Herzen. Da ging eine schlimme Zeit für das arme Stiefkind an. »Was will der Unnütz in den Stuben«, sprachen sie, »wer Brot essen will, muß es erst verdienen, fort mit der Küchenmagd.« Da nahmen ihm die Schwestern seine schönen Kleider, gaben ihm einen grauen alten Kittel anzuziehen, und dann lachten sie es aus und führten es in die Küche. Nun mußte es so schwere Arbeit tun, früh vor Tag aufstehen, Wasser tragen, Feuer anmachen, kochen und waschen. Dabei taten ihm die Schwestern alles Herzeleid an, spotteten und schütteten ihm die Erbsen und Linsen in die Asche, so daß es sitzen und sie wieder auslesen mußte. Abends, wenn es müd war, kam es in kein Bett, sondern mußte sich neben dem Herd in die Asche legen. Und weil es immer staubig und schmutzig aussah, nannten sie es Aschenputtel.

Es trug sich zu, daß der Vater einmal in die Messe ziehen wollte, da fragte er die beiden Stieftöchter, was er ihnen mitbringen sollte? »Schöne Kleider«, sagte die eine, und: »Perlen und Edelsteine«, die zweite. »Nun, Aschenputtel«, sprach er, »was willst du haben?« – »Vater, das erste Reis, das Euch auf Eurem Heimweg an den Hut stößt«, antwortete Aschenputtel. Er kaufte nun für die beiden Stiefschwestern die Kleider, Perlen und Edelsteine, und auf dem Rückweg, als er durch einen grünen Busch ritt, streifte ihn ein Haselreis und stieß ihm den Hut ab. Da brach er das Reis, und als er nach Haus kam, gab er den Stieftöchtern, was sie sich gewünscht hatten, und dem Aschenputtel gab er das Reis von dem Haselbusch. Aschenputtel nahm es, ging damit zu seiner Mutter Grab und pflanzte es darauf und weinte so sehr, daß das Reis von seinen Tränen begossen ward. Es wuchs aber und ward ein schöner Baum. Aschenputtel ging alle Tage dreimal darunter, weinte und betete, und allemal kam ein Vöglein auf den Baum und gab ihm, was es sich wünschte.

Es begab sich aber, daß der König ein Fest anstellte, das drei Tage dauern sollte, damit sich sein Sohn eine Braut aussuchen könnte. Die zwei Stiefschwestern waren auch dazu eingeladen, riefen Aschenputtel und sprachen: »Nun kämm uns die

Haare, bürst uns die Schuhe und schnall uns die Schnallen, wir tanzen auf des Königs Fest.« Das tat Aschenputtel und weinte, weil es auch gern zum Tanz mitgegangen wär, und bat die Stiefmutter gar sehr, sie möchte es ihm erlauben. »Du, Aschenputtel«, sprach sie, »hast nichts am Leib und hast keine Kleider und kannst nicht tanzen und willst zur Hochzeit!« Als es noch weiter bat, sprach sie endlich: »Ich will dir eine Schüssel Linsen in die Asche schütten, und wenn du die in zwei Stunden wieder ausgelesen hast, so sollst du mitgehen.« Nun schüttete sie ihm die Linsen in die Asche, aber das Mädchen ging vor die Hintertüre nach dem Garten zu und rief: »Ihr zahmen Täubchen, ihr Turteltäubchen, all ihr Vöglein unter dem Himmel, kommt und helft mir lesen:

> Die guten ins Töpfchen,
> die schlechten ins Kröpfchen!«

Da kamen zum Küchenfenster zwei weiße Täubchen herein und danach die Turteltäubchen, und endlich schwirrten und schwärmten alle Vögelein unter dem Himmel herein und ließen sich um die Asche nieder.

Und die Täubchen nickten mit dem Köpfchen und fingen an: pik, pik, pik, pik, und da fingen die übrigen auch an: pik, pik, pik, pik, und lasen alle guten Körnlein in die Schüssel.

Wie eine Stunde herum war, waren sie schon fertig und flogen alle wieder hinaus, da brachte es die Schüssel der Stiefmutter und freute sich und glaubte, nun mit auf die Hochzeit gehen zu dürfen. Aber sie sprach: »Nein, du, Aschenputtel, du hast keine Kleider und kannst nicht tanzen, du sollst nicht mitgehen.« Als es nun weinte, sprach sie: »Wenn du mir zwei Schüsseln voll Linsen in einer Stunde aus der Asche rein lesen kannst, so sollst du mitgehen«, und dachte dabei, das kann es nimmermehr. Nun schüttete sie zwei Schüsseln Linsen in die Asche, aber das Mädchen ging vor die Hintertüre nach dem Garten zu und rief: »Ihr zahmen Täubchen, ihr Turteltäubchen, all ihr Vöglein unter dem Himmel, kommt und helft mir lesen:

> Die guten ins Töpfchen,
> die schlechten ins Kröpfchen!«

Da kamen zum Küchenfenster zwei weiße Täubchen herein und danach die Turteltäubchen, und endlich schwirrten und schwärmten alle Vöglein unter dem Himmel herein und ließen sich um die Asche nieder. Und die Täubchen nickten mit ihren Köpfchen und fingen an: pik, pik, pik, pik, und da fingen die übrigen auch an: pik, pik, pik, pik, und lasen alle guten Körner in die Schüsseln. Und eh' eine halbe Stunde herum war, waren sie schon fertig und flogen alle wieder hinaus; da brachte es der Stiefmutter die Schüsseln und freute sich und glaubte nun mitgehen zu dürfen. Aber sie sprach: »Es hilft alles nichts, du kommst nicht mit, du

hast keine Kleider und kannst nicht tanzen, und wir müßten uns nur schämen.«
Darauf ging sie mit ihren zwei Töchtern fort.

Als nun niemand mehr daheim war, ging Aschenputtel zu seiner Mutter Grab
unter den Haselbaum und rief:

>»Bäumchen, rüttel dich und schüttel dich!
Wirf Gold und Silber über mich!«

Da warf ihm der Vogel ein golden und silbern Kleid herunter und mit Seide und
Silber ausgestickte Pantoffeln. Das zog es an und ging zur Hochzeit. Ihre Schwestern aber und die Stiefmutter kannten es nicht und meinten, es müßt ein fremdes
Königsfräulein sein, so schön sah es in den reichen Kleidern aus. An Aschenputtel
dachten sie gar nicht und glaubten, es läg daheim im Schmutz. Der Königssohn
kam ihm entgegen und nahm es bei der Hand und tanzte mit ihm. Er wollte auch
mit sonst niemand tanzen, also daß er ihm die Hand nicht los ließ, und wenn ein
anderer kam, es aufzufordern, sprach er: »Das ist meine Tänzerin.«

Es tanzte, bis Abend war, da wollte es nun nach Haus gehen. Der Königssohn
aber sprach: »Ich gehe mit und begleite dich«, denn er wollte sehen, wem das
schöne Mädchen angehörte. Sie entwischte ihm aber und sprang in das Taubenhaus. Nun wartete der Königssohn, bis der Vater kam, und sagte ihm, das fremde
Mädchen wär in das Taubenhaus gesprungen. Da dachte er: sollte es Aschenputtel
sein, und sie mußten ihm Axt und Hacken bringen, damit er das Taubenhaus
entzwei schlagen konnte; aber es war niemand darin. Und als sie ins Haus kamen,
lag Aschenputtel in seinen schmutzigen Kleidern in der Asche, und sein trübes
Öllämpchen brannte im Schornstein. Denn es war geschwind durch das Taubenhaus gesprungen und zu dem Haselbäumchen gegangen, da hatte es die schönen
Kleider ausgetan und aufs Grab gelegt, und der Vogel hatte sie wieder weggenommen, es aber hatte sich in seinem grauen Kittelchen in die Küche zur Asche
gesetzt.

Am andern Tag, als das Fest von neuem anhub und die Eltern und Stiefschwestern wieder fort waren, ging Aschenputtel zu dem Haselbaum und sprach:

>»Bäumchen, rüttel dich und schüttel dich!
Wirf Gold und Silber über mich!«

Da warf der Vogel ein noch viel stolzeres Kleid herab als am vorigen Tag. Als es
damit auf die Hochzeit kam, erstaunte jedermann über seine Schönheit, der Königssohn aber hatte schon auf es gewartet, nahm es bei der Hand und tanzte nur
allein mit ihm. Wenn die andern kamen und es aufforderten, sprach er: »Das ist
meine Tänzerin.« Als es nun Abend war, wollte es fort, und dcr Königssohn ging
mit und wollte sehen, in welches Haus es ginge, aber es sprang ihm fort und in den

Garten hinter dem Haus. Darin stand ein schöner, großer Birnbaum voll herrlichem Obst, auf den stieg es gar behend, und der Königssohn wußte nicht, wo es hingekommen war. Er wartete aber, bis der Vater kam, und sprach zu ihm: »Das fremde Mädchen ist mir entwischt, und ich glaube, daß es auf den Birnbaum gesprungen ist.« Der Vater dachte, sollte es Aschenputtel sein! Und ließ sich die Axt holen und hieb den Baum um, aber es war niemand darauf. Und als sie in die Küche kamen, lag Aschenputtel da in der Asche, wie gewöhnlich, denn es war auf der andern Seite vom Baum herabgesprungen, hatte dem Vogel auf dem Haselbäumchen die schönen Kleider wieder gebracht und sein grau Kittelchen angezogen.

Am dritten Tag, als die Eltern und Schwestern dahin waren, ging Aschenputtel wieder zu seiner Mutter Grab und sprach zu dem Bäumchen:

>»Bäumchen, rüttel dich und schüttel dich!
>Wirf Gold und Silber über mich!«

Nun warf ihm der Vogel ein Kleid herab, das war so prächtig, wie es noch keins gehabt, und die Pantoffeln waren ganz golden. Als es zu der Hochzeit kam, wußten sie alle nicht, was sie vor Verwunderung sagen sollten, der Königssohn tanzte ganz allein mit ihm, und wenn es einer aufforderte, sprach er: »Es ist meine Tänzerin.«

Als es nun Abend war, wollte Aschenputtel fort, und der Königssohn wollte es begleiten, aber es sprang ihm fort. Doch verlor es seinen linken, ganz goldenen Pantoffel, denn der Königssohn hatte Pech auf die Treppe streichen lassen, und daran blieb er hängen.

Nun nahm er den Schuh und ging am andern Tag damit zu dem Mann und sagte: Die, welcher dieser goldene Schuh passe, die solle seine Gemahlin werden. Da freuten sich die beiden Schwestern, weil sie schöne Füße hatten. Die Älteste ging mit dem Schuh in die Kammer und wollte ihn anprobieren, und die Mutter stand dabei. Aber sie konnte mit der großen Zehe nicht hineinkommen, und der Schuh war ihr zu klein, da reichte ihr die Mutter ein Messer und sprach: »Hau die Zehe ab, wenn du Königin bist, so brauchst du nicht mehr zu Fuß zu gehen.« Das Mädchen hieb die Zehe ab, zwängte nun den Schuh hinein und ging zum Königssohn. Der nahm sie als seine Braut auf sein Pferd und ritt mit ihr fort. Sie mußten aber an dem Haselbäumchen, das auf dem Grabe stand, vorbei, da saßen die zwei Täubchen drauf und riefen:

>»Rucke di guck! rucke di guck!
>Blut ist im Schuck (Schuh),
> der Schuck ist zu klein,
>   die rechte Braut sitzt noch daheim!«

Da blickte er auf ihren Fuß und sah, wie das Blut herausquoll. Nun wendete er sein Pferd um, brachte die falsche Braut wieder nach Haus und sagte: »Das ist nicht die rechte, die andere Schwester soll den Schuh anziehen.« Sie ging in die Kammer und kam mit den Zehen in den Schuh, aber hinten die Ferse war zu groß. Da reichte ihr die Mutter ein Messer und sprach: »Hau ein Stück von der Ferse ab, wenn du Königin bist, brauchst du nicht mehr zu Fuß zu gehen.« Das Mädchen hieb ein Stück von der Ferse ab, zwängte den Fuß in den Schuh und ging zum Königssohn. Der nahm sie als seine Braut aufs Pferd und ritt mit ihr fort. Als sie an dem Haselbäumchen vorbeikamen, saßen die zwei Täubchen darauf und riefen:

> »Rucke di guck! rucke di guck!
> Blut ist im Schuck,
> der Schuck ist zu klein,
> die rechte Braut sitzt noch daheim!«

Er blickte nieder auf ihren Fuß und sah, wie das Blut aus dem Schuh quoll und an den weißen Strümpfen ganz rot heraufgestiegen war. Da wendete er sein Pferd und brachte die falsche Braut wieder zurück. »Das ist nicht die rechte«, sprach er, »habt ihr keine andere Tochter?« – »Nein«, sagte der Mann, »nur von meiner verstorbenen Frau ist noch ein kleines, garstiges Aschenputtel da, das kann aber nicht die Braut sein.« Der Königssohn sprach, er sollt' es heraufschicken, die Mutter aber antwortete: »Ach nein, das ist viel zu schmutzig, das darf sich nicht sehen lassen.« Er aber wollt' es durchaus haben, und Aschenputtel mußte gerufen werden. Da wusch es sich erst Hände und Angesicht rein, ging dann hin und neigte sich vor dem Königssohn, der ihm seinen goldenen Schuh reichte. Nun streifte es den schweren Schuh vom linken Fuß ab, setzte diesen auf den goldenen Pantoffel und drückte ein wenig, so stand es darin, als wär er ihm angegossen. Und als es sich aufbückte, erkannte er es im Angesicht und sprach: »Das ist die rechte Braut!« Die Stiefmutter und die beiden Schwestern erschraken und wurden bleich vor Ärger, aber er nahm Aschenputtel aufs Pferd und ritt mit ihm fort. Als sie an dem Haselbäumchen vorbei kamen, riefen die zwei weißen Täubchen:

> »Rucke di guck! rucke di guck!
> kein Blut im Schuck,
> der Schuck ist nicht zu klein,
> die rechte Braut, die führt er heim!«

Und als sie das gerufen, kamen sie beide hergeflogen und setzten sich dem Aschenputtel auf die Schultern, eine rechts, die andere links, und blieben da sitzen.

Als die Hochzeit mit dem Königssohn sollte gehalten werden, kamen die falschen Schwestern, wollten sich einschmeicheln und teil an seinem Glück nehmen. Als es nun zur Kirche ging, war die älteste zur rechten, die jüngste zur linken Seite, da pickten die Tauben einer jeden das eine Auge aus, hernach, als sie herausgingen, war die älteste zur linken und die jüngste zur rechten, da pickten die Tauben einer jeden das andere Auge aus und waren sie also für ihre Bosheit und Falschheit mit Blindheit auf ihr Lebtag gestraft.

1819

Der Meisterdieb

Eines Tages saß vor einem ärmlichen Haus ein alter Mann mit seiner Frau und wollte von der Arbeit ein wenig ausruhen. Da kam auf einmal ein prächtiger, mit vier Rappen bespannter Wagen herbeigefahren, aus dem ein reichgekleideter Herr stieg. Der Bauer stand auf, trat zu dem Herrn und fragte, was sein Verlangen wäre und worin er ihm dienen könnte. Der Fremde reichte dem Alten die Hand und sagte: »Ich wünsche nichts, als einmal ein ländliches Gericht zu genießen. Bereitet mir Kartoffeln, wie Ihr sie zu essen pflegt, dann will ich mich zu Euerm Tisch setzen und sie mit Freude verzehren.« Der Bauer lächelte und sagte: »Ihr seid ein Graf oder Fürst oder gar ein Herzog, vornehme Herrn haben manchmal solch ein Gelüst. Euer Wunsch soll aber erfüllt werden.« Die Frau ging in die Küche, und sie fing an, Kartoffeln zu waschen und zu reiben und wollte Klöße daraus bereiten, wie sie die Bauern essen. Während sie bei der Arbeit stand, sagte der Bauer zu dem Fremden: »Kommt einstweilen mit mir in meinen Hausgarten, wo ich noch etwas zu schaffen habe.«

In dem Garten hatte er Löcher gegraben und wollte jetzt Bäume einsetzen. »Habt Ihr keine Kinder«, fragte der Fremde, »die Euch bei der Arbeit behilflich sein könnten?« – »Nein«, antwortete der Bauer. »Ich habe freilich einen Sohn gehabt«, setzte er hinzu, »aber der ist schon seit langer Zeit in die weite Welt gegangen. Es war ein ungeratener Junge, klug und verschlagen, aber er wollte nichts lernen und machte lauter böse Streiche; zuletzt lief er mir fort, und seitdem habe ich nichts von ihm gehört.« Der Alte nahm ein Bäumchen, setzte es in ein Loch und stieß einen Pfahl daneben; und als er Erde hineingeschaufelt und sie festgestampft hatte, band er den Stamm unten, oben und in der Mitte mit einem Strohseil fest an den Pfahl. »Aber sagt mir«, sprach der Herr, »warum bindet Ihr den krummen, knorrigen Baum, der dort in der Ecke fast bis auf den Boden gebückt liegt, nicht auch an einen Pfahl wie diesen, damit er gerade wächst?« Der Alte lächelte und sagte: »Herr, Ihr redet, wie Ihr's versteht; man sieht wohl, daß Ihr Euch mit der Gärtnerei nicht abgegeben habt. Der Baum dort ist alt und verknorzt, den kann niemand mehr gerad machen. Bäume muß man ziehen, solange sie jung sind«. – »Es ist wie bei Euerm Sohn«, sagte der Fremde, »hättet Ihr den gezogen, wie er noch jung war, so wäre er nicht fortgelaufen; jetzt wird er auch hart und knorzig geworden sein.« – »Freilich«, antwortete der Alte, »es ist schon lange, seit er fortgegangen ist; er wird sich verändert haben.« – »Würdet Ihr ihn noch erkennen, wenn er vor Euch träte?« fragte der Fremde. »Am Gesicht schwerlich«, antwortete der Bauer, »aber er hat ein Zeichen an sich, ein Muttermal auf der Schulter, das wie eine Bohne aussieht.« Als er das gesagt hatte, zog der Fremde den Rock aus, entblößte seine Schulter und zeigte dem Bauern die Bohne. »Herr Gott«, rief der Alte, »du bist wahrhaftig mein Sohn«, und die Liebe zu seinem Kind regte sich in seinem Herzen. »Aber«, setzte er hinzu, »wie kannst du mein Sohn sein, du bist ein großer Herr geworden und lebst in Reichtum und Überfluß? Auf welchem Weg bist du dazu gelangt?« – »Ach, Vater«, erwiderte der Sohn, »der junge Baum war an keinen Pfahl gebunden und ist krumm gewachsen. Jetzt ist er zu alt; er wird nicht wieder gerade. Wie ich das alles erworben habe? Ich bin ein Dieb geworden. Aber erschreckt Euch nicht, ich bin ein Meisterdieb. Für mich gibt es weder Schloß noch Riegel. Wonach mich gelüstet, das ist mein. Glaubt nicht, daß ich stehle wie ein gemeiner Dieb, ich nehme nur vom Überfluß der Reichen. Arme Leute sind sicher: Ich gebe ihnen lieber, als daß ich ihnen etwas nehme. So auch, was ich ohne Mühe, List und Gewandtheit haben kann, das rühre ich nicht an.« – »Ach, mein Sohn«, sagte der Vater, »es gefällt mir doch nicht, ein Dieb bleibt ein Dieb; ich sage dir, es nimmt kein gutes Ende.« Er führte ihn zu der Mutter, und als sie hörte, daß es ihr Sohn war, weinte sie vor Freude. Als er ihr aber sagte, daß er ein Meisterdieb geworden wäre, so flossen ihr zwei Ströme über das Gesicht. Endlich sagte sie: »Wenn er auch ein Dieb geworden ist, so ist er doch mein Sohn, und meine Augen haben ihn noch einmal gesehen.«

Sie setzten sich an den Tisch, und er aß mit seinen Eltern wieder einmal die schlechte Kost, die er lange nicht gegessen hatte. Der Vater sprach: »Wenn unser Herr, der Graf drüben im Schlosse, erfährt, wer du bist und was du treibst, so nimmt er dich nicht auf die Arme und wiegt dich darin, wie er tat, als er dich am Taufstein hielt, sondern er läßt dich am Galgenstrick schaukeln.« – »Seid ohne Sorge, mein Vater, er wird mir nichts tun, denn ich verstehe mein Handwerk. Ich will heute noch selbst zu ihm gehen.«

Als die Abendzeit sich näherte, setzte sich der Meisterdieb in seinen Wagen und fuhr nach dem Schloß. Der Graf empfing ihn mit Artigkeit, weil er ihn für einen vornehmen Mann hielt. Als aber der Fremde sich zu erkennen gab, so erbleichte er und schwieg eine Zeitlang ganz still. Endlich sprach er: »Du bist mein Patenkind, deshalb will ich Gnade für Recht ergehen lassen und nachsichtig mit dir verfahren. Weil du dich rühmst, ein Meisterdieb zu sein, so will ich deine Kunst auf die Probe stellen, wenn du aber nicht bestehst, so mußt du mit des Seilers Tochter Hochzeit halten, und das Gekrächze der Raben soll deine Musik dabei sein.« – »Herr Graf«, antwortete der Meister, »denkt Euch drei Stücke aus, so schwer Ihr wollt, und wenn ich Eure Aufgabe nicht löse, so tut mit mir, wie Euch gefällt.« Der Graf sann einige Augenblicke nach, dann sprach er: »Wohlan, zum ersten sollst du mir mein Leibpferd aus dem Stall stehlen, zum andern sollst du mir und meiner Gemahlin, wenn wir eingeschlafen sind, das Bettuch unter dem Leib wegnehmen, ohne daß wir's merken, und dazu meiner Gemahlin den Trauring vom Finger; zum dritten und letzten sollst du mir den Pfarrer und Küster aus der Kirche wegstehlen. Merke dir alles wohl, denn es geht dir an den Hals.«

Der Meister begab sich in die zunächstliegende Stadt. Dort kaufte er einer alten Bauersfrau die Kleider ab und zog sie an. Dann färbte er sich das Gesicht braun und malte sich noch Runzeln hinein, so daß ihn kein Mensch wiedererkannt hätte. Endlich füllte er ein Fäßchen mit altem Ungarwein, in welchen ein starker Schlaftrunk gemischt war. Das Fäßchen legte er auf eine Kiepe, die er auf den Rücken nahm, und ging mit bedächtigen, schwankenden Schritten zu dem Schloß des Grafen. Es war schon dunkel, als er anlangte; er setzte sich in dem Hof auf einen Stein, fing an zu husten wie eine alte, brustkranke Frau und rieb die Hände, als wenn er fröre. Vor der Türe des Pferdestalls lagen Soldaten um ein Feuer. Einer von ihnen bemerkte die Frau und rief ihr zu: »Komm näher, altes Mütterchen, und wärme dich bei uns. Du hast doch kein Nachtlager und nimmst es an, wo du es findest.« Die Alte trippelte herbei, bat, ihr die Kiepe vom Rücken zu heben, und setzte sich zu ihnen ans Feuer. »Was hast du da in deinem Fäßchen, du alte Schachtel?« fragte einer. »Einen guten Schluck Wein«, antwortete sie, »ich ernähre mich mit dem Handel, für Geld und gute Worte gebe ich euch gerne ein Glas.« – »Nur her damit«, sagte der Soldat, und als er ein Glas gekostet hatte, rief er: »Wenn der Wein gut ist, so trink ich lieber ein Glas mehr«, ließ sich nochmals einschenken, und die andern folgten seinem Beispiel. »Heda, Kameraden«, rief einer denen zu, die in dem Stall saßen, »hier ist ein Mütterchen, das hat Wein, der so alt ist wie sie selber, nehmt auch einen Schluck, der wärmt euch den Magen noch besser als unser Feuer.« Die Alte trug ihr Fäßchen in den Stall. Einer hatte sich auf das gesattelte Leibpferd gesetzt, ein anderer hielt den Zaum in der Hand, ein dritter hatte den Schwanz gepackt. Sie schenkte ein, soviel verlangt ward, bis die Quelle versiegte. Nicht lange, so fiel dem einen der Zaum aus der Hand, er sank nieder und fing an zu schnarchen, der andere ließ den Schwanz los, legte sich nieder und schnarchte noch lauter. Der, welcher im Sattel saß, blieb zwar sitzen, bog sich aber mit dem Kopf fast bis auf den Hals des Pferdes, schlief und blies mit dem Mund wie ein Schmiedebalg. Die Soldaten draußen waren schon längst eingeschlafen, lagen auf der Erde und regten sich nicht, als wären sie von Stein. Als der Meisterdieb sah, daß es ihm geglückt war, gab er dem einen statt des Zaums ein Seil in die Hand und dem andern, der den Schwanz gehalten hatte, einen Strohwisch; aber was sollte er mit dem, der auf dem Rücken des Pferdes saß, anfangen? Herunterwerfen wollte er ihn nicht, er hätte erwachen und ein Geschrei erheben können. Er wußte aber guten Rat, er schnallte die Sattelgurte auf, knüpfte ein paar Seile, die in Ringen an der Wand hingen, an den Sattel fest und zog den schlafenden Reiter mit dem Sattel in die Höhe, dann schlug er die Seile um den Pfosten und machte sie fest. Das Pferd hatte er bald von der Kette losgebunden, aber wenn er über das steinerne Pflaster des Hofs geritten wäre, so hätte man den Lärm im Schloß gehört. Er umwickelte ihm also zuvor die Hufe mit alten Lappen, führte es dann vorsichtig hinaus, schwang sich auf und jagte davon.

Als der Tag angebrochen war, sprengte der Meister auf dem gestohlenen Pferd zu dem Schloß. Der Graf war eben aufgestanden und blickte aus dem Fenster. »Guten Morgen, Herr Graf«, rief er ihm zu, »hier ist das Pferd, das ich glücklich aus dem Stall geholt habe. Schaut nur, wie schön Eure Soldaten da liegen und schlafen, und wenn Ihr in den Stall gehen wollt, so werdet Ihr sehen, wie bequem sich's Eure Wächter gemacht haben.« Der Graf mußte lachen, dann sprach er: »Einmal ist dir's gelungen, aber das zweite Mal wird's nicht so glücklich ablaufen. Und ich warne dich, wenn du mir als Dieb begegnest, so behandle ich dich auch wie einen Dieb.« Als die Gräfin abends zu Bette gegangen war, schloß sie die Hand mit dem Trauring fest zu, und der Graf sagte: »Alle Türen sind verschlossen und verriegelt, ich bleibe wach und will den Dieb erwarten. Steigt er aber zum Fenster ein, so schieße ich ihn nieder.«

Der Meisterdieb aber ging in der Dunkelheit hinaus zu dem Galgen, schnitt einen armen Sünder, der da hing, von dem Strick ab und trug ihn auf dem Rücken nach dem Schloß. Dort stellte er eine Leiter an das Schlafgemach, setzte den Toten auf seine Schultern und fing an hinaufzusteigen. Als er so hoch gekommen war, daß der Kopf des Toten in dem Fenster erschien, drückte der Graf, der in seinem Bett lauerte, eine Pistole auf ihn los; alsbald ließ der Meister den armen Sünder herabfallen, sprang selbst die Leiter herab, und versteckte sich in einer Ecke. Die Nacht war von dem Mond so weit erhellt, daß der Meister deutlich sehen konnte,

wie der Graf aus dem Fenster auf die Leiter stieg, herabkam und den Toten in den Garten trug. Dort fing er an, ein Loch zu graben, in das er ihn legen wollte. Jetzt, dachte der Dieb, ist der günstige Augenblick gekommen, schlich behende aus seinem Winkel und stieg die Leiter hinauf, geradezu ins Schlafgemach der Gräfin. »Liebe Frau«, fing er mit der Stimme des Grafen an, »der Dieb ist tot, aber er ist doch mein Patenkind und mehr ein Schelm als ein Bösewicht gewesen. Ich will ihn der öffentlichen Schande nicht preisgeben; auch mit den armen Eltern habe ich Mitleid. Ich will ihn, bevor der Tag anbricht, selbst im Garten begraben, damit die Sache nicht ruchbar wird. Gib mir das Bettuch, so will ich die Leiche einhüllen und ihn wie einen Hund verscharren.« Die Gräfin gab ihm das Tuch. »Weißt du was«, sagte der Dieb weiter, »ich habe eine Anwandlung von Großmut, gib mir noch den Ring; der Unglückliche hat sein Leben gewagt, so mag er ihn ins Grab mitnehmen.« Sie wollte dem Grafen nicht entgegen sein, und obgleich sie es ungern tat, so zog sie doch den Ring vom Finger und reichte ihn hin. Der Dieb machte sich mit beiden Stücken fort und kam glücklich nach Haus, bevor der Graf im Garten mit seiner Totengräberarbeit fertig war.

Was zog der Graf für ein langes Gesicht, als am andern Morgen der Meister kam und ihm das Bettuch und den Ring brachte. »Kannst du hexen?« sagte er zu ihm. »Wer hat dich aus dem Grab geholt, in das ich selbst dich gelegt habe, und hat dich wieder lebendig gemacht?« – »Mich habt Ihr nicht begraben«, sagte der Dieb, »sondern den armen Sünder am Galgen«, und erzählte ausführlich, wie es zugegangen war; der Graf mußte ihm zugestehen, daß er ein gescheiter und listiger Dieb wäre. »Aber noch bist du nicht zu Ende«, setzte er hinzu, »du hast noch die dritte Aufgabe zu lösen, und wenn dir das nicht gelingt, so hilft dir alles nichts.« Der Meister lächelte und gab keine Antwort.

Als die Nacht angebrochen war, kam er mit einem langen Sack auf dem Rücken, einem Bündel unter dem Arm und einer Laterne in der Hand zu der Dorfkirche gegangen. In dem Sack hatte er Krebse, in dem Bündel aber kurze Wachslichter. Er setzte sich auf den Gottesacker, holte einen Krebs heraus und klebte ihm ein Wachslichtchen auf den Rücken; dann zündete er das Lichtchen an, setzte den Krebs auf den Boden und ließ ihn kriechen. Er holte einen zweiten aus dem Sack, machte es mit diesem ebenso und fuhr fort, bis auch der letzte aus dem Sack war.

Hierauf zog er ein langes schwarzes Gewand an, das wie eine Mönchskutte aussah, und klebte sich einen grauen Bart an das Kinn. Als er endlich ganz unkenntlich war, nahm er den Sack, in dem die Krebse gewesen waren, ging in die Kirche und stieg auf die Kanzel. Die Turmuhr schlug eben zwölf. Als der letzte Schlag verklungen war, rief er mit lauter, gellender Stimme: »Hört an, ihr sündigen Menschen, das Ende aller Dinge ist gekommen, der Jüngste Tag ist nahe: hört an, hört an. Wer mit mir in den Himmel will, der krieche in den Sack. Ich bin Petrus, der die Himmelstüre öffnet und schließt. Seht ihr, draußen auf dem Gottesacker wandeln die Gestorbenen und sammeln ihre Gebeine zusammen. Kommt, kommt und kriecht in den Sack, die Welt geht unter.«

Das Geschrei erschallte durch das ganze Dorf. Der Pfarrer und der Küster, die zunächst an der Kirche wohnten, hatten es zuerst vernommen, und als sie die Lichter erblickten, die auf dem Gottesacker umherwandelten, merkten sie, daß etwas Ungewöhnliches vorging, und traten in die Kirche ein. Sie hörten der Predigt eine Weile zu, da stieß der Küster den Pfarrer an und sprach: »Es wäre nicht übel, wenn wir die Gelegenheit benutzten und zusammen vor dem Einbruch des Jüngsten Tags auf eine leichte Art in den Himmel kämen.« – »Freilich«, erwiderte der Pfarrer, »das sind auch meine Gedanken gewesen; habt Ihr Lust, so wollen wir uns auf den Weg machen.« – »Ja«, antwortete der Küster, »aber Ihr, Herr Pfarrer, habt den Vortritt, ich folge nach.« Der Pfarrer schritt also vor und stieg auf die Kanzel, wo der Meister den Sack öffnete. Der Pfarrer kroch zuerst hinein, dann der Küster. Gleich band der Meister den Sack fest zu, packte ihn am Bausch und schleifte ihn die Kanzeltreppe hinab. Sooft die Köpfe der beiden Toren auf die Stufen aufschlugen, rief er: »Jetzt geht's schon über die Berge.« Dann zog er sie auf gleiche Weise durch das Dorf, und wenn sie durch Pfützen kamen, rief er: »Jetzt geht's schon durch die nassen Wolken«, und als er sie endlich die Schloßtreppe hinaufzog, so rief er: »Jetzt sind wir auf der Himmelstreppe und werden bald im Vorhof sein.« Als er oben angelangt war, schob er den Sack in den Taubenschlag, und als die Tauben flatterten, sagte er: »Hört ihr, wie die Engel sich freuen und mit den Fittichen schlagen?« Dann schob er den Riegel vor und ging fort. Am andern Morgen begab er sich zu dem Grafen und sagte ihm, daß er auch die dritte Aufgabe gelöst und den Pfarrer und Küster aus der Kirche weggeführt hätte. »Wo hast du sie gelassen?« fragte der Herr. »Sie liegen in einem Sack oben auf dem Taubenschlag und bilden sich ein, sie wären im Himmel.« Der Graf stieg selbst hinauf und überzeugte sich, daß er die Wahrheit gesagt hatte. Als er den Pfarrer und Küster aus dem Gefängnis befreit hatte, sprach er: »Du bist ein Erzdieb und hast deine Sache gewonnen. Für diesmal kommst du mit heiler Haut davon, aber mache, daß du aus meinem Land fortkommst, denn wenn du es erneut betreten solltest, so kannst du auf deine Erhöhung am Galgen rechnen.«

Der Erzdieb nahm Abschied von seinen Eltern, ging wieder in die weite Welt, und niemand hat wieder etwas von ihm gehört. 1843

Hurleburlebutz

Ein König verirrte sich auf der Jagd, da trat ein kleines weißes Männchen vor ihn: »Herr König, wenn Ihr mir Eure jüngste Tochter geben wollt, so will ich Euch wieder aus dem Wald führen.« Der König sagte es in seiner Angst zu, das Männchen brachte ihn auf den Weg, nahm dann Abschied und rief noch nach: »In acht Tagen komm ich und hol meine Braut.«

Daheim aber war der König traurig über sein Versprechen, denn die jüngste Tochter hatte er am liebsten; das sahen ihm die Prinzessinnen an und wollten wissen, was ihm Kummer mache. Da mußt' er's endlich gestehen, er habe die jüngste von ihnen einem kleinen weißen Waldmännchen versprochen, und das komme in acht Tagen und hole sie ab. Sie sprachen aber, er solle guten Muts sein, das Männchen wollten sie schon anführen. Danach, als der Tag kam, kleideten sie eine Kuhhirtstochter mit ihren Kleidern an, setzten sie in ihre Stube und befahlen ihr: »Wenn jemand kommt und will dich abholen, so gehst du mit!« Sie selber aber gingen alle aus dem Hause fort.

Kaum waren sie weg, so kam ein Fuchs in das Schloß und sagte zu dem Mädchen: »Setz dich auf meinen rauhen Schwanz, Hurleburlebutz! Hinaus in den Wald!« Das Mädchen setzte sich dem Fuchs auf den Schwanz, und so trug er es hinaus in den Wald.

Wie sie aber auf einen schönen grünen Platz kamen, wo die Sonne recht hell und warm schien, sagte der Fuchs: »Steig ab und laus mich!« Das Mädchen gehorchte, der Fuchs legte seinen Kopf auf ihren Schoß und ward gelaust; bei der Arbeit sprach das Mädchen: »Gestern um die Zeit war's doch schöner in dem Wald!« – »Wie bist du in den Wald gekommen?« fragte der Fuchs. »Ei, da hab ich mit meinem Vater die Kühe gehütet.« – »Also bist du nicht die Prinzessin! Setz dich auf meinen rauhen Schwanz, Hurleburlebutz! Zurück in das Schloß!«

Da trug sie der Fuchs zurück und sagte zum König: »Du hast mich betrogen, das ist eine Kuhhirtstochter, in acht Tagen komm ich wieder und hol mir deine.« Am achten Tag aber kleideten die Prinzessinnen eine Gänsehirtstochter prächtig an, setzten sie hin und gingen fort. Da kam der Fuchs wieder und sprach: »Setz dich auf meinen rauhen Schwanz, Hurleburlebutz! Hinaus in den Wald!« Wie sie in dem Wald auf den sonnigen Platz kamen, sagte der Fuchs wieder: »Steig ab und laus mich!« Und als das Mädchen den Fuchs lauste, seufzte es und sprach: »Wo mögen jetzt meine Gänse sein!« – »Was weißt du von Gänsen?« – »Ei, die hab ich alle Tage mit meinem Vater auf die Wiesen getrieben.« – »Also bist du nicht des Königs Tochter! Setz dich auf meinen rauhen Schwanz, Hurleburlebutz! Zurück in das Schloß!«

Der Fuchs trug sie zurück und sagte zum König: »Du hast mich wieder betrogen, das ist eine Gänsehirtstochter, in acht Tagen komm ich noch einmal, und wenn du mir dann deine Tochter nicht gibst, so soll dir's übel gehen.« Dem König ward angst, und wie der Fuchs wiederkam, gab er ihm die Prinzessin. »Setz dich auf meinen rauhen Schwanz, Hurleburlebutz! Hinaus in den Wald!« Da mußte sie auf dem Schwanz des Fuchses hinausreiten, und als sie auf den Platz im Sonnenschein kamen, sprach er auch zu ihr: »Steig ab und laus mich!« Als er ihr aber seinen Kopf auf den Schoß legte, fing die Prinzessin an zu weinen und sagte: »Ich bin eines Königs Tochter und soll einen Fuchs lausen, säß ich jetzt daheim in meiner Kammer, so könnt ich meine Blumen im Garten sehen!« Da hörte der Fuchs, daß er die rechte Braut hatte, verwandelte sich in das kleine weiße Männchen, und das war nun ihr Mann, bei dem mußt' sie in einer kleinen Hütte wohnen, ihm kochen und nähen, und es dauerte eine gute Zeit.

Das Männchen aber tat ihr alles zuliebe.

Einmal sagte das Männchen zu ihr: »Ich muß fortgehen, aber es werden bald drei weiße Tauben geflogen kommen, die werden ganz niedrig über die Erde hinstreifen, davon fang die mittlere, und wenn du sie hast, schneid ihr gleich den Kopf ab, hüt dich aber, daß du keine andere ergreifst als die mittlere, sonst entsteht ein groß Unglück daraus.«

Das Männchen ging fort; es dauerte auch nicht lang, so kamen drei weiße Tauben dahergeflogen. Die Prinzessin gab acht, ergriff die mittlere, nahm ein Messer und schnitt ihr den Kopf ab. Kaum aber lag der auf dem Boden, so stand ein schöner junger Prinz vor ihr und sprach: »Mich hat eine Fee verzaubert, sieben Jahr lang sollt' ich meine Gestalt verlieren und sodann als eine Taube an meiner Gemahlin vorbeifliegen, zwischen zwei andern, da müsse sie mich fangen und mir den Kopf abhauen, und fange sie mich nicht oder eine unrechte und ich sei einmal vorbeigeflogen, so sei alles vorbei und keine Erlösung mehr möglich; darum hab ich dich gebeten, ja recht achtzuhaben, denn ich bin das graue Männlein und du meine Gemahlin.« Da war die Prinzessin vergnügt, und sie gingen zusammen zu ihrem Vater, und als der starb, erbten sie das Reich. 1812

Die vier kunstreichen Brüder

Es war ein armer Mann, der hatte vier Söhne. Wie die nun herangewachsen waren, sprach er zu ihnen: »Liebe Kinder, ihr müßt in die Welt, ich habe nichts, das ich euch geben könnte, macht euch auf in die Fremde, lernt ein Handwerk und seht, wie ihr euch durchschlagt.« Da ergriffen die vier Brüder den Wanderstab, nahmen Abschied von ihrem Vater und zogen zusammen zum Tor hinaus. Als sie ein Stück Wegs gemacht hatten, kamen sie an einen Kreuzweg, der nach vier verschiedenen Gegenden führte. Da sprach der älteste: »Hier müssen wir uns trennen, aber heut über vier Jahre wollen wir uns an dieser Stelle wieder treffen und in der Zeit unser Glück versuchen.«

Nun ging jeder seinen Weg, und dem ältesten begegnete ein Mann, der fragte ihn, wo er hinaus wollte und was er vorhätte. »Ich will ein Handwerk lernen«, antwortete er. Da sprach der Mann: »Geh mit mir und werde ein Dieb.« – »Nein«, antwortete er, »das ist jetzt kein ehrliches Handwerk mehr und das End vom Lied, daß einer als Schwengel in der Feldglocke gebraucht wird.« – »Oh«, sprach der Mann, »vor dem Galgen brauchst du dich nicht zu fürchten, ich will dich bloß lehren, das zu holen, was sonst kein Mensch kriegen kann und wo dir niemand auf die Spur kommt.« Da ließ er sich überreden und ward bei dem Mann ein gelernter Dieb und so geschickt, daß vor ihm nichts sicher war, was er einmal haben wollte. Der zweite Bruder begegnete einem Mann, der dieselbe Frage an ihn tat, was er in der Welt lernen wolle. »Ich weiß es noch nicht«, antwortete er. »So geh mit mir und werde ein Sterngucker, nichts besser als das, es bleibt einem nichts verborgen.« Er ließ sich das gefallen und ward ein so geschickter Sterngucker, daß sein Meister, als er ausgelernt hatte und weiter ziehen wollte, ihm ein Glas gab und zu ihm sprach: »Damit kannst du sehen, was auf Erden und am Himmel vorgeht, und kann dir nichts verborgen bleiben.« Der dritte Bruder begegnete einem Jäger, der nahm ihn mit in die Lehre und gab ihm in allem, was zur Jägerei gehörte, so guten Unterricht, daß er ein ausgelernter Jäger ward. Der Meister schenkte ihm beim Abschied eine Büchse und sprach: »Die fehlt nicht, was du damit aufs Korn nimmst, das triffst du auch.« Der jüngste Bruder begegnete gleichfalls einem Manne, der ihn anredete und nach seinem Vorhaben fragte. »Hast du nicht Lust, ein Schneider zu werden?« – »Ach nein«, sprach der Junge, »das Krummsitzen von morgens bis abends, das Hin- und Herfegen mit der Nadel und das Bügeleisen will mir nicht in den Sinn.« – »Ei was«, antwortete der Mann, »bei mir lernst du eine ganz andere Schneiderkunst.«

Da ließ er sich überreden, ging mit und lernte die Kunst des Mannes aus dem Fundament.

Beim Abschied gab ihm dieser eine Nadel und sprach: »Damit kannst du zusammennähen, was dir vorkommt, es sei so weich wie ein Ei oder so hart wie Stahl, und es wird so zu einem Stück, daß keine Naht mehr zu sehen ist.«

Zu der bestimmten Zeit, nach Jahresfrist, kamen die vier Brüder an dem Kreuzwege zusammen, herzten und küßten sich und kehrten heim zu ihrem Vater. Sie erzählten ihm, wie es ihnen ergangen wäre und daß jeder das seinige gelernt hätte. Nun saßen sie gerade vor dem Haus unter einem großen Baum, da sprach der Vater: »Ich will euch einmal versuchen und sehen, was ihr könnt.« Danach schaute er auf und sagte zu dem zweiten Sohn: »Oben im Gipfel dieses Baums sitzt ein Buchfinkennest, sag mir doch, wieviel Eier liegen darin?« Der Sterngucker nahm sein Glas, schaute hinauf und sprach: »Fünf liegen darin.« – »Jetzt«, sagte der Vater zum ältesten, »holst du die Eier, ohne daß der Vogel, der darauf sitzt und brütet, gestört wird.« Der kunstfertige Dieb stieg hinauf und nahm dem Vöglein, das gar nichts davon merkte und ruhig sitzen blieb, die fünf Eier unter dem Leib weg und brachte sie dem Vater herab. Der Vater nahm sie, legte an jede Ecke des Tisches eins und das fünfte in die Mitte und sprach zum Jäger: »Du schießest mir mit einem Schuß die fünf Eier in der Mitte entzwei.« Der Jäger legte seine Büchse an und schoß die Eier, wie's der Vater verlangt hatte, alle fünf, und zwar in einem Schuß. »Nun kommt die Reihe an dich«, sprach dieser zu dem vierten Sohn; »du nähst die Eier wieder zusammen und auch die jungen Vöglein, die darin sind, so daß ihnen der Schuß nichts schadet.« Der Schneider holte seine Nadel und nähte nach Vorschrift. Als er fertig war, mußte der Dieb sie wieder auf den Baum ins Nest tragen und dem Vogel, ohne daß er etwas gewahr ward, wieder unterlegen. Das Tierchen brütete sie vollends aus, und nach ein paar Tagen krochen die Jungen hervor und hatten da, wo der Schneider sie zusammengenäht, ein rot Streifchen um den Hals.

»Ja«, sprach der Alte zu seinen Söhnen, »ihr habt eure Zeit wohl benutzt und was Rechtschaffenes gelernt, ich kann nicht sagen, wem von euch der Vorzug gebührt. Wenn ihr nur eure Kunst bald anwenden könnt!« Nicht lang danach kam ein großer Lärm ins Land, die Königstochter wär von einem Drachen entführt. Der König war Tag und Nacht darüber in Sorgen und ließ bekannt machen: Wer sie zurückbrächte, sollte sie zur Gemahlin haben. Die vier Brüder sprachen untereinander: »Das wäre eine Gelegenheit, wo wir uns könnten sehen lassen«, und beschlossen, die Königstochter zu befreien. »Wo sie ist, will ich bald wissen«, sprach der Sterngucker, schaute durch sein Glas und sprach: »Ich sehe sie, sie sitzt weit von hier, auf einem Felsen im Meer, bei dem Drachen, der sie hütet.« Da ging er zu dem König und bat ihn um ein Schiff für sich und seine Brüder und fuhr mit ihnen fort und über das Meer, bis sie zur Stätte hinkamen. Die Königstochter saß da, und der Drache lag in ihrem Schoß und schlief.

Der Jäger sprach: »Ich darf ihn nicht schießen, ich würde die schöne Jungfrau zugleich töten.« – »So will ich mein Heil versuchen«, sagte der Dieb und stahl sie unter dem Drachen weg, so leis und behend, daß das Untier nichts merkte, son-

dern fortschnarchte. Sie eilten voll Freude mit ihr aufs Schiff und segelten in das Meer hinein.

Da kam der Drache, der wach geworden war und die Königstochter nicht mehr gefunden hatte, wütend hinter ihnen her durch die Luft geschnaubt. Als er eben über dem Schiff war und sich herablassen wollte, da legte der Jäger seine Büchse an und schoß ihm gerade ins Herz, daß er tot herabfiel. Es war aber ein so gewaltiges Untier, daß es im Herabfallen das ganze Schiff zertrümmerte und sie nur noch auf ein paar Brettern in der offenen See schwammen. Da war der Schneider nicht faul, nahm seine wunderbare Nadel, nähte sich mit ein paar großen Stichen einige Bretter zusammen, setzte sich darauf, schiffte hin und sammelte alle Stücke des Schiffs. Dann nähte er sie so behend zusammen, daß gar bald das Schiff wieder segelfertig war und sie glücklich heimfahren konnten.

Als sie dem König seine Tochter wiederbrachten, da war große Freude, und er sprach zu den vier Brüdern: »Einer von euch soll sie zur Gemahlin haben, aber welcher das ist, macht unter euch aus.« Da entstand Streit unter ihnen, und der Sterngucker sprach: »Hätte ich nicht die Königstochter gesehen, so wären alle eure Künste für nichts gewesen, darum ist sie mein.« Der Dieb sprach: »Was hätte das Sehen geholfen, wenn ich sie nicht unter dem Drachen weggenommen hätte, darum ist sie mein.« Der Jäger sprach: »Ihr wärt doch samt der Königstochter von dem Untier zerrissen worden, wenn ich es nicht getötet hätte, darum ist sie mein.« Der Schneider sprach: »Und hätte ich euch mit meiner Kunst nicht das Schiff wieder zusammengebracht, ihr wärt alle jämmerlich ertrunken, darum ist sie mein.«

Da tat der König den Ausspruch: »Jeder von euch hat recht, und weil ein jeder die Jungfrau nicht haben kann, so soll sie keiner von euch haben; aber ich will jedem zur Belohnung ein halbes Königreich geben.« Da sprachen die Brüder: »Es ist auch besser, als daß wir uneins werden.« Der König gab jedem ein halbes Königreich, und sie lebten mit ihrem Vater in aller Glückseligkeit. 1819

Die kluge Bauerntochter

Es war einmal ein armer Bauer, der hatte kein Land, nur ein kleines Häuschen und eine einzige Tochter, da sprach die Tochter: »Wir sollten den Herrn König um ein Stückchen Rodland bitten.« Da der König von ihrer Armut hörte, schenkte er ihnen auch ein Eckchen Rasen, den hackten sie und ihr Vater um und wollten ein wenig Korn und derart Frucht säen; und als sie ihn beinah herum hatten, da fanden sie in der Erde einen Mörser von purem Gold. »Hör«, sagte der Vater zu dem Mädchen, »weil unser Herr König so gnädig ist gewesen und hat uns diesen Acker geschenkt, so müssen wir ihm den Mörser wiedergeben.« Die Tochter aber wollt' es nicht bewilligen und sagte: »Vater, wenn wir den Mörser haben und haben den Stößer nicht, dann müssen wir auch den Stößer schaffen, darum schweigt lieber still.« Er wollt' ihr aber nicht gehorchen, nahm den Mörser, trug ihn zum Herrn König und sagte, den hätt' er gefunden in der Heide. Der König nahm den Mörser und fragte, ob er nichts mehr gefunden? »Nein«, sprach der Bauer; da sagte der König, er sollte nun auch den Stößer herbeischaffen. Der Bauer sprach, den hätten sie nicht gefunden. Aber das half ihm soviel, als hätt' er's in den Wind gesagt, er ward ins Gefängnis gesetzt und sollte so lange da sitzen, bis er den Stößer herbeigeschafft hätte. Die Bedienten mußten ihm täglich Wasser und Brot bringen, was man so in dem Gefängnis kriegt, da hörten sie, wie der Mann alsfort schrie: »Ach! hätt' ich auf meine Tochter gehört! Ach, ach hätt' ich auf meine Tochter gehört!« Da gingen die Bedienten zum König und sprachen das, wie der Gefangene alsfort schrie: »Ach! hätt' ich doch auf meine Tochter gehört!« und wollte nicht essen und nicht trinken. Da befahl er den Bedienten, sie sollten ihn vor ihn bringen, und fragte der Herr König, warum er immerfort schreie: »Ach! hätt' ich auf meine Tochter gehört!« – »Was hat Eure Tochter denn gesagt?« – »Ja, sie hat gesprochen, ich sollt' den Mörser nicht bringen, sonst müßt' ich auch den Stößer schaffen.« – »Habt Ihr denn so eine kluge Tochter, so laßt sie einmal herkommen.« Also mußte sie vor den König kommen; der fragte sie, ob sie denn so klug wäre? Und sagte, er wollt' ihr ein Rätsel aufgeben, wenn sie das treffen könnte, dann wollt' er sie heiraten. Da sprach sie ja, sie wollt's erraten. Da sagte der König: »Komm zu mir, nicht gekleidet, nicht nackend, nicht geritten, nicht gefahren, nicht in dem Weg, nicht außer dem Weg, und wenn du das kannst, will ich dich heiraten.« Da ging sie hin, und zog sich aus splitternackend, da war sie nicht gekleidet, nahm ein großes Fischgarn und setzte sich hinein und wickelte sich hinein, da war sie nicht nackend, und borgte einen Esel fürs Geld und band dem Esel das Fischgarn an den Schwanz, daran er sie fortschleppen mußte, und war das nicht geritten und nicht gefahren, und mußte sie der Esel in der Fahrspur schleppen, so daß sie nur mit der großen Zehe auf die Erde kam, und war das nicht in dem Weg und nicht außer dem Weg. Und wie sie so daher kam, sagte der König, sie hätte das Rätsel getroffen und sei alles erfüllt. Da ließ er ihren Vater los aus dem Gefängnis und nahm sie zu sich als seine Gemahlin und befahl ihr das ganze königliche Gut an.

Nun waren etliche Jahre herum, als der Herr König einmal auf die Parade zog. Da trug es sich zu, daß Bauern mit ihren Wagen vor dem Schloß hielten, die hatten Holz verkauft; etliche mit Ochsen und etliche mit Pferden. Da war ein Bauer, der hatte drei Pferde, davon kriegte eines ein junges Füllchen, das lief weg und legte sich an einen Wagen, wo zwei Ochsen davor waren, mittendrein. Als nun die Bauern zusammenkamen, fingen sie an sich zu zanken, schmeißen und lärmen, und der Ochsenbauer wollte das Füllchen behalten und sagte, die Ochsen hätten's gehabt, und der andere sagte, nein, seine Pferde hätten's gehabt, und es wär sein. Der Zank kam vor den König, und der tat den Ausspruch: Wo das Füllen gelegen hätte, da sollt' es bleiben, und also bekam's der Ochsenbauer, dem's doch nicht gehörte. Da ging der andere weg, weinte und lamentierte über sein Füllchen. Nun hatte er gehört, daß die Frau Königin so gnädig sei, weil sie auch von armen Bauersleuten gekommen wäre, ging zu ihr und bat sie, ob sie ihm nicht helfen könnte, daß er sein Füllchen wieder bekäme. Sagte sie: »Ja, wenn Ihr mir versprecht, daß Ihr mich nicht verraten wollt, will ich's Euch sagen: Morgen früh, wenn der König auf der Wachtparade ist, stellt Euch hin mitten in die Straße, wo er vorbeikommen muß, nehmt ein großes Fischgarn und tut, als fischtet Ihr, und fischt also fort und schüttet es aus, als wenn Ihr's voll hättet«, und sagte ihm auch, was er antworten sollte, wenn er vom König gefragt würde. Also stand der Bauer am andern Tag da und fischte auf einem trockenen Platz. Wie der König vorbeikam und das sah, schickte er seinen Läufer hin, der sollte fragen, was der närrische Mann vorhabe. Da gab er zur Antwort: »Ich fische.« Fragte der Läufer, wie er fischen könnte, es wär ja kein Wasser da. Sagte der Bauer: »So gut als zwei Ochsen können ein Füllen kriegen, so gut kann ich auch auf dem trockenen Platz fischen.« Da ging der Läufer hin und brachte dem König die Antwort, da ließ er den Bauer vor sich kommen und sagte ihm, das hätte er nicht von sich, von wem er das hätte? Und sollt's gleich bekennen. Der Bauer aber wollt's nicht tun und sagte immer, Gott bewahr! Er hätt' es von sich. Sie banden ihn aber auf ein Gebund Stroh und schlugen und drangsalten ihn so lange, bis er's bekannte, daß er's von der Frau Königin hätte.

Als der König nach Haus kam, sagte er zu seiner Frau: »Warum bist du so falsch mit mir, ich will dich nicht mehr zur Gemahlin, deine Zeit ist um, geh wieder hin, woher du gekommen bist, in dein Bauernhäuschen.« Doch erlaubte er ihr eins: Sie sollte sich das Liebste und Beste mitnehmen, was sie wüßte, und das sollte ihr Abschied sein. Sie sagte: »Ja, lieber Mann, wenn du's so befiehlst, will ich es auch tun.« Und fiel über ihn her und küßte ihn und sprach, sie wollte Abschied von ihm nehmen. Dann ließ sie einen starken Schlaftrunk kommen, Abschied mit ihm zu trinken. Der König tat einen großen Zug, sie aber trank nur ein wenig, da geriet er bald in einen tiefen Schlaf. Und als sie das sah, rief sie einen Bedienten und nahm ein schönes weißes Linnentuch und schlug ihn da hinein, und die Bedienten mußten ihn in einen Wagen vor der Türe tragen, und fuhr sie ihn heim in ihr

Häuschen. Da legte sie ihn auf ihr Bettchen, und er schlief Tag und Nacht in einem fort, und als er aufwachte, sah er sich um und sagte: »Ach, Gott! Wo bin ich denn?«, rief seinen Bedienten, aber es war keiner da. Endlich kam seine Frau vors Bett und sagte: »Lieber Herr König, Ihr habt mir befohlen, ich sollte das Liebste und Beste aus dem Schloß mitnehmen, nun hab ich nichts Besseres und Lieberes als dich, da hab ich dich mitgenommen.« Der König sagte: »Liebe Frau, du sollst mein sein und ich dein«, und nahm sie wieder mit ins königliche Schloß und ließ sich aufs neue mit ihr vermählen, und werden ja wohl noch auf heutigen Tag leben.   1819

Jorinde und Joringel

Es war einmal ein altes Schloß mitten in einem großen, dicken Wald, darinnen wohnte eine alte Frau ganz allein, das war eine Erzzauberin. Am Tage machte sie sich zur Katze oder zur Nachteule, des Abends aber wurde sie wieder ordentlich wie ein Mensch gestaltet. Sie konnte das Wild und die Vögel herbeilocken, und dann schlachtete sie's, kochte und briet es. Wenn jemand auf hundert Schritte dem Schloß nahe kam, so mußte er stille stehn und konnte sich nicht von der Stelle bewegen, bis sie ihn lossprach; wenn aber eine keusche Jungfrau in diesen Kreis kam, so verwandelte sie dieselbe in einen Vogel und sperrte sie dann in einen Korb ein, in die Kammern des Schlosses. Sie hatte wohl siebentausend solcher Körbe mit so raren Vögeln im Schlosse.

Nun war einmal eine Jungfrau, die hieß Jorinde; sie war schöner als alle anderen Mädchen. Die und ein gar schöner Jüngling namens Joringel hatten sich zusammen versprochen. Sie waren in den Brauttagen, und sie hatten ihr größtes Vergnügen eins am andern. Damit sie nun einsmalen vertraut zusammen reden könnten, gingen sie in den Wald spazieren. »Hüte dich«, sagte Joringel, »daß du nicht so nahe ans Schloß kommst!« Es war ein schöner Abend, die Sonne schien zwischen den Stämmen der Bäume hell ins dunkle Grün des Waldes, und die Turteltaube sang kläglich auf den alten Maibuchen.

Jorinde weinte zuweilen, setzte sich hin im Sonnenschein und klagte. Joringel klagte auch; sie waren so bestürzt, als wenn sie hätten sterben sollen. Sie sahen sich um, waren irre und wußten nicht, wohin sie nach Hause gehen sollten. Noch halb stand die Sonne über dem Berg, und halb war sie unter; Joringel sah durchs Gebüsch und sah die alte Mauer des Schlosses nah bei sich, er erschrak und wurde todbang. Jorinde sang:

> »Mein Vöglein mit dem Ringlein rot
> singt Leide, Leide, Leide.
> Es singt dem Täublein seinen Tod,
> singt Leide, Lei-zicküt! Zicküt! Zicküt!«

Joringel sah nach Jorinde. Jorinde war in eine Nachtigall verwandelt, die sang Zicküt! Zicküt! Eine Nachteule mit glühenden Augen flog dreimal um sie herum und schrie dreimal Schu – hu – hu – hu! Joringel konnte sich nicht regen; er stand da wie ein Stein, konnte nicht weinen, nicht reden, nicht Hand noch Fuß regen. Nun war die Sonne unter. Die Eule flog in einen Strauch, und gleich darauf kam eine alte, krumme Frau aus diesem hervor, gelb und mager, große rote Augen, krumme Nase, die mit der Spitze ans Kinn reichte. Sie murmelte, fing die Nach-

tigall und trug sie auf der Hand fort. Joringel konnte nichts sagen, nicht von der Stelle kommen. Die Nachtigall war fort, endlich kam das Weib wieder und sagte mit dumpfer Stimme: »Grüß dich, Zachiel! Wenn's Möndel ins Körbel scheint, bind los, Zachiel, zu guter Stund!« Da wurde Joringel los; er fiel vor dem Weib auf die Knie und bat, sie möchte ihm seine Jorinde wiedergeben; aber sie sagte, er solle sie nie wieder haben, und ging fort. Er rief, er weinte, er jammerte, aber alles umsonst. Uu! Was soll mir geschehn? Joringel ging fort und kam endlich in ein fremdes Dorf; da hütete er die Schafe lange Zeit. Oft ging er rund um das Schloß herum, aber nicht zu nahe dabei; endlich träumte er einmal des Nachts, er fände eine blutrote Blume, in deren Mitte eine schöne große Perle war; die Blume brach er ab, ging damit zum Schlosse. Alles, was er mit der Blume berührte, ward von der Zauberei frei; auch träumte er, er hätte seine Jorinde dadurch wiederbekommen. Des Morgens, als er erwachte, fing er an, durch Berg und Tal zu suchen, ob er eine solche Blume fände. Er suchte bis an den neunten Tag, da fand er die blutrote Blume am Morgen früh. In der Mitte war ein großer Tautropfen, so groß wie die schönste Perle. Diese Blume trug er Tag und Nacht bis zum Schloß. Wie er auf hundert Schritt nahe zum Schloß kam, da ward er nicht fest, sondern ging fort bis ans Tor. Joringel freute sich, berührte die Pforte mit der Blume, und sie sprang auf; er ging hinein, durch den Hof, horchte, wo er die vielen Vögel vernähme. Endlich hörte er's; er ging und fand den Saal, da war die Zauberin und fütterte die Vögel in den siebentausend Körben. Wie sie den Joringel sah, ward sie bös, sehr bös, schalt, spie Gift und Galle gegen ihn aus, aber sie konnt' auf zwei Schritte nicht an ihn kommen. Er kehrte sich nicht an sie und ging, besah die Körbe mit den Vögeln; da waren aber viele Hundert Nachtigallen. Wie sollte er nun seine Jorinde wiederfinden? Indem er so zusah, merkte er, daß die Alte heimlich ein Körbchen mit einem Vogel nimmt und damit nach der Türe geht. Flugs sprang er hinzu, berührte das Körbchen mit der Blume, und auch das alte Weib. Nun konnte sie nicht mehr zaubern, und Jorinde stand da, hatte ihn um den Hals gefaßt, so schön, wie sie ehemals war. Da machte er auch alle die andern Vögel wieder zu Jungfrauen, und da ging er mit seiner Jorinde nach Hause, und sie lebten lange vergnügt zusammen.

1819

Der gescheite Hans

Hansens Mutter spricht: »Wohin, Hans?« Hans antwortet: »Zur Gretel.« – »Mach's gut, Hans.« – »Schon gut machen. Adies, Mutter.« – Hans kommt zur Gretel. »Guten Tag, Gretel.« – »Guten Tag, Hans. Was bringst du Gutes?« – »Bring nichts, gegeben han.«

Gretel schenkt dem Hans eine Nadel, Hans spricht: »Adies, Gretel.« – »Adies, Hans.« – Hans nimmt die Nadel und steckt sie in einen Heuwagen und geht hinterher nach Haus. »Guten Abend, Mutter.« – »Guten Abend, Hans, wo bist du gewesen?« – »Bei der Gretel.« – »Was hast du ihr gebracht?« – »Nichts gebracht, gegeben hat.« – »Was hat sie dir gegeben?« – »Nadel gegeben.« – »Wo hast du die Nadel, Hans?« – »In Heuwagen gesteckt.« – »Das hast du dumm gemacht, mußt's an Ärmel stecken.« – »Tut nichts, besser machen.«

»Wohin, Hans?« – »Zur Gretel.« – »Mach's gut, Hans.« – »Schon gut machen.

Adies, Mutter.« – Hans kommt zur Gretel: »Guten Tag, Gretel.« – »Guten Tag, Hans. Was bringst du Gutes?« – »Bring nichts, gegeben han.«

Gretel schenkt dem Hans ein Messer. »Adies, Gretel.« – »Adies, Hans.« – Hans nimmt das Messer, steckt's an den Ärmel und geht nach Haus. »Guten Abend, Mutter.« – »Guten Abend, Hans, wo bist du gewesen?« – »Bei der Gretel.« – »Was hast du ihr gebracht?« – »Nichts gebracht, gegeben hat.« – »Was hat sie dir gegeben?« – »Messer gegeben.« – »Wo hast du das Messer, Hans?« – »An den Ärmel gesteckt.« – »Das hast du dumm gemacht, mußt's in die Tasche stecken.« – »Tut nichts, besser machen.«

»Wohin, Hans?« – »Zur Gretel.« – »Mach's gut, Hans.« – »Schon gut machen. Adies, Mutter.« – Hans kommt zur Gretel: »Guten Tag, Gretel.« – »Guten Tag, Hans. Was bringst du Gutes?« – »Bring nichts, gegeben han.«

Gretel schenkt dem Hans eine junge Ziege. »Adies, Gretel.« – »Adies, Hans.« Hans nimmt die Ziege, bindet ihr die Beine und steckt sie in die Tasche. Wie er nach Haus kommt, ist sie erstickt. »Guten Abend, Mutter.« – »Guten Abend, Hans, wo bist du gewesen?« – »Bei der Gretel.« – »Was hast du ihr gebracht?« – »Nichts gebracht, gegeben hat.« – »Was hat sie dir gegeben?« – »Ziege gegeben.« – »Wo hast du die Ziege, Hans?« – »In die Tasche gesteckt.« – »Das hast du dumm gemacht, Hans, mußt's an ein Seil binden.« – »Tut nichts, besser machen.«

»Wohin, Hans?« – »Zur Gretel.« – »Mach's gut, Hans.« – »Schon gut machen. Adies, Mutter.« – Hans kommt zur Gretel: »Guten Tag, Gretel.« – »Guten Tag, Hans. Was bringst du Gutes?« – »Bring nichts, gegeben han.«

Gretel schenkt dem Hans ein Stück Speck. Hans bindet den Speck an ein Seil und schleift's hinter sich, die Hunde kommen und fressen es ab. Wie er nach Haus kommt, ist das Seil leer. »Guten Abend, Mutter.« – »Guten Abend, Hans, wo bist du gewesen?« – »Bei der Gretel.« – »Was hast du ihr gebracht?« – »Nichts gebracht, gegeben hat.« – »Was hat sie dir gegeben?« – »Stück Speck gegeben.« – »Wo hast du den Speck, Hans?« – »Ans Seil gebunden, heimgeführt, fort gewesen.« – »Das hast du dumm gemacht, Hans, mußt's auf dem Kopf tragen.« – »Tut nichts, besser machen.«

»Wohin, Hans?« – »Zur Gretel.« – »Mach's gut, Hans.« – »Schon gut machen. Adies, Mutter.« – Hans kommt zur Gretel: »Guten Tag, Gretel.« – »Guten Tag, Hans. Was bringst du Gutes?« – »Bring nichts, gegeben han.«

Gretel schenkt dem Hans ein Kalb, Hans setzt es auf den Kopf, und es zertritt ihm das Gesicht. – »Guten Abend, Mutter.« – »Guten Abend, Hans, wo bist du gewesen?« – »Bei der Gretel.« – »Was hast du ihr gebracht?« – »Nichts gebracht, gegeben hat.« – »Was hat sie dir gegeben?« – »Kalb gegeben.« – »Wo hast du das Kalb, Hans?« – »Auf den Kopf gesetzt, Gesicht zertreten.« – »Das hast du dumm gemacht, Hans, mußt's leiten und an die Raufe stellen.« – »Tut nichts, besser machen.«

»Wohin, Hans?« – »Zur Gretel.« – »Mach's gut, Hans.« – »Schon gut machen.

Adies, Mutter.« – »Guten Tag, Gretel.« – »Guten Tag, Hans. Was bringst du Gutes?« – »Bring nichts, gegeben han.«

Gretel sagt: »Ich will mit dir gehen.« Hans bindet die Gretel an ein Seil, leitet sie, führt sie vor die Raufe und knüpft sie fest. »Guten Abend, Mutter.« – »Guten Abend, Hans, wo bist du gewesen?« – »Bei der Gretel.« – »Was hat sie dir gegeben?« – »Gretel mitgegangen.« – »Wo hast du die Gretel?« – »Geleitet, vor die Raufe geknüpft, Gras vorgeworfen.« – »Das hast du dumm gemacht, mußt ihr die Augen freundlich zuwerfen.« – »Tut nichts, besser machen.«

Hans geht in den Stall, sticht allen Kälbern und Schafen die Augen aus und wirft sie der Gretel ins Gesicht; da wird Gretel bös, reißt sich los und läuft fort und ist Hansens Braut gewesen.

1819

Der Gevatter Tod

Es hatte ein armer Mann zwölf Kinder und mußte Tag und Nacht arbeiten, damit er ihnen nur Brot geben konnte. Als nun das dreizehnte zur Welt kam, wußte er sich in seiner Not nicht zu helfen, lief hinaus und wollte den ersten, der ihm begegnete, zu Gevatter bitten. Der erste, der ihm begegnete, das war der liebe Gott, der wußte schon, was er auf dem Herzen hatte, und sprach zu ihm: »Armer Mann, du dauerst mich, ich will dein Kind aus der Taufe heben und will für es sorgen, daß es glücklich wird auf Erden.« Der Mann sprach: »Wer bist du?« – »Ich bin der liebe Gott.« – »So begehr ich dich nicht zum Gevatter, denn du gibst den Reichen und läßt die Armen hungern.« So sprach der Mann, weil er nicht wußte, wie weise Gott Reichtum und Armut verteilt; wendete sich ab von dem Herrn und ging weiter. Da trat der Teufel zu ihm und sprach: »Was suchst du? Ich bin der Pate deines Kinds und will ihm Gold geben und alle Lust der Welt.« Der Mann fragte: »Wer bist du?« – »Ich bin der Teufel.« – »So begehr ich dich nicht zum Gevatter, du betrügst und verführst die Menschen«, und ging weiter. Da kam der Tod auf ihn zugeschritten und sprach: »Nimm mich zum Gevatter.« – »Wer bist du?« fragte der Mann. »Ich bin der Tod, der alles gleich macht.« Da sprach der Mann: »Du bist der rechte, du holst den Reichen und den Armen ohne Unterschied, du sollst mein Gevattersmann sein.« Der Tod antwortete: »Ich will dein Kind reich und berühmt machen auf der Welt, denn wer mich zum Freund hat, dem kann's nicht fehlen.« Sprach der Mann: »Künftigen Sonntag ist die Taufe, da stell dich zu rechter Zeit ein.« Der Tod erschien, wie er versprochen hatte, und hielt das Kind über die Taufe.

Als der Knabe nun zu Jahren gekommen war, trat zu einer Zeit der Pate ein, nahm ihn mit sich hinaus in den Wald, und als sie ganz allein waren, sprach er: »Jetzt sollst du dein Patengeschenk haben. Ich mache dich zu einem berühmten Arzt. Wenn du zu einem Kranken gerufen wirst, so will ich dir jedesmal erscheinen. Stehe ich zu Füßen des Kranken, so sprich keck, ich will ihn wieder gesund machen, und gib ihm nur von einem gewissen Kraut ein, das ich dir zeigen will, so wird er genesen; stehe ich aber zu Häupten des Kranken, so ist er mein, und dann sprich: ›Alle Hilfe ist umsonst, der muß sterben.‹« Dann zeigte ihm der Tod das Kraut und sprach: »Hüte dich, daß du es nicht gegen meinen Willen gebrauchst.«

Es dauerte nicht lange, so war der Arzt in der ganzen Welt berühmt. »Wenn der den Kranken nur ansieht, weiß er gleich, ob er wieder gesund wird oder ob er sterben muß«, so hieß es von ihm, und weit und breit kamen die Leute und holten ihn und gaben ihm Gold, soviel, als er verlangte, also daß er bald große Reichtümer besaß. Nun trug es sich zu, daß der König auch krank ward, da wurde nach ihm geschickt, er sollte sagen, ob er sterben müßte. Wie der Arzt

nun zu dem Bette trat, sah er den Tod zu Häupten des Kranken stehen, und da war für ihn kein Kraut mehr gewachsen. Der Arzt aber dachte, vielleicht kannst du den Tod überlisten, weil's dein Herr Pate ist, wird er's so übel nicht nehmen, packte den König an und legte ihn verkehrt, so daß der Tod an seine Füße zu stehen kam; darauf gab er ihm das Kraut ein, und der König erholte sich und ward wieder gesund.

Der Tod aber kam zu dem Arzt, machte ein böses, finsteres Gesicht und sprach: »Diesmal soll dir's hingehen, weil ich dein Pate bin, aber unterstehst du dich noch einmal, mich zu betrügen, so geht dir's selbst an den Hals.« Bald darauf ward des Königs Tochter krank, und niemand konnte ihr helfen. Der alte König weinte Tag und Nacht, daß ihm die Augen erblindeten, endlich ließ er bekannt machen, wer sie vom Tod errette, der solle zum Lohn ihr Gemahl werden und die Krone erben. Nun kam der Arzt auch, aber der Tod stand zu Häupten, doch als er die Schönheit der Königstochter sah und an das Versprechen des Königs dachte, so vergaß er alle Warnungen, und ob ihn gleich der Tod ganz fürchterlich anschaute, so kehrte er doch die Kranke herum und gab ihr sein Kraut, so daß sich das Leben in ihr neu zu regen anfing.

Der Tod aber, als er sich zum zweitenmal um sein Eigentum betrogen sah, trat zu dem Arzt und sprach: »Nun folge mir«, packte ihn hart mit seiner eiskalten Hand und führte ihn in eine unterirdische Höhle, in der viel tausend und tausend Lichter in unübersehbaren Reihen brannten. Etliche waren groß, etliche halb, etliche klein; jeden Augenblick verloschen einige und brannten neue wieder auf, also daß die Flämmchen hin und her zu hüpfen schienen. »Siehst du«, sprach der Tod, »das sind die Lebenslichter der Menschen. Die großen gehören Kindern, die halben Eheleuten in ihren guten Jahren, die kleinen gehören Greisen. Doch haben auch Kinder und junge Menschen oft nur ein kleines Licht. Ist's abgebrannt, so ist ihr Leben zu Ende, und sie sind mein Eigentum.« Der Arzt sprach: »Zeige mir nun auch mein Licht.« Da deutete der Tod auf ein ganz kleines Endchen, das eben auszugehen drohte, und sagte: »Siehst du!« Da erschrak der Arzt und sprach: »Ach, lieber Pate, zündet mir ein neues an, damit ich meines Lebens erst genießen kann, König werde und Gemahl der schönen Königstochter.« — »Ich kann nicht«, antwortete der Tod, »erst muß ein's verlöschen, ehe ein neues anbrennt.« — »So setzet das alte auf ein neues, das gleich fortbrennt, wenn jenes zu Ende ist«, sprach der Arzt. Da stellte sich der Tod an, als wollte er seinen Wunsch erfüllen, langte ein frisches großes Licht herbei, aber beim Unterstecken versah er's, um sich zu rächen, absichtlich, und das Stückchen fiel und verlosch. Da sank der Arzt mit um und war nun selbst in die Hand des Todes gefallen.   1819

Simeliberg

Es waren zwei Brüder, einer war reich, der andere arm. Der Reiche aber gab dem Armen nichts, und er mußte sich vom Kornhandel kümmerlich ernähren, da ging es ihm oft so schlecht, daß er für seine Frau und Kinder kein Brot hatte. Einmal fuhr er mit seinem Karren durch den Wald, da erblickte er zur Seite einen großen kahlen Berg, und weil er den noch nie gesehen hatte, hielt er still und betrachtete ihn mit Verwunderung. Wie er so stand, sah er zwölf wilde, große Männer daherkommen. Weil er nun glaubte, das wären Räuber, schob er seinen Karren ins

Gebüsch und stieg auf einen Baum und wartete, was da geschehen würde. Die zwölf Männer gingen aber vor den Berg und riefen: »Berg Semsi! Berg Semsi! Tu dich auf.« Alsbald tat sich der kahle Berg in der Mitte voneinander, und die zwölfe gingen hinein, und wie sie drin waren, schloß er sich zu. Über eine kleine Weile aber tat er sich wieder auf, und die Männer kamen mit schweren Säcken auf den Rücken heraus, und wie sie alle wieder am Tageslicht waren, sprachen sie: »Berg Semsi! Berg Semsi! Tu dich zu!«

Da fuhr der Berg zusammen und war kein Eingang mehr an ihm zu sehen, und die zwölfe gingen fort.

Als sie ihm nun ganz aus den Augen waren, stieg der Arme vom Baum herunter und war neugierig, was wohl im Berge Heimliches verborgen wäre. Also ging er davor und sprach: »Berg Semsi! Berg Semsi! Tu dich auf!«, und der Berg tat sich auch vor ihm auf. Da trat er hinein, und der ganze Berg war eine Höhle voll Silber und Gold, und hinten lagen große Haufen Perlen und leuchtende Edelsteine wie Korn aufgeschüttet. Der Arme wußte gar nicht, was er anfangen sollte, und ob er sich etwas von den Schätzen nehmen dürfte. Endlich füllte er sich die Taschen mit Gold, die Perlen und Edelsteine aber ließ er liegen. Als er wieder herauskam, sprach er gleichfalls: »Berg Semsi! Berg Semsi! Tu dich zu!« Da schloß sich der Berg, und er fuhr nun mit seinem Karren nach Haus.

Nun brauchte er nicht mehr zu sorgen und konnte mit seinem Golde für Frau und Kind Brot und auch Wein dazu kaufen, lebte fröhlich und redlich, gab den Armen und tat jedermann Gutes.

Als aber das Gold alle war, ging er zu seinem Bruder, lieh einen Scheffel und holte sich von neuem, doch rührte er von den großen Schätzen nichts an. Wie er sich zum drittenmal etwas holen wollte, borgte er bei seinem Bruder wieder den Scheffel. Der Reiche aber war schon lange neidisch über sein Vermögen und den schönen Haushalt, den er sich eingerichtet hatte, und konnte nicht begreifen, woher der Reichtum käme und was sein Bruder mit dem Scheffel anfing. Da dachte er eine List aus und bestrich den Boden mit Pech, und wie er das Maß wieder bekam, so war ein Goldstück darin hängen geblieben. Alsbald ging er zu seinem Bruder und fragte ihn: »Was hast du mit dem Scheffel gemessen?« — »Korn und Gerste«, sagte der andere. Da zeigte er ihm das Goldstück und drohte ihm, wenn er nicht die Wahrheit sagte, so wollt' er ihn beim Gericht verklagen. Er erzählte ihm nun alles, wie es zugegangen war; der Reiche aber ließ gleich einen Wagen anspannen, fuhr hinaus und dachte ganz andere Schätze mitzubringen. Wie er vor den Berg kam, rief er: »Berg Semsi! Berg Semsi! Tu dich auf!« Der Berg tat sich auf, und er ging hinein. Da lagen die Reichtümer alle vor ihm, und er wußte lange nicht, wozu er am ersten greifen sollte, endlich lud er Edelsteine auf, soviel er tragen konnte, und wollte sie hinausbringen. Er kehrte also um, weil aber Herz und Sinn ganz voll von den Schätzen waren, hatte er darüber den Namen des Bergs vergessen und rief: »Berg Simeli! Berg Simeli! Tu dich auf!« Aber das war der rechte Name nicht, und der Berg regte sich nicht und blieb verschlossen. Da ward ihm angst, aber je länger er nachsann, desto mehr verwirrten sich seine Gedanken, und halfen ihm alle Schätze nichts mehr. Am Abend tat sich der Berg auf, und die zwölf Räuber kamen herein, und als sie ihn sahen, waren sie froh und riefen: »Vogel, haben wir dich endlich, meinst du, wir hätten's nicht gemerkt, daß du zweimal hereingekommen bist, aber wir konnten dich nicht fangen, zum drittenmal sollst du nicht wieder heraus.« Da rief er: »Ich war's nicht; mein Bruder war's!«, aber er mochte bitten um sein Leben und sagen, was er wollte, sie schlugen ihm das Haupt ab.   1819

König Drosselbart

Ein König hatte eine Tochter, die war wunderschön, aber stolz und übermütig, so daß ihr kein Freier gut genug war und sie einen nach dem andern abwies und noch dazu Spott mit ihnen trieb. Einmal ließ der König ein großes Fest anstellen und lud dazu alle heiratslustigen Männer ein, die wurden in eine Reihe nach ihrem Rang und Stand geordnet; erst kamen die Könige, dann die Herzöge, die Fürsten, Grafen und Freiherrn, zuletzt die Edelleute. Nun wurde die Königstochter durch die Reihen geführt, aber an jedem hatte sie etwas auszusetzen. Der eine war ihr zu dick: »Das Weinfaß!« sprach sie. Der andere zu lang: »Lang und schwank hat keinen Gang!« Der dritte zu kurz: »Kurz und dick hat kein Geschick!« Der vierte zu blaß: »Der bleiche Tod!« Der fünfte zu rot: »Der Zinshahn!« Der sechste war nicht gerad genug: »Grünes Holz, hinterm Ofen getrocknet!« Und so hatte sie an einem jeden etwas auszusetzen, besonders aber machte sie sich über einen guten König lustig, der ganz oben stand und dem das Kinn ein wenig krumm gewachsen war. »Ei«, rief sie und lachte, »der hat ein Kinn wie die Drossel einen Schnabel!« Und seit der Zeit bekam er den Namen Drosselbart.

Der alte König aber, als er sah, daß seine Tochter nichts tat, als über die Leute spotten, und alle Freier, die da versammelt waren, verschmähte, ward er zornig und schwur, sie sollte den ersten besten Bettler zum Mann nehmen, der vor seine Türe käme.

Ein paar Tage darauf hub ein Spielmann an, unter dem Fenster zu singen, um damit ein geringes Almosen zu erwerben. Als es der König hörte, sprach er: »Laßt ihn heraufkommen!« Da trat ein schmutziger Spielmann herein, sang vor dem König und seiner Tochter und bat, als er fertig war, um eine milde Gabe. Der König sprach: »Dein Gesang hat mir so wohl gefallen, daß ich dir meine Tochter zur Frau geben will.« Die Königstochter erschrak, aber der König sagte: »Ich habe den Eid getan, dich dem ersten besten Bettelmann zu geben, den will ich auch halten.« Es half keine Einrede, der Pfarrer ward geholt, und sie mußte sich gleich mit dem Spielmann trauen lassen. Als das geschehen war, sprach der König: »Nun schickt sich's nicht weiter, daß du in meinem Schloß bleibst, du kannst nur mit deinem Manne fortziehen.«

Der Bettelmann nahm sie mit hinaus, und sie kamen in einen großen Wald; da fragte sie:

>»Ach, wem gehört der schöne Wald?«
>»Der gehört dem König Drosselbart:
>hätt'st du'n genommen, so wär er dein!«
>»Ich arme Jungfer zart,
>ach, hätt' ich genommen den König Drosselbart!«

Darauf kamen sie über eine Wiese, da fragte sie wieder:

> »Wem gehört die schöne, grüne Wiese?«
> »Sie gehört dem König Drosselbart:
> hätt'st du'n genommen, so wär sie dein!«
> »Ich arme Jungfer zart,
> ach, hätt' ich genommen den König Drosselbart!«

Dann kamen sie durch eine große Stadt, da fragte sie wieder:

> »Wem gehört wohl die schöne große Stadt?«
> »Sie gehört dem König Drosselbart:
> hätt'st du'n genommen, so wär sie dein!«
> »Ich arme Jungfer zart,
> ach, hätt' ich genommen den König Drosselbart!«

»Das gefällt mir gar nicht«, sprach der Spielmann, »daß du dir immer einen andern zum Mann wünschest, bin ich dir nicht gut genug?« Endlich kamen sie an ein ganz kleines Häuschen, da sprach sie:

> »Ach Gott! Was für ein Häuselein!
> Wem mag das elende, winzige Häuschen sein?«

Der Spielmann antwortete: »Das ist mein und dein Haus, wo wir zusammen wohnen.« – »Wo sind die Diener?« sprach die Königstochter. »Was, Diener!« antwortete der Bettelmann. »Du mußt dir selber tun, was du willst getan haben. Mach nur gleich Feuer an und stell Wasser auf, daß du mir mein Essen kochst, ich bin ganz müd.« Die Königstochter verstand aber nichts vom Feueranmachen und Kochen, und der Bettelmann mußte selber mit Hand anlegen, daß es noch so leidlich ging. Als sie die schmale Kost gegessen hatten, legten sie sich zu Bett, aber am Morgen trieb er sie schon ganz früh heraus, weil sie das Haus besorgen sollte. Ein paar Tage lebten sie auf diese Art schlecht genug und zehrten ihren Vorrat auf. Da sprach der Mann: »Frau, so geht's nicht länger, daß wir hier zehren und nichts verdienen. Du sollst Körbe flechten.« Er ging aus, schnitt Weiden und brachte sie heim, da fing sie an zu flechten, aber die harten Weiden stachen ihr die zarten Hände wund. »Ich sehe, das geht nicht«, sprach der Mann, »spinn lieber, vielleicht kannst du das besser.« Sie setzte sich hin und versuchte zu spinnen, aber der harte Faden schnitt ihr bald in die weichen Finger, daß das Blut daran herunterlief. »Siehst du«, sprach der Mann, »du taugst zu keiner Arbeit, mit dir bin ich schlimm angekommen. Nun will ich's versuchen und einen Handel mit Töpfen und irdenem Geschirr anfangen, du sollst dich auf den Markt setzen und die Ware feil halten.« – »Ach«, dachte sie, »wenn auf den Markt Leute aus meines Vaters Reich kommen und sehen mich da sitzen und feil halten, wie werden sie mich verspotten!« Aber es half nichts, sie mußte hin, wenn sie nicht Hungers sterben wollten. Das erstemal ging's gut, denn die Leute kauften der Frau, weil sie so schön war, gern ihre Ware ab und bezahlten, was sie forderte, ja viele gaben ihr das Geld und ließen ihr die Töpfe noch dazu. Nun lebten sie von dem Erworbenen, so lang es dauerte, da handelte der Mann wieder eine Menge neues Geschirr ein, und sie setzte sich an eine Ecke des Markts und stellte es um sich her und hielt feil. Da kam plötzlich ein trunkener Husar dahergejagt und ritt geradezu in die Töpfe hinein, daß alles in tausend Scherben zersprang. Sie fing an zu weinen und wußte nicht vor Angst, was sie anfangen sollte. »Ach, wie wird mir's ergehen!« rief sie. »Was wird mein Mann dazu sagen!« Sie lief heim und erzählte ihm das Unglück. »Wer setzt sich auch an die Ecke des Markts mit irdenem Geschirr!« sprach der Mann. »Laß nur das Weinen, ich sehe wohl, du bist zu keiner ordentlichen Arbeit zu gebrauchen; da bin ich in unseres Königs Schloß gewesen und habe gefragt, ob sie nicht eine Küchenmagd brauchen könnten, und sie haben mir versprochen, sie wollten dich dazu nehmen, dafür bekommst du freies Essen.«

Nun ward die Königstochter eine Küchenmagd, mußte dem Koch zur Hand gehen und die sauerste Arbeit tun. Sie machte sich an beiden Seiten in den Taschen ein Töpfchen fest, darin trug sie, was sie von dem Übriggebliebenen erhielt, nach Haus, und sie lebten zusammen davon. Es trug sich zu, daß die Hochzeit des ältesten Königssohns sollte gefeiert werden, da ging die arme Frau hinauf, stellte sich vor die Saaltüre und sah zu. Als nun alles voll Pracht und Herrlichkeit war, da dachte sie mit betrübtem Herzen an ihr Schicksal und verwünschte ihren Hochmut und Übermut, der sie in diese Armut gestürzt hatte. Von den köstlichen Speisen, die da ein und aus getragen wurden, erhielt sie von den Dienern manchmal etwas geschenkt, das tat sie in ihre Töpfchen und wollte es heim tragen. Auf einmal trat der Königssohn in goldenen Kleidern daher, und als er die schöne Frau in der Türe stehen sah, ergriff er sie bei der Hand und wollte mit ihr tanzen, aber sie wollte nicht und erschrak, denn sie sah, daß es der König Drosselbart war, der um sie gefreit und den sie mit Spott abgewiesen hatte. Als sie sich sträubte, zog er sie herein, da ging das Band auf, welches die Taschen hielt, und die Töpfe fielen heraus, daß die Suppe floß und die Brocken umher sprangen. Und wie das die Leute sahen, entstand ein allgemeines Gelächter und Spotten, und sie war so beschämt, daß sie sich lieber tausend Klafter unter die Erde gewünscht hätte. Sie sprang zur Türe und wollte entfliehen, aber auf der Treppe holte sie ein Mann ein und brachte sie zurück, und wie sie ihn ansah, war es der König Drosselbart selbst, der sprach: »Fürchte dich nicht, ich und der Spielmann, der mit dir in dem elenden Häuschen gewohnt hat, sind eins, dir zur Liebe habe ich mich so verstellt, und der Husar, der dir die Töpfe entzwei geritten hat, bin ich auch gewesen. Das alles ist geschehen, um deinen stolzen Sinn zu beugen und dich für deinen Hochmut,

Mann nahm den Hut ab und setzte den Kleinen auf einen Acker am Weg, da sprang und kroch er ein wenig zwischen den Schollen hin und her und schlüpfte dann auf einmal in ein Mausloch, das er sich gesucht hatte. »Guten Abend, ihr Herrn, ihr habt mich gehabt!« rief er heraus. Sie liefen herbei, stachen mit Stöcken in die Höhlung, aber das war vergebliche Mühe. Daumesdick kroch immer weiter zurück, bald war es auch stichdunkel, so daß sie voll Ärger und mit leerem Beutel wieder heim wandern mußten.

Als Daumesdick merkte, daß sie fort waren, kroch er aus dem unterirdischen Gang wieder hervor. »Es ist hier auf dem Acker in der Dunkelheit so gefährlich gehen«, sprach er, »wie leicht bricht einer Hals und Bein!« Zum Glück stieß er an ein leeres Schneckenhaus: »Gottlob, da kann ich die Nacht sicher zubringen!« und setzte sich hinein. Nicht lang, als er eben einschlafen wollte, so hörte er zwei Männer vorübergehen, davon sprach der eine: »Wie wir's nur anfangen, um dem reichen Pfarrer sein Geld und sein Silber zu holen?« – »Das könnt ich dir sagen«, sprach Daumesdick dazwischen. »Was war das!« rief der eine Dieb erschrocken. »Ich hörte jemand sprechen.« Sie blieben stehen und horchten, da sprach Daumesdick wieder: »Nehmt mich mit, so will ich euch helfen.« – »Wo bist du denn?« – »Sucht nur hier auf der Erde und merkt, wo die Stimme herkommt«, antwortete er. Da fanden ihn endlich die Diebe und hoben ihn in die Höhe. »Du kleiner Wicht, was willst du uns helfen!« sprachen sie. »Seht«, antwortete er, »ich krieche zwischen den Eisenstäben in die Kammer des Pfarrers hinein und reich euch heraus, was ihr haben wollt.« – »Nun«, sagten sie, »wir wollen sehen, was du kannst.« Als sie bei dem Pfarrhaus waren, kroch Daumesdick in die Kammer, schrie aber gleich aus Leibeskräften: »Wollt ihr alles haben, was hier ist?« Die Diebe erschraken und sagten: »So sprich doch leise, damit niemand aufwacht!« Aber Daumesdick tat, als hätte er sie nicht verstanden, und schrie von neuem: »Was wollt ihr? Wollt ihr alles haben, was hier ist?« Das hörte die Köchin, die in der Stube daran schlief, richtete sich im Bett auf und horchte. Die Diebe aber waren vor Schrecken ein Stück Wegs zurückgelaufen, endlich faßten sie wieder Mut, dachten, der kleine Kerl will uns necken, kamen zurück und flüsterten ihm hinein: »Nun mach Ernst, und reich uns etwas heraus.« Da schrie Daumesdick noch einmal, so laut er konnte: »Ich will euch ja alles geben, reicht nur die Hände herein.« Das hörte nun die horchende Magd ganz deutlich, sprang aus dem Bett und stolperte zur Türe herein. Die Diebe gingen los und rannten, als wär Feuer hinter ihnen, die Magd aber, als sie nichts bemerken konnte, ging, ein Licht anzuzünden. Wie sie damit kam, machte sich Daumesdick, ohne daß er gesehen wurde, hinaus in die Scheune; die Magd aber, nachdem sie alle Winkel durchgesucht und nichts gefunden hatte, legte sich endlich wieder zu Bett und glaubte, sie hätte mit offnen Augen und Ohren doch nur geträumt.

Daumesdick war in den Heuhälmchen herumgeklettert und hatte einen schönen Platz zum Schlafen darin gefunden, da wollte er sich ausruhen, bis es Tag wäre, und dann zu seinen Eltern wieder heimgehen. Aber was mußt' er nicht für andere Dinge erfahren! Ja, es gibt viel Trübsal und Not auf der Welt! Die Magd stieg, wie gewöhnlich, als der Tag graute, schon aus dem Bett, um das Vieh zu füttern. Ihr erster Gang war in die Scheune, wo sie einen Arm voll Heu packte, und gerade dasjenige, worin der arme Daumesdick lag und schlief. Er schlief aber so fest, daß er nichts gewahr wurde und nicht eher aufwachte, als bis er in dem Maul der Kuh war, die ihn mit dem Heu aufgerafft hatte. »Ach Gott«, rief er, »wie bin ich in die Walkmühle geraten!« Aber er merkte bald, wo er war. Da hieß es aufpassen, daß er nicht zwischen die Zähne kam und zerdrückt wurde, und danach mußte er doch mit in den Magen hinabrutschen. »In dem Stübchen sind die Fenster vergessen«, sprach er, »und bricht keine Sonne hindurch; ein Licht wird auch nicht wohl zu haben sein!« Überhaupt gefiel ihm das Quartier schlecht, und was das schlimmste war, es kam immer mehr neues Heu zur Tür hinein, und der Platz ward immer enger. Da rief er endlich in der Angst, so laut er konnte: »Bringt mir kein neu Futter mehr! Bringt mir kein neu Futter mehr!« Die Magd melkte gerade die Kuh, und als sie sprechen hörte, ohne jemand zu sehen, und es dieselbe Stimme war, die sie auch in der Nacht gehört hatte, erschrak sie so, daß sie von ihrem Stühlchen herabglitschte und die Milch verschüttete. Sie lief in der größten Hast zu ihrem Herrn und rief: »Ach Gott, Herr Pfarrer, die Kuh hat geredet.« Der Pfarrer antwortete der Magd: »Du bist verrückt!«, ging aber doch selbst in den Stall, nachzusehen, was da wäre. Aber kaum hatte er den Fuß hineingesetzt, so rief Daumesdick eben aufs neue: »Bringt mir kein neu Futter mehr! Bringt mir kein neu Futter mehr!« Da erschrak der Pfarrer selbst, meinte, es wär ein böser Geist, und hieß die Kuh töten. Nun ward sie geschlachtet, der Magen aber, worin Daumesdick steckte, hinaus auf den Mist geworfen. Daumesdick suchte sich herauszuarbeiten, aber das war nicht leicht. Endlich brachte er es so weit, daß er Platz bekam, aber als er eben sein Häuptlein herausstrecken wollte, kam das Unglück von neuem: Ein Wolf sprang vorbei und schlang den ganzen Magen mit einem hungrigen Schluck. Daumesdick verlor den Mut nicht; vielleicht, dachte er, läßt der Wolf mit sich reden, und rief ihm aus dem Wanst zu: »Lieber Wolf, ich weiß dir einen herrlichen Fraß.« — »Wo ist der zu holen?« sprach der Wolf. »In dem und dem Haus, da mußt du durch die Gosse hineinkriechen und wirst Kuchen, Speck und Wurst finden, soviel du essen willst«, und beschrieb ihm genau seines Vaters Haus. Der Wolf ließ sich das nicht zweimal sagen, drängte sich in der Nacht zur Gosse hinein und fraß in der Vorratskammer nach Herzenslust. Als er satt war, wollte er wieder fort, aber er war so dick geworden, daß er denselben Weg nicht wieder hinaus konnte. Daumesdick hatte eben darauf gerechnet und fing nun an, in dem Leib des Wolfs einen gewaltigen Lärm zu machen, tobte und schrie, was er konnte. »Willst du still sein!« sprach der Wolf. »Du weckst die Leute auf.« — »Ei was«, antwortete der Kleine, »du hast dich satt gefressen, ich will mich auch lustig machen!« und fing von neuem an, aus allen Kräften zu schreien. Davon erwachten nun sein Vater und seine Mutter, liefen an die Kammer und schauten durch die Spalte hinein. Wie sie sahen, daß ein Wolf darin hauste, erschraken sie, und der Mann holte die Axt und die Frau die Sense. »Bleib dahinten«, sprach der Mann, als sie in die Kammer traten, »wenn ich ihm einen Schlag gegeben und er ist noch nicht tot, daß du auf ihn haust und ihm den Leib zerschneidest.« Da hörte Daumesdick die Stimme seines Vaters und rief: »Lieber Vater, ich bin hier, ich stecke im Leib des Wolfs!« Sprach der Vater voll Freuden: »Gottlob, unser liebstes Kind hat sich wieder gefunden«, und hieß die Frau die Sense wegtun, damit es nicht beschädigt würde. Danach holte er aus und schlug dem Wolf einen Schlag auf den Kopf, daß er tot niederstürzte, dann suchten sie Messer und Schere, schnitten ihm den Leib auf und zogen ihr liebes Kind wieder hervor. »Ach«, sprach der Vater, »was haben wir für Sorge um dich ausgestanden!« – »Ja, Vater, ich bin viel in der Welt herumgekommen, gottlob, daß ich wieder frische Luft schöpfe.« – »Wo bist du denn all gewesen?« – »Ach, Vater, ich war in einem Mauseloch, in einer Kuh Bauch und eines Wolfes Wanst, nun bleib ich bei euch.« – »Und wir verkaufen dich um alle Reichtümer der Welt nicht wieder.« Da herzten und küßten sie ihren lieben Daumesdick, gaben ihm zu essen und trinken und ließen ihm neue Kleider machen, denn seine waren ihm auf der Reise verdorben.

1819

Allerleirauh

Es war einmal ein König, dessen Frau hatte Haare von lauterem Gold und war so schön, daß sich ihresgleichen nicht mehr auf Erden fand. Es geschah, daß sie krank lag, und als sie fühlte, daß sie bald sterben würde, rief sie den König und sprach: »Wenn du nach meinem Tode dich wieder vermählen willst, so nimm keine, die nicht ebenso schön ist, als ich bin, und die nicht solche goldenen Haare hat, wie ich habe; das mußt du mir versprechen.« Nachdem es ihr der König versprochen hatte, tat sie die Augen zu und starb.

Der König war lange Zeit gar nicht zu trösten und dachte nicht daran, eine zweite Frau zu nehmen. Endlich sprachen seine Räte: »Es geht nicht anders, der König muß sich wieder vermählen, damit wir eine Königin haben.« Nun wurden Boten weit und breit umhergeschickt, um eine Braut zu suchen, die so schön wäre, als es die verstorbene Königin gewesen. Es war aber keine Königstochter in der Welt so schön, und wenn sie's auch gewesen wäre, so waren doch solche goldenen Haare nicht mehr zu finden. Also kamen die Boten unverrichteter Sache wieder heim.

Nun hatte der König eine Tochter, die war gerade so schön wie ihre verstorbene Mutter und hatte auch solche goldenen Haare. Als sie herangewachsen war, sah sie der König einmal an und sah, daß sie in allem seiner verstorbenen Gemahlin gliche, da fühlte er eine heftige Liebe zu ihr und sprach zu seinen Räten: »Ich will meine Tochter heiraten, denn sie ist das Ebenbild meiner verstorbenen Frau, und sonst kann ich doch keine Braut auf Erden finden.« Als die Räte das hörten, erschraken sie und sprachen: »Gott hat verboten, daß der Vater seine Tochter heiratet, und aus der Sünde kann nichts Gutes entspringen.« Die Tochter erschrak auch, hoffte aber, den König noch von seinem Vorhaben abzubringen. Da sagte sie zu ihm: »Eh' ich Euern Wunsch erfülle, muß ich erst drei Kleider haben, eins so golden wie die Sonne, eins so silbern wie der Mond und eins so glänzend als die Sterne. Ferner verlang ich einen Mantel von tausenderlei Pelz und Rauhwerk zusammengesetzt, zu welchem ein jedes Tier in Euerm Reich ein Stück von seiner Haut gegeben hat.« Dabei dachte sie, das anzuschaffen ist ganz unmöglich, und dann muß mein Vater von seinen Gedanken ablassen. Der König aber ließ nicht ab, und die geschicktesten Jungfrauen in seinem Reich mußten die drei Kleider weben, eins so golden wie die Sonne, eins so silbern wie der Mond und eins so glänzend wie die Sterne; und seine Jäger mußten alle Tiere in seinem Reich auffangen und ihnen ein Stück von ihrer Haut abziehen, daraus ward ein Mantel von tausenderlei Rauhwerk gemacht. Und wie alles fertig war, ließ es der König zu ihr bringen und sprach: »Morgen soll die Hochzeit sein.«

Als nun die Königstochter sah, daß keine Hoffnung mehr war, ihres Vaters Herz umzuwenden, so stand sie, wie alles schlief, in der Nacht auf, nahm von ihren Kostbarkeiten dreierlei, einen goldenen Ring, ein goldenes Spinnrädchen und ein goldenes Haspelchen; die drei Kleider von Sonne, Mond und Sterne tat sie in eine Nußschale, zog den Mantel von allerlei Rauhwerk an und machte sich Gesicht und Hände mit Ruß schwarz. Dann befahl sie sich Gott und ging fort und ging die

ganze Nacht, bis sie in einen großen Wald kam. Und weil sie so müd war, setzte sie sich in einen hohlen Baum und schlief ein.

Sie schlief aber noch immer, als es schon hoher Tag war. Da trug es sich zu, daß der König, dem der Wald gehörte, darin jagte und seine Hunde zu dem Baum kamen, die schnupperten und liefen daran herum und bellten. Sprach der König zu den Jägern: »Seht doch, was dort für ein Wild sich versteckt hat.« Die Jäger gingen hin und kamen wieder und sprachen: »In dem hohlen Baum liegt ein wunderliches Tier, das wir nicht kennen und noch nicht gesehen haben; an seiner Haut ist tausenderlei Pelz, es liegt aber und schläft.« Sprach der König: »Seht zu, ob ihr's lebendig fangen könnt, dann bindet's auf den Wagen und nehmt's mit.« Da packten es die Jäger, davon erwachte das Mädchen, erschrak und sprach: »Ich bin ein armes Kind, das Vater und Mutter verlassen haben, erbarmt euch mein und nehmt mich mit.« Da sprachen sie: »Ja, Allerleirauh, du bist gut für die Küche, komm nur mit, da kannst du die Asche zusammenkehren.« Also setzten sie es auf den Wagen und fuhren es heim ins königliche Schloß. Dort wiesen sie ihm ein Ställchen unter der Treppe, wo kein Tageslicht hinkam, und sagten: »Rauhtierchen, da kannst du wohnen und schlafen.« Dann wurde es in die Küche geschickt, da trug es Holz und Wasser, schürte das Feuer, rupfte das Federvieh, belas das Gemüs, kehrte die Asche und tat alle schlechte Arbeit.

Da lebte Allerleirauh lange Zeit recht armselig. Ach, du schöne Königstochter, wie soll's mit dir noch werden! Es geschah aber einmal, daß ein Fest im Schloß gefeiert wurde, da sprach sie zum Koch: »Darf ich ein wenig hinaufgehen und zusehen? Ich will mich außen vor die Türe stellen.« Antwortete der Koch: »Ja, geh nur hin, aber in einer halben Stunde mußt du wieder hier sein und die Asche zusammentragen.« Da nahm sie ihr Öllämpchen, ging in ihr Ställchen, zog den Pelzrock aus und wusch sich den Ruß von dem Gesicht und den Händen ab, daß ihre Schönheit hervorkam, recht wie die Sonne aus den Wolken. Dann machte sie die Nuß auf und holte ihr Kleid hervor, das wie die Sonne glänzte. Und wie das geschehen war, ging sie hinauf zum Fest, und alle traten ihr aus dem Weg, denn niemand kannte sie, und meinten nicht anders, als daß es eine Königstochter wäre. Der König aber kam ihr entgegen und reichte ihr die Hand und tanzte mit ihr und dachte in seinem Herzen: »So schön habe ich noch keine gesehen.« Als der Tanz zu Ende war, verneigte sie sich, und wie sich der König umsah, war sie verschwunden, und niemand wußte, wohin. Die Wächter wurden gerufen, die vor dem Schlosse standen, aber sie hatten niemand erblickt.

Sie war aber in ihr Ställchen gelaufen, hatte geschwind ihr Kleid ausgezogen, Gesicht und Hände schwarz gemacht und den Pelzmantel umgetan und war wieder Allerleirauh. Als sie nun in die Küche kam und an ihre Arbeit gehen und die Asche zusammenkehren wollte, sprach der Koch: »Laß das gut sein bis morgen und koch da die Suppe für den König, ich will auch einmal ein bißchen oben zugucken; aber laß mir kein Haar hineinfallen, sonst kriegst du in Zukunft nichts mehr zu essen!« Da ging der Koch fort, und Allerleirauh kochte die Suppe für den König und kochte eine Brotsuppe, so gut es konnte, und wie sie fertig war, holte es in dem Ställchen seinen goldenen Ring und legte ihn in die Schüssel, in welche die Suppe angerichtet ward. Als der Tanz zu Ende war, ließ sich der König die Suppe bringen und aß sie, und sie schmeckte ihm so gut, daß er meinte, niemals eine so gute Suppe gegessen zu haben. Wie er aber auf den Grund kam, sah er da einen goldenen Ring liegen und konnte nicht begreifen, wie er dahin geraten war. Da befahl er, der Koch sollte vor ihn kommen; der Koch erschrak, wie er den Befehl hörte, und sprach zu Allerleirauh: »Gewiß hast du ein Haar in die Suppe fallen lassen. Wenn's wahr ist, so kriegst du Schläge.« Als er vor den König kam, fragte dieser, wer die Suppe gekocht hätte? Antwortete der Koch: »Ich habe sie gekocht.« Der König aber sprach: »Das ist nicht wahr, denn sie war anders und besser gekocht.« Antwortete er: »Ich muß es gestehen, daß ich sie nicht gekocht habe, sondern das Rauhtierchen.« Sprach der König: »Laß es heraufkommen«; und als Allerleirauh kam, fragte er: »Wer bist du?« – »Ich bin ein armes Kind, das keinen Vater und Mutter mehr hat«, antwortete es. Fragte er weiter: »Wozu bist du in meinem Schloß?« Antwortete es: »Ich bin zu nichts gut, als daß mir die Stiefel um den Kopf geworfen werden.« Fragte er weiter: »Wo hast du den Ring her, der in der Suppe war?« Antwortete es: »Von dem Ring weiß ich nichts.« Also konnte der König nichts erfahren und mußte es wieder fortschicken.

Über eine Zeit war wieder ein Fest, da bat Allerleirauh den Koch wie voriges Mal um Erlaubnis, zusehen zu dürfen. Antwortete er: »Ja, aber komm in einer halben Stunde wieder und koch dem König die Brotsuppe, die er so gerne ißt.« Da lief es in sein Ställchen, wusch sich geschwind und nahm aus der Nuß das Kleid, das so silbern war wie der Mond, und tat es an. Da ging sie wie eine Königstochter hinauf, und der König trat ihr entgegen und freute sich, daß er sie wiedersah, und weil eben der Tanz anhub, so tanzten sie zusammen. Wie aber der Tanz zu Ende war, verschwand sie wieder so schnell, daß der König nicht bemerken konnte, wo sie hinging. Sie sprang aber in ihr Ställchen und machte sich wieder zum Rauhtierchen und ging in die Küche, die Brotsuppe zu kochen. Als der Koch oben war, holte es das goldene Spinnrad und tat es in die Schüssel, so daß die Suppe darüber angerichtet wurde. Danach ward sie dem König gebracht, der aß sie, und sie schmeckte ihm so gut wie das vorige Mal und ließ den Koch kommen, der mußte wieder gestehen, daß Allerleirauh die Suppe gekocht. Allerleirauh kam da wieder vor den König, aber sie antwortete, daß sie nur dazu da sei, daß ihr die Stiefel an den Kopf geworfen würden und daß sie von dem goldenen Spinnrädchen gar nichts wisse.

Als der König zum drittenmal ein Fest anstellte, da ging es nicht anders als die vorigen Male. Der Koch sprach zwar: »Du bist eine Hexe, Rauhtierchen, und tust immer etwas in die Suppe, davon sie so gut wird und dem König besser schmeckt als meine«; doch weil es so bat, so ließ er es auf die bestimmte Zeit hingehen. Nun zog es sein Kleid an, was wie die Sterne glänzte, und trat damit in den Saal. Der König tanzte wieder mit der schönen Jungfrau und meinte, daß sie noch niemals so schön gewesen wäre. Und während er tanzte, steckte er ihr, ohne daß sie es merkte, einen goldenen Ring an den Finger und hatte befohlen, daß der Tanz recht lang währen sollte. Wie er zu Ende war, wollte er sie an den Händen festhalten, aber sie riß sich los und sprang so geschwind unter die Leute, daß sie vor seinen Augen verschwand. Sie lief, was sie konnte, in ihr Ställchen unter der Treppe, weil sie aber zu lange und über die halbe Stunde geblieben war, so konnte sie das schöne Kleid nicht ausziehen, sondern warf nur den Mantel von Pelz darüber, und in der Eile machte es sich auch nicht ganz rußig, sondern ein Finger blieb weiß. Allerleirauh lief nun in die Küche und kochte dem König die Brotsuppe und legte, wie der Koch fort war, das goldene Haspelchen hinein. Der König, als er es auf dem Grund fand, ließ Allerleirauh wieder rufen, da erblickte er den weißen Finger und sah den Ring, den er im Tanze ihr angesteckt hatte. Da ergriff er sie an der Hand und hielt sie fest, und als sie sich losmachen und fortspringen wollte, tat sich der Pelzmantel ein wenig auf, und das Sternenkleid schimmerte hervor. Da faßte der König den Mantel und riß ihn ab, und die goldenen Haare und der ganze herrliche Anzug kamen hervor, und sie konnte sich nicht mehr verbergen und wischte Ruß und Asche aus ihrem Gesicht. Da war sie die schönste Königstochter, die je auf Erden gegangen ist. Der König aber sprach: »Du bist meine liebe Braut, und wir scheiden nimmermehr voneinander.« Darauf ward die Hochzeit gefeiert, und sie lebten vergnügt bis an ihren Tod.   1819

Der Hund und der Sperling

Ein Schäferhund hatte keinen guten Herrn, sondern einen, der ihn Hunger leiden ließ. Wie er's nicht mehr aushalten konnte, ging er ganz traurig fort. Auf der Straße begegnete ihm ein Sperling, der sprach: »Bruder Hund, warum bist du so traurig?« Antwortete der Hund: »Ich bin so hungrig und habe nichts zu fressen.« Da sprach der Sperling: »Lieber Bruder, komm mit in die Stadt, so will ich dich satt machen.« Also gingen sie zusammen in die Stadt, und als sie vor einen Fleischerladen kamen, sprach der Sperling zum Hund: »Da bleib stehen, ich will dir ein Stück Fleisch herunterpicken«; setzte sich auf den Laden, schaute sich um, ob ihn auch niemand bemerkte, und pickte, zog und zerrte so lang an einem Stück, das am Rande lag, bis es herunterrutschte. Da packte es der Hund, lief damit in eine Ecke und fraß es auf. Sprach der Sperling: »Nun komm mit zu einem andern Laden, da will ich dir noch ein Stück herunterpicken, damit du satt wirst.« Als der Hund das zweite Stück auch gefressen hatte, fragte der Sperling: »Bruder Hund, bist du nun satt?« – »Ja, Fleisch bin ich satt«, antwortete er, »aber ich habe noch kein Brot gekriegt.« Sprach der Sperling: »Das sollst du auch haben, komm nur mit.« Da führte er ihn an einen Bäckerladen und pickte an ein paar Brötchen, bis sie herunterrollten, und wie der Hund mehr wollte, führte er ihn zu einem andern und holte ihm noch einmal Brot herab. Wie das verzehrt war, sprach der Sperling: »Bruder Hund, bist du nun satt?« – »Ja«, antwortete er, »nun wollen wir ein bißchen vor die Stadt gehen.«

Nun gingen sie beide hinaus auf die Landstraße, es war aber warmes Wetter, und als sie ein Eckchen gegangen waren, sprach der Hund: »Ich bin müd und möchte gern schlafen.« – »Ja, schlaf nur«, antwortete der Sperling, »ich will mich derweil auf einen Zweig setzen.« Der Hund legte sich also auf die Straße und schlief fest ein. Während er da schlief, kam ein Fuhrmann herangefahren, der hatte einen Wagen mit drei Pferden und hatte zwei Fässer Wein geladen. Der Sperling aber sah, daß er nicht ausbiegen wollte, sondern in der Fahrspur blieb, in welcher der Hund lag, da rief er: »Fuhrmann, tu's nicht, oder ich mach dich arm!« Der Fuhrmann aber brummte vor sich hin: »Du wirst mich nicht arm machen!«, knallte mit der Peitsche und trieb den Wagen über den Hund, daß ihn die Räder totfuhren. Da rief der Sperling: »Du hast mir meinen Bruder Hund totgefahren, das soll dich Karren und Gaul kosten.« – »Ja, Karren und Gaul!« sagte der Fuhrmann. »Was könntest du mir schaden!« und fuhr fort. Da kroch der Sperling unter das Wagentuch und pickte an dem einen Spundloch so lange, bis er den Spund losbrachte, da lief der ganze Wein heraus, ohne daß es der Fuhrmann merkte. Und als er einmal umblickte, sah er, daß der Wagen tröpfelte, untersuchte und fand, daß das eine Faß leer war. »Ach, ich armer Mann!« rief er. »Noch nicht arm genug!« sprach der Sperling und flog dem einen Pferd auf den Kopf und pickte ihm die Augen aus. Als der Fuhrmann das sah, zog er seine Hacke heraus und wollte den Sperling treffen, aber der Sperling flog in die Höhe, und der Fuhrmann traf seinen Gaul auf den Kopf, daß er tot hinfiel. »Ach, ich armer Mann!« rief er. »Noch nicht arm genug!« sprach der Sperling, und als der Fuhrmann mit den zwei Pferden weiterfuhr, kroch der Sperling wieder unter das Tuch und pickte auch den Spund am zweiten Faß los, daß aller Wein herausschwappte. Als es der Fuhrmann gewahr wurde, rief er wieder: »Ach, ich armer Mann!« Aber der Sperling antwortete: »Noch nicht arm genug!«, setzte sich dem zweiten Pferd auf den Kopf und pickte ihm die Augen aus. Der Fuhrmann lief herbei und holte mit seiner Hacke aus, aber der Sperling flog in die Höhe, da traf der Schlag das Pferd, daß es hinfiel: »Ach, ich armer Mann!« – »Noch nicht arm genug«, sprach der Sperling, setzte sich auch dem dritten Pferd auf den Kopf und pickte ihm nach den Augen. Der Fuhrmann in seinem Zorn, ohne umzusehen, schlug auf den Sperling los, traf ihn aber nicht, sondern schlug auch sein drittes Pferd tot. »Ach, ich armer Mann!« rief er. »Noch nicht arm genug!« antwortete der Sperling. »Jetzt will ich dich daheim arm machen!« und flog fort.

Der Fuhrmann mußte den Wagen stehen lassen und ging voll Zorn und Ärger heim. »Ach«, sprach er zu seiner Frau, »was hab ich Unglück gehabt, der Wein ist ausgelaufen, und die Pferde sind alle drei tot.« – »Ach, Mann«, antwortete sie,

»was für ein böser Vogel ist ins Haus gekommen! Er hat alle Vögel auf der Welt zusammengebracht, und die sind droben über unsern Weizen hergefallen und fressen ihn auf!« Da stieg er hinauf, und viel tausend Vögel saßen auf dem Boden und hatten den Weizen aufgefressen, und der Sperling saß mitten drin. Da rief der Fuhrmann: »Ach, ich armer Mann!« – »Noch nicht arm genug«, antwortete der Sperling, »Fuhrmann, es kostet dir noch dein Leben!« und flog hinaus.

Da hatte der Fuhrmann all sein Gut verloren, ging hinab in seine Stube und setzte sich bös und giftig hinter den Ofen. Der Sperling aber saß draußen vor dem Fenster und rief: »Fuhrmann, es kostet dir dein Leben!« Da griff der Fuhrmann die Hacke und warf sie nach dem Sperling, aber er schmiß das Fenster entzwei und traf den Vogel nicht. Der Sperling hüpfte nun herein, setzte sich auf den Ofen und rief: »Fuhrmann, es kostet dir dein Leben!« Dieser, ganz toll und blind vor Wut, schlug den Ofen entzwei, und so fort, wie der Sperling von einem Ort zum andern fliegt, sein ganzes Hausgerät, Spieglein, Stühle, Bänke, Tische und zuletzt die Wände seines Hauses, und kann ihn nicht treffen. Endlich aber erwischte er ihn doch, da sprach seine Frau: »Soll ich ihn tot schlagen?« – »Nein«, rief er, »das ist zu gelind, der soll viel mörderlicher sterben, ich will ihn verschlingen!« und verschlingt ihn auf einmal. Der Sperling aber fängt an in seinem Leibe zu flattern, flattert wieder herauf, dem Mann in den Mund, da streckt er den Kopf heraus und ruft: »Fuhrmann, es kostet dir doch dein Leben!« Der Fuhrmann reicht seiner Frau die Hacke und spricht: »Frau, schlag mir den Vogel im Munde tot.« Die Frau schlägt zu, schlägt aber fehl und dem Fuhrmann gerade auf den Kopf, so daß er tot hinfällt. Der Sperling aber fliegt auf und davon. 1819

Spindel, Weberschiffchen und Nadel

Es war einmal ein Mädchen, dem starb Vater und Mutter, als es noch ein kleines Kind war. Am Ende des Dorfes wohnte in einem Häuschen ganz allein seine Patin, die sich von Spinnen, Weben und Nähen ernährte. Die Alte nahm das verlassene Kind zu sich, hielt es zur Arbeit an und erzog es in aller Frömmigkeit. Als das Mädchen fünfzehn Jahre alt war, erkrankte sie, rief das Kind an ihr Bett und sagte: »Liebe Tochter, ich fühle, daß mein Ende herannaht, ich hinterlasse dir das Häuschen, darin bist du vor Wind und Wetter geschützt, dazu Spindel, Weberschiffchen und Nadel, damit kannst du dir dein Brot verdienen.« Sie legte noch die Hände auf seinen Kopf, segnete es und sprach: »Behalt nur Gott in dem Herzen, so wird dir's wohl gehen.« Darauf schloß sie die Augen, und als sie zur Erde bestattet wurde, ging das Mädchen bitterlich weinend hinter dem Sarg und erwies ihr die letzte Ehre.

Das Mädchen lebte nun in dem kleinen Haus ganz allein, war fleißig, spann, webte und nähte, und auf allem, was es tat, ruhte der Segen der guten Alten. Es war, als ob sich der Flachs in der Kammer von selbst mehrte, und wenn sie ein Stück Tuch oder einen Teppich gewebt oder ein Hemd genäht hatte, so fand sich gleich ein Käufer, der es reichlich bezahlte, so daß sie keine Not empfand und andern noch etwas mitteilen konnte.

Um diese Zeit zog der Sohn des Königs im Land umher und wollte sich eine Braut suchen. Eine arme sollte er nicht wählen, und eine reiche wollte er nicht. Da sprach er: »Die soll meine Frau werden, die zugleich die ärmste und die reichste ist.« Als er in das Dorf kam, wo das Mädchen lebte, fragte er, wie er überall tat, wer in dem Ort die reichste und ärmste wäre. Sie nannten ihm die reichste zuerst; die ärmste, sagten sie, wäre das Mädchen, das in dem kleinen Haus ganz am Ende wohnte.

Die Reiche saß vor der Haustür in vollem Putz, und als der Königssohn sich näherte, stand sie auf, ging ihm entgegen und neigte sich vor ihm. Er sah sie an, sprach kein Wort und ritt weiter.

Als er zu dem Haus der Armen kam, stand das Mädchen nicht an der Türe, sondern saß in seinem Stübchen. Er hielt das Pferd an und sah durch das Fenster, durch das die helle Sonne schien, das Mädchen an dem Spinnrad sitzen und emsig spinnen. Es blickte auf, und als es bemerkte, daß der Königssohn hereinschaute, ward es über und über rot, schlug die Augen nieder und spann weiter. Ob der Faden diesmal ganz gleich ward, weiß ich nicht, aber es spann so lange, bis der Königssohn wieder weggeritten war. Dann trat es ans Fenster, öffnete es und sagte: »Es ist so heiß in der Stube«, aber es blickte ihm nach, solange es noch die weißen Federn an seinem Hut erkennen konnte.

Das Mädchen setzte sich wieder in seine Stube zur Arbeit und spann weiter. Da kam ihm ein Spruch in den Sinn, den die Alte manchmal gesagt hatte, wenn es bei der Arbeit saß, und es sang so vor sich hin:

>»Spindel, Spindel, geh du aus,
> bring den Freier in mein Haus.«

Was geschah? Die Spindel sprang ihm augenblicklich aus der Hand und zur Türe hinaus; und als es vor Verwunderung aufstand und ihr nachblickte, so sah es, daß sie lustig in das Feld hineintanzte und einen glänzenden goldenen Faden hinter sich herzog. Nicht lange, so war sie ihm aus den Augen verschwunden. Das Mädchen, da es keine Spindel mehr hatte, nahm das Weberschiffchen in die Hand, setzte sich an den Webstuhl und fing an zu weben.

Die Spindel aber tanzte immer weiter, und eben als der Faden zu Ende war, hatte sie den Königssohn erreicht.

»Was sehe ich?« rief er. »Die Spindel will mir wohl den Weg zeigen?« Er drehte sein Pferd um und ritt an dem goldenen Faden zurück. Das Mädchen aber saß an seiner Arbeit und sang:

»Schiffchen, Schiffchen, webe fein,
führ den Freier mir herein.«

Alsbald sprang ihr das Schiffchen aus der Hand und sprang zur Türe hinaus. Vor der Türschwelle aber fing es an, einen Teppich zu weben, schöner, als man je einen gesehen hat. Auf beiden Seiten blühten Rosen und Lilien, und in der Mitte auf goldenem Grund stiegen grüne Ranken herauf, darin sprangen Hasen und Kaninchen. Hirsche und Rehe streckten die Köpfe dazwischen; oben in den Zweigen saßen bunte Vögel; es fehlte nichts, als daß sie gesungen hätten. Das Schiffchen sprang hin und her, und es war, als wüchse alles von selber.

Weil das Schiffchen fortgelaufen war, hatte sich das Mädchen zum Nähen hingesetzt; es hielt die Nadel in der Hand und sang:

»Nadel, Nadel, spitz und fein,
mach das Haus dem Freier rein.«

Da sprang ihr die Nadel aus den Fingern und flog in der Stube hin und her, so schnell wie der Blitz. Es war nicht anders, als wenn unsichtbare Geister arbeiteten. Alsbald überzogen sich Tisch und Bänke mit grünem Tuch, die Stühle mit Samt, und an den Fenstern hingen seidene Vorhänge herab. Kaum hatte die Nadel den letzten Stich getan, so sah das Mädchen schon durch das Fenster die weißen Federn von dem Hut des Königssohns, den die Spindel an dem goldenen Faden herbeigeholt hatte. Er stieg ab, schritt über den Teppich in das Haus herein, und als er in die Stube trat, stand das Mädchen da in seinem ärmlichen Kleid, aber es glühte darin wie eine Rose im Busch. »Du bist die Ärmste und auch die Reichste«, sprach er zu ihr, »komm mit mir, du sollst meine Braut sein.« Sie schwieg, aber sie reichte ihm die Hand. Da gab er ihr einen Kuß, führte sie hinaus, hob sie auf sein Pferd und brachte sie in das königliche Schloß, wo die Hochzeit mit großer Freude gefeiert ward. Spindel, Weberschiffchen und Nadel wurden in der Schatzkammer verwahrt und in großen Ehren gehalten. 1843

Der junge Riese

Ein Bauersmann hatte einen Sohn, der war so groß wie ein Daumen und ward gar nicht größer und wuchs in etlichen Jahren nicht haarbreit. Einmal wollte der Bauer ins Feld gehen und pflügen, da sagte der Kleine: »Vater, ich will mit hinaus.« – »Nein«, sprach der Vater, »bleib du nur hier, draußen bist du zu nichts nutz, du könntest mir auch verloren gehen.« Da fing der Däumling an zu weinen, und wollte der Vater Ruhe haben, mußt' er ihn mitnehmen. Also steckte er ihn in die Tasche, und auf dem Felde tat er ihn heraus und setzte ihn in eine frische Furche.

Wie er da so saß, kam über den Berg ein großer Riese daher. »Siehst du dort den großen Butzemann?« sagte der Vater und wollte den Kleinen schrecken, damit er artig wäre. »Der kommt und holt dich.« Der Riese aber hatte lange Beine, und wie er noch ein paar Schritte getan, da war er bei der Furche, nahm den kleinen Däumling heraus und ging mit ihm fort. Der Vater stand dabei, konnte vor Schreck kein Wort sprechen und glaubte, sein Kind wäre nun verloren, also daß er's sein Lebtag nicht wiedersehen würde.

Der Riese aber nahm es mit sich und ließ es an seiner Brust saugen, und der Däumling wuchs und ward groß und stark nach Art der Riesen, und als zwei Jahre herum waren, ging der Alte mit ihm in den Wald und wollt' ihn versuchen und sprach: »Zieh dir da eine Gerte heraus.« Da war der Knabe schon so stark, daß er einen jungen Baum mit den Wurzeln aus der Erde riß. Der Riese aber dachte, das muß noch besser kommen, und nahm ihn wieder mit, säugte ihn noch zwei Jahre, und als er ihn da in den Wald führte, sich zu versuchen, riß er schon einen viel größeren Baum heraus. Das war aber dem Riesen noch nicht genug, und er säugte ihn noch zwei Jahre, ging dann mit ihm in den Wald und sprach: »Nun reiß einmal eine ordentliche Gerte aus.« Da riß der Junge den dicksten Eichenbaum aus der Erde, daß es krachte, und war ihm nur ein Spaß. Wie der alte Riese das sah, sprach er: »Nun ist's gut, du hast ausgelernt«, und führte ihn zurück auf den Acker, wo er ihn geholt hatte. Sein Vater pflügte gerade wieder, da ging der junge Riese auf ihn zu und sprach: »Sieht Er wohl, Vater, wie's gekommen ist, ich bin dein Sohn.« Da erschrak der Bauer und sagte: »Nein, du bist mein Sohn nicht, geh weg von mir.« – »Freilich bin ich dein Sohn, laß Er mich einmal pflügen, ich kann's so gut wie Er auch.« – »Nein, du bist mein Sohn nicht, du kannst auch nicht pflügen, geh nur weg von mir.« Weil er sich aber vor dem großen Mann fürchtete, ließ er den Pflug los, ging weg und setzte sich zur Seite ans Land. Da nahm der Junge das Geschirr und wollte pflügen und drückte bloß mit der einen Hand darauf, aber der Druck war schon so gewaltig, daß der Pflug tief in die Erde ging. Der Bauer konnte das nicht mit ansehen und rief ihm zu: »Wenn du pflügen willst, mußt du nicht so gewaltig drücken, das gibt ja schlechte Arbeit!« Der Junge aber spannte die Pferde aus und spannte sich selber vor den Pflug und sagte: »Geh Er nur nach Haus, Vater, und sag Er der Mutter, sie sollt' eine rechte Schüssel voll zu essen kochen; ich will derweil den Acker schon herumreißen.«

Da ging der Bauer heim und bestellte es bei seiner Frau, und die kochte eine tüchtige Schüssel voll, der Junge aber pflügte das Land, zwei Morgen Feld, ganz allein, und dann spannte er sich auch selber vor die Egge und eggte alles mit zwei Eggen zugleich. Wie er fertig war, ging er in den Wald und riß zwei Eichenbäume aus, legte sie auf die Schultern und hinten und vorn eine Egge drauf und hinten und vorn auch ein Pferd und trug das alles wie ein Bund Stroh nach Haus. Wie er in den Hof kam, erkannte ihn seine Mutter nicht und fragte: »Wer ist der entsetzliche, große Mann?« Der Bauer sagte: »Das ist unser Sohn.« Sie sprach: »Nein, unser Sohn ist das nimmermehr, so groß haben wir keinen gehabt, unser war ein kleines Ding. Geh nur weg, wir wollen dich nicht.« Der Junge aber schwieg still, zog seine Pferde in den Stall, gab ihnen Hafer und Heu und brachte alles in Ordnung; und wie er fertig war, ging er in die Stube, setzte sich auf die Bank und sagte: »Mutter, nun hätt' ich Lust zu essen, ist's bald fertig?« Da sagte sie ja, getraute sich nicht, ihm zu widersprechen, und brachte zwei große, große Schüsseln voll herein, daran hätten sie und ihr Mann acht Tage lang satt gehabt. Er aber aß sie allein auf und fragte, ob sie nicht mehr hätten? »Nein«, sagte sie, »das ist alles, was wir haben.« – »Das war ja nur zum Schmecken, ich muß noch mehr haben.« Da ging sie hin und setzte einen großen Schweinekessel voll übers Feuer, und wie es gar war, trug sie es herein. »Nun, da ist noch ein bißchen«, sagte er und aß das alles noch hinein; es war aber doch noch nicht genug. Da sprach er: »Vater, ich seh wohl, bei Ihm werd ich nicht satt, will Er mir einen Stab von Eisen verschaffen, der stark ist, daß ich ihn vor meinen Knien nicht zerbrechen kann, so will ich wieder fort gehen.«

Da war der Bauer froh und spannte seine zwei Pferde vor den Wagen, fuhr zum Schmied und holte einen Stab so groß und dick, als ihn die zwei Pferde nur fahren konnten. Der Junge aber nahm ihn vor die Knie, und ratsch! zerbrach er ihn wie eine Bohnenstange in der Mitte entzwei. Der Vater spannte da vier Pferde vor und holte einen Stab so groß und dick, als ihn die vier Pferde fahren konnten. Den nahm der Sohn auch, knickte ihn vor dem Knie entzwei, warf ihn hin und sprach: »Vater, der kann mir nicht helfen. Er muß besser vorspannen und einen stärkern Stab holen.« Da spannte der Vater acht Pferde vor und holte einen so groß und dick, als ihn die acht Pferde nur fahren konnten. Wie der Sohn den kriegte, brach er gleich oben ein Stück davon ab und sagte: »Vater, ich sehe, Er kann mir doch keinen Stab anschaffen, ich will nur so weggehen.«

Da ging er fort und gab sich für einen Schmiedegesellen aus. Er kam in ein Dorf, darin wohnte ein Schmied, der war ein Geizmann, gönnte keinem Menschen etwas und wollte alles haben; zu dem trat er nun in die Schmiede und fragte ihn, ob er keinen Gesellen brauche. »Ja«, sagte der Schmied und sah ihn an und dachte, das ist ein tüchtiger Kerl, der wird gut vorschlagen und sein Brot verdienen: »Wieviel willst du Lohn haben?« – »Gar keinen Lohn will ich haben«, sagte er, »nur alle vierzehn Tage, wenn die andern Gesellen ihren bezahlt kriegen, will ich dir zwei Streiche geben, die mußt du aushalten.« Das war der Geizmann von Herzen zufrieden und dachte damit viel Geld zu sparen. Am andern Morgen sollte der fremde Gesell zuerst vorschlagen, wie aber der Meister den glühenden Stab bringt und er den ersten Schlag tut, da fliegt das Eisen voneinander, und der Amboß sinkt in die Erde, so tief, daß sie ihn gar nicht wieder herausbringen konnten. Da ward der Geizmann bös und sagte: »Ei was, dich kann ich nicht brauchen, du schlägst gar zu grob, was willst du für den einen Zuschlag haben?« Da sprach er: »Ich will dir nur einen ganz kleinen Streich geben, weiter nichts.« Und er hob seinen Fuß auf und gab ihm einen Tritt, daß er über vier Fuder Heu hinausflog. Darauf nahm er den dicksten Eisenstab aus der Schmiede als einen Stock in die Hand und ging weiter.

Als er eine Weile weitergezogen war, kam er zu einem Amt und fragte den Amtmann, ob er keinen Großknecht nötig hätte. Ja, sagte der Amtmann, er könnte einen brauchen, er sehe aus wie ein tüchtiger Kerl, der schon was vermöchte, wieviel er Jahreslohn haben wollte. Da sprach er wieder, er wollt' gar keinen Lohn, aber alle Jahre wollt' er ihm drei Streiche geben, die müßte er aushalten. Das war der Amtmann zufrieden, denn er war auch so ein Geizhals. Am andern Morgen sollten die Knechte ins Holz fahren, und die andern waren schon auf, er aber lag noch im Bett. Da rief ihn einer an: »Nun steh auf, es ist Zeit, wir wollen ins Holz, du mußt mit.« – »Ach«, sagte er ganz grob und trotzig, »geht ihr nur hin, ich komme doch eher wieder als ihr alle miteinander.« Da gingen die andern zum Amtmann und erzählten ihm, der Großknecht läge noch im Bett und wollte nicht mit ins Holz fahren. Der Amtmann sagte, sie sollten ihn noch einmal wecken und ihn heißen, die Pferde vorspannen. Der Großknecht sprach aber wie vorher: »Geht ihr nur hin, ich komme doch eher wieder als ihr alle miteinander.« Darauf blieb er noch zwei Stunden liegen, da stieg er endlich aus den Federn, holte sich aber erst zwei Scheffel voll Erbsen vom Boden, kochte sie und aß sie in guter Ruhe, und wie das alles geschehen war, ging er hin, spannte die Pferde vor und fuhr ins Holz. Bald vor dem Holz war ein Hohlweg, wo er durch mußte, da fuhr er den Wagen erst vorwärts, dann mußten die Pferde stillhalten, und er ging hinter den Wagen und nahm Bäume und Reisig und machte da eine große Hucke (Verhau), so daß kein Pferd durchkommen konnte. Wie er nun vors Holz kam, fuhren die andern eben mit ihren beladenen Wagen heraus und wollten heim, da sprach er zu ihnen: »Fahrt nur hin, ich komme doch eher als ihr nach Haus.« Er fuhr aber nur ein bißchen ins Holz und riß gleich zwei von den allergrößten Bäumen aus der Erde, die lud er auf den Wagen und drehte um. Wie er vor die Hucke kam, standen die andern noch da und konnten nicht durch, da sprach er: »Seht ihr wohl, wärt ihr bei mir geblieben, wärt ihr ebenso gerade nach Haus gekommen und hättet noch eine Stunde schlafen können.« Er wollte nun zufahren, aber seine vier Pferde konnten sich nicht durcharbeiten, da spannte er sie aus, legte sie oben auf den Wagen, spannte sich selber vor, húf, zog er alles durch, und das ging so leicht, als hätt' er Federn geladen. Wie er drüben war, sprach er zu den andern: »Seht ihr wohl, ich bin eher durchgekommen als ihr«, und fuhr fort, und die andern mußten stehen bleiben. In dem Hof aber nahm er einen Baum in die Hand und zeigte ihn dem Amtmann und sagte: »Ist das nicht ein schönes Klafterstück?« Da sprach der Amtmann zu seiner Frau: »Der Knecht ist gut, wenn er auch lang schläft, er ist doch eher wieder da als die andern.«

Nun diente er dem Amtmann ein Jahr; wie das herum war und die andern Knechte ihren Lohn kriegten, sprach er, nun wär's Zeit, er wollte auch gern seinen Lohn sich nehmen. Dem Amtmann ward aber angst dabei, daß er die Streiche kriegen sollte, und bat ihn gar zu sehr, er möchte sie ihm schenken, lieber wollte er selbst Großknecht werden und er sollte Amtmann sein. »Nein«, sprach er, »ich will kein Amtmann werden, ich bin Großknecht und will's bleiben, ich will aber austeilen, was bedungen ist.« Der Amtmann wollt' ihm geben, was er nur verlangte, aber es half nichts, der Großknecht sprach zu allem nein. Da wußte sich der Amtmann keinen Rat und bat ihn nur um vierzehn Tage Frist, er wollte sich auf etwas besinnen; da sprach der Großknecht, die sollt' er haben. Der Amtmann berief alle seine Schreiber zusammen, die sollten sich bedenken und ihm einen Rat geben. Die besannen sich lange, endlich sagten sie, man müßte den Großknecht ums Leben bringen; er sollte große Mühlsteine um den Brunnen im Hof anfahren lassen und dann ihn heißen hinabsteigen und den Brunnen rein machen, und wenn er unten wäre, wollten sie ihm die Mühlsteine auf den Kopf werfen. Der Rat gefiel dem Amtmann, und da ward alles eingerichtet und wurden die größten Mühlsteine herangefahren. Wie nun der Großknecht im Brunnen stand, rollten sie die Steine hinab, und die schlugen hinunter, daß das Wasser in die Höh spritzte. Da meinten sie gewiß, der Kopf wär ihm eingeschlagen, aber er rief: »Jagt doch die Hühner vom Brunnen weg, die kratzen da oben Sand und werfen mir die Körner in die Augen, daß ich nicht sehen kann.« Da rief der Amtmann: bsch! bsch! Und tat, als scheuche er die Hühner weg. Wie nun der Großknecht fertig war, stieg er hinauf und sagte: »Seht einmal, ich hab doch ein schön Halsband um«, da waren es die Mühlensteine, die trug er um den Hals. Wie der Amtmann das sah, ward ihm wieder angst, denn der Großknecht wollt' ihm nun seinen Lohn geben; da bat er wieder um vierzehn Tage Bedenkzeit und ließ die Schreiber zusammenkommen, die gaben endlich den Rat, er sollt' ihn in die verwünschte Mühle schicken und ihn heißen, dort in der Nacht noch Korn mahlen, da sei noch kein Mensch morgens lebendig herausgegangen. Der Anschlag gefiel dem Amtmann; also rief er ihn noch denselben Abend und sagte, er sollte acht Malter Korn in die Mühle fahren und in der Nacht noch mahlen, sie hätten's nötig. Da ging der Großknecht auf den Boden und tat zwei Malter in seine rechte Tasche, zwei in die linke, vier nahm er in einem Quersack halb auf den Rücken, halb auf die Brust und ging so nach der verwünschten Mühle. Der Müller aber sagte ihm, bei Tag könnt er recht gut da mahlen, aber nicht in der Nacht, da sei die Mühle verwünscht, und wer da noch hineingegangen, der sei am Morgen tot darin gefunden worden. Er sprach: »Ich will schon durchkommen, macht Euch nur fort und legt Euch aufs Ohr.« Darauf ging er in die Mühle und schüttete das Korn auf, und wie's bald elf schlagen wollte, ging er in die Müllerstube und setzte sich auf die Bank. Als er ein bißchen da gesessen hatte, tat sich auf einmal die Tür auf und kam eine große, große Tafel herein, und auf die Tafel stellte sich Wein und Braten und viel gutes Essen, alles von selber, denn es war niemand da, der's auftrug. Und danach rückten sich die Stühle herbei, aber es kamen keine Leute, bis auf einmal sah er Finger, die hantierten mit den Messern und Gabeln und legten Speisen auf die Teller, aber sonst konnt' er nichts sehen. Nun war er hungrig und sah die Speisen, da setzte er sich auch an die Tafel und aß mit und ließ sich's gut schmecken. Wie er aber satt war und die andern ihre Schüsseln auch ganz leer gemacht hatten, da wurden die Lichter auf einmal alle ausgeputzt, das hörte er deutlich, und wie's nun stockfinster war, so kriegte er so etwas wie eine Ohrfeige ins Gesicht; da sprach er: »Wenn noch einmal so etwas kommt, so teil ich auch wieder aus«; und wie er zum zweiten Mal

234 *Der junge Riese*

eine kriegte, da schlug er gleichfalls mit hinein. Und so ging das fort die ganze Nacht, er ließ sich nicht schrecken und schlug, nicht faul, um sich herum; bei Tagesanbruch aber hörte alles auf. Wie der Müller aufgestanden war, wollt' er nach ihm sehen und verwunderte sich, daß er noch lebte. Da sprach er: »Ich habe Ohrfeigen gekriegt, aber ich habe auch Ohrfeigen ausgeteilt und mich satt gegessen.« Der Müller freute sich und sagte, nun wäre die Mühle erlöst, und er wollt' ihm gern zur Belohnung viel Geld geben. Er sprach aber: »Geld will ich nicht, ich habe doch genug.« Dann nahm er sein Mehl auf den Rücken und ging nach Haus und sagte dem Amtmann, er habe die Sache ausgerichtet und wollte nun seinen bedungenen Lohn haben. Wie der Amtmann das hörte, da ward ihm erst recht angst, und er wußte sich nicht zu lassen und ging in der Stube auf und ab, daß ihm die Schweißtropfen von der Stirn herunter liefen. Da machte er das Fenster auf nach ein wenig frischer Luft, eh' er sich's aber versah, hatte ihm der Großknecht einen Tritt gegeben, daß er durchs Fenster in die Luft hinein flog, immer fort, bis ihn niemand mehr sehen konnte. Da sprach der Großknecht zur Frau des Amtmanns, nun müßte sie den andern Streich hinnehmen, die sagte aber: »Ach nein, ich kann's nicht aushalten«, und machte auch ein Fenster auf, weil ihr die Schweißtropfen die Stirn herunter liefen. Da gab er ihr gleichfalls einen Tritt, daß sie auch hinausflog, und noch viel höher als ihr Mann; und der rief ihr zu: »Komm doch zu mir!« Sie aber rief: »Komm du doch zu mir, ich kann nicht zu dir«; und sie schwebten da in der Luft und konnten keins zum andern, und ob sie da noch schweben, das weiß ich nicht. Der junge Riese aber nahm seine Eisenstange und ging weiter. 1819

Der arme Müllerbursch und das Kätzchen

In einer Mühle dienten einmal drei Müllerburschen, worin nur ein alter Müller lebte, ohne Frau und Kind. Wie sie nun etliche Jahre bei ihm gedient hatten, sagte er zu ihnen: »Zieht einmal fort, und wer mir das beste Pferd nach Haus bringt, dem will ich die Mühle geben.« Der dritte von den Burschen war aber der Kleinknecht, der ward von den andern für albern gehalten, dem gönnten sie die Mühle nicht; und er wollte sie hernach nicht einmal! Da gingen alle drei miteinander hinaus, und wie sie vor das Dorf kamen, sagten die zwei zu dem albernen Hans: »Du kannst nur hier bleiben, du kriegst doch dein Lebtag keinen Gaul.« Der Hans aber ging doch mit, und als es Nacht war, kamen sie an eine Höhle, da hinein legten sie sich schlafen. Die zwei Klugen warteten, bis Hans eingeschlafen war, dann stiegen sie auf, machten sich fort, ließen das Hänschen liegen und meinten's recht fein ge-

macht zu haben. Ja, es wird euch doch nicht gut gehen! Wie nun die Sonne kam und Hans aufwachte, lag er in einer tiefen Höhle. Er guckte sich überall um und rief: »Ach Gott! Wo bin ich!« Da erhob er sich und kraxelte die Höhle hinauf, ging in den Wald und dachte: »Wie soll ich nun zu einem Pferd kommen?« Indem er so in Gedanken dahin ging, begegnete ihm ein kleines buntes Kätzchen, sprach: »Hans, wo willst du hin?« – »Ach, du kannst mir doch nicht helfen.« – »Was dein Begehren ist, weiß ich wohl«, sprach das Kätzchen, »du willst einen hübschen Gaul haben, komm mit mir und sei sieben Jahre lang mein treuer Knecht, so will ich dir einen geben, schöner, als du dein Lebtag einen gesehen hast.« Da nahm sie ihn mit in ihr verwünschtes Schlößchen, er mußt' ihr dienen und alle Tage Holz klein machen, dazu kriegte er eine Axt von Silber und die Keile und Säge von Silber, und der Schläger war von Kupfer.

Nun, da machte er's klein, blieb bei ihm, hatte sein gutes Essen und Trinken, sah aber niemand als das bunte Kätzchen.

Einmal sagte es zu ihm: »Geh hin und mäh meine Wiese und mach das Gras trocken«, und gab ihm von Silber eine Sense und von Gold einen Wetzstein, hieß ihn aber auch alles wieder richtig abliefern. Da ging der Hans hin und tat, was es geheißen hatte, und als er fertig war und die Sense, den Wetzstein und das Heu nach Haus brachte, fragte er, ob es ihm noch nicht seinen Lohn geben wollte. »Nein«, sagte die Katze, »du sollst mir erst noch einerlei tun. Da ist Bauholz von Silber, Zimmeraxt, Winkeleisen und was nötig ist, alles von Silber, daraus bau mir erst ein kleines Häuschen.« Da baute der Hans das Häuschen fertig und sagte, er hätte nun alles getan und noch kein Pferd. Die sieben Jahre aber waren ihm herumgegangen wie ein halbes. Fragte die Katze: Ob er ihre Pferde sehen wollte? »Ja«, sagte Hans. Da machte sie ihm das Häuschen auf, und wie sie die Türe so aufmacht, da stehen zwölf Pferde. Ach, die waren gewesen ganz stolz! Die hatten geblänkt und gespiegelt, daß sich sein Herz im Leib darüber freute. Nun gab sie ihm zu essen und zu trinken und sprach: »Geh nun heim, dein Pferd geb ich dir nicht mit, in drei Tagen aber komm ich und bring dir's nach.« Also ging Hans heim, und sie zeigte ihm den Weg zur Mühle. Sie hatte ihm aber nicht einmal ein neu Kleid gegeben, sondern er mußte sein altes lumpiges Kittelchen behalten, das er mitgebracht hatte und das ihm in den sieben Jahren überall zu kurz geworden war.

Wie er nun heimkam, da waren die beiden andern Müllerburschen auch wieder da, jeder hatte zwar ein Pferd mitgebracht, aber des einen seins war blind, des andern seins lahm. Sie fragten ihn: »Hans, wo hast du dein Pferd?« – »In drei Tagen wird's nachkommen.« Da lachten sie und sagten: »Ja, du Hans, wo willst du dein Pferd herkriegen, das wird was Rechtes sein!« Hans ging in die Stube, der Müller sagte aber, er solle nicht an den Tisch kommen, er wäre zu zerrissen und zerlumpt, man müßte sich schämen, wenn jemand hereinkäme. Da gaben sie ihm sein bißchen Essen hinaus, und wie sie abends schlafen gingen, wollten ihm die zwei andern kein Bett geben, und er mußte endlich ins Gänseställchen kriechen und sich auf ein wenig Stroh hineinlegen. Am Morgen, wie er aufwacht, sind schon die drei Tage herum, und es kommt eine Kutsche mit sechs Pferden, ei, die glänzten, daß es schön war, und ein Bedienter, der brachte noch ein siebentes, das war für den armen Müllerbursch.

Aus der Kutsche aber stieg eine prächtige Königstochter und ging in die Mühle hinein, und die Königstochter war das kleine bunte Kätzchen, dem der arme Hans sieben Jahre gedient hatte. Sie fragte den Müller, wo der dritte Mahlbursch, der Kleinknecht, wäre? Da sagte der Müller: »Den können wir nicht in die Mühle nehmen, der ist so zerrissen und liegt im Gänsestall.« Da sagte die Königstochter, sie sollten ihn gleich holen. Also holten sie ihn heraus, und er mußte sein Kittelchen zusammenpacken, um sich zu bedecken; da schnallte der Bediente prächtige Kleider aus und mußte ihn waschen und anziehen, und wie er fertig war, konnte kein König schöner aussehen.

Danach wollte die Jungfrau die Pferde sehen, welche die andern Mahlburschen mitgebracht hatten; eins war blind, das andere lahm. Da ließ sie den Bedienten das siebente Pferd bringen. Wie der Müller das sah, sprach er, so eins wär ihm noch nicht auf den Hof gekommen. »Und das ist für den dritten Mahlbursch«, sprach sie. »Da muß er die Mühle haben«, sagte der Müller. Die Königstochter aber sprach, das wär sein Pferd, er solle die Mühle auch behalten; und nimmt ihren treuen Hans und setzt ihn in die Kutsche und fährt mit ihm fort. Sie fahren erst nach dem kleinen Häuschen, das er mit dem silbernen Werkzeug gebaut hat, da ist es ein großes Schloß und ist alles darin von Silber und Gold, und da hat sie ihn geheiratet und war er reich, so reich, daß er für sein Lebtag genug hatte. Darum soll keiner sagen, daß wer albern ist, deshalb nichts Rechtes werden könne. 1819

Fitchers Vogel

Es war einmal ein Hexenmeister, der nahm die Gestalt eines armen Mannes an, ging vor die Häuser und bettelte und fing die schönen Mädchen. Kein Mensch wußte, wo er sie hinbrachte, denn sie kamen nimmermehr wieder zum Vorschein. Nun trat er auch einmal vor die Türe eines Mannes, der drei schöne Töchter hatte, als ein armer, schwacher Bettler und trug eine Kiepe auf dem Rücken, als wollte er die milden Gaben darin sammeln. Er bat um ein bißchen Essen, und als die älteste herauskam und ihm ein Stück Brot reichen wollte, rührte er sie nur an, und alsbald mußte sie in seine Kiepe springen. Dann trug er sie mit starken Schritten fort und durch einen Wald hindurch in sein Haus, wo alles prächtig war. Da gab er ihr, was sie nur wünschte, und sprach: »Es wird dir wohlgefallen bei mir, denn du hast alles, was dein Herz begehrt.« Das dauerte ein paar Tage, da sagte er: »Ich muß fortreisen und dich eine kurze Zeit allein lassen, da sind die Hausschlüssel, du kannst überall herumgehen und alles sehen, nur nicht in eine Stube, die dieser kleine Schlüssel aufschließt, das verbiet ich dir bei Lebensstrafe. Da hast du auch ein Ei, das verwahre mir sorgfältig und trag es lieber beständig bei dir, denn wenn es verloren ging, wär's ein großes Unglück.«

Sie nahm die Schlüssel und das Ei und versprach, alles wohl auszurichten. Als er aber fort war, konnte sie der Neugierde nicht widerstehen, und nachdem sie das ganze Haus gesehen, ging sie auch zu der verbotenen Türe und öffnete sie. Wie erschrak sie aber, als sie hineintrat: da stand in der Mitte ein großes, blutiges Becken, und darin lagen tote, zerhauene Menschen. Sie erschrak so sehr, daß das Ei, das sie in der Hand hielt, hineinplumpte. Zwar holte sie es geschwind wieder heraus und wischte das Blut ab, aber es half nichts, denn es kam den Augenblick wieder zum Vorschein: sie wischte und schabte, aber sie konnte es nicht herunterkriegen. Nicht lange, so kam der Mann von der Reise zurück und sprach: »Nun gib mir die Schlüssel und das Ei wieder.« Sie reichte es ihm mit Zittern hin, er sah beides an und sah, daß sie in der Blutkammer gewesen war. Da sprach er: »Bist du gegen meinen Willen in der Kammer gewesen, so sollst du nun gegen deinen wieder hinein. Dein Leben ist zu Ende.« Darauf ergriff er sie, führte sie hinein, zerhackte sie, daß ihr rotes Blut auf der Erde floß, und warf sie zu den übrigen ins Becken.

»Jetzt will ich mir die zweite holen«, sprach der Hexenmeister, ging wieder in Gestalt eines armen Mannes vor das Haus und bettelte. Da brachte ihm die zweite ein Stück Brot, und er fing sie wie die erste durch ein bloßes Anrühren, trug sie hinaus und mordete sie in der Blutkammer, weil sie hineingeschaut hatte. Da ging er, die dritte Schwester noch zu fangen, und brachte sie auch hinaus. Die dritte aber war klug und listig; als er ihr nun die Schlüssel und das Ei gegeben hatte und fortgereist war, hob sie das Ei erst auf und verschloß es und ging dann in die verbotene Kammer. Ach, was sah sie! Ihre beiden lieben Schwestern jämmerlich ermordet in dem Becken liegen. Aber sie hub an und suchte ihre Glieder zusammen und legte sie zurecht, Kopf, Leib, Arm und Beine. Und als nichts mehr fehlte, da fingen die Glieder an, sich zu regen, und schlossen sich aneinander, und beide Mädchen öffneten die Augen und wurden wieder lebendig. Da freuten sie sich, küßten und herzten einander, aber die jüngste führte sie heraus und versteckte sie. Als der Mann zurückkam, forderte er die Schlüssel und das Ei, und als er an diesem keine Spur von Blut entdecken konnte, sprach er: »Du hast die Probe bestanden, du sollst meine Braut sein.« – »Ja«, antwortete sie, »aber du mußt mir versprechen, vorher einen Korb voll Gold meinem Vater und meiner Mutter auf deinem Rücken hinzutragen, derweil will ich die Hochzeit bestellen.« Darauf ging sie in ihr Kämmerlein, wo sie ihre Schwestern versteckt hatte, und sprach: »Ja, will ich euch erretten, aber sobald ihr nach Haus kommt, bestellt mir Hilfe.« Dann setzte sie beide in einen Korb und deckte sie mit Gold ganz zu, daß nichts von ihnen zu sehen war, und rief den Hexenmeister herein und sprach: »Nun trag den Korb fort, aber daß du unterwegs nicht stehen bleibst und ruhen willst! Ich schaue hier durch mein Fensterlein und habe acht.«

Nun hob der Hexenmeister den Korb auf seinen Rücken und ging mit fort, er wurde ihm aber so schwer, daß ihm der Schweiß über das Angesicht lief und er glaubte, tot gedrückt zu werden. Da wollt' er sich ein wenig ruhen, aber gleich rief eine im Korb: »Ich schaue durch mein Fensterlein, daß du ruhst, willst du gleich weiter!« Er meinte, die Braut rief ihm das zu, und machte sich wieder auf. Hernach wollte er sich wieder setzen, aber es rief gleich: »Ich schaue durch mein Fensterlein, daß du ruhst, willst du gleich weiter!« Und sooft er stillstand, rief es, und da mußte er fort und brachte außer Atem den Korb mit Gold und den beiden Mädchen in ihrer Eltern Haus.

Daheim aber ordnete die Braut das Hochzeitfest an. Sie nahm einen Totenkopf mit grinsenden Zähnen und setzte ihm einen Schmuck auf und trug ihn oben vors Bodenloch und ließ ihn da herausschauen. Dann lud sie die Freunde des Hexenmeisters zum Fest ein, und wie das geschehen war, steckte sie sich in ein Faß mit Honig, schnitt das Bett auf und wälzte sich darin, daß sie aussah wie ein wunderlicher Vogel und kein Mensch sie erkennen konnte. Da ging sie zum Haus hinaus, und unterwegs begegnete ihr ein Teil der Hochzeitgäste, die fragten:

>>Du Fitchers-Vogel, wo kommst du her?<<
>>Ich komme von Fitze Fitchers Hause her.<<
>>Was macht denn da die junge Braut?<<
>>Hat gekehrt von unten bis oben das Haus
Und guckt zum Bodenloch heraus.<<

Darauf begegnete ihr der Bräutigam, der zurückkam, der fragte auch:

>>Du Fitchers-Vogel, wo kommst du her?<<
>>Ich komme von Fitze Fitchers Hause her.<<
>>Was macht denn da meine junge Braut?<<
>>Hat gekehrt von unten bis oben das Haus
Und guckt zum Bodenloch heraus.<<

Der Bräutigam schaute hinauf und sah den geputzten Totenkopf, da meinte er, es wäre seine Braut, und nickte ihr zu und grüßte sie freundlich. Wie er aber samt seinen Gästen ins Haus gegangen war, da kam die Hilfe von den Schwestern an, und sie schlossen alle Türen des Hauses zu, daß niemand entfliehen konnte, und steckten es an, also daß der Hexenmeister mit seinem ganzen Gesindel verbrennen mußte.

1819

Der gelernte Jäger

Es war einmal ein junger Bursch, der hatte das Schlosserhandwerk gelernt und sprach zu seinem Vater, er müßte in die Welt gehen und sich versuchen. »Ja«, sagte der Vater, »das bin ich zufrieden« und gab ihm etwas Geld auf die Reise. Also zog er herum. Nach einiger Zeit, da gefiel ihm das Schlosserhandwerk nicht mehr und stand ihm auch nicht mehr an, aber er kriegte Lust zur Jägerei. Da begegnete ihm auf der Wanderschaft ein Jäger in grünem Kleide, der fragte, wo er her käm und hin wollte? Er wär ein Schlossergesell, sagte der Bursch, aber das Handwerk gefiele ihm nicht mehr, hätte Lust zur Jägerei, ob er sie ihn lehren wollte. – »O ja, wenn du mit mir gehen willst.« Da ging der junge Bursch mit und vermietete sich etliche Jahre bei ihm und lernte die Jägerei. Danach wollt' er sich weiter versuchen, und der Jäger gab ihm nichts zum Lohn als eine Windbüchse, die hatte aber die Eigenschaft, wenn er damit schoß, so traf er unfehlbar.

Da ging er nun fort und kam in einen sehr großen Wald, von dem konnt' er in einem Tag das Ende nicht finden. Wie's Abend war, setzte er sich auf einen hohen Baum, damit er aus den wilden Tieren käme. Gegen Mitternacht zu, deuchte ihn, schimmerte ein kleines Lichtchen von weitem; da sah er durch die Äste darauf hin und behielt in acht, wo es war. Doch nahm er erst noch seinen Hut und warf ihn nach dem Licht zu herunter, daß er danach gehen wollte, wenn er herabgestiegen wär, als nach einem Zeichen. Nun kletterte er herunter, ging auf seinen Hut los, setzte ihn wieder auf und zog geradewegs fort. Je weiter er ging, desto größer ward das Licht, und wie er nahe dabei kam, sah er, daß es ein gewaltiges Feuer war, und saßen drei Riesen dabei und hatten einen Ochsen am Spieß und ließen ihn braten. Nun sprach der eine: »Ich muß doch schmecken, ob das Fleisch bald gar ist«, riß ein Stück herab und hielt's an den Mund, indem schoß es ihm der Jäger aus der Hand. »Nun ja«, sprach der Riese, »da weht mir der Wind das Stück aus der Hand!« und nahm sich ein anderes. Wie er eben anbeißen wollte, schoß es ihm der Jäger abermals weg; da gab der Riese dem, der neben ihm saß, eine Ohrfeige und rief zornig: »Was reißt du mir mein Stück weg!« – »Ich habe dir nichts weggerissen«, sprach der andere, »es wird dir's ein Scharfschütz weggeschossen haben.« Der Riese nahm sich das dritte Stück, er konnt's aber nicht in der Hand behalten, der Jäger schoß es ihm heraus. Da sprachen die Riesen: »Das muß ein guter Schütze sein, der den Bissen vor dem Maul wegschießen kann, so einer wär uns nützlich«, und riefen laut: »Komm herbei, du Scharfschütze, setz dich ans Feuer und iß dich satt, wir wollen dir nichts tun; aber kommst du nicht und wir holen dich mit Gewalt, so bist du verloren.«

Da trat der Bursch herzu und sagte, er wär ein gelernter Jäger, und wonach er mit seiner Büchse ziele, das treffe er auch sicher und gewiß. Da sprachen sie, wenn er mit ihnen gehe, solle er's gut haben, und erzählten ihm, vor dem Wald sei ein groß Wasser, dahinter ständ ein Turm, und in dem Turm säß eine schöne Königstochter, die wollten sie gern rauben. »Ja«, sprach er, »die will ich bald geschafft haben.« Sagten sie weiter: »Es ist aber etwas noch dabei, es liegt ein kleines Hündchen dort, das fängt gleich an zu bellen, wenn sich jemand nähert, und sobald das bellt, wacht auch alles am königlichen Hofe auf, darum können wir nicht hineinkommen. Unterstehst du dich, das Hündchen totzuschießen?« – »Ja«, sprach er, »das ist mir ein kleiner Spaß.« – Danach setzte er sich auf ein Schiff und fuhr über das Wasser, und wie er bald an Land war, kam das Hündchen gelaufen und wollte bellen, aber er kriegte seine Windbüchse und schoß es tot. Wie die Riesen das sahen, freuten sie sich und meinten, sie hätten die Königstochter nun schon gewiß. Er sprach aber zu ihnen, sie sollten außen bleiben, bis er ihnen riefe. Da ging er in das Schloß, und es war mäuschenstill und schlief alles; wie er das erste Zimmer aufmachte, hing da ein Säbel an der Wand, der war von purem Silber und ein goldener Stern darauf und des Königs Name; daneben aber stand ein Tisch, und auf dem Tisch lag ein versiegelter Brief, den brach er auf, und stand darin, wer den Säbel hätte, könnte alles ums Leben bringen, was ihm vorkäme. Da nahm er den Säbel von der Wand, hing ihn um und ging weiter. Da kam er in das Zimmer, wo die Königstochter lag und schlief, und sie war so schön, daß er still stand und sie betrachtete und den Atem anhielt.

Wie er sich weiter umschaute, da standen unter dem Bett ein Paar Pantoffeln, auf dem rechten stand ihres Vaters Name mit einem Stern und auf dem linken ihr Name mit einem Stern. Sie hatte auch ein großes Halstuch um, von Seide mit Gold ausgestickt, auf der rechten Seite ihres Vaters Name, auf der linken ihr Name, alles mit goldenen Buchstaben.

Da nahm der Jäger eine Schere und schnitt den rechten Zipfel ab und stopfte ihn in seinen Ranzen, und dann nahm er auch den rechten Pantoffel mit des Königs Namen und steckte ihn hinein. Nun lag die Jungfrau noch immer und schlief, und sie war ganz in ihr Hemd eingenäht, da schnitt er auch ein Stückchen von dem Hemd ab und steckte es zu dem andern, doch tat er das alles, ohne sie anzurühren. Dann ging er wieder fort und ließ sie schlafen, und als er wieder ans Tor kam, standen da die Riesen noch draußen, warteten auf ihn und dachten, er würde die Königstochter bringen. Er rief ihnen aber zu, sie sollten sich auch herein machen, die Jungfrau wäre schon in seiner Gewalt; die Türe könnte er ihnen aber nicht aufmachen, da wär ein Loch, durch welches sie kriechen müßten. Nun kam der erste näher, da wickelte der Jäger des Riesen Haar um seine Hand, zog den Kopf herein und hieb ihn mit seinem Säbel in einem Streich ab und zog ihn dann vollends herein. Dann rief er den zweiten und hieb ihm gleichfalls das Haupt ab und endlich auch dem dritten und war froh, daß er die schöne Jungfrau von ihren Feinden befreit hatte, und schnitt ihnen die Zungen aus und steckte sie in seinen Ranzen. Da dacht' er, ich will heimgehen zu meinem Vater und ihm zeigen, was ich

schon getan habe, dann will ich in der Welt herumziehen, das Glück, das mir Gott bescheren will, wird mich schon erreichen.

Der König in dem Schloß aber, als er aufwachte, sah drei Riesen da tot liegen; ging in die Schlafkammer seiner Tochter, weckte sie auf und fragte, wer das wohl gewesen, der die Riesen ums Leben gebracht. Da sagte sie: »Lieber Vater, ich weiß es nicht, ich habe geschlafen.« Wie sie nun aufstand und ihre Pantoffeln anziehen wollte, da war der rechte weg, und wie sie ihr Halstuch betrachtete, war es durchschnitten und fehlte der rechte Zipfel, und wie sie ihr Hemd ansah, war ein Stückchen heraus. Der König ließ den ganzen Hof zusammenkommen, Soldaten und alles, was da war, und fragte, wer seine Tochter befreit und die Riesen ums Leben gebracht hätte?

Nun hatte er einen Hauptmann, der war einäugig und ein häßlicher Mensch, der sagte, er hätte es getan. Da sprach der alte König, so er das vollbracht, sollte er auch seine Tochter heiraten. Die Jungfrau aber sagte: »Lieber Vater, dafür, daß ich den heiraten soll, will ich lieber in die Welt gehen, so weit, als mich meine Beine tragen.« Da sprach der König, wenn sie den nicht heiraten wollte, sollte sie die königlichen Kleider ausziehen und Bauernkleider antun und fortgehen; und sie sollte zu einem Töpfer gehen und einen irden Geschirrhandel anfangen. Da tat sie ihre königlichen Kleider aus und ging zu einem Töpfer und borgte sich einen Kram irden Werk; versprach ihm auch, wenn sie's am Abend verkauft hätte, es zu bezahlen. Nun sagte der König, sie sollte sich an eine Ecke damit setzen und es verkaufen, dann bestellte er etliche Bauernwagen, die sollten mitten durchfahren, daß alles in tausend Stücke ging. Wie nun die Königstochter ihren Kram auf die Straße hingestellt hatte, kamen die Wagen und zerbrachen ihn zu lauter Scherben. Fing sie an zu weinen und sprach: »Ach Gott! Wie will ich nun den Töpfer bezahlen.« Der König aber hatte sie damit zwingen wollen, den Hauptmann zu heiraten, statt dessen ging sie wieder zum Töpfer und fragte ihn, ob er ihr noch einmal borgen wolle. Er antwortete nein, sie sollt' erst das Vorige bezahlen. Da ging sie zu ihrem Vater und schrie und sagte, sie wollte in die Welt hineingehen. Da sprach er, sie sollt' hingehen in den Wald, da wollt' er ihr ein Häuschen bauen, darin sollt' sie ihr Lebtag sitzen und für jedermann kochen, dürfte aber kein Geld nehmen. Also ließ er ihr ein Häuschen im Wald bauen, vor die Türe ein Schild, darauf stand geschrieben: »Heute umsonst, morgen für Geld.« Da saß sie lange Zeit, und sprach es sich in der Welt herum, da säß eine Jungfrau, die kochte umsonst, und das ständ vor der Türe an einem Schild. Das hörte auch der Jäger und dachte: Ei, das wär etwas für dich, du bist doch arm und hast kein Geld; nahm also seine Windbüchse und seinen Ranzen, worin noch alles steckte, was er damals im Schloß als Wahrzeichen hineingetan hatte, und ging in den Wald und fand auch das Häuschen mit dem Schild: »Heute umsonst, morgen für Geld.« Er hatte aber den Degen umhängen, womit er den drei Riesen den Kopf abgehauen hatte, trat so in das Häuschen hinein und ließ sich etwas zu essen geben. Er freute sich über das schöne Mädchen, es war aber auch bildschön. Sie fragte ihn, wo er herkäm und hin wollte, da sagte er: »Ich reise in der Welt herum.« Da fragte sie ihn, wo er den Degen her hätte, da stände ja ihres Vaters Name darauf! Fragte er, ob sie des Königs Tochter wäre? »Ja«, sagte sie. »Mit diesem Säbel«, sprach er, »hab ich drei Riesen den Kopf abgehauen« und holte zum Zeichen ihre Zungen aus dem Ranzen, dann zeigte er ihr auch den Pantoffel, den Zipfel vom Halstuch und das Stück vom Hemd. Da war sie voller Freude und sagte, er wär derjenige, der sie erlöst hätte. Darauf gingen sie zusammen zum alten König, und sie führte ihn in ihre Kammer und sagte ihm, der Jäger sei der rechte, der sie erlöst hätte von den Riesen. Und wie der alte König die Wahrzeichen alle sah, da konnt' er nicht mehr zweifeln und sagte, das wär ihm lieb, und er sollte sie nun auch zur Gemahlin haben; darüber war die Jungfrau von Herzen froh. Darauf kleideten sie ihn, als wenn er ein fremder Herr wäre, und der König ließ ein Gastmahl anstellen. Als sie nun zu Tisch gingen, kam der Hauptmann auf die linke Seite der Königstochter, der Jäger aber auf die rechte, und der Hauptmann meinte, das sei ein fremder Herr und wär zu Besuch gekommen. Wie sie gegessen und getrunken hatten, sprach der alte König zum Hauptmann, er wollt' ihm etwas aufgeben, das sollt' er erraten: Wenn einer spräch, er hätte drei Riesen ums Leben gebracht und er gefragt würde, wo die Zungen der Riesen wären, und er müßt' zusehen, und wären keine in ihren Köpfen, wie das zuginge? Da sagte der Hauptmann: »Sie werden keine gehabt haben.« – »Ei!«, sagte der König, »jed' Getier hat eine Zunge«, und fragte weiter, was der wert wäre, daß ihm widerführe? Da sprach der Hauptmann: »Der gehört in Stücke zerrissen zu werden.« Da sagte der König, er hätte sich selber sein Urteil gesprochen, und ward der Hauptmann gefangengesetzt und dann in vier Stücke zerrissen, die Königstochter aber mit dem Jäger vermählt, der holte seinen Vater und seine Mutter, und die lebten in Freude bei ihrem Sohn, und nach des alten Königs Tod bekam er das Reich.   1819

246 *Blaubart*

Blaubart

In einem Walde lebte ein Mann, der hatte drei Söhne und eine schöne Tochter. Einmal kam ein goldener Wagen mit sechs Pferden und einer Menge Bedienten angefahren, hielt vor dem Haus still, und ein König stieg aus und bat den Mann, er möchte ihm seine Tochter zur Gemahlin geben. Der Mann war froh, daß seiner Tochter ein solches Glück widerfuhr, und sagte gleich ja; es war auch an dem Freier gar nichts auszusetzen, als daß er einen ganz blauen Bart hatte, so daß man einen kleinen Schrecken kriegte, sooft man ihn ansah. Das Mädchen erschrak auch anfangs davor und scheute sich, ihn zu heiraten, aber auf Zureden ihres Vaters willigte es endlich ein. Doch weil es so eine Angst fühlte, ging es erst zu seinen drei Brüdern, nahm sie allein und sagte: »Liebe Brüder, wenn ihr mich schreien hört, wo ihr auch seid, so laßt alles stehen und liegen und kommt mir zu Hilfe.« Das versprachen ihm die Brüder und küßten es. »Leb wohl, liebe Schwester, wenn wir deine Stimme hören, springen wir auf unsere Pferde und sind bald bei dir.«

Darauf setzte es sich in den Wagen zu dem Blaubart und fuhr mit ihm fort. Wie es in sein Schloß kam, war alles prächtig, und was die Königin nur wünschte, das geschah, und sie wären recht glücklich gewesen, wenn sie sich nur an den blauen Bart des Königs hätte gewöhnen können, aber immer, wenn sie den sah, erschrak sie innerlich davor. Nachdem das einige Zeit gewährt, sprach er: »Ich muß eine große Reise machen, da hast du die Schlüssel zu dem ganzen Schloß, du kannst überall aufschließen und alles besehen, nur die Kammer, wozu dieser kleine goldene Schlüssel gehört, verbiete ich dir; schließt du die auf, so ist dein Leben verfallen.«

Sie nahm die Schlüssel, versprach ihm zu gehorchen, und als er fort war, schloß sie nacheinander die Türen auf und sah so viel Reichtümer und Herrlichkeiten, daß sie meinte, aus der ganzen Welt wären sie hier zusammengebracht. Es war nun nichts mehr übrig als die verbotene Kammer, der Schlüssel war von Gold, da gedachte sie, in dieser ist vielleicht das Allerkostbarste verschlossen. Die Neugierde fing an, sie zu plagen, und sie hätte lieber all das andere nicht gesehen, wenn sie nur gewußt, was in dieser wäre. Eine Zeitlang widerstand sie der Begierde, zuletzt aber ward diese so mächtig, daß sie den Schlüssel nahm und zu der Kammer hinging. »Wer wird es sehen, daß ich sie öffne«, sagte sie zu sich selbst, »ich will auch nur einen Blick hineintun.« Da schloß sie auf, und wie die Türe aufging, schwomm ihr ein Strom Blut entgegen, und an den Wänden herum sah sie tote Weiber hängen, und von einigen waren nur die Gerippe noch übrig. Sie erschrak so heftig, daß sie die Türe gleich wieder zuschlug, aber der Schlüssel sprang dabei heraus und fiel in das Blut. Geschwind hob sie ihn auf und wollte das Blut abwischen, aber es war umsonst, wenn sie es auf der einen Seite abgewischt, kam es auf der andern wieder zum Vorschein. Sie setzte sich den ganzen Tag hin und rieb daran und versuchte alles mögliche, aber es half nichts, die Blutflecken waren nicht abzubringen; endlich am Abend legte sie ihn ins Heu, das sollte in der Nacht das Blut ausziehen.

Am andern Tag kam der Blaubart zurück, und das erste war, daß er die Schlüssel von ihr forderte. Ihr Herz schlug, sie brachte die andern und hoffte, er werde es nicht bemerken, daß der goldene fehlte. Er aber zählte sie alle, und wie er fertig war, sagte er: »Wo ist der zu der heimlichen Kammer?«

Dabei sah er ihr ins Gesicht.

Sie ward blutrot und antwortete: »Er liegt oben, ich habe ihn verlegt, morgen will ich ihn suchen.« – »Geh lieber gleich, liebe Frau, ich werde ihn noch heute brauchen.« – »Ach, ich will dir's nur sagen, ich habe ihn im Heu verloren, da muß ich erst suchen.« – »Du hast ihn nicht verloren«, sagte der Blaubart zornig, »du hast ihn dahin gesteckt, damit die Blutflecken herausziehen sollen, denn du hast mein Gebot übertreten und bist in der Kammer gewesen, aber jetzt sollst du hinein, wenn du auch nicht willst.«

Da mußte sie den Schlüssel holen, der war noch voller Blutflecken. »Nun bereite dich zum Tode, du sollst noch heute sterben«, sagte der Blaubart, holte sein großes Messer und nahm sie mit. »Laß mich nur noch vor meinem Tod mein Gebet tun«, sagte sie. »So geh, aber eil dich, denn ich habe keine Zeit, lange zu warten.« Da lief sie die Treppe hinauf und rief, so laut sie konnte, zum Fenster hinaus: »Brüder, meine lieben Brüder, kommt, helft mir!« Die Brüder saßen im Wald beim kühlen Wein, da sprach der jüngste: »Mir ist, als hätt' ich unserer Schwester Stimme gehört. Auf, wir müssen ihr zu Hilfe eilen!« Da sprangen sie auf ihre Pferde und ritten, als wären sie der Sturmwind. Ihre Schwester aber lag in Angst auf den Knien; da rief der Blaubart unten: »Nun, bist du bald fertig?«

Dabei hörte sie, wie er auf der untersten Stufe sein Messer wetzte; sie sah hinaus, aber sie sah nichts als von Ferne einen Staub, als käm eine Herde gezogen.

Da schrie sie noch einmal: »Brüder, meine lieben Brüder! Kommt, helft mir!« Und ihre Angst ward immer größer.

Der Blaubart aber rief: »Wenn du nicht bald kommst, so hol ich dich, mein Messer ist gewetzt!«

Da sah sie wieder hinaus und sah ihre drei Brüder durch das Feld reiten, als flögen sie wie Vögel in der Luft, da schrie sie zum drittenmal in der höchsten Not und aus allen Kräften: »Brüder, meine lieben Brüder! Kommt, helft mir!« Und der jüngste war schon so nah, daß sie seine Stimme hörte: »Tröste dich, liebe Schwester, noch einen Augenblick, so sind wir bei dir!« Der Blaubart aber rief: »Nun ist's genug gebetet, ich will nicht länger warten, kommst du nicht, so hol ich dich!« – »Ach, nur noch für meine drei lieben Brüder laß mich beten.« Er hörte aber nicht, kam die Treppe heraufgegangen und zog sie hinunter, und eben hatte er sie an den Haaren gefaßt und wollte ihr das Messer in das Herz stoßen, da schlugen die drei Brüder an die Haustüre, drangen herein und rissen sie ihm aus der Hand, dann zogen sie ihre Säbel und hieben ihn nieder. Da ward er in der Blutkammer aufgehängt zu den andern Weibern, die er getötet, die Brüder aber nahmen ihre liebste Schwester mit nach Haus, und alle Reichtümer des Blaubarts gehörten ihr.

1812

Von dem Tod des Hühnchens

Auf eine Zeit ging das Hühnchen mit dem Hähnchen in den Nußberg, und sie machten miteinander aus, wer einen Nußkern fände, sollte ihn mit dem andern teilen. Nun fand das Hühnchen eine große, große Nuß, sagte aber nichts davon und wollte den Kern allein essen. Er war aber so dick, daß es ihn nicht hinunterschlucken konnte und er ihm im Hals stecken blieb, daß ihm angst wurde, es müßte ersticken, und es schrie: »Hähnchen, ich bitt dich, lauf, was du kannst, und hol mir Wasser, sonst ersticke ich.« Das Hähnchen lief, was es konnte, zum Brunnen und sprach: »Born, du sollst mir Wasser geben, das Hühnchen liegt auf dem Nußberg und will ersticken an einem großen Nußkern.« Der Brunnen antwortete: »Lauf erst hin zur Braut und laß dir rote Seide geben.« Das Hähnchen lief zur Braut: »Braut, du sollst mir rote Seide geben, rote Seide will ich dem Brunnen geben, der Brunnen soll mir Wasser geben, das Wasser will ich dem Hühnchen bringen, das liegt auf dem Nußberg und will ersticken an einem großen Nußkern.« Die Braut antwortete: »Lauf erst und hol mir mein Kränzlein, das blieb an einer Weide hängen.«

Da lief das Hähnchen zur Weide und zog das Kränzlein von dem Ast und bracht' es der Braut, und die Braut gab ihm rote Seide dafür, die bracht' es dem Brunnen, der gab ihm Wasser dafür, da bracht' das Hähnchen das Wasser zum Hühnchen, wie es aber hinkam, war dieweil das Hühnchen erstickt und lag da tot und regte sich nicht.

Da war das Hähnchen so traurig, daß es laut schrie, und kamen alle Tiere und beklagten das Hühnchen, und sechs Mäuse bauten einen kleinen Wagen, das Hühnchen darin zum Grab zu fahren, und als der Wagen fertig war, spannten sie sich davor, das Hähnchen aber fuhr. Auf dem Weg aber kam der Fuchs: »Wo willst du hin, Hähnchen?« – »Ich will mein Hühnchen begraben.« – »Darf ich mitfahren?«

»Ja, aber setz dich hinten auf den Wagen,
vorne können's meine Pferdchen nicht vertragen.«

Da setzte sich der Fuchs hinten auf, dann der Wolf, der Bär, der Hirsch, der Löwe und alle Tiere in dem Wald. So ging die Fahrt fort, da kamen sie an einen Bach. »Wie sollen wir nun hinüber?« sagte das Hähnchen. Da war ein Strohhalm, der sagte: »Ich will mich quer drüber legen, da könnt ihr über mich fahren«; wie aber die sechs Mäuse darauf waren, rutschte der Strohhalm und fiel ins Wasser, und die sechs Mäuse fielen alle hinein und ertranken. Die Not ging von neuem an, da kam eine Kohle und sagte: »Ich bin groß genug, ich will mich darüber legen, und ihr sollt über mich fahren.« Die Kohle legte sich auch an das Wasser, aber sie berührte es unglücklicherweise ein wenig, da zischte sie, verlöschte und war tot. Wie das ein Stein sah, wollte er dem Hähnchen helfen und legte sich über das Wasser, da zog nun das Hähnchen den Wagen selber. Wie es ihn aber bald drüben hatte und war mit dem toten Hühnchen auf dem Land und wollte die andern, die hintenauf saßen, auch herauf ziehen, da waren ihrer zuviel geworden, und der Wagen fiel zurück, und alles fiel miteinander in das Wasser und ertrank. Da war das Hähnchen noch allein mit dem toten Hühnchen und grub ihm da ein Grab und legte es hinein und machte einen Hügel darüber, auf den setzte es sich und grämte sich so lang, bis es auch starb; und da war alles tot.

1819

Märchen von einem, der auszog,
das Fürchten zu lernen

Ein Vater hatte zwei Söhne, davon war der älteste klug und gescheit und wußte sich in alles wohl zu schicken, der jüngste aber war dumm, konnte nichts begreifen und lernen, und wenn ihn die Leute sahen, sprachen sie: »Mit dem wird der Vater noch seine Last haben!« Wenn nun etwas zu tun war, so mußte es der älteste allzeit ausrichten; hieß ihn aber der Vater noch spät oder gar in der Nacht etwas holen und der Weg ging dabei über den Kirchhof oder sonst einen schaurigen Ort, so antwortete er wohl: »Ach Vater, es gruselt mir!«, denn er fürchtete sich. Oder wenn abends beim Feuer Geschichten erzählt wurden, wobei einem die Haut schaudert, so sprachen die Zuhörer manchmal: »Ach, es gruselt mir!« Der jüngste saß in einer Ecke und hörte das mit an und konnte nicht begreifen, was es heißen sollte. »Immer sagen sie: Es gruselt mir! Es gruselt mir! Mir gruselt's nicht; das wird wohl eine Kunst sein, von der ich auch nichts verstehe.«

Nun geschah es, daß der Vater einmal zu ihm sprach: »Hör du in der Ecke dort, du wirst groß und stark und mußt auch etwas lernen, womit du dein Brot verdienst. Siehst du, wie sich dein Bruder Mühe gibt, aber an dir ist Hopfen und Malz verloren.« — »Ach Vater«, antwortete er, »ich will gern was lernen. Ja, wenn's anginge, so möchte ich lernen, daß mir's gruselte, davon verstehe ich noch gar nichts.« Der älteste lachte, als er das hörte, und dachte bei sich: »Du lieber Gott, was ist mein Bruder ein Dummbart, aus dem wird mein Lebtag nichts — was ein Häkchen werden will, muß sich bei Zeiten krümmen.« Der Vater seufzte und antwortete ihm: »Das Gruseln sollst du schon noch lernen, aber dein Brot wirst du damit nicht verdienen.«

Bald danach kam der Küster zum Besuch ins Haus, da klagte ihm der Vater seine Not und erzählte, wie sein jüngster Sohn in allen Dingen so schlecht beschlagen wäre, er wisse nichts und lerne nichts. »Denkt Euch, als ich ihn gefragt, womit er sein Brot verdienen wolle, hat er gar verlangt, das Gruseln zu lernen!« — »Ei«, antwortete der Küster, »das kann er bei mir lernen, tut ihn nur zu mir, ich will ihn schon abhobeln.« Der Vater war es zufrieden, weil er dachte, der Junge wird doch ein wenig abgehobelt, und der Küster nahm ihn zu sich ins Haus, und er mußte ihm die Glocke läuten. Nach ein paar Tagen weckte er ihn um Mitternacht, hieß ihn aufstehn, in den Kirchturm steigen und läuten. Da wirst du schon lernen, was Gruseln ist, dachte er, doch um ihm noch einen rechten Schrecken einzujagen, ging er heimlich voraus und stellte sich ins Schalloch, da sollte der Junge meinen, es wär ein Gespenst. Der Junge stieg ruhig den Turm hinauf. Als er oben hinkam, sah er eine Gestalt im Schalloch. »Wer steht dort?« rief er, aber es regte und bewegte sich nicht. Da sprach er: »Was willst du hier in der Nacht? Mach, daß du

252 *Märchen von einem, der auszog, das Fürchten zu lernen*

fortkommst, oder ich werf dich hinunter.« Der Küster dachte, es wird so arg nicht gemeint sein, schwieg und blieb unbeweglich stehen. Da rief ihn der Junge zum drittenmal an, und als er noch immer keine Antwort erhielt, nahm er einen Anlauf und stieß das Gespenst hinab, daß es Hals und Bein brach. Darauf läutete er die Glocke, und wie das geschehen war, stieg er wieder hinab, legte sich, ohne ein Wort zu sprechen, ins Bett und schlief fort. Die Küsterfrau wartete auf ihren Mann lange Zeit, aber der kam immer nicht wieder, da ward ihr endlich angst, daß sie den Jungen weckte und fragte: »Weißt du nicht, wo mein Mann geblieben ist? Er ist mit auf den Turm gestiegen.« – »Nein«, antwortete der Junge, »aber da hat einer im Schalloch gestanden, und weil er nicht weggehn und keine Antwort geben wollte, so habe ich ihn hinuntergeschmissen. Geht einmal hin, so werdet Ihr sehen, ob er's ist.«

Die Frau eilte voll Angst auf den Kirchhof und fand ihren Mann tot auf der Erde liegen. Da lief sie schreiend zu dem Vater des Jungen und weckte ihn und sprach: »Ach, was hat Euer Taugenichts für ein Unglück angerichtet, meinen Mann hat er zum Schalloch hinuntergestürzt, daß er tot auf dem Kirchhof liegt!« Der Vater erschrak, kam herbeigelaufen und schalt den Jungen: »Was sind das für gottlose Streiche! Die muß dir der Böse eingegeben haben!« – »Ei Vater«, antwortete er, »ich bin ganz unschuldig; er stand da in der Nacht, wie einer, der Böses vorhat, ich wußte nicht, wer's war, ich hab's ihm ja dreimal gesagt, warum ist er nicht weggegangen?« – »Ach«, sprach der Vater, »mit dir erleb ich nur Unglück, geh mir vor den Augen weg, ich will dich nicht mehr ansehn.« – »Ja, Vater, recht gern, wartet nur, bis Tag ist, da will ich ausgehn und das Gruseln lernen, so versteh ich doch auch eine Kunst, die mich ernähren kann.« – »Lerne, was du willst«, sprach der Vater, »mir ist alles einerlei, da hast du fünfzig Taler, damit geh mir aus den Augen und sag keinem Menschen, wo du her bist und wer dein Vater ist, denn ich muß mich deiner schämen.« – »Ja, Vater, wie Ihr's haben wollt, wenn Ihr nicht mehr verlangt, das kann ich leicht in acht behalten.«

Als nun der Tag anbrach, steckte der Junge seine fünfzig Taler in die Tasche, ging hinaus auf die große Landstraße und sprach immer vor sich hin: »Wenn mir's nur gruselte! Wenn mir's nur gruselte!« Da ging ein Mann neben ihm, der hörte das Gespräch mit an, und als sie ein Stück weiter waren, daß man den Galgen sehen konnte, sagte er zu dem Jungen: »Siehst du, dort ist der Baum, wo siebene mit des Seilers Tochter Hochzeit gehalten haben, setz dich darunter und wart, bis die Nacht kommt, so wirst du schon das Gruseln lernen.« – »Wenn weiter nichts dazu gehört«, antwortete der Junge, »das will ich gern tun, lern ich aber so geschwind das Gruseln, so sollst du meine fünfzig Taler haben, komm nur morgen früh wieder zu mir.«

Da ging der Junge zu dem Galgen und setzte sich darunter und wartete, bis der Abend kam. Und weil ihn fror, machte er sich ein Feuer an, aber um Mitternacht ging der Wind so kalt, daß er trotz des Feuers nicht warm werden wollte. Und als der Wind die Gehenkten gegeneinander stieß, daß sie sich hin und her bewegten, da dachte er: Du frierst unten bei dem Feuer, was mögen die da oben erst frieren und zappeln. Und weil er mitleidig war, legte er die Leiter an, stieg hinauf, knüpfte einen nach dem andern los und holte sie alle siebene herab. Darauf schürte er das Feuer und blies es an und setzte sie herum, daß sie sich wärmen sollten. Aber sie saßen da und regten sich nicht, und das Feuer ergriff ihre Kleider. Da sprach er: »Nehmt euch in acht, sonst häng ich euch wieder hinauf.« Die Toten aber hörten nicht, schwiegen und ließen ihre Lumpen fort brennen. Da ward er bös und sprach: »Wenn ihr nicht achtgeben wollt, so kann ich euch nicht helfen, ich will nicht mit euch verbrennen«, und hing sie der Reihe nach wieder hinauf. Nun setzte er sich zu seinem Feuer und schlief ein, und am andern Morgen kam der Mann zu ihm, wollte die fünfzig Taler haben und sprach: »Nun weißt du, was Gruseln ist?« – »Nein«, antwortete er, »woher sollt' ich's wissen? Die da droben haben das Maul nicht aufgetan und waren so dumm, daß sie die paar alten Lappen, die sie am Leib haben, brennen ließen.« Da sah der Mann, daß er die fünfzig Taler heute nicht davontragen würde, und ging fort und sprach: »So einer ist mir noch nicht vorgekommen.«

Der Junge ging auch seines Weges und fing wieder an, vor sich hin zu reden: »Ach, wenn mir's nur gruselte! Ach, wenn mir's nur gruselte!« Das hörte ein Fuhrmann, der hinter ihm her schritt, und fragte: »Wer bist du?« – »Ich weiß nicht«, antwortete der Junge. Der Fuhrmann fragte weiter: »Wo bist du her?« – »Ich weiß nicht.« – »Wer ist dein Vater?« – »Das darf ich nicht sagen.« – »Was brummst du so in den Bart hinein?« – »Ei«, antwortete der Junge, »ich wollte, daß mir's gruselte; aber niemand kann mir's lehren.« – »Laß das dumme Geschwätz«, sprach der Fuhrmann, »komm, geh mit mir, ich will sehn, daß ich dich unterbringe.« Nun ging der Junge mit dem Fuhrmann. Abends gelangten sie zu einem Wirtshaus, wo sie übernachten wollten, da sprach er beim Eintritt in die Stube wieder ganz laut: »Wenn mir's nur gruselte! Wenn mir's nur gruselte!« Der Wirt, der das hörte, lachte und sprach: »Wenn dich danach lüstet, dazu sollte hier wohl Gelegenheit sein.« – »Ach, schweig still«, sprach die Wirtsfrau, »so mancher Vorwitzige hat schon sein Leben eingebüßt, es wäre Jammer und Schade um die schönen Augen, wenn die das Tageslicht nicht wieder sehen sollten.« Der Junge aber sagte: »Wenn es noch so schwer ist, ich will's einmal lernen, dazu bin ich ja ausgezogen.« Er ließ dem Wirt auch keine Ruhe, bis dieser erzählte, nicht weit davon stände ein verwünschtes Schloß, worin einer wohl lernen könnte, was Gruseln wäre, wenn er drei Nächte darin wachen wollte. Der König hätte dem, der's wagen wollte, seine Tochter zur Frau versprochen, und die wäre die schönste Jungfrau, welche die Sonne beschien; in dem Schloß steckten große Schätze, von Geistern bewacht, die würden dann frei. Schon viele wären wohl hinein, aber noch keiner wieder herausgekommen. Da ging der Junge am andern Morgen vor den König und sprach: »Wenn's erlaubt wäre, so wollte ich wohl drei Nächte in dem verwünschten Schloß wachen.« Der König sah ihn an, und weil er ihm gefiel, sprach er: »Du darfst dir noch dreierlei ausbitten, aber von leblosen Dingen, das du mit ins Schloß nimmst.« Da antwortete er: »So bitt ich um ein Feuer, eine Drehbank und eine Schnitzbank mit dem Messer.«

Der König ließ ihm das alles bei Tag in das Schloß tragen. Als es Nacht werden wollte, ging der Junge hinauf, machte sich in einer Kammer ein helles Feuer an, stellte die Schnitzbank mit dem Messer daneben und setzte sich auf die Drehbank. »Ach, wenn mir's nur gruselte«, sprach er, »aber hier werd ich's auch nicht lernen.« Gegen Mitternacht wollte er sich sein Feuer einmal aufschüren; wie er so hineinblies, da schrie's plötzlich aus einer Ecke: »Au, miau! Was uns friert!« – »Ihr Narren«, rief er, »was schreit ihr? Wenn euch friert, kommt, setzt euch ans Feuer und wärmt euch.« Und wie er das gesagt hatte, kamen zwei große schwarze Katzen in einem gewaltigen Sprung herbei und setzten sich ihm zu beiden Seiten und sahen ihn mit ihren feurigen Augen ganz wild an. Über ein Weilchen, als sie sich gewärmt hatten, sprachen sie: »Kamerad, wollen wir eins in der Karte spielen?« – »Ja«, antwortete er, »aber zeigt einmal eure Pfoten her.« Da streckten sie die Krallen aus. »Ei«, sagte er, »was habt ihr lange Nägel! Wartet, die muß ich euch erst abschneiden.« Damit packte er sie beim Kragen, hob sie auf die Schnitzbank und schraubte ihnen die Pfoten fest. »Euch hab ich auf die Finger gesehen«, sprach er, »da vergeht mir die Lust zum Kartenspiel«, und schlug sie tot und warf sie hinaus ins Wasser. Als er aber die zwei zur Ruhe gebracht und sich wieder an sein Feuer setzen wollte, da kamen aus allen Ecken und Enden schwarze Katzen und schwarze Hunde an glühenden Ketten, immer mehr und mehr, daß er sich nicht mehr bergen konnte; die schrien greulich, traten ihm auf sein Feuer, zerrten es auseinander und wollten es ausmachen. Das sah er ein Weilchen ruhig mit an, als es ihm aber zu arg ward, faßte er sein Schnitzmesser: »Ei, du Gesindel! Fort mit dir!« und hieb hinein. Ein großer Teil sprang fort, die andern schmiß er tot und trug sie hinaus in den Teich. Als er wiedergekommen war, blies er aus den Funken sein Feuer frisch an und wärmte sich. Und als er so saß, wollten ihm die Augen nicht länger offen bleiben, und er bekam Lust zu schlafen. Da blickte er um sich und sah in der Ecke ein großes Bett, ging und legte sich hinein. Als er aber die Augen eben zutun wollte, so fing das Bett von selbst an zu fahren und fuhr im ganzen Schloß herum. »Recht so«, sprach er, »nur immerzu.« Da fing das Bett an zu fahren, als wären sechs Pferde vorgespannt, fort über Schwellen und Treppen auf und ab! hopp; hopp! warf es um, das unterste zu oberst, und er lag mitten drunter. Da schleuderte er Decken und Kissen in die Höhe, stieg heraus und sagte: »Nun mag fahren, wer Lust hat!« Legte sich an sein Feuer und schlief, bis es Tag war. Am Morgen kam der König, und als er ihn da auf der Erde liegen sah, meinte er, die Gespenster hätten ihn umgebracht und er wäre tot. Da sprach er: »Es ist doch schade um den schönen Menschen!« Das hörte der Junge, richtete sich auf und sprach: »Soweit ist's noch nicht!« Da verwunderte sich der König, freute sich aber und fragte, wie es ihm gegangen wäre. »Recht gut«, antwortete er, »eine Nacht wäre herum, die zwei andern werden auch herumgehen.« Als er nun zum Wirt kam, machte der große Augen und sprach: »Ich dachte nicht, daß ich dich wieder lebendig sehen würde, hast du nun gelernt, was Gruseln ist?« – »Nein«, sagte er, »ich weiß es nicht, wenn mir's nur einer sagen könnte!«

Die zweite Nacht ging er wieder hinauf ins alte Schloß, setzte sich zum Feuer und sprach: »Wenn mir's nur gruselte.« Wie Mitternacht herankam, fing ein Lärm und Gepolter an, erst sachte, dann immer stärker, dann war's ein bißchen still, endlich kam mit lautem Geschrei ein halber Mensch den Schornstein herab und fiel vor ihn hin. »Heda!« rief er. »Noch ein halber gehört dazu, das ist zuwenig.« Da ging der Lärm von frischem an, es tobte und heulte und fiel die andere Hälfte auch herab. »Wart«, sprach er, »ich will dir erst das Feuer ein wenig anblasen.« Wie er das getan und sich wieder umsah, da waren die beiden Stücke zusammengefahren und saß da ein greulicher Mann auf seinem Platz. »So ist's nicht gemeint«, sprach der Junge, »die Bank ist mein.« Der Mann wollte ihn wegdrängen, aber der Junge ließ sich's nicht gefallen, schob ihn mit Gewalt weg und setzte sich wieder auf seinen Platz. Da fielen noch mehr Männer herab, die hatten neun Totenbeine und zwei Totenköpfe, setzten auf und spielten Kegel. Der Junge bekam auch Lust und fragte: »Hört ihr, kann ich mit sein?« – »Ja, wenn du Geld hast.« – »Geld genug«, antwortete er, »aber eure Kugeln sind nicht recht rund.« Da nahm er sie, setzte sie in die Drehbank und drehte sie rund. »Jetzt werden sie besser schüppeln«, sprach er, »heida! Nun geht's lustig!« Er spielte mit und verlor etwas von seinem Geld, als es aber zwölf Uhr schlug, war alles vor seinen Augen verschwunden, und er legte sich nieder und schlief ruhig ein. Am andern Morgen kam der König und wollte sich erkundigen: »Wie ist dir's diesmal gegangen?« fragte er. »Ich hab gekegelt«, antwortete er, »und ein paar Heller verloren.« – »Hat dir denn nicht gegruselt?« – »Ei was«, sprach er, »lustig hab ich mich gemacht, wenn ich nur wüßte, was das Gruseln wäre!«

In der dritten Nacht setzte er sich wieder auf seine Bank und sprach ganz verdrießlich: »Wenn es mir nur gruselte!« Als es spät ward, kamen sechs große Männer und brachten eine Totenlade hereingetragen. Da sprach er: »Haha, das ist gewiß mein Vetterchen, das erst vor ein paar Tagen gestorben ist«, winkte mit dem Finger und rief: »Komm, Vetterchen, komm!« Sie stellten den Sarg auf die Erde, er aber ging hinzu und nahm den Deckel ab, da lag ein toter Mann darin; er fühlte ihm ans Gesicht, aber es war kalt wie Eis. »Wart«, sprach er, »ich will dich ein bißchen wärmen«, ging ans Feuer, wärmte seine Hand und legte sie ihm aufs Gesicht, aber der Tote blieb kalt. Nun nahm er ihn heraus, setzte sich ans Feuer und legte ihn auf seinen Schoß und rieb ihm die Arme, um ihn zu erwärmen. Als auch das nichts helfen wollte, fiel ihm ein: Wenn zwei zusammen im Bett liegen, so wärmen sie sich, brachte ihn ins Bett, deckte ihn zu und legte sich neben ihn. Über ein Weilchen ward auch der Tote warm und fing an, sich zu regen. Da sprach der

Junge: »Siehst du, Vetterchen, hätt' ich dich nicht gewärmt!« Der Tote aber hub an und rief: »Jetzt will ich dich erwürgen.« – »Was«, sagte er, »ist das mein Dank? Nun sollst du wieder in deinen Sarg«, hob ihn auf, warf ihn hinein und machte den Deckel zu. Da kamen die sechs Männer und trugen ihn wieder fort. »Es will mir nicht gruseln«, sagte er, »hier lerne ich's mein Lebtag nicht.«

Da trat ein Mann herein, der war größer als alle anderen und sah fürchterlich aus, doch war er schon alt und hatte einen langen, weißen Bart und sprach: »O du Wicht, nun sollst du bald lernen, was Gruseln ist, denn du sollst sterben.« – »Nicht so schnell«, antwortete er, »da muß ich auch dabei sein.« Sprach der Mann: »Dich will ich schon packen!« – »Nun sachte, mach dich nicht gar zu breit, so stark, wie du bist, bin ich auch, und wohl noch stärker.« – »Das will sehn«, sprach der Alte, »bist du stärker als ich, so will ich dich lassen, komm, wir wollen's versuchen.« Da führte er ihn durch dunkle Gänge zu einem Schmiedefeuer und nahm eine Axt und schlug den einen Amboß mit einem Schlag in die Erde. »Das kann ich noch besser«, sprach der Junge und ging zu dem andern Amboß, und der Alte stellte sich neben hin und wollte zusehen, und sein weißer Bart hing herab. Da faßte der Junge die Axt und zerspaltete den Amboß auf einen Hieb und klemmte den Bart mit hinein. »Nun hab ich dich«, sprach der Junge, »jetzt ist das Sterben an dir.«

Dann faßte er eine Eisenstange und schlug auf ihn los, bis der Alte wimmerte und bat, er möge aufhören, er wollte ihm große Reichtümer geben. Der Junge zog die Axt raus und ließ den Alten los, der führte ihn wieder ins Schloß zurück und zeigte ihm im Keller drei Kasten voll Gold. »Davon«, sprach er, »ist ein Teil den Armen, der andere dem König, der dritte dein.« Indem schlug es zwölfe, und der Geist verschwand, also daß der Junge im Finstern stand. »Ich werde mir doch heraushelfen können«, sprach er, tappte herum, suchte den Weg in die Kammer und schlief bei seinem Feuer ein. Am andern Morgen kam der König und sagte: »Nun wirst du gelernt haben, was Gruseln ist.« – »Nein«, antwortete er, »was ist's nur? Mein toter Vetter war da, und ein bärtiger Mann ist gekommen, der hat mir da unten viel Gold gezeigt, aber das Gruseln hat mich keiner gelehrt.« Der König sprach: »Du hast das Schloß erlöst und sollst meine Tochter heiraten.« – »Das ist all recht gut«, antwortete er, »aber ich weiß immer noch nicht, was Gruseln ist.«

Da ward das Gold gehoben und die Hochzeit gehalten, aber der junge König, so lieb er seine Gemahlin hatte und so vergnügt er war, sagte doch immer: »Wenn mir nur gruselte, wenn mir nur gruselte!« Das verdroß sie endlich. Ihr Kammermädchen sprach: »Ich will Hilfe schaffen, das Gruseln soll er schon noch lernen.« Und ging hinaus und ließ sich einen ganzen Eimer voll Gründlinge holen. Und nachts, als der junge König schlief, mußte seine Gemahlin ihm die Decke wegziehen und den Eimer voll kalt Wasser mit den Gründlingen über ihn herschütten, daß die kleinen Fische um ihn herum zappelten. Da wachte er auf und rief: »Ach, was gruselt mir, was gruselt mir, liebe Frau! Ja, nun weiß ich, was Gruseln ist.« 1819

Das blaue Licht

Es war einmal ein König, der hatte einen Soldaten zum Diener, wie der ganz alt wurde und unbrauchbar, schickte er ihn fort und gab ihm nichts. Da wußte er nicht, womit er sein Leben fristen sollte, ging traurig fort den langen Tag und kam abends in einen Wald. Wie er ein Weilchen gegangen war, sah er ein Licht, dem näherte er sich, und kam zu einem kleinen Haus, darin wohnte eine alte Hexe. Er bat um ein Nachtlager und ein wenig Essen und Trinken, sie schlug's ihm aber ab, endlich sagte sie: »Ich will dich doch aus Barmherzigkeit aufnehmen, du mußt mir aber morgen meinen ganzen Garten umgraben.« Der Soldat versprach's und ward also beherbergt.

Am andern Tag hackte er der Hexe den Garten um und hatte damit Arbeit bis zum Abend. Nun wollte sie ihn wegschicken, er sprach aber: »Ich bin so müd, laß mich noch die Nacht hier bleiben.« Sie wollte nicht, endlich gab sie's zu, doch sollt'

er ihr andern Tags ein Fuder Holz klein spalten. Der Soldat hackte den zweiten Tag das Holz und hatte sich abends so abgearbeitet, daß er wieder nicht fort konnte, also bat er um die dritte Nacht; dafür sollte er aber den folgenden Tag das blaue Licht aus dem Brunnen holen.

Da führte ihn die Hexe an einen Brunnen und band ihn an ein lang Seil, daran ließ sie ihn hinab; und als er unten war, fand er das blaue Licht und machte das Zeichen, daß sie ihn wieder hinaufziehen sollte. Sie zog ihn auch in die Höhe, wie er aber am Rand war, so nah, daß man sich die Hände reichen konnte, wollte sie das Licht haben, um ihn dann wieder hinunterfallen zu lassen. Aber er merkte ihre bösen Gedanken und sagte: »Nein, eher geb ich das blaue Licht nicht, als bis ich mit meinen Füßen auf dem Erdboden stehe.« Da erboste die Hexe und stieß ihn mitsamt dem Licht hinunter in den Brunnen und ging fort. Der Soldat unten in dem dunkeln, feuchten Morast war traurig, denn ihm stand sein Ende bevor, da fiel ihm seine Pfeife in die Hand, die war noch halb voll, und er dachte, die willst du zum letzten Vergnügen doch noch ausrauchen. Also steckte er sie an dem blauen Licht an und fing an zu rauchen; als der Dampf ein wenig herumzog, so kam ein

geworden.« Die Eltern verboten es ihr streng und sagten: »Die Frau Trude ist eine böse Frau, die gottlose Dinge treibt, und wenn du zu ihr hingehst, so bist du unser Kind nicht mehr.« Aber das Mädchen kehrte sich nicht an das Verbot seiner Eltern und ging doch zu der Frau Trude. Und als es zu ihr kam, fragte die Frau Trude: »Warum bist du so bleich?« – »Ach«, antwortete es und zitterte am Leibe, »ich habe mich so erschrocken über das, was ich gesehen habe.« – »Was hast du gesehen?« – »Ich sah auf Eurer Stiege einen schwarzen Mann.« – »Das war mein Köhler.« – »Dann sah ich einen grünen Mann.« – »Das war mein Jäger.« – »Danach sah ich einen blutroten Mann.« – »Das war mein Metzger.« – »Ach, Frau Trude, mir grauste, ich sah durchs Fenster und sah statt Euch den Teufel mit feurigem Schopf.« – »Oho«, sagte sie, »so hast du die Hexe in ihrem rechten Schmuck gesehen, ich habe schon lange auf dich gewartet und nach dir verlangt, du sollst mir leuchten.« Da verwandelte sie das Mädchen in einen Holzblock, warf ihn ins Feuer, setzte sich daneben, wärmte sich daran und sprach: »Das leuchtet einmal hell!«

1837

Das Wasser des Lebens

Es war einmal ein König, der ward krank und glaubte niemand, daß er mit dem Leben davonkäme. Er hatte aber drei Söhne, die waren darüber betrübt, gingen hinunter in den Schloßgarten und weinten. Da begegnete ihnen ein alter Mann, der fragte sie nach ihrem Kummer. Sie erzählten ihm, ihr Vater wär so krank, daß er wohl sterben würde, denn es wollte ihm nichts helfen. Da sprach der Alte: »Ich weiß ein Mittel, das ist das Wasser des Lebens, wenn er davon trinkt, so wird er wieder gesund; es ist aber schwer zu finden.« Da sagte der älteste: »Ich will es schon finden«, ging zum kranken König und bat ihn, er möcht ihm erlauben auszuziehen, um das Wasser des Lebens zu suchen, das ihn allein heilen könne. »Nein«, sprach der König, »dabei sind zu große Gefahren, lieber will ich sterben.« Er bat aber so lange, bis es der König erlaubte. Der Prinz dachte auch in seinem Herzen: »Hol ich das Wasser, so bin ich meinem Vater der liebste und erbe das Reich.«

Also machte er sich auf, und als er eine Zeit lang fortgeritten war, stand da ein Zwerg auf dem Weg, der rief ihn an und sprach: »Wohinaus so geschwind?« — »Du Knirps«, sagte der Prinz ganz stolz, »das brauchst du nicht zu wissen«; und ritt weiter. Das kleine Männchen aber war zornig geworden und hatte einen bösen Wunsch getan. Wie nun der Prinz fortritt, kam er in eine Bergschlucht, und je weiter, je enger taten sich die Berge zusammen, und endlich ward der Weg so eng, daß er keinen Schritt weiter konnte, und auch das Pferd konnte er nicht wenden und selber nicht absteigen und mußte da eingesperrt stehen bleiben. Indessen wartete der kranke König auf ihn; aber er kam nicht und kam nicht. Da sagte der zweite Prinz: »So will ich ausziehen und das Wasser suchen«, und dachte bei sich, das ist mir eben recht, ist der tot, so fällt das Reich mir zu. Der König wollt' ihn auch anfangs nicht ziehen lassen, endlich aber mußte er's doch zugeben. Der Prinz zog also gleichen Wegs fort und begegnete demselben Zwerg, der hielt ihn wieder an und fragte: »Wohinaus so geschwind?« — »Du Knirps«, sagte der Prinz, »das brauchst du nicht zu wissen«, und ritt in seinem Stolz fort. Aber der Zwerg verwünschte ihn, und er geriet wie der andere in eine Bergschlucht und konnte nicht vorwärts und rückwärts. So geht's aber den Hochmütigen.

Wie nun der zweite Prinz ausblieb, sagte der jüngste, er wollte ausziehen und das Wasser holen, und der König mußt' ihn endlich auch gehen lassen. Als er den Zwerg auf dem Wege fand und der fragte: »Wohinaus so geschwind?«, so antwortete er ihm: »Ich suche das Wasser des Lebens, weil mein Vater sterbenskrank ist.« — »Weißt du denn, wo das zu finden ist?« — »Nein«, sagte der Prinz. »So will ich dir's sagen, weil du mir ordentlich Rede gestanden hast; es quillt aus einem Brunnen in einem verwünschten Schloß, und damit du dazu gelangst, geb ich dir da eine eiserne Rute und zwei Laiberchen Brot. Mit der Rute schlag dreimal an das eiserne

Tor am Schloß, so wird es aufspringen; inwendig werden dann zwei Löwen liegen und den Rachen aufsperren, wenn du ihnen aber das Brot hineinwirfst, wirst du sie stillen, und dann eil dich und hol von dem Wasser des Lebens, ehe es zwölf schlägt, sonst geht das Tor wieder zu, und du bist eingesperrt.«

Da dankte ihm der Prinz und nahm die Rute und das Brot, ging hin, und war da alles, wie der Zwerg gesagt hatte. Das Tor sprang beim dritten Rutenschlag auf, und als die Löwen besänftigt waren, ging er in das Schloß hinein und fand einen großen schönen Saal und darin verwünschte Prinzen, denen zog er die Ringe ab; und dann nahm er ein Schwert und ein Brot, das lag da. Und weiter kam er in ein Zimmer, darin war eine schöne Jungfrau, die freute sich, als sie ihn sah, küßte ihn und sagte, er hätte sie erlöst und sollte ihr ganzes Reich haben; in einem Jahr sollt' er kommen und die Hochzeit mit ihr feiern. Dann sagte sie ihm auch, wo der Brunnen wäre mit dem Lebenswasser, er müßte sich aber eilen und daraus schöpfen, eh' es zwölf schlüge. Da ging er weiter und kam endlich in ein Zimmer, darin stand ein schönes, frischgedecktes Bett, und weil er müd war, wollt' er sich erst ein wenig ausruhen. Also legte er sich und schlief ein. Wie er aber erwachte, schlug es drei viertel auf zwölf. Da sprang er ganz erschrocken auf, lief zu dem Brunnen und schöpfte sich einen Becher, der daneben stand, voll und eilte, daß er fortkam. Wie er eben zum eisernen Tor hinausging, da schlug's zwölf, und das Tor fuhr zu, so heftig, daß es ihm noch ein Stück von der Ferse wegnahm.

Er aber war froh, daß er das Wasser des Lebens hatte, und ging heimwärts und wieder an dem Zwerg vorbei. Als dieser das Schwert und das Brot sah, sprach er: »Damit hast du großes Gut gewonnen, mit dem Schwert kannst du ganze Heere schlagen, das Brot aber wird niemals alle.« Da dachte der Prinz, ohne deine Brüder willst du zum Vater nicht nach Haus kommen, und sprach: »Lieber Zwerg, kannst du mir nicht sagen, wo meine zwei Brüder sind, die waren früher als ich nach dem Wasser des Lebens ausgezogen und sind nicht wiedergekommen.« – »Zwischen zwei Bergen sind sie eingeschlossen«, sprach der Zwerg, »dahin hab ich sie verwünscht, weil sie so übermütig waren.« Da bat der Prinz so lange, bis sie der Zwerg wieder losließ, aber er sprach noch: »Hüte dich vor ihnen, sie haben ein böses Herz.«

Wie sie nun kamen, da freute er sich und erzählte ihnen alles, wie es ihm ergangen wäre, daß er das Wasser des Lebens gefunden und einen Becher voll mitgenommen und eine schöne Prinzessin erlöst habe, die wolle ein Jahr lang auf ihn warten, dann sollte Hochzeit gehalten werden, und er bekäm ein großes Reich. Danach ritten sie zusammen fort und gerieten in ein Land, wo Hunger und Krieg war, und der König glaubte schon, er sollte verderben in der Not. Da ging der Prinz zu ihm und gab ihm das Brot, damit speiste und sättigte er sein ganzes Reich, und dann gab ihm der Prinz auch das Schwert, und damit schlug er die Heere seiner Feinde und konnte nun in Ruhe und Frieden leben. Da nahm der Prinz sein Brot und sein Schwert wieder zurück, und die drei Brüder ritten weiter; sie kamen

aber noch in zwei Länder, wo Hunger und Krieg herrschten, und da gab der Prinz den Königen jedesmal sein Brot und Schwert und hatte nun drei Reiche gerettet. Und danach setzten sie sich auf ein Schiff und fuhren übers Meer. Während der Fahrt sprachen die beiden ältesten unter sich: »Der jüngste hat das Wasser gefunden und wir nicht, dafür wird ihm unser Vater das Reich geben, das uns gebührt, und er wird uns unser Glück wegnehmen.« Da wurden sie rachsüchtig und verabredeten miteinander, daß sie ihn verderben wollten. Sie warteten aber, bis er einmal fest eingeschlafen war, da gossen sie das Wasser des Lebens aus dem Becher und nahmen es für sich, ihm aber gossen sie bitteres Meerwasser hinein.

Als sie nun daheim ankamen, brachte der jüngste dem kranken König seinen Becher, damit er daraus trinken und gesund werden sollte. Kaum aber hatte er ein wenig von dem bittern Meerwasser getrunken, da ward er noch kränker als zuvor. Und wie er darüber jammerte, kamen die beiden ältesten Söhne und klagten den jüngsten an und sagten, er habe ihn vergiften wollen. Das rechte Wasser des Lebens hätten sie gefunden und mitgebracht und reichten es dem König. Kaum hatte er davon getrunken, so fühlte er seine Krankheit verschwinden und ward stark und gesund wie in seinen jungen Tagen. Danach gingen die beiden zu dem jüngsten, spotteten sein und sagten: »Nun, hast du das Wasser des Lebens gefunden? Du hast die Mühe gehabt und wir den Lohn, du hättest die Augen auftun sollen, wir haben dir's genommen, wie du auf dem Meere eingeschlafen warst. Übers Jahr holt sich einer von uns deine schöne Königstochter; aber hüte dich, daß du davon nichts dem Vater verrätst, er glaubt dir doch nicht, und wenn du ein Wort sagst, so sollst du auch noch dein Leben verlieren, schweigst du aber, so soll dir's geschenkt sein.«

Der alte König aber war zornig über seinen jüngsten Sohn und glaubte, er hätte ihm nach dem Leben getrachtet, also ließ er den Hof versammeln und das Urteil über ihn sprechen, daß er heimlich sollte erschossen werden. Als der Prinz nun einmal auf die Jagd ritt und nichts davon wußte, mußte des Königs Jäger mitgehen. Draußen, als sie ganz allein im Wald waren und der Jäger so traurig aussah, sagte der Prinz zu ihm: »Lieber Jäger, was fehlt dir?« Der Jäger sprach: »Ich kann's nicht sagen und soll es doch.« Da sprach der Prinz: »Sag's nur heraus, was es ist, ich will dir's verzeihen.« – »Ach«, sagte der Jäger, »ich soll Euch totschießen, der König hat mir's befohlen.« Da erschrak der Prinz und sprach: »Lieber Jäger, laß mich leben, da geb ich dir mein königliches Kleid, gib mir dafür dein schlechtes.« Der Jäger sagte: »Das will ich gern tun, ich hätte doch nicht nach Euch schießen können.« Da nahm der Jäger des Prinzen Kleid und der Prinz das schlechte vom Jäger und ging fort in den Wald hinein.

Über eine Zeit, da kamen beim alten König drei Wagen mit Geschenken an Gold und Edelsteinen für seinen jüngsten Sohn, sie waren aber von den drei Königen geschickt, denen der Prinz das Schwert und das Brot geliehen, womit sie die Feinde geschlagen und ihr Land ernährt hatten. Das fiel dem alten König aufs Herz, und er dachte, sein Sohn könnte doch unschuldig gewesen sein, und sprach zu seinen Leuten: »Ach, wär er noch am Leben, wie tut mir's so herzlich leid, daß ich ihn habe töten lassen.« – »So hab ich ja recht getan«, sprach der Jäger, »ich hab ihn nicht tot schießen können«, und sagte dem König, wie es zugegangen wäre. Da war der König froh und ließ bekannt machen in allen Reichen, sein Sohn solle wieder kommen, er nehme ihn in Gnaden auf.

Die Königstochter aber ließ eine Straße vor ihrem Schloß machen, die war ganz golden und glänzend, und sagte ihren Leuten, wer darauf geradewegs zu ihr geritten käme, das wäre der Rechte, und den sollten sie einlassen, wer aber daneben käme, der wär der Rechte nicht, und den sollten sie auch nicht einlassen. Als nun die Zeit bald herum war, dachte der älteste, er wollte sich eilen, zur Königstochter gehen und sich für ihren Erlöser ausgeben, da bekäm er sie zur Gemahlin und das Reich dazu. Also ritt er fort; als er vor das Schloß kam und die schöne goldene Straße sah, dachte er: »Ei, das wäre jammerschade, wenn du darauf rittest«, lenkte ab und ritt rechts nebenher. Wie er aber vors Tor kam, sagten die Leute zu ihm, er wär der Rechte nicht, er solle wieder fortgehen.

Bald darauf machte sich der zweite Prinz auf. Wie der zur goldenen Straße kam und das Pferd den einen Fuß darauf gesetzt hatte, dachte er: »Ei, es wäre jammerschade, das könnte etwas abtreten«, lenkte ab und ritt links nebenher. Wie er aber vors Tor kam, sagten die Leute, er wär der Rechte nicht, er solle wieder fortgehen. Als nun das Jahr ganz herum war, wollte der dritte aus dem Wald fort zu seiner Liebsten reiten und bei ihr sein Leid vergessen. Also machte er sich auf und dachte immer an sie und wär gern schon bei ihr gewesen und sah die goldene Straße gar nicht. Da ritt sein Pferd mitten darüber hin, und als er vors Tor kam, ward es aufgetan, und die Königstochter empfing ihn mit Freuden und sagte, er wär ihr Erlöser und der Herr des Königreichs, und ward die Hochzeit gehalten mit großer Glückseligkeit. Und als sie vorbei war, erzählte sie ihm, daß ihn sein Vater habe zu sich entboten und ihm verziehen. Da ritt er hin und sagte ihm alles, wie seine Brüder ihn betrogen und er doch dazu geschwiegen hätte. Der alte König wollte sie strafen, aber sie hatten sich aufs Meer gesetzt und waren fortgeschifft und kamen ihr Lebtag nicht wieder.

1819

Hans Dumm

Es war ein König, der lebte mit seiner Tochter, die sein einziges Kind war, vergnügt. Auf einmal aber brachte die Prinzessin ein Kind zur Welt, und niemand wußte, wer der Vater war. Der König wußte lange nicht, was er anfangen sollte. Am Ende befahl er, die Prinzessin solle mit dem Kind in die Kirche gehen, da sollte ihm eine Zitrone in die Hand gegeben werden, und wem es die reiche, solle der Vater des Kinds und Gemahl der Prinzessin sein. Das geschah nun, doch war der Befehl gegeben, daß niemand als schöne Leute in die Kirche sollten eingelassen werden. Es war aber in der Stadt ein kleiner, schiefer und buckelichter Bursch, der nicht recht klug war und darum der Hans Dumm hieß, der drängte sich ungesehen zwischen den andern auch in die Kirche, und wie das Kind die Zitrone austeilen sollte, so reichte es sie dem Hans Dumm. Die Prinzessin war erschrocken, der König war so aufgebracht, daß er sie und das Kind mit dem Hans Dumm in eine Tonne stecken und aufs Meer setzen ließ. Die Tonne schwamm bald fort, und wie sie allein auf dem Meere waren, klagte die Prinzessin und sagte: »Du garstiger, buckelichter, naseweiser Bub bist an meinem Unglück schuld, was hast du dich in die Kirche gedrängt, das Kind ging dich nichts an.« – »O ja«, sagte Hans Dumm, »das ging mich wohl etwas an, denn ich habe es einmal gewünscht, daß du ein Kind bekämst, und was ich wünsche, das trifft ein.« – »Wenn das wahr ist, so wünsch uns doch was zu essen hierher.« – »Das kann ich auch«, sagte Hans Dumm, wünschte sich aber eine Schüssel recht voll Kartoffeln. Die Prinzessin hätte gern etwas Besseres gehabt, aber weil sie so hungrig war, half sie ihm die Kartoffeln essen. Nachdem sie satt waren, sagte Hans Dumm: »Nun will ich uns ein schönes Schiff wünschen!« Und kaum hatte er das gesagt, so saßen sie in einem prächtigen Schiff, darin war alles zum Überfluß, was man nur verlangen konnte. Der Steuermann fuhr grad ans Land, und als sie ausstiegen, sagte Hans Dumm: »Nun soll ein Schloß dort stehen!« Da stand ein prächtiges Schloß, und Diener in Goldkleidern kamen und führten die Prinzessin und das Kind hinein, und als sie mitten in dem Saal waren, sagte Hans Dumm: »Nun wünsch ich, daß ich ein junger und kluger Prinz werde!« Da verlor sich sein Buckel, und er war schön und gerad und freundlich, und er gefiel der Prinzessin gut und ward ihr Gemahl.

So lebten sie lange Zeit vergnügt; da ritt einmal der alte König aus, verirrte sich und kam zu dem Schloß. Er verwunderte sich darüber, weil er es noch nie gesehen, und kehrte ein. Die Prinzessin erkannte gleich ihren Vater, er aber erkannte sie nicht, er dachte auch, sie sei schon längst im Meer ertrunken. Sie bewirtete ihn prächtig, und als er wieder nach Haus wollte, steckte sie ihm heimlich einen goldenen Becher in die Tasche. Nachdem er aber fortgeritten war, schickte sie ein paar Reiter nach, die mußten ihn anhalten und untersuchen, ob er den goldenen

Becher nicht gestohlen, und wie sie ihn in seiner Tasche fanden, brachten sie ihn mit zurück. Er schwor der Prinzessin, er habe ihn nicht gestohlen, und wisse nicht, wie er in seine Tasche gekommen sei. »Darum«, sagte sie, »muß man sich hüten, jemand gleich für schuldig zu halten«, und gab sich als seine Tochter zu erkennen. Da freute sich der König, und sie lebten vergnügt zusammen, und nach seinem Tod ward Hans Dumm König.

1812

Katz und Maus in Gesellschaft

Eine Katze und eine Maus waren einig geworden, zusammen zu leben und gemeinschaftlich Haus zu halten. Als nun der Winter sich näherte, trugen sie Vorsorge und kauften ein Töpfchen mit Fett, und weil sie keinen besseren und sichereren Ort wußten, stellten sie es unter den Altar der Kirche, da sollte es stehen, bis sie es nötig brauchten. Einstmals aber hatte die Katze Gelüste danach, ging zur Maus und sprach: »Hör, Mäuschen, ich bin von meiner Base zu Gevatter gebeten, sie hat ein Söhnchen geboren, weiß und braun gefleckt, das soll ich über die Taufe halten, laß mich ausgehen und hüte heut allein das Haus.« – »Ja, ja«, sagte die Maus, »geh hin, und wenn du was Gutes issest, denk an mich, von dem süßen, roten Kindbetterwein tränk ich auch gern ein Tröpfchen.« Die Katze aber hatte keine Base und sollte auch nicht Gevatter stehen, sondern ging geradenwegs in die Kirche und leckte die fette Haut ab, spazierte danach um die Stadt herum und kam erst am Abend nach Haus. »Du wirst dich recht verlustiert haben«, sagte die Maus, »wie hat denn das Kind geheißen?« – »Hautab«, antwortete die Katze. – »Hautab? Das ist ein seltsamer Name, den hab ich noch nicht gehört.«

Bald danach hatte die Katze wieder ein Gelüste, ging zur Maus und sprach: »Ich bin aufs neue zu Gevatter gebeten, das Kind hat einen weißen Ring um den Leib, da kann ich's nicht abschlagen, du mußt mir den Gefallen tun und allein die Wirtschaft treiben.« Die gute Maus sagte ja, die Katze aber ging hin und fraß den Fettopf bis zur Hälfte leer. Als sie heim kam, fragte die Maus: »Wie ist denn das Kind getauft worden?« – »Halbaus.« – »Halbaus? Was du sagst! Den Namen hab ich mein Lebtag noch nicht gehört, der steht auch gewiß nicht im Kalender.«

Der Katze aber hatte das Leckerwerk zu gut geschmeckt, und das Maul wässerte ihr wieder danach. Da sprach sie: »Ich bin zum drittenmal zu Gevatter gebeten, das Kind ist schwarz und hat bloß weiße Pfoten, sonst kein weißes Haar am ganzen Leib, das trifft sich alle paar Jahr nur einmal, du lässest mich doch ausgehen?« – »Hautab, Halbaus«, sagte die Maus, »es sind so kuriose Namen, die machen mich so nachdenksam, doch geh nur hin.« Die Maus hielt alles daheim in Ordnung und räumte auf, dieweil fraß die Katze den Fettopf rein aus und kam satt und dick erst in der Nacht wieder. »Wie heißt denn das dritte Kind?« – »Ganzaus.« – »Ganzaus? Ei! Ei! Das ist der allerbedenklichste Name«, sagte die Maus. »Ganzaus? Was soll der bedeuten? Gedruckt ist er mir noch nicht vorgekommen!« Damit schüttelte sie den Kopf und legte sich schlafen.

Zum viertenmal wollte niemand die Katze zu Gevatter bitten. Als der Winter aber gekommen war und draußen nichts mehr zu finden war, sagte die Maus zur Katze: »Komm, wir wollen zum Vorrat gehen, den wir in der Kirche unter dem Altar versteckt haben, das soll uns schmecken!« – »Ja«, sagte die Katze spöttisch, »es wird schmecken, als wenn du die Zunge zum Fenster hinaus streckst.«

Wie sie nun hinkamen, war alles leer. – »Ach!« sagte die Maus, »nun kommt's an den Tag, du hast alles gefressen, wie du zu Gevatter ausgegangen bist: erst Haut ab, dann Halb aus, dann …« – »Schweig still«, sagte die Katze, »oder ich freß dich, wenn du noch ein Wort sprichst.« – »Ganz aus«, hatte die arme Maus im Mund, und hatt' es kaum gesprochen, so sprang die Katze auf sie zu und schluckte sie hinunter.

1819

Sechse kommen durch die ganze Welt

Es war einmal ein Mann, der verstand allerlei Künste. Er diente im Krieg und hielt sich brav und tapfer, aber als der Krieg zu Ende war, bekam er den Abschied und drei Heller Zehrgeld auf den Weg. »Wart«, sprach er, »mit mir geht man nicht so um! Find ich die rechten Leute, so soll mir der König noch den Reichtum des ganzen Landes herausgeben.« Da ging er voll Zorn in den Wald und sah einen darin stehen, der hatte sechs Bäume ausgerupft, als wären's Kornhalme. Sprach er zu ihm: »Willst du mein Diener sein und mit mir ziehn?« – »Ja«, antwortete er, »aber erst will ich meiner Mutter das Bündel Holz heimbringen«, und nahm einen von den Bäumen und wickelte ihn um die fünf andern, hob das Bündel auf die Schulter und trug es fort. Dann kam er wieder und ging mit seinem Herrn, der sprach: »Wir zwei sollten wohl durch die ganze Welt kommen.« Und als sie ein Weilchen gegangen waren, fanden sie einen Jäger, der lag auf den Knien, hatte die Büchse angelegt und zielte. Sprach der Herr zu ihm: »Jäger, was willst du schießen?« Er antwortete: »Zwei Meilen von hier sitzt eine Fliege auf einem Eichenästchen, der will ich das linke Auge herausschießen.« – »Geh mit mir«, sprach der Mann, »wenn wir drei zusammen sind, sollten wir wohl durch die ganze Welt kommen.« Da ging der Jäger mit ihm, und sie kamen zu sieben Windmühlen, deren Flügel trieben ganz hastig herum, und ging doch links und rechts kein Wind und bewegte sich kein Blättchen. Da sprach der Mann: »Ich weiß nicht, was die Windmühlen treibt, es regt sich ja kein Lüftchen!« und ging mit seinen Dienern weiter, und als sie zwei Meilen fortgegangen waren, sahen sie einen auf einem Baum sitzen, der hielt das eine Nasenloch zu und blies aus dem andern. »Was treibst du da oben?« fragte der Mann. Er antwortete: »Zwei Meilen von hier stehen sieben Windmühlen, seht, die blase ich an, daß sie gehen.« – »Oh, geh mit mir«, sprach der Mann, »wenn wir vier zusammen sind, sollten wir wohl durch die ganze Welt kommen.« Da stieg der Bläser herab und ging mit, und über eine Zeit sahen sie einen, der stand da auf einem Bein und hatte das andere abgeschnallt und neben sich gelegt. »Ei«, sprach der Herr, »du hast dir's ja bequem gemacht zum Ausruhen.« – »Ich bin ein Läufer«, antwortete er, »und damit ich nicht gar zu schnell springe, habe ich mir das eine Bein abgeschnallt; denn wenn ich mit zwei Beinen laufe, so geht's geschwinder, als ein Vogel fliegt.« – »Oh, geh mit mir, wenn wir fünf zusammen sind, sollten wir wohl durch die ganze Welt kommen.« Da ging er mit, und gar nicht lang, so begegneten sie einem, der hatte ein Hütchen auf, hatte es aber ganz auf dem einen Ohr sitzen. Da sprach der Herr zu ihm: »Manierlich, manierlich! Setz deinen Hut doch ein bißchen gerade, du siehst ja aus wie ein Hans Narr.« – »Ich darf's nicht tun«, sprach der andere, »denn setz ich meinen Hut gerade, so kommt ein gewaltiger, entsetzlicher Frost, und die Vögel unter dem

Himmel erfrieren und fallen tot zur Erde.« – »Oh, geh mit mir«, sprach der Herr,
»wenn wir sechs zusammen sind, sollten wir wohl durch die ganze Welt kommen.«

Nun gingen die sechse in die Stadt, wo der König hatte bekannt machen lassen,
wer mit seiner Tochter um die Wette laufe und den Sieg davontrage, der solle ihr
Gemahl werden; wer aber verliere, müsse auch seinen Kopf hergeben. Da meldete
sich der Mann und sprach: »Ich will aber meinen Diener für mich laufen lassen.«
Der König antwortete: »Dann mußt du auch noch dessen Leben zum Pfand setzen,
also daß sein und dein Kopf für den Sieg haften.« Nun ward das verabredet und
festgemacht, da schnallte der Mann dem Läufer das andere Bein an und sprach zu
ihm: »Nun sei hurtig und hilf, daß wir siegen.« Es war aber bestimmt, daß, wer am
ersten Wasser aus einem fern gelegenen Brunnen brächte, Sieger sein sollte. Nun
bekam der Läufer einen Krug und die Königstochter auch einen, und sie fingen zu

andere dorthin. Ein Feldwebel rief um Gnade: er hätte neun Wunden und wäre ein braver Kerl, der den Schimpf nicht verdiene. Da ließ der Bläser ein wenig nach, so daß er ohne Schaden wieder herab kam, dann sprach er zu ihm: »Nun geh heim zum König und sag ihm, er sollt' nur noch mehr Reiterei schicken, ich wollte sie alle in die Luft hineinblasen.« Der König, als er den Bescheid vernahm, sprach: »Laßt sie gehen, sie haben etwas an sich!« Da brachten die sechs den Reichtum heim, teilten ihn unter sich und lebten vergnügt bis an ihr Ende.   1819

Rotkäppchen

Es war einmal eine kleine süße Dirn, die hatte jedermann lieb, der sie nur ansah, am allerliebsten aber ihre Großmutter, die wußte gar nicht, was sie alles dem Kind geben sollte. Einmal schenkte sie ihm ein Käppchen von rotem Samt, und weil ihm das so wohl stand und es nichts anderes mehr tragen wollte, hieß es nur das Rotkäppchen. Da sagte einmal seine Mutter zu ihm: »Komm, Rotkäppchen, da hast du ein Stück Kuchen und eine Flasche Wein, die bring der Großmutter hinaus; weil sie krank und schwach ist, wird sie sich daran laben; sei aber hübsch artig und grüß sie von mir, geh auch ordentlich und lauf nicht vom Weg ab, sonst fällst du und zerbrichst das Glas, dann hat die kranke Großmutter nichts.«

Rotkäppchen sagte: »Ja, ich will alles recht gut ausrichten«, und versprach's der Mutter in die Hand. Die Großmutter aber wohnte draußen im Wald, eine halbe Stunde vom Dorf. Wie nun Rotkäppchen in den Wald kam, begegnete ihm der Wolf. Rotkäppchen aber wußte nicht, was er für ein böses Tier war, und fürchtete sich nicht vor ihm. »Guten Tag, Rotkäppchen«, sprach er. – »Schönen Dank, Wolf.« – »Wo willst du so früh hinaus, Rotkäppchen?« – »Zur Großmutter.« – »Was trägst du unter der Schürze?« – »Kuchen und Wein, für die kranke und schwache Großmutter; gestern haben wir gebacken, da soll sie sich stärken.« – »Rotkäppchen, wo wohnt deine Großmutter?« – »Noch eine gute Viertelstunde im Wald, unter den drei großen Eichbäumen, da steht ihr Haus, unten sind die Nußhecken, das wirst du ja wissen«, sagte Rotkäppchen. Der Wolf dachte bei sich, das junge, zarte Mädchen, das ist ein guter, fetter Bissen für dich, wie fängst du's an, daß du den kriegst? Da ging er ein Weilchen neben Rotkäppchen her, dann sprach er: »Rotkäppchen, sieh einmal die schönen Blumen, die im Walde stehen, warum guckst du nicht um dich; ich glaube, du hörst gar nicht darauf, wie die Vöglein so lieblich singen? Du gehst ja für dich hin als wie zur Schule und ist so lustig haußen in dem Wald.«

Rotkäppchen schlug die Augen auf, und als es sah, wie die Sonne durch die

Bäume hin und her sprang und alles voll schöner Blumen stand, dachte es: Ei, wenn ich der Großmutter einen Strauß mitbringe, der wird ihr lieb sein; es ist noch früh, daß ich doch zu rechter Zeit ankomme, sprang in den Wald und suchte Blumen. Und wenn es eine gebrochen hatte, meint' es, dort stünd noch eine schönere, und lief danach und lief immer weiter in den Wald hinein. Der Wolf aber ging geradeswegs nach dem Haus der Großmutter und klopfte an die Türe. »Wer ist draußen?« – »Das Rotkäppchen, ich bring dir Kuchen und Wein, mach mir auf.« – »Drück nur auf die Klinke«, rief die Großmutter, »ich bin zu schwach und kann nicht aufstehen.« Der Wolf drückte an der Klinke, und er trat hinein, ohne ein Wort zu sprechen, geradezu an das Bett der Großmutter, und verschluckte sie. Dann nahm er ihre Kleider, tat sie an, setzte sich ihre Haube auf, legte sich in ihr Bett und zog die Vorhänge vor.

Rotkäppchen aber war herumgelaufen nach Blumen, und als es so viel hatte, daß es keine mehr tragen konnte, fiel ihm die Großmutter wieder ein, und es machte sich auf den Weg zu ihr. Wie es ankam, stand die Türe auf, darüber verwunderte es sich, und wie es in die Stube kam, sah's so seltsam darin aus, daß es dachte: Ei du mein Gott, wie ängstlich wird mir's heut zumut, und bin sonst so gern bei der Großmutter. Drauf ging es zum Bett und zog die Vorhänge zurück, da lag die Großmutter und hatte die Haube tief ins Gesicht gesetzt und sah so wunderlich aus. »Ei, Großmutter, was hast du für große Ohren!« – »Daß ich dich besser hören kann.« – »Ei, Großmutter, was hast du für große Augen!« – »Daß ich dich besser sehen kann.« – »Ei, Großmutter, was hast du für große Hände!« – »Daß ich dich besser packen kann.« – »Aber Großmutter, was hast du für ein entsetzlich großes Maul!« – »Daß ich dich besser fressen kann.« Und wie der Wolf das gesagt hatte, sprang er aus dem Bett und auf das arme Rotkäppchen und verschlang es.

Wie der Wolf den fetten Bissen im Leib hatte, legte er sich wieder ins Bett, schlief ein und fing an, überlaut zu schnarchen. Der Jäger ging eben vorbei und dachte bei sich: Wie kann die alte Frau so schnarchen, du mußt einmal nachsehen, ob ihr etwas fehlt. Da trat er in die Stube, und wie er vors Bett kam, so lag der Wolf darin, den er lange gesucht hatte. Nun wollte er seine Büchse anlegen, da fiel ihm ein, vielleicht hat er die Großmutter gefressen und ich kann sie noch erretten, und schoß nicht, sondern nahm eine Schere und schnitt dem schlafenden Wolf den Bauch auf. Wie er ein paar Schnitte getan, da sah er das rote Käppchen leuchten, und wie er noch ein wenig geschnitten, da sprang das Mädchen heraus und rief: »Ach, wie war ich erschrocken, was war's so dunkel in dem Wolf seinem Leib!« Und dann kam die Großmutter auch lebendig heraus. Rotkäppchen aber holte große schwere Steine, damit füllten sie dem Wolf den Leib, und wie er aufwachte, wollte er fortspringen, aber die Steine waren so schwer, daß er gleich niedersank und sich tot fiel.

Da waren alle drei vergnügt, der Jäger nahm den Pelz vom Wolf, die Großmutter aß den Kuchen und trank den Wein, den Rotkäppchen gebracht hatte, und Rotkäppchen dachte bei sich: Du willst dein Lebtag nicht wieder allein vom Weg ab in den Wald laufen, wenn dir's die Mutter verboten hat.

Es wird auch erzählt, daß einmal, als Rotkäppchen der alten Großmutter wieder Gebackenes brachte, ein anderer Wolf ihm zugesprochen und es vom Weg hat ableiten wollen. Rotkäppchen aber hütete sich und ging gerad fort ihres Wegs und sagte der Großmutter, daß sie den Wolf gesehen, daß er ihm guten Tag gewünscht, aber so bös aus den Augen geguckt! »Wenn's nicht auf offner Straße gewesen, er hätt' mich gefressen.« – »Komm«, sagte die Großmutter, »wir wollen die Türe verschließen, daß er nicht herein kann.« Bald danach klopfte der Wolf an und rief: »Mach auf, Großmutter, ich bin das Rotkäppchen, ich bring dir Gebackenes.« Sie schwiegen aber still und machten die Türe nicht auf, da ging der Böse etliche Mal um das Haus und sprang endlich aufs Dach und wollte warten, bis Rotkäppchen abends nach Haus ging, dann wollt' er ihm nachschleichen und wollt's in der Dunkelheit fressen. Aber die Großmutter merkte, was er im Sinn hatte. Nun stand vor dem Haus ein großer Steintrog, da sprach sie zu dem Kind: »Hol den Eimer, Rotkäppchen, gestern hab ich Würste gekocht, da trag das Wasser, worin sie gekocht sind, in den Trog.« Rotkäppchen trug so lange, bis der große, große Trog ganz voll war. Da stieg der Geruch von den Würsten dem Wolf in die Nase, er schnupperte und guckte hinab, endlich machte er den Hals so lang, daß er sich nicht mehr halten konnte und anfing zu rutschen; so rutschte er vom Dach herab und gerade in den großen Trog hinein und ertrank. Rotkäppchen aber ging fröhlich nach Haus, und tat ihm niemand etwas zu Leid.   1819

Die zertanzten Schuhe

Es war einmal ein König, der hatte zwölf Töchter, eine immer schöner als die andere, die hatten ihre zwölf Betten zusammen in einem Saal, und wenn sie waren schlafen gegangen, wurde die Türe verschlossen und verriegelt, und doch waren jeden Morgen ihre Schuhe zertanzt und wußte niemand, wo sie gewesen und wie es zugegangen war. Da ließ der König ausrufen, wer's könnte ausfindig machen, wo sie in der Nacht tanzten, der sollte sich eine davon zur Frau wählen und nach seinem Tod König sein; wer sich aber meldete und es nach drei Tagen und Nächten nicht herausbrächte, der hätte sein Leben verwirkt. Es kam bald ein Königssohn, der ward wohl aufgenommen und abends in das Zimmer geführt, das vor dem Schlafsaal der zwölf Töchter war, da stand sein Bett, und da sollte er achthaben, wo sie hingingen und tanzten; und damit sie nichts heimlich treiben konnten oder zu einem andern Ort hinausgingen, war auch die Saaltüre offen gelassen.

Der Königssohn aber schlief ein, und als er am Morgen aufwachte, waren alle zwölfe zum Tanz gewesen, denn ihre Schuhe standen da und hatten Löcher in den Sohlen. Den zweiten und dritten Abend ging's ebenso, und da ward ihm sein Haupt abgeschlagen; und so kamen noch viele und meldeten sich zu dem Wagestück, sie mußten aber alle ihr Leben lassen.

Nun trug sich's zu, daß ein armer Soldat, der eine Wunde hatte und nicht mehr dienen konnte, nach der Stadt zuging, wo der König wohnte. Da begegnete ihm eine alte Frau, die fragte ihn, wo er hin wollte. »Ich weiß selber nicht recht«, sprach er, »aber ich hätte wohl Lust, König zu werden und auszumachen, wo die Königstöchter ihre Schuhe vertanzen.« – »Ei«, sagte die Alte, »das ist so schwer nicht, du mußt nur den Wein nicht trinken, den dir die eine abends bringt, und mußt tun, als wärst du fest eingeschlafen.« Darauf gab sie ihm ein Mäntelchen und sprach: »Wenn du das umhängst, so bist du unsichtbar und kannst den zwölfen dann nachschleichen.«

Wie der Soldat so guten Rat bekommen hatte, ward's Ernst bei ihm, so daß er sich ein Herz faßte, vor den König ging und sich als Freier meldete. Er ward so gut aufgenommen wie die andern auch und wurden ihm königliche Kleider angetan. Abends zur Schlafenszeit wurde er in das Vorzimmer geführt, und als er zu Bett gehen wollte, kam die älteste und brachte ihm einen Becher Wein, aber er hatte sich einen Schwamm unter das Kinn gebunden und ließ den Wein da hineinlaufen und trank keinen Tropfen. Dann legte er sich nieder, und als er ein Weilchen gelegen hatte, fing er an zu schnarchen wie im tiefsten Schlaf. Das hörten die zwölf Königstöchter, lachten, und die älteste sprach: »Der hätte auch sein Leben sparen können!« Danach standen sie auf, öffneten Schränke, Kisten und Kasten und holten prächtige Kleider heraus, putzten sich vor den Spiegeln, sprangen herum und freuten sich auf den Tanz. Nur die jüngste sagte: »Ich weiß nicht, ihr freut euch, aber mir ist so wunderlich zu Mute, gewiß widerfährt uns ein Unglück.« – »Du Schneegans«, sagte die älteste, »du fürchtest dich immer, hast du vergessen, wieviel Königssöhne schon umsonst da gewesen sind; dem Soldaten hätt' ich nicht einmal brauchen einen Schlaftrunk zu geben, er wär doch nicht aufgewacht.«

Wie sie alle fertig waren, sahen sie erst nach dem Soldaten, aber der rührte und regte sich nicht, und wie sie nun glaubten, ganz sicher zu sein, ging die älteste an ihr Bett und klopfte daran; alsbald sank es in die Erde und öffnete sich eine Falltür. Da sah der Soldat, wie sie hinunterstiegen, eine nach der andern, die älteste voran; es war keine Zeit zu verlieren, er richtete sich auf, hing sein Mäntelchen um und stieg hinter der jüngsten mit hinab. Mitten auf der Treppe trat er ihr ein wenig aufs Kleid; da erschrak sie und rief: »Es ist nicht richtig, es hält mich was am Kleid.« – »Stell dich nicht so einfältig«, sagte die älteste, »du bist an einem Haken hängen geblieben.« Da gingen sie vollends hinab, und wie sie unten waren, standen sie in einem wunderprächtigen Baumgang, da waren alle Blätter von Silber und schimmerten und glänzten. Der Soldat dachte, du willst dir ein Wahrzeichen mitneh-

men, und brach einen Zweig davon ab, da kam ein gewaltiger Knall aus dem Baume. Die jüngste rief wieder: »Es ist nicht richtig, habt ihr den Knall gehört, das ist noch nie hier geschehen.« Die älteste aber sprach: »Das sind Freudenschüsse, weil wir unsere Prinzen bald erlöst haben!« Sie kamen darauf in einen Baumgang, wo alle Blätter von Gold, und endlich in einen dritten, wo sie klarer Diamant waren; von beiden brach er einen Zweig ab, wobei es jedesmal knallte, daß die jüngste vor Schrecken zusammenfuhr, aber die älteste blieb dabei, es wären Freudenschüsse. Da gingen sie weiter bis zu einem großen Wasser, darauf standen zwölf Schifflein, und in jedem Schifflein saß ein schöner Prinz, die hatten auf die zwölfe gewartet, und jeder nahm eine zu sich, der Soldat aber setzte sich mit der jüngsten hinein, da sprach der Prinz: »Ich bin doch so stark als sonst, aber heute ist das

Schiff viel schwerer, und ich muß rudern, was ich kann.« – »Wovon sollt' das kommen«, sprach die jüngste, »als vom warmen Wetter, es ist mir auch so heiß zu Mut.« Jenseits des Wassers aber stand ein schönes helleuchtendes Schloß, woraus eine lustige Musik erschallte von Pauken und Trompeten; da hinüber ruderten sie, gingen ein, und jeder Prinz tanzte mit seiner Liebsten; der Soldat aber tanzte unsichtbar mit, und wenn eine einen Becher mit Wein hielt, so trank er ihn aus, daß er leer war, wenn sie ihn an den Mund brachte; und der jüngsten ward auch angst darüber, aber die älteste brachte sie immer zum Schweigen. Sie tanzten da bis drei Uhr am andern Morgen, wo alle Schuhe durchgetanzt waren und sie aufhören mußten. Die Prinzen fuhren sie über das Wasser wieder hinüber, und der Soldat setzte sich diesmal vorne hin zur ältesten. Am Ufer nahmen sie von ihren Prinzen Abschied und versprachen, in der folgenden Nacht wiederzukommen.

Als sie an der Treppe waren, lief der Soldat voraus, legte sich ins Bett, und als die zwölf langsam und müd heraufgetrippelt kamen, schnarchte er schon wieder laut, so daß sie sprachen: »Nun, vor dem sind wir sicher.« Da taten sie ihre schönen Kleider aus, hoben sie auf, stellten die zertanzten Schuhe unter das Bett und legten sich nieder. Am andern Morgen wollte der Soldat nichts sagen, sondern das wunderliche Wesen noch mehr ansehen und ging die zweite und dritte Nacht wieder mit, und da war alles wie das erstemal, und sie tanzten jedesmal, bis die Schuhe entzwei waren. Nur das drittemal nahm er noch einen Becher mit zum Wahrzeichen.

Zu der Stunde nun, wo er antworten sollte, nahm er die drei Zweige und den Becher und ging vor den König, und die zwölfe standen hinter der Türe und horchten, was er sagen würde. Wie der König nun fragte: »Wo haben meine zwölf Töchter ihre Schuhe in der Nacht vertanzt?«, antwortete er: »Mit zwölf Prinzen in einem unterirdischen Schloß«, und erzählte alles und holte die Wahrzeichen hervor. Da rief der König seine Töchter und fragte sie, ob der Soldat die Wahrheit gesagt hätte, und da sie sahen, daß sie verraten waren und Leugnen nichts half, erzählten sie alles. Darauf fragte ihn der König, welche er zur Frau haben wollte? Er antwortete: »Ich bin nicht mehr jung, so gebt mir die älteste.« Da ward noch am selben Tage die Hochzeit gehalten und ihm das Reich nach des Königs Tode versprochen. Aber die Prinzen wurden auf soviel Tage wieder verwünscht, als sie Nächte mit den zwölfen getanzt hatten.

1819

Der Eisenofen

Zur Zeit, wo das Wünschen noch geholfen hat, ward ein Königssohn von einer alten Hexe verwünscht, daß er im Walde in einem großen Eisenofen sitzen sollte. Da brachte er nun viele Jahre zu und konnte ihn niemand erlösen. Einmal kam eine Königstochter in den Wald, die hatte sich irr gegangen und konnt' ihres Vaters Reich nicht wieder finden; neun Tage war sie so herum gegangen und stand zuletzt vor dem eisernen Kasten. Da fragte er sie: »Wo kommst du her, und wo willst du hin?« Sie antwortete: »Ich habe meines Vaters Königreich verloren und kann nicht wieder nach Haus kommen.« Da sprach's aus dem Eisenofen: »Ich will dir wieder nach Haus verhelfen in einer kurzen Zeit, wenn du dich willst unterschreiben zu tun, was ich verlange. Ich bin ein größerer Königssohn als du eine Königstochter und will dich heiraten.«

Da erschrak sie und dachte: »Lieber Gott, was soll ich mit dem Eisenofen anfangen!« Weil sie aber gern wieder zu ihrem Vater heim wollte, unterschrieb sie sich doch zu tun, was er verlangte. Er sprach aber: »Du sollst wiederkommen, ein Messer mitbringen und ein Loch in das Eisen schrappen.« Dann gab er ihr jemand zum Gefährten, der ging nebenher und sprach nicht, er brachte sie aber in zwei Stunden nach Haus. Nun war große Freude im Schloß, als die Königstochter wieder kam, und der alte König fiel ihr um den Hals und küßte sie. Sie war aber sehr betrübt und sprach: »Lieber Vater, wie mir's gegangen ist! Ich wär nicht wieder nach Haus gekommen aus dem großen wilden Walde, wenn ich nicht wär bei einen eisernen Ofen gekommen, dem habe ich mich müssen dafür unterschreiben, daß ich wollte wieder zu ihm zurückkehren, ihn erlösen und heiraten.« Da erschrak der alte König so sehr, daß er beinahe in eine Ohnmacht gefallen wäre, denn er hatte nur die eine Tochter. Beratschlagten sich also, sie wollten die Müllerstocher, die schön war, an ihre Stelle nehmen; führten die hinaus, gaben ihr ein Messer und hießen sie an dem Eisenofen schaben. Sie schrappte auch vierundzwanzig Stunden, konnte aber nicht das geringste herabbringen; wie nun der Tag anbrach, rief's in dem Eisenofen: »Mich deucht, 's ist Tag draußen!« Da antwortete sie: »Das deucht mich auch, ich meint', ich hört meines Vaters Mühle rappeln.« – »So bist du ja eine Müllerstochter, dann geh gleich hinaus und laß die Königstochter herkommen.« Da ging sie hin und sagte dem alten König, der draußen wollte sie nicht, er wollte seine Tochter. Da erschrak der alte König, und die Tochter weinte; sie hatten aber noch eine schöne Schweinehirtentochter, die war noch schöner als die Müllerstochter, der wollten sie ein Stück Geld geben, damit sie für die Königstochter zum eisernen Ofen ging. Also ward sie hinausgebracht und mußte auch vierundzwanzig Stunden schrappen, sie bracht' aber nichts davon. Wie nun der Tag anbrach, rief's im Ofen: »Mich deucht, es ist Tag drau-

284 *Der Eisenofen*

ßen!« Da antwortete sie: »Das deucht mich auch, ich meint', ich hört meines Vaters Hörnchen tüten!« – »So bist du ja eine Schweinehirtentochter, dann geh gleich hinaus und laß die Königstochter kommen; und sag ihr, es sollt' ihr widerfahren, was ich ihr versprochen hätte, und wenn sie nicht käme, sollte im ganzen Reich alles zerfallen und einstürzen und kein Stein auf dem andern bleiben.«

Als die Königstochter das hörte, fing sie an zu weinen, es war aber nun nicht anders, sie mußte ihr Versprechen halten. Da nahm sie Abschied von ihrem Vater, steckte ein Messer ein und ging zu dem Eisenofen in den Wald hinaus. Wie sie nun angekommen war, hub sie an zu schrappen, und das Eisen gab ihr nach, und wie zwei Stunden vorbei waren, hatte sie schon ein kleines Loch geschabt. Da guckte sie hinein und sah einen so schönen Königssohn. Ach, der glitzerte, daß er ihr recht in der Seele gefiel. Nun, da schrappte sie noch weiter fort und machte das Loch so groß, daß er heraus konnte. Da sprach er: »Du bist mein, und ich bin dein, du bist meine Braut und hast mich erlöst.« Sie bat sich aus, daß sie noch einmal dürfte zu ihrem Vater gehen, und der Königssohn erlaubte es ihr, sie sollte aber nicht mehr mit ihrem Vater sprechen als drei Worte, und dann sollte sie wiederkommen. Also ging sie heim, sie sprach aber mehr als drei Worte, da verschwand alsbald der Eisenofen und war weit weg über gläserne Berge und schneidende Schwerter; doch war der Königssohn erlöst und nicht mehr darin eingeschlossen. Danach nahm sie Abschied von ihrem Vater und etwas Geld mit, aber nicht viel, ging wieder in den Wald und suchte den Eisenofen, doch der war nicht wieder zu finden. Neun Tage suchte sie, da ward ihr Hunger so groß, daß sie sich nicht zu helfen wußte, denn sie hatte nichts mehr zu leben. Und wie es Abend wurde, setzte sie sich auf einen kleinen Baum und gedachte darauf die Nacht hinzubringen, weil sie sich vor den wilden Tieren fürchtete. Als nun Mitternacht herankam, sah sie von ferne ein kleines Lichtchen, dacht' sie: »Ach, da wär ich wohl erlöst«, stieg vom Baum und ging dem Lichtchen nach, auf dem Weg aber betete sie. Da kam sie zu einem kleinen alten Häuschen, da war viel Gras herum gewachsen und stand ein kleines Häufchen Holz davor. Dachte sie: »Ach, wo kommst du hier hin«; guckte durchs Fenster hinein, so sah sie nichts darin als dicke und kleine Itschen (Kröten), aber einen Tisch, schön gedeckt mit Wein und Braten, und Teller und Becher waren von Silber. Da nahm sie sich ein Herz und klopfte an; alsbald rief die Dicke:

>»Jungfer grün und klein,
Hutzelbein!
Hutzelbeins Hündchen!
Hutzel hin und her!
Laß geschwind sehen, wer draußen wär.«

Da kam eine kleine Itsche herbeigegangen und machte ihr auf. Wie sie eintrat, hießen alle sie willkommen, und sie mußte sich setzen. »Wo kommt Ihr her? Wo wollt Ihr hin?« Da erzählte sie alles, wie es ihr gegangen wäre, und weil sie das Gebot übertreten, nicht mehr als drei Worte zu sprechen, wäre der Ofen weg samt dem Prinzen; nun wollte sie so lange suchen und über Berg und Tal wandern, bis sie ihn fände. Da sprach die alte Dicke:

>»Jungfer grün und klein,
>Hutzelbein!
>Hutzelbeins Hündchen!
>Hutzel hin und her!
>Bring mir die große Schachtel her!«

Da ging die Kleine hin und brachte die Schachtel herbeigetragen, hernach gaben sie ihr Essen und Trinken und brachten sie zu einem schönen, gemachten Bett, das war wie Seide und Samt, da legte sie sich hinein und schlief in Gottes Namen. Als der Tag kam, stand sie auf, und gab ihr die alte Itsche drei Nadeln aus der großen Schachtel, die sollte sie mitnehmen. Sie würden ihr nötig sein, denn sie müßte über einen hohen gläsernen Berg und über drei schneidende Schwerter und über ein großes Wasser. Wenn sie das durchsetzte, würde sie ihren Liebsten wiederkriegen. Nun gab sie ihr mit drei Teile (Stücke), die sollte sie recht in acht nehmen, nämlich drei große Nadeln, ein Pflugrad und drei Nüsse. Hiermit reise sie ab, und wie sie vor den gläsernen Berg kam, der so glatt war, steckte sie die drei Nadeln als hinter die Füße und dann wieder vorwärts und gelangte so hinüber, und als sie hinüber war, steckte sie sie an einen Ort, den sie wohl in acht nahm. Danach kam sie vor die drei schneidenden Schwerter, da stellte sie sich auf ihr Pflugrad und rollte hinüber.

Endlich kam sie vor ein großes Wasser, und wie sie übergefahren war, in ein großes, schönes Schloß. Sie ging hinein und hielt um einen Dienst an, sie wär eine arme Magd und wollte sich gern vermieten. Sie wußte aber, daß der Königssohn drinnen war, den sie erlöst hatte aus dem eisernen Ofen im großen Wald. Also ward sie angenommen zum Küchenmädchen für geringen Lohn. Nun hatte der Königssohn schon wieder eine andere an der Seite, die wollte er heiraten, denn er dachte, sie wäre längst gestorben. Abends nun, wie sie aufgewaschen hatte und fertig war, fühlte sie in ihre Tasche und fand die drei Nüsse, welche ihr die alte Itsche gegeben hatte. Biß eine auf und wollte den Kern essen, siehe da war ein stolzes königliches Kleid drin. Wie's nun die Braut hörte, kam sie und hielt um das Kleid an und wollte es kaufen; es wär kein Kleid für eine Dienstmagd. Da sprach sie, ja sie wollt's nicht verkaufen, doch wenn sie ihr einerlei (ein Ding) wollte erlauben, so sollte sie's haben, nämlich eine Nacht in der Kammer ihres Bräutigams zu schlafen. Die Braut erlaubt' es ihr, weil das Kleid so schön war und sie noch keins so hatte. Wie's nun Abend war, sagte sie zu ihrem Bräutigam: »Das närrische Mädchen will in deiner Kammer schlafen.« – »Wenn du's zufrieden bist, bin ich's auch«, sprach er. Sie gab aber dem Mann ein Glas Wein, in das sie einen Schlaftrunk getan hatte. Also gingen beide in die Kammer schlafen, und er schlief so fest, daß sie ihn nicht erwecken konnte. Sie weinte aber die ganze Nacht und rief: »Ich hab dich erlöst aus einem wilden Wald und aus einem eisernen Ofen, du hast mich erlöst, und ich hab dich erlöst durch ein verwünschtes Schloß, über einen gläsernen Berg, über drei schneidende Schwerter und über ein großes Wasser, ehe ich dich gefunden habe, und willst mich doch nicht hören.« Die Bedienten saßen vor der Stubentüre und hörten, wie sie so die ganze Nacht weinte, und sagten's am Morgen ihrem Herrn. Und wie sie am andern Abend aufgewaschen hatte, biß sie die zweite Nuß auf, da war noch ein weit schöneres Kleid drin. Wie das die Braut sah, wollte sie es auch kaufen. Aber Geld wollte das Mädchen nicht und bat sich aus, daß es noch einmal in der Kammer des Bräutigams schlafen dürfte. Sie gab ihm aber wieder einen Schlaftrunk, und er schlief so fest, daß er nichts hören konnte. Das Küchenmädchen weinte aber die ganze Nacht und rief: »Ich hab dich erlöst aus einem wilden Walde und aus einem eisernen Ofen, du hast mich erlöst, und ich habe dich erlöst, durch ein verwünschtes Schloß, über einen gläsernen Berg, über drei schneidende Schwerter und über ein großes Wasser, ehe ich dich gefunden habe, und willst mich doch nicht hören.« Die Bedienten saßen vor der Stubentüre und hörten, wie sie so die ganze Nacht weinte, und sagten's am Morgen ihrem Herrn. Und wie sie am dritten Abend aufgewaschen hatte, biß sie die dritte Nuß auf, da war ein noch schöneres Kleid darin, das starrte von purem Gold. Wie die Braut das sah, wollte sie es haben, das Mädchen aber gab es nur hin, wenn sie zum drittenmal dürfte in der Kammer des Bräutigams schlafen. Der Königssohn aber hütete sich und ließ den Schlaftrunk vorbeilaufen. Wie sie nun anfing zu weinen und zu rufen: »Liebster Schatz, ich habe dich erlöst aus dem grausamen, wilden Walde und aus einem eisernen Ofen, du hast mich erlöst, und ich habe dich erlöst«, so sprang der Prinz auf und sprach: »Du bist mein, und ich bin dein.«

Darauf setzte er sich noch in der Nacht mit ihr in einen Wagen, und der falschen Braut nahmen sie die Kleider weg, daß sie nicht aufstehen konnte. Als sie zu dem großen Wasser kamen, da schifften sie hinüber, und vor den drei schneidenden Schwertern, da setzten sie sich aufs Pflugrad, und vor dem gläsernen Berg, da steckten sie die drei Nadeln hinein; und so gelangten sie endlich zu dem alten kleinen Häuschen. Aber wie sie hineintraten, war's ein großes Schloß, die Itschen waren alle erlöst und lauter Königskinder und waren in voller Freude. Da ward Vermählung gehalten, und sie blieben in dem Schloß, das war viel größer als ihres Vaters Schloß. Weil aber der Alte jammerte, daß er allein bleiben sollte, so fuhren sie weg und holten ihn zu sich und hatten zwei Königreiche und lebten in gutem Ehestand.

1819

Der Zaunkönig

In den alten Zeiten, da hatte jeder Klang noch Sinn und Bedeutung. Wenn der Hammer des Schmieds ertönte, so rief er: »Smiet mi to! Smiet mi to!« Wenn der Hobel des Tischlers schnarrte, so sprach er: »Dor häst! Dor, dor häst!« Fing das Räderwerk der Mühle an zu klappern, so sprach es: »Help, Herr Gott! Help, Herr Gott!« Und war der Müller ein Betrüger und ließ die Mühle an, so sprach sie hochdeutsch und fragte erst langsam: »Wer ist da? Wer ist da?« Dann antwortete sie schnell: »Der Müller, der Müller!« Und endlich ganz geschwind: »Stiehlt tapfer, stiehlt tapfer, vom Achtel drei Sechstel.«

Zu dieser Zeit hatten auch die Vögel ihre eigene Sprache, die jedermann verstand, jetzt lautet es nur wie ein Zwitschern, Kreischen und Pfeifen und bei einigen wie Musik ohne Worte. Es kam aber den Vögeln in den Sinn, sie wollten nicht länger ohne Herrn sein und einen unter sich zu ihrem König wählen. Nur einer von ihnen, der Kiebitz, war dagegen: Frei hatte er gelebt, und frei wollte er sterben, und angstvoll hin und her fliegend, rief er: »Wo bliew ick? Wo bliew ick?« Er zog sich zurück in einsame und unbesuchte Sümpfe und zeigte sich nicht wieder unter seinesgleichen.

Die Vögel wollten sich nun über die Sache besprechen, und an einem schönen Maimorgen kamen sie alle aus Wäldern und Feldern zusammen, Adler und Buchfink, Eule und Krähe, Lerche und Sperling, was soll ich sie alle nennen? Selbst der Kuckuck kam und der Wiedehopf, sein Küster, der so heißt, weil er sich immer ein paar Tage früher hören läßt; auch ein ganz kleiner Vogel, der noch keinen Namen hatte, mischte sich unter die Schar. Das Huhn, das zufällig von der ganzen Sache nichts gehört hatte, verwunderte sich über die große Versammlung. »Wat, wat, wat is den dar to don?« gackerte es, aber der Hahn beruhigte seine liebe Henne und sagte: »Luter riek Lüd«, erzählte ihr auch, was sie vorhätten. Es ward aber beschlossen, daß der König sein sollte, der am höchsten fliegen könnte. Ein Laubfrosch, der im Gebüsch saß, rief, als er das hörte, warnend: »Natt, natt, natt, natt, natt, natt!«, weil er meinte, es würden deshalb viel Tränen vergossen werden. Die Krähe aber sagte: »Quark ok!«, es sollte alles friedlich abgehen.

Es ward nun beschlossen, sie wollten gleich an diesem schönen Morgen aufsteigen, damit niemand hinterher sagen könnte: »Ich wäre wohl noch höher geflogen, aber der Abend kam, da konnte ich nicht mehr.« Auf ein gegebenes Zeichen erhob sich also die ganze Schar in die Lüfte. Der Staub stieg da von dem Felde auf, es war ein gewaltiges Sausen und Brausen und Fittichschlagen, und es sah aus, als wenn eine schwarze Wolke dahinzöge. Die kleineren Vögel aber blieben bald zurück, konnten nicht weiter und fielen wieder auf die Erde. Die größeren hielten's länger aus, aber keiner konnte es dem Adler gleichtun, der stieg so hoch, daß er der Sonne hätte die Augen aushacken können. Und als er sah, daß die andern nicht zu ihm herauf konnten, so dachte er: Was willst du noch höher fliegen, du bist doch der König, und fing an, sich wieder herabzulassen. Die Vögel unter ihm riefen ihm alle gleich zu: »Du mußt unser König sein, keiner ist höher geflogen als du.« – »Ausgenommen ich«, schrie der kleine Kerl ohne Namen, der sich in die Brustfedern des Adlers verkrochen hatte. Und da er nicht müde war, so stieg er auf und stieg so hoch, daß er Gott auf seinem Stuhle konnte sitzen sehen. Als er aber so weit gekommen war, legte er seine Flügel zusammen, sank herab und rief unten mit feiner, durchdringender Stimme: »König bün ick! König bün ick!«

»Du unser König?« schrien die Vögel zornig. »Durch Ränke und Listen hast du es dahin gebracht.« Sie machten eine andere Bedingung, der sollte ihr König sein, der am tiefsten in die Erde fallen könnte. Wie klatschte da die Gans mit ihrer breiten Brust wieder auf das Land! Wie scharrte der Hahn schnell ein Loch! Die Ente kam am schlimmsten weg, sie sprang in einen Graben, verrenkte sich aber die Beine und watschelte fort zum nahen Teiche mit dem Ausruf: »Pracherwerk! Pracherwerk!« Der Kleine ohne Namen aber suchte ein Mäuseloch, schlüpfte hinab und rief mit seiner feinen Stimme heraus: »König bün ick! König bün ick!«

»Du unser König?« riefen die Vögel noch zorniger. »Meinst du, deine Listen sollten gelten?« Sie beschlossen, ihn in seinem Loch gefangenzuhalten und auszuhungern. Die Eule ward als Wache davorgestellt. Sie sollte den Schelm nicht herauslassen, so lieb ihr das Leben wäre. Als es aber Abend geworden war und die Vögel von der Anstrengung beim Fliegen große Müdigkeit empfanden, gingen sie mit Weib und Kind zu Bett. Die Eule allein blieb bei dem Mäuseloch stehen und blickte mit ihren großen Augen unverwandt hinein. Indessen war sie auch müde geworden und dachte: Ein Auge kannst du wohl zutun, du wachst ja noch mit dem andern, und der kleine Bösewicht soll nicht aus seinem Loch heraus. Also tat sie das eine Auge zu und schaute mit dem andern steif auf das Mäuseloch. Der kleine Kerl guckte mit dem Kopf heraus und wollte wegwitschen, aber die Eule trat gleich davor, und er zog den Kopf wieder zurück. Dann tat die Eule das eine Auge wieder auf und das andere zu und wollte so die ganze Nacht abwechseln. Aber als sie das eine Auge wieder zumachte, vergaß sie, das andere aufzutun, und sobald die beiden Augen zu waren, schlief sie ein. Der Kleine merkte das bald und schlüpfte weg.

Von der Zeit an darf sich die Eule nicht mehr am Tage sehen lassen, sonst sind die andern Vögel hinter ihr her und zerzausen ihr das Fell. Sie fliegt nur zur Nachtzeit aus, haßt aber und verfolgt die Mäuse, weil sie solche bösen Löcher machen. Auch der kleine Vogel läßt sich nicht gerne sehen, weil er fürchtet, es ginge ihm an den Kragen, wenn er erwischt würde. Er schlüpft in den Zäunen herum, und wenn er ganz sicher ist, ruft er wohl zuweilen: »König bün ick!« Und deshalb nennen ihn die andern Vögel aus Spott »Zaunkönig«.

Niemand aber war froher als die Lerche, daß sie dem Zaunkönig nicht zu gehorchen brauchte. Wie sich die Sonne blicken läßt, steigt sie in die Lüfte und ruft: »Ach, wo is dat schön! Schön ist dat! Schön! Schön! Ach, wo is dat schön!« 1840

Die Krähen

Es hatte ein rechtschaffener Soldat etwas Geld verdient und zusammengespart, weil er fleißig war und es nicht, wie die andern, in den Wirtshäusern durchbrachte. Nun waren zwei von seinen Kameraden, die hatten eigentlich ein falsches Herz und wollten ihn um sein Geld bringen; sie stellten sich aber äußerlich ganz freundschaftlich an. Auf eine Zeit sprachen sie zu ihm: »Hör, was sollen wir hier in der Stadt liegen, wir sind ja eingeschlossen darin, als wären wir Gefangene, und gar einer wie du, der könnt sich daheim was Ordentliches verdienen und vergnügt leben.« Mit solchen Reden setzten sie ihm so lange zu, bis er endlich einwilligte und mit ihnen ausreißen wollte; die zwei andern hatten aber nichts anders im Sinn, als ihm draußen sein Geld abzunehmen. Wie sie nun ein Stück Wegs fortgegangen waren, sagten die zwei: »Wir müssen uns da rechts einschlagen, wenn wir an die Grenze kommen wollen.« – »Ei! Gott bewahre, da geht's gerade wieder in die Stadt zurück, links müssen wir weiter.« – »Was, willst du dich mausig machen?« riefen die zwei, drangen auf ihn ein, schlugen ihn, bis er niederfiel, und nahmen ihm sein Geld aus den Taschen. Das war aber noch nicht genug, sie stachen ihm auch die Augen aus, schleppten ihn zum Galgen und banden ihn daran fest. Da ließen sie ihn und gingen mit dem gestohlenen Geld in die Stadt zurück.

Der arme Blinde wußte aber nicht, an welchem schlechten Ort er war, fühlte um sich und merkte, daß er unter einem Balken Holz saß. Da meinte er, es wäre ein Kreuz, sprach: »Es ist doch gut von ihnen, daß sie mich wenigstens unter ein Kreuz gebunden haben, Gott ist bei mir«, und fing an, recht zu Gott zu beten. Wie es ungefähr Nacht werden mochte, hörte er etwas flattern; das waren aber drei Krähen, die ließen sich auf dem Balken nieder. Danach hörte er, wie eine sprach: »Schwester, was bringt Ihr Gutes? Ja, wenn die Menschen wüßten, was wir wissen! Die Königstochter ist krank, und der alte König hat sie demjenigen versprochen, der sie heilt, das kann aber keiner, denn sie wird nur gesund, wenn die Kröte in dem Teich dort zu Asche verbrannt wird und sie die Asche trinkt.« Da sprach die zweite: »Ja, wenn die Menschen wüßten, was wir wissen! Heute nacht fällt ein Tau vom Himmel, so wunderbar und heilsam, wer blind ist und bestreicht seine Augen damit, der erhält sein Gesicht wieder.« Da sprach auch die dritte: »Ja, wenn die Menschen wüßten, was wir wissen! Die Kröte hilft nur einem, und der Tau hilft nur wenigen, aber in der Stadt ist große Not, da sind alle Brunnen vertrocknet, und niemand weiß, daß der große viereckige Stein auf dem Markt muß weggenommen und darunter gegraben werden, dort quillt das schönste Wasser.«

Wie die drei Krähen das gesagt hatten, hörte er es wieder flattern, und sie flogen da fort! Er aber machte sich allmählich von seinen Banden los, und dann bückte er sich und brach ein paar Gräserchen ab und bestrich seine Augen mit dem Tau, der

292　*Die Krähen*

darauf gefallen war. Alsbald ward er wieder sehend und waren Mond und Sterne am Himmel und sah er, daß er neben dem Galgen stand. Danach suchte er Scherben und sammelte von dem köstlichen Tau, soviel er zusammenbringen konnte, und wie das geschehen war, ging er zum Teich, grub das Wasser davon ab und holte die Kröte heraus, und dann verbrannte er sie zu Asche und ging damit an des Königs Hof. Da ließ er nun die Königstochter von der Asche einnehmen, und als sie gesund war, verlangte er sie, wie es versprochen war, zur Gemahlin. Dem König aber gefiel er nicht, weil er so schlechte Kleider anhatte, und er sprach, wer seine Tochter haben wollte, der müßte der Stadt erst Wasser verschaffen, und damit hoffte er ihn los zu werden. Er aber ging hin, hieß die Leute den viereckigen Stein auf dem Markt wegheben und darunter nach Wasser graben. Das taten sie auch und kamen bald zu einer schönen Quelle, da war Wasser zum Überfluß. Der König aber konnte ihm nun seine Tochter nicht länger abschlagen, und er wurde mit ihr vermählt, und lebten sie in einer vergnügten Ehe.

Auf eine Zeit, als er durchs Feld spazieren ging, begegneten ihm seine beiden ehemaligen Kameraden, die so treulos an ihm gehandelt hatten. Sie kannten ihn nicht, er aber erkannte sie gleich, ging auf sie zu und sprach: »Seht, das ist euer ehemaliger Kamerad, dem ihr so schändlich die Augen ausgestochen habt, aber der liebe Gott hat mir's zum Glück gedeihen lassen.« Da fielen sie ihm zu Füßen und baten um Gnade, und weil er ein gutes Herz hatte, erbarmte er sich ihrer und nahm sie mit sich und gab ihnen auch Nahrung und Kleider. Er erzählte ihnen danach, wie es ihm ergangen und wie er zu diesen Ehren gekommen wäre; als die zwei das vernahmen, hatten sie keine Ruhe und wollten sich auch eine Nacht unter den Galgen setzen: Ob sie vielleicht auch etwas Gutes hörten? Wie sie nun unter dem Galgen saßen, flatterte auch bald etwas über ihren Häuptern und kamen die drei Krähen. Die eine sprach zur andern: »Hört, Schwestern, es muß uns jemand behorcht haben, denn die Prinzessin ist gesund, die Kröte ist fort aus dem Teich, ein Blinder ist sehend geworden, und in der Stadt haben sie einen frischen Brunnen gegraben. Kommt, laßt uns suchen, vielleicht finden wir ihn.« Da flatterten sie herab und fanden die beiden, und eh' sie sich helfen konnten, saßen sie ihnen auf den Köpfen und hackten ihnen die Augen aus und hackten weiter so lange ins Gesicht, bis sie ganz tot waren. Da blieben sie liegen unter dem Galgen. Als sie nun in ein paar Tagen nicht wiederkamen, dachte ihr ehemaliger Kamerad: Wo mögen die zwei herumirren, und ging hinaus, sie zu suchen. Da fand er aber nichts mehr als ihre Gebeine, die trug er vom Galgen weg und legte sie in ein Grab. 1819

Die Geschenke des kleinen Volkes

Ein Schneider und ein Goldschmied wanderten zusammen und vernahmen eines Abends, als die Sonne hinter die Berge gesunken war, den Klang einer fernen Musik, die immer deutlicher ward. Sie tönte ungewöhnlich, aber so anmutig, daß sie alle Müdigkeit vergaßen und rasch weiterschritten. Der Mond war schon aufgestiegen, als sie zu einem Hügel gelangten, auf dem sie eine Menge kleiner Männer und Frauen erblickten, die sich bei den Händen gefaßt hatten und mit größter Lust und Freudigkeit im Tanze herumwirbelten. Sie sangen dazu auf das lieblichste; und das war die Musik, die die Wanderer gehört hatten. In der Mitte saß ein Alter, der etwas größer war als die übrigen, der einen buntfarbigen Rock trug und dem ein eisgrauer Bart über die Brust herabhing. Die beiden blieben voll Verwunderung stehen und sahen dem Tanz zu. Der Alte winkte, sie sollten eintreten, und das kleine Volk öffnete bereitwillig seinen Kreis. Der Goldschmied, der einen Höcker hatte und wie alle Bucklingen keck genug war, trat herzu; der Schneider empfand zuerst einige Scheu und hielt sich zurück, doch als er sah, wie es so lustig herging, faßte er sich ein Herz und kam nach. Alsbald schloß sich der Kreis wieder, und die Kleinen sangen und tanzten in den wildesten Sprüngen weiter, der Alte aber nahm ein breites Messer, das an seinem Gürtel hing, wetzte es, und als es hinlänglich geschärft war, blickte er sich nach den Fremdlingen um. Es ward ihnen angst, aber sie hatten nicht lange Zeit, sich zu besinnen, der Alte packte den Goldschmied und schor in der größten Geschwindigkeit ihm Haupthaar und Bart glatt hinweg; ein gleiches geschah hierauf dem Schneider. Doch ihre Angst verschwand, als der Alte nach vollbrachter Arbeit beiden freundlich auf die Schulter klopfte, als wollte er sagen, sie hätten es gut gemacht, daß sie ohne Sträuben alles willig hätten geschehen lassen. Er zeigte mit dem Finger auf einen Haufen Kohlen, der zur Seite lag, und deutete ihnen durch Gebärden an, daß sie ihre Taschen damit füllen sollten. Beide gehorchten, obgleich sie nicht wußten, wozu ihnen die Kohlen dienen sollten, und gingen dann weiter, um ein Nachtlager zu suchen. Als sie ins Tal gekommen waren, schlug die Glocke des benachbarten Klosters zwölf Uhr. Augenblicklich verstummte der Gesang, alles war verschwunden, und der Hügel lag in einsamem Mondschein.

Die beiden Wanderer fanden eine Herberge und deckten sich auf dem Strohlager mit ihren Röcken zu, vergaßen aber wegen ihrer Müdigkeit, die Kohlen zuvor herauszunehmen. Ein schwerer Druck auf ihren Gliedern weckte sie früher als gewöhnlich. Sie griffen in die Taschen und wollten ihren Augen nicht trauen, als sie sahen, daß sie nicht mit Kohlen, sondern mit reinem Gold angefüllt waren; auch Haupthaar und Bart war glücklich wieder in aller Fülle vorhanden. Sie waren nun reiche Leute geworden, doch besaß der Goldschmied, der seiner habgierigen

Natur gemäß die Taschen besser gefüllt hatte, noch einmal soviel als der Schneider. Ein Habgieriger, wenn er viel hat, verlangt noch mehr, der Goldschmied machte dem Schneider den Vorschlag, noch einen Tag zu verweilen, am Abend wieder hinauszugehen, um sich bei dem Alten auf dem Berge noch größere Schätze zu holen. Der Schneider wollte nicht und sagte: »Ich habe genug und bin zufrieden. Jetzt werde ich Meister, heirate meinen angenehmen Gegenstand (wie er seine Liebste nannte) und bin ein glücklicher Mann.« Doch wollte er, ihm zu Gefallen, den Tag noch bleiben.

Abends hing der Goldschmied noch ein paar Taschen über die Schulter, um recht einsacken zu können, und machte sich auf den Weg zu dem Hügel. Er fand, wie in der vorigen Nacht, das kleine Volk bei Gesang und Tanz, der Alte schor ihn abermals glatt und deutete ihm an, Kohlen mitzunehmen. Er zögerte nicht einzustecken, was nur in seine Taschen gehen wollte, kehrte ganz glückselig heim und deckte sich mit dem Rock zu. »Wenn das Gold auch drückt«, sprach er, »ich will das schon ertragen«, und schlief endlich mit dem süßen Vorgefühl ein, morgen als steinreicher Mann zu erwachen. Als er die Augen öffnete, erhob er sich schnell, um die Taschen zu untersuchen, aber wie erstaunte er, als er nichts herauszog als schwarze Kohlen, er mochte so oft hineingreifen, als er wollte. »Noch bleibt mir das Gold, das ich die Nacht vorher gewonnen habe«, dachte er und holte es herbei, aber wie erschrak er, als er sah, daß es ebenfalls wieder zu Kohle geworden war. Er schlug sich mit der schwarzbestäubten Hand an die Stirne, da fühlte er, daß der ganze Kopf kahl und glatt war wie der Bart. Aber sein Mißgeschick war noch nicht zu Ende, er merkte erst jetzt, daß ihm zu dem Höcker auf dem Rücken noch ein zweiter, ebenso großer vorn auf der Brust gewachsen war. Da erkannte er die Strafe seiner Habgier und begann laut zu weinen. Der gute Schneider, der davon aufgeweckt ward, tröstete den Unglücklichen, so gut es gehen wollte, und sprach: »Du bist mein Geselle auf der Wanderschaft gewesen, du sollst bei mir bleiben und mit von meinem Schatz zehren.« Er hielt Wort, aber der arme Goldschmied mußte sein Lebtag die beiden Höcker tragen und seinen kahlen Kopf mit einer Mütze bedecken.

1850

Der Dreschflegel vom Himmel

Es zog einmal ein Bauer mit einem Paar Ochsen zum Pflügen aus. Als er aufs Land kam, da fingen den beiden Tieren die Hörner an zu wachsen, wuchsen fort, und als er nach Haus wollte, waren sie so groß, daß er nicht mit ihnen zum Tor hinein konnte. Zu gutem Glück kam gerade ein Metzger daher, dem überließ er sie, und schlossen sie den Handel dergestalt, daß er sollte dem Metzger ein Maß Rübsamen bringen, der wollt' ihm dann für jedes Korn einen Brabanter Taler aufzählen. Das heiß ich mir gut verkauft!

Der Bauer ging nun heim und trug das Maß Rübsamen auf dem Rücken herbei. Unterwegs verlor er aber aus dem Sack ein Körnchen. Der Metzger bezahlte ihn dem Handel gemäß richtig aus. Hätte der Bauer das eine Korn nicht verloren, so hätte er einen Brabanter Taler mehr gehabt. Indessen, wie er wieder des Wegs zurückkam, war aus dem Korn ein Baum gewachsen, der reichte bis an den Himmel. Da dachte der Bauer: Weil die Gelegenheit da ist, mußt du doch sehen, was die Engel da droben machen, und ihnen einmal unter die Augen gucken. Also stieg er hinauf und sah, daß die Engel oben Hafer droschen, und schaute das mit an. Wie er so schaute, merkte er, daß der Baum, worauf er stand, anfing zu wackeln, und guckte hinunter und sah, daß ihn eben einer umhauen wollte. Wenn du da herabstürztest, das wär ein böses Ding, dachte er, und in der Not wußt' er sich nicht besser zu helfen, als daß er die Spreu vom Hafer nahm, die haufenweis dalag, und daraus einen Strick drehte, auch griff er nach einer Hacke und einemDreschflegel, die da herum im Himmel lagen, und ließ sich an dem Seil herunter. Er kam aber unten auf der Erde gerade in ein tiefes, tiefes Loch, und da war es ein rechtes Glück, daß er die Hacke hatte, denn er nahm sie und hackte sich eine Treppe, stieg darauf in die Höhe und brachte den Dreschflegel zum Wahrzeichen mit, so daß niemand an seiner Erzählung mehr zweifeln konnte.   1837

Der Teufel und seine Großmutter

Es war ein großer Krieg, und der König gab seinen Soldaten wenig Sold, so daß sie nicht davon leben konnten. Da taten sich drei zusammen und wollten ausreißen. Einer sprach zum andern: »Wenn wir aber gekriegt werden, hängt man uns an den Galgenbaum; wie wollen wir das machen?« Sprach der andere: »Da steht ein großes Kornfeld, wenn wir hineinkriechen, findet uns kein Mensch, das Heer kommt nicht hinein.« Da krochen sie hinein und saßen zwei Tage und zwei Nächte im Korn, hatten aber so großen Hunger, daß sie beinah gestorben wären, denn sie durften nicht heraus. Da sprachen sie: »Was hilft uns unser Ausreißen, wir müssen elendig im Korn sterben.« Indem kam ein feuriger Drache über das Kornfeld durch die Luft geflogen, der sah sie liegen und fragte: »Was tut ihr drei da im Korn?« Sie antworteten: »Wir sind drei ausgerissene Soldaten, wir konnten von unserem Sold nicht länger im Heer leben, nun müssen wir hier Hungers sterben, weil das Heer rund herum liegt und wir nicht entrinnen können.« – »Wollt ihr mir sieben Jahre dienen«, sagte der Drache, »so will ich euch mitten durchs Heer führen, daß euch niemand kriegen soll.« – »Wir haben keine Wahl und sind's zufrieden«, antworteten sie.

Da nahm sie der Drache in seine Klauen und unter seine Fittiche und brachte sie durch die Luft über das Heer weg in Sicherheit. Danach ließ er sie wieder zur Erde, er war aber der Teufel und gab ihnen ein kleines Peitschchen, womit sie sich Geld peitschen konnten, soviel sie wollten. »Damit«, sprach er, »könnt ihr große Herren werden und im Wagen fahren; nach Verlauf der sieben Jahre aber seid ihr mein eigen«, und hielt ihnen ein Buch vor, in das mußten sie alle drei unterschreiben. »Doch will ich euch«, sagte er, »dann erst noch ein Rätsel geben. Könnt ihr das raten, sollt ihr frei und aus meiner Gewalt sein.«

Da ging der Drache von ihnen ab, und sie reisten fort mit ihren Peitschchen, hatten Geld die Fülle, ließen sich Herrenkleider machen und zogen in der Welt herum. Wo sie waren, lebten sie in Freuden und Herrlichkeit, fuhren mit Pferden und Wagen, aßen und tranken, und die sieben Jahre strichen in kurzer Zeit um. Als es nun bald ans Ende kam, wurde ihnen angst und bang, zwei waren ganz betrübt, der dritte aber nahm's auf die leichte Schulter und sprach: »Brüder, fürchtet nichts, vielleicht können wir das Rätsel raten.«

Wie sie so zusammen saßen, kam eine alte Frau daher, die fragte, warum sie so traurig wären. »Ach, was liegt Euch daran, Ihr könnt uns doch nicht helfen.« – »Wer weiß das, erzählt mir's nur.« Da erzählten sie's ihr, daß sie fast sieben Jahr dem Teufel gedient, der hätte ihnen Geld wie Heu geschafft, sie hätten sich ihm aber verschrieben und wären sein Eigentum, wenn sie nach den sieben Jahren nicht ein Rätsel auflösen könnten. Die Alte sprach: »Soll euch geholfen werden, so

muß einer von euch zum Wald hineingehen, und da wird er an eine zerfallene Klippe kommen, die aussieht wie ein Häuschen.« Die zwei traurigen dachten, das wird uns doch nicht retten, und blieben vor dem Wald, der dritte lustige machte sich auf und fand alles so, wie die Frau gesagt hatte. In dem Häuschen aber saß eine steinalte Frau, die war des Teufels Großmutter und fragte ihn, woher er käme und was er wollte? Da erzählte er ihr alles, und weil er ein gar schöner Mensch war, hatte sie Erbarmen und hob einen großen Stein auf. »Darunter sitz ganz still. Wenn der Drache kommt, will ich ihn um die Rätsel fragen.«

Um zwölf Uhr nachts kam der Drache geflogen und wollte sein Essen, da deckte ihm seine Großmutter den Tisch und trug Trank und Speise auf, daß er vergnügt war, und sie aßen und tranken zusammen. Da fragte sie ihn im Gespräch, wie's den Tag ergangen wäre, wieviel Seelen er gekriegt hätte? »Ich hab noch drei Soldaten, die sind mein«, sprach er. »Ja, drei Soldaten«, sagte sie, »haben etwas an sich, die können dir noch entkommen.« Sprach der Teufel höhnisch: »Die sind mir gewiß, denen gebe ich ein Rätsel auf, das sie nimmermehr raten können.« – »Was ist das für ein Rätsel?« fragte sie. »Das will ich dir sagen: In der großen Nordsee liegt eine tote Meerkatze, das soll ihr Braten sein; und von einem Walfisch die Rippe, das soll ihr silberner Löffel sein; und ein alter Pferdefuß, das soll ihr Weinglas sein.«

Da ging der Teufel fort zu schlafen, und die alte Großmutter hob den Stein auf und ließ den Soldaten heraus. »Hast du auch alles wohl in acht genommen?« – »Ja«, sprach er, »nun weiß ich mir schon zu helfen.« Darauf mußte er einen andern Weg durchs Fenster schnell zu seinen Gesellen gehen, damit ihn der Teufel nicht merkte. Wie er nun zu den andern kam, erzählte er ihnen, was er gehört hatte, und sie konnten nun raten, was sonst keine Seele geraten hätte; da waren sie alle fröhlich und guter Dinge und peitschten sich Geld genug.

Als nun die sieben Jahre völlig herum waren, kam der Teufel mit dem Buch, zeigte die Unterschriften und sprach: »Ich will euch nun in die Hölle mitnehmen, da sollt ihr eine Mahlzeit haben. Könnt ihr mir raten, was ihr für einen Braten werdet zu essen kriegen, so sollt ihr frei und los sein und das Peitschchen dazu behalten.« Da fing der erste Soldat an: »In der großen Nordsee liegt eine tote Meerkatze, das wird wohl der Braten sein.« Der Teufel ärgerte sich, machte hm, hm, hm, und fragte den zweiten: »Was soll euer Löffel sein?« Da antwortete er: »Von einem Walfisch die Rippe, das soll unser silberner Löffel sein.« Der Teufel schnitt ein Gesicht, knurrte wieder dreimal hm, hm, hm, und sprach zum dritten: »Was soll euer Weinglas sein?« – »Ein alter Pferdefuß, das soll unser Weinglas sein.« Da flog der Teufel fort, ließ sie im Stich und hatte keine Gewalt mehr über sie; aber die drei behielten das Peitschchen, schlugen Geld hervor, soviel sie wollten, und lebten vergnügt bis an ihr Ende.

1819

Die zwölf Brüder

Es war einmal ein König und eine Königin, die lebten in Frieden miteinander und hatten zwölf Kinder, das waren aber lauter Buben. Nun sprach der König zu seiner Frau: »Wenn das dreizehnte Kind, das du zur Welt bringst, ein Mädchen ist, so sollen die zwölf Buben sterben, damit sein Reichtum groß wird und es das Königreich allein erhält.« Er ließ auch zwölf Särge machen, die waren schon mit Hobelspänen gefüllt, und in jedem lag das Totenkißchen, und ließ sie in eine verschlossene Stube bringen, davon gab er der Königin den Schlüssel und sprach, sie sollte niemand davon etwas sagen.

Die Mutter aber saß nun den ganzen Tag und trauerte, so daß der kleinste Sohn, der immer bei ihr war und den sie nach der Bibel Benjamin nannte, zu ihr sprach: »Liebe Mutter, warum bist du so traurig?« – »Liebstes Kind«, antwortete sie, »ich darf dir's nicht sagen.« Er ließ ihr aber keine Ruhe, bis sie ging und die Stube aufschloß und ihm die zwölf Totenladen, mit Hobelspänen schon gefüllt, zeigte und sprach: »Mein liebster Benjamin, die hat dein Vater für dich und deine elf Brüder machen lassen, denn wenn ich ein Mädchen zur Welt bringe, so sollt ihr allesamt getötet und in den Särgen da begraben werden.« Da sagte der Sohn: »Weine nicht, liebe Mutter, wir wollen uns helfen und wollen fortgehen.« Sie sprach: »Geh mit deinen elf Brüdern hinaus in den Wald, und einer setze sich immer auf den höchsten Baum, der zu finden ist, und halte Wacht und schaue nach dem Turm hier im Schloß. Gebär ich ein Söhnlein, so will ich eine weiße Fahne aufstecken, dann dürft ihr wieder kommen; gebär ich ein Töchterlein, so will ich eine rote Fahne aufstecken, dann flieht fort, und der liebe Gott behüt euch. Alle Nacht will ich aufstehn und für euch beten: im Winter, daß ihr an einem Feuer euch wärmen könnt, im Sommer, daß ihr nicht in der Hitze schmachtet.«

Nachdem sie also ihre Söhne gesegnet hatte, gingen sie hinaus in den Wald. Einer hielt um den andern Wacht, saß auf der höchsten Eiche und schaute nach dem Turm. Als elf Tage herum waren und die Reihe an Benjamin kam, da sah er, wie eine Fahne aufgesteckt wurde, es war aber nicht die weiße, sondern die rote Blutfahne, die verkündigte, daß sie alle sterben sollten. Wie die Brüder das nun hörten, wurden sie zornig und sprachen: »Sollen wir um eines Mädchens willen den Tod leiden; nun schwören wir, daß, wo uns eins begegnet, wir uns rächen und sein rotes Blut fließen lassen.«

Darauf gingen sie tiefer in den großen Wald hinein, und mitten drin, wo er am dunkelsten war, fanden sie ein kleines verwünschtes Häuschen, das leer stand. Da sprachen sie: »Hier wollen wir wohnen, und du, Benjamin, du bist der jüngste und schwächste, du sollst daheim bleiben und haushalten, wir wollen ausgehen und Essen holen.« Nun zogen sie in den Wald und schossen Hasen, wilde Rehe, Vögel und Täuberchen und was zu essen stand; das brachten sie dem Benjamin, der mußt's ihnen zurecht machen, damit sie ihren Hunger stillen konnten. In dem Häuschen lebten sie zehn Jahre zusammen, und die Zeit ward ihnen nicht lang.

Das Töchterchen, das ihre Mutter, die Königin, geboren, war nun herangewachsen, war gar schön und hatte einen goldenen Stern auf der Stirne. Einmal, als große Wäsche war, sah es darunter zwölf Mannshemden und fragte seine Mutter: »Wem gehören diese zwölf Hemden, für den Vater sind sie doch viel zu klein?« Da antwortete sie mit schwerem Herzen: »Liebes Kind, die gehören deinen zwölf Brüdern.« Sprach das Fräulein: »Wo sind denn meine zwölf Brüder, von denen habe ich noch niemals gehört.« Sie antwortete: »Das weiß Gott, wo sie sind, sie irren in der Welt herum.« Da nahm sie das Mädchen und schloß ihm das Zimmer auf und zeigte ihm die zwölf Särge mit den Hobelspänen und den Totenkißchen. »Die«, sprach sie, »waren für sie bestimmt, aber sie sind heimlich fortgegangen, eh' du geboren warst«, und erzählte ihm, wie sich alles zugetragen hatte. Da sagte das Mädchen: »Liebe Mutter, weine nicht, ich will gehen und meine Brüder suchen.«

Nun nahm es die zwölf Hemden und ging fort und geradezu in den großen Wald hinein. Es ging den ganzen Tag, und am Abend kam es zu dem verwünschten Häuschen. Da trat es hinein und fand einen jungen Knaben, der fragte: »Wo kommst du her und wo willst du hin?« und erstaunte, daß sie so gar schön war, königliche Kleider trug und einen Stern auf der Stirne hatte. Da antwortete sie: »Ich bin eine Königstochter und suche meine zwölf Brüder und will gehen, so weit der Himmel blau ist, bis ich sie finde.« Und zeigte ihm die zwölf Hemden, die ihnen gehörten. Da sah Benjamin, daß es seine Schwester war, und sprach: »Ich bin Benjamin, dein jüngster Bruder!« Und sie fing an zu weinen vor Freude und Benjamin auch, und sie küßten und herzten einander vor großer Liebe. Hernach sprach er: »Liebe Schwester, es ist noch ein Vorbehalt da, wir hatten beschlossen und verabredet, daß ein jedes Mädchen, das uns begegnete, sterben sollte, weil wir um ein Mädchen unser Königreich verlassen mußten.« Da sagte sie: »Ich will gern sterben, wenn ich damit meine zwölf Brüder erlösen kann.« – »Nein«, antwortete er, »du sollst nicht sterben, setz dich unter diese Bütte, bis die elf Brüder kommen, dann will ich schon einig mit ihnen werden.« Also tat sie; und wie es Nacht ward, kamen die andern von der Jagd, und die Mahlzeit war bereit. Und als sie am Tisch saßen und aßen, fragten sie: »Was gibt's Neues?« Sprach Benjamin: »Wißt ihr nichts?« – »Nein«, antworteten sie. Sprach er weiter: »Ihr seid im Wald gewesen, und ich bin daheim geblieben und weiß doch mehr als ihr.« – »So erzähl uns«, riefen sie. Antwortete er: »Versprecht ihr mir auch, daß das erste Mädchen, das uns begegnet, nicht soll getötet werden?« – »Ja«, riefen sie alle, »das soll Gnade haben, erzähl uns nur.« Da sprach er: »Unsere Schwester ist da«, und hub die Bütte auf, und die Königstochter kam hervor in ihren königlichen Kleidern mit

dem goldenen Stern auf der Stirne und war so schön zart und fein. Da freuten sie sich alle, fielen ihr um den Hals und küßten sie und hatten sie von Herzen lieb.

Nun blieb sie bei Benjamin zu Haus und half ihm in der Arbeit. Die elf zogen in den Wald, suchten Wild: Rehe, Hasen, Vögel und Täuberchen, damit sie zu essen hatten, und die Schwester und Benjamin sorgten, daß es zubereitet wurde. Sie suchte das Holz zum Kochen und die Kräuter zum Gemüs und stellte zu am Feuer, also daß die Mahlzeit immer fertig war, wenn die elf kamen. Sie hielt auch sonst Ordnung im Häuschen und deckte die Bettlein hübsch weiß und rein, und die Brüder waren immer zufrieden und lebten in großer Einigkeit mit ihr.

Auf eine Zeit hatten die beiden daheim eine schöne Kost zurecht gemacht, und wie sie nun alle beisammen waren, setzten sie sich, aßen und tranken und waren voller Freude. Es war aber ein kleines Gärtchen an dem verwünschten Häuschen, darin standen zwölf Lilienblumen, die man auch Studenten heißt; nun wollte sie ihren Brüdern ein Vergnügen machen, brach die zwölf Blumen ab und dachte jedem aufs Essen eine zu schenken. Wie sie aber die Blumen abgebrochen hatte, in demselben Augenblick waren die zwölf Brüder in zwölf Raben verwandelt und flogen über den Wald hin fort, und das Haus mit dem Garten war auch verschwunden. Da war nun das arme Mädchen allein in dem wilden Wald, und wie es sich umsah, so stand eine alte Frau neben ihm, die sprach: »Ei, ei, mein Kind, was hast du angefangen? Warum hast du die zwölf weißen Blumen nicht stehen lassen, das waren deine Brüder, die sind nun auf immer in Raben verwandelt.« Das Mädchen sprach weinend: »Ist denn kein Mittel, sie zu erlösen?« – »Nein«, sagte die Alte, »es ist keins auf der ganzen Welt als eins, das ist aber so schwer, daß du sie damit nicht befreien wirst, denn du mußt sieben Jahre stumm sein, darfst nicht sprechen und nicht lachen, und sprichst du ein einziges Wort, und es fehlt nur eine Stunde an den sieben Jahren, so ist alles umsonst, und deine Brüder werden von dem Wort getötet.«

Da sprach das Mädchen in seinem Herzen: »Ich will meine Brüder gewiß erlösen«, und ging und suchte einen hohen Baum, setzte sich darauf und spann und sprach nicht und lachte nicht. Nun trug's sich zu, daß ein König in dem Wald jagte, der hatte einen großen Windhund, der lief zu dem Baum, wo das Fräulein drauf saß, sprang herum, schrie und bellte hinauf. Da kam der König herbei und sah die schöne Königstochter mit dem goldnen Stern auf der Stirne und war so entzückt über ihre Schönheit, daß er hinauf rief, ob sie seine Gemahlin werden wollte. Sie gab keine Antwort, nickte aber ein wenig mit dem Kopf; da stieg er selbst hinauf, trug sie herab, setzte sie auf sein Pferd, und da ward die Hochzeit, obgleich die Braut stumm war und nicht lachte, mit großer Pracht und Freude gefeiert. Als sie ein paar Jahre miteinander vergnügt gelebt, fing die Mutter des Königs, die eine böse Frau war, an, die junge Königin zu verleumden, und sprach zum König: »Es ist ein gemeines Bettelmädchen, das du dir mitgebracht, wer weiß, was für Böses sie heimlich treibt. Wenn sie stumm ist und nicht sprechen kann, so könnte sie doch einmal lachen, aber wer nicht lacht, der hat ein böses Gewissen.« Der König wollte zuerst nicht daran glauben, aber sie trieb es so lang, bis er sich endlich überreden ließ und sie zum Tod verurteilte.

Nun ward im Hof ein großes Feuer angezündet, darin sollte sie verbrannt werden, und der König stand oben und sah's mit weinenden Augen an, weil er sie noch immer so lieb hatte. Und als sie schon an den Pfahl festgebunden war und das Feuer schon nach ihren Kleidern die Zungen streckte, da war eben der letzte Augenblick von den sieben Jahren verflossen, und in der Luft ließ sich ein Geschwirr hören. Zwölf Raben kamen hergezogen und senkten sich nieder, und wie sie die Erde berührten, waren es ihre zwölf Brüder, die sie erlöst hatte. Sie rissen das Feuer auseinander, löschten die Flammen, machten ihre liebe Schwester frei und küßten und herzten sie. Nun durfte sie ihren Mund auftun und reden und erzählte dem König, wie es gekommen war, daß sie stumm gewesen und niemals gelacht hatte, der freute sich, daß sie unschuldig war, und sie lebten nun alle zusammen in Lust und Einigkeit bis an ihren Tod. Die böse Stiefmutter ward in ein Faß gesteckt, das mit siedendem Öl und giftigen Schlangen angefüllt war, und starb eines bösen Todes.

1819

306 *Der Bauer und der Teufel*

Der Bauer und der Teufel

Es war einmal ein kluges und verschmitztes Bäuerlein, von dessen Streichen viel zu erzählen wäre. Die schönste Geschichte ist aber doch, wie er den Teufel einmal drangekriegt und zum Narren gehabt hat.

Das Bäuerlein hatte eines Tages seinen Acker bestellt und rüstete sich zur Heimfahrt, als die Dämmerung schon eingetreten war. Da erblickte er mitten auf seinem Acker einen Haufen feuriger Kohlen, und als er voll Verwunderung hinzuging, so saß oben auf der Glut ein kleiner schwarzer Teufel. »Du sitzest wohl auf einem Schatz?« sprach das Bäuerlein. »Jawohl«, antwortete der Teufel, »auf einem Schatz, der mehr Gold und Silber enthält, als du dein Lebtag gesehen hast.« – »Der Schatz liegt auf meinem Feld und gehört mir«, sprach das Bäuerlein. »Er ist dein«, antwortete der Teufel, »wenn du mir zwei Jahre lang die Hälfte von dem gibst, was dein Acker hervorbringt; Geld habe ich genug, aber ich trage Verlangen nach den Früchten der Erde.« Das Bäuerlein ging auf den Handel ein. »Damit aber kein Streit bei der Teilung entsteht«, sprach es, »so soll dir gehören, was über der Erde ist, und mir, was unter der Erde ist.« Dem Teufel gefiel das wohl, aber das listige Bäuerlein hatte Rüben gesät. Als nun die Zeit der Ernte kam, so erschien der Teufel und wollte seine Frucht holen, er fand aber nichts als die gelben, welken Blätter, und das Bäuerlein, ganz vergnügt, grub seine Rüben aus. »Einmal hast du den Vorteil gehabt«, sprach der Teufel, »aber für das nächstemal soll das nicht gelten. Dein ist, was über der Erde wächst, und mein, was darunter ist.« – »Mir auch recht«, antwortete das Bäuerlein. Als aber die Zeit zur Aussat kam, säte das Bäuerlein nicht wieder Rüben, sondern Weizen. Die Frucht ward reif, das Bäuerlein ging auf den Acker und schnitt die vollen Halme bis zur Erde ab. Als der Teufel kam, fand er nichts als die Stoppeln und fuhr wütend in eine Felsenschlucht hinab. »So muß man die Füchse prellen«, sprach das Bäuerlein, ging hin und holte sich den Schatz.

1843

Vom süßen Brei

Es war einmal ein armes, frommes Mädchen, das lebte mit seiner Mutter allein, und sie hatten nichts mehr zu essen. Da ging das Kind hinaus in den Wald und begegnete ihm darin eine alte Frau, die wußte seinen Jammer schon und schenkte ihm ein Töpfchen, zu dem sollt' es sagen: »Töpfchen, koch!«, so kochte es guten,

süßen Hirsebrei, und wenn es sagte: »Töpfchen, steh«, so hörte es wieder auf zu kochen. Das Mädchen brachte den Topf seiner Mutter heim, und nun waren sie ihrer Armut und ihres Hungers ledig und aßen süßen Brei, sooft sie wollten.

Auf eine Zeit war das Mädchen ausgegangen, da sprach die Mutter: »Töpfchen, koch!«, da kocht' es, und sie ißt sich satt. Nun will sie, daß das Töpfchen wieder aufhören soll, aber sie weiß das Wort nicht. Also kocht es fort, und der Brei steigt über den Rand hinaus und kocht immerzu, die Küche und das ganze Haus voll, und das zweite Haus und dann die Straße, als wollt's die ganze Welt satt machen, und ist die größte Not, und kein Mensch weiß sich da zu helfen. Endlich, wie nur noch ein einziges Haus übrig ist, da kommt das Kind heim und spricht nur: »Töpfchen, steh!«, da steht es und hört auf zu kochen, und wenn sie wieder in die Stadt wollten, haben sie sich durchessen müssen.   1819

Die Gänsemagd

Es lebte einmal eine alte Königin, der war ihr Gemahl schon lange Jahre gestorben, und sie hatte eine schöne Tochter; wie die erwuchs, wurde sie weit über Feld auch an einen Königssohn versprochen. Als nun die Zeit kam, wo sie vermählt werden sollten und das Kind in das fremde Reich abreisen mußte, packte ihr die Alte gar viel köstliches Gerät und Geschmeide ein: Gold und Silber, Becher und Kleinode, kurz alles, was ihr zu einem königlichen Brautschatz gehörte, denn sie hatte ihr Kind von Herzen lieb. Auch gab sie ihr eine Kammerjungfer bei, welche mitreiten und die Braut in die Hände des Bräutigams überliefern sollte, und jede bekam ein Pferd zur Reise, aber das Pferd der Königstochter hieß Falada und konnte sprechen. Wie nun die Abschiedsstunde da war, begab sich die alte Mutter in ihre Schlafkammer, nahm ein Messerlein und schnitt damit in ihre Finger, daß sie bluteten; darauf hielt sie ein weißes Läppchen unter und ließ drei Tropfen Blut hineinfallen, gab sie der Tochter und sprach: »Liebes Kind, verwahr sie wohl, sie werden dir unterwegs not tun.«

Also nahmen beide voneinander betrübten Abschied, das Läppchen steckte die Königstochter in ihren Busen vor sich, setzte sich aufs Pferd und zog nun fort zu ihrem Bräutigam. Da sie eine Stunde geritten waren, empfand sie heißen Durst und rief ihrer Kammerjungfer: »Steig ab und schöpfe mir mit meinem Becher, den du aufzuheben hast, Wasser aus dem Bach, ich möchte gern einmal trinken.« — »Ei, wenn Ihr Durst habt«, sprach die Kammerjungfer, »so steigt selber ab, legt Euch ans Wasser und trinkt, ich mag Eure Magd nicht sein!« Da stieg die Königstochter vor großem Durst herunter, neigte sich über das Wässerlein im Bach und trank und durfte nicht aus dem goldnen Becher trinken. Da sprach sie: »Ach Gott!« Da antworteten die drei Blutstropfen: »Wenn das deine Mutter wüßte, das Herz im Leibe tät ihr zerspringen.« Aber die Königsbraut war gar demütig, sagte nichts und stieg wieder zu Pferd. So ritten sie etliche Meilen weiter fort, und der Tag war warm, daß die Sonne stach, und sie dürstete bald von neuem. Da sie nun an einen Wasserfluß kamen, rief sie noch einmal ihrer Kammerjungfer: »Steig ab und gib mir aus meinem Goldbecher zu trinken!« Denn sie hatte aller bösen Worte längst vergessen. Die Kammerjungfer sprach aber noch hochmütiger: »Wollt Ihr trinken, so trinkt allein, ich mag nicht Eure Magd sein.« Da stieg die Königstochter hernieder vor großem Durst und legte sich über das fließende Wasser, weinte und sprach: »Ach Gott!« Und die Blutstropfen antworteten wiederum: »Wenn das deine Mutter wüßte, das Herz im Leibe tät ihr zerspringen!« Und wie sie so trank und sich recht überlehnte, fiel ihr das Läppchen, worin die drei Tropfen waren, aus dem Busen und floß mit dem Wasser fort, ohne daß sie es in ihrer großen Angst merkte. Die Kammerjungfer hatte aber zugesehen und freute sich, daß sie Macht über die Braut bekäme, denn damit, daß diese die Blutstropfen verloren hatte, war sie schwach geworden. Als sie nun wieder auf ihr Pferd steigen wollte, das da hieß Falada, sagte die Kammerfrau: »Auf Falada gehör ich, und auf meinen Gaul gehörst du«, und das mußte sie sich gefallen lassen, dann hieß sie die Kammerfrau auch noch die königlichen Kleider ausziehen und ihre schlechten anlegen, und endlich mußte sie sich unter freiem Himmel verschwören, daß sie am königlichen Hof keinem Menschen davon sprechen wollte, und wenn sie diesen Eid nicht abgelegt hätte, wäre sie auf der Stelle umgebracht worden. Aber Falada sah das alles an und nahm's wohl in acht.

Die Kammerfrau stieg nun auf Falada und die wahre Braut auf das schlechte Roß, und so zogen sie weiter, bis sie endlich in dem königlichen Schloß eintrafen. Da war große Freude über ihre Ankunft, und der Königssohn sprang ihnen entgegen, hob die Kammerfrau vom Pferde und meinte, sie wäre seine Gemahlin, und sie wurde die Treppe hinaufgeführt, die wahre Königstochter aber mußte unten stehenbleiben. Da schaute der alte König am Fenster und sah sie im Hofe halten, nun war sie fein und zart und sehr schön, ging hin ins königliche Gemach und fragte die Braut nach der, die sie bei sich hätte und da unten im Hof stände, und wer sie wäre? »Ei, die hab ich mir unterwegs mitgenommen zur Gesellschaft, gebt der Magd was zu arbeiten, daß sie nicht müßig steht.« Aber der alte König hatte keine Arbeit für sie und wußte nichts, als daß er sagte: »Da hab ich so einen kleinen Jungen, der hütet die Gänse, dem mag sie helfen!« Der Junge hieß Kürdchen (Conrädchen), dem mußte die wahre Braut helfen Gänse hüten.

Bald aber sprach die falsche Braut zu dem jungen König: »Liebster Gemahl, ich bitte Euch, tut mir einen Gefallen!« Er antwortete: »Das will ich gerne tun.« — »Nun, so laßt mir den Schinder rufen und da dem Pferd, worauf ich her geritten bin, den Hals abhauen, weil es mich unterwegs geärgert hat.« Eigentlich aber fürchtete sie sich, daß das Pferd sprechen möchte, wie sie mit der Königstochter umgegangen wäre. Nun war das so weit geraten, daß es geschehen und der treue Falada sterben sollte, da kam es auch der rechten Königstochter zu Ohr, und sie versprach dem Schinder heimlich ein Stück Geld, das sie ihm bezahlen wollte, wenn er ihr einen kleinen Dienst erwiese. In der Stadt war ein großes, finsteres Tor, wo sie abends und morgens mit den Gänsen durch mußte, unter das finstere Tor möchte er dem Falada seinen Kopf hinnageln, daß sie ihn doch noch einmal sehen könnte. Also versprach das der Schinderknecht zu tun, hieb den Kopf ab und nagelte ihn unter das finstere Tor fest. Des Morgens früh, als sie und Kürdchen unterm Tor hinaustrieben, sprach sie im Vorbeigehen:

>»O du Falada, da du hangest«,
da antwortete der Kopf:
>»O du Jungfer Königin, da du gangest,
>wenn das deine Mutter wüßte,

ihr Herz tät ihr zerspringen!«

Da zog sie still weiter zur Stadt hinaus, und sie trieben die Gänse aufs Feld. Und wenn sie auf der Wiese angekommen war, saß sie hier und machte ihre Haare auf, die waren eitel Silber, und Kürdchen sah sie und freute sich, wie sie glänzten, und wollte ihr ein Paar ausraufen. Da sprach sie:

> »Weh, weh! Windchen,
> nimm Kürdchen sein Hütchen
> und laß'n sich mit jagen,
> bis ich mich geflochten und geschnatzt
> und wieder aufgesatzt.«

Und da kam ein so starker Wind, daß er dem Kürdchen sein Hütchen wegwehte über alle Lande, daß es ihm nachlief, und bis es wiederkam, war sie mit dem Kämmen und Aufsetzen fertig, und er konnte keine Haare kriegen. Da war Kürdchen bös und sprach nicht mit ihr, und so hüteten sie die Gänse, bis daß es Abend wurde, dann gingen sie nach Haus.

Den andern Morgen, wie sie unter dem finstern Tor hinaustrieben, sprach die Jungfrau:

> »O du Falada, da du hangest«,

es antwortete:

> »O du Jungfer Königin, da du gangest,
> wenn das deine Mutter wüßte,
> das Herz tät ihr zerspringen!«

Und in dem Feld setzte sie sich wieder auf die Wiese und fing an, ihr Haar zu auszukämmen, und Kürdchen lief und wollte danach greifen, da sprach sie schnell:

> »Weh, weh! Windchen,
> nimm dem Kürdchen sein Hütchen
> und laß'n sich mit jagen,
> bis ich mich geflochten und geschnatzt
> und wieder aufgesatzt.«

Da wehte der Wind und wehte ihm das Hütchen vom Kopf weit weg, daß es nachzulaufen hatte, und als es wiederkam, hatte sie längst ihr Haar zurecht, und es konnte keins davon erwischen, und sie hüteten die Gänse, bis es Abend wurde.

Abends aber, nachdem sie heimkamen, ging Kürdchen vor den alten König und sagte: »Mit dem Mädchen will ich nicht länger Gänse hüten.« — »Warum denn?« sprach der alte König. »Ei, das ärgert mich den ganzen Tag.« Da befahl ihm der

alte König zu erzählen, wie's ihm denn mit ihr ginge. Da sagte Kürdchen: »Des Morgens, wenn wir unter dem finstern Tor mit der Herde durchkommen, so ist da ein Gaulskopf an der Wand, zu dem redet sie:

›Falada, da du hangest‹,
da antwortet der Kopf:
›O du Königsjungfer, da du gangest,
wenn das deine Mutter wüßte,
das Herz tät ihr zerspringen!‹«

Und so erzählte Kürdchen weiter, was auf der Gänsewiese geschähe und wie es da dem Hut im Wind nachlaufen müßte.

Der alte König befahl ihm aber, den nächsten Tag wieder hinaus zu treiben, und er selbst, wie es Morgen war, setzte sich hinter das finstere Tor und hörte da, wie sie mit dem Haupt des Falada sprach; und dann ging er ihr auch nach in das Feld und barg sich in einem Busch auf der Wiese. Da sah er nun bald mit seinen eigenen Augen, wie die Gänsemagd und der Gänsejunge die Herde getrieben brachten, und nach einer Weile sie sich setzte und ihre Haare losflocht, die strahlten von Glanz. Gleich sprach sie wieder:

»Weh, weh! Windchen,
faß Kürdchen sein Hütchen
und laß'n sich mit jagen,
bis daß ich mich geflochten und geschnatzt
und wieder aufgesatzt.«

Da kam ein Windstoß und fuhr mit Kürdchens Hut weg, daß es weit zu laufen hatte, und die Magd kämmte und flocht ihre Locken still fort, welches der alte König alles beobachtete. Darauf ging er unbemerkt zurück, und als abends die Gänsemagd heimkam, rief er sie beiseite und fragte: Warum sie dem allem so täte? »Das darf ich Euch und keinem Menschen sagen, denn so hab ich mich unter freiem Himmel verschworen, weil ich sonst um mein Leben wäre gekommen.« Er aber drang in sie und ließ ihr keinen Frieden. »Willst du mir's nicht erzählen«, sagte der alte König endlich, »so darfst du's doch dem Kachelofen erzählen.« – »Ja, das will ich wohl«, antwortete sie. Damit mußte sie in den Ofen kriechen und schüttete ihr ganzes Herz aus, wie es ihr bis dahin ergangen und wie sie von der bösen Kammerjungfer betrogen worden war. Aber der Ofen hatte oben ein Loch, da lauerte ihr der alte König zu und vernahm ihr Schicksal von Wort zu Wort. Da war's gut, und Königskleider wurden ihr alsbald angetan, und es schien ein Wunder, wie sie so schön war. Der alte König rief seinen Sohn und offenbarte ihm, daß er die falsche Braut hätte, die wäre bloß ein Kammermädchen, die wahre aber stände hier, als die gewesene Gänsemagd. Der junge König aber war herzensfroh, als er ihre Schönheit und Tugend erblickte, und ein großes Mahl wurde angestellt, zu dem alle Leute und guten Freunde gebeten wurden, obenan saß der Bräutigam, die Königstochter zur einen Seite und die Kammerjungfer zur andern, aber die Kammerjungfer war verblendet und erkannte jene nicht mehr in dem glänzenden Schmuck. Als sie nun gegessen und getrunken hatten und guten Muts waren, gab der alte König der Kammerfrau ein Rätsel auf: was eine solche wert wäre, die den Herrn so und so betrogen hätte, erzählte damit den ganzen Verlauf und fragte: »Welches Urteils ist diese würdig?« Da sprach die falsche Braut: »Die ist nichts Besseres wert, als splitternackt ausgezogen in ein Faß, inwendig mit spitzen Nägeln beschlagen, geworfen zu werden, und zwei weiße Pferde, davor gespannt, müssen sie, Gaß auf, Gaß ab, zu Tode schleifen!« – »Das bist du«, sprach der alte König, »und dein eigen Urteil hast du gesprochen, und danach soll dir widerfahren«, welches auch vollzogen wurde. Der junge König vermählte sich aber mit seiner rechten Gemahlin, und beide beherrschten ihr Reich in Frieden und Seligkeit.

1819

Die Alte im Wald

Es fuhr einmal ein armes Dienstmädchen mit seiner Herrschaft durch einen großen Wald, und als sie mitten darin waren, kamen Räuber aus dem Dickicht hervor und ermordeten, wen sie fanden. Da kam alles miteinander um, nur das Mädchen nicht, das war aus dem Wagen gesprungen und hatte sich hinter einen Baum verborgen. Wie die Räuber mit ihrer Beute fort waren, trat es herbei und sah das große Unglück, da fing es an bitterlich zu weinen und sagte: »Was soll ich armes Mädchen nun anfangen, ich weiß mich nicht zu finden in dem Wald, kein Haus ist da, so muß ich gewiß verhungern!« Es ging herum, suchte einen Weg, konnte aber keinen finden bis zum Abend, da setzte es sich unter einen Baum, befahl sich Gott und wollt' da sitzen bleiben und nicht weggehen, möchte geschehen, was immer wollte. Als es aber ein bißchen da gesessen, kam ein weiß Täubchen heruntergeflogen, mit einem kleinen goldnen Schlüsselchen im Schnabel, das legte es ihm in die Hand und sprach: »Siehst du dort den großen Baum, daran ist ein kleines Schloß, das schließ mit dem Schlüsselchen auf, so wirst du Speise genug finden und keinen Hunger mehr leiden.«

Da ging es zu dem Baum und schloß ihn auf und fand Milch in einem kleinen Schüsselchen und Weißbrot zum Einbrocken dabei, daß es sich satt essen konnte. Als es satt war, sprach es: »Jetzt ist die Zeit, wo die Hühner daheim aufliegen, ich bin so müd, könnt ich mich auch in mein Bett legen!« Da kam das Täubchen wieder geflogen und hatt' ein anderes goldenes Schlüsselchen im Schnabel und sagt': »Schließ dort den Baum auf, da wirst du ein Bett finden.« Da schloß es auf und fand ein schönes weiches Bettchen, da betete es zum lieben Gott, er sollt' es behüten in der Nacht, legte sich und schlief ein. Am Morgen kam das Täubchen zum drittenmal, brachte wieder ein Schlüsselchen und sprach: »Schließ dort den Baum auf, da wirst du Kleider finden«; und wie es aufschloß, fand es Kleider mit Gold und Edelsteinen besetzt, so herrlich, wie sie keine Königstochter hat. Also lebte es da eine Zeitlang, und kam das Täubchen alle Tage und sorgte für alles, was es bedurfte, und war das ein stilles, gutes Leben.

Einmal aber kam das Täubchen und sprach: »Willst du mir etwas zulieb tun?« – »Von Herzen gern«, sagte das Mädchen. Da sprach das Täubchen: »Ich will dich zu einem kleinen Häuschen führen, da geh hinein, mittendrin am Herd wird eine alte Frau sitzen und guten Tag sagen. Aber gib ihr beileibe keine Antwort, sie mag anfangen, was sie will, sondern geh zu ihrer rechten Hand weiter, da ist eine Türe, die mach auf, so wirst du in eine Stube kommen, wo eine große Menge von Ringen allerlei Art auf dem Tisch liegt, darunter sind prächtige mit glitzernden Steinen, die laß aber liegen, und such einen schlichten heraus, der auch darunter sein muß, und bring ihn zu mir her, so geschwind du kannst.« Da ging das Mädchen hin zu dem Häuschen und öffnete es, da saß eine Alte, die machte große Augen, wie sie es sah, und sprach: »Guten Tag, mein Kind.« Es gab ihr keine Antwort und ging auf die Türe zu. »Ei! Wo hinaus?« rief sie und faßt' es beim Rock und wollt' es festhalten. »Das ist mein Haus, da darf niemand herein, wenn ich's nicht haben will.« Aber es schwieg immer still, machte sich von ihr los und ging gerade in die Stube hinein. Da lag nun auf dem Tisch eine übergroße Menge von Ringen, die glitzerten und glimmerten ihm vor den Augen, es warf sie herum und suchte nach dem schlichten, konnt' ihn aber nicht finden. Wie es so suchte, sah es die Alte, wie sie daher schlich und einen Vogelkäfig in der Hand hatte und damit fort wollte; da ging es auf sie zu und nahm ihr den Käfig aus der Hand, und wie es ihn aufhob und hineinsah, saß ein Vogel darin, der hatte den schlichten Ring im Schnabel. Da war es froh und lief damit zum Haus hinaus und dachte, das weiße Täubchen würde kommen und den Ring holen, aber es kam nicht. Da lehnte es sich an einen Baum und wollte auf es warten, und wie es so stand, da deuchte ihm, der Baum würde weich und biegsam und senkte seine Zweige herab. Und auf einmal schlangen sich die Zweige um es herum und waren zwei Arme, und wie es sich umsah, war der Baum ein schöner Mann, der es umfaßte und herzlich küßte und sagte: »Du hast mich erlöst, die Alte ist eine Hexe, die mich in einen Baum verwandelt hatte, und alle Tage ein paar Stunden war ich eine weiße Taube, und so lang sie den Ring besaß, konnte ich meine menschliche Gestalt nicht wieder erhalten.« Da waren auch seine Bedienten und Pferde von dem Zauber frei und keine Bäume mehr, und standen neben ihm, da fuhren sie fort in sein Reich, denn er war eines Königs Sohn, heirateten sich und lebten glücklich.

1819

Der singende Knochen

In einem großen Wald lief ein mächtiges Wildschwein herum, das die Äcker um-
wühlte, das Vieh tötete und den Menschen mit seinen Hauern den Leib aufriß, also
daß sich niemand mehr in die Nähe des Waldes wagte und es zu einer Plage für das
ganze Land ward. Der König bot auf, was er konnte, aber noch jeder, der es
einfangen oder töten wollte, war schlimm weggekommen, so daß niemand kühn
genug war, das Wagnis zu übernehmen. Endlich ließ der König bekanntmachen,
wer das Wildschwein erlege, solle seine einzige Tochter zur Gemahlin haben.

Nun waren zwei Brüder im Reich, Söhne eines armen Mannes, die meldeten sich
dazu: der älteste, der listig und klug war, aus Hochmut; der jüngste, der unschuldig und dumm war, aus gutem Herzen. Der König hieß sie von verschiedenen
Seiten in den Wald gehen und ihr Heil versuchen. Da ging der jüngste von Morgen

aus, der älteste von Abend. Als der jüngste hineingekommen war, trat ein kleines
Männlein zu ihm, das hielt eine schwarze Lanze in der Hand und sprach: »Siehst
du, mit dieser Lanze kannst du ohne Furcht auf das Wildschwein eingehen und es
töten; die geb ich dir, weil dein Herz gut ist.« Nun nahm er den Spieß, dankte dem
Männlein und ging getrost weiter. Bald sah er das Tier wütend heranrennen, aber
er hielt den Spieß vor, und es rannte sich in seiner blinden Wut so gewaltig hinein,
daß es sich selbst das Herz durchschnitt. Da nahm er seinen Fang auf die Schulter,
ging vergnügt heimwärts und wollte ihn dem König bringen.

Der andere Bruder hatte auf seinem Weg ein Haus gefunden, wo sich die Menschen mit Tanz und Wein lustig machten, und war da eingegangen. »Das Wildschwein«, dachte er, »läuft dir doch nicht fort, du willst dir hier erst ein Herz trinken.« Der jüngste kam nun bei seinem Heimweg daran vorbei, und als ihn der älteste sah, mit der Beute beladen, ward er neidisch und sann darauf, ihm zu schaden. Da rief er: »Komm doch herein, lieber Bruder, und ruh dich ein wenig aus und trink einen Becher Wein zur Stärkung.« Der jüngste, der in seiner Unschuld an nichts Böses dachte, ging hinein und erzählte ihm, wie es zugegangen war und daß er mit einer schwarzen Lanze das Schwein getötet hätte. Nun hielt ihn der älteste zurück bis gegen Abend, wo sie zusammen sich aufmachten. Als sie aber in der Dunkelheit zu der Brücke über einen Bach kamen, ließ der älteste den jüngsten vorangehen, und mitten drauf gab er ihm einen Schlag, daß er tot hinabstürzte. Dann begrub er ihn unter der Brücke, nahm das Schwein und brachte es vor den König, mit dem Vorgeben, er habe es getötet, und erhielt darauf die Tochter des Königs zur Gemahlin. Als der jüngste Bruder nicht wiederkommen wollte, sagte er: »Das Schwein wird ihm den Leib aufgerissen haben.« Und das glaubte jedermann.

Weil aber vor Gott nichts verborgen bleibt, so sollte auch diese schwarze Tat an des Tages Licht kommen. Nach langen Jahren trieb ein Hirt seine Herde über die Brücke und sah unten im Sande ein schneeweißes Knöchlein liegen und dachte, das gäbe ein gutes Mundstück. Da stieg er hinab, hob es auf und schnitzte ein Mundstück für sein Horn daraus, und als er es zum erstenmal ansetzen und darauf blasen wollte, so fing das Knöchlein an, von selbst zu singen:

> »Ach, du liebes Hirtelein,
> du bläst auf meinem Knöchelein!
> Mein Bruder hat mich erschlagen,
> unter der Brücke begraben,
> um das wilde Schwein
> für des Königs Töchterlein.«

»Ei, was für ein Hörnlein, das von selber singt!« sprach der Hirt, wußte nicht, was es zu bedeuten hatte, brachte es aber vor den König. Da fing das Knöchlein wieder an, dieselben Worte zu singen; der König verstand wohl, was es sagen wollte, ließ unter der Brücke graben, und das ganze Gerippe des Erschlagenen kam hervor. Der böse Bruder konnte sein Verbrechen nicht leugnen und ward lebendig ins Wasser geworfen und ersäuft, die Gebeine des Gemordeten aber wurden auf dem Kirchhof in ein schönes Grab zur Ruhe gelegt. 1819

Die Goldkinder

Es war ein armer Mann und eine arme Frau, die hatten nichts als eine kleine Hütte und nährten sich vom Fischfang, und es ging bei ihnen von Hand zu Mund. Es geschah aber, daß der Mann, als er einmal beim Wasser saß und sein Netz auswarf, einen Fisch herauszog, der ganz golden war. Und als er den Fisch voll Verwunderung betrachtete, hub dieser an zu reden und sprach: »Hör, Fischer, wirfst du mich wieder hinab ins Wasser, so mach ich deine kleine Hütte zu einem prächtigen Schloß.« Da antwortete der Fischer: »Was hilft mir ein Schloß, wenn ich nichts zu essen habe!« Sprach der Goldfisch weiter: »Dafür soll auch gesorgt sein, es wird ein Schrank im Schloß sein, wenn du den aufschließest, so stehen Schüsseln darin mit Gesottenem und Gebratenem, soviel du dir wünschest.« – »Wenn das ist«, sprach der Mann, »so kann ich dir wohl den Gefallen tun.« – »Ja«, sagte der Fisch, »es ist aber die Bedingung dabei, daß du keinem Menschen auf der Welt, wer es auch immer sein mag, entdeckst, woher dein Glück gekommen; sprichst du ein einziges Wort, so ist alles vorbei.«

Nun warf der Mann den wunderbaren Fisch wieder ins Wasser und ging heim. Wo aber sonst seine Hütte gestanden, da stand jetzt ein großes Schloß. Da machte er ein paar Augen, trat hinein und sah seine Frau, mit schönen Kleidern geputzt, in einer prächtigen Stube sitzen. Sie war ganz vergnügt und sprach: »Mann, wie ist das auf einmal gekommen? Das gefällt mir wohl.« – »Ja«, sagte der Mann, »es

gefällt mir auch, aber es hungert mich auch gewaltig, gib mir erst etwas zu essen.«
Sprach die Frau: »Ich habe nichts und weiß in dem neuen Haus nichts zu finden.«
– »Oh«, sagte der Mann, »dort sehe ich einen großen Schrank, den schließ einmal
auf.« Wie sie den Schrank aufschloß, stand da Kuchen, Fleisch, Obst, Wein und
lachte einen ordentlich an. Da rief die Frau voll Freude: »Herz, was begehrst du
nun?« Und sie aßen und tranken zusammen. Wie sie satt waren, fragte die Frau:
»Aber, Mann, wo kommt all dieser Reichtum her?« – »Ach«, antwortete er, »frag
mich nicht darum, ich darf dir's nicht sagen, denn wenn ich's jemand entdecke, so
ist unser Glück wieder dahin.« – »Nun«, sprach sie, »wenn ich's nicht wissen soll, so
begehr ich's auch nicht zu wissen.« Das war aber ihr Ernst nicht, sondern es ließ ihr
keine Ruhe Tag und Nacht, und sie quälte und stichelte den Mann so lang, bis er's
heraus sagte, es käme alles von einem wunderlichen goldenen Fisch, den er gefangen und wieder dafür in Freiheit gelassen hätte. Und wie's heraus war, da
verschwand alsbald das schöne Schloß mit dem Schrank, und sie saßen wieder in
der alten Fischerhütte.

Der Mann mußte von vorne anfangen, seinem Gewerbe nachgehen und fischen.
Das Glück wollte es aber, daß er den goldenen Fisch noch einmal herauszog.
»Hör«, sprach der Fisch, »wenn du mich wieder ins Wasser wirfst, so will ich dir
noch einmal das Schloß mit dem Schrank voll Gesottenem und Gebratenem zurückgeben; nur halt dich fest und verrat beileibe nicht, von wem du's hast, sonst
geht's wieder verloren.« – »Ich will mich schon hüten«, antwortete der Fischer und
warf den Fisch in sein Wasser hinab. Daheim war nun alles wieder in voriger
Herrlichkeit und die Frau in einer Freude über das Glück, aber die Neugierde ließ
ihr doch keine Ruhe, daß sie nach ein paar Tagen wieder zu fragen anhub, wie es
zugegangen wäre und wie er es angefangen habe? Der Mann schwieg eine Zeitlang
still dazu, endlich aber machte sie ihn so ungeduldig, daß er herausplatzte und das
Geheimnis verriet. In dem Augenblick verschwand das Schloß, und sie saßen
wieder in der alten Hütte. »Nun hast du's«, sagte der Mann, »jetzt können wir
wieder am Hungertuch nagen.« – »Ach«, sprach die Frau, »ich will den Reichtum
lieber nicht, wenn ich nicht weiß, von wem er kommt, da habe ich doch keine Ruhe
dabei.«

Der Mann ging wieder fischen, und über eine Zeit, so war's nicht anders, er holte
den Goldfisch zum drittenmal heraus. »Hör«, sprach der Fisch, »ich sehe wohl, ich
soll in deine Hände fallen, nimm mich mit nach Haus und zerschneid mich in sechs
Stücke, zwei davon gib deiner Frau zu essen, zwei deinem Pferd, und zwei leg in die
Erde, so wirst du Segen davon haben.« Der Mann nahm den Fisch mit nach Haus
und tat, wie er ihm gesagt hatte. Es geschah aber, daß aus den zwei Stücken, die in
die Erde gelegt waren, zwei goldene Lilien aufwuchsen und daß das Pferd zwei
goldene Füllen bekam und des Fischers Frau zwei Kinder gebar, die ganz golden
waren.

Die Kinder wuchsen heran und wurden groß und schön, und die Lilien und die

Pferde wuchsen mit ihnen. Nun sprachen sie: »Vater, wir wollen uns auf unsere goldenen Rosse setzen und ausziehen in die Welt.« Da antwortete er betrübt: »Wie will ich's aushalten, wenn ihr fortzieht und ich nicht weiß, wie's euch geht?« Da sagten sie: »Die zwei goldenen Lilien bleiben hier, daran könnt ihr sehen, wie's uns geht: sind sie frisch, so sind wir gesund; sind sie welk, so sind wir krank, fallen sie um, so sind wir tot.«

Sie ritten fort und kamen in ein Wirtshaus, darin war viel Volk, und als das die zwei Goldkinder sah, fing es an zu lachen und zu spotten. Wie der eine das Gespött hörte, so schämte er sich, wollte nicht in die Welt, kehrte um und kam wieder heim zu seinem Vater. Der andere aber ritt fort und gelangte zu einem großen Wald. Und als er hineinreiten wollte, sprachen die Leute: »Es geht nicht, daß Ihr durchreitet, der Wald ist voll Räuber, die werden übel mit Euch umgehen, und gar, wenn sie sehen, daß Ihr und Euer Pferd golden seid, werden sie Euch tot schlagen.« Er aber ließ sich nicht schrecken und sprach: »Ich muß und soll hindurch!« Da nahm er Bärenfelle und überzog sich und sein Pferd damit, daß nichts mehr vom Gold zu sehen war, und ritt getrost in den Wald hinein. Und als er ein wenig fortgeritten war, so hörte er es in den Gebüschen rauschen und vernahm Stimmen, die miteinander sprachen. Von der einen Seite rief's: »Da ist einer«, von der anderen aber: »Laß ihn laufen, das ist ein Bärenhäuter und arm und kahl wie eine Kirchenmaus, was sollen wir mit ihm anfangen!« So ritt das Goldkind glücklich durch den Wald und geschah ihm kein Leid.

Es trug sich zu, daß er in ein Dorf kam, darin sah er ein Mädchen, das war so schön, daß er nicht glaubte, es könne ein schöneres auf der Welt sein. Und weil er eine so große Liebe zu ihm empfand, so ging er zu ihm und sagte: »Ich habe dich von ganzem Herzen lieb, willst du meine Frau werden?« Er gefiel aber auch dem Mädchen so sehr, daß es einwilligte und sprach: »Ja, ich will deine Frau werden und dir treu sein mein Lebelang.« Nun hielten sie Hochzeit zusammen, und als sie eben in der größten Freude waren, kam der Vater der Braut heim, und als er sah, daß seine Tochter Hochzeit machte, verwunderte er sich und sprach: »Wo ist der Bräutigam?« Sie zeigten ihm das Goldkind, das hatte aber noch seine Bärenfelle um, da sprach er zornig: »Nimmermehr soll der Bärenhäuter meine Tochter haben!« und wollte ihn ermorden. Da bat ihn die Braut, was sie konnte, und sprach: »Er ist einmal mein Mann, und ich habe ihn von Herzen lieb«, bis er sich endlich besänftigen ließ. Doch kam's ihm nicht aus den Gedanken, so daß er am andern Morgen früh aufstand und seiner Tochter Mann sehen wollte, ob er ein gemeiner und verlumpter Bettler wäre, wie er aber hinblickte, sah er einen herrlichen, goldenen Mann im Bette, und die abgeworfenen Bärenfelle lagen auf der Erde. Da ging er zurück und dachte: »Wie gut ist's, daß ich meinen Zorn bändigte.«

Dem Goldkind aber hatte geträumt, es zöge hinaus auf die Jagd nach einem prächtigen Hirsch; und als er erwachte, sprach er zu seiner Braut: »Nun will ich auf die Jagd.« Ihr aber war angst, und sie bat ihn dazubleiben und sagte: »Leicht kann dir ein großes Unglück begegnen«, aber er antwortete: »Ich soll und muß fort.« Da stand er auf und zog hinaus in den Wald, und gar nicht lange, so hielt auch ein stolzer Hirsch vor ihm, ganz nach seinem Traume. Er legte an und wollte ihn schießen, aber der Hirsch sprang fort. Da jagte er ihm nach, über Gräben und durch Gebüsche, und ward nicht müd den ganzen Tag; am Abend aber verschwand der Hirsch vor seinen Augen. Und als das Goldkind sich umsah, so stand es vor einem kleinen Haus, darin saß eine Hexe. Er klopfte an, und ein Mütterchen kam heraus und fragte: »Was wollt Ihr so spät noch mitten in dem großen Wald?« Er sprach: »Habt Ihr keinen Hirsch gesehen?« – »Ja«, antwortete sie, »den Hirsch kenne ich wohl«, und ein Hündlein, das mit ihr aus dem Haus gekommen war, bellte dabei den Mann heftig an. »Willst du schweigen, du böse Kröte«, sprach er, »sonst schieß ich dich tot.« Da rief die Hexe zornig: »Was, mein Hündlein willst du mir töten«, und verwandelte ihn alsbald, daß er dalag wie ein Stein, und seine Braut erwartete ihn umsonst und dachte: Es ist gewiß eingetroffen, was mir so angst machte und so schwer auf dem Herzen lag.

Daheim aber stand der andere Bruder bei den Goldlilien, als plötzlich eine davon umfiel. »Ach Gott«, sprach er, »meinem Bruder ist ein großes Unglück zugestoßen, ich muß fort, ob ich ihn vielleicht errette.« Da sagte der Vater: »Bleib hier, wenn ich dich auch verliere, was soll ich anfangen!« Er aber antwortete: »Ich soll und muß fort!« Da setzte er sich auf sein goldenes Pferd und ritt fort und kam in den großen Wald, wo sein Bruder lag und Stein war. Die alte Hexe kam aus

ihrem Haus, rief ihn an und wollte ihn auch berücken, aber er näherte sich nicht, sondern sprach: »Ich schieße dich nieder, wenn du meinem Bruder das Leben nicht wieder gibst.« Da mußte sie, so ungern sie's auch tat, den Stein wieder anrühren und ihm sein menschliches Leben wieder geben. Die beiden Goldkinder aber freuten sich, als sie sich wiedersahen, küßten und herzten sich und ritten zusammen fort aus dem Wald, der eine zu seiner Braut, der andere heim zu seinem Vater. Da sprach der Vater: »Ich wußte wohl, daß du deinen Bruder erlöst hattest, denn die goldene Lilie ist auf einmal wieder aufgestanden und hat fortgeblüht.« Nun lebten sie vergnügt, und es ging ihnen wohl bis an ihr Ende.   1819

Die weiße Schlange

Es war ein mächtiger und weiser König, der ließ sich jeden Mittag, wenn von der Tafel alles abgetragen und niemand mehr zugegen war, von einem seiner ersten Diener noch eine verdeckte Schüssel bringen, davon aß er ganz allein, deckte sie selbst wieder zu, und kein Mensch wußte, was darunter lag. Nun trug sich zu, daß der Diener, als ihm der König einmal die Schüssel fortzutragen gab, der Neu-

gierde nicht widerstehen konnte, sie in seine Kammer mitnahm, wo er sie aufdeckte, und eine weiße Schlange darin fand. Als er sie ansah, bekam er so große Lust, daß er sich nicht enthalten konnte, ein Stückchen davon abzuschneiden und zu essen. Kaum aber hatte es seine Zunge berührt, so hörte er deutlich, was die Sperlinge und andere Vögel vor dem Fenster zueinander sagten, und merkte wohl, daß er die Tiersprache verstehe.

Es geschah aber, daß der Königin gerade an demselben Tag einer ihrer schönsten Ringe fort kam und der Verdacht auf diesen Diener fiel. Der König schalt ihn hart aus und drohte, wenn er den Dieb nicht bis Morgen zu nennen wisse, so solle er als der Täter angesehen und gerichtet werden. Da erschrak der Diener gar sehr und wußte nicht, wie er sich helfen sollte. In seiner Unruhe ging er auf den Hof hinab, da saßen die Enten an einem fließenden Wasser nebeneinander, ruhten sich und hielten ein vertrauliches Gespräch. Nun hörte er, wie eine sagte: »Wie liegt mir's so schwer im Magen! Ich habe einen Ring, der unter der Königin Fenster lag, in der Hast mit geschluckt!« Da faßte er die Ente beim Kragen, trug sie zum Koch und sprach: »Schlacht doch diese fette zuerst ab!« Der Koch schnitt ihr den Hals ab, und als er sie ausnahm, fand er den Ring der Königin im Magen liegen. Der Diener brachte ihn dem König, der sich gar sehr darüber freute, und weil er sein Unrecht gern wieder gut machen wollte, sprach er zu ihm: »Fordere, was du willst, und sage, was für eine Ehrenstelle du an meinem Hofe wünschest.« Aber er schlug alles aus und bat nur um ein Pferd und Geld zur Reise, weil er in die Welt ziehen wollte.

Nun ritt er fort und kam zu einem Teich, da hatten sich drei Fische im Rohr gefangen, die schnappten nach Wasser und klagten, daß sie so elendig umkommen müßten. Weil er nun ihre Worte verstand und Mitleid mit ihnen hatte, so stieg er ab und setzte sie wieder ins Wasser. Da riefen die Fische heraus: »Wir wollen dir's gedenken und dir's vergelten!« Er ritt weiter, nicht lang, so hörte er einen Ameisenkönig zu seinen Füßen sprechen: »Wenn der Mensch nur mit seinem großen Tier weg wäre, das zertritt mir so viele von meinen Leuten.« Er blickte zur Erde und sah, daß sein Pferd in einen Ameisenhaufen getreten hatte, da lenkte er ab, und der Ameisenkönig rief: »Wir wollen dir's gedenken und dir's vergelten!« Er ritt weiter und kam in einen Wald, da saßen zwei Raben-Eltern auf dem Nest, warfen ihre Jungen heraus und sprachen: »Ihr seid groß genug und könnt euch selbst ernähren, wir können euch nicht mehr satt machen.« Da lagen die Jungen auf der Erde, schlugen mit ihren kleinen Fittichen und schrien: »Wie sollen wir uns ernähren, wir können noch nicht fliegen und etwas suchen, wir müssen Hungers sterben.« Er stieg ab, zog den Degen und tötete sein Pferd und warf's den jungen Raben vor, die kamen herbeigehüpft, sättigten sich und sprachen: »Wir wollen dir's gedenken und dir's vergelten!«

Nun ging er zu Fuß weiter, und als er lange Wege gegangen war, kam er in eine große Stadt. Da ritt einer herum und machte bekannt, wer Gemahl der jungen Königstochter werden wolle, müsse eins ausführen, das sie ihm aufgäbe; unternähme er's aber und vollbrächte es nicht, so hätte er das Leben verloren. Es wollte sich aber niemand mehr melden, so viele hatten schon ihr Leben eingebüßt. Der Jüngling dachte, was hast du zu verlieren? Du willst es wagen! Trat vor den König und seine Tochter und meldete sich als Freier.

Da ward er hinausgeführt ans Meer, ein Ring hinabgeworfen und ihm aufgegeben, den Ring wieder herauszuholen. Auch wurde ihm gesagt, daß, wenn er untertauche und käme ohne ihn in die Höhe, so würde er wieder ins Wasser gestürzt und müßte darin sterben. Darauf ward er allein gelassen, und als er an dem Ufer stand und überlegte, was er wohl tun solle, um den Ring zu erlangen, sah er, wie die drei Fische, die er aus dem Rohr ins Wasser geworfen, dahergeschwommen kamen; der mittelste hatte eine Muschel im Mund, die legte er an den Strand, dem Jüngling zu Füßen, und als er sie öffnete, lag der Ring darin. Voll Freude brachte er ihn dem König und verlangte seine Tochter, diese aber, als sie hörte, daß er kein Königssohn wäre, wollte ihn nicht. Sie ging hinaus in den Garten, schüttete zehn Säcke voll Hirse ins Gras und sprach: »Die soll er auflesen, daß kein Körnchen fehlt, und fertig sein morgen, eh' die Sonne aufgeht.« Nun hätte es der Jüngling nicht vollbracht, wenn ihm nicht die treuen Tiere beigestanden hätten. Aber in der Nacht kam der Ameisenkönig mit seinen viel tausend Ameisen, die lasen in der Nacht alle Hirse, trugen sie in die Säcke und waren, eh' die Morgensonne aufging, fertig, so daß kein Körnchen weggekommen war. Als die Königstochter in den Garten kam und das sah, verwunderte sie sich und sprach: »Ob er gleich auch dieses vollbracht hat und jung und schön ist, so will ich ihn doch nicht eher heiraten, als bis er mir einen Apfel vom Baum des Lebens bringt.« Aber die aus dem Nest geworfenen Raben, die er gefüttert, waren groß geworden und hatten gehört, was die Königstochter verlangte. Da flogen sie fort, und bald kam einer, trug den Apfel im Schnabel und ließ ihn dem Jüngling in die Hand fallen. Als er ihn der Königstochter brachte, nahm sie ihn mit Freuden und wurde seine Gemahlin, und als der alte König starb, erhielt er die Krone.   1819

Das eigensinnige Kind

Es war einmal ein Kind eigensinnig und tat nicht, was seine Mutter haben wollte. Darum hatte der liebe Gott kein Wohlgefallen an ihm und ließ es krank werden, und kein Arzt konnte ihm helfen, und in kurzem lag es auf dem Totenbettchen. Als es nun ins Grab versenkt war und Erde über es hingedeckt, so kam auf einmal sein Ärmchen wieder hervor und reichte in die Höhe, und wenn sie es hineinlegten und frische Erde darüber taten, so half das nicht, es kam immer wieder heraus. Da mußte die Mutter selbst zum Grabe gehn und mit der Rute aufs Ärmchen schlagen, und wie sie das getan hatte, zog es sich hinein und hatte nun erst Ruhe unter der Erde.   1819

Schneewittchen

Es war einmal mitten im Winter, und die Schneeflocken fielen wie Federn vom Himmel herab, da saß eine Königin an einem Fenster, das einen Rahmen von schwarzem Ebenholz hatte, und nähte. Und wie sie so nähte und nach dem Schnee aufblickte, stach sie sich mit der Nadel in den Finger, und es fielen drei Tropfen Blut in den Schnee. Und weil das Rote im weißen Schnee so schön aussah, dachte sie bei sich: »Hätt' ich ein Kind so weiß wie Schnee, so rot wie Blut und so schwarz wie der Rahmen!« Bald darauf bekam sie ein Töchterlein, das war so weiß wie Schnee, so rot wie Blut und so schwarzhaarig wie Ebenholz und wurde darum das Schneewittchen (Schneeweißchen) genannt. Und wie das Kind geboren war, starb die Königin. Über ein Jahr nahm sich der König eine andere Gemahlin, sie war eine schöne Frau, aber stolz auf ihre Schönheit und konnte nicht leiden, daß sie von jemand darin sollte übertroffen werden. Sie hatte einen wunderbaren Spiegel, wenn sie vor den trat und sich darin beschaute, sprach sie:

> »Spieglein, Spieglein an der Wand:
> wer ist die schönste im ganzen Land?«

so antwortete er:

> »Ihr, Frau Königin, seid die schönste im Land.«

Da war sie zufrieden, denn sie wußte, daß der Spiegel die Wahrheit sagte.

Schneewittchen aber wuchs heran und wurde immer schöner, und als es sieben Jahr alt war, war es so schön wie der klare Tag und schöner als die Königin selbst. Wie diese nun ihren Spiegel wieder fragte:

> »Spieglein, Spieglein an der Wand,
> wer ist die schönste im ganzen Land?«

antwortete er:

> »Frau Königin, Ihr seid die schönste hier,
> aber Schneewittchen ist tausendmal schöner als Ihr.«

Als die Königin das hörte, erschrak sie und ward blaß vor Zorn und Neid. Von Stund an, wenn sie Schneewittchen erblickte, kehrte sich ihr das Herz im Leibe herum, so haßte sie es. Und der Neid und Hochmut wuchsen und wurden so groß in ihr, daß sie ihr Tag und Nacht keine Ruh mehr ließen. Da rief sie einen Jäger und sprach: »Führ das Kind hinaus in den wilden Wald, ich will's nicht mehr vor meinen Augen sehen. Dort sollst du's töten und mir Lunge und Leber zum Wahrzeichen mitbringen.« Der Jäger gehorchte und führte Schneewittchen hinaus. Als

er nun den Hirschfänger gezogen hatte und ihm sein unschuldiges Herz durchstoßen wollte, fing es an zu weinen und sprach: »Ach, lieber Jäger, schenk mir mein Leben; ich will in den Wald laufen und nimmermehr wieder heimkommen.« Und weil es so schön war, hatte der Jäger Mitleid und sprach: »So lauf hin, du armes Kind.« Die wilden Tiere werden dich bald gefressen haben, dachte er, und doch war's ihm, als wär ein Stein von seinem Herzen gewälzt, weil er es nicht zu töten brauchte. Und weil gerade ein junger Frischling daher gesprungen kam, stach er ihn ab, nahm Lunge und Leber heraus und brachte sie als Wahrzeichen der Königin mit. Die ließ sie in ihrer Gier gleich in Salz kochen, aß sie auf und meinte, sie hätte Schneewittchens Lunge und Leber gegessen.

Nun war das arme Schneewittchen in dem großen Wald mutterselig allein und ward ihm so angst, daß es alle Blättchen an den Bäumen ansah und dachte, wie es sich helfen und retten sollte. Da fing es an zu laufen und lief über die spitzen Steine und durch die Dornen, und die wilden Tiere sprangen an ihm vorbei, aber sie taten ihm nichts. Es lief, so lang nur die Füße noch fort konnten, bis es bald Abend werden wollte, da sah es ein kleines Häuschen und ging hinein, sich zu ruhen. In dem Häuschen war alles klein, aber so zierlich und reinlich, daß es nicht zu sagen ist. Da stand ein weiß gedecktes Tischlein mit sieben kleinen Tellern, jedes Tellerlein mit seinem Löffelein, ferner sieben Messerlein und Gäblein und sieben Becherlein. An der Wand waren sieben Bettlein nebeneinander aufgestellt und schneeweiße Laken darüber. Schneewittchen, weil es so hungrig und durstig war, aß von jedem Tellerlein ein wenig Gemüs und Brot und trank aus jedem Becherlein einen Tropfen Wein; denn es wollte nicht einem allein alles wegnehmen. Hernach, weil es so müde war, legte es sich in ein Bettchen, aber keins paßte für es, das eine war zu lang, das andere zu kurz, bis endlich das siebente recht war, und darin blieb es liegen, befahl sich Gott und schlief ein.

Als es nun ganz dunkel war, kamen die Herren von dem Häuslein, das waren sieben Zwerge, die in den Bergen nach Erz hackten und gruben. Sie zündeten ihre sieben Lichtlein an, und wie es nun hell im Häuslein ward, sahen sie, daß jemand darin gewesen, denn es stand nicht so alles in der Ordnung, wie sie es verlassen hatten. Der erste sprach: »Wer hat auf meinem Stühlchen gesessen?« Der zweite: »Wer hat von meinem Tellerchen gegessen?« Der dritte: »Wer hat von meinem Brötchen genommen?« Der vierte: »Wer hat von meinem Gemüschen gegessen?« Der fünfte: »Wer hat mit meinem Gäbelchen gestochen?« Der sechste: »Wer hat mit meinem Messerchen geschnitten?« Der siebente: »Wer hat aus meinem Becherlein getrunken?« Dann sah sich der erste um und sah, daß auf seinem Bett eine kleine Delle war, da sprach er: »Wer hat in mein Bettchen getreten?« Die andern kamen gelaufen und riefen: »Ei, in meinem hat auch jemand gelegen!« Der siebente aber, als der in sein Bett sah, erblickte Schneewittchen, das lag darin und schlief. Nun rief er die andern, die kamen herbeigelaufen und schrien vor Verwunderung, holten ihre sieben Lichtlein und beleuchteten das Schneewittchen.

»Ei du mein Gott! Ei du mein Gott!« riefen sie. »Was ist das Kind schön!« und
hatten so große Freude, daß sie es nicht aufweckten, sondern im Bettlein fort-
schlafen ließen. Der siebente Zwerg aber schlief bei seinen Gesellen, bei jedem eine
Stunde, da war die Nacht herum.

Als es Morgen war, erwachte Schneewittchen, und wie es die sieben Zwerge sah,
erschrak es. Sie waren aber freundlich und fragten: »Wie heißt du?« – »Ich heiße
Schneewittchen«, antwortete es. »Wie bist du in unser Haus gekommen?« sprachen weiter die Zwerge. Da erzählte es ihnen, wie es seine Stiefmutter hätte wollen
umbringen, der Jäger ihm aber das Leben geschenkt, und da wär es gelaufen den
ganzen Tag, bis es endlich ihr Häuslein gefunden. Die Zwerge sprachen: »Willst du
unsern Haushalt versehen: kochen, betten, waschen, nähen und stricken, und
willst du alles ordentlich und reinlich halten, so kannst du bei uns bleiben, und es
soll dir an nichts fehlen.« Das versprach ihnen Schneewittchen. Da hielt es ihnen
haus, morgens gingen sie in die Berge und suchten Erz und Gold, abends kamen
sie nach Haus, und da mußte ihr Essen bereitet sein. Den Tag über war das
Mädchen allein, da warnten es die guten Zwerge und sprachen: »Hüt dich vor deiner Stiefmutter, die wird bald wissen, daß du hier bist, und laß niemand herein.«

Die Königin aber, nachdem sie Schneewittchens Lunge und Leber glaubte gegessen zu haben, dachte nicht anders, als wieder die Erste und Allerschönste zu
sein, und trat vor ihren Spiegel und sprach:

> »Spieglein, Spieglein an der Wand,
> wer ist die schönste im ganzen Land?«

Da antwortete der Spiegel:

> »Frau Königin, Ihr seid die schönste hier;
> aber Schneewittchen über den Bergen
> bei den sieben Zwergen
> ist noch tausendmal schöner als Ihr!«

Da erschrak sie, denn sie wußte, daß der Spiegel keine Unwahrheit sprach, und
merkte, daß der Jäger sie betrogen hatte und Schneewittchen noch am Leben war.
Und da sie hörte, daß es über den sieben Bergen bei den sieben Zwergen war, sann
sie aufs neue, wie sie es umbringen wollte, denn so lange sie nicht die schönste war
im ganzen Land, ließ ihr der Neid keine Ruhe. Und als sie lange nachgedacht hatte,
färbte sie sich das Gesicht und kleidete sich wie eine alte Krämerin an und war ganz
unkenntlich. In dieser Gestalt ging sie über die sieben Berge hinaus zu dem Zwergenhaus, klopfte an die Türe und rief: »Gute Ware feil, feil!« Schneewittchen
guckte zum Fenster heraus und rief: »Guten Tag, liebe Frau, was habt Ihr denn zu
verkaufen?« – »Gute Ware, schöne Ware«, antwortete sie, »Schnürriemen von

allen Farben.« Dabei holte sie einen bunten von Seide hervor und zeigte ihn. Die gute Frau kann ich hereinlassen, dachte Schneewittchen, die meint's redlich; riegelte die Türe auf und kaufte sich den bunten Schnürriemen. »Wart, Kind«, sprach die Alte, »wie bist du geschnürt! Komm, ich will dich einmal ordentlich schnüren.« Schneewittchen dachte an nichts Böses, stellte sich vor sie und ließ sich mit dem neuen Schnürriemen schnüren; aber die Alte schnürte mit schnellen Fingern und schnürte so fest, daß dem Schneewittchen der Atem verging und es für tot hinfiel. »Nun ist's aus mit deiner Schönheit«, sprach das böse Weib und ging fort.

Nicht lange darauf, zur Abendzeit, kamen die sieben Zwerge nach Haus, aber wie erschraken sie, als sie ihr liebes Schneewittchen auf der Erde liegen fanden, das sich nicht regte und nicht bewegte, als wär es tot! Sie hoben es in die Höhe, da sahen sie, daß es zu fest geschnürt war, und schnitten den Schnürriemen entzwei: da fing es an, ein wenig zu atmen, und ward nach und nach wieder lebendig. Als die Zwerge von ihm hörten, was geschehen war, sprachen sie: »Die alte Krämerfrau war niemand als die Königin, hüt dich und laß keinen Menschen herein, wenn wir nicht bei dir sind.«

Das böse Weib aber, als es nach Haus gekommen war, ging vor den Spiegel und fragte:

>>Spieglein, Spieglein an der Wand,
wer ist die schönste im ganzen Land?«

Da antwortete er:

>>Frau Königin, Ihr seid die schönste hier;
aber Schneewittchen über den Bergen
bei den sieben Zwergen
ist noch tausendmal schöner als Ihr.«

Als sie das hörte, lief ihr das Blut all zum Herzen, so erschrak sie, denn sie sah, daß Schneewittchen doch wieder lebendig geworden war. Nun sann sie aufs neue, was sie anfangen wollte, um es zu töten, und machte einen giftigen Kamm. Dann verkleidete sie sich und nahm wieder die Gestalt einer armen Frau, aber einer ganz anderen, an. So ging sie hinaus über die sieben Berge zum Zwergenhaus, klopfte an die Türe und rief: »Gute Ware feil, feil!« Schneewittchen schaute heraus und sprach: »Ich darf niemand hereinlassen.« Die Alte aber rief: »Sieh einmal die schönen Kämme«, zog den giftigen heraus und zeigte ihn. Der gefiel dem Kind so gut, daß es sich betören ließ und die Tür öffnete. Als es den Kamm gekauft hatte, sprach die Alte: »Nun will ich dich auch kämmen.« Schneewittchen dachte an nichts Böses, aber die Alte steckte ihm den Kamm in die Haare, alsbald wirkte das Gift darin so heftig, daß es tot niederfiel. »Nun wirst du liegen bleiben«, sprach sie und ging fort. Zum Glück aber war es bald Abend, wo die sieben Zwerglein nach Haus kamen; als sie das Schneewittchen wie tot auf der Erde liegen sahen, dachten

sie gleich, die böse Stiefmutter hätte es wieder umbringen wollen, suchten und fanden den giftigen Kamm; und wie sie ihn herausgezogen, kam es wieder zu sich und erzählte ihnen, was vorgegangen war. Da warnten sie es noch einmal, auf seiner Hut zu sein und niemand die Türe zu öffnen.

Die Königin aber stellte sich daheim vor den Spiegel und sprach:

>>Spieglein, Spieglein an der Wand,
wer ist die schönste im ganzen Land?<<

Da antwortete er, wie vorher:

>>Frau Königin, Ihr seid die schönste hier;
aber Schneewittchen über den Bergen
bei den sieben Zwergen
ist noch tausendmal schöner als Ihr.<<

Bei diesen Worten zitterte und bebte sie vor Zorn und sprach: >>So soll das Schneewittchen noch sterben, und wenn es mein Leben kostet!<< Darauf ging sie in eine ganz verborgene einsame Kammer, wo niemand hinkam, und machte da einen giftigen, giftigen Apfel. Äußerlich sah er schön aus mit roten Backen, daß jeder, der ihn erblickte, eine Lust danach bekam, aber wer ein Stückchen davon aß, der mußte sterben. Als der Apfel fertig war, färbte sie sich das Gesicht und verkleidete sich in eine Bauersfrau, und so ging sie über die sieben Berge zu dem Zwergenhaus und klopfte an. Schneewittchen streckte den Kopf zum Fenster heraus und sprach: >>Ich darf keinen Menschen einlassen, die Zwerge haben mir's verboten.<< — >>Nun, wenn du nicht willst<<, antwortete die Bäurin, >>so ist's auch gut. Meine Äpfel will ich schon loswerden. Da, einen will ich dir schenken.<< — >>Nein<<, sprach Schneewittchen, >>ich darf nichts annehmen.<< — >>Ei, du fürchtest dich wohl vor Gift; da, den roten Backen beiß du ab, ich will den weißen essen<<, sprach die Alte. Der Apfel war aber so künstlich gemacht, daß nur der rote Backen vergiftet war.

Schneewittchen lusterte den schönen Apfel an, und als es sah, daß die Bäurin davon aß, so konnte es nicht länger widerstehen, streckte die Hand hinaus und ließ ihn sich geben. Kaum aber hatte es einen Bissen davon im Mund, so fiel es tot zur Erde nieder. Da sprach die Königin: »Diesmal wird dich niemand erwecken«, ging heim und fragte den Spiegel:

»Spieglein, Spieglein an der Wand,
wer ist die schönste im ganzen Land?«

Da antwortete der Spiegel endlich:

»Ihr, Frau Königin, seid die schönste im Land.«

Und ihr neidisches Herz hatte Ruhe, so gut es Ruhe haben konnte. Die Zwerglein, wie sie abends nach Haus kamen, fanden das Schneewittchen auf der Erde liegen, und regte sich kein Atem mehr, und es war tot. Sie hoben es auf, suchten, ob sie was Giftiges fänden, schnürten es auf, kämmten ihm die Haare, wuschen es mit Wasser und Wein, aber es half alles nichts, das liebe Kind war tot und blieb tot. Sie legten es darauf in eine Bahre und setzten sich alle sieben daran und beweinten es und weinten drei Tage lang. Da wollten sie es begraben, aber es sah noch frisch aus wie ein lebender Mensch und hatte noch seine schönen roten Backen, und sie sprachen: »Das können wir nicht in die schwarze Erde versenken.« Sie ließen einen Sarg von Glas machen, daß man es recht sehen könnte, legten es hinein und schrieben mit goldenen Buchstaben seinen Namen darauf und daß es eine Königstochter wäre. Dann setzten sie den Sarg hinaus auf den Berg, und einer von ihnen blieb immer dabei und bewachte ihn. Und die Tiere kamen auch und beweinten das Schneewittchen, erst eine Eule, dann ein Rabe, zuletzt ein Täubchen.

Nun lag Schneewittchen lange, lange Zeit in dem Sarg und verweste nicht, sondern sah noch aus, als wenn es lebte und da schlief, denn es war noch so weiß wie Schnee, so rot wie Blut und so schwarzhaarig wie Ebenholz. Es geschah aber, daß ein Königssohn in den Wald geriet und zu dem Zwergenhaus kam, da zu übernachten. Der sah auf dem Berg den Sarg und Schneewittchen darin und las, was mit goldenen Buchstaben darauf geschrieben war. Da sprach er zu den Zwergen: »Laßt mir den Sarg, ich will euch geben, was ihr dafür haben wollt.« Aber die Zwerge antworteten: »Wir geben ihn nicht um alles Gold in der Welt.« Da sprach er: »So schenkt mir ihn, denn ich kann nicht leben, ohne Schneewittchen zu sehen, ich will es ehren und hochhalten wie mein Liebstes.« Wie er so sprach, empfanden die guten Zwerglein Mitleid mit ihm und gaben ihm den Sarg. Der Königssohn ließ ihn nun von seinen Dienern auf den Schultern forttragen. Da geschah es, daß sie über einen Strauch stolperten, und von dem Schüttern fuhr der giftige Apfelgrütz, den das Schneewittchen abgebissen hatte, aus dem Hals, und es ward wieder

lebendig und richtete sich auf. Da sprach es: »Ach Gott! Wo bin ich?« Aber der Königssohn sagte voll Freude: »Du bist bei mir«, und erzählte ihm, was sich zugetragen hatte, und sprach: »Ich habe dich lieber als alles auf der Welt, komm mit mir in meines Vaters Schloß, du sollst meine Gemahlin werden.« Da war ihm das Schneewittchen gut und ging mit ihm, und zu ihrer Hochzeit ward alles mit großer Pracht und Herrlichkeit angeordnet.

Zu dem Fest war aber auch Schneewittchens gottlose Stiefmutter eingeladen. Wie sie sich nun mit schönen Kleidern angetan hatte, trat sie vor den Spiegel und sprach:

> »Spieglein, Spieglein an der Wand,
> wer ist die schönste im ganzen Land?«

Da antwortete der Spiegel:

> »Frau Königin, Ihr seid die schönste hier,
> aber die junge Königin ist tausendmal schöner als Ihr!«

Wie das böse Weib das hörte, erschrak sie und ward ihr so angst, so angst, daß sie es nicht sagen konnte. Sie wollte gar nicht auf die Hochzeit kommen, und doch trieb sie der Neid, daß sie die junge Königin sehen wollte. Und wie sie hineintrat, sah sie, daß es niemand anders als Schneewittchen war, und vor Schrecken konnte sie sich nicht regen. Aber es standen schon eiserne Pantoffeln überm Kohlenfeuer, und wie sie glühten, wurden sie hereingebracht, und sie mußte die feuerroten Schuhe anziehen und darin tanzen, daß ihr die Füße jämmerlich verbrannt wurden, und eher durfte sie nicht aufhören, als bis sie sich zu Tode getanzt hatte.

1819

Frau Holle

Eine Witwe hatte zwei Töchter, davon war die eine schön und fleißig, die andere häßlich und faul. Sie hatte aber die häßliche und faule, weil sie ihre rechte Tochter war, viel lieber, und die andere mußte alle Arbeit tun und war recht das Aschenputtel im Haus. Es mußte sich täglich hinaus auf die große Straße an einen Brunnen setzen und so viel spinnen, daß ihm das Blut aus den Fingern sprang. Nun trug es sich zu, daß die Spule einmal ganz blutig war, da bückte es sich damit in den Brunnen und wollte sie abwaschen, sie sprang ihm aber aus der Hand und fiel hinab. Weinend lief es zur Stiefmutter und erzählte ihr das Unglück, sie schalt es aber heftig und war so unbarmherzig, daß sie sprach: »Hast du die Spule hinunterfallen lassen, so hol sie auch wieder herauf!« Da ging das Mädchen zu dem Brunnen zurück und wußte nicht, was es anfangen sollte, und sprang in seiner Angst in den Brunnen hinein. Als es erwachte und wieder zu sich selber kam, war es auf einer schönen Wiese, da schien die Sonne und waren vieltausend Blumen. Auf der Wiese ging es fort und kam zu einem Backofen, der war voller Brot; das Brot aber rief: »Ach! zieh mich raus, zieh mich raus, sonst verbrenn ich, ich bin schon längst ausgebacken!« Da trat es fleißig herzu und holte alles heraus. Danach ging es weiter und kam zu einem Baum, der hing voll Äpfel, und rief ihm zu: »Ach! schüttel mich! schüttel mich! Wir Äpfel sind alle miteinander reif!« Da schüttelt' es den Baum, daß die Äpfel fielen, als regneten sie, so lang, bis keiner mehr oben war, danach ging es wieder fort. Endlich kam es zu einem kleinen Haus, daraus guckte eine alte Frau, weil sie aber so große Zähne hatte, ward ihm angst, und es wollte fortlaufen. Die alte Frau aber rief ihm nach: »Fürcht dich nicht, liebes Kind, bleib bei mir, wenn du alle Arbeit im Haus ordentlich tun willst, so soll dir's gutgehn. Nur mußt du acht geben, daß du mein Bett gut machst und es fleißig aufschüttelst, daß die Federn fliegen, dann schneit es in der Welt; ich bin die Frau Holle.« Weil die Alte so gut ihm zusprach, willigte das Mädchen ein und begab sich in ihren Dienst. Es besorgte auch alles nach ihrer Zufriedenheit und schüttelte ihr das Bett immer gewaltig auf, dafür hatte es auch ein gut Leben bei ihr, kein böses Wort und alle Tage Gesottenes und Gebratenes. Nun war es eine Zeitlang bei der Frau Holle, da ward es traurig in seinem Herzen, und ob es hier gleich viel tausendmal besser war als zu Haus, so hatte es doch ein Verlangen dahin; endlich sagte es zu ihr: »Ich habe den Jammer nach Haus kriegt, und wenn es mir auch noch so gut hier geht, so kann ich doch nicht länger bleiben.« Die Frau Holle sagte: »Du hast recht, und weil du mir so treu gedient hast, so will ich dich selbst wieder hinaufbringen.« Sie nahm es darauf bei der Hand und führte es vor ein großes Tor. Das ward aufgetan, und wie das Mädchen darunter stand, fiel ein gewaltiger Goldregen, und alles Gold blieb an ihm hängen, so daß es über und über davon bedeckt war. »Das sollst du haben, weil du so fleißig gewesen bist«, sprach die Frau Holle und gab ihm auch noch die Spule wieder, die ihm in den Brunnen gefallen war. Darauf ward das Tor verschlossen, und das Mädchen befand sich oben auf der Welt, nicht weit von seiner Mutter Haus, und als es in den Hof kam, saß der Hahn auf dem Brunnen und rief:

»Kikeriki!
Unsere goldene Jungfrau ist wieder hie!«

Da ging es hinein zu seiner Mutter, und weil es so mit Gold bedeckt ankam, ward es gut aufgenommen.

Als die Mutter hörte, wie es zu dem Reichtum gekommen, wollte sie der andern häßlichen und faulen Tochter gern dasselbe Glück verschaffen, und sie mußte sich auch an den Brunnen setzen und spinnen; damit ihr die Spule blutig ward, stach sie sich in die Finger und zerstieß sich die Hand an der Dornenhecke. Danach warf sie sie in den Brunnen und sprang selber hinein. Sie kam, wie die andere, auf die schöne Wiese und ging auf demselben Pfad weiter. Als sie zu dem Backofen gelangte, schrie das Brot wieder: »Ach! zieh mich raus, zieh mich raus, sonst verbrenn ich, ich bin schon längst ausgebacken!« Die Faule aber antwortete: »Da hätt' ich Lust, mich schmutzig zu machen!« und ging fort. Bald kam sie zu dem Apfelbaum, der rief: »Ach! schüttel mich! schüttel mich! Wir Äpfel sind alle miteinander reif!« Sie antwortete aber: »Du kommst mir recht, es könnt mir einer auf den Kopf fallen!« und ging weiter. Als sie vor der Frau Holle Haus kam, fürchtete sie sich nicht, weil sie von ihren großen Zähnen schon gehört hatte, und verdingte sich gleich bei ihr. Am ersten Tag tat sie sich Gewalt an und war fleißig und folgte der Frau Holle, wenn sie ihr etwas sagte, denn sie gedachte an das viele Gold, das sie ihr schenken würde; am zweiten Tag aber fing sie schon an zu faulenzen, am dritten noch mehr, da wollte sie morgens gar nicht aufstehen, sie machte auch der Frau Holle das Bett schlecht und schüttelte es nicht recht, daß die Federn aufflogen. Das ward die Frau Holle bald müd und sagte der Faulen den Dienst auf. Die war es wohl zufrieden und meinte, nun werde der Goldregen kommen, die Frau Holle führte sie auch zu dem Tor. Als sie aber darunter stand, ward statt des Golds ein großer Kessel voll Pech ausgeschüttet. »Das ist zur Belohnung deiner Dienste«, sagte die Frau Holle und schloß das Tor zu. Da kam die Faule heim, ganz mit Pech bedeckt, und das hat ihr Lebtag nicht wieder abgehen wollen. Der Hahn aber auf dem Brunnen, als er sie sah, rief:

»Kikeriki!
Unsere schmutzige Jungfrau ist wieder hie!«

1819

Der König vom goldenen Berg

Ein Kaufmann, der hatte zwei Kinder, einen Buben und ein Mädchen, die waren beide noch klein und konnten noch nicht laufen. Es fuhren aber zwei reichbeladene Schiffe von ihm auf dem Meer, und sein ganzes Vermögen war darin, und wie er meinte, dadurch viel Geld zu gewinnen, kam die Nachricht, sie wären versunken. Da war er nun statt eines reichen Mannes ein armer Mann und hatte nichts mehr übrig als einen Acker vor der Stadt. Um sich nun sein Unglück ein bißchen aus den Gedanken zu schlagen, ging er dahinaus. Und wie er da so auf und ab ging, stand auf einmal ein kleines schwarzes Männchen neben ihm und fragte, warum er

so traurig wäre und was er sich so sehr zu Herzen nähme. Da sprach der Kaufmann: »Wenn du mir helfen könntest, wollt' ich dir es wohl sagen.« – »Wer weiß«, sagte das schwarze Männchen, »sag mir's nur, vielleicht helf ich dir.« Da erzählte der Kaufmann, daß ihm sein ganzer Reichtum auf dem Meer zu Grunde gegangen wäre, und habe er nichts mehr übrig als diesen Acker. »Oh, da bekümmere dich nicht«, sagte das Männchen, »wenn du mir versprichst, das, was dir zu Haus am ersten wider's Bein stößt, in zwölf Jahren hierher auf den Platz zu bringen, sollst du Geld haben, soviel du willst.« Der Kaufmann dachte, das ist ein geringes, was kann das anders sein als dein Hund, aber an seinen kleinen Jungen dachte er nicht und sagte ja und gab dem schwarzen Mann Handschrift und Siegel darüber und ging nach Haus.

Als er nach Haus kam, da hatte sich sein kleiner Junge so gefreut, daß er sich an den Bänken hielt, zu ihm hinwackelte und ihn an den Beinen fest packte. Da erschrak der Vater und wußte nun, was er verschrieben hatte. Weil er aber immer noch kein Geld sah, dachte er, es wär nur ein Spaß von dem Männchen gewesen. Ungefähr einen Monat nachher ging er auf den Boden und wollte das alte Zinn zusammensuchen und verkaufen, um noch etwas daraus zu lösen, da sah er einen großen Haufen Geld liegen. Wie er das Geld sah, war er vergnügt, kaufte wieder ein, ward ein größerer Kaufmann als vorher und ließ Gott einen guten Mann sein. Unterdessen ward der Junge groß und ein gescheiter Mensch. Je mehr aber die zwölf Jahre herbeikamen, desto ängstlicher ward der Kaufmann, so daß man ihm die Angst im Gesicht sehen konnte. Da fragte ihn der Sohn einmal, was ihm fehle; der Vater wollt' es nicht sagen, aber er hielt so lange an, bis er ihm endlich sagte, er habe ihn, ohne daß er es gewußt, einem schwarzen Männchen versprochen für viel Geld und habe seine Handschrift mit Siegel darüber gegeben, und nun müsse er ihn, wenn zwölf Jahre herum wären, ausliefern. Da sprach der Sohn: »O Vater, laßt Euch nicht bang sein, das soll schon gut werden, der Schwarze hat keine Macht über mich.«

Da ließ sich der Sohn von dem Geistlichen segnen, und als die Stunde kam, gingen sie zusammen hinaus auf den Acker, und der Sohn machte einen Kreis und stellte sich mit seinem Vater hinein. Da kam das schwarze Männchen und sprach zu dem Alten: »Hast du, was du mir versprochen hast?« Der schwieg aber still, und der Sohn sprach: »Was willst du hier?« Da sagte das schwarze Männchen: »Ich habe mit deinem Vater zu sprechen und nicht mit dir.« – Der Sohn sprach: »Du hast meinen Vater betrogen und verführt, gib die Handschrift heraus.« – »Nein«, sagte das schwarze Männchen, »mein Recht geb ich nicht auf.« Da redeten sie noch lange miteinander, endlich wurden sie einig, der Sohn, weil er nicht dem Erbfeind und nicht mehr seinem Vater zugehöre, solle sich in ein Schiffchen setzen, das auf einem abwärts fließenden Wasser stehe, und der Vater solle es mit seinem eigenen Fuß fortstoßen, und da solle der Sohn dem Wasser überlassen bleiben. Da nahm er Abschied von seinem Vater und setzte sich in ein Schiffchen, und der Vater mußte es mit seinem eigenen Fuß fortstoßen. Und das Schiffchen drehte sich herum, daß der untere Teil oben war, die Decke aber im Wasser, und der Vater glaubte, sein Sohn wär verloren, ging heim und trauerte um ihn.

Das Schiffchen aber floß ganz ruhig fort und ging nicht unter, und der Jüngling saß sicher darin, und so floß es lange, bis es endlich an einem unbekannten Ufer festsitzen blieb. Da stieg er ans Land, sah ein schönes Schloß vor sich liegen und ging drauf los. Wie er aber hineintrat, war es verwünscht und alles leer, bis er zuletzt in einer Kammer eine Schlange antraf. Die Schlange aber war eine verwünschte Jungfrau, die freute sich, wie sie ihn sah, und sprach zu ihm: »Kommst du, mein Erlöser, auf dich habe ich schon zwölf Jahre gewartet, dies Reich ist verwünscht, und du mußt es erlösen. Heute nacht kommen zwölf Männer, schwarz und mit Ketten behangen, die werden dich fragen, was du hier machst, da schweig aber still und gib ihnen keine Antwort und laß sie mit dir machen, was sie wollen;

sie werden dich quälen, schlagen und stechen, laß alles geschehen, nur rede nicht. Um zwölf Uhr müssen sie wieder fort. Und in der zweiten Nacht werden wieder zwölf andere kommen, in der dritten vierundzwanzig, die werden dir den Kopf abhauen; aber um zwölf Uhr ist ihre Macht vorbei, und wenn du dann ausgehalten und kein Wörtchen gesprochen hast, so bin ich erlöst und komme zu dir und stehe dir bei und habe das Wasser des Lebens, damit bestreich ich dich, und dann bist du wieder lebendig und gesund wie zuvor.«

Da sprach er: »Gern will ich dich erlösen«, und es geschah nun alles so, wie sie gesagt hatte: Die schwarzen Männer konnten ihm kein Wort abzwingen, und in der dritten Nacht ward die Schlange zu einer schönen Königstochter, die kam mit dem Wasser des Lebens und machte ihn wieder lebendig. Und dann fiel sie ihm um den Hals und küßte ihn, und ward Jubel und Freude im ganzen Schloß, und ihre Hochzeit wurde gehalten, und er war König vom goldenen Berge.

Also lebten sie vergnügt zusammen, und die Königin gebar einen schönen Knaben, und acht Jahre waren schon herum, da fiel ihm sein Vater ein, daß sein Herz davon bewegt ward, und er wünschte, ihn einmal heimzusuchen. Die Königin wollte ihn aber nicht fortlassen und sagte: »Ich weiß schon, daß das mein Unglück ist.« Er ließ ihr aber keine Ruhe, bis sie einwilligte. Beim Abschied gab sie ihm noch einen Wünschring und sprach: »Nimm diesen Ring und steck ihn an deinen Finger, wo du dich hinwünschest, wirst du alsbald hinversetzt, nur mußt du mir versprechen, daß du ihn nicht gebrauchst, um mich von hier weg zu deinem Vater zu wünschen.« Da versprach er's, steckte den Ring an seinen Finger und wünschte sich heim vor die Stadt, wo sein Vater lebte. Alsbald war er auch davor, aber nicht darin; wie er nun vors Tor kam, wollten ihn die Schildwachen nicht einlassen, weil er so seltsam und reich gekleidet war. Da ging er auf einen Berg, wo ein Schäfer hütete, mit diesem tauschte er die Kleider und zog den alten Schäferrock an und ging also ungestört in die Stadt ein. Als er zu seinem Vater kam, gab er sich zu erkennen, der aber sprach, er glaube nimmermehr, daß er sein Sohn sei, er hätte zwar einen gehabt, der sei längst tot, weil er aber sehe, daß er ein armer, dürftiger Schäfer sei, so wolle er ihm einen Teller voll zu essen geben. Da sprach der Schäfer zu seinen Eltern: »Ich bin wahrhaftig euer Sohn, wißt ihr kein Mal an meinem Leibe, woran ihr mich erkennen könnt?« – »Ja«, sagte die Mutter, »unser Sohn hatte eine Himbeere unter dem rechten Arm.« Da streifte er das Hemd von seinem Arm, und da sahen sie die Himbeere und waren nun überzeugt, daß es ihr Sohn war. Darauf erzählte er ihnen, er wäre König vom goldenen Berge und eine Königstochter seine Gemahlin, und sie hätten einen schönen Sohn von sieben Jahren. Da sprach der Vater: »Nie und nimmermehr ist das wahr! Das ist ein schöner König, der in einem zerlumpten Schäferrock einhergeht.« Da ward er zornig, drehte seinen Ring herum, ohne an sein Versprechen zu denken, und wünschte beide, seine Gemahlin und seinen Prinzen, zu sich. In dem Augenblick waren sie auch da, aber die Königin, die klagte und weinte und sagte, er hätte sein

Wort gebrochen und sie unglücklich gemacht. Er besänftigte sie und redete sie zufrieden, und sie stellte sich auch, als gäbe sie nach, aber sie hatte Böses im Sinn.

Da führte er sie hinaus vor die Stadt auf den Acker und zeigte ihr das Wasser und wo das Schiffchen war abgestoßen worden, und dann sprach er: »Ich bin müd, setz dich nieder, ich will ein wenig auf deinem Schoß schlafen.« Da legte er seinen Kopf auf ihren Schoß, und sie lauste ihn ein wenig, bis er einschlief. Als er eingeschlafen war, zog sie den Ring von seinem Finger, und den Fuß, den sie unter ihm stehen hatte, zog sie auch heraus und ließ nur den Pantoffel unter ihm liegen; dann nahm sie ihren Prinzen und wünschte sich wieder in ihr Königreich. Als er aufwachte, da lag er da ganz verlassen, und seine Gemahlin mit dem Prinzen war fort und der Ring vom Finger auch, nur der Pantoffel stand noch da zum Wahrzeichen. »Nach Haus zu deinen Eltern kannst du nicht wieder gehen«, dachte er, »die sagen, du wärst ein Hexenmeister, du willst aufpacken und gehen, bis du in dein Königreich kommst.« Also ging er fort und kam endlich zu einem Berg, wo drei Riesen ihres Vaters Erbe teilen wollten, und als sie ihn vorbeigehen sahen, riefen sie ihn und sagten, kleine Menschen hätten klugen Sinn, er sollt' ihnen die Erbschaft verteilen: Das war ein Degen, wenn einer den in die Hand nahm und sprach: »Köpf alle runter, nur meiner nicht«, so lagen alle Köpfe auf der Erde; zweitens ein Mantel, wer den anzog, war unsichtbar; drittens ein Paar Stiefel, wenn man die an den Füßen hatte und sich wohin wünschte, so war man gleich da. Er sprach, sie müßten ihm die drei Stücke einmal geben, damit er sie probieren könne, ob sie auch alle noch in gutem Stand wären. Da gaben sie ihm den Mantel, den tat er um und wünschte sich zu einer Fliege, alsbald war er eine Fliege. »Der Mantel ist gut«, sprach er, »nun gebt mir einmal das Schwert.« Sie sagten: »Nein, das geben wir nicht, denn wenn du sprächst: ›Köpf alle runter, nur meiner nicht!‹ so wären unsere Köpfe alle herab, und du hättest deinen noch«; doch gaben sie es ihm, wenn er's an den Bäumen probieren wollte. Das tat er, und das Schwert war auch gut. Nun wollt' er noch die Stiefel haben, sie sprachen aber: »Nein, die können wir nicht geben, wenn du die anhättest und sprächst, du wolltest oben auf dem Berg sein, so stünden wir da unten und hätten nichts.« — »Nein«, sprach er, »das will ich nicht tun«, da gaben sie ihm die Stiefel auch noch. Wie er nun alle drei Stücke hatte, da wünschte er sich auf den goldenen Berg, und alsbald war er dort und die Riesen verschwunden, und war also ihr Erbe geteilt. Als er nah beim Schloß war, hörte er Geigen und Flöten, und die Leute sagten ihm, seine Gemahlin halte Hochzeit mit einem andern Prinzen. Da zog er seinen Mantel an und machte sich zur Fliege, ging ins Schloß hinein und stellte sich hinter seine Gemahlin, und niemand sah ihn. Wenn sie ihr nun ein Stück Fleisch auf den Teller legten, nahm er's weg und aß es, und wenn sie ihr ein Glas Wein einschenkten, nahm er's weg und trank's; sie gaben ihr immer, und sie hatte doch immer nichts auf dem Teller. Da schämte sie sich, stand auf, ging in ihre Kammer und weinte, er aber ging hinter ihr her. Da sprach

sie vor sich: »Ist denn der Teufel über mir, oder mein Erlöser kam nie!« Da gab er ihr ein paar derbe Ohrfeigen und sagte: »Kam dein Erlöser nie, er ist über dir, du Betrügerin! Habe ich das an dir verdient?« Darauf ging er hin und sagte, die Hochzeit wär aus, er wäre wieder gekommen, da wurde er verlacht von den Königen, Fürsten und Räten, die da waren. Er aber gab kurze Worte und fragte, ob sie sich entfernen wollten oder nicht? Da wollten sie ihn fangen, aber er zog sein Schwert und sprach: »Köpf alle runter, nur meiner nicht!« Da lagen alle gleich im Blut danieder, und er war wieder König vom goldenen Berge.   1819

344   *Der König vom goldenen Berg*

Des Teufels rußiger Bruder

Ein abgedankter Soldat hatte nichts zu leben und wußte sich nicht mehr zu helfen. Da ging er hinaus in den Wald, und als er ein Weilchen gegangen war, begegnete ihm ein kleines Männchen, das war aber der Teufel. Das Männchen sagte zu ihm: »Was fehlt dir? Du siehst ja so trübselig aus.« Da sprach der Soldat: »Ich habe Hunger und kein Geld.« Der Teufel sagte: »Willst du dich bei mir vermieten und mein Knecht sein, so sollst du für dein Lebtag genug haben. Sieben Jahre sollst du mir dienen, dann bist du wieder frei, aber eins sag ich dir, du darfst dich nicht waschen, nicht kämmen, nicht schnippen, keine Nägel und Haare abschneiden und kein Wasser aus den Augen wischen.« Der Soldat sprach: »Wohlan, so soll's sein!« und ging mit dem Männchen fort, das führte ihn nun geradeswegs in die Hölle hinein. Da sagte es ihm, was er zu tun habe: Er müßte das Feuer schüren unter den Kesseln, wo die Höllenbraten drin säßen, das Haus rein halten, den Kehrdreck hinter die Türe tragen und überall auf Ordnung sehen, aber guckt' er ein einziges Mal in die Kessel hinein, so sollt's ihm schlimm gehen. Der Soldat sprach: »Es ist gut, ich will's schon besorgen.«

Da ging nun der alte Teufel wieder hinaus auf seine Wanderung, und der Soldat trat seinen Dienst an, legte Feuer zu, kehrte und trug den Kehrdreck hinter die Türe. Wie der alte Teufel wiederkam, war er zufrieden und ging zum zweitenmal fort. Der Soldat schaute sich nun einmal recht um, da standen die Kessel rings herum in der Hölle und war ein gewaltiges Feuer darunter, und es kochte und brutzelte darin. Da hätt' er für sein Leben gern hineingeschaut, es war ihm aber so streng verboten. Endlich konnt' er sich nicht mehr anhalten, ging herbei und hob vom ersten Kessel ein klein bißchen den Deckel auf und guckte hinein. Da sah er seinen ehemaligen Unteroffizier darin sitzen: »Aha! Vogel«, sprach er, »treff ich dich hier! Du hast mich gehabt, jetzt hab ich dich!«, ließ geschwind den Deckel fallen, schürte das Feuer und legte noch frisch zu. Danach ging er zum zweiten Kessel, hob ihn auch ein wenig auf und guckte, da saß sein Fähnrich darin: »Aha! Vogel, treff ich dich hier, du hast mich gehabt, jetzt hab ich dich«, machte den Deckel wieder zu und trug noch einen Klotz herbei, der sollt' ihm erst recht heiß machen. Nun wollt' er auch sehen, wer im dritten Kessel säße, da war's gar sein General: »Aha! Vogel, treff ich dich hier! Du hast mich gehabt, jetzt hab ich dich!«, holte den Blasbalg und ließ das Höllenfeuer recht unter ihm flackern. Also tat er sieben Jahre seinen Dienst in der Hölle, wusch sich nicht, kämmte sich nicht, schnippte sich nicht, schnitt sich die Nägel und Haare nicht und wischte sich kein Wasser aus den Augen, und die sieben Jahr waren ihm so kurz, daß er meinte, es wär nur ein halb Jahr gewesen.

Wie nun die Zeit vollends herum war, kam der Teufel und sagte: »Nun, Hans, was hast du gemacht?« – »Ich hab das Feuer unter den Kesseln geschürt, ich hab gekehrt und den Kehrdreck hinter die Türe getragen.« – »Aber du hast auch in die Kessel geguckt; dein Glück ist, daß du noch Holz zugelegt hast, sonst wär dein Leben verloren; jetzt ist deine Zeit herum, willst du wieder heim?« – »Ja«, sagte der Soldat, »ich wollt' auch gern sehen, was mein Vater daheim macht.« Sprach der Teufel: »Damit du deinen verdienten Lohn kriegst, geh und raff dir deinen Ranzen voll Kehrdreck und nimm's mit nach Haus, du sollst auch gehen ungewaschen und ungekämmt, mit langen Haaren am Kopf und am Bart, mit ungeschnittenen Nägeln und mit trüben Augen, und wenn du gefragt wirst, woher du kämst, sollst du sagen: aus der Hölle; und wenn du gefragt wirst, wer du wärst, sollst du sagen: des Teufels rußiger Bruder und mein König auch.« Der Soldat schwieg still und tat, was der Teufel sagte, aber er war mit seinem Lohn gar nicht zufrieden.

Wie er nun wieder auf die Welt kam und im Wald war, hob er seinen Ranzen vom Rücken und wollt' ihn ausschütten; wie er ihn aber öffnete, so war der Kehrdreck pures Gold geworden. Als er das sah, war er vergnügt und ging in die Stadt hinein. Vor dem Wirtshaus stand der Wirt, und wie er ihn herankommen sah, erschrak er, weil Hans so entsetzlich aussah, ärger als eine Vogelscheuche, und rief ihn an: »Woher kommst du?« – »Aus der Hölle.« – »Wer bist du?« – »Des Teufels rußiger Bruder und mein König auch.« Nun wollte der Wirt ihn nicht einlassen. Wie er ihm aber das Gold zeigte, ging er und klinkte dem Hans selber die Türe auf. Da ließ er sich die beste Stube geben, köstlich aufwarten, aß und trank sich satt, wusch sich aber nicht und kämmte sich nicht, wie ihm der Teufel geheißen hatte, und legte sich endlich schlafen. Dem Wirt aber war der Ranzen voll Gold vor den Augen und ließ ihm keine Ruh, bis er in der Nacht hinschlich und ihn wegstahl.

Wie nun Hans am andern Morgen aufstand, den Wirt bezahlen und weitergehen wollte, da war sein Ranzen weg. Er faßte sich aber kurz, dachte, du bist ohne Schuld unglücklich gewesen, und kehrte wieder um, geradezu in die Hölle; da klagte er es dem alten Teufel und bat ihn um Hilfe. Der Teufel sagte: »Setz dich, ich will dich waschen, kämmen, schnippen, die Haare und Nägel schneiden und die Augen auswischen«, und als er fertig mit ihm war, gab er ihm den Ranzen wieder voll Kehrdreck und sprach: »Geh hin und sag dem Wirt, er sollt' dir dein Gold wieder herausgeben, sonst wollt' ich kommen und ihn abholen an deinen Platz.« Hans ging hinauf und sprach zum Wirt: »Du hast mein Gold gestohlen, gibst du's nicht wieder, so kommst du in die Hölle an meinen Platz und sollst aussehen wie ich.« Da gab ihm der Wirt das Gold und noch mehr dazu und bat ihn, nur still davon zu sein, und Hans war nun ein reicher Mann.

Hans machte sich auf den Weg heim zu seinem Vater, kaufte sich einen schlechten Linnenkittel auf den Leib, ging herum und machte Musik, denn das hatte er bei dem Teufel in der Hölle gelernt. Es war aber ein alter König im Land, vor dem mußt' er spielen, und der geriet darüber in solche Freude, daß er dem Hans seine

älteste Tochter zur Ehe versprach. Als die aber hörte, daß sie so einen gemeinen Kerl im weißen Kittel heiraten sollte, sprach sie: »Eh' ich das tät, wollt' ich lieber ins tiefste Wasser gehen.« Da gab ihm der König die jüngste, die wollt's ihrem Vater zu Liebe gern tun, und also bekam des Teufels rußiger Bruder die Königstochter, und als der alte König gestorben war, auch das ganze Reich.

1819

Doktor Allwissend

Es war einmal ein armer Bauer namens Krebs, der fuhr mit zwei Ochsen ein Fuder Holz in die Stadt und verkaufte es für zwei Taler an einen Doktor. Wie ihm nun das Geld ausbezahlt wurde, saß der Doktor gerade zu Tisch, da sah der Bauer, was er schön aß und trank, und das Herz ging ihm danach auf, und er wär auch gern ein Doktor gewesen. Also blieb er noch ein Weilchen stehen und fragte endlich, ob er nicht auch könnte ein Doktor werden. »O ja«, sagte der Doktor, »das ist bald geschehen. Zuerst kauf dir ein Abc-Buch, so eins, wo vorne ein Göckelhahn drin ist; mach deinen Wagen und deine zwei Ochsen zu Geld und schaff dir damit Kleider an und was sonst zur Doktorei gehört; drittens laß dir ein Schild malen mit den Worten: Ich bin der Doktor Allwissend, und das oben über deine Haustür nageln.« Der Bauer tat alles, wie's ihm geheißen war. Als er nun ein wenig gedoktert, aber noch nicht viel, ward einem reichen großen Herrn Geld gestohlen. Da ward ihm von dem Doktor Allwissend gesagt, der in dem und dem Dorfe wohnte und wissen müßte, wo das Geld hingekommen wäre. Also ließ der Herr seinen Wagen anspannen, fuhr hinaus ins Dorf und fragte bei ihm an, ob er der Doktor Allwissend wäre? Ja, der wär er. – So sollte er mitgehen und das gestohlene Geld wiederschaffen. O ja, aber die Grete, seine Frau, müßte auch mit. Der Herr war das zufrieden, ließ sie beide in dem Wagen sitzen, und sie fuhren zusammen fort. Als sie auf den adligen Hof kamen, war der Tisch gedeckt; da sollt' er erst mitessen. Ja, aber seine Frau, die Grete, auch, sagte er und setzte sich mit ihr an den Tisch. Wie nun der erste Bediente mit einer Schüssel schönem Essen kam, stieß der Bauer seine Frau an und sagte: »Grete, das war der erste.« Und meinte, es wär derjenige, welcher das erste Essen brächte. Der Bediente aber meinte, er hätte damit sagen wollen, das ist der erste Dieb, und weil er's nun wirklich war, ward ihm angst, und er sagte draußen zu seinen Kameraden: »Der Doktor weiß alles, wir kommen übel an, er hat gesagt, ich wär der erste.« Der zweite wollte gar nicht herein, er mußte aber doch. Wie der nun mit seiner Schüssel herein kam, stieß der Bauer seine Frau an: »Grete, das ist der zweite.« Dem Bedienten ward ebenfalls angst, und er machte, daß er hinauskam. Dem dritten ging's nicht besser, der

Bauer sagte wieder: »Grete, das ist der dritte.« Der vierte mußte eine verdeckte Schüssel hereintragen, und der Herr sprach zum Doktor, er solle seine Kunst zeigen und raten, was darunter läg, es waren aber Krebse. Der Bauer sah die Schüssel an, wußt' nicht, wie er sich helfen sollte, und sprach: »Ach, ich armer Krebs!« Wie der Herr das hörte, rief er: »Da! Er weiß es, nun weiß er auch, wer das Geld hat.«

Dem Bedienten aber ward gewaltig angst, und er blinzelte den Doktor an, er möge einmal herauskommen. Wie er nun hinauskam, gestanden sie ihm alle vier, sie hätten das Geld gestohlen, sie wollten's ja gern herausgeben und ihm eine schwere Summe dazu, wenn er sie nicht verraten wollte; es ging ihnen sonst an den Hals. Sie führten ihn auch hin, wo das Geld versteckt lag. Damit war der Doktor zufrieden, ging wieder hinein und sprach: »Herr, nun will ich in meinem Buch suchen, wo das Geld steckt.« Der fünfte Bediente aber kroch in den Ofen, und wollt' hören, ob der Doktor noch mehr wüßte. Der saß aber und schlug sein Abc-Buch auf, blätterte darin hin und her und suchte den Göckelhahn. Weil er ihn nun nicht gleich finden konnte, sprach er: »Du bist doch darin und mußt auch heraus.« Da meinte der im Ofen, er wär gemeint, sprang voller Schrecken heraus und rief: »Der Mann weiß alles!« Nun zeigte der Doktor Allwissend dem Herrn, wo das Geld lag, sagte aber nicht, wer's gestohlen hatte, bekam von beiden Seiten viel Geld zur Belohnung und ward ein berühmter Mann.   1819

Strohhalm, Kohle und Bohne

In einem Dorfe wohnte eine arme alte Frau, die hatte ein Gericht Bohnen zusammengebracht und wollte sie kochen. Sie machte also auf ihrem Herd ein Feuer zurecht, und damit es desto schneller brennen sollte, zündete sie es mit einer Hand voll Stroh an. Als sie die Bohnen in den Topf schüttete, entfiel ihr unbemerkt eine,

die auf dem Boden neben einen Strohhalm zu liegen kam; bald danach sprang auch eine glühende Kohle vom Herd zu ihnen herab. Da fing der Strohhalm an und sprach: »Liebe Freunde, von wannen kommt ihr her?« Die Kohle antwortete: »Ich bin zu gutem Glück dem Feuer entsprungen, und hätte ich das nicht mit Gewalt durchgesetzt, so war mir der Tod gewiß: ich wäre zu Asche verbrannt.« Die Bohne sagte: »Ich bin auch noch mit heiler Haut davongekommen, aber hätte mich die Alte in den Topf gebracht, ich wäre ohne Barmherzigkeit zu Brei gekocht worden, wie meine Kameraden.« – »Wäre mir denn ein besser Schicksal zuteil geworden?« sprach das Stroh. »Alle meine Brüder hat die Alte in Feuer und Rauch aufgehen lassen, sechzig hat sie auf einmal gepackt und ums Leben gebracht.

Glücklicherweise bin ich ihr zwischen den Fingern durchgeschlüpft.« – »Was sollen wir aber nun anfangen?« sprach die Kohle. »Ich meine«, antwortete die Bohne, »weil wir so glücklich dem Tode entronnen sind, so wollen wir uns als gute Gesellen zusammenhalten und, damit uns hier nicht wieder ein neues Unglück ereilt, gemeinschaftlich auswandern und in ein fremdes Land ziehen.«

Der Vorschlag gefiel den beiden andern, und sie machten sich miteinander auf den Weg. Bald aber kamen sie an einen kleinen Bach, und da keine Brücke oder Steg da war, so wußten sie nicht, wie sie hinüberkommen sollten. Der Strohhalm fand guten Rat und sprach: »Ich will mich querüber legen, so könnt ihr auf mir wie auf einer Brücke hinübergehen.« Der Strohhalm streckte sich also von einem Ufer zum andern, und die Kohle, die von hitziger Natur war, trippelte auch ganz keck auf die neugebaute Brücke. Als sie aber in die Mitte gekommen war und unter ihr das Wasser rauschen hörte, ward ihr doch angst, sie blieb stehen und getraute sich nicht weiter. Der Strohhalm aber fing an zu brennen, zerbrach in zwei Stücke und fiel in den Bach: die Kohle rutschte nach, zischte, wie sie ins Wasser kam, und gab den Geist auf. Die Bohne, die vorsichtigerweise noch auf dem Ufer zurückgeblieben war, mußte über die Geschichte lachen, konnte nicht aufhören und lachte so gewaltig, daß sie zerplatzte. Nun war es ebenfalls um sie geschehen, wenn nicht zu gutem Glück ein Schneider, der auf der Wanderschaft war, sich an dem Bach ausgeruht hätte. Weil er ein mitleidiges Herz hatte, so holte er Nadel und Zwirn heraus und nähte sie zusammen. Die Bohne bedankte sich bei ihm aufs schönste, aber da er schwarzen Zwirn gebraucht hatte, so haben seit der Zeit alle Bohnen eine schwarze Naht.

1837

Von dem Mäuschen, Vögelchen und der Bratwurst

Es waren einmal ein Mäuschen, ein Vögelchen und eine Bratwurst in Gesellschaft geraten, hatten einen Haushalt geführt, lange wohl und köstlich im Frieden gelebt und trefflich an Gütern zugenommen. Des Vögelchens Arbeit war, daß es täglich im Wald fliegen und Holz beibringen mußte. Die Maus sollte Wasser tragen, Feuer anmachen und Tisch decken, die Bratwurst aber sollte kochen.

Wem zu wohl ist, den gelüstet immer nach neuen Dingen! Also eines Tages stieß dem Vöglein unterwegs ein anderer Vogel auf, dem es seine treffliche Gelegenheit erzählet und gerühmet. Derselbe andere Vogel schalt es aber einen armen Tropfen, der große Arbeit, die beiden zu Haus aber gute Tage hätten. Denn, wenn die Maus ihr Feuer angemacht und Wasser getragen hatte, so begab sie sich in ihr Kämmerlein zur Ruhe, bis man sie heiße, den Tisch decken. Das Würstlein blieb

beim Hafen, sah zu, daß die Speise wohl kochte, und wann es bald Essenszeit war, schlingte es sich einmal viere durch den Brei oder das Gemüs, so war es geschmalzen, gesalzen und bereitet. Kam dann das Vöglein heim und legte seine Bürde ab, so saßen sie zu Tisch, und nach gehabtem Mahl schliefen sie sich die Haut voll bis den andern Morgen, und das war ein herrlich Leben.

Das Vöglein anderes Tages wollte aus Anstiftung nicht mehr ins Holz, sprechend: es wäre lang genug Knecht gewest und hätte gleichsam ihr Narr sein müssen, sie sollten einmal umwechseln und es auf eine andere Weise auch versuchen. Und wiewohl die Maus heftig dafür bat, auch die Bratwurst, so war der Vogel doch Meister, es mußte gewagt sein, spielten derowegen und kam das Los auf die Bratwurst, die mußte Holz tragen, die Maus ward Koch, und der Vogel sollte Wasser holen.

Was geschicht? Das Bratwürstchen zog fort gen Holz, das Vöglein machte Feuer an, die Maus stellte den Topf zu und erwarteten allein, bis Bratwürstchen heim käme und Holz für den andern Tag brächte. Es blieb aber das Würstlein so lang unterwegs, daß ihnen beiden nichts Guts vorkam und das Vöglein ein Stück Luft hinaus entgegen flog. Unfern aber findet es einen Hund am Weg, der das arme Bratwürstlein als freie Beute angetroffen, angepackt und niedergemacht.

Das Vöglein beschwerte sich auch dessen als eines offenbaren Raubs sehr gegen den Hund, aber es half kein Wort, denn sprach der Hund, er hätte falsche Briefe bei der Bratwurst gefunden, deswegen wäre sie ihm des Lebens verfallen gewesen.

Das Vöglein, traurig, nahm das Holz auf sich und heim und erzählte, was es gesehn und gehöret. Sie waren sehr betrübt, verglichen sich aber, das Beste zu tun und beisammen zu bleiben. Derowegen so deckte das Vöglein den Tisch, und die Maus rüstete das Essen und wollte anrichten, und in den Hafen wie zuvor das Würstlein, und durch das Gemüs schlingen und schlupfen, dasselbe zu schmelzen; aber ehe sie in die Mitte kam, ward sie angehalten und mußte Haut und Haar und dabei das Leben lassen.

Als das Vöglein kam und wollte das Essen auftragen, da war kein Koch vorhanden. Das Vöglein warf bestürzt das Holz hin und her, rufte und suchte, konnte aber seinen Koch nicht mehr finden. Aus Unachtsamkeit kam das Feuer in das Holz, also daß eine Brunst entstund; das Vöglein eilte Wasser zu langen, da entfiel ihm der Eimer in den Brunnen, und es mit hinab, daß es sich nicht konnte mehr erholen und da ersaufen mußte.

1819

Die Bremer Stadtmusikanten

Es hatte ein Mann einen Esel, der ihm schon lange Jahre treu gedient, dessen Kräfte aber nun zu Ende gingen, so daß er zur Arbeit immer untauglicher ward. Da wollt' ihn der Herr aus dem Futter schaffen, aber der Esel merkte, daß kein guter Wind wehte, lief fort und machte sich auf den Weg nach Bremen; dort, dachte er, kannst du ja Stadtmusikant werden. Als er ein Weilchen fortgegangen war, fand er einen Jagdhund auf dem Wege liegen, der jappte wie einer, der sich müd gelaufen. »Nun, was jappst du so?« sprach der Esel. »Ach«, sagte der Hund, »weil ich alt bin und jeden Tag schwächer werde und auf der Jagd nicht mehr fort kann, hat mich mein Herr wollen totschlagen, da habe ich Reißaus genommen; aber womit soll ich nun mein Brot verdienen?« – »Weißt du was«, sprach der Esel, »ich gehe nach Bremen, dort Stadtmusikant zu werden, geh mit und laß dich auch bei der Musik annehmen.« Der Hund war's zufrieden, und sie gingen weiter. Es dauerte nicht lange, so saß da eine Katze auf dem Weg und machte ein gar trübselig Gesicht. »Nun, was ist dir denn in die Quere gekommen?« sprach der Esel. »Ei«, antwortete die Katze, »wer kann da lustig sein, wenn's einem an den Kragen geht? Weil ich nun zu Jahren komme, meine Zähne stumpf werden und ich lieber hinter dem Ofen sitze und spinne, als nach den Mäusen herumjage, hat mich meine Frau ersäufen wollen; ich hab mich zwar noch fortgemacht, aber nun ist guter Rat teuer; wo soll ich hin?« – »Geh mit uns nach Bremen, du verstehst dich doch auf die Nachtmusik, da kannst du ein Stadtmusikant werden.« Die Katze war's zufrieden und ging mit. Darauf kamen die drei Landesflüchtigen an einem Hof vorbei, da saß auf dem Tor der Haushahn und schrie aus Leibeskräften. »Du schreist einem durch Mark und Bein«, sprach der Esel, »was hast du vor?« – »Da hab ich gut Wetter prophezeit«, sprach der Hahn, »weil unserer lieben Frauen Tag ist, wo sie dem Christkindlein die Tücher gewaschen hat und sie trocknen will, aber weil morgen zum Sonntag Gäste kommen, so hat die Hausfrau doch kein Erbarmen und der Köchin gesagt, sie wollte mich morgen in der Suppe essen, und da soll ich mir heut abend den Kopf abschneiden lassen. Nun schrei ich aus vollem Hals, so lang ich noch kann.« – »Ei was, du Rotkopf«, sagte der Esel, »zieh lieber mit uns fort, wir gehen nach Bremen, etwas Besseres als den Tod findest du überall. Du hast eine gute Stimme, und wenn wir zusammen musizieren, so muß es eine Art haben.« Der Hahn ließ sich den Vorschlag gefallen, und sie gingen alle vier zusammen fort.

Sie konnten aber die Stadt Bremen an einem Tag nicht erreichen und kamen abends in einen Wald, wo sie übernachten wollten. Der Esel und der Hund legten sich unter einen großen Baum, und die Katze und der Hahn machten sich hinauf, der Hahn flog bis in die Spitze, wo's am sichersten für ihn war, und sah sich, ehe er einschlief, noch einmal nach allen vier Winden um. Da deuchte ihn, er säh in der Ferne ein Fünkchen brennen, und rief seinen Gesellen zu, es müßte nicht gar weit ein Haus sein, denn es scheine ein Licht. Sprach der Esel: »So müssen wir uns aufmachen und noch hingehen, denn hier ist die Herberge schlecht«, und der Hund sagte: »Ja, ein paar Knochen und etwas Fleisch täten mir auch gut!« Nun machten sie sich auf den Weg nach der Gegend, wo das Licht war, und sahen es bald heller schimmern, und es ward immer größer, bis sie vor ein hell erleuchtetes Räuberhaus kamen. Der Esel, als der größte, machte sich ans Fenster und schaute hinein. »Was siehst du, Grauschimmel?« fragte der Hahn. »Was ich sehe?« antwortete der Esel, »einen gedeckten Tisch mit schönem Essen und Trinken, und Räuber sitzen daran und lassen's sich wohl sein.« – »Das wär was für uns«, sprach der Hahn. »Ia, Ia, ach wären wir da!« sagte der Esel. Da ratschlagten die Tiere, wie's anzufangen wäre, um die Räuber fortzubringen, endlich fanden sie ein Mittel. Der Esel mußte sich mit den Vorderfüßen auf das Fenster stellen, der Hund auf des Esels Rücken, die Katze auf den Hund klettern, und endlich flog der Hahn hinauf und setzte sich der Katze auf den Kopf. Wie das geschehen war, fingen sie insgesamt auf ein Zeichen an, ihre Musik zu machen; der Esel schrie, der Hund bellte, die Katze miaute, und der Hahn krähte, indem stürzten sie durch das Fenster in die Stube hinein, daß die Scheiben klirrend niederfielen. Die Räuber, die schon über das entsetzliche Geschrei erschrocken waren, meinten nicht anders, als ein Gespenst käm herein, und entflohen in größter Furcht in den Wald. Nun

setzten sich die vier Gesellen an den Tisch, nahmen mit dem vorlieb, was übriggeblieben war, und aßen, als wenn sie vier Wochen hungern sollten.

Wie die vier Spielleute fertig waren, löschten sie das Licht aus und suchten sich eine Schlafstätte, jeder nach seiner Natur und Bequemlichkeit. Der Esel legte sich auf den Mist, der Hund hinter die Türe, die Katze auf den Herd bei der warmen Asche, und der Hahn setzte sich auf den Hahnenbalken, und weil sie müd waren von ihrem Weg, schliefen sie auch bald ein.

Als Mitternacht vorbei war und die Räuber von weitem sahen, daß kein Licht mehr im Haus war, auch alles ruhig schien, sprach der Hauptmann: »Wir hätten uns doch nicht sollen ins Bockshorn jagen lassen«, und hieß einen hingehen und das Haus untersuchen. Der Abgeschickte fand alles still, ging in die Küche, wollte ein Licht anzünden und nahm ein Schwefelhölzchen, und weil er die glühenden, feurigen Augen der Katze für lebendige Kohlen ansah, hielt er es daran, daß es Feuer fangen sollte. Aber die Katze verstand keinen Spaß, sprang ihm ins Gesicht, spie und kratzte. Da erschrak er gewaltig, lief und wollte zur Hintertüre hinaus, aber der Hund, der da lag, sprang auf und biß ihm ins Bein, und als er über den Hof an dem Mist vorbei rannte, gab ihm der Esel noch einen tüchtigen Schlag mit dem Hinterfuß, der Hahn aber, der vom Lärmen aus dem Schlaf geweckt und munter geworden war, rief vom Balken herab: »Kikeriki!« Da lief der Räuber, was er konnte, zu seinem Hauptmann zurück und sprach: »Ach, in dem Haus sitzt eine greuliche Hexe, die hat mich angehaucht und mit ihren langen Fingern mir das Gesicht zerkratzt, und vor der Türe steht ein Mann mit einem Messer, der hat mich ins Bein gestochen, und auf dem Hof liegt ein schwarzes Ungetüm, das hat mit einer Holzkeule auf mich losgeschlagen, und oben auf dem Dach, da sitzt der Richter, der rief: ›Bringt mir den Schelm her!‹ Da machte ich, daß ich fortkam.« Von nun an getrauten sich die Räuber nicht mehr in das Haus, den vier Bremer Musikanten gefiel's aber so wohl darin, daß sie nicht wieder heraus wollten, und der das zuletzt erzählt hat, dem ist der Mund noch warm. 1819

Hänsel und Gretel

Vor einem großen Walde wohnte ein armer Holzhacker, der hatte nichts zu beißen und zu brechen und kaum das tägliche Brot für seine Frau und seine zwei Kinder, Hänsel und Gretel. Endlich kam die Zeit, da konnte er auch das nicht schaffen, und wußte keine Hilfe mehr für seine Not. Wie er sich nun abends vor Sorge im Bett herumwälzte, sprach seine Frau zu ihm: »Höre, Mann, morgen früh nimm die beiden Kinder, gib jedem noch ein Stückchen Brot, dann führ sie hinaus in den Wald, mitten hinein, wo er am dicksten ist, da mach ihnen ein Feuer an, und dann geh weg und laß sie dort allein, wir können sie nicht länger ernähren.« — »Nein, Frau«, sagte der Mann, »das kann ich nicht über mein Herz bringen, meine eigenen lieben Kinder den wilden Tieren im Wald zu bringen, die sie bald würden zerrissen haben.« — »Nun, wenn du das nicht tust«, sprach die Frau, »so müssen wir alle miteinander Hungers sterben.« Und ließ ihm keine Ruhe, bis er einwilligte.

Die zwei Kinder waren auch noch vor Hunger wach gewesen und hatten mit angehört, was die Mutter zum Vater gesagt hatte. Gretel dachte, nun ist es um mich geschehen, und fing erbärmlich an zu weinen, Hänsel aber sprach: »Sei still, Gretel, und gräm dich nicht, ich will uns helfen.« Damit stand er auf, zog sein Röcklein an, machte die Untertüre auf und schlich hinaus. Da schien der Mond hell, und die weißen Kieselsteine glänzten wie lauter Batzen. Hänsel bückte sich und steckte so viele in sein Rocktäschlein als nur hinein wollten, dann ging er zurück ins Haus. »Tröste dich, Gretel, und schlaf nur ruhig«, sprach er, legte sich wieder ins Bett und schlief ein.

Morgens früh, ehe die Sonne noch aufgegangen war, kam die Mutter und weckte sie alle beide: »Steht auf, ihr Kinder, wir wollen in den Wald gehen. Da hat jedes von euch ein Stücklein Brot, aber haltet's zu Rate und hebt's euch für den Mittag auf.« Gretel nahm das Brot unter die Schürze, weil Hänsel die Steine in der Tasche hatte, dann machten sie sich auf den Weg zum Wald hinein. Wie sie ein Weilchen gegangen waren, stand Hänsel still und guckte nach dem Haus zurück, bald darauf wieder und immer wieder. Der Vater sprach: »Hänsel, was guckst du zurück und hältst dich auf, hab acht und heb deine Beine auf.« — »Ach, Vater, ich seh nach meinem weißen Kätzchen, das sitzt oben auf dem Dach und will mir ade sagen.« Die Mutter sprach: »Ei, Narr, das ist dein Kätzchen nicht, das ist die Morgensonne, die auf den Schornstein scheint.« Hänsel aber hatte nicht nach dem Kätzchen gesehen, sondern immer einen von den blanken Kieselsteinen aus seiner Tasche auf den Weg geworfen.

Wie sie mitten in den Wald gekommen waren, sprach der Vater: »Nun sammelt Holz, ihr Kinder, ich will ein Feuer anmachen, daß wir nicht frieren.« Hänsel und

Gretel trugen Reisig zusammen, einen kleinen Berg hoch. Da steckten sie es an, und wie die Flamme recht groß brannte, sagte die Mutter: »Nun legt euch ans Feuer und schlaft, wir wollen in dem Wald das Holz fällen, wartet, bis wir wiederkommen und euch abholen.«

Hänsel und Gretel saßen an dem Feuer, bis Mittag, da aß jedes sein Stücklein Brot. Sie glaubten, der Vater wär noch im Wald, weil sie die Schläge seiner Axt hörten, aber das war ein Ast, den er an einen Baum gebunden hatte und den der Wind hin und her schlug. Nun warteten sie bis zum Abend, aber Vater und Mutter blieben aus, und niemand wollte kommen und sie abholen. Wie es nun finstere Nacht wurde, fing Gretel an zu weinen, Hänsel aber sprach: »Wart nur ein Weilchen, bis der Mond aufgegangen ist.« Und als der Mond aufgegangen war, faßte er die Gretel bei der Hand, und da lagen die Kieselsteine und schimmerten wie neugeschlagene Batzen und zeigten ihnen den Weg. Da gingen sie die ganze Nacht durch, und wie es Morgen war, kamen sie wieder bei ihres Vaters Haus an. Der Vater freute sich von Herzen, als er seine Kinder wiedersah; denn es hatte ihm doch weh getan, wie er sie allein gelassen; die Mutter stellte sich auch, als wenn sie sich freute, heimlich aber war sie bös.

Nicht lange danach war wieder kein Brot im Hause, und Hänsel und Gretel hörten, wie abends die Mutter zum Vater sagte: »Einmal haben die Kinder den Weg zurückgefunden, und da habe ich's gut sein lassen; aber jetzt ist wieder nichts als nur noch ein halber Laib Brot im Haus, du mußt sie morgen tiefer in den Wald führen, daß sie den Weg nicht zurückfinden. Es ist sonst keine Hilfe für uns mehr.«

Dem Mann fiel's schwer aufs Herz, und er gedachte, es wäre doch besser, wenn du den letzten Bissen mit deinen Kindern teiltest, weil er es aber einmal getan hatte, so dürfte er nicht nein sagen. Als die Kinder das Gespräch gehört hatten, stand Hänsel auf und wollte wieder Kieselsteine auflesen, wie er aber an die Türe kam, da hatte sie die Mutter zugeschlossen. Doch tröstete er die Gretel und sprach: »Schlaf nur, lieb Gretel, der liebe Gott wird uns schon helfen.«

Morgens früh erhielten sie ihr Stücklein Brot, noch kleiner als das vorige Mal. Auf dem Wege bröckelte es Hänsel in der Tasche, stand oft still und warf ein Bröcklein auf die Erde. »Was bleibst du immer stehen, Hänsel, und guckst dich um«, sagte der Vater, »geh deiner Wege.« − »Ach! Ich seh nach meinem Täubchen, das sitzt auf dem Dach und will mir ade sagen.« − »Du Narr«, sagte die Mutter, »das ist dein Täubchen nicht, das ist die Morgensonne, die auf den Schornstein oben scheint.« Hänsel aber zerbröckelte all sein Brot und warf die Bröcklein auf den Weg.

Die Mutter führte sie noch tiefer in den Wald hinein, wo sie ihr Lebtag nicht gewesen waren, da sollten sie wieder bei einem großen Feuer sitzen und schlafen, und abends wollten die Eltern kommen und sie abholen. Zu Mittag teilte Gretel ihr Brot mit Hänsel, weil der seins all auf den Weg gestreut hatte. Aber der Mittag verging und der Abend verging, und niemand kam zu den armen Kindern. Hänsel tröstete die Gretel und sagte: »Wart, wenn der Mond aufgeht, dann seh ich die Bröcklein Brot, die ich ausgestreut habe, die zeigen uns den Weg nach Haus.« Der Mond ging auf, wie aber Hänsel nach den Bröcklein sah, da waren sie weg. Die viel tausend Vöglein in dem Wald, die hatten sie gefunden und aufgepickt. Hänsel meinte doch den Weg nach Haus zu finden und zog die Gretel mit sich, aber sie verirrten sich bald in der großen Wildnis und gingen die Nacht und den ganzen Tag, da schliefen sie vor Müdigkeit ein. Dann gingen sie noch einen Tag, aber kamen nicht aus dem Wald heraus und waren so hungrig; denn sie hatten nichts zu essen als ein paar kleine Beerlein, die auf der Erde standen.

Als sie am dritten Tage wieder bis zu Mittag gegangen waren, da kamen sie an ein Häuslein, das war ganz aus Brot gebaut und war mit Kuchen gedeckt, und die Fenster waren von hellem Zucker. »Da wollen wir uns niedersetzen und uns sattessen«, sagte Hänsel. »Ich will vom Dach essen, iß du vom Fenster, Gretel, das ist fein süß für dich.«

Wie nun Gretel an dem Zucker knusperte, rief drinnen eine feine Stimme:

>>Knusper, knusper, Kneischen,
wer knuspert an meinem Häuschen!<<

Die Kinder antworteten:

>>Der Wind, der Wind,
das himmlische Kind!<<

Und aßen weiter. Gretel brach sich eine ganze runde Fensterscheibe heraus, und
Hänsel riß sich ein gewaltig Stück Kuchen vom Dach ab. Da ging die Türe auf und
eine steinalte Frau, die sich auf eine Krücke stützte, kam heraus. Hänsel und Gretel
erschraken so gewaltig, daß sie fallen ließen, was sie in Händen hatten. Die Alte
aber wackelte mit dem Kopf und sagte: >>Ei, ihr lieben Kinder, wo seid ihr denn
hergelaufen, kommt herein, ihr sollt's gut haben<<, faßte beide an der Hand und
führte sie in ihr Häuschen. Da ward gutes Essen aufgetragen, Milch und Pfann-
kuchen mit Zucker, Äpfel und Nüsse, und dann wurden zwei schöne Bettlein
bereitet, da legten sich Hänsel und Gretel hinein, und meinten, sie wären wie im
Himmel.

Die Alte aber war eine böse Hexe, die lauerte den Kindern auf und hatte, um sie
zu locken, ihr Brothäuslein gebaut, und wenn eins in ihre Gewalt kam, da machte
sie es tot, kochte es und aß es, und das war ihr ein Festtag. Da war sie nun recht
froh, wie Hänsel und Gretel ihr zugelaufen kamen. Früh, ehe sie noch erwacht
waren, stand sie schon auf, ging an ihre Bettlein, und wie sie die zwei so lieblich
ruhen sah, freute sie sich und murmelte: >>Das wird ein guter Bissen für mich sein!<<
Darauf packte sie den Hänsel und steckte ihn in einen kleinen Stall. Wie er nun
aufwachte, war er von einem Gitter umschlossen, wie man junge Hühnlein ein-
sperrt, und konnte nur ein paar Schritte gehen. Die Gretel aber schüttelte sie und
rief: >>Steh auf, du Faullenzerin, hol Wasser und geh in die Küche und koch was
Gutes zu essen. Dort steckt dein Bruder in einem Stall, den will ich erst fettmachen,
und wenn er fett ist, dann will ich ihn essen. Jetzt sollst du ihn füttern.<< Gretel
erschrak und weinte, mußte aber tun, was die Hexe verlangte. Da ward nun alle
Tage dem Hänsel das beste Essen gekocht, daß er fett werden sollte, Gretel aber
bekam nichts als die Krebsschalen, und alle Tage kam die Alte und sagte: >>Hänsel,
streck deine Finger heraus, daß ich fühle, ob du bald fett genug bist.<< Hänsel
streckte ihr aber immer ein Knöchlein heraus, da verwunderte sie sich, daß er gar
nicht zunehmen wolle.

Nach vier Wochen sagte sie eines Abends zu Gretel: >>Sei flink, geh und trag
Wasser herbei, dein Brüderchen mag nun fett sein oder nicht, morgen will ich es
schlachten und sieden. Ich will derweil den Teig anmachen, daß wir auch dazu

backen können.« Da ging Gretel mit traurigem Herzen und trug das Wasser, worin Hänsel sollte gesotten werden. Früh morgens mußte Gretel aufstehen, Feuer anmachen und den Kessel mit Wasser aufhängen. »Gib nun acht«, sagte die Hexe, »ich will Feuer in den Backofen machen und das Brot hineinschieben.« Gretel stand in der Küche und weinte und dachte, hätten uns lieber die wilden Tiere im Walde gefressen, so wären wir zusammen gestorben und müßten nun nicht das Herzeleid tragen, und ich müßte nicht selber das Wasser zu dem Tod meines lieben Bruders sieden. »Du lieber Gott, hilf uns armen Kindern aus der Not.«

Da rief die Alte: »Gretel, komm gleich hierher zu dem Backofen!« Wie Gretel kam, sagte sie: »Guck hinein, ob das Brot schon hübsch braun und gar ist, meine Augen sind schwach, ich kann nicht so weit sehen, und wenn du auch nicht kannst, so setz dich auf das Brett, so will ich dich hineinschieben, da kannst du darin herumgehen und nachsehen.« Wenn aber Gretel darin war, da wollte sie zumachen, und Gretel sollte in dem heißen Ofen backen, und sie wollte sie auch aufessen. Das dachte die böse Hexe und darum hatte sie Gretel gerufen. Gott gab es aber dem Mädchen ein, daß es sprach: »Ich weiß nicht, wie ich das anfangen soll, zeige mir's erst und setz dich auf, ich will dich hineinschieben.« Da setzte sich die Alte auf das Brett, und weil sie leicht war, schob Gretel sie hinein, so weit sie konnte, und dann machte sie geschwind die Türe zu und steckte den eisernen Riegel vor. Nun fing die Alte an in dem heißen Backofen zu schreien und zu jammern, Gretel aber lief fort, und sie mußte elendiglich verbrennen.

Da lief Gretel zum Hänsel, machte ihm sein Türchen auf und rief: »Spring heraus, Hänsel, wir sind erlöst!« Da sprang Hänsel heraus wie ein eingesperrtes Vöglein aus dem Bauer. Und sie weinten vor Freude und küßten sich einander. Das ganze Häuschen aber war voll von Edelgesteinen und Perlen, damit füllten sie ihre Taschen, gingen fort und suchten den Weg nach Haus. Sie kamen aber vor ein großes Wasser und konnten nicht hinüber. Da sah das Schwesterchen ein weißes Entchen hin und her schwimmen, dem rief es zu: »Ach, liebes Entchen, nimm uns auf deinen Rücken.« Als das Entchen das hörte, kam es geschwommen und trug die Gretel hinüber, und hernach holte es auch den Hänsel. Danach fanden sie bald ihre Heimat. Der Vater freute sich herzlich, als er sie wiedersah; denn er hatte keinen vergnügten Tag gehabt, seit seine Kinder fort waren. Die Mutter aber war gestorben. Nun brachten die Kinder Reichtümer genug mit, und sie brauchten für Essen und Trinken nicht mehr zu sorgen.

1819

Die treuen Tiere

Es war einmal ein Mann, der hatte gar nicht viel Geld, und mit dem wenigen, das ihm übrig blieb, zog er in die weite Welt. Da kam er in ein Dorf, wo die Jungen zusammenliefen, schrien und lärmten. »Was habt ihr vor, ihr Jungen?« fragte der Mann. »Ei«, antworteten sie, »da haben wir eine Maus, die muß uns tanzen, seht einmal, was das für ein Spaß ist, wie die herumtrippelt!« Den Mann aber dauerte das arme Tierchen, und er sprach: »Laßt die Maus laufen, ihr Jungen, ich will euch auch Geld geben.« Da gab er ihnen Geld, und sie ließen die Maus gehen; die lief, was sie konnte, in ein Loch hinein. Der Mann ging fort und kam in ein anderes Dorf, da hatten die Jungen einen Affen, der mußte tanzen und Purzelbäume machen, und sie lachten darüber und ließen dem Tier keine Ruh. Da gab ihnen der Mann auch Geld, damit sie den Affen losließen. Danach kam der Mann in ein

drittes Dorf, da hatten die Jungen einen Bären und ließen ihn tanzen, und wenn er dazu brummte, war's ihnen eben recht. Da kaufte ihn der Mann auch los, und der Bär war froh, daß er wieder auf seine vier Beine kam und trabte fort.

Der Mann aber hatte nun sein bißchen übriges Geld ausgegeben und keinen roten Heller mehr in der Tasche. Da sprach er zu sich selber: »Der König hat so viel in seiner Schatzkammer, was er nicht braucht, Hungers kannst du nicht sterben, du willst da etwas nehmen, und wenn du wieder zu Geld kommst, kannst du's ja wieder hineinlegen.« Also machte er sich über die Schatzkammer und nahm sich ein wenig davon; allein beim Herausschleichen ward er von den Leuten des Königs erwischt. Sie sagten, er wäre ein Dieb, und führten ihn vor Gericht, da ward er verurteilt, daß er in einem Kasten sollte aufs Wasser gesetzt werden. Der Kastendeckel war voller Löcher, damit Luft hinein konnte, auch ward ihm ein Krug Wasser und ein Laib Brot mit hineingegeben. Wie er nun so auf dem Wasser schwamm und recht in Angst war, hört er was krabbeln am Schloß, nagen und schnauben. Auf einmal springt das Schloß auf und der Deckel in die Höh, und stehen da Maus, Affe und Bär, die hatten's getan. Weil er ihnen geholfen, wollten sie ihm wieder helfen. Nun wußten sie aber nicht, was sie noch weiter tun sollten und ratschlagten miteinander. Indem kam ein weißer Stein auf dem Wasser dahergeschwommen, der sah aus wie ein rundes Ei. Da sagte der Bär: »Der kommt zu rechter Zeit, das ist ein Wunderstein, wem der eigen ist, der kann sich wünschen, wozu er nur Lust hat.« Da fing der Mann den Stein, und wie er ihn in der Hand hielt, wünschte er sich ein Schloß mit Garten und Marstall, und kaum hatte er den Wunsch gesagt, so saß er in dem Schloß mit dem Garten und dem Marstall, und war alles so schön und prächtig, daß er sich nicht genug verwundern konnte.

Nach einiger Zeit zogen Kaufleute des Wegs vorbei. »Sieh einmal einer«, riefen sie, »was da für ein herrliches Schloß steht, und das letztemal, wie wir vorbeikamen, lag da noch schlechter Sand.« Weil sie nun neugierig waren, gingen sie hinein und erkundigten sich bei dem Mann, wie er alles so geschwind hätte bauen können. Da sprach er: »Das hab ich nicht getan, sondern mein Wunderstein.« – »Was ist das für ein Stein?« fragten sie. Da ging er hin und holte ihn und zeigte ihn den Kaufleuten. Die hatten große Lust dazu und fragten, ob er nicht zu erhandeln wäre, auch boten sie ihm alle ihre schönen Waren dafür. Dem Manne stachen die Waren in die Augen, und weil das Herz unbeständig ist, ließ er sich betören und meinte, die schönen Waren seien mehr wert als sein Wunderstein, und gab ihn hin. Kaum aber hatte er ihn aus den Händen gegeben, da war auch alles Glück dahin, und er saß auf einmal wieder in dem verschlossenen Kasten auf dem Fluß mit einem Krug Wasser und einem Laib Brot. Die treuen Tiere, Maus, Affe und Bär, wie sie sein Unglück sahen, kamen wieder und wollten ihm helfen, aber sie konnten nicht einmal das Schloß aufsprengen, weil's viel fester war als das erste Mal. Da sprach der Bär: »Wir müssen den Wunderstein wiederschaffen, oder es ist alles umsonst.«

Weil nun die Kaufleute in dem Schloß noch wohnten, gingen die Tiere miteinander hin, und wie sie nah dabei kamen, sagte der Bär: »Maus, geh hin und guck durchs Schlüsselloch und sieh, was anzufangen ist, du bist klein, dich merkt kein Mensch.« Die Maus war willig, kam aber wieder und sagte: »Es geht nicht, ich hab hineingeguckt, der Stein hängt unter dem Spiegel an einem roten Bändchen, und hüben und drüben sitzen ein paar große Katzen mit feurigen Augen, die sollen ihn bewachen.« Da sagten die andern: »Geh nur wieder hinein und warte, bis der Herr im Bett liegt und schläft, dann schleich dich durch ein Loch hinein und kriech' aufs Bett und zwick ihn an der Nase und beiß ihm seine Haare ab.« Die Maus ging wieder hinein und tat, wie die andern gesagt hatten, und der Herr wachte auf, rieb sich die Nase, war ärgerlich und sprach: »Die Katzen taugen nichts, sie lassen mir die Mäuse die Haare vom Kopf abbeißen« und jagte sie alle beide fort. Da hatte die Maus gewonnenes Spiel.

Wie nun der Herr die andere Nacht wieder eingeschlafen war, machte sich die Maus hinein, knusperte und nagte an dem roten Band, woran der Stein hing, so lang, bis es entzwei war und herunterfiel, dann schleifte sie's bis zu der Haustür. Da

ward aber der armen kleinen Maus recht sauer, und sie sprach zum Affen, der schon auf der Lauer stand: »Nimm du nun deine Pfote und hol's ganz heraus!« Das war dem Affen ein Leichtes. Er trug den Stein, und sie gingen so miteinander bis zum Fluß; da sagte der Affe: »Wie sollen wir aber nun zu dem Kasten kommen?« Der Bär sagte: »Das ist bald geschehen, ich geh ins Wasser und schwimme, Affe, setz du dich auf meinen Rücken, halt dich aber mit deinen Händen fest und nimm den Stein ins Maul; Mäuschen, du kannst dich in mein rechtes Ohr setzen.« Also taten sie und schwammen den Fluß hinab. Nach einiger Zeit war's dem Bären so still, fing an zu schwatzen und sagte: »Hör, Affe, wir sind doch brave Kameraden, was meinst du?« – Der Affe aber antwortete nicht und schwieg still. »Ei!« sagte der Bär, »willst du mir keine Antwort geben? Das ist ein schlechter Kerl, der nicht antwortet!« Wie der Affe das hört, tut er das Maul auf, läßt den Stein ins Wasser fallen und sagt: »Ich konnt' ja nicht antworten, ich hatte den Stein im Mund, jetzt ist er fort, daran bist du allein schuld.« – »Sei nur ruhig«, sagte der Bär, »wir wollen schon etwas erdenken.« Da beratschlagten sie und riefen die Laubfrösche, Unken und alles Ungeziefer, das im Wasser lebt, zusammen und sagten: »Es kommt ein gewaltiger Feind, macht, daß ihr viele Steine zusammenschafft, so wollen wir euch eine Mauer bauen und euch schützen.« Da erschraken die Tiere und brachten Steine von allen Seiten herbeigeschleppt; endlich kam auch ein alter, dicker Quakfrosch recht aus dem Grund heraufgerudert und hatte das rote Band mit dem Wunderstein im Mund. Wie der Bär das sah, war er vergnügt: »Da haben wir, was wir wollen«, nahm dem Frosch seine Last ab, sagte den Tieren, es sei schon gut, und machte einen kurzen Abschied. Darauf fuhren die drei hinab zu dem Mann im Kasten, sprengten den Deckel mit Hilfe des Steins und kamen noch zu rechter Zeit, denn er hatte das Brot schon aufgezehrt und das Wasser getrunken und war schon halb verschmachtet. Wie er aber den Stein in die Hände bekam, da wünscht' er sich wieder frisch und gesund und in sein schönes Schloß mit dem Garten und Marstall und lebte vergnügt, und die drei Tiere blieben bei ihm und hatten's gut ihr Leben lang.

1819

Hans mein Igel

Es war ein reicher Bauer, der hatte mit seiner Frau keine Kinder. Öfters, wenn er mit den andern Bauern in die Stadt ging, spotteten sie und fragten, warum er keine Kinder hätte. Da ward er einmal zornig, und als er nach Haus kam, sprach er: »Ich will ein Kind haben, und sollt's ein Igel sein.« Da kriegte seine Frau ein Kind, das war oben ein Igel und unten ein Junge, und als sie das Kind sah, erschrak sie und sprach: »Siehst du, du hast uns verwünscht!« Da sprach der Mann: »Was kann das alles helfen, getauft muß der Junge werden, aber wir können keinen Gevatter dazu nehmen.« Die Frau sprach: »Wir können ihn auch nicht anders taufen als Hans mein Igel.« Als er getauft war, sagte der Pfarrer: »Der kann wegen seiner Stacheln in kein ordentlich Bett kommen.« Da ward hinter dem Ofen ein wenig Stroh zurecht gemacht und Hans mein Igel darauf gelegt. Er konnte auch an der Mutter nicht trinken, denn er hätte sie mit seinen Stacheln gestochen. So lag er da hinter dem Ofen acht Jahre, und sein Vater war ihn müde und dachte, wenn er nur stürbe; aber er starb nicht, sondern blieb da liegen.

Nun trug es sich zu, daß in der Stadt ein Markt war, und der Bauer wollte darauf gehen. Da fragte er seine Frau, was er ihr sollte mitbringen. »Ein wenig Fleisch und ein paar Wecke, was zum Haushalt gehört«, sprach sie. Darauf fragte er die Magd, die wollte ein Paar Pantoffeln und Zwickelstrümpfe. Endlich sagte er auch: »Hans

mein Igel, was willst du denn haben?« – »Väterchen«, sprach er, »bring mir doch einen Dudelsack mit.« Wie nun der Bauer wieder nach Haus kam, gab er der Frau, was er ihr mitgebracht hatte, Fleisch und Wecke, dann gab er der Magd die Pantoffeln und die Zwickelstrümpfe, endlich ging er hinter den Ofen und gab dem Hans mein Igel den Dudelsack. Und wie Hans mein Igel den hatte, sprach er: »Väterchen, geh doch vor die Schmiede und laß mir meinen Göckelhahn beschlagen, dann will ich fortreiten und will nimmermehr wiederkommen.« Da war der Vater froh, daß er ihn los werden sollte, und ließ ihm den Hahn beschlagen, und als er fertig war, setzte sich Hans mein Igel darauf, ritt fort, nahm auch Schweine und Esel mit, die wollt' er draußen im Walde hüten. Im Wald aber mußte der Hahn mit ihm auf einen hohen Baum fliegen, da saß er und hütete die Esel und Schweine, und saß lange Jahre, bis die Herde ganz groß war, und wußte sein Vater nichts von ihm. Wenn er aber auf dem Baum saß, blies er seinen Dudelsack und machte Musik, die war sehr schön. Einmal kam ein König vorbeigefahren, der hatte sich verirrt und hörte die Musik; da verwunderte er sich darüber und schickte seinen Bedienten hin, er sollte sich einmal umgucken, wo die Musik herkäme. Der guckte sich um, sah aber nichts als ein kleines Tier auf dem Baum oben sitzen, das war wie ein Göckelhahn, auf dem ein Igel saß, und machte die Musik. Da sprach der König zum Bedienten, er sollte fragen, warum es da säße und ob es nicht wüßte, wo der Weg in sein Königreich ging. Da stieg Hans mein Igel vom Baum und sprach, er wollte den Weg zeigen, wenn der König ihm wollte verschreiben und versprechen, was ihm zuerst begegnete am königlichen Hofe, wenn er nach Haus käme. Da dachte der König, das kannst du leicht tun, Hans mein Igel versteht's doch nicht, und kannst schreiben, was du willst. Da nahm der König Feder und Tinte und schrieb etwas auf, und als es geschehen war, zeigte Hans mein Igel ihm den Weg, und er kam glücklich nach Haus. Seine Tochter aber, wie sie ihn von weitem sah, war so voll Freuden, daß sie ihm entgegenging und ihn küßte. Er dachte an Hans mein Igel und erzählte ihr, wie es ihm gegangen wäre, und daß er an ein wunderliches Tier, das auf einem Hahn geritten und schöne Musik gemacht, hätte verschreiben sollen, was ihm daheim zuerst begegnen würde; er hätte aber geschrieben, er sollt's nicht haben, denn Hans mein Igel könnt es doch nicht lesen. Darüber war die Prinzessin froh und sagte, das wäre gut, denn sie wäre doch nimmermehr hingegangen.

Hans mein Igel aber hütete die Esel und Schweine, war immer lustig, saß auf dem Baum und blies auf seinem Dudelsack. Nun geschah es, daß ein anderer König gefahren kam mit seinen Bedienten und Läufern, und hatte sich verirrt und wußte nicht wieder nach Haus zu kommen, weil der Wald so groß war. Da hörte er gleichfalls die schöne Musik von weitem und sprach zu seinem Läufer, was das wohl wäre, er sollt' einmal zusehen, woher es käme. Da ging der Läufer hin unter den Baum und sah den Göckelhahn sitzen und Hans mein Igel oben drauf. Der Läufer fragte ihn, was er da oben vorhätte. »Ich hüte meine Esel und Schweine; was ist Euer Begehren?« Der Läufer sagte, sie hätten sich verirrt und könnten nicht wieder ins Königreich, ob er ihnen den Weg nicht zeigen wollte. Da stieg Hans mein Igel mit dem Hahn vom Baum herunter und sagte zu dem alten König, er wollt' ihm den Weg zeigen, wenn er ihm zu eigen geben wollte, was ihm zu Haus vor seinem königlichen Schloß das erste begegnen würde. Der König sagte ja und unterschrieb sich dem Hans mein Igel, er sollt' es haben. Als das geschehen war, ritt er auf dem Göckelhahn voraus und zeigte ihm den Weg und gelangte er glücklich wieder in sein Königreich. Wie er auf den Hof kam, war große Freude darüber. Nun hatte er eine einzige Tochter, die war sehr schön, die kam ihm entgegen, fiel ihm um den Hals und küßte ihn und freute sich, daß ihr alter Vater wieder kam. Sie fragte ihn auch, wo er so lang in der Welt gewesen wäre, da erzählte er ihr, er hätte sich verirrt und wär beinahe gar nicht wiedergekommen, aber als er durch einen großen Wald gefahren, hätte einer halb wie ein Igel, halb wie ein Mensch rittlings auf einem Hahn in einem hohen Baum gesessen und schöne Musik gemacht, der hätte ihm fortgeholfen und den Weg gezeigt, dafür habe er ihm versprochen, was ihm am königlichen Hofe zuerst begegnete, und das wäre sie, und das täte ihm nun so leid. Da versprach sie ihm aber, sie wollte gern mit ihm gehen, wenn er käme, ihrem alten Vater zuliebe.

Hans mein Igel aber hütete seine Schweine, und die Schweine bekamen wieder Schweine und diese wieder und wurden ihrer so viele, daß der ganze Wald voll war. Da ließ Hans mein Igel seinem Vater sagen, sie sollten alle Ställe im Dorf leer

machen und räumen, er käme mit einer so großen Herde Schweine, daß jeder schlachten sollte, der nur schlachten könnte. Da war sein Vater betrübt, als er das hörte, denn er dachte, Hans mein Igel wäre schon lang gestorben. Hans mein Igel aber setzte sich auf seinen Göckelhahn, trieb die Schweine vor sich her ins Dorf und ließ schlachten. Hu, da war ein Gemetzel und ein Hacken, daß man's zwei Stunden weit hören konnte. Danach sagte Hans mein Igel: »Väterchen, laß mir meinen Göckelhahn noch einmal vor der Schmiede beschlagen, dann reit ich fort und komm mein Lebtag nicht wieder.« Da ließ der Vater den Göckelhahn beschlagen und war froh, daß Hans mein Igel nicht wiederkommen wollte.

Hans mein Igel ritt fort in das erste Königreich, da hatte der König befohlen, wenn einer käme auf einem Hahn geritten und hätte einen Dudelsack bei sich, dann sollten alle auf ihn schießen, hauen und stechen, damit er nicht ins Schloß käme. Als nun Hans mein Igel dahergeritten kam, drangen sie mit den Bajonetten auf ihn ein, er aber gab dem Hahn die Sporen, flog auf, über das Tor hin vor des Königs Fenster, setzte sich da und rief ihm zu: Er sollt' ihm geben, was er versprochen hätte, sonst wollt' er ihm und seiner Tochter das Leben nehmen. Da gab der König seiner Tochter gute Worte, sie möchte zu ihm hinausgehen, damit sie ihm und sich das Leben rettete. Da zog sie sich weiß an, und ihr Vater gab ihr einen Wagen mit sechs Pferden und herrlichen Bedienten, Geld und Gut. Sie setzte sich hinein, und Hans mein Igel mit seinem Hahn und Dudelsack neben sie, dann nahmen sie Abschied und zogen fort, und der König dachte, er kriegte sie nicht wieder zu sehen. Es ging aber anders, als er dachte, denn als sie ein Stück Wegs von der Stadt waren, da zog sie Hans mein Igel aus und stach sie mit seiner Igelhaut, bis sie ganz blutig war, sagte: »Das ist der Lohn für Eure Falschheit, geh hin, ich will dich nicht«, und jagte sie damit nach Haus, und war sie beschimpft ihr Leben lang.

Hans mein Igel aber ritt weiter auf seinem Göckelhahn und mit seinem Dudelsack nach dem zweiten Königreich, wo er dem König auch den Weg gezeigt hatte. Der aber hatte bestellt, wenn einer käm wie Hans mein Igel, sollten sie das Gewehr vor ihm präsentieren, ihn frei hereinführen, Vivat rufen und ihn ins königliche Schloß bringen. Wie ihn nun die Prinzessin sah, war sie erschrocken, weil er doch gar so wunderlich aussah, sie dachte aber, es wäre nicht anders, sie hätte es ihrem Vater versprochen. Da ward Hans mein Igel von ihr bewillkommt, mußte mit an die königliche Tafel gehen, und sie setzte sich zu seiner Seite, und sie aßen und tranken. Wie's nun Abend ward, daß sie wollten schlafen gehen, da fürchtete sie sich sehr vor seinen Stacheln, er aber sprach, sie sollte sich nicht fürchten, es geschäh ihr kein Leid, und sagte zu dem alten König, er sollte vier Mann bestellen, die sollten wachen vor der Kammertüre und ein großes Feuer anmachen, und wenn er in die Kammer hineingehe und sich ins Bett legen wolle, würde er aus seiner Igelshaut herauskriechen und sie vor dem Bett liegen lassen; dann sollten die Männer hurtig herbeispringen und sie ins Feuer werfen, auch dabei bleiben, bis sie vom Feuer verzehrt wäre. Wie die Glocke nun elf schlug, da ging er in die Kammer und streifte die Igelshaut ab und ließ sie vor dem Bett liegen, da kamen die Männer und holten sie geschwind und warfen sie ins Feuer, und als sie das Feuer verzehrt hatte, da war er erlöst und lag da im Bett ganz als ein Mensch gestaltet, aber er war kohlschwarz wie gebrannt. Der König schickte zu seinem Arzt, der wusch ihn mit guten Salben und balsamierte ihn, da ward er weiß und war ein schöner junger Herr. Wie das die Prinzessin sah, war sie froh, und sie standen auf mit Freuden, aßen und tranken und ward die Vermählung gehalten, und Hans mein Igel bekam das Königreich von dem alten König.

Wie etliche Jahre herum waren, fuhr er mit seiner Gemahlin zu seinem Vater und sagte, er wäre sein Sohn, der Vater aber sprach, er hätte keinen, er hätte nur einen gehabt, der wär aber wie ein Igel mit Stacheln geboren worden und in die Welt gegangen. Da gab er sich zu erkennen, und der alte Vater freute sich und ging mit ihm in sein Königreich.

1819

Das singende, springende Löweneckerchen

Es war einmal ein Mann, der hatte eine große Reise vor, und beim Abschied fragte er seine drei Töchter, was er ihnen mitbringen sollte. Da wollte die älteste Perlen, die zweite Diamanten, die dritte aber sprach: »Lieber Vater, ich wünsche mir ein singendes, springendes Löweneckerchen (Lerche).« Der Vater sagte: »Ja, wenn ich es kriegen kann, sollst du es haben«, küßte alle drei und zog fort. Als nun die Zeit kam, daß er wieder auf dem Heimweg war, hatte er Perlen und Diamanten für die zwei ältesten, aber das singende, springende Löweneckerchen für die jüngste hatte er umsonst allerorten gesucht, und das tat ihm leid, denn sie war sein liebstes Kind. Da führte ihn sein Weg durch einen Wald, und mitten darin war ein prächtiges Schloß, und nah am Schloß stand ein Baum, ganz oben auf der Spitze des Baums aber sah er ein Löweneckerchen singen und springen: »Ei, du kommst mir noch recht!« sagte er und war froh und rief seinem Diener, er solle hinaufsteigen und das Tierchen fangen. Wie der aber an den Baum herantrat, sprang ein Löwe darunter auf, schüttelte sich und brüllte, daß das Laub an den Bäumen zitterte. »Wer mir mein singendes, springendes Löweneckerchen stehlen will, den freß ich auf!« Da sagte der Mann: »Das hab ich nicht gewußt, daß der Vogel dir gehört; kann ich mich nicht von dir loskaufen?« – »Nein!« sprach der Löwe. »Da ist nichts, was dich retten kann, als wenn du mir zu eigen versprichst, was dir daheim zuerst begegnet; willst du aber das tun, so schenk ich dir das Leben und den Vogel für deine Töchter obendrein.« Der Mann aber wollte nicht und sprach: »Das könnte meine jüngste Tochter sein, die hat mich am liebsten und läuft mir immer entgegen, wenn ich nach Haus komme.« Dem Diener aber war angst, und er sagte: »Es könnte ja auch eine Katze oder ein Hund sein!« Da ließ sich der Mann überreden, nahm mit traurigem Herzen das singende, springende Löweneckerchen und versprach dem Löwen zu eigen, was ihm daheim zuerst begegnen würde.

Wie er nun zu Haus eintrat, war das erste, was ihm begegnete, niemand anders als seine jüngste, liebste Tochter; die kam gelaufen und küßte und herzte ihn, und als sie sah, daß er ein singendes, springendes Löweneckerchen mitgebracht hatte, freute sie sich noch mehr. Der Vater aber konnte sich nicht freuen, sondern fing an zu weinen und sagte: »O weh! mein liebes Kind, den kleinen Vogel hab ich teuer gekauft, dafür hab ich dich einem wilden Löwen versprechen müssen. Wenn er dich hat, wird er dich zerreißen und fressen«, und erzählte ihr alles, wie es zugegangen war, und bat sie, nicht hinzugehen, es möcht auch kommen, was wollte. Sie aber tröstete ihn und sprach: »Liebster Vater, weil Ihr's versprochen habt, muß es auch gehalten werden; ich will hingehen und den Löwen schon besänftigen, daß ich wieder gesund zu Euch heim komme.« Am andern Morgen ließ sie sich den Weg zeigen, nahm Abschied und ging getrost in den Wald hinein. Der Löwe aber war ein verzauberter Königssohn und bei Tag ein Löwe, und mit ihm wurden alle seine Leute zu Löwen, in der Nacht aber hatten sie ihre natürliche Gestalt wieder. Als sie nun ankam, tat er gar freundlich und ward Hochzeit gehalten, und in der Nacht war er ein schöner Mann, und da wachten sie in der Nacht und schliefen am Tag und lebten eine lange Zeit vergnügt miteinander.

Einmal kam er und sagte: »Morgen ist ein Fest in deines Vaters Haus, weil deine älteste Schwester sich verheiratet, und wenn du Lust hast hinzugehen, sollen dich meine Löwen hinführen.« Da sagte sie, ja, sie möchte gern ihren Vater wiedersehen, und fuhr hin und wurde von den Löwen begleitet. Da war große Freude, als sie ankam, denn sie hatten alle geglaubt, sie wäre schon lange tot und von dem Löwen zerrissen worden. Sie erzählte aber, wie gut es ihr ging, und blieb bei ihnen, so lang die Hochzeit dauerte, dann fuhr sie wieder zurück in den Wald.

Wie die zweite Tochter heiratete und sie wieder zur Hochzeit eingeladen war, sprach sie zum Löwen: »Diesmal will ich nicht allein sein, du mußt mitgehen.« Der Löwe aber wollte nicht und sagte, das wäre zu gefährlich für ihn, denn wenn dort ein Strahl eines brennendes Lichts ihn anrühre, so würd er in eine Taube verwandelt und müßte sieben Jahre lang mit den Tauben fliegen. Sie ließ ihm aber keine Ruh und sagte, sie wollt' ihn schon hüten und bewahren vor allem Licht.

Also zogen sie zusammen und nahmen auch ihr kleines Kind mit. Sie aber ließ dort einen Saal mauern, so stark und dick, daß kein Strahl durchdrang, darin sollt' er sitzen, wenn die Hochzeitslichter angesteckt würden. Die Tür aber war von frischem Holz gemacht, das sprang und bekam einen kleinen Ritz, den kein Mensch bemerkte. Nun ward die Hochzeit mit Pracht gefeiert, wie aber der Zug

aus der Kirche zurückkam mit den vielen Fackeln und Lichtern an dem Saal vorbei, da fiel ein dünner, dünner Strahl auf den Königssohn, und wie dieser ihn berührt hatte, in dem Augenblick war er auch verwandelt, und als sie hinein kam und ihn suchte, sah sie ihn nicht, aber eine weiße Taube saß da, die sprach zu ihr: »Sieben Jahre muß ich nun in die Welt fortfliegen, alle sieben Schritte aber will ich einen roten Blutstropfen und eine weiße Feder fallen lassen, die sollen dir den Weg zeigen, und wenn du mir da nachfolgst, kannst du mich erlösen.«

Da flog die Taube zur Tür hinaus, und sie folgte ihr nach, und alle sieben Schritte fiel ein rotes Blutströpfchen und ein weißes Federchen herab und zeigte ihr den Weg. So ging sie immerzu in die weite Welt hinein und schaute nicht um sich und ruhte nicht, und waren die sieben Jahre fast herum; da freute sie sich und meinte, sie wären erlöst, und war noch so weit davon. Einmal, als sie fortging, fiel kein Federchen mehr und auch kein rotes Blutströpfchen, und als sie die Augen aufschlug, da war die Taube verschwunden. Und weil sie dachte, Menschen können dir da nicht helfen, so stieg sie zur Sonne hinauf und sagte zu ihr: »Du scheinst in alle Ritzen und über alle Spitzen; hast du keine weiße Taube fliegen sehen?« – »Nein«, sagte die Sonne, »ich habe keine gesehen, aber da schenk ich dir ein Schächtelchen, das mach auf, wenn du in großer Not bist.« Da dankte sie der Sonne und ging weiter, bis es Abend war und der Mond schien, da fragte sie ihn: »Du scheinst ja die ganze Nacht, durch alle Felder und Wälder: hast du keine weiße Taube fliegen sehen?« – »Nein«, sagte der Mond, »ich habe keine gesehen, aber da schenk ich dir ein Ei, das zerbrich, wenn du in großer Not bist.« – Da dankte sie dem Mond und ging weiter, bis der Nachtwind wehte, da sprach sie zu ihm: »Du wehst ja durch alle Bäume und unter alle Blätterchen weg, hast du keine weiße Taube fliegen sehen?« – »Nein«, sagte der Nachtwind, »ich habe keine gesehen, aber ich will die drei andern Winde fragen, die haben sie vielleicht gesehen.« Der Ostwind und der Westwind kamen und sagten, sie hätten nichts gesehen, der Südwind aber sprach: »Die weiße Taube hab ich gesehen, sie ist zum roten Meer geflogen, da ist sie wieder ein Löwe geworden, denn die sieben Jahre sind herum, und der Löwe steht dort im Kampf mit einem Lindwurm, der Lindwurm ist aber eine verzauberte Königstochter.« Da sagte der Nachtwind zu ihr: »Ich will dir Rat geben, geh zum roten Meer, am rechten Ufer da stehen große Ruten, die zähl, und die elfte schneid dir ab und schlag den Lindwurm damit, dann kann ihn der Löwe bezwingen, und beide bekommen auch ihren menschlichen Leib wieder. Dann schau dich um, und du siehst den Vogel Greif am roten Meer sitzen, schwing dich auf seinen Rücken mit deinem Liebsten, der Vogel wird euch übers Meer nach Haus tragen. Da hast du auch eine Nuß, wenn du mitten über dem Meer bist, laß sie herabfallen, alsbald wird sie aufgehen und ein großer Nußbaum aus dem Wasser hervorwachsen, auf dem sich der Greif ruht, und könnte er nicht ruhen, wär er nicht stark genug, euch hinüberzutragen, und wenn du es vergißt, die Nuß herabfallen zu lassen, wirft er euch ins Meer hinunter.«

Da ging sie hin und fand alles, wie der Nachtwind gesagt hatte, und schnitt die elfte Rute ab, damit schlug sie den Lindwurm, alsbald bezwang ihn der Löwe, und da hatten beide ihren menschlichen Leib wieder. Und wie sich die Königstochter, die vorher ein Lindwurm gewesen war, frei sah, nahm sie den Mann in den Arm, setzte sich auf den Vogel Greif und führtc ihn mit sich fort. Also stand die arme Weitgewanderte und war wieder verlassen, sie sprach aber: »Ich will noch so weit gehen, als der Wind weht, und so lang, als der Hahn kräht, bis ich ihn finde.« Und ging fort, lange, lange Wege, bis sie endlich zu dem Schloß kam, wo beide zusammenlebten, da hörte sie, daß bald ein Fest wäre, wo sie Hochzeit miteinander machen wollten. Sie sprach aber: »Gott hilft mir doch noch!« und nahm das Schächtelchen, das ihr die Sonne gegeben hatte, da lag ein Kleid darin, so glänzend wie die Sonne selber. Da nahm sie es heraus und zog es an, und ging hinauf in das Schloß, und alle Leute sahen sie an und die Braut selber; und das Kleid gefiel ihr so gut, daß sie dachte, es könnte ihr Hochzeitkleid geben, und fragte, ob es nicht feil wäre? »Nicht für Geld und Gut«, antwortete sie, »aber für Fleisch und Blut.« Die Braut fragte, was sie damit meine? Da sagte sie: »Laßt mich eine Nacht in der Kammer schlafen, wo der Bräutigam schläft.« Die Braut wollte nicht und wollte doch gern das Kleid haben, endlich willigte sie ein, aber der Kammerdiener mußte dem Königssohn einen Schlaftrunk geben. Als es nun Nacht war und der Prinz schon schlief, ward sie in die Kammer geführt, da setzte sie sich ans Bett und sagte: »Ich bin dir nachgefolgt sieben Jahre, bin bei Sonne, Mond und den Winden gewesen und hab nach dir gefragt und hab dir geholfen gegen den Lindwurm, willst du mich denn ganz vergessen?« Der Königssohn aber schlief so tief, daß es ihm nur vorkam, als rausche der Wind draußen in den Tannenbäumen.

Wie nun der Morgen anbrach, da ward sie wieder hinausgeführt und mußte das goldene Kleid hergeben; und als auch das nichts geholfen hatte, ward sie traurig, ging hinaus auf eine Wiese, setzte sich da hin und weinte. Und wie sie so saß, da fiel ihr das Ei noch ein, das ihr der Mond gegeben hatte, und sie schlug es auf; ei! da kam eine Glucke heraus mit zwölf Küchlein ganz von Gold, die liefen herum und piepten und krochen der Alten wieder unter die Flügel, so daß nichts Schöneres auf der Welt zu sehen war. Da stand sie auf, trieb sie auf der Wiese vor sich her, so lange, bis die Braut aus dem Fenster sah, und da gefielen ihr die kleinen Wesen so gut, daß sie gleich herab kam und fragte, ob sie nicht feil wären? »Nicht für Geld und Gut, aber für Fleisch und Blut. Laßt mich noch eine Nacht in der Kammer schlafen, wo der Bräutigam schläft.« Die Braut sagte ja und wollte sie betrügen, wie am vorigen Abend, als aber der Königssohn zu Bett ging, fragte er seinen Kammerdiener, was das Murmeln und Rauschen in der Nacht gewesen sei. Da erzählte der Kammerdiener alles, daß er ihm einen Schlaftrunk hätte geben müssen, weil ein armes Mädchen heimlich in der Kammer geschlafen hätte, und heute nacht solle er ihm wieder einen geben. Sagte der Königssohn: »Gieße den Trank neben das Bett aus«, und zur Nacht wurde sie wieder hereingeführt, und als sie anfing, wieder zu erzählen, wie es ihr traurig ergangen wär, da erkannt' er gleich an der Stimme seine liebe Gemahlin, sprang auf und sprach: »So bin ich erst recht erlöst, mir ist gewesen wie in einem Traum, denn die fremde Königstochter hat mich bezaubert, daß ich dich vergessen mußte, aber Gott hat mir noch zu rechter Stunde geholfen.« Da gingen sie beide in der Nacht heimlich aus dem Schloß, denn sie fürchteten sich vor dem Vater der Königstochter, der ein Zauberer war, und setzten sich auf den Vogel Greif, der trug sie über das rote Meer, und als sie in der Mitte waren, ließ sie die Nuß fallen. Alsbald wuchs ein großer Nußbaum, darauf ruhte sich der Vogel aus, und dann führte er sie nach Haus, wo sie ihr Kind fanden, das war groß und schön geworden, und sie lebten von nun an vergnügt bis an ihr Ende.

1819

Die wunderliche Gasterei

Auf eine Zeit lebte eine Blutwurst und eine Leberwurst in Freundschaft, und die Blutwurst bat die Leberwurst zu Gast. Wie es Essenszeit war, ging die Leberwurst auch ganz vergnügt zu der Blutwurst, als sie aber in die Haustüre trat, sah sie allerlei wunderliche Dinge, auf jeder Stiege der Treppe, deren viele waren, immer etwas anderes; da war etwa ein Besen und eine Schippe, die sich miteinander schlugen, dann ein Affe mit einer großen Wunde am Kopf und dergleichen mehr.

Die Leberwurst war ganz erschrocken und bestürzt darüber, doch nahm sie sich ein Herz, trat in die Stube und wurde von der Blutwurst freundschaftlich empfangen. Die Leberwurst hub an, sich nach den seltsamen Dingen zu erkundigen, die draußen auf der Treppe wären, die Blutwurst tat aber, als hörte sie es nicht oder als sei es nicht der Mühe wert, davon zu sprechen, aber sie sagte etwa von der Schippe und dem Besen: »Es wird meine Magd gewesen sein, die auf der Treppe mit jemand geschwätzt hat«, und brachte die Rede auf etwas anderes.

Die Blutwurst ging darauf hinaus und sagte, sie müsse in der Küche nach dem Essen sehen, ob alles ordentlich angerichtet werde und nichts in die Asche geworfen. Wie die Leberwurst derweil in der Stube auf- und abging und immer die wunderlichen Dinge im Kopf hatte, kam jemand, ich weiß nicht, wer's gewesen ist, herein und sagte: »Ich warne dich, Leberwurst, du bist in einer Blut- und Mörderhöhle, mach dich eilig fort, wenn dir dein Leben lieb ist.« Die Leberwurst besann sich nicht lang, schlich zur Tür hinaus und lief, was sie konnte; sie stand auch nicht eher still, bis sie aus dem Haus mitten auf der Straße war. Da blickte sie sich um und sah die Blutwurst oben im Bodenloch stehen mit einem langen, langen Messer, das blinkte, als wär's frisch gewetzt, und damit drohte sie und rief herab:

»Hätt' ich dich, so wollt' ich dich!«

1819

Die Sterntaler

Es war einmal ein kleines Mädchen, dem war Vater und Mutter gestorben, und es war so arm, daß es kein Kämmerchen mehr hatte, darin zu wohnen, und kein Bettchen mehr, darin zu schlafen, und gar nichts mehr als die Kleider, die es auf dem Leib trug, und ein Stückchen Brot, das es in der Hand hielt und das ihm ein mitleidiges Herz noch geschenkt hatte. Es war aber gar gut und fromm. Und weil es so von aller Welt verlassen war, ging es im Vertrauen auf den lieben Gott hinaus ins Feld, da begegnete ihm ein armer Mann, der sprach: »Ach, gib mir doch etwas zu essen, ich bin so hungrig.« Es reichte ihm das ganze Stückchen Brot und sagte: »Gott segne dir's!« und ging weiter. Da kam ein Kind, das jammerte und sprach: »Es friert mich so an meinem Kopf, schenk mir doch etwas, womit ich ihn bedecken kann!« Da tat es seine Mütze ab und gab sie ihm. Und als es noch ein bißchen gegangen war, kam wieder ein Kind und hatte kein Leibchen an und fror, da gab es ihm seins; und noch weiter, da bat eins um ein Röcklein, das gab es auch von sich hin. Endlich kam es in einen Wald, und es war schon dunkel geworden, da kam noch eins und bat um ein Hemdlein, und das fromme Mädchen dachte: Es ist dunkle Nacht, da kannst du wohl dein Hemd weggeben; und gab es auch noch hin. Und wie es so stand und gar nichts mehr hatte, fielen auf einmal die Sterne vom Himmel und waren lauter harte, blanke Taler, und ob es gleich sein Hemdlein weggegeben, so hatte es ein neues an vom allerfeinsten Linnen. Da sammelte es sich die Taler hinein und war reich für sein Lebtag.

1819

Der goldene Schlüssel

Zur Winterszeit, als einmal ein tiefer Schnee lag, mußte ein armer Junge hinausgehen und Holz auf einem Schlitten holen. Wie er es nun zusammengesucht und aufgeladen hatte, wollte er, weil er so erfroren war, noch nicht nach Haus gehen, sondern erst Feuer anmachen und sich ein bißchen wärmen. Da scharrte er den Schnee weg, und wie er so den Erdboden aufräumte, fand er einen kleinen goldnen Schlüssel. Nun glaubte er, wo der Schlüssel wäre, müßte auch das Schloß dazu sein, grub in der Erde und fand ein eisernes Kästchen. Wenn der Schlüssel nur paßt! dachte er. Es sind gewiß kostbare Sachen in dem Kästchen. Er suchte, aber es war kein Schlüsselloch da. Endlich fand er eins, das man kaum sehen konnte, zu dem auch der Schlüssel glücklich paßte. Er drehte einmal herum, und nun müssen wir warten, bis er vollends aufgeschlossen und den Deckel aufgemacht hat, dann können wir erfahren, was für wunderbare Sachen in dem Kästchen lagen.   1837

Allerleirauh *219*

Aschenputtel *176*

Blaubart *246*

Das blaue Licht *258*

Das eigensinnige Kind *326*

Das kluge Gretel *28*

Das singende, springende
  Löweneckerchen *371*

Das tapfere Schneiderlein *31*

Das Waldhaus *171*

Das Wasser des Lebens *263*

Daumesdick *214*

Der arme Müllerbursch und das
  Kätzchen *235*

Der Bauer und der Teufel *306*

Der Dreschflegel vom Himmel *296*

Der Eisenhans *110*

Der Eisenofen *283*

Der faule Heinz *58*

Der Froschkönig oder Der eiserne
  Heinrich *17*

Der Geist im Glas *117*

Der gelernte Jäger *241*

Der gescheite Hans *202*

Der Gevatter Tod *205*

Der goldene Schlüssel *380*

Der Hund und der Sperling *223*

Der junge Riese *229*

Der König vom goldenen Berg *340*

Der Meisterdieb *183*

Der Okerlo *146*

Der Räuberbräutigam *68*

Der Riese und der Schneider *63*

Der singende Knochen *318*

Der starke Hans *130*

Der Teufel mit den drei goldenen
  Haaren *104*

Der Teufel und seine Großmutter *298*

Der Trommler *137*

Der undankbare Sohn *10*

Der Wolf und die sieben jungen Geißlein *80*

Der wunderliche Spielmann *46*

Der Zaunkönig *288*

Der Zaunkönig und der Bär *20*

Des Schneiders Daumerling Wanderschaft *6*

Des Teufels rußiger Bruder *345*

Die Alte im Wald *315*

Die Boten des Todes *66*

Die Bremer Stadtmusikanten *353*

Die drei Federn *90*

Die drei Männlein im Walde *23*

Die drei Schlangenblätter *38*

Die Gänsemagd *309*

Die Geschenke des kleinen Volkes *294*

Die goldene Gans *156*

Die Goldkinder *320*

Die kluge Bauerntochter *197*

Die kluge Else *52*

Die Krähen *291*

Die Nixe im Teich *94*

Die sechs Schwäne *42*

Die sieben Raben *55*

Die sieben Schwaben *127*

Die Sterntaler *378*

Die treuen Tiere *363*

Die vier kunstreichen Brüder *193*

Die weiße Schlange *324*

Die weiße und die schwarze Braut *123*

Die Wichtelmänner *153*

Die wunderliche Gasterei *377*

Die zertanzten Schuhe *279*

Die zwölf Brüder *301*

Die zwölf Jäger *60*

Doktor Allwissend *348*

Dornröschen *149*

Einäuglein, Zweiäuglein und Dreiäuglein *83*

Fitchers Vogel *238*

Frau Holle *337*

Frau Trude *261*

Hänsel und Gretel *357*

Hans Dumm *268*

Hans im Glück *99*

Hans mein Igel *366*

Herr Korbes *121*

Hurleburlebutz *190*

Jorinde und Joringel *200*

Katz und Maus in Gesellschaft *270*

König Drosselbart *210*

Märchen von der Unke *93*

Märchen von einem, der auszog, das
Fürchten zu lernen *251*

Rapunzel *159*

Rotkäppchen *276*

Rumpelstilzchen *49*

Schneeweißchen und Rosenrot *11*

Schneewittchen *328*

Sechse kommen durch die ganze Welt *272*

Simeliberg *207*

Spindel, Weberschiffchen und Nadel *226*

Strohhalm, Kohle und Bohne *350*

Tischchen deck dich, Goldesel und Knüppel
aus dem Sack *72*

Vom Fundevogel *168*

Vom süßen Brei *307*

Von dem Fischer un siine Fru *163*

Von dem Mäuschen, Vögelchen und der
Bratwurst *351*

Von dem Tod des Hühnchens *249*

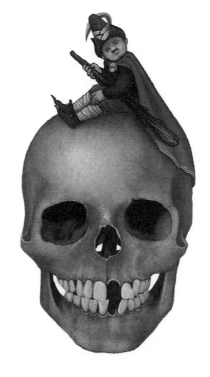

Für Jochen
N.H.